The Art of Teaching Writing

The Art of Teaching Writing

NEW EDITION

Lucy McCormick Calkins

Teachers College, Columbia University

Photography by Peter Cunningham

HEINEMANN
Portsmouth, New Hampshire

IRWIN PUBLISHING
Toronto, Canada

HEINEMANN
A division of Reed Elsevier Inc.
361 Hanover Street   Portsmouth, NH 03801-3912
Offices and agents throughout the world

Published simultaneously in Canada by
IRWIN PUBLISHING
1800 Steeles Avenue West   Concord, Ontario, Canada L4K 2P3

Editor: Philippa Stratton   Copy editor: Linda Howe
Production: Donna Bouvier and   Text design: Joni Doherty
            J. B. Tranchemontagne   Cover design: Jenny Jensen Greenleaf
Photos © 1994 by Peter Cunningham

Acknowledgments for borrowed material begin on page 549.

All the photographs in this book were taken at Maugham and Stillman Schools in Tenafly, New Jersey, and at P.S. 148 in New York City's District 30.

Library of Congress Cataloging-in-Publication Data
Calkins, Lucy McCormick.
    The art of teaching writing / Lucy McCormick Calkins.—New ed.
      p.   cm.
    Includes bibliographical references.
    ISBN 0-435-08809-2 (paper)   ISBN 0-435-08817-3 (cloth)
    1. English language—Composition and exercises—Study and teaching.   I. Title.
PE1404.C29   1994
808'.042'0712—dc20   93-21095
                                                                     CIP

Canadian Cataloguing in Publication Data
Calkins, Lucy McCormick
    The art of teaching writing

Includes bibliographical references.
ISBN 0-7725-2116-6

1. English language—Composition and exercises—
Study and teaching (Elementary).   I. Title.

LB1576.C35 1994   372.6'23044   C94-930513-8

Printed in the United States of America on acid-free paper
05 04 03 02 01   15 14 13 12   (paper)
05 04 03 02 01   11 10 9 8 7   (cloth)

*F*or Miles

who fills this book

with stories

and

my life

with

miracles

Contents

SECTION IV THE CHANGING CURRICULUM IN THE WRITING WORKSHOP

SECTION V WRITING WORKSHOP TEACHING IN A LARGER CONTEXT

ACKNOWLEDGMENTS

In her essay "Eleven" Sandra Cisneros writes, "What they don't understand about birthdays and what they never tell you is that when you're eleven, you're also ten, and nine, and eight, and seven, and six, and five, and four, and three, and two, and one. . . . Because the way you grow old is kind of like an onion or like the rings inside a tree trunk or like my little wooden dolls that fit one inside the other, each year inside the next one."

This is exactly how I feel about this new edition of *The Art of Teaching Writing*. It has grown like an onion, or like the rings inside a tree. When I look now at the completed manuscript, I am amazed to see that the ideas about teaching and learning that are most important to me are those that were part of the fiber of my own childhood. It was my parents, Evan and Virginia Calkins, who first demonstrated to me that when we're given the opportunity to initiate and pursue our own important projects, the line between work and play becomes very thin indeed. I am grateful to them for giving my eight brothers and sisters and me the opportunity to live our lives as if one person can make a difference and to believe in the old-fashioned value of having a mission.

When I was first teaching, it was hard to believe I could make a difference. How fortunate I was to find a community of like-minded educators who allowed me to remember my dreams. Bud Church, Joy Mermin, Sue Devokaitis, Chris Wood, and Peggy Walker Stevens were my lifelines, helping me hold on to the values that led me to teaching in the first place. We sang and studied, hiked and read together, and then, within that context, worked to make our dreams for education come true. We founded and led an alternative elementary and middle school, and that school, with its nature trails and gardens, and its classrooms filled with reading lofts and easels, is ever present in my vision for education.

But I think the most lasting lessons I learned from Center School were those about the importance of community. Freud said that a healthy person needs two things: work and love. Early on in my involvement in education I learned that it's when the two come together that I am happiest. I have never forgotten that lesson.

For almost fifteen years now I have learned alongside a cadre of literacy educators known as the Teachers College Writing Project. It has been the privilege of my life to teach and inquire side by side with these colleagues, who are among the most brilliant, original, and dedicated teacher-educators in the world. I thank each of the people who share in this endeavor. I could not imagine more important or more satisfying work than the work we do together, helping teachers in schools throughout New York City and its suburbs develop new images for how classrooms can look, sound, and feel, and for what it means to teach. I will not list each of my Writing Project colleagues by name; you know who you are, and you know what a source of wisdom and inspiration our collaboration has been for me.

A number of my Writing Project colleagues have made particularly dramatic contributions to this edition of *The Art of Teaching Writing*. I want to thank Randy Bomer, Co-Director of the Teachers College Writing Project, for his leadership of our Project and for being an extraordinary thought-companion. How I admire his clear, principled thinking, his commitment to inquiry, and his genius for turning conversation into collaboration. I am also grateful to Kathy Doyle for her wisdom, energy, and generosity. Many of the ideas in this edition came to life for me while I learned alongside Kathy and her students at the Maugham School in Tenafly, New Jersey. Shirley McPhillips, staff developer in Tenafly and a leader among the Writing Project staff members for a decade now, has enriched my thinking about reading and writing in innumerable ways. Finally, I will forever be grateful to Lydia Bellino, a teacher-educator at the Shelter Rock School in Manhasset, Long Island. The biggest ideas in these chapters emerged in conversation with Lydia. Her thinking on literacy education grows out of her extraordinary ability to take enormous and complicated notions and explore what they might mean in the very real world of children, curriculum, and teaching.

Others have also helped with this edition or the earlier one. I'm grateful to Mary Ellen Giacobbe, JoAnn Curtis, Martha Horn, Ralph Fletcher, Kathy Bearden, and Isoke Nia for their contributions. Joanne Hindley and Laurie Pessah have each been especially instrumental in my recent learning, and I thank them for their help in my thinking and in my life. Shelley Harwayne and Georgia Heard were very helpful in the process of writing the first edition of this book. Shelley was at the time a staff developer in District 15, Brooklyn, and the seemingly effortless brilliance of her teaching astonished me then, as it has since. Georgia's clarity and strength have graced my life; her contributions extend far beyond the province of poetry.

All that I do now relies on a foundation that was built while I worked alongside two mentors, Don Graves and Don Murray. Their ideas are seminal to this book, but here I want to thank them also for the undeserved support they gave me when I was new to writing and teaching. They saw more in me than I saw in myself, and that made all the difference. Don Graves has been a lifelong friend and mentor; he believed in me when I was an earnest, awkward eleven-year-old. Later, when I was a novice researcher, he invited me to work with him as a colleague, "an equal." I am grateful to him for demonstrating and inviting me into a life of passionate research. Don Murray entered my life at a later stage; I knew him first as my hero, and I continue to put him on a pedestal. At the crucial junctures in my writing life, I still turn to Murray, as a student turns to her teacher, and I still leave those interactions feeling as if I can write for several years with his comments to guide me. It was Don Murray who nudged me to follow Philippa Stratton's advice and write this new edition of *The Art of Teaching Writing.*

Philippa, who was Editor-in-Chief at Heinemann for well over a decade, has been a guiding light for the entire field of literacy education. When I look over my reading lists, I'm astonished to see that almost every book I mention was published by Heinemann; this is because Philippa has recruited, championed, and coached her authors. The first edition of *The Art of Teaching Writing* was one of Heinemann's early accomplishments, and this next edition is Philippa's final project at Heinemann. She has been an extraordinary resource for me, flying to New York to discuss early drafts, helping me reassemble the team that created both the first edition of *The Art of Teaching Writing* and my more recent *Living Between the Lines.* That team includes Linda Howe and Donna Bouvier, two of the most careful wordsmiths I've ever known. I've begun to believe I could not write a book without them.

While Donna, Linda, and Philippa worked with me on the details of this manuscript at Heinemann, colleagues in the Writing Project worked with me in my office. Mary Beth Solomon has assisted in innumerable ways. Kate Montgomery has conferred with me about every draft of every chapter, and her wisdom has made this a far better book. Kathy Collins, at the helm of the Project, has been a miracle worker, steering us into smooth waters and allowing me to be as productive as possible.

It has also been a help to know that caring, insightful educators are working with my children. I am grateful to the faculty of both the Growing Tree Nursery School in Ridgefield and the Wooster School in Danbury, Connecticut, and in particular to Barb Costello, Nancy Craig, and Marian Sundloff.

It is traditional to end the acknowledgments by thanking one's spouse for not minding the long hours of deskwork. I want, instead, to thank my husband, John Skorpen, for calling me away from the desk. I'm grateful for mountain meadows full of wildflowers, moonlit ski trails, and cascading waterfalls. I'm grateful for the laughter and sense of adventure that fill our home. And I am grateful, above all, for John's company in parenting Miles and Evan. Our sons have given John and me the greatest adventure of our lives.

Miles is six and Evan, four. What a joy it has been over the past two years to watch and learn from Miles as he finds his wings as a reader and writer, and what fun it will be to learn in brand-new ways from Evan, as he now moves into this phase of literacy development.

The Art of
Teaching Writing

I

The Essentials of Writing

1

Making Meaning on the Page and in Our Lives

If our teaching is to be an art, we must draw from all we know, feel, and believe in order to create something beautiful. To teach well, we do not need more techniques and strategies as much as we need a vision of what is essential. It is not the number of good ideas that turns our work into art but the selection, balance, and design of those ideas.

Artists know this. Artistry does not come from the *quantity* of red and yellow paint or from the *amount* of clay or marble but from the organizing *vision* that shapes the use of these materials. It comes from a sense of priority and design.

Eight years ago, when I wrote the first edition of *The Art of Teaching Writing*, I conveyed my sense of the essentials of teaching writing this way:

> For me, it is essential that children are deeply involved in writing, that they share their texts with others, and that they perceive themselves as authors. I believe these three things are interconnected. A sense of authorship comes from the struggle to put something big and vital into print, and from seeing one's own printed words reach the hearts and minds of readers. (1986, p. 9)

I have written this new edition of *The Art of Teaching Writing* because I've come to believe that authorship does not begin in the struggle to put something big into print; rather, it begins in living with a sense of awareness. James Dickey's definition of a writer—"someone who is enormously taken by things anyone else would walk by"—is an important reminder to those of us who assume that we begin to write by brainstorming ideas, listing topics, and outlining possible directions for a piece. Writing does not begin with deskwork but with lifework. When the author Cynthia

Rylant was asked to describe her writing process, she refused to talk about writing as something she does at a desk. "We are talking about . . . being an artist every single day of one's life," she said. "This is about going fishing as an artist and having relatives over for supper as an artist and walking the aisles of a Woolworth's as an artist."

Byrd Baylor would add, "We're talking about driving down the highway as an artist." Byrd is the author of *I'm in Charge of Celebrations,* a book about the days she has circled on her calendar in which she commemorates important occasions. The first such occasion—Green Cloud Day—occurred as Byrd was driving her pickup truck along the Arizona highway. "I'd decided to take the longer route because the skies are so beautiful along that road," she says. "But it'd never before been like it was that day." As Byrd drove along, she was astonished to see the clouds turn green. She stopped the truck and stood alongside the highway, her face turned up toward the clouds overhead. A van filled with teenagers came along and pulled over to see what it was that had caught her attention. Soon the entire group of them, a tribe of green cloud worshippers, stood alongside the road, mouths open, gaping at the green clouds. As they stood there, one green cloud took on the shape of a parrot. "No one in the entire universe has seen what we are seeing today," they told each other and vowed to meet in the same place at the same time the next year.

Byrd Baylor is wise to turn this into a metaphor for the writing life. We human beings *are* in charge of celebrations. Writing allows us to hold our life in our hands and make something of it. We grow a piece of writing not only by jotting notes and writing rough drafts, but also by noticing, wondering, remembering, questioning, yearning. "I must write," Anne Morrow Lindbergh says. "I must write at all costs, for writing is more than living. It is being conscious of living."

Seven-year-old Luke lives like a writer. When he asks his brother, "Why are you so happy?" and he answers, "Jacob 1992," he cups his hands around his surprising response and makes something of it (Figure 1–1):

> I asked my little brother why he was so happy. He said, "Jacob 1992."
> I think that means "I'm happy because I'm me and because there will never be another October the 16th, 1992." What my little brother said was poetry.

The richness in Luke's writing comes from his struggle to put something big and vital into print, but it also comes from lingering with a bit of

FIGURE 1–1 Emily's writing

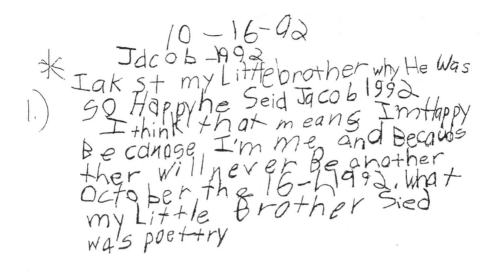

life and layering it with meaning. Writing for him is not a process of *recording* details but one of *making significance* of them.

Fifteen-year-old Jose meets once a week in an after-school writing club led by his fifth-grade teacher, Maria Maher. In his notebook, Jose wrote about his memories of the day their class rabbit gave birth to a litter of naked little babies. He wrote about the mother rabbit's huge belly, about the anticipation in his classroom as they waited for the great event, about how his teacher told them this would be a wonderful thing. In the end, however, Jose's teacher was called to the office during the birth, and a substitute teacher took the class. Jose writes about what he saw through the substitute teacher's eyes (Figure 1–2):

> It was Mrs. Kenny that made me notice the blood. It shocked me. She said it was a painful process and during a birth there was always blood. She scared me. I stopped watching it. I was mad at Ms. Maher for lying and pretending it was a wonderful thing. I hated the bunnies for hurting their mom.
>
> I remember going home and telling my mom. She told me Ms. Maher didn't lie or pretend. She told me how when she had me and Raphael and Christopher that it did hurt and it did bleed but it was also the most wonderful experience in the world.

FIGURE 1–2   Jose's notebook entry

It was this Kenny that made me notice the blood. It shocked me. She said it was a painful process and during a birth there was always blood. She scared me. I stopped watching it. I was mad at the mother for lying and pretending it was a wonderful thing. I hated the bunnies for hurting their mom.

I remember going home and telling my mom. She told me my mother didn't lie or pretend. She told me how when she had me and Raphael and Christopher that it did hurt and it did bleed but it was also the most wonderful experience in the world.

Already in this one entry Jose has lingered with his topic, layering the story of the birth with his comments about it. The next day he returned to this same subject, gathered more memories, thoughts, and wonderings about it, and wrote this entry (Figure 1–3):

> My cousin is 15 and pregnant. She must be so scared. She must know how much it's going to hurt. How wonderful will it be for a 15-year-old girl who is scared and alone? Some guy is out there and he's the father of her child, and he's nowhere to be found. I will *never* do that to a girl. It isn't right to leave a girl with that responsibility. Alone, it will be painful. Together, it could be wonderful.

FIGURE 1–3   Another entry by Jose

My cousin is 15 and pregnant. She must be so scared. She must know how much its going to hurt. How wonderful will it be for a 15 year old girl who is scared and alone? Some guy is out there and his the father of her child and his no where to be found. I will never do that to a girl. It isn't right to leave a girl with that responsibility. Alone it will be painful. Together it could be wonderful.

Jose may continue to gather entries associated with this topic, or he may move on to develop a different piece of writing. But already, for Jose as for Emily, writing has been a journey toward insight.

In her book, *Roxaboxen*, Alice McLerran tells about how, as a little girl, she and her friends invented a kingdom. Roxaboxen, as the kingdom was called, started out as a scraggly desert hill with nothing but cacti, sand, and some broken-down boxes. Then Marian dug up a rusty tin box. Everyone gathered around and declared it treasure. And it was. Inside the box there were smooth black stones. After that, there were treasure hunting days, and a town grew, with streets lined with white stones, and a jail, and a cemetery (although the only one who died was a dried-up old lizard the children found). The kingdom of Roxaboxen began with Marian holding a rusty tin box in her hands and declaring it a treasure. That is why I write.

I write to hold what I find in my life in my hands and to declare it a treasure. I'm not very good at doing this. When I sit down at my desk, I'm like my students. "Nothing happens in my life," I say. I feel empty-handed. I want to get up and rush around, looking for something Big and Significant to put on the page.

And yet, as a writer I have come to know that significance cannot be found, it must be grown. Looking back in my notebook I find a brief entry about how my son Miles uses one of my cotton T-shirts as his "pretend blanket," replacing his original blanket, which has disintegrated. My inclination is to dismiss the entry as trivial, as something only a mother could care about, but then I remember the writer Vicki Vinton saying, "It is an illusion that writers live more significant lives than non-writers; the truth is, writers are just more in the habit of *finding* the significance that is there in their lives."

Vicki's words hang over my desk, as do the words of the poet Theodore Roethke, who said, "If our lives don't feel significant, sometimes it's not *our lives,* but our response to our lives, which needs to be richer." It's not only these quotations that nudge me to believe I can find significance in my son's "pretend blanket." I'm also instructed by memories of times when I've begun with something small, and seen significance emerge on my page. From my experiences as a writer and from the experiences of other authors, I have developed a small repertoire of strategies to draw on when I want to take a seed idea and grow it into a speech, a story, a book. This, for me, is what the writing process is all about.

Revision for me, then, is quite literally a time *to see again,* so I take my short entry about my son sleeping with my T-shirt and this time I add detail.

I write about seeing my sleeping son's face pressed against my T-shirt, and I write about later seeing him pat my T-shirt, scrunched up in the seat beside him on the way to school. As I write, I realize that Miles must be clinging to the idea of being a baby and to his relationship with me. As I write more, I realize that he won't hold my T-shirt in the car beside him much longer, that soon he won't even glance back at me when I let him off at school, that soon he won't want me to bring him to school because I don't have the "right" kind of car. . . . Miles is not the only one who is clinging to the idea of him as a baby. He is six and his brother is four. They are growing up—I miss them already.

This is how I write. I take a moment—an image, a memory, a phrase, an idea—and I hold it in my hands and declare it a treasure. I begin by writing about my son's frayed blanket and end up realizing I'm suffering from empty nest syndrome.

When I wrote the first edition of this book, I saw writing as a process of choosing a topic, turning the topic into the best possible draft, sharing the draft with friends, then revising it. But I've come to think that it's very important that writing is not only a process of *recording*, it is also a process of *developing* a story or an idea. In this new edition I describe writing episodes that do not begin with a topic and a draft but instead with a noticing, a question. When writing begins with something that has not yet found its significance, it is more apt to become a process of *growing meaning*.

In this new edition I argue that as human beings we write to communicate, plan, petition, remember, announce, list, imagine . . . but above all, we write to hold our lives in our hands and to make something of them. There is no plot line in the bewildering complexity of our lives but that which we make for ourselves. Writing allows us to turn the chaos into something beautiful, to frame selected moments, to uncover and celebrate the organizing patterns of our existence.

As human beings we have a deep need to represent our experience. By articulating our experience, we reclaim it for ourselves. We need to make our truths beautiful. This is why early peoples inscribed their stories on stony cave walls with pictographs. It is why my closets are filled with boxes of musty old journals. It is why I found pages of poetry under my stepdaughter Kira's mattress when she went off to college. It is why my four-year-old son, Evan, uses magic markers, pens, lipstick, and pencils to leave his mark on bathroom walls, on the backs of old envelopes, on his brother's charts and drawings. These markings give Evan a way to hold onto his world, to be instructed and moved by what he finds in it. As John Cheever explains, "When I began to write, I found this was the best way to make sense out of my life."

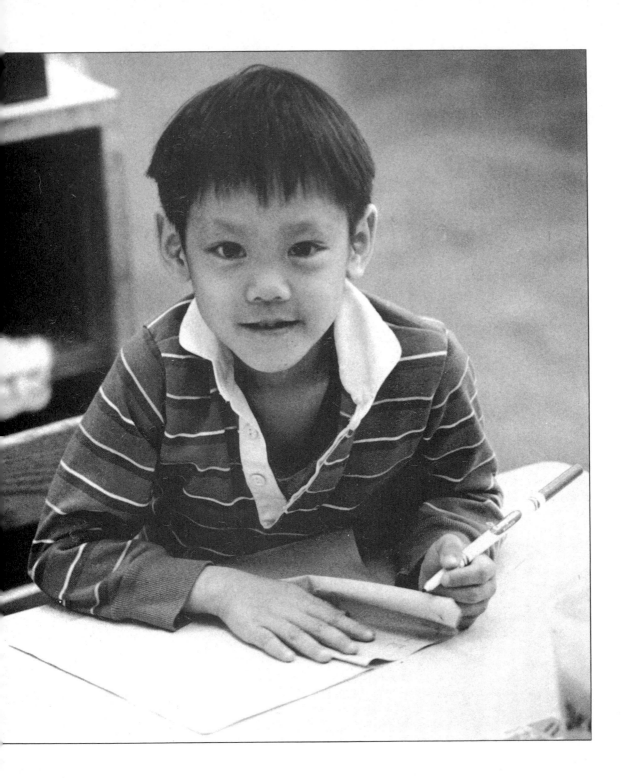

2

Tap the Energy for Writing

In our schools, students often tell us they don't want to write. But they need not bother to tell us. We can feel their resistance as they eke out tense, tight lines of words and as they ask, "How long does it have to be?" Their resistance to writing reminds us of our own. When students ask, "Do we *have* to write?" we remember sitting before the empty page thinking, "I have nothing to say," and, with growing desperation, "My life is boring." Those of us who finally did pour our hearts and souls onto the page remember receiving only marginal responses: "Awk" and "Run-on."

When Students Become Deeply Involved in Their Writing, They Don't Need Motivating Activities

When we, as teachers, do not have good memories of writing to draw upon, we are apt to accept our students' resistance to writing as a given. When we assume that writing will always be a dreaded activity, we spend all our time pushing, luring, motivating, and bribing.

I am embarrassed to recall how I used to initiate writing: "We're going to write in our journals for five minutes this morning," and then, as if anticipating mutiny, I'd hasten to add, "It's just five minutes . . . Spelling won't count . . . Just put down anything . . . No one will read it; it's private. . . ." Although I didn't realize it at the time, the conditions I established for my students' writing almost guaranteed they wouldn't tap into the natural and enduring reasons for writing. When I said, "No one will read it," I ensured that my students wouldn't know the joy and the intimacy of feeling seen and heard through their writing. When I said, "It's just five minutes," I made certain that my students wouldn't know the thrill of reaching for the exact word or of being surprised by what emerged on their pages. But worst of all, my hesitancy and defensiveness conveyed a sense that writing was something to complain about, that I expected their resistance.

I can recall other well-intended efforts to lure students into what I assumed would be the dreaded activity of writing. I remember bringing a hornet's nest to school when I was a first-year teacher. Displaying it proudly, I told all my students that they could look at it, touch it, smell it . . . and then write about it.

Over the years, I invented lots of variations on those first efforts to "stimulate" student writing; I assigned lots of topics, gave out lots of starting sentences, used lots of song-and-dance routines. Now I believe all these efforts created, for the most part, only short-lived fizzles of energy for writing. Before long, I'd have to dream up yet another way to "stimulate" students to write. Within such a cycle, it would be absurd to talk about coaching students to write better, about helping them understand the role of drafting and revision in writing, or about building a place for peer conferring in the classroom. If the need to motivate student writing requires all of a teacher's time and attention, if a teacher is constantly straining against a giant boulder of student resistance, then the teacher's hands are already full. But the biggest problem with my bringing a hornet's nest to school and asking my students to smell it, look at it, and then write about it is that I was indirectly agreeing with those who come to us saying, "I have nothing to write about" or "Nothing ever happens to me." By supplying a topic from my experience and giving it to my students, I indirectly taught them that their lives aren't worth writing about, that they don't have their own cherished bits of life, their own moments, their own hornet's nests.

In retrospect, I realize that back then, my teaching was based on the assumption that youngsters would write only if they were forced or bribed or coerced or cajoled into doing so. Because I had not, at the time, experienced the power of writing in my own life, I didn't yet understand that there is a world of difference between "motivating writing" and helping people become deeply and personally involved in their own writing. And so I spent most of my time conjuring up motivating activities, all based on the assumption that my students would write only if I jump-started them. Now I believe that this is a devastating assumption for a teacher of literacy to hold. We cannot teach writing well unless we trust that there are real, human reasons to write.

Let me be clear. I have seen teachers who do not regard themselves as writers and yet teach writing in wondrous ways. If we ourselves are immersed in an ongoing way in our own writing, we have a fabulous resource to draw from when we teach. But it is not necessary to expect that all of us, as teachers, will regularly draft, revise, and publish our own essays and poems. What *is* necessary, however, is that we have memories of a time when we loved writing and that we draw on those memories when we teach writing. If we have even once in our lives experienced the power of writing, our teaching will be forever changed.

Often when I work with teachers at the Teachers College Writing Project's annual summer institute on the teaching of writing, I suggest that we each map our journeys as readers and writers, remembering and lingering over the important moments. When we retrace our lifelines, most of us find that we can remember a time when writing meant everything to us. It may have been a letter we finally dared to mail, a poem for a loved one, a letter to the editor, or an article for the paper. It is tremendously important that we, as teachers of writing, fill ourselves with memories of times when writing mattered to us . . . and that we let our teaching be informed by those memories. If we keep such memories foremost in our minds, then when Jessica whines, "How long does it have to be?" we stand a chance of responding with, "I can't believe you are asking that, Jessica. What's going on?"

I am not arguing that all our students are secretly yearning for the chance to write poems and plays and essays. I am not suggesting that classrooms will all fill with applause after we announce, "Boys and girls, we're going to spend time every day writing." I'm not naive. But I do know that when we teachers have known the power of writing for ourselves, when we've fashioned our own poems and stories and letters and memoirs, then we can look at the resistance in our students' faces and clenched hands and know it is there *not* because writing is inherently a dreaded activity, but because writing has been taught in ways that make it so. When our students resist writing, it's usually because writing has been treated as little more than a place to display—to expose—their command of spelling, penmanship, and grammar. For too many students writing is, as researcher Mina Shaughnessy says, "but a line that moves haltingly across the page, exposing as it goes all that the writer doesn't know. Writing puts us on the line and we don't want to be there" (1977, p. 7). It doesn't have to be that way.

When we have experienced for ourselves the human reasons for writing, then instead of assuming that writing will always be a dreaded activity—and therefore pushing, luring, motivating, bribing, and requiring our students to write—we ask, "How can I establish conditions within which my students will want to write?"

We Care About Writing When It Is Personal and Interpersonal

If we want to know how to create conditions that are as supportive of writing as the art studio is of art, the library of research, and the gymnasium of basketball, it helps to think about the times in our lives when writing meant the world to us. Time and again, colleagues have told me that for them writing matters the most when it is personal (when it is self-sponsored and grows out of purposes in their own lives) and when it is interpersonal. Not surprisingly, for us human beings the work that is deeply personal, that is woven into the fabric of our lives, is also interpersonal. We care about writing when we write with, for, and about the people who matter to us, and when we write about or "off of" the issues and experiences that matter to us. Youngsters aren't any different. They, too, will care about writing when it is personal and interpersonal.

During the first day of kindergarten, a little girl sat apart from the other children, sniffling and crying. "I want Mommy," she said when her teacher, Martha Horn, tried to work with her. The next day Maria drew a primitive picture and wrote an assortment of letters. Maria's teacher was delighted, and at the end of the writing workshop, she asked if Maria would sit in the place of honor, the author's chair, and share her story. Maria held up her picture and told her story:

> The girl is sad.
> She has no friends.

Several children raised their hands. "I like your picture," one said.

"I like your writing," another said.

Then a tiny boy with big solemn eyes looked up at Maria and said, "I'll be your friend." That little boy is a wise teacher of writing.

As writers, what we all need more than anything else in the world is listeners, listeners who will respond with silent empathy, with sighs of recognition, with laughter and tears and questions and stories of their own. Writers need to be heard.

As François Mauriac says, "Each of us is like a desert, and a literary work is like a cry from the desert, or like a pigeon let loose with a message in its claws, or like a bottle thrown into the sea. The point is: To be heard—even if by one single person."

When I entered the field of writing about fifteen years ago, I learned firsthand about the power of this kind of listening from Pulitzer Prize–winning writer Donald Murray. After I read Murray's *A Writer Teaches Writing,* I wrote to him. He suggested that we meet to talk about my writing. That Saturday and, as it turned out, one Saturday a month for the next two years, I drove two and a half hours to the University of New Hampshire for a fifteen-minute conference with Murray. I then drove two and a half hours back to Connecticut. As a teacher of writing, I often think back to that. Five hours of driving for a fifteen-minute conference. What did Murray teach me that was so important?

He taught me that I had something to say. He was fascinated by what I knew about classroom teaching, and his interest helped me believe in my profession and in myself. I began to sense that I had a unique and powerful story to tell. Of course, I've since learned that Murray makes everyone feel this way, but that doesn't take away from the power of his listening attention.

It's not surprising, then, that when I teach classrooms full of young writers, I try to listen to them as Murray listened to me. In Chapter 11, I talk about the ways in which many other teachers and I have learned to structure our classrooms so that we can listen to our students. Clearly, writing workshops need to be modeled after art studios and researchers' laboratories; we need to invite students to pursue their own important projects in an environment that is ongoing and stable and then move around among them—watching, demonstrating, and giving pointers. As I move about the room, I pull my chair alongside one child after another in order to listen intently. "You know so much," I say to one child. "What you're teaching me is amazing stuff." Then, moments later, I'm crouching beside another desk. "You need to tell this to the world. It's huge. It's so big. Write it down."

When we respond to young writers in these ways, we are teaching important lessons. Our children's lives are brim full of concerns and stories, and yet when we ask them to write about their experiences they often say, "Nothing happens in my life." When we suggest that they choose their own topics for writing, they often write about superheroes or retell television dramas. In word and deed, our children ask, "Does my life really matter?" Too often, children come to school bursting with concerns: a newborn brother, their grandmother's farm in Puerto Rico, a letter from their father, and never tell their teachers or other classmates about these things. In *A Place Called School*, John Goodlad writes, "Data . . . suggest to me a picture of rather well-intentioned teachers going about their business somewhat detached from and not quite connecting with the 'other lives' of their students. What the students see as primary concerns in their daily lives, teachers view as dissonance in conducting school and classroom business" (1984, p. 80). The image Goodlad conveys is of two cogs in a wheel, spinning separately but not touching. Teachers teach, and children watch, glassy-eyed and detached. Goodlad goes on to say that schools tend to be characterized by emotional neutrality. "Classes at all levels," observes Goodlad, "tend not to be marked with exuberance, joy, laughter, abrasiveness, praise . . . but by emotional neutrality" (p. 112). In most classrooms the teacher's focus is on a unit of study, a textbook, a prepackaged curriculum, and not on children.

When we help children know that their lives do matter, we are teaching writing. When Kendra tells me about the Name-the-Kitten contest she has scheduled for her family, I respond that she could write a whole book about naming her cat. When Tamara wants not only to *tell* me about her cartwheels but also to show me and teach me how to do them, I groan. She laughs, claps her hands, and announces that she's going to put directions for doing cartwheels onto paper, so I can practice at home. Our listening attention allows these young writers to listen to their own lives.

As we take lessons from our children, we demonstrate to them that their lives are worth writing about. We help our students know what they know— and this is essential in a writing workshop. It is no wonder that Don Murray describes his teaching this way:

> I am tired, but it is a good tired, for my students have generated energy as well as absorbed it. I've learned something of what it is to be a childhood diabetic, to raise oxen, to work across from your father at 115 degrees in a steel drum factory, to be a welfare mother with three children, to build a bluebird trail . . . to bring your father home to die of cancer. I have been instructed in other lives, heard the voices of my students they had not heard before, shared their satisfaction in solving the problems of writing with clarity and grace. . . .

> I feel guilty when I do nothing but listen. I confess my fear that I'm
> too easy, that I have too low standards, to a colleague, Don Graves.
> He assures me I am a demanding teacher, for I see more in my students
> than they do—to their surprise, not mine.
>
> I hear voices from my students they have never heard from them-
> selves. I find they are authorities on subjects they think ordinary. . . .
> It is a matter of faith, faith that my students have something to say and
> a language in which to say it. (1982, pp. 157, 160)

Teaching writing is a matter of faith. We demonstrate that faith when
we listen well, when we refer to our students as writers, when we expect
them to love writing and to pour heart and soul into it. I will never forget,
when I was working with Don Murray on my own writing, how it felt when
he casually made comments such as, "Writers like you . . ." or "When you
send this out. . . ." I held those phrases close to my heart, repeating them
over and over. I remember even more how it felt to have Murray listening
to my ideas and to my teaching, as they lived on my page.

When children receive this kind of listening attention, when their
stories and information and ideas and lives are heard and celebrated
and channeled onto the page in this way, they respond as I did when
Don Murray mailed me a letter addressed to "Author Lucy Calkins." I
saved and framed the envelope, made a gigantic desk out of a wooden door,
and told my friends not to phone on Sundays because that was my writing
day. When we listen intently to children and their subjects, they respond
in similar ways. They race off to get more paper; they toil over a list of all
the chapters they plan to write; they buy themselves new notebooks, and,
gathering around us, say, "Listen to what I've got" and "Will you hear my
story?"

As we move around the room hearing our students' stories, our teaching changes our children—and it changes us. Each child becomes infinitely
precious to us. "What fascinating, amazing kids I have," we think. When
we feel this way, we stand a chance of making a difference in their lives.
"We cannot affect another person unless we are affected by them," my
friend Ralph Peterson, author of *Life in a Crowded Place*, once said, and
it seems to me that he is saying something essential about teaching writing. Yes, we need to bring paper and books and display areas and plants
into our workshops, but the most important thing we need to bring is
ourselves.

When teachers asked the author Avi, "What do we do if our kids
won't write?" Avi answered, "First you have to love them. If you can
convince your children that you love them, then there's nothing you can't

teach them." We fall in love with our students when we know their stories: when we know that Reginald rides the subway for an hour to get to school and sometimes falls asleep during that hour and wakes up to find he's traveled far past his subway stop, when we know that Brian and Sam have organized a club, Project Snuffy, dedicated to the proposition of convincing Brian's parents that he should have a dog of his own, when we learn that Samantha's family takes care of eleven foster children.

The reason that the teaching of writing has become such a powerful force in reforming schools is that once we know Reginald's and Brian's, Sam's and Samantha's stories, these youngsters begin to affect us and our teaching. We cannot avoid seeing them among the sea of children, and when faces and lives and stories emerge, our teaching is forever different. Once Maria sits at the front of her classroom and reads, "The girl is sad. She has no friends," her classroom is never the same again. There is a moment of real eye contact, a moment of person-to-person interaction between Maria and her teacher and between Maria and the other children. The curriculum no longer stands between them, and this changes everything in a school.

These are the wonderful moments when everything clicks. We reach the end of *Where the Red Fern Grows* and for a moment the class is silent, tears glistening in everyone's eyes. Or a cluster of children come in tearfully from recess holding the limp body of a dead chipmunk. They ask if they can have a funeral for the poor chipmunk, and we nod, putting aside the spelling test and math dittos. Or one child reenacts a scene from *James and the Giant Peach* and others join in until the whole class is focused on reliving their favorite story. These moments are the reasons we chose teaching, yet we often arm ourselves against them. We focus so intently on the curriculum that when a child finds a moth fluttering inside his desk, we view the ripples of energy it produces in a classroom as interference. We continue with our curriculum, and the classroom settles back into emotional flatness.

When Maria writes "The girl is sad. She has no friends," and then reads what she has written, all of this changes. Maria is no longer a child reading at such-and-such a grade level; she is no longer a child with such-and-such a score on the achievement test. Maria emerges as herself.

It is not only Maria but also her classmates and her teacher who emerge during this interaction. All of a sudden the curriculum and manuals and kits and workbooks and programs recede, and what comes forward is the relationship between one child and another child, between a child and her teacher.

In the workshop children write about what is alive and vital and real for them—and other writers in the room listen and extend and guide, laugh and cry and marvel.

3
Rehearsal
Living the Writerly Life

My son entered nursery school in the middle of the year, so neither he nor I received a proper introduction to the school's rituals. In particular, we didn't realize that Fridays were for show-and-tell. Apparently, on Miles's first Friday, everyone gathered in a circle. One child had a robot, another a dog that walked and barked, another a Spiderman figure. Only Miles was empty-handed. Each child, in turn, sat in a special chair and showed an item to the admiring circle. Miles's turn came. He took his seat in the special chair. The group looked at him expectantly. "Ummm . . ." Miles said slowly, looking out at the circle. Then he fished around in his pocket. With great seriousness, he produced a little yellow thread from his blanket. "I brought this thread," he said, turning ceremoniously so everyone could see it. Then he began rolling the thread on his hand like a miniature snowball. "If you roll it like this and like this," he said, "you can make a love ball." And Miles gave the love ball to Jonathan, who was becoming his friend.

The next Friday came. Again Miles's companions brought toys that beep and bop, and again, Miles was empty-handed. This time when he reached into his pocket, he produced a small white stone. "In my family, we have memory rocks," he said. "You save a special rock from the top of the mountain, or from the beach, and when you hold it and close your eyes, you can remember the mountaintop and the sea." Then Miles added, "I didn't even know this was a memory rock! I found it in my pocket today. I got it when I went to the big church and it was very boring, so I picked it up from the floor." Squinching his face up, his hand closed around the stone, Miles said, "Now when I close my eyes, I can remember just how boring church really was."

My hope is that in our writing workshops all of us—teachers and children alike—will be able to take the small threads and small stones of experience and of thought, declare them significant, and make something of them.

Finding the Words to Describe the Writing Process

The story of my son turning one of the threads from his blanket into a love ball is one of many metaphors I've used to tell young writers about the writing process. Sometimes I've told children about how the poet Lucille Clifton likens writing to quilting, or I tell them about Naomi Shihab Nye, who writes, in "Valentine for Ernest Mann,"

> You can't order a poem like you order a taco.
> Walk up to the counter, say, "I'll take two"
> and expect it to be handed back to you
> on a shiny plate.
>
> Still, I like your spirit.
> Anyone who says, "Here's my address,
> write me a poem," deserves something in reply.
> So I'll tell you a secret instead:
> poems hide. In the bottoms of our shoes,
> they are sleeping. They are shadows
> drifting across our ceilings the moment
> before we wake up. What we have to do
> is live in a way that lets us find them . . .
>
> Maybe if we re-invent whatever our lives give us,
> we find poems. Check your garage, the odd sock
> in your drawer, the person you almost like, but
> not quite.
>
> And let me know.

Sometimes instead of using metaphor to convey the writing process, I talk to students about research in the field. I tell them, for example, that through the work of scholars such as Donald Murray, Ken Macrorie, Peter Elbow, and Janet Emig, and through what writers report about their composing processes, we have begun to recognize that just as researchers often follow a scientific method, writers often follow a process of craft when they work. Some theorists describe the writing process as prewriting, writing, and rewriting; some speak of circling out and circling back; some of collecting and connecting. I prefer Donald Murray's terms: rehearsal, drafting, revision, and editing.

Whether we write a poem about shadows or an article about a geological expedition, we often move through these same stages. Some of us spend longer on rehearsal, others on revision. Some revisions fit between the lines of a draft, others require a sequence of drafts. We may edit a great deal when working on an expository essay and not at all when writing a letter. Or the opposite may be true. In our own way and at our own pace, most of us follow a cycle in our writing: rehearsal, drafting, revision, and editing. In this chapter, I describe rehearsal; in Chapter 4, I focus on drafting and revision. Later, in Chapter 18, I focus on editing.

Rehearsal: An Overview

For me, rehearsal is, above all, a way of living. People who write regularly live with a sense of "I am one who writes," and this consciousness engenders an extra-susceptibility, an extra-awareness. "Stories happen to those who tell them," Thucydides said. Just as photographers are always seeing potential pictures, so too, writers see potential stories and poems and essays everywhere and gather them in entries and jotted notes. This is rehearsal.

"What do you do when you sit down to write a picture book?" I recently asked Karla Kuskin, the award-winning author of *The Philharmonic Gets Dressed* and *Near the Window Tree: Poems and Notes*.

"I *don't* sit down to write," she answered. "My writing starts with catching glimpses and snatches." Then, to explain, Kuskin added, "On my way here, I saw a big, beautiful yellow truck with a sign, 'Manhasset Imperial Sewage.' I noticed it, and that sign may become the seed of a story." Then Kuskin went on to say, "*The Philharmonic Gets Dressed* began on my daughter's birthday when she lifted up the dress on her new doll to check out its underpants. Watching her, I suddenly remembered my childhood fascination with underwear, and the chant, "I see London, I see France, I see Karla's underpants' . . . and my book began."

Karla Kuskin is not alone. After reviewing hundreds of interviews with writers for his *Writers at Work* series, Malcolm Cowley says that although each writer's process is idiosyncratic, each writer begins with a precious particle and then grows meaning from it. This is true for Cynthia Voigt, whose trilogy about Dicey and her family began when Voigt saw the strained faces of some children as they sat alone in a parked car outside a mall, peering out into the parking lot. It is true for Betsy Byars, who says in her memoir (1991) that her books grow out of drawers full of clippings and letters and jotted notes and photographs. "It's a mystery why I kept a clipping about a man who ate thirty-nine watermelons or this photograph of two beagles in sombreros or this story about a woman who put her very old hamster into the freezer to give him a merciful death," she says, but then adds, "Plenty of good scraps are as important in writing a book as in the making of a quilt" (pp. 26, 39). Patricia MacLachlan talks about her writing process by likening herself to Cassie, the heroine in *Cassie Binegar,* who hides under a huge, ugly tablecloth in order to study what feet reveal about the people conversing above her. "I am possessed by the image of that child," MacLachlan says, "hiding under the tablecloth in order to watch and listen and become a writer, peering at truths from a safe place." Then she adds, "I know that child because I was that child, studying the world in order to learn who I was and how I fit in" (1993).

The Writer's Notebook as a Tool for Rehearsal

The recognition that writing begins not as deskwork but as lifework has radical implications for how we and our students rehearse for writing. Whereas some educators imagine that rehearsal for writing begins with listing and choosing among topics, brainstorming ideas, mapping alternative forms, and experimenting with various leads, most writers say that rehearsal for writing is not a string of exercises that warms up a writer just prior to the process of drafting but a way of life. Rehearsal is not even something that occurs in conjunction with any one piece of writing; it is a state of readiness out of which one writes.

The best way to develop the kind of wide-awakeness that is so fundamental to the writing life is to write often. Throughout the field of teaching writing, one educator after another has begun to advocate that students jot down things they notice and wonder about, their memories and ideas, their favorite words and responses to reading into a container of some sort. Donald Murray speaks of that container as a day book, Donald Graves as a journal, Betsy Byars as a bureau drawer, and my colleagues and I as a writer's notebook, but in each instance, these containers differ from the popular understanding of journals. Whether one calls them a day book, a bureau drawer, or a notebook, they are, above all, places for *rehearsal.* They are seed beds out of which rough drafts grow.

The poet Donald Hall has written an autobiographical work he calls *String Too Short to Be Saved.* I like to think of a writer's notebook as a collection of strings too short to save. It's a place for bits of life that may or may not emerge someday as major pieces of writing. When our youngsters begin the writing process by collecting bits and pieces—entries—in their notebooks rather than by listing and choosing among possible topics for writing, they are more apt to experience writing as a process of growing meaning. Instead of entering writing with a subject in hand that already

FIGURE 3–1   Angelica's entry

Once I saw a tulip in something and always wondered if it rained if it would fill up with water, then I saw a[n] image, it was a tulip filled with water and somebody drinking it

feels big enough to be a story or an essay, Angelica begins with this entry (Figure 3–1):

> Once I saw a tulip in something and always wondered if it rained if it would fill up with water, then I saw a[n] image, it was a tulip filled with water and somebody drinking it.

Michelle has used her notebook in a similar way—to record a tiny flash of her imagination, a moment she would not have put onto the page had her teacher said, "Choose a topic for a story." She wrote:

> Will I ever do a Diet Coke commercial since it's my favorite drink or will I open myself to prune juice?

If Michelle or Angelica had begun writing by choosing a topic for a story, she wouldn't have written about drinking water from a tulip or wondering whether she'd make commercials for prune juice. They have written about these tiny morsels of life because the notebook has served as a tool that encourages them to do so.

Whereas Michelle and Angelica will probably take these seed ideas and gather more related entries in their notebooks before they try their hand at rough drafts, Dan, a second grader in Kathy Mason's classroom, has already starred the following two entries (Figure 3–2):

> WHAT HAPPENED?
>
> What happened to the dinosaurs?
> What happened to the ice man?

FIGURE 3–2 Dan's starred entries

What happend?
What happend to the dinosaurs?
What happend to the ice man?

What happend to my brother?
What happend to my dad's time?
What happend to my moms time?
I guss all just sit here
With no parents to hug me
and give me love. I feel
licke a little orphan Boy.
I wish they had time to
spend time with me
like othre parents do.

The worlds exploding
People are fihting People
are having wars. Familes
are Breaking up. Poeple
are stealing things. People
our killing People. People
are Dying. Poepl make
Povlootion. Peopl are makeing
too much Buildings
What I mean the
Worlds exploding

What happened to my brother?
What happened to my dad's time?
What happened to my mom's time?
I guess I'll just sit here
With no parents to hug me,
and give me love.
I feel like a little orphan boy.
I wish they had time to spend with me
Like other parents do.

THE WORLD'S EXPLODING

People are fighting
People are having wars
Families are breaking up
People are stealing things
People are killing people
People are dying
People make pollution
People are making too much buildings.
What I mean . . .
The world's exploding.

Dan wants to make something of these pieces. His revision process will involve polishing these rough drafts into finished pieces of writing.

Michelle, Angelica, and Dan all came to their classroom and to their writing desk without drawers full of good scraps, without precious particles.

Like many of our students, they had never grown stories or essays out of what they saw and remembered and wondered about. For this reason they probably didn't enter the class with a writer's eye, already seeing potential stories in their lives. Instead, they told us, "My life is boring" and "I have nothing to write about." Although Thucydides' words, "Stories happen to those who tell them," are true, the reverse is also true. Stories don't happen to those who don't perceive of themselves as story makers, reporters, poets, or essayists. And so when my colleagues and I work with youngsters, often our first goal is to fill these youngsters with a sense of "I've got so much to say" and "My life is full of possible stories."

The First Days: Introducing Our Students to the Writing Workshop and to the Writer's Wide-Awakeness

Isoke Nia, one of the staff members of the Teachers College Writing Project, recently gathered a group of youngsters around her. From her knobby, handwoven satchel, Isoke pulled out a black book. Perhaps it was the way Isoke cradled the book in her arms, perhaps it was the way the book itself looked, with its corners covered in a bold African fabric; I don't know. But I do know that the book seemed alive. "What do you suppose I have in here?" Isoke asked.

"Words," a child said.

I might have been impatient with that answer, wanting an answer more specific than "words." But Isoke, a wiser teacher than I, instead reached out to cherish that child's suggestion. "Words," she repeated. "Words." She spoke as if this was the most precious gem in the world. "Yes, I have words. Words. And what else?"

Others in the group probably gained confidence when they saw that their friend's guess had been well received, because now there was a flurry of suggestions.

"Stories."

"Memories."

"Poems."

"Yes, yes," Isoke answered, holding the notebook closer in her arms as if each suggestion reminded her again of the riches contained in it. "And what else?"

"Secrets."

"Secrets," Isoke said. "Secrets. And?" She turned the pages of her notebook, and those closest to her craned their necks to see inside.

The children spoke quickly, their voices piling on top of each other. "Purple ink." "Snapshots." "Newspaper clippings." "A dried flower." "Lists."

Isoke continued to cradle her notebook, and it seemed as if she was also cradling each of the ideas the children had given her, and each of the children. "My notebook has all of my life in it because I keep my notebook beside me always," she said. "I don't carry those cute little purses some women carry because I need a bag that is big enough to hold my notebook. I needed my notebook to be there after I left my daughter off at college last week, and I told her father to drive because I had some thinking to do. And I needed my notebook to be there after I saw a homeless woman filling a line of paper plates with food for a swarm of homeless cats." And she continued to demonstrate the way writing weaves through all of her life. "The other night at a dinner party I didn't have my notebook, and the speeches made me remember so many things that I had to borrow everybody's napkins to write on," she said, and opened her notebook to the pages onto which she'd taped her napkin notes.

Isoke used this writing workshop as a time to demonstrate the role writing plays in her life and to invite students to join her in living the writerly life. In doing this, Isoke relied on the theory of language development that parents of young children know instinctively. Mothers and fathers don't drill their toddlers on blends and word endings but instead engage them in purposeful conversations, fully expecting that their children will convey meaning as best they can. So too, Isoke didn't drill her students on the component skills of good writing or on possible rehearsal strategies but instead invited the students to join her in using writing in genuine, purposeful ways.

Within a few days, each of Isoke's students will have brought in his or her own notebook and many will have added magazine pictures, fabric, postcards, or drawings to their covers as a way of saying, "This is my book. This is my life."

But this won't happen accidentally. It will happen because Isoke knows that when she launches a writing workshop, she needs to be sure that notebooks become a valued tool in her students' lives. She'll help her students realize that choosing one's own perfect notebook is an enormous decision, and she'll show them the diversity of choices available to them. She'll watch for the one child who begins to personalize her notebook with a careful drawing, a photograph, a quote to live by . . . and she'll make a big fuss over this. She'll watch for the one child who invents a bag for his notebook or finds a way to clip the notebook onto his belt or makes a small portable satellite notebook to carry with him to lunch . . . and she'll make a big fuss over this, too. She may ask everyone who has chosen a notebook to wave them overhead so she can admire all their gorgeous, precious books.

Just as Isoke knows (even before it happens) that a few of her students will bond with their notebooks immediately, she also knows (even before it happens) that a few will leave their notebooks at home or tear out pages to use for their math homework. Both extremes will become opportunities for teaching. When half the class has forgotten their notebooks, Isoke may go to one of the students and (acting as if she doesn't recognize the extent of the problem) she may stop in her tracks, open-mouthed in amazement and say, "You *forgot* your notebook?" Turning to the class she might say, "Oh no, what will Diana *do* without her notebook? Geez, that is awful . . . I am *so sorry*. . . . Is there someone at home who could bring it in?" What Isoke will *not* do is to reassure the student by saying, "That's okay. Write on loose-leaf paper for now and paste it in your notebook tomorrow." Isoke is establishing norms in her classroom. She does this not by listing her expectations on the chalkboard but by living as if they already existed.

During the first few weeks in the writing workshop especially, Isoke will need to show children what it means to carry a notebook with them everywhere and to jot in it often. When children ready themselves to see a film or hear a guest speaker or listen to a story, Isoke will want to be sure she has her notebook open and her pen poised, and she'll want to search through the class, asking, "Where are your notebooks? How can you listen without having your notebook there to catch the ideas and memories and facts that interest you?" At the end of the day, when Isoke wonders if any of her students have remembered to pack their notebooks in their knapsacks, she'll probably say, "I've got my notebook in my bag, and I know you all have yours in your packs and purses. Tomorrow and every day, let's begin by sharing the wonderful noticings and memories and words and ideas we've each put into our notebooks the night before." Isoke acts as if writing is the most important thing in the world to her students, and she refers to them as authors, because she wants her students to be members of what researcher Frank Smith calls "the literacy club."

"We get our identities," Smith says, "not by looking in the bathroom mirror and asking, 'Who am I?' but by the clubs we belong to, the groups we're members of" (1988). The teacher of literacy sponsors a club, a conversation, in his or her classroom, and then does everything possible to bring students into that conversation and that community.

Each of us, as teachers, will need to invent our own ways of launching our writing workshops. In *Living Between the Lines,* I tell about how my colleagues and I often begin the workshop by asking students to push back the desks and form a storytelling circle. When we want to invite and cajole our students to bring their memories, treasures, and noticings into the storytelling circle, we often begin by reading aloud a book such as Mem Fox's *Wilfrid Gordon McDonald Partridge,* in which the old people living in a nursing home find that everyday bits of their lives—chicken eggs and shells—hold memories. "What treasures from *your* lives hold memories?" we ask. In the reading list at the end of this chapter I have included books that could, in a similar fashion, evoke stories and memories. In *Living Between the Lines,* I tell about how Shelley Harwayne, a colleague, used her own memories to invite storytelling. She told a circle of children about how her mother had used dried bones from a chicken's neck as jacks and a roll of cow hairs as a ball when she was a child. When Shelley finished telling her story, she asked, "Does my story bring out any memories of stories you've heard in your family or images of anything you've made?" And then, of course, the circle was filled with the contagious energy that comes from a tumbling richness of stories, one resonating against another. There were exclamations of, "That happened to me, too," and "Wow, did you *really* do that?" and there was in the room a growing sense of "what a group we are" and "what lives, what stories." Later, after a week or more of sharing stories in the whole group and in small groups, Shelley said, "We've got *so much* to say . . . why don't we each begin gathering some of these amazing bits in writers' notebooks?"

In her book *In the Middle,* Nancie Atwell (1987) writes about how she began a writing workshop by inviting her students to join her in living the literate life. She drew her eighth graders around her and said, "I'm a writer and a reader. Writing and reading and teaching them to you are my life." Nancie describes her teaching this way:

> I write with my students. I show them my drafts. I ask for their responses in writing conferences. I tell them writing is a new habit, one that is changing my life. I tear my hair over my writing, but I keep on writing because I can't stop.
>
> I read with my students. I show them what I'm reading and I talk about and lend my books. I tell them reading is an old habit, one that shaped my life and gives it so much meaning I don't know if I could go on living if I suddenly couldn't read. . . . I love these things so much I can't imagine that my students won't love them, too. From the first day

of school I expect they'll participate in written language as real writers and readers do—as I do. (pp. 48, 49)

Each of us, as teachers, will constantly need to reinvent our own ways of inviting students to live like writers. But we will all draw on some of the principles that underlie what Isoke Nia, Shelley Harwayne, and Nancie Atwell have done. During the first days of their writing workshops, each of these teachers invited students to join them in collecting "drawers full of scraps," in seeing their lives as full of precious particles—they invited their students to come together as a richly literate community.

Good teaching is very rich, and I want to pause for a moment to name and savor some of the lessons that can be learned from these glimpses of teaching.

- When we teach writing, we will probably not begin by talking *about* writing, but rather, by demonstrating the power and purposes writing has in our lives, and by inviting students to discover ways that writing can enrich their lives as well.
- Rehearsal for writing *can* involve brainstorming possible topics or mapping possible directions for a piece, but the more important thing is that students realize rehearsal involves living wide-awake lives—seeing, hearing, noticing, wondering—and gathering all of this in bureau drawers or notebooks or daybooks.
- Teachers help students to see and value the precious particles in their lives not by giving lectures and assignments, but by demonstrating this quality of attentiveness in our own lives and by establishing rituals in our classrooms that encourage it in our students' lives.
- Our teaching conveys messages of which we're not even aware. We may think our teaching is, above all, informing students about how the little things an author sees can ignite an idea for a story, but our most important lesson may, in fact, be carried instead by the way we call our students together: "*Authors,* let's gather in a circle," or by the way we refer to Robert McCloskey, as "an author, like you."
- At the beginning of the school year and of the writing workshop, each teacher must, above all, build a learning community. By paying careful attention to the tone of our teaching, we can establish an atmosphere of graciousness and care and respect in our classrooms.

Rituals That Encourage Students to Write Often Throughout Their Lives

When we teach writing, we first establish simple, predictable writing work-shops and then move about the classroom extending what our students do. Our teaching is characterized not by the words we say but by the ongoing structures and rituals that shape the writing workshop. I will describe these ongoing structures in great detail in Section III, but for now it is enough to say that once a writing workshop is under way, we will want to institute a few carefully chosen rituals that will help students see their lives as full of invitations to write. Since Isoke wants her students to write in their note-books every night, she is wise to institute a morning ritual of sharing, with a partner, whatever one has written the night before. This ritual will exert a much stronger influence on her students than anything she could say to them. Whereas Isoke and her students begin by opening their notebooks and sharing their entries, other classroom communities may decide to begin the day in silence, while members of the class take time to record their lives and their thoughts on the page. Still other classrooms may begin with a variation of show-and-tell, with students meeting in small groups to share and to savor the stuff of their lives.

Betty Lyons, a first-grade teacher in Manhasset, Long Island, begins many of her autumn writing workshops with "Notebook News." "Who has tried something new in their notebook?" she asks, in order to launch each session of Notebook News. "My brother told a joke and so I put it in my notebook," one child says. "I found a box of wrapping paper at my grandma's house and made a cover for my notebook," another child says, and adds, "and I got my grandma to put down the song she sang me when I was a baby." Yet another child tells of riding the subway with a notebook in hand. When young writers share the ways they weave notebooks into their lives, their teacher doesn't need to spend her time lecturing them on the value of writing often, for varied reasons, and in various places.

Other teachers have invented still other rituals for encouraging students to write in their notebooks. Some teachers begin each class meeting, at least in the autumn of the year, by hearing about and celebrating the diversity in their students' notebooks. "How many of you have written a very, very short entry—a line, a word, a little list?" The children raise their hands high, celebrating what they have done, even if it is just a single word. "How many of you have written an entry that reached all the way to the bottom of your page *and* went around to yet another page?" "How many of you have written about a memory? a question? something you've noticed? a dream? a book? How many of you have written a poem? a letter? a plan? a story?"

Some teachers celebrate the diverse ways in which students choose to rehearse for writing by suggesting that every writer read aloud a single word from his or her notebook. This happens quickly, so that first one writer reads into the circle, then the next, and then the next, until the classroom fills up with the bits of life that are there, in the notebooks. One of the wonderful things about this ritual is that it allows teachers to accept and to celebrate *whatever* students do. When a child brings us a notebook with just a single word in it, the brilliant teachers of the world say, "What a word!" and they say, "It's such a *big* word, isn't it?" Later, there will be times and ways for saying, "You can do so much more than this," but at the start of the year, when we're most apt to feel overwhelmed by all that our students do not yet know, the wisest thing is to celebrate and extend.

Still other teachers suggest that each notebook be opened to a particular page and laid out in great ceremony as part of a Notebook Museum, and that all the writers in the room move about admiring the different ways in which writers use their notebooks to rehearse for writing. Later, these students will gather to respond to the questions "What did you notice?" and "What new idea will you try, based on what you saw today?"

I have referred to the Notebook Museum or to Notebook News not as *activities*, but as *rituals*. Wise teachers know that using any one of these ideas, often and with variations, is far more powerful than using all of them. For example, the writers who display their notebooks in a museum and take note of what others have done can eventually use this ritual for very specific purposes. Students can form a museum for displaying long entries, and they can be encouraged to study what others have done. Who has written long entries? What can we notice by paying attention to those entries? What questions do we want to ask the authors of those entries?

Because these ideas are best used as rituals, teachers will want to select from among them carefully, and to imagine ways to make the ritual significant in the classroom and to keep it alive over time. Although it may not be wise to have a museum display at the start of every day's writing workshop, this may be a wonderful way to begin or end each week. Alternatively, perhaps the idea of a museum is best used when it fits whatever is on the front burner of the classroom community. In Chapter 20, I suggest that as teachers, we will also want to think about how a ritual that works in the writing workshop might be used later within the math or social studies or science curriculum.

Our writing workshops will always be shaped by a few carefully chosen rituals and structures, but this is particularly necessary at the start of the year. As all of us know and all of us forget, everything is particularly difficult at the start of a writing workshop. We cannot assume that students know how to gather in a circle or how to answer their own questions ("Pen or pencil?" "Two sides of the page or one?" "Page numbers or no page numbers?"). So it is particularly important, at the start of the year, that we institute only a few rituals and structures in the classroom and take the time to attend to these with care. If our teaching is too complicated, we focus on our lesson plans rather than on our students.

Recommended Literature on Launching Notebook Writing and Inviting Students to Live as Writers

Children's Literature

Aragon, Jane Chelsea. *Salt hands.* New York: E. P. Dutton, 1989.

Arnosky, James. *Secrets of a wildlife watcher.* New York: Lothrop, Lee & Shepard, 1983.

Avi. *Nothing but the truth: A documentary novel.* New York: Orchard Books, 1991.

Baylor, Byrd. *The best town in the world.* New York: Aladdin Books, 1982.

————. *The other way to listen.* New York: Macmillan, 1978.

————. *The way to start a day.* New York: Charles Scribner's Sons, 1978.

————. *Your own best secret place.* New York: Macmillan, 1991.

Bliss, Corinne Demas. *Matthew's meadow.* San Diego: Harcourt Brace Jovanovich, 1992.

Blyler, Allison. *Finding foxes.* New York: Philomel Books, 1991.

Booth, David. *Til all the stars have fallen.* New York: Viking Children's Books, 1990.

Brinckloe, Julie. *Fireflies.* New York: Macmillan Children's Book Group, 1985.

Carlstrom, Nancy. *Light: Stories of a small bright kindness.* Boston: Little, Brown, 1990.

Charlip, Remy, and Jerry Joyner. *Thirteen*. New York: Macmillan, 1984.

Cisneros, Sandra. *The house on Mango Street*. New York: Vintage Books, 1989.

Collins, Pat Lowery. *I am an artist*. New York: Millbrook Press, 1992.

DeSaix, Frank. *The girl who danced with dolphins*. New York: Farrar, Straus & Giroux, 1991.

DeFelice, Cynthia. *When Grampa kissed his elbow*. New York: Macmillan, 1992.

Fleischman, Paul. *Rondo in C*. New York: HarperCollins Children's Books, 1988.

Fox, Mem. *Wilfrid Gordon McDonald Partridge*. Brooklyn, NY: Kane/Miller Book Publishers, 1989.

George, Jean Craighead. *Dear Rebecca, Winter is here*. New York: HarperCollins, 1993.

Goffstein, M. B. *Family scrapbook*. New York: Farrar, Straus & Giroux, 1978.

Goldstein, Bobbye. *Inner chimes: Poems on poetry*. New York: Boyds Mills Press, 1992.

Golenbock, Peter. *Teammates*. San Diego: Harcourt Brace Jovanovich, 1992.

Greenfield, Eloise. *First pink light*. New York: Black Butterfly Children's Books, 1976.

Greenfield, Eloise, and Lessie Jones Little. *Childtimes*. New York: Thomas Y. Crowell, 1979.

Hall, Donald. *The man who lived alone*. Boston: Godine, 1984.

Hartmann, Wendy. *All the magic in the world*. New York: Dutton Children's Books, 1993.

Innocenti, Roberto. *Rose Blanche*. New York: Stewart Tabori & Chang, 1991.

Klein, Robin. *Penny Pollard's diary*. New York: Oxford University Press, 1987.

Lasky, Kathryn. *My island grandma*. New York: F. Warne, 1979.

Little, Jean. *Hey world, here I am!* New York: HarperCollins Children's Books, 1989.

MacLachlan, Patricia. *Through Grandpa's eyes*. New York: HarperCollins, 1980.

McCloskey, Robert. *Time of wonder*. New York: Puffin Books, 1989.

McLerran, Alice. *Roxaboxen.* New York: Lothrop, Lee & Shepard, 1990.

Merriam, Eve. *The wise woman and her secret.* New York: Simon & Schuster Books for Young Readers, 1991.

Mills, Patricia. *Until the cows come home.* New York: North-South Books, 1993.

Ray, Deborah. *Star-gazing sky.* New York: Crown Publishers, 1991.

Reading Is Fundamental. *Once upon a time.* New York: Crown Books for Young Readers, 1991.

Ringold, Faith. *Tar beach.* New York: Crown Books for Young Readers, 1991.

Ryder, Joanne. *Step into the night.* New York: Macmillan Children's Book Group, 1988.

Rylant, Cynthia. *All I see.* New York: Orchard Books, 1988.

———. *Soda jerk.* New York: Orchard Books, 1990.

———. *Waiting to waltz: A childhood.* Scarsdale, NY: Bradbury Press, 1984.

Zolotow, Charlotte. *Snippets.* New York: HarperCollins Children's Books, 1993.

Professional Literature

Bomer, Randy. *A time for meaning: Learning literacy with people aged 10–20.* Portsmouth, NH: Heinemann, in press.

Calkins, Lucy McCormick, with Shelley Harwayne. *Living between the lines.* Portsmouth, NH: Heinemann, 1991.

Dillard, Annie. *The writing life.* New York: Harper & Row, 1989.

Elbow, Peter. *Writing with power: Techniques for mastering the writing process.* New York: Oxford University Press, 1981.

Goldberg, Natalie. *Wild mind: Living the writer's life.* New York: Bantam, 1990.

Harwayne, Shelley. *Lasting impressions: Weaving literature into the writing workshop.* Portsmouth, NH: Heinemann, 1992.

Heard, Georgia. *For the good of the earth and sun.* Portsmouth, NH: Heinemann, 1989.

Hopkins, Lee Bennett. *Pass the poetry please.* New York: HarperCollins Children's Books, 1987.

Jackson, Jacqueline. *Turn not pale, beloved snail.* Boston: Little, Brown, 1974.

Murray, Donald. *Expecting the unexpected: Teaching myself—and others—to read and write.* Portsmouth, NH: Boynton/Cook–Heinemann, 1989.

4
Drafting and Revision
Letting Our Words Instruct and Surprise Us

When I finished writing the text of the first edition of this book, I turned my attention to the acknowledgments. I turned out pages and pages thanking all my colleagues. Then, when I was almost done, I knew it was time to thank my husband. I picked up my pen and wrote, "My thanks go to my husband, John Skorpen, for not minding the long hours of deskwork, for supporting me as I toil away. . . ." Sitting back, I reread what I'd written: "My thanks go to . . . John . . . for *not minding* the long hours of deskwork," and thought, "This is hogwash." I looked back through the lens of those early words to John and thought, "So what *do* I have to thank him for?" This time, I picked up my pen and wrote,

> Although it is traditional to end the Acknowledgments with a paragraph giving special thanks to one's spouse for not protesting over the long hours of deskwork, I want, instead, to thank my husband, John Skorpen, for calling me away from the desk. I'm grateful for the days of hiking in the Wind River Range and of exploring Caribbean islands, and I am grateful for the quiet adventures with our cat, dog, home, and family. (xi)

This is why I write. I put words on the page in order to use them as a lens, in order to look through them to what I want to say. I often begin by writing the clichéd, expected phrases ("My thanks go to my husband, John Skorpen, for not minding the long hours") but then, pulling back, I realize that no, these words aren't exactly honest, and so I focus in again to try to tell the truth. This, to me, is the writing process. I shift between drafting and revision frequently as I write. For me, revision does not mean repairing a draft; it means using the writing I have already done to help me see more, feel more, think more, learn more.

Exploratory Writing in the Notebook:
Moving Between Drafts and Revision

Because I approach the blank page knowing that at this stage, the words I write are meant to give me a leg up toward what I want to say, I don't fret over whether I'm writing well. Like an artist at a sketch pad, I try to capture the contours and nuances of my subject. I write quickly, since nothing is permanent. This is drafting. "Get it down," William Faulkner writes. "Take chances. It may be bad, but it is the only way you can do anything really good." And so I write notebook entries about silly worries, about small moments, about uninspired ideas . . . but as I write these, I'm leaning forward to learn. I know these entries are meant as beginnings. I'm watching for something to snag my curiosity, to move me.

When an entry or a line catches my attention, I may decide to see if I can develop it, to see if I can grow something out of it. And so I tend to dedicate a few pages of my notebook, a few days of my writing life, to pursuing that one subject. I write, watch, remember, read, talk, question, imagine, pretend . . . and all of this writing brings new layers of meaning around my original idea. This, to me, is what the writing process is all about.

Later, I decide to take bits of this writing and turn them into a poem, a speech, a chapter. Now revision changes. As Murray says in *Learning by Teaching* (1982), "The writing stands apart from the writer, and the writer interacts with it, first to find out what the writing has to say, and then to help the writing say it clearly and gracefully." Now as I listen to language, I attend to the rhythm of words, I trim away excess.

One Child's Writing Process

Jennifer is eight. She'd already gathered lots of entries when my friend Laurie Pessah came alongside her desk, and she'd already decided which ones mattered most to her—those about her younger brother being a pest. With Laurie's help, Jennifer folded over a page in her notebook to create a divider, wrote "My Brother Is a Pest" on the folded page, and began collecting entries about her topic. In one entry she recorded her brother's birthday and horoscope, recalled an incident when, as a toddler, he had run around the house dragging toilet paper in hopes that someone would wipe his bottom, and discussed the way her brother and his friends get into trouble together. In another entry, she remembered one time when her brother had saved her from unfair punishment. After writing this entry, Jennifer crossed out the last three words of her initial title, "My Brother Is

FIGURE 4–1 Jennifer's poem "My Brother Is a Bother"

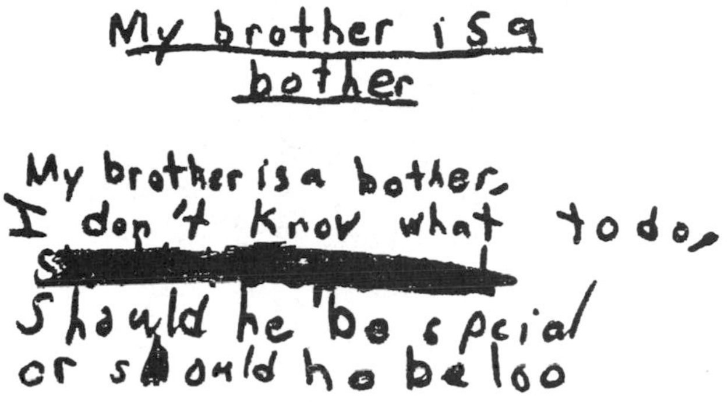

My brother is a
bother

My brother is a bother.
I don't know what to do,
Should he be special
or should he be loo

a Pest," so that it now read "My Brother." Then she returned to her work, gathering and rethinking memories of her life with her little brother. She wrote about a time when she and her brother were locked out of their apartment. Her brother raced up and down the apartment stairwell until finally he slipped and hurt his leg, and Jennifer tried to comfort him.

Luckily, after about a week of gathering these entries and rethinking her relationship with her brother, Jennifer's teacher urged her to ask, "What do I want to make of all this?" Jennifer reread her entries and decided to make an anthology of poems about her brother. She started to do so (Figure 4–1):

MY BROTHER IS A BOTHER

My brother is a bother,
I don't know what to do,
Should he be special
Or should he be loo

The irony is that although Jennifer had spent a week gathering together little vignettes about her brother, when it came time to draft a poem, she laid all her entries aside and wrote in the silly rhymes that constituted her image of poetry. In a conference, Laurie Pessah suggested that Jennifer needed to regard her entries as dough rolled out before her: "Pretend you have cookie-cutters, poetry-cutters. Lift out the poemlike parts from your entries," she said, "and then reshape them." Laurie also gave Jennifer some published poems to read. Ten days later Jennifer had revised and edited her anthology. By this time, she'd also changed the title of her anthology again. Instead of naming it "My Brother the Bother" or even just "My Brother," she named it "I Love Him Anyways." Here are three of her poems (see also Figure 4–2):

LOCKED OUT

Jonathan
do you remember
we were locked out?
Sitting
looking down
lonely
you had me
I had you.
Running down the stairs
like the flash
you tripped and fell.
I got scared.
I tried to calm you
like a mother
calms her baby.
You sprained your ankle
limping along.
I'm glad you're all right.

CURTAIN DOWN

Jonathan
do you remember
you knocked down
the curtain?
It fell all the way down
as if the sky was falling.

I was punished
you could have been freed.
After a while
you confessed
and you set me free.

THE BATHROOM LESSON

Jonathan
do you remember
going to the bathroom?
Not knowing how to wipe.

You ran
around the house
with the end of the tissue
hanging
like a long, long tail.

Looking for mommy
to show you what to do.
I would have helped you
but you went
to mom and dad.

Our students' writing will not always occur in the sequence that Jennifer's writing demonstrates. Sometimes writers will bypass their notebooks altogether. They may read a published poem, or imagine a poem, or live a poem, and then sit down with an empty page in front of them and produce a poem. Sometimes the purpose for writing will come first, such as a contest deadline or a grandmother's birthday, which could prompt a child to reread her notebook looking for material for the particular project. Then, too, occasionally a youngster will write an entry or a draft that seems publishable just as it is.

Although the lifeline of Jennifer's writing should not be regarded as a model for every student, I think it is worth lingering over what Jennifer has done because I would want to encourage most of my students, especially in grades two and higher, to experiment with processes that are somewhat similar to hers.

One thing to notice is that there was no starting or finishing point to Jennifer's rehearsal for writing. Like writers the world over, Jennifer lives with a writer's wide-awakeness. She writes often, using whatever material she has

FIGURE 4–2   Poems from Jennifer's anthology

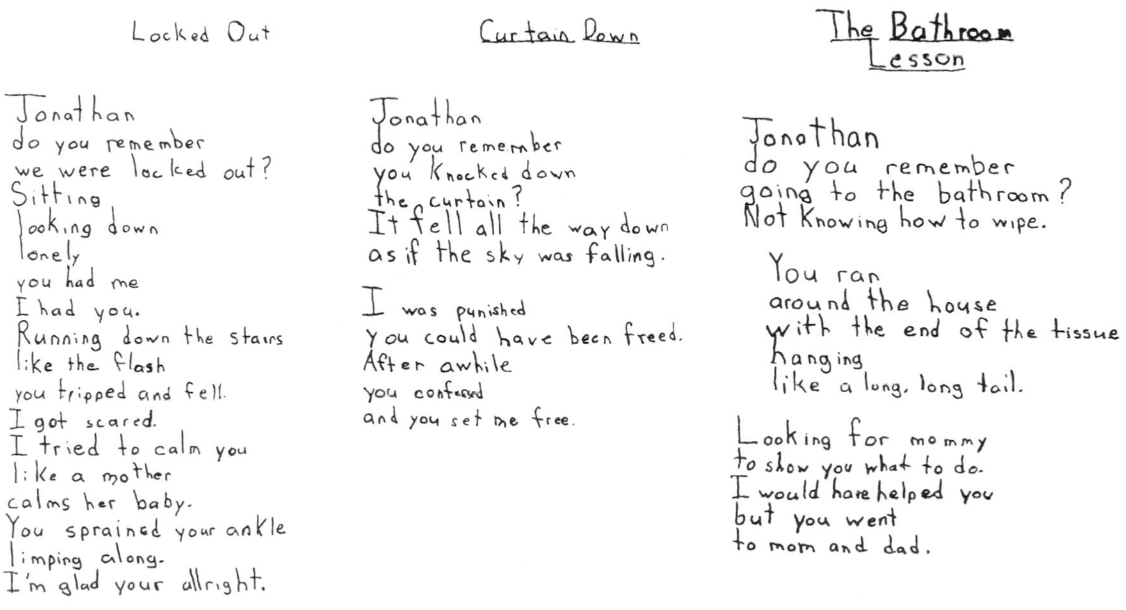

Locked Out

Jonathan
do you remember
we were locked out?
Sitting
looking down
lonely
you had me
I had you.
Running down the stairs
like the flash
you tripped and fell.
I got scared.
I tried to calm you
like a mother
calms her baby.
You sprained your ankle
limping along.
I'm glad your allright.

Curtain Down

Jonathan
do you remember
you knocked down
the curtain?
It fell all the way down
as if the sky was falling.

I was punished
you could have been freed.
After awhile
you confused
and you set me free.

The Bathroom Lesson

Jonathan
do you remember
going to the bathroom?
Not knowing how to wipe.

You ran
around the house
with the end of the tissue
hanging
like a long, long tail.

Looking for mommy
to show you what to do.
I would have helped you
but you went
to mom and dad.

at hand. As she gathers entries in her notebook (or on napkins and loose papers), she knows they may become material for major pieces of writing. All along her notebook feels very different from a conventional journal. The notebook becomes especially powerful, however, after Jennifer reads through her entries and decides she'll gather them around a particular topic, "My Brother Is a Pest." Now every entry Jennifer selects is about her brother. This was easy for Jennifer, but it may not always be easy for all our students.

When Youngsters Don't Know How to Collect Entries About Their Subjects

Often our students will choose entries they like and a topic that matters, yet neither they nor we will be able to imagine generating more entries about that particular topic. Recently, some teachers and I encountered this problem. "Anna," I said, pulling my chair alongside a tiny Latina child, "what are you up to?" She glanced shyly at me and then watched with solemn eyes as four observing teachers joined us. Speaking in a tiny whisper, Anna said, "I was just trying to write an entry." Looking at her notebook, I saw that she already had an extensive collection of entries. "Do you want to write a new entry," I asked, "or do you want to move toward a poem or a story?"

Anna looked at me and said, "But . . ." I thought she was asking, "How?" Putting my hand on Anna's arm, I turned for a moment to the other teachers. "I'm going to help Anna find an entry in her notebook that she wants to develop."

Returning to Anna, I said, "Anna, my friend, I want to show you what I do with my notebook. After I've collected entries for a few weeks, like you have here, I reread my notebook thinking, 'What's in here that catches my heart? What's in here that matters especially?'" Anna and I turned to the first pages of her notebook and began retracing her journey. "Sometimes it's not a whole entry, even, that catches my attention. Sometimes it's a few lines, part of an entry." I suggested that Anna take her time rereading and rethinking what she'd written. Ten minutes later she was at my side. "I found it," she said. The observing teachers and I repositioned ourselves so we could see what she'd chosen. There had been some poignant entries in Anna's notebook, and we were eager to see her choice. This was the one Anna had selected (Figure 4–3):

> Yesterday I was in a restaurant and I saw my friend Luisa. I said "Hi" and she said "Hi." Then I finished eating and I played with her. I said I have to leave and then she said "OK." When I got home I was looking at TV then it was time to go to bed. So I brushed my teeth and went to sleep.

FIGURE 4–3   Anna's entry

The Restarnt

Yesterday I was in a resturnt
and I saw my friend Luisa
I said Hi and she said Hi
then I finsh eating and I.
Playd with her. I said I have to
kv and then she said ok when I
got home I was looking at tv then
it was time to go to bed. So I bursh
my teeth and whent to sleep

After glancing at the entry, the observing teachers eyed each other and me skeptically. I could read their minds, for their question was mine as well: "Does it really make sense for Anna to write more entries based on *this* entry?" I wanted to say, "Anna, could I look through your notebook again?" and I wanted to draw her attention to other entries I'd liked in her notebook, but the presence of the observing teachers made me a better teacher than usual. Looking at Anna's entry, I thought, "If someone had asked me, 'Do you *really* want to write about your son using your T-shirt as a pretend blanket?' I would have answered, 'You're right. It's a silly entry,' and I would have felt empty-handed all over again." Writing begins with a leap of faith, with a decision to make meaning from a chosen thread, and the truth of the matter is that *anything* can start us on the road toward significance.

Looking at Anna, I realized something else as well. She'd chosen this entry as her most significant. She'd looked through pages of other entries and chosen this one. Clearly, it had layers of significance I couldn't see. And so I took a leap of faith that matched hers.

"It's big, isn't it?" I said. Anna's eyes filled with tears, and she nodded. I waited for her to say more, but she just sat there. And so I paraphrased what she'd written in hopes this would draw out more of the story. "You went into the deli," I said, my voice trailing off so that she would take over telling the story.

Anna looked at me. I waited. She continued to look at me.

"And you said 'hi' and she said 'hi' . . ." I said, again letting my voice trail off so she could pick up the thread of the story.

Anna looked at me.

I thought, "This isn't working," so I tried a different tack. "Anna," I said, looking into her eyes. "Anna, I can tell this is *really* big." I paused. "But Anna, can you tell me, what's the big thing about it?"

Slowly, the story came out. Apparently, Anna had gone into a restaurant and seen her one and only friend in this country sitting with someone else. With fear in her stomach, Anna sent up a trial balloon. She said "Hi." Thank God, Luisa said "Hi" back. They played together. And they are still friends.

Once I understood the significance of her entry, it was easy to suggest that Anna might want to do what writers do: live with an awareness of her topic and become a magnet, gathering more and more memories and thoughts and stories about it.

Anna made herself a six-page notebook, and on the cover she listed some of the entries she could write:

- I could write about other times Luisa has gone off with kids.
- I could write how it was before I had Luisa for a friend.
- I could write why she's a good friend.

Anna was on her way. Over the next few days, she lived toward her topic. After gathering more entries, she would look over all she'd written and ask herself, "Do I want to write a letter to my friend? Or a picture book about a girl who was afraid of losing her best friend?" Then, on yellow paper, she'd begin a draft.

In our New York City classrooms, class sizes are so big that we are not able to confer this closely with each of our students, so we need to find ways to help other students progress on the coattails of youngsters like Anna. One way to do this is to let other students in on the events of our individual conferences. Another way is to involve the whole class in peer conferring. After telling a group of youngsters who did not know Anna about her writing, I told them that soon they would each meet in pairs, with one child acting as the writer and the other as the writing teacher. First, I gave everyone a lesson in being a good writing teacher for each other.

"Let's say we're all going to act as writing teachers for Samantha," I said, bringing Samantha to the front of the classroom. "What could we say to get Samantha rereading her notebook in search of an entry or a passage she wants to develop?" Soon Samantha was reading selected entries aloud to the class.

"You should choose *that* one," one of her friends interjected, and I stepped into the discussion. "Hold on, hold on," I cautioned, and I told the children that if I'd told Anna which entry I thought had the most potential, she'd never have written about her restaurant entry. If we're going to be good writing teachers, we need to help Samantha listen to her own writing; we need to help her select the entry she will develop.

Samantha, like so many children, did not have a resounding opinion. "Well," she said, her voice full of tentativeness, "maybe I could, um, maybe, write about my grandpa . . . ?" Her voice trailed off.

I don't tend to insist that a child act enthusiastic about her topic. Instead of requiring enthusiasm on Samantha's part—"It's up to you. Is your grandpa *really* important to you?"—I interpret Samantha's tentative indication of interest as both a plea and a question. Samantha is probably asking whether the kids and I can imagine that her grandpa *might* be a worthwhile subject. And so I tell my apprentices, the students who are learning from me to be writing teachers, "Our job is to be *really interested* in Samantha's topic and to get her talking about it to us so *she* can become really interested in it, too."

At this point, the children and I stopped to recall what it was <u>good writing teachers did to help each other select and develop seed ideas</u> for their writing. We listed our ideas on the chalkboard:

- Writing teachers invite writers to reread all their entries, looking for something that feels alive.
- The writer, not the writing teacher, identifies an entry that has potential.
- The writing teacher responds with interest, encouraging the writer to talk more about his or her topic.
- The writer and the writing teacher list or imagine possible entries the writer might write as he or she lives with the topic.

As the children headed off to work with each other in pairs, Samantha returned to her notebook. She folded over a page and began collecting entries about her grandpa. She wrote and wrote and wrote, filling pages with long, rambling entries such as the ones shown in Figure 4–4. When Samantha reread her entries, she decided to shape them into a poem:

MY GRANDFATHER

When I saw him
I came running
to see him I
ran in the hospital
I notice that the
hospital was white and blue
but I didn't care
about the hospital
in that time I
only cared about
my grandfather

FIGURE 4–4   Samantha's entries about her grandfather

Yesterday my mother was crying
and the famliy was crying because
My Ganafather was very sick so he
had to go to the. Hosptil I was
Sad to becaure he's comeing
Back to the house in decmber May
be he's comeing on tuseday or on
monday. when I went to the hosptil
to see my Grandfather. I had to say
I was 12 years old becaure if I did'nt
Say the I was 12years old they didn't
Let me go upsires to see my
Grandfather. ~~when I saw him I
gave him a big big big big hug and I
gave him a kiss   and he hug me tite~~
I brang him cupcakes

Before he uast to be better but
now he ssick and he uast to be
a litte bit fatter but now he's
Skine before he uast to eat but
now he's not eating that moch
So I'm afaid he myte dide.

We used to go Shopping together
we used to eat ice cream togethe
when it was my brithday I put cream
on his face then he _Laugh_ we spead
go time together. he bout a suit
for him and he bout me a toy
I got happy becaure he bout
me a teddy bear everytime I
hug that teddy bear it reminds
me of him. I wish he could be
better than he's now

when I came in
the room I gave
him a big kiss
and I gave him a big hug
he was happy to see me
because he was alone
in a room.

Samantha was proud of her poem, but when I came alongside her desk, she'd also begun to turn her entries into a letter. This is how the letter began:

Dear Grandfather,
Remember that we used to tickle each other? Remember that time when I put cream on your face and we all laughed?

Revision for Samantha is not unlike the revision process an artist experiences. The jeweler shapes some silver into earrings, some into a necklace. The sculptor finds, in her wood or marble, a lion or a horse. Samantha, in a similar way, has found in her material the beginning of a poem and a letter. Of course, it is true for the writer as for the jeweler and the sculptor that the magic is never in the material alone but in the artist's ability to reimagine it.

Recommended Literature on Drafting and Revision

Bomer, Randy. *A time for meaning: Learning literacy with people aged 10–20*. Portsmouth, NH: Heinemann, in press.

Calkins, Lucy McCormick, with Shelley Harwayne. *Living between the lines*. Portsmouth, NH: Heinemann, 1991.

Cowley, Malcolm, ed. *Writers at work: The Paris Review interviews*. New York: Viking Press, 1959.

Dillard, Annie. *The writing life*. New York: Harper & Row, 1989.

Elbow, Peter. *Writing with power: Techniques for mastering the writing process*. New York: Oxford University Press, 1981.

Goldberg, Natalie. *Writing down the bones: Freeing the writer within*. Acton, CA: Shambhala Publications, 1986.

Morrison, Toni. The site of memory. In *Inventing the truth: The art and craft of memoir*, ed. William Zinsser. Boston: Houghton Mifflin, 1987.

Murray, Donald. *Expecting the unexpected: Teaching myself—and others—to read and write*. Portsmouth, NH: Boynton/Cook–Heinemann, 1989.

———. *Write to learn*. New York: Holt, Rinehart and Winston, 1990.

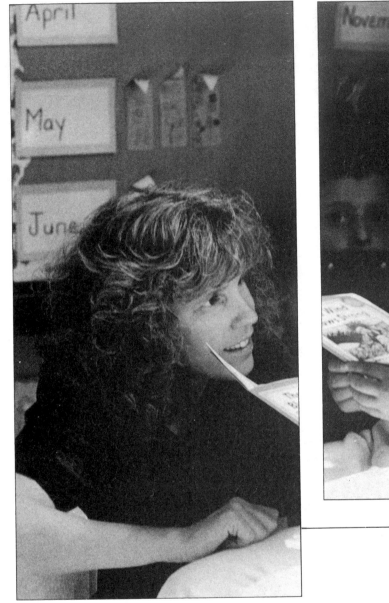

II

Let Children
Show Us
How to Teach

5
Lessons from Children

My family and I travel every summer to Barking Waters, a lakeside cabin in Northern Michigan where I spent my childhood summers. I remember, when Miles was two weeks old, lying back on the rope hammock with his tiny body against my chest, the giant pines forming a canopy overhead. Looking up at the pines and the Michigan sky, I thought about all the summers that stretched ahead for Miles and for me.

I told Miles that someday I'd take him on the Indian trail that edges the lake, and we'd pick blackberries. I know just the place. And I told him that someday I'd show him how to catch the wind just right so we could sail around Fox Island. I thought, at the time, that what I was doing with Miles was a metaphor for what we, as teachers of reading and writing, do. I was inviting Miles to share my world and my ways of living in that world.

When I returned several years later to Barking Waters with John, Miles, and my infant son Evan, I lay back in the rope hammock, wiggled my toes against Miles's toes, and felt Evan's bald head against my cheek. This time, when I looked up at the pine trees forming a canopy overhead, I did not tell my boys that someday I'd show them the blackberry patch at the end of the Indian trail, or that I'd teach them how to catch the wind just right so we could sail all the way around Fox Island. What my sons have taught me is that it doesn't matter if we make it all the way to the blackberry patch; look, there are tiny red mushrooms in this patch of moss, and wait, creatures live under this log. They've taught me it's not important whether we sail all the way around Fox Island, for listen, there is a loon calling to us, and look, the lake glistens like diamonds.

And this, of course, is the real metaphor for literacy learning. If we adults listen and watch closely, our children will invite us to share *their* worlds and *their* ways of living in the world. And then, when children become our teachers, showing us what they see and delight in and wonder about and reach toward, then, and only then, will we be able to extend what they know and enrich their ways of knowing.

Wise teaching, like wise parenting, begins with watching and listening and delighting in the learner. That is why, when the Edward Gould Foundation came to me and said, "If we could help you give anything you dream of to the New York City teachers with whom you work, what would it be?" my answer was that I wanted to give these teachers an opportunity to be kid-watchers, to be teacher-researchers, to be students of their students.

The foundation officers were surprised. They expected me to ask for funds to support a summer writing experience for teachers. And it is true that when we, as teachers, have opportunities to write our own poems and stories and essays, this experience changes us forever as teachers of writing. But I think that it is equally or even more essential for us to learn to take lessons from our children.

Teaching is always a mystery. We see a child endlessly recopying her writing and titling each new copy "Draft 2," "Draft 3," and so on. What is this child's concept of revision? What lures this writer to act in these ways? We see a student who has written insightful, detailed entries on his topic leave all of these behind in order to produce a stilted final draft. Why? What's going on?

The important thing to realize is that our students can be our teachers. We can pull our chairs alongside their desks and say, "I notice that your writing is totally different when you write entries and when you write finished pieces. . . . Can you explain why your writing changes so much?" We can bring out the final draft and ask, "What were you aiming to do when you wrote this?" and "What do you think makes for good writing?"

It's often hard to imagine how we can make time to study what our students do when they write. When our classes are filled (as they often are) with thirty or more students, it's difficult to find ways to take our cues from students. We need to petition and work for more humane class sizes, but in the meantime, we need to remember that we have no choice but to teach responsively. The basketball coach *must* get his players out onto the court and respond to what he sees. The piano teacher *must* listen, the art teacher *must* watch . . . and, as writing teachers, we *must* let students show us how to teach them.

Over the years, wonderful teachers have developed ways to build in rituals for studying their children. In some schools, teachers organize their professional networks rather like "rounds" in medical schools. At each meeting, one teacher tells the story of one child and shows that child's work, and then the entire group of professionals gathers around to marvel over and CFg learn from and wonder about the child. In other schools, writing workshops usually begin with a few minutes of silent time in which the teacher moves among the writers, making silent notes of what she sees them doing. Later, her notes may lead to a mini-lesson about what to do when you're stuck, or about the importance of rereading your work, asking, "Does this make sense?"

The most important thing that will happen as we move among our children or as we gather to study their work is this: We will delight in them. What a treat it is to hear children inventing metaphors and words of their own, to watch them savoring the sounds of language. If we listen well, we'll hear even our littlest writers speaking in poetry.

"Your pancake's drowning in syrup," I said this morning to Evan, who is now four years old.

"It's not *drownin'*," he answered. "It's *yummin'* in syrup!"

Five-year-old Michelle Bellino lagged behind her mother, my colleague Lydia Bellino, as they walked through the empty mall. Everywhere, they could hear gates being pulled over store entrances. The fountain stood dry. A man stepped into it and started sweeping up the coins. "Mom! Mom!" Michelle said, catching her mother's hand. "He's sweeping away our wishes."

It's a delight, too, to watch children inventing their own explanations for the conventions of written language. Jonah earnestly reread his story adding exclamation marks throughout, one for each ordinary sentence and whole strings of fat, dark exclamation marks when the chase begins and when the hero dies. "I'm adding excitement," he explains.

Meredith diligently counts nine dots in the ellipsis that follows the "ringggg" of her alarm clock. "That's how many minutes went by," she explains.

When five-year-old Brad brought his story about rabbits ("RBTS") to his teacher, she commented, "I notice you put an *s* for two rabbits*!*"

"Yup," he nodded, and turning to leave he said, "One *s* for two rabbits, two *s*'s for three rabbits!"

Although Brad's understanding of plurals is still embryonic, his teacher can celebrate the fact that Brad *expects* written language to be logical. Because Brad is thinking about the rules behind the spellings he sees and invents, he is well on his way to becoming knowledgeable about the conventions of written language.

Brad's teacher may want him to explain his theory to the class, which may lead the entire community to wonder together over the logic behind plural words and to chart different ways to indicate plurals. Alternatively, Brad's teacher may support the boy's wise guess and explain to him that, in fact, the English language *doesn't* follow his logic. Then, again, Brad's teacher may simply smile over his delightful explanation and watch him head off to his writing and reading, knowing he'll continue to make and revise explanations for the conventions of written language.

When we move among our students' desks as they write, or when we take one tableful of writers' notebooks and writing folders home to read, our children will show us what they know about why and how people write. They'll show us their images of good writing, their understandings of why writers keep notebooks, their concepts of revision and editing. I am always amazed and intrigued and baffled by what children show me.

Sometimes it helps to have a sense of what children have shown other teachers and of the meanings those teachers have attributed to their behavior. Sometimes we become better "readers" of our classrooms when we hear the stories of other children in other classrooms. For this reason I will spend time in the next few chapters sketching portraits of writers and classrooms throughout the elementary and middle-school grades.

I do so with some trepidation. About fifteen years ago, when Donald Graves, Susan Sowers, and I set out to study the composing processes of children in grades 1 through 4, we expected to discover universal sequences and stages of development that paralleled Piaget's stages. Instead, we found a huge range of differences across children. Amy, a gifted fourth-grade writer and artist, seemed to look her subject in the eye as she wrote brilliant first drafts. She resisted her teacher's emphasis on revision as much as possible, but when she was finally pressed to revise, her new drafts were not reformulations of her early ones but whole new views of her subject. Susie, on the other hand, took to revision like a fish takes to water. She'd tinker with her lead sentences and her endings, and try moving closer to her subject and then stepping farther back from it. Was one child farther along on a developmental continuum than the other? We didn't think so. They were just different people with different ways of seeing and learning and writing. And these differences existed in a single classroom, under the auspices of a single approach to teaching writing. How much more varied our children will be when they come from different schools, different approaches to teaching writing, different cultures, different genders. It is with good reason, therefore, that Don Graves, Jerry Harste, and other colleagues who study writing development have resisted all efforts to create grade-level expectations or to suggest that children's writing will develop in any fixed order. I respect their views.

Having said all this, I must also say that the range of writing I tend to see in kindergarten is different from what I tend to see in fourth-grade classrooms, or even in second-grade classrooms. And it may be helpful if I describe, in tentative ways, the kinds of writing behaviors and continuums of growth I often see in writing workshops like those described in this book. Readers will want to pay careful attention to the grade levels that lead into and follow your own grades. As we all know, within a third-grade classroom there will be many children whose writing resembles what we see in both second- and fourth-grade classrooms.

My goal in doing this is to help all of us be better observers of children. When I wander in the forest, I find I am a more astute observer of trees if I know something about the categories of trees and the ways in which they tend to be similar and different. I hope, and trust, that the following chapters will, in similar ways, help all of us be surprised and instructed by our students.

6

The Foundations of Literacy
Writing in the Home, the Nursery School, and the Kindergarten

"Teaching writing in nursery school? I don't believe in it," a friend announced, punctuating her remark with loud sighs and a shake of her head. "Children need time to be children, to grow through play and song, dance and art."

I agree. Children need time to be children, to grow through natural childhood activities. It is not children but adults who have separated writing from art, song, and play; it is adults who have turned writing into an exercise on lined paper, into a matter of rules, lessons, and cautious behavior. Children view writing quite differently. For them, it is exploration with marker and pen. Long before they come to school, youngsters leave their mark on foggy car windows and wet beaches (Graves 1983). They leave their mark on the backs of old envelopes, on living room walls, on shopping lists, and on their big sister's homework. We, as adults, may not believe in writing for preschool children—but the children believe in it.

The Philosophy Behind Early Writing

The young child's writing is an outgrowth of the infant's gestures. As L. S. Vygotsky points out, "Gestures are writing in air, and written signs frequently are simply gestures that have been fixed" (Vygotsky 1962). The baby moves her arms, and our faces light into smiles. "She's waving to us," we say. Because we attach meaning to what could be called meaningless gestures, the gestures assume meaning. Babies learn the power of their gestures by our response to them.

In a similar way, babies learn the power of speech. The baby bangs on the kitchen table with a spoon and says, "Maw Maw." Although the baby may be making sounds for the pure pleasure of it, we, as proud parents, want to believe our brilliant baby is saying something significant. "More, more. He's asking for more," we say, and rush to bring our child Cheerios or bananas. Our response leads the youngster to know the power of language.

Children learn the power of language because they are surrounded by people who use language for real world reasons and expect children to do so as well. And they do. Children have nearly invariable success in learning the complex and subtle skills of talking. "By the age of four to six, the child . . . controls the phonetic system of his language; he handles the grammatical core; he knows and uses the basic vocabulary of his language," Philip Morrison writes (1964, pp. 63–70).

We can invite our children inside the world of written language if we take our cue from how babies learn to talk. As Courtney Cazden emphasizes, oral language development "takes place on a non-sequenced, whole-task basis" (1972, p. 138). We wouldn't think of dissecting oral language into component parts, of ranking phonemes from simplest to most complex and then teaching them to children one at a time. The sounds coming from such a household would be very strange indeed, with the little toddler going about saying /p/ /p/ /p/ /p/ (Holdaway 1979, p. 21). We laugh at the idea of drilling children on the components of oral language before allowing them to try whole words. Why, then, do so many people still think it is helpful to drill young children on all the sounds of the alphabet before inviting them to use the sound-symbol correspondences they know to make meaning on the page?

Those of us who work with young children as writers also need to remember that when children are first learning to talk, error is not an issue. The baby says "Dadadada" and we wouldn't think of responding, "Oh, no! He is saying Daddy incorrectly. He isn't ready for whole words yet, he needs to drill on the *da* sound." We do not even regard "Dadadada" as wrong, but rather as an approximation of adult language. When the baby says "Dadadada," we marvel at what the child can do. We phone relatives across the country and, holding the receiver close to the youngster in hopes of a repeat performance, we celebrate the child's brilliance.

In homes and nursery schools people have begun to trust that children can learn written language in the same ways. Children learn to write when they see us writing for real purposes. By watching us, children can learn that writing is not only doable, it is also worth doing. They need to see us copying favorite lines from a book, pausing to record a fact, or venting our feelings onto the page. They need to know that we write letters, poems, notebook entries, lists, speeches, lesson plans, shopping lists, Post-it notes, postcards, contracts, petitions, recipes. And children need to be invited and expected to join us in all of this purposeful writing.

"I'll try to remember to get you some batteries," I tell my four-year-old son Evan. "But if you want to make sure I remember, add them to the shopping list."

"Wait, let's write down the steps for turning on the computer," I say. "Then we'll remember."

"Let's hang our Christmas lists on the refrigerator," I tell my sons, assuming, of course, that they'll make them. "Then if folks phone to find out what you want, the lists will be right here."

I say these things in words and I say them in deeds. My children have marker pens and paper beside their blocks, their books, their beds. I assume that writing will weave through their lives, just as it weaves through mine. And it does. Long before my sons knew sound-letter correspondences, they lived the lives of literate people. Miles began carrying pencils behind his ear before he did anything very much with those pencils. For several years now, he has carried his notebook with him everywhere. He constructs new ones constantly, filling up only a portion of each, often with drawings rather than writing. To me, the important thing is that Miles regards his pens and papers as necessary to his life. He ties notebooks to his belt and wedges them into the pocket of his carpenter's apron. He has shoeboxes and plastic bags and backpacks filled with pens and spiral notebooks and graph paper and protractors. He hears the weather on television and makes himself a weather map. He goes to school collecting phone numbers and addresses in his phone directory and address book. He posts signs alongside the road announcing club meetings and book sales (of all my books!) and contests.

Launching a Writing Workshop in the Primary-Level Classroom

In nursery schools and kindergarten classrooms, teachers have found their own ways to demonstrate purposeful writing and to invite children to join them. On the first day of school in many nursery school and kindergarten classrooms, many teachers say to children, "Sign in on this paper."

"How is this possible?" some readers will ask. "What about the children who can't sign their names? Shouldn't we be certain that every student has the necessary skills before we put them on the spot?"

The first thing to remember is that when we ask a baby, "Are you hungry?" or "How's your day been?" we don't check to be sure the baby has the necessary skills to answer us, nor do we worry about putting the child on the spot. Instead, we ask these questions fully expecting that the baby will participate in the conversation as best she can. We know that by speaking with the baby as if she *can* carry on her half of the conversation, we teach her to do just that.

The other thing to remember is that ninety percent of children come to school believing they can write. This shouldn't be a surprise; children believe they can sweep the kitchen floor, too, long before they actually can. They believe they can be pilots and chefs and parents and clowns and animal trainers and teachers. . . . Why are we willing to refer to our child as an engineer and to climb aboard that child's "train" and not equally willing to suggest that the child sign in on the attendance sheet?

In *The Whole Language Evaluation Book* (Goodman, Goodman, and Hood 1989), teacher Wendy Hood describes her children's responses to an invitation to sign in. For most of Wendy's children, who come from low socioeconomic backgrounds in small, densely populated housing units, English is a second language. Wendy describes the first day of her kindergarten classroom this way:

> Outside the kindergarten classroom stands a large painting easel covered with butcher paper. It greets the kindergartners on their first day. "Sign in, Please. Firmen Aquí," it reads at the top. I hold a fresh box of crayons out to the children as they approach. "Hi, my name is Wendy," I say to each. "Which crayon would you like to use to write your name here?" One by one the kids sign in, some easily, some with only a little encouragement, and some very reluctantly.
>
> As the wide-eyed kindergartners move away from the easel, my instructional aide, Terry, greets them: "Can I help you find your name tag?" She watches or helps them as needed and then directs them to tables set with paper, pencils, and crayons. "Draw a picture of anything you like," she says as they choose their seats.
>
> Outside two children still stand, crayon in hand, facing the easel, looking almost as anxious as the two mothers standing close behind them. One mom leans close to her little boy. Softly, patiently, she whispers as he writes, "D . . . a . . . n . . . i . . . e . . . l." I greet Daniel, who smiles and rushes into the room to pick out his own name tag.
>
> Tears begin to come to the lone little girl's eyes as her mother says to her in Spanish, "You remember how. Come on now. V. . . ." The girl stands, sadly frozen. Mom wraps her hand around the little girl's and moves her hand to shape a V. Now the tears are flowing. "That's a fine V," I say to them both. Veronica sniffles as I slip my arm around her and we walk away from her mother, away from the easel, and into the room. Although there is only one name tag left, Veronica does not choose it for herself.
>
> As the kids finish their drawings, Terry and I wander about the room looking at the pictures, talking to the children, and asking them to

"write that that's a truck" or whatever. Most of them do write, or pretend to write. "Read it to me," I say. And most of them do. I respond in writing: "Where is the truck going?" This is the beginning of our journal writing.

After writing my responses I ask the children if I may keep their papers. I invite them to choose a book to read on the rug. One by one they complete their journal pages and meander, sometimes by way of the toy areas, to the rug area and the bookshelf. When all the children are there, we put away our books and begin our group time.

So the day goes. After group time we move to directed activities, followed by choices time, followed by supervised clean-up, followed by a final group time. When the bell rings to go home, moms, dads, and various other relatives greet their excited children. "Did you like your first day of school?" they all ask in their own way. "Yes," the kids reply. "What did you do today?" the proud families ask. "Play!" (pp. 27–28)

Our teaching is always a matter of selection, and what we choose to do often reveals more than we could imagine about our attitudes toward children and their literacy. On my son Miles's first day of kindergarten at his former school, his warm, loving teacher gave him a rexograph sheet and directed him to color one balloon red, one blue, and one green. Miles's teacher told me how pleased she was with the activity because it taught the children about following directions and allowed her to see if children knew their colors. It was also an activity no one would fail. How revealing it is to juxtapose these two incidents of teaching.

Both of these teachers are undoubtedly gifted, dedicated, caring professionals. But the details of their teaching reveal that they have very different philosophies. Miles's teacher regarded writing, at least for children and probably for herself, as taxing, difficult work. Often during the school year she told my son, "Just scribble if you don't want to write." When I mentioned that I'd love to write with the children, she suggested we postpone writing, except with a selected few children, until the entire class had "received enough help" that they knew all their upper- and lowercase letters.

I suspect that my son's teacher wanted, above all, to ensure that her children didn't encounter difficulty. She would rather have their work be a bit purposeless than have it be difficult. For her, difficulty was something to be avoided. She placed a high priority on having children learn to follow directions, on "socializing" them. It was probably not an accident that the first activity of the school year demonstrated to her whether children could follow directions and to children that school is a place for following the teachers' directions, even in drawing.

Wendy Hood's teaching represents entirely different assumptions. Wendy writes herself and regards writing as a joyful, natural human activity. Just as parents expect their babies to talk as best they can and know they will grow into talkers, Wendy expects her children to write (as best they can) and knows they'll grow to love writing. Wendy envisions her kindergarten classroom, above all, as a richly literate community. She feels sure that when her children see real reasons to read and write, when they are regarded as members of the club of readers and writers (Smith 1988) they will have a meaningful context for acquiring the component skills. She is not afraid that her children will "fail" as writers because she can't imagine such a thing as "failure." Her children will come to her with a range of starting points. Veronica's "V" is as acceptable as any other child's signature. Finally, Wendy Hood doesn't shy away from difficulty; she shies away from meaninglessness. She believes hard work is gratifying when it's done for one's own important purposes.

Wendy Hood's method is one of many ways to launch children into writing; others are described in the professional books I list at the end of this chapter. Many teachers and parents give children books made of blank sheets of paper stapled together. "You can draw and write," we say. Children take these books and spread out all over the room—on the floor, in favorite nooks and crannies, at tables. Some will be unsure how to begin. "What do you want your story to be about?" I ask Regina. She says, "My dog." I answer, "Why don't you draw him?" and then turn to the next child. Relieved that she's only expected to draw after all, Regina settles into making her picture. When I return, the dog looks fairly complete, but Regina is continuing to work on it. I interrupt her by gently putting my hand on hers, bringing it away from the picture. "You can continue drawing later," I say to Regina, "but for now, while I'm here, why don't we put the writing down? What should we say?" Regina, hearing the "we" and figuring I'll do the writing, isn't the least bit anxious anymore. She answers with a long, involved story, and I ask, "Regina, what's the *one thing* we should put down for now?"

"My dog," she says.

"Mmmmmy . . . dog," I say, repeating her words slowly but not turning them into a staccato of separate sounds. "Mmmmyy." And then I hand her the thin marker pen. "Here you go."

She looks up at me, surprised. Her look probably says, "What should I do? I can't write," but I don't know what it says because I deliberately fix my eyes on her paper, as if waiting expectantly for what she'll write. Often, when children cannot engage my glance, they turn to the page and do whatever they can do. I want to see if this will happen, and I want to do everything possible to make it happen. I want Regina to be independent of me. If she *does* write, I'll accept whatever she puts down and respond with, "Okay, Regina. Will you read that to me?"

If she puts nothing on the page but instead seems stymied and unable to continue, I'll ask her to join me saying the word slowly. "Mmmyyy," we say, my voice deliberately softer than hers. "Mmmyy," we say again. "What sound do you hear?"

For this particular sound, Regina will probably respond with the correct letter, but if the letter she chooses is incorrect (as it's apt to be for other sounds), I don't worry about it at this point. If she won't make any guess, I might give her laminated alphabet cards and ask, "Which of these letters could it be?" or I might encourage nearby children to pitch in and help. After I've helped Regina write something on her page to represent the word *my*, I'll encourage her to be more independent with her next word. "What comes next?" I ask. Rereading what she has written so far, I say, "My . . ."

Filling in the end of the phrase, she says, "Dog," and then we say "dog" slowly together, listening to it.

"What a writer you are!" I say, and deliberately move to a child at a distant table, who is probably well along on his illustrations.

Writing Throughout the Classroom

We may decide to launch writing instead within some of the other areas of the classroom. The block area, for example, offers wonderful reasons for writing. One child may need to write a sign saying "Don't wreck it" to protect her created world. Another child may need road signs, street signs, billboards, shop signs. Still another child may need a map or an entrance ticket or names on animal cages. In Joanne Hindley's classroom at the Manhattan New School, children make careful drawings of their favorite block creations, and when the structures come down, they put their drawing (or map), along with whatever functional writing accompanied their structures, into a class book.

The area that is probably best suited to functional writing, however, is the dramatic play area. When I taught in the primary grades, I called this area "dress-up." It was filled with cradles, sinks, stoves, cupboards, and other equipment that channeled children toward "playing house." It's not hard to find reasons to write within a housekeeping corner; if children are given a variety of paper and nudged to write, one child will make a menu, another a book for the dolls or a note on the refrigerator or a recipe or a shopping list. If there is a pad of paper beside the make-believe phone, there will be writing there, and of course, every bedroom needs a bookshelf. But more and more, we are realizing that it's not ideal to equip the dramatic play area with stoves and cradles, because these channel children's play in only one direction. When we instead give children some wooden spools and boards, big boxes, and varied paper, they will create a space ship, a bank, a post office, a museum. If we as teachers and parents take these imagined worlds seriously, each one presents amazing opportunities for study and learning and, of course, for writing.

In their imagined bank, our children write checks, fill out deposit slips, and keep ledgers. For their museums they have made display cases and guidebooks. Each of these worlds can invite new genres of writing. It's a mistake, however, to think that all that matters is the written texts that emerge from this play. The dramatic play itself is a form of composition, an occasion for world-building. In her brilliant book *The Multiple Worlds of Child Writers*, Anne Haas Dyson talks about how young story creators became characters within imagined worlds. They shift from speaking as if they were inside the story ("Oh, how beautiful I am") to speaking as narrators ("This is going to be her baby"). Dyson points out that authors need to assume all of these voices and shift between them.

> An author may first be the real-world director of the unfolding imaginary world, an actor speaking a character's words, feeling a character's emotions; then, inside a remembered world, a reflective storyteller reliving past experiences where the roots of the story may lie. (1989, p. 11)

What About the Kids Who Don't Know Their Alphabet Letters?

It's hard to imagine some of our youngsters writing checks and deposit slips, let alone guidebooks for a museum. "What about all the children who don't know any of their alphabet letters yet?" teachers ask. First of all, some of these children will, for a time, draw rather than write. There will be some youngsters who develop whole story lines based on their drawings. In our eagerness to see writing on the children's papers, it is easy to dismiss these picture stories, and this is especially so because the drawings are rudimentary. It is, however, very helpful if we can focus on what children are doing rather than on what we wish they would do. Usually more is happening in their drawings than meets the eye. A kindergarten teacher told JoAnn Curtis, a former

Writing Project staff member, that she had given up on one youngster in despair. "It's not that he doesn't write," the teacher said. "I'd settle for drawings. But all he does is draw the same thing over and over." When JoAnn looked at the child's most recent book, she found that the teacher was right. On each page, the boy had drawn a little square person standing in midair—and that was all. Only the final page was different. On it there was a funny-looking shape that could have been a flower. Because JoAnn wondered about the drawings (and because she had no encouraging words to say to the teacher), she asked the boy to tell her about the book. To her astonishment, he responded by opening to page one and then reading the entire book to her, turning the pages as he went along.

"Once upon a time Mr. Toastman wanted to make a flower," he said, "so he got a seed." The boy showed her page one, with Mr. Toastman and the seed. "You can't see the seed," he explained. Then, on page two, Mr. Toastman got some dirt (and sure enough, there was a smudge on his hand), and on page three, he got some more dirt (a bigger smudge). The book ends with the seed growing into a flower.

How much this child has learned! Although he doesn't seem to know sound-letter correspondences, he knows the lilt of story language and the pacing of story plots. He is able to create beginnings and endings, character names, and story sequences. He has the confidence to take a single idea, a simple picture, to declare it significant, and to make it so.

Whereas some children will choose to draw rather than write for a while, others will write make-believe alphabet letters. I do not *suggest* that children do either of these things. Their intention is to tell their story, to write, and I wouldn't want to say, "Let's pretend we are writing." Nor do I refer to writing that looks like the footprints of a chicken as "scribble writing" or "pretend writing." Instead, I give these hieroglyphics the same respect I give to the baby's "dadadada." Just as I say to the babbling baby, "Daddy? You want your daddy?" I say to Tiziana when she shows me her paper, "Will you read it to me?" Here is what she wrote:

$$\mathcal{N} \quad \mathcal{N} \quad \mathcal{N} \quad \mathcal{N} \quad \mathcal{N}$$
$$\mathcal{N} \quad \mathcal{N} \quad \mathcal{N} \quad \mathcal{N} \quad 3$$

While Tiziana reads her story to me, I take note of how much she already knows. She knows that speech can be encoded in little marks on the page and that the marks go from left to right, then return to the left

FIGURE 6–1 Evan's story

and repeat the pattern. At an earlier stage Tiziana probably peppered letters randomly around her page, or began on the right and proceeded to the left.

The fact that we watch and celebrate what children can do doesn't mean that we necessarily maintain a hands-off policy when our children write. It *does* mean that our teaching is in response to what children do. If a child often begins writing on the right rather than the left side of a page, we may for a while want to put a sticker or an "X" to suggest a starting point for the child's next few pieces. When Evan brought me the story shown in Figure 6–1, I let him know I wasn't quite sure where to begin reading and showed him how pages are laid out in a book. I extended what Evan had done, but I also celebrated the fact that he used what he knows— the letters from his name, and a scattering of other letters—to hold his message.

On another day, if Evan is writing while I'm at his side, I might teach him about particular letter-sound correspondences. If he wants to write "I love you" to his cousin Matthew, I might write an "I" on another piece of paper so he can copy it onto his own, and if he doesn't know how to write "you," I might bring out the small alphabet he keeps on the table while he writes and show him the letter "u" in it. Alternatively, I might tell him "you" is spelled in a weird way and write it (y-o-u) on another bit of paper for him to copy. In classrooms, children as well as teachers can help each other in all of these ways, and of course, this peer collaboration deserves our support. How wonderful it is to see writing becoming a richly social activity. "How do you spell /b/?" one child will ask another, and soon five youngsters will be leaning across the table writing capital and lowercase b's and d's, arguing over which is which.

When David read the following story to me (see Figure 6–2), I noticed that, like Evan, he used what he knew to write his story:

FIGURE 6-2   David's story

I took the A train to Botanical Gardens.

I also noticed that as David read, he carefully matched each spoken word of the story with a letter on the page. Although he doesn't yet understand that particular letters have particular sounds, David has an early notion of a correspondence between words and print.

Responding to Early Writing: An Alternative to Compliments

David's writing, like Tiziana's and Evan's, will be treated with the respect we give to a baby's earliest words. Parents instinctively know that the way to support "dadadada" is not to heap praise onto the baby but to signal for Daddy to come over. The same is true for children's earliest writing. We support David's writing by asking him to sit in the author's chair and read his story aloud, just as children with longer, more conventional stories do. Listeners can ask David questions about his trip to the Botanical Gardens, and they can suggest that he add more to the story, either by turning a single page into a long book or by adding more lines to his page.

Recently I was in a kindergarten classroom in Upper Manhattan. Two children were fooling around with the water fountain. Seeing this, five-year-old Latrice ran to her writing folder and pulled out her writing. The piece looked like nothing more than rows of circles to me, but to Latrice, it was a list of class rules. "Look at this!" she said sternly, waving her page in front of the misbehaving boys. "Can't you read? It says, 'No fooling around in the water fountain'!"

Latrice believes her writing has power in the world because her teacher empowers her writing and that of her classmates. Instead of complimenting Latrice, instead of putting smiling stickers on her stories and hanging them up for display, the wise teacher lets children's writing do some real work in the world. When a teacher asks, "What will you do with your story?" it is a far better compliment than any amount of praise, and it's the kind of compliment that lets children see that writing has its own rewards. And so children's greeting cards are mailed, their letters answered, their stories read aloud, their plays performed, their recipes followed, their songs sung, their posters and notices hung, their poems chanted and given as gifts and learned by heart.

When we respect children's early writing, we create a mood of appreciation in the classroom. It is a beautiful sight to enter these rooms and see clusters of children sharing their writing. Some may be lying together on the floor; perhaps two children will be sitting, arms linked, on a single chair. Everywhere youngsters are writing and reading writing. In the library corner, homemade stapled-together books are propped up on the shelves between the hardbound books, and everywhere children's writing is being used for important purposes. Children have labeled the areas of the room, they've written notes for putting away materials, they've made rules about caring for the hamster. When Hindy List, director of a Mentor Schools program within our Writing Project, went into one such classroom to select several pieces of early writing to duplicate, a small boy came running after her as she was leaving. He waved his piece and called, "Here, take mine, I'm an author too!"

What a wonderful teacher that boy must have! His drawings were wobbly and sparse, and he seemed unsure whether lollipops or letters were preferable for the writing, but that youngster knew he belonged to the world of authors. What a gift!

Sometimes people ask me what I think is the most important message I could convey to teachers of young children. My answer is simple: I want teachers to delight in what youngsters do and to respond in real ways to what they are trying to do. I want teachers to have a wonderful time watching and admiring and working with young writers.

It is easy to enjoy teaching writing because the children do such terrific and funny things. I think of Ariel, who came to her teacher with a big wad of paper and said, "Would you staple my story together? Whenever I staple it, I do it the Jewish way [Hebrew books are read right to left and back to front]. Would you staple it the regular way?"

Another time a child brought one of my colleagues a story about a peanut butter factory. He'd divided his page into four frames and on each one he'd drawn a picture of the factory. Solemnly the boy told my colleague about how they slop the peanut butter about and then add nuts. After a while he paused. "It isn't real, you know," he whispered. "But don't tell her," and he motioned to the teacher. "She thinks it is."

I think also of Michelle. Shelley Harwayne met Michelle in the hallway of P.S. 230 in Brooklyn. Michelle was looking at a ragged bit of paper and saying something as she walked.

"What do you have there?" Shelley asked her, crouching down so she was at eye level.

"The Bible," she said. "My Mama gave it to me. She said it'll make me strong; it'll make me strong if I say the words, if I read it."

Michelle was right—she did have a little piece of the Bible in her hand.

"Would you read it to me?" Shelley asked.

Holding the torn page upside down, Michelle looked at it and read, "Spinach, rice, beans." Then she looked at Shelley and said, "They make you strong, right?"

But my favorite story of all is the book "Baby," written by five-year-old Marisol (Figure 6–3). There was not a single bit of print in Marisol's "Baby" story. Marisol "read" the story to Writing Project staff member JoAnn Curtis, which is how I know the oral version.

FIGURE 6–3 "Baby" by Marisol

"The lady is going to have a baby."

"They drove to the hospital."

"And she had the baby. They were so happy and they loved the baby so much…

"They decided to get married!"

The wonderful thing is that, when allowed and encouraged to participate in meaningful ways in their language-rich worlds, young children are amazingly capable language learners. Growth happens very quickly. By the time children are five years old, they already know an average of ten thousand vocabulary words. That means that by the time they are five they have learned an average of twenty new vocabulary words a day, without forgetting them, every day of their lives! Their growth as writers is equally dazzling. Once children regard themselves as writers, they go through their lives like vacuum cleaners, sucking up knowledge of written language. They learn sound-symbol correspondences not because their entire class spends a week drilling on the "M" sound by eating M & M's and marshmallows, cutting pictures of items that begin with M's out of magazines, and chanting poems full of marvelous monkeys that munch on muffins. Instead a child learns the M from seeing McDonald's Golden Arches rising up over the horizon as she drives with her family down the highway . . . and from using those same arches later to label her block building with the word MIN (mine). Because writers need to know sound-letter correspondences, they learn the "S" sound from stop signs, and add it beside their drawing of a snake.

As teachers and parents we support this appetite for learning the conventions of written language when we trust that children can learn phonics just as they learned the complex grammar of our language. No one drilled children in the rules that call for "my big red wagon" rather than "my red big wagon." Children simply pick this up because they are talkers, immersed in a sea of language. In the same way, we can trust that children will pick up sound-symbol correspondences if we allow them to be readers and writers from the first day of school on, immersed in real experiences with sounds and letters. We can help that immersion to happen not only by reading and writing with our students (and our sons and daughters), but also by playfully fooling around with sounds and letters. And so with them we make invisible letters in the sky using a finger as the pencil and the air as the page and guessing what we each have written. Then we laugh and try it again. We play a game in which we try to get our bodies into the shapes of a J or an N, and see if people can read our embodied letters . . . and we laugh some more and fall into a loving heap. While I was driving Evan to nursery school last week, he curled his bootlace around to make an O. We named his lace an "alphabet lace" and spent the whole drive making his lace into S's and M's and D's and hearts. In a similar way, a walk down the school corridor can be an alphabet walk if we read everything around us and then look again at what we have read, asking ourselves a million times, "What do we notice?" and "What surprises us?" Instead of mastering one alphabet letter at a time, we immerse ourselves in all the letters and sounds. We play with alphabet puzzles, sing and chant poems, read and write as best we can, and make alphabet books, and we talk and talk and talk as we do all of this. "How do you make an M?" one child asks, and another child answers with an M drawn in the sky.

"What?" the first child asks, and this time the answer is drawn on her back.

"Wait—is it this?" she asks. "Is it a camel?"

"It's mountains."

All of these discussions are terribly important for youngsters who regard themselves as writers. My son is eager to know the "S" sound because he's posting a sign in front of our house announcing a soccer club starting tomorrow. He *must* know how to write "dollars," because how else can he make money for his make-believe bank (and of course, a bank is necessary if there is to be a bank robbery).

All of this learning is immediately evident in what children write. In no time at all, the child who came to school knowing very few sound-symbol correspondences will be labeling her drawings using the consonants she knows. It's very common for preschool and kindergartners to write like this:

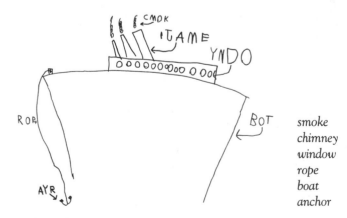

smoke
chimney
window
rope
boat
anchor

This is one of Evan's first stories:

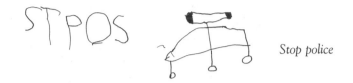

Stop police

When Evan wrote this story, he began by asking me, "How do you spell 'stop'?" Years ago, I would have responded by suggesting he sound it out, but I've come to realize that it's more helpful to say, "Have you ever seen that word?" or "Close your eyes. Can you picture it?" or "Just give it a go, Evan." Sounding out a word is one way—but surely not the only way—for a child to figure out spellings. Because Evan has yet to learn independence as a speller, I will probably tell him, "I won't be giving you spellings." I want him to realize he does have resources of his own to draw upon. At a later stage, when he's spelling independently and fluently and wants help with a particular word, I might well decide to give it to him. The important thing for now is that we and our children realize that once they know a handful of sound-symbol correspondences, they can write anything they wish. One of my son's older cousins—a kindergartner—said to him, "I can spell 'Yes.' Y-E-S."

"So?" my son shrugged. "I can spell *anything.*" And he can. In thousands of kindergarten classrooms, children write letters to their friends and teachers like the one shown in Figure 6–4. Children in these classrooms write their own absence notes (Figure 6–5). The calendar that hangs over my desk at Teachers College (Figure 6–6) was made by a five-year-old.

FIGURE 6–4   Letter to a teacher

Mrs. Seltzer,
When you die,
I will take your place.
I love you.
Love, Beth

FIGURE 6–5 Absence note

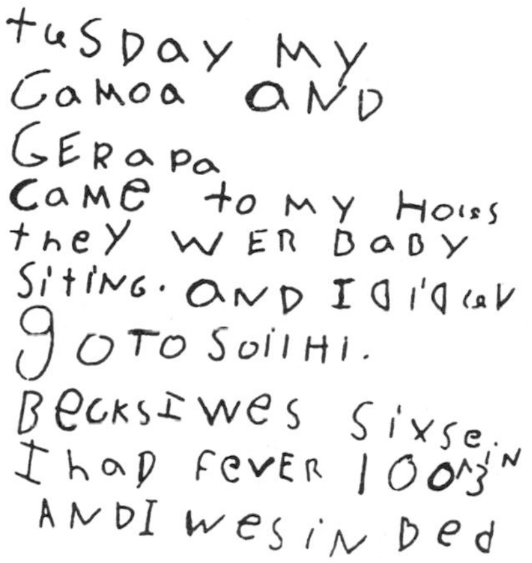

tuSDay My
Camoa aND
GERapa
Came to my Hoiss
they WER DaBy
SitiNG. aND I Di'd caV
go To SoilHi.
BecksIwes Sixse
I had feveR 100 Ʒin
ANDI wes iN Ded

Tuesday my grandma and grandpa came
to my house. They were babysitting.
And I didn't have to go to school
because I was sick. I had a fever, 100
and 3, and I was in bed.

FIGURE 6–6 A calendar

Last week, after Miles (who is now six) watched the videotape *Johnny Tremain,* he decided to form a club called "The Sons of Liberty." He phoned all his neighborhood friends—Megan, Kelly, Gordon, and Lindsay—and arranged a time for them to gather for the club's first hike. Then he made this list of everything he'd need for the first club meeting:

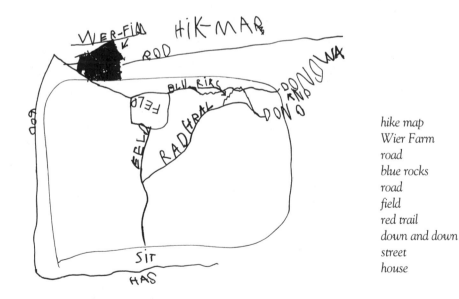

SONS-OF-LABER tu
IMANUFNI-ANG-GLAS
IGNOT-BUKS
5SIEANS-BUKS-BUES-AND-ANUNLS
IKARM-MRU
IPILE-OF-CHESE
IBIKS-OF-CRAKERS
IMOVE-OF-JOHNY-HR-MAN

one magnifying glass
six notebooks
five science books
    about bugs and
    animals
1 camera
1 pile of cheese
1 box of crackers
1 movie of Johnny
    Tremain

Miles also made a map of where they'd go on the hike:

WER-FIM HIK-MAR
ROD
BLU-RIRC
FIELD
FELD
RADHRAL
DONO-WA
DONO
SIT
HAS

hike map
Wier Farm
road
blue rocks
road
field
red trail
down and down
street
house

The first club meeting was so successful that Miles decided to arrange another. This time he used the computer to survey his friends about their hopes for the next club meeting:

Dere club,
   chek wich dae you
can mete:
      _____ sadrdae pm
      _____ sundae pm
chek wich you wont
to duw:
      _____ hike
      _____ play in side
      _____ bld woodn botes
      _____ go to new pond
            tepe
Rite yor name: _____

After Miles tallied results from the survey, he sent out a final notice.

KLB METING   SUNDAE 1:00
WE'L GO TO NEW POND TEPE. BRING
YR NOTBOK.
                    MILES

It's not Miles's spellings that make my heart sing but his belief that writing is necessary. For his club meeting, he needs a pile of cheese, a box of crackers, and notebooks for everyone. His final memo to his friends reads, "Bring your notebook." Miles writes to dream, to plan, to envision, to map, to learn, and to play, and so does his brother.

I know my sons have learned that writing is for dreaming and planning, learning and playing, not because of the time we've spent sounding out and spelling labels for their drawings. They've learned to value writing because when we climb to the very top of the hill behind our house and lean back against Story Rock, the giant boulder there, we crown our trek with a story made up from the leaves and sky overhead, the world below us, and each other. They've learned to value writing because, when the clouds were racing before the full moon, we took our paper and pens out into the night with us and tried to capture the magic. They've learned to value writing because when we hold our own Storm Party, we not only have whipped cream on our corn muffins and candlelight, we also have poems read against the backdrop of wind and rain. Writing for us is part of living and loving. As Byrd Baylor reminds us, we human beings *are* in charge of celebration.

Literature to Read to Young Children

Bemmelmans, Ludwig. *Madeline.* New York: Viking Press, 1958.

Brown, Margaret Wise. *Goodnight moon.* New York: HarperCollins Children's Books, 1991.

Burton, Virginia Lee. *Mike Mulligan and his steam shovel.* New York: Houghton Mifflin, 1987.

Conrad, Pam. *The tub people.* New York: HarperCollins Children's Books, 1989.

Degen, Bruce. *Jamberry.* New York: HarperCollins Children's Books, 1983.

de Paola, Tomie. *Now one foot, now the other.* New York: Putnam Publishing Group, 1992.

De Veaux, Alexis. *An enchanted hair tale.* New York: HarperCollins Children's Books, 1987.

Dorros, Arthur. *Abuela.* New York: Dutton Children's Books, 1991.

Fleming, Denise. *In the tall, tall grass.* New York: Henry Holt & Co., 1991.

Freeman, Don. *Corduroy.* New York: Viking Press, 1968.

Gag, Wanda. *Millions of cats.* New York: Putnam Publishing Group, 1977.

Geringer, Laura. *A three hat day.* New York: HarperCollins Children's Books, 1978.

Gordon, Gaelyn. *Duckat.* New York: Scholastic, 1992.

Greenfield, Eloise. *Honey, I love and other love poems.* New York: HarperCollins Children's Books, 1978.

Griffith, Helen V. *Grandaddy and Janetta.* New York: Greenwillow, 1993.

Henkes, Kevin. *Chrysanthemum.* New York: Greenwillow, 1991.

Hoffman, Mary. *Amazing Grace.* New York: Dial Books, 1991.

Hopkins, Lee Bennett. *Good books, good times!* New York: HarperCollins Children's Books, 1990.

Huck, Charlotte. *Princess Furball.* New York: Greenwillow, 1989.

Jonas, Ann. *The quilt.* New York: Greenwillow, 1984.

Kellogg, Steven. *Can I keep him?* New York: Dial Books, 1976.

Kuskin, Karla. *Dogs and dragons, trees and dreams: A collection of poems.* HarperCollins Children's Books, 1980.

Leaf, Margaret. *Eyes of the dragon.* New York: Lothrop, Lee & Shepard, 1987.

Marshall, James. *Rats on the roof and other stories.* New York: Dial Books, 1991.

Martin, Bill, Jr. *Chicka chicka boom boom.* New York: Simon & Schuster, 1989.

Minarik, Else Holmelund. *Little bear's friend.* New York: HarperCollins Children's Books, 1960.

Numeroff, Laura Joffe. *If you give a mouse a cookie.* New York: HarperCollins Children's Books, 1985.

Parish, Peggy. *Amelia Bedelia helps out.* New York: Greenwillow Books, 1979.

Say, Allen. *El Chino.* Boston: Houghton Mifflin, 1990.

Seeger, Pete. *Abiyoyo: Based on a South African lullaby and folk story.* New York: Macmillan Children's Book Group, 1985.

Sendak, Maurice. *Where the wild things are.* New York: Harper & Row, 1963.

Slobodkina, Esphyr. *Caps for sale.* New York: Scholastic, 1989.

Steig, William. *Amos and Boris.* New York: Farrar, Straus & Giroux, 1971.

Steptoe, John. *Stevie.* New York: HarperCollins Children's Books, 1986.

Tejima, Keizabur. *Owl lake.* New York: Philomel Books, 1987.

Wells, Rosemary. *First tomato / The island light / Moss pillows.* New York: Dial Books, 1992.

Williams, Karen Lynn. *Galimoto.* New York: Lothrop, Lee & Shepard, 1990.

Williams, Vera B. *Music, music for everyone!* New York: Greenwillow, 1984.

Zolotow, Charlotte. *The hating book.* New York: HarperCollins Children Books, 1989.

All the books listed below and those listed in Chapter 7 are also recommended.

Literature for Young Children to Read Independently or Collaboratively

Ahlberg, Janet, and Allan Ahlberg. *Each peach pear plum: An "I spy" story.* New York: Viking, 1979.

Bang, Molly. *Ten, nine, eight.* New York: Greenwillow Books, 1983.

Barton, Bryan. *I want to be an astronaut.* New York: Harper Trophy, 1992.

Brown, Margaret Wise. *The runaway bunny.* New York: HarperCollins Children's Books, 1991.

Carle, Eric. *The very hungry caterpillar.* New York: Putnam Publishing Group, 1981.

Christelow, Eileen. *Five little monkeys jumping on the bed.* New York: Clarion Books, 1991.

de Paola, Tomie. *The knight and the dragon.* New York: G. P. Putnam's Sons, 1980.

Eastman, Philip D. *Are you my mother?* New York: Beginner Books, a division of Random House, 1960.

Ginsburg, Mirra. *Good morning, chick.* New York: Morrow, 1989.

Guarino, Deborah. *Is your mama a llama?* New York: Scholastic, 1989.

Hogrogian, Nonny. *One fine day.* New York: Macmillan Children's Book Group, 1974.

Hutchins, Pat. *Rosie's walk.* New York: Macmillan Children's Book Group, 1971.

Johnson, Crockett. *Harold and the purple crayon.* New York: HarperCollins Children's Books, 1958.

Mahy, Margaret. *The boy who was followed home.* New York: Dial Books, 1986.

Martin, Bill, Jr. *Brown bear, brown bear, what do you see?* New York: Holt, Rinehart & Winston, 1983.

Shaw, Nancy. *Sheep in a jeep.* New York: Houghton Mifflin, 1991.

Stadler, John. *Hooray for snail.* New York: Thomas Y. Crowell, 1984.

The books listed in Chapter 7 are also recommended.

Recommended Professional Literature

Bissex, Glenda. GNYS AT WRK: *A child learns to write and read.* Cambridge, MA: Harvard University Press, 1980.

Cambourne, Brian. *The whole story: Natural learning and the acquisition of literacy in the classroom.* New York: Scholastic, 1988.

Clay, Marie. *What did I write?* Portsmouth, NH: Heinemann, 1975.

Dyson, Anne Haas. *The multiple worlds of child writers: Friends learning to write.* New York: Teachers College Press, 1989.

Fisher, Bobbi. *Joyful learning: A whole language kindergarten.* Portsmouth, NH: Heinemann, 1991.

Harste, Jerome, Virginia Woodward, and Carolyn Burke. *Language stories and literacy lessons.* Portsmouth, NH: Heinemann, 1984.

Holdaway, Donald. *The foundations of literacy.* Portsmouth, NH: Heinemann, 1979.

Karclitz, Ellen Blackburn. *The author's chair and beyond.* Portsmouth, NH: Heinemann, 1993.

Mills, Heidi, Timothy O'Keefe, and Diane Stephens. *Looking closely: Exploring the role of phonics in one whole language classroom.* Urbana, IL: National Council of Teachers of English, 1992.

Newkirk, Thomas. *More than stories: The range of children's writing.* Portsmouth, NH: Heinemann, 1989.

Newman, Judith. *The craft of children's writing.* Portsmouth, NH: Heinemann, 1985.

Paley, Vivian Gussin. *Mollie is three: Growing up in school.* Chicago: University of Chicago Press, 1986.

————. *Wally's stories.* Chicago: University of Chicago Press, 1979.

Routman, Regie. *Transitions: From literature to literacy.* Portsmouth, NH: Heinemann, 1988.

Temple, Charles, Ruth Nathan, Nancy Burris, and Frances Temple. *The beginnings of writing.* Boston: Allyn and Bacon, 1982.

Wells, Gordon. *The meaning makers: Children learning language and using language to learn.* Portsmouth, NH: Heinemann, 1986.

The books listed in Chapter 7 are also recommended.

7
Growing Up Writing
Grades K, 1, and 2

Children can write sooner than we ever dreamed was possible. Most children come to school knowing a handful of letters, and with these they can write labels and calendars, letters and stories, poems and songs. They will learn to write by writing and by living with a sense of "I am one who writes." This self-perception will give children the eyes to see, and they will notice the conventions of written language everywhere. They will learn about punctuation, spelling, purposes for writing, and the many rhythms of written language from billboards and environmental labels and books. They will ask about the monogram letters on their bath towels and the words on their sweatshirts. They will imitate their big sister's cursive writing, they will gather knowledge from all the writing and all the writers in their world. Their growth as writers is spectacular. All over the world, there are six- and seven-year-olds who write with voice, skill, and confidence.

Sometimes it helps us as teachers and as parents if we can anticipate some of the continuums along which growth in writing may happen. In this chapter, we'll reflect on:

- Changes that occur as children's writing is supported by, and eventually separated from, their drawings.
- The growth that happens as children's spellings become more conventional.
- Changes that happen as the temporal dimensions of children's writing processes expand, allowing children to move toward more rehearsal and revision.

Changes That Occur as Children's Writing Is Supported by, and Eventually Separated from, Their Drawings

Five-year-old Chris opens his book to a blank page and takes hold of his pencil. Cheerfully I ask, "What are you going to write?" The boy stares at me as if astounded by the stupidity of my question. "How should I know?" he says. "I haven't drawed it yet."

For a few minutes, Chris glances around the classroom and then he begins to draw. He makes the standard figure of a person; his dad has taught him to draw people, so now he follows the formula with care. Partway through the drawing, Chris announces, "This is gonna be my brother. He's fighting," and he adds a giant fist to the person as if to symbolize the fight. Then he draws a second person, again with an oversized hand. "We're fighting," he adds and begins to write.

Like many four-, five-, and six-year-olds, Chris rehearses for writing by drawing. This does not mean that his drawings are important only as preludes to writing. In fact, the drawings are far more important to Chris than the writing; the drawings take up most of his time and most of his paper, and they convey most of his story. When I say that Chris's drawings are rehearsals for writing, I also do not mean that his drawings accomplish the purposes we, as adults, normally connect with rehearsal. As he draws, Chris does not weigh one topic against another, nor does he anticipate an audience's response to his story or plan the direction his writing will take. In the block area, Chris does not begin with armchair speculation over what he will build. Instead he piles one block on top of another until he announces, "I'm makin' a tower." So, too, in the writing area he does not begin by thinking about his final product but by drawing the conventional person; then, in the middle of drawing, he announces, "This is gonna be my brother."

For older children, rehearsal for writing will involve living one's life as a writer, noticing all that it contains. Rehearsal will also involve rereading one's notebook to consider various topics, planning a story, thinking about making something for someone, worrying over the audiences' responses, and gathering notebook entries with an eye toward future writing. In order to do this, the writer must have a wide-lens sense of time. The writer must be able to anticipate that the work begun today will exist tomorrow. Chris, like many kindergarten, first-, and second-grade children, tends to operate more in the present tense, in the here and now. He doesn't spend a lot of time anticipating his tomorrows. He doesn't fret about whether his writing topic is "good enough" any more than he frets about whether his block tower will be acceptable. He **writes** the way he plays with blocks—for the sake of the activity more than for the creation of a final product.

For Chris, drawing plays an important role. The act of drawing and the picture itself both provide a supportive scaffolding within which he can construct his piece of writing. When he writes, Chris is like a newborn foal; he stands on shaky legs. When he does not have a visual memory of a word, he sounds it out: "Fighting." He isolates a sound, /f/, then asks, "How do you spell /f/?" When no one answers, he scans the alphabet, guesses at a letter, and puts it down on his paper. Meanwhile, he's forgotten what he wanted to write. What a relief it must be to return to the drawing, to darkening his brother's fist! As he carefully fills in the hand, Chris remembers what he wanted to write, and so he returns to print. Back and forth he switches, from drawing to writing, then back to drawing again, moving from the relief and stability of one medium to the challenge of the other.

Alongside a crayoned picture of two cars crashing another child writes "BOOM." This child is able to convey her story through a single word, and she can do this only because the word is lodged within the context of the picture. Most of the child's meaning is carried by the picture. Not just the act of drawing but the picture itself provides a supportive framework for young writers. In time, children learn to create autonomous, explicit texts, but during their early forays into writing, they often embed much of their meaning in the picture rather than in the text, as in the example in Figure 7–1. In nine words and a picture, this youngster has made a powerful statement about the meaning of life.

FIGURE 7–1   Meaning embedded in drawing

*When you get to be a big person . . .
cemetery.*

Drawings must also help youngsters with the problem of selection. The world involves such a rapid flux of activities and ideas, and writing is so slow, so limited, that selection is a problem even for skilled writers. How much more true this must be for beginning writers! In their drawings, children take one bit of the world and hold it still for a moment; then, with the picture lying in front of them, they begin work on the accompanying words.

Kindergarten children's drawings often hold the world totally still. Their pictures tend to be a collection of objects placed here and there on the page: a boy, a dog, a house. It is a great day when a thin line appears on the bottom of the paper. With common ground comes the possibility of relationship: the boy and the dog are beside the house. Will they enter it? Do they live there? For a while, the action is only implicit: the drawings show only a static frontal lineup. But soon, through spaghetti arms, or through lines, dots, and arrows, as in the pictures in Figure 7–2, action enters into the drawing.

About fifteen years ago, Don Graves, Susan Sowers, and I spent several years conducting a major study of children and their writing. As part of this study, Sowers found that when action enters children's drawing, their texts tend to change from "all-about" books into narratives or chronologically ordered books. Action entered into children's drawings especially after they began drawing their figures in profile. Now horses could be led on a rope, people could kiss and dance together, dogs could drink out of their bowls. Characters could interact with each other and with their settings . . . and different written texts resulted.

FIGURE 7–2 Action depicted in drawing

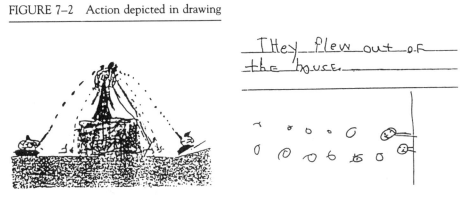

Because of the many ways in which drawing contributes to early writing, I encourage kindergarten and first-grade teachers to provide their children with thin marker pens and with an assortment of unlined and experience-chart paper, with some stapled into small, informal books, and some left as individual sheets.

Having spoken so extensively about the ways in which drawing can support children's early writing, let me also say that in *some* first- and most second-grade classrooms I discourage teachers and children from regarding drawing as an integral part of the writing process. In some primary classrooms, I ask teachers, "Why not steer them away from drawings?"

Let me be clear that when I suggest, at some point, that children move away from writing only captions under drawings, I'm not advocating moving away from artwork. Although it is not always necessary for writing to weave in and out of drawing, it is certainly necessary for our classrooms to support all kinds of artistic exploration. I selected my sons' nursery school largely because of the centrality of the "cut and color" table at that school, and because, instead of having teacher-directed art projects, the school encourages free exploration with pens, paints, and clay. I think it's very important that the painting easel always be available as an option in primary classrooms. There is no question in my mind that the habits of mind one develops in composing a diorama or a clay sculpture are very similar to the habits of mind one develops in writing. In both instances, the composer needs to ask, "How shall I go about making something lovely? What medium might work best?" The artist, like the writer, explores one possibility and then another, drafting and revising. With paint, clay, and fabric, the artist, like the writer, creates imaginary worlds and invites others to live inside them.

Teachers are sometimes baffled to find that first I recommend drawing as a way of rehearsing for writing and then later, I discourage it. The point is that no solution works for every child and no solution works forever. We can introduce drawing as a form of rehearsal, but then we must watch for signs indicating that a child no longer needs to weave drawing and writing together.

I would want to be sure, for example, that drawings do not limit rather than extend the range of my children's writing. One boy was very skillful at drawing the Pink Panther, so that character starred in every book he wrote, even though he had nothing to say about the Pink Panther. I'd also want to be sure that children weren't drawing *after* they wrote and hurrying through the writing in order to be able to draw. I'd also want to watch that the presence of drawings didn't curtail my children's writing, so that they write nothing more extended than captions, or so they grow up relying on drawings to carry much of their content. Words, as well as pictures, can be a way to set the scene and describe characters. There would be many instances, then, when I might encourage children to write in little books consisting of five or six small sheets of lined paper, for example, rather than on pages with white space for drawings. The paper itself can lure children toward writing self-standing, autonomous texts.

Once children do not rely on drawings as their primary form of rehearsal for writing, I'd want them to see that talking can perform the same function. Whereas drawing is a predominant form of rehearsal for many first graders, talking is particularly effective for second graders. Let me explain.

In kindergarten and first grade, many children convey their meaning more easily through drawing than through print. Drawing, therefore, can provide a supportive scaffolding for the writing. Because more information is embedded in the pictures than in the print, drawing provides a horizon and leads the child deeper into the writing. In a sense, our goal at this stage is to help children's writing catch up with their drawing.

By second grade, writing has often surpassed drawing. Although these children may still find it easier to draw than to write, many find it easier to embed meaning into a written text than into a drawing. In early first grade, then, the goal is to have writing catch up to drawing; by second grade the goal is often to have writing catch up to talking. The goal is fluency and voice, for the lilt of oral language to come through in a child's writing.

In second grade, chatting about one's subject with an interested friend seems to be an ideal method for rehearsal. Because the focus of these discussions is on content, the writer's attention is drawn away from conventions and rules, which is helpful for children who sometimes obsess about the "right way" to do things. Because the discussions are interactive, writers learn not only that they have something to say and a voice with which to say it, but also that somebody values what they have to say. When I work with second graders, I often encourage them to interview each other before they write. "Find a partner," I tell the children, "and a quiet place in the classroom. Then take turns telling each other about your topics." Soon there are no quiet places in the classroom!

The first interviews are invariably happy disasters. Roger says, "I'm going to write about my grandma's new car. She is going to take me for a ride in it." Mark cuts him off to announce, "I'm going to write about a big dinosaur and he eats a lady up. In his mouth, he just chews her up." End of interview.

In the next chapter and elsewhere in this book, I suggest ways to extend our children's abilities to confer with each other. But for now, it's enough to say that even if children simply chat with each other about their topics and their writing, these discussions are important.

Young Children's Growth in Spelling and Punctuation

Children who begin by writing with wiggly lines and lollipops will very soon begin writing with the letters they know best. In Chapter 6, we saw David using the letters D, A, V, I, and D to represent "I took the A train to Botanical Gardens." David was matching each of his words to a letter, but he wasn't deliberately matching particular letters with particular words. Even when children do try to match letters with sounds, they usually do this first by relying on the *names* of letters, as when Miles labeled his boat's windows YNDO (see Chapter 6). At first glance this spelling may look like a string of random letters, but a closer look suggests that Miles has accurately used his knowledge of letter names. The letter Y is called "*w*ye"; it's not surprising, therefore, that Miles uses a Y rather than a W (double-u) as the initial sound when he wants to write "window."

There is a similar explanation for why Miles spells *chimney* as JAME. He uses a J for the initial sound in *chimney* because the name of the letter he uses starts with a |ch| sound (*ch*ay). Miles might have begun the word *chimney* with an H (ait*ch*) for the same reason. Like many young writers, Miles is relying on the names, not the sounds, of letters. Therefore, he ends the word *chimney* with an E and begins the word *smoke* with a C.

Early on, children often represent only the first and final sounds of a word on the page. The word *today*, for example, might be spelled TA. Spellings fill out as children learn more sound-symbol correspondences, as they become more able to segment words into sounds (or phonemes), and as they gradually develop a bank of sight words (and parts of words). When we first launch children into invented spelling, it's important to remember that learning to spell is not only about learning to match sounds with letters, it's also about learning to hear sounds in the first place. If we go around the classroom breaking every word into sounds for our kids to encode, we are taking over a big part of the writer's job. We are better off inviting children to join us in saying words slowly ("Let's stretch out the word *today* like a rubber band and listen to the sounds") than taking the words and breaking them into separate sounds for them. Of course, children will not always understand what it means to listen for the sounds in a word. A colleague of mine, Martha Horn, pulled her chair alongside Renee's desk. Renee, who was four, was drawing a picture of Santa Claus.

"Do you want to write something?" Martha asked her, but Renee didn't seem to understand. Martha tried again. "Can you say *Santa* slowly, listening to the sounds?" Soon Martha and Renee were sounding out S-S-S-S-S-anta. "What sounds do you hear?" Martha asked.

Renee whispered the word to herself again, listening intently to it. "Sa-a-nta," she said. "S-a-a-a-nnnn-ta." Then she looked proudly at Martha and announced, "I hear 'Ho Ho Ho.'"

Over time, children's spellings not only become more complete, they also become more conventional. As teachers, we don't have to wait for children to spell *you* and *the* and *a* conventionally. As I discuss later (Chapter 18), we will probably not suggest that children sound out common sight vocabulary words. Instead, we'll say something like, "*You?* —you know how to spell *you*—y-o-u." Alternatively, we might say, "Close your eyes and see if you can picture how the word *you* is spelled in your books."

Almost as soon as children begin to write, they will begin to spell certain words automatically, from memory, and this is necessary if they are to become fluent spellers. It helps if we consciously remind them that their memory of how words look—as well as sound—can be a resource when they write. Many children, for example, have a visual sense of words like *school* or *today* and they need to know that their image of a word is an important resource to draw on when they spell.

Sometimes teachers and parents are so intently focused on watching children's spellings fill out, we don't realize the other developments that are also evident in their early writings. In the child's message to her teacher shown in Figure 7–3 (which the teacher found taped to her pocketbook) there are no spaces between words.

Once children begin to realize that words need to be separated, they often go to the extreme and write one word on each line so their stories look like the one in Figure 7–4. Other children insert dashes, dots, or slashes into their texts to separate words. Not uncommonly, they are not sure where one word ends and another begins. *Ham and eggs* is written HAMANAGS, *Steve Austin* is STE FSDN. *All of a sudden* is ALLUVA SDN, and *other reasons* is OTRSNS.

Then, too, when kindergarten and first-grade children write, they often use darkened letters, oversized print, or capitals to add the sound of a voice to their words. After six-year-old Brad put the word *pull* into his story, he returned to it and carefully darkened each of the letters.

FIGURE 7–3 No spaces between words

DOFRGTYR
RNROL+AP *Don't forget the rock 'n' roll tape.*

FIGURE 7–4 An early effort to add space between words

ONES
I HAD
I STRO
BERY
PIENT
AND
IT GROO
STRO
BERY
INTIL
BAGS
KEM
TO THAI BLRY

Once I had a strawberry plant, and it grew strawberries until the bugs came to eat the berries.

"Why did you do that?" Don Graves wondered.

"Because I want them to know to really PULL," Brad answered. Hearing this, Brad's teacher showed the boy how to use exclamation marks; soon they were spreading from child to child throughout the classroom. "I like them," one child told me. "You use them when you yell and when you are excited. Usually I put them at the end of every line, but if it's somebody birthday or the guy's dying, I put them at the end of every word." Another youngster told me exclamation marks are really called "happy marks."

Quotation marks are equally popular in kindergarten and first-grade classrooms, for they, too, give voice to print. One six-year-old put comic-strip balloons around spoken sections of her stories until her teacher, Mary Ellen Giacobbe, showed her the conventional way to represent speech. Like exclamation marks, quotations spread quickly. Even very young children want their characters to talk like real people. By the end of the year, thirty percent of Mary Ellen's first graders were using quotation marks correctly in their stories.

In addition to changes in the use of conventions, observers of young children will quickly notice changes in the voicing behaviors that accompany writing. For Andrea, as for many young writers, writing is deeply embedded in oral language. Speech—like drawing—provides a scaffolding within which the text can be constructed. A tremendous amount of talk surrounds the production of even just a few written words, as this transcript shows:

> Andrea is singing to herself as she draws. "My little caterpillar, my little caterpillar, little, little, little . . ."
> > *She voices as part of language play.*
>
> "There, that's my caterpillar," she says as she finishes her drawing. "Now, let's see . . ."
> > *This is procedural talk. Perhaps it orients Andrea, helping her organize the task before her.*
>
> "I've got two pages done, now, let's see."
> > *She gauges her progress. Talk keeps her company.*
>
> "I-like-my-caterpillar."
> > *She isolates what she will write and says it slowly.*

Eventually, some of this externalized talk will become a silent sort of inner commentary, accompanying Andrea as she writes.

Children Move Toward Rehearsal and Revision

I remember working once in a creative movement class with a group of five- and six-year-olds. With my wand, I turned each child into an icicle, and then I became an icicle too. "The sun is coming out," I said, speaking slowly, quietly. "Its rays are warming us. Slowly, slowly, slowly, we begin to drip, drip." As I spoke, I let one of my hands drip drip out of its frozen icicle posture. I continued, still speaking slowly. "We drip . . . drip . . . drip. . . ." Then the fingers on my other hand began melting . . . and I heard thuds all over the room. Looking up, I saw twenty children, twenty melted icicles, lying like puddles on the floor.

The incident seemed at the time to be emblematic of young children's all-or-nothing sense of time. It's not surprising that children who go from being an icicle to being a puddle without drip-drip-drip-dripping sometimes put the entire sequence of events in their story onto the first page of their books. The story may begin, for example, "There was an explosion and everyone died," or "We went to the beach and the diner and the park and came home." It's not surprising that these children's writing processes, like their products, often do not extend over a sequence of days. Many young children, when given a book with six blank pages, will write six different stories, one on each page, or, if no one stops them, they'll write a story on page one and then leave the book behind as they head off to the next adventure. It is progress, indeed, for children to begin a book on day one and page one and continue it on day two, page two.

All of this is a far cry from the way we saw eight-year-old Jennifer, in Chapter 4, developing her poems about her brother. She gathered entries on various topics in her notebook, decided to stay with the subject of her pesky brother, lived with this topic for a week, reread her collection of entries, decided to write poems, and then began rough drafts and revisions of those poems.

Teachers often ask, "When should I encourage children to keep notebooks and to live toward a particular piece of writing? When should I introduce revision?" In a sense, these teachers are asking, "When should I extend the time dimensions of my children's writing?"

There are no answers to questions like these. Some teachers in kindergarten and first grade, especially, will feel that it's enough to encourage invented spelling and purposeful writing, and they'll decide to leave notebooks (rehearsal) and revision for another year. Other teachers will introduce notebooks and revision only as options in these early grades. Still other teachers will encourage all their children to live like writers, noticing and cherishing and recording the details of their lives in notebooks. All of these choices are reasonable as long as we bear in mind that young children will invent their own special understandings of notebooks and revision and that their writing processes will not match those of their third- or sixth-grade friends. In the next two sections, I'll explore—for teachers who are interested—some ways in which notebooks and revision might be brought into primary classrooms.

Notebooks in the Primary Grades

When I put my sons' blue jeans in the hamper at night and hear the thunk thunk of shelled acorns, pretty stones, and small creatures cascading from their pockets, it strikes me that my sons' pockets are their real-life notebooks.

Very young children are the best writers in the world—except for the writing part of being a writer. Georgia Heard, a colleague of mine and the author of *For the Good of the Earth and Sun*, spent the Fourth of July with her three-year-old nephew. I figured they'd watch fireworks together, but Georgia and her nephew had something different in mind. After the child got on his pajamas, after he was all washed and ready for bed, he and Georgia went out onto the porch. The two of them, the child and the poet, sat very still, waiting and waiting and waiting for the slugs to come out. They watched as each slug left a trail of slime along the porch. When it was time for Georgia's nephew to go to bed, he whispered goodnight to each tiny slug, gently touched their horns, and then scampered off, not knowing he'd shared a bit of the writerly life that night.

We grown-ups do not have to teach young children to cherish the little stuff of their lives. We do not have to remind them to cup their hands around the bits of their lives and declare them treasures. We don't have to teach children that they can collect strings of wonderful words, or that they can linger to wonder and to question.

What we *do* need is to teach children that their wonderings and questions and curiosity are part of what it means to write well. We need to teach them that even though we rush them here and there, we only halfway mean for them to "hurry up," that truly, we know they should be telling us to "slow down," to "look, listen, wait. . . ." We need to teach children that when they notice a new kind of fruit at the grocer's or marvel that a tree can grow from such a small patch of earth, this is part of writing. We need to teach them that what they see and collect and wonder about will enrich their poems and stories and posters.

To me, it makes all the sense in the world to value our children's wide-awakeness by telling them that they can gather the little treasures of their lives in notebooks. Kathy Mason, a first/second-grade teacher in Phoenix, Arizona, introduces her children to the idea of "lifebooks" by reading aloud Byrd Baylor's *I'm in Charge of Celebrations*. Afterward, she and her youngsters sit under a tree, looking and listening, finding something to celebrate. In Kathy's classroom, children can choose to write in tiny poem books, or on the clipboard beside their lizard's cage, or in small, homemade books, or on posters or musical score sheets—and they can also choose to write in their lifebooks. Because the lifebooks are with the children all day, because they go home with the children every night, and to the nursing home where the children have buddies and onto the playground and to lunch, they are often the place where children *first* write down their lives. But this writing coexists alongside a wide range of other writing.

Once young children realize that notebooks (or lifebooks) aren't collections of stories "with beginnings, middles, and ends," but are, instead, places for gathering the bits and pieces of their lives, the notebooks take on a feeling very diffcrent from the journals so many primary children are encouraged to keep. Justine, a second grader in Kathy Mason's class, wrote a letter to me about her notebook. For Justine, the notebook is all about an attitude toward life. "I love the sun, moon, stars, flowers, grass, and trees," she wrote. "I like to write, read, play, and sing." This reverence for life shines through her notebook. This is one page of it (Figure 7–5):

TODAY

Today is November 30th my celebration day. It is the last day of November. There will never be a November 30, 1992. So I am going to make the best of it and today is the day, the last day of November.

FIGURE 7–5   A page of Justine's notebook

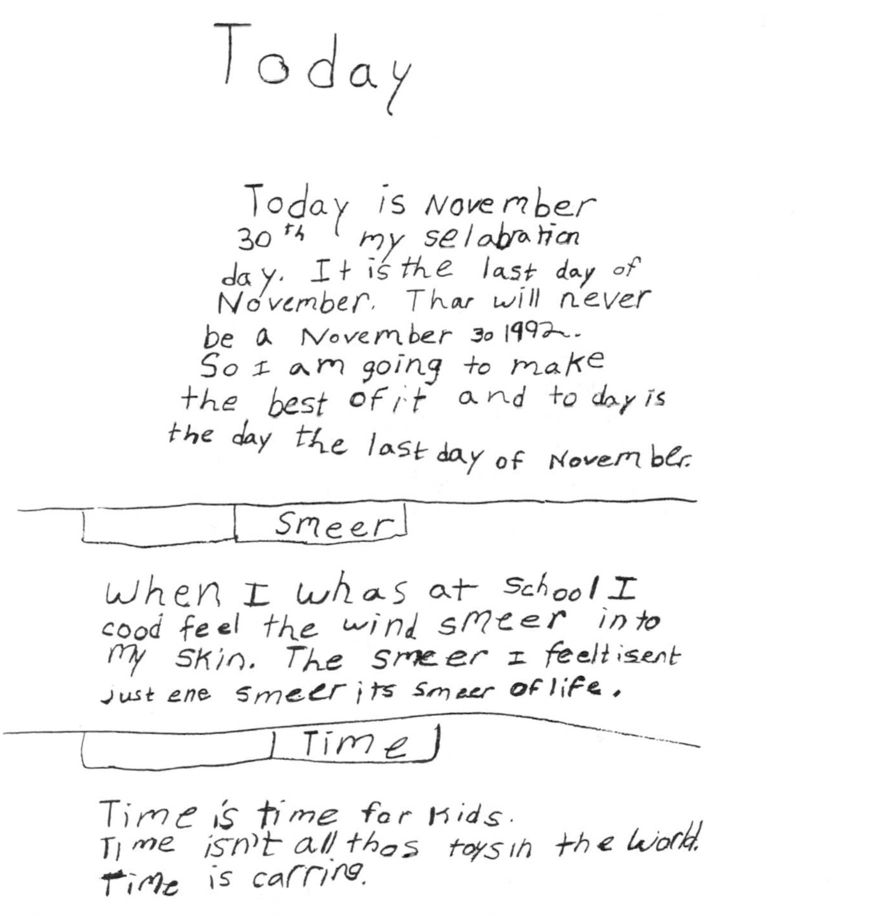

Today

Today is November 30th my selabration day. It is the last day of November. Thar will never be a November 30 1992. So I am going to make the best of it and to day is the day the last day of November.

Smeer

When I whas at school I cood feel the wind smeer into my skin. The smeer I feelt isent just ene smeer its smeer of life.

Time

Time is time for kids. Time isn't all thos toys in the world. Time is carring.

SMEER

When I was at school I could feel the wind smeer into my skin. The smeer I felt isn't just any smeer. Its smeer of life.

TIME

Time is time for kids.
Time isn't all those toys in the world.
Time is caring.

In the page of Emily's notebook shown in Figure 7–6, she records and values a comment made by one of the residents at the nursing home and reflects on her mother's collection of plates:

FIGURE 7–6   A page of Emily's notebook

Bessie is in a nursing home.
She is 82. She said
"My brains don't think
any more."

My mothers cloecter plates

My mom has cloecter plates. She keeps them in a glass cuboard. I always wonder about them. They all have mothers on them, and with thoose mothers there is a chiled. And ever chiled is a girl.
On the back of the plates it says the mothers name and the little girls name.
My mom has two special plates. One is called Jessica and Kate The uther is Jennifer and Emily My name is Emily. My little sisters name is Kate.

BESSIE

Bessie is in a nursing home. She is 82. She said, "My brains don't think anymore."

MY MOTHER'S COLLECTOR PLATES

My mom has collector plates. She keeps them in a glass cupboard. I always wonder about them. They all have mothers on them, and with those mothers there is a child. And every child is a girl. On the back of the plates it says the mother's name and the little girl's name. My mom has two special plates. One is called Jessica and Kate. The other is Jennifer and Emily. My name is Emily. My little sister's name is Kate.

Emily may at some point decide to write a story or an article for the school newspaper about her class's involvement with the nursing home. She may someday write about the people in her life who have collections. If she does either of these projects, Kathy Mason will help her reread her notebook and gather together all the entries that relate to the topic she chooses to pursue. It is more likely, however, that Emily will not consciously draw upon these entries when she writes for publication (although I can't imagine she won't do so unconsciously). The notebook enriches her writing life whether or not she deliberately develops her entries into finished pieces of writing.

Kathy Mason, like many other wonderful primary teachers, begins the year by launching her entire class into notebook writing, but other teachers move toward notebooks in different ways. Dora Ferriulio, for example, began the year expecting that her children would write one-draft-only stories and poems and songs. By January, Dora's first graders were cranking out underdeveloped little stories at such a rapid clip that Dora decided to introduce notebooks to some of her youngsters as a way of encouraging them to slow down and deepen their writing process. Dora suggested that these children spread all their completed pieces out on the floor. Then the children walked through this giant lacework of pieces thinking, "What do I *often* write about?" and "Which of these pieces and topics matter especially to me?"

In this very physical, embodied way, Dora introduced her children to the idea of rereading one's collection of first-draft writing in order to ask, "What should I develop more?" After each child found a topic that had already become something of an obsession to him or her, each child made a small notebook and set out to collect more entries on the chosen topic.

FIGURE 7–7 Entries from Hannah's notebook

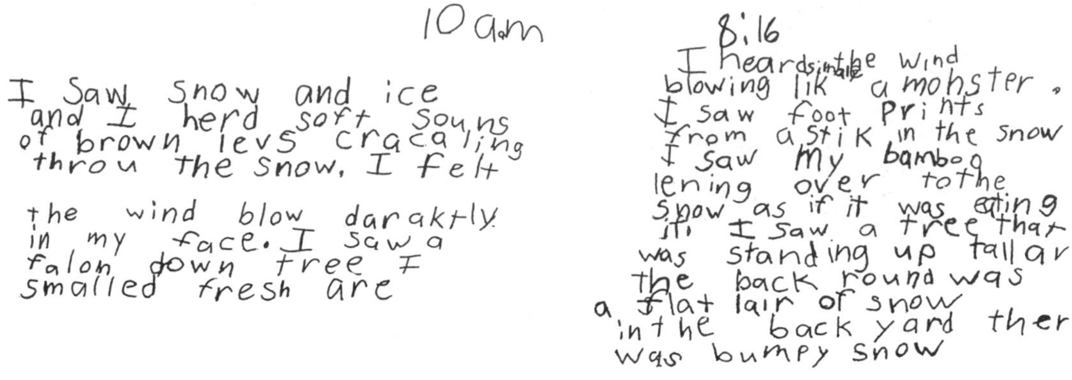
10 am

I saw snow and ice and I herd soft souns of brown levs cracaling throu the snow, I felt the wind blow darakly in my face. I saw a falon down tree I smalled fresh are

8:16

I heards the wind blowing lik a monster. I saw foot prints from a stik in the snow I saw my bamboo lening over tothe snow as if it was eating it. I saw a tree that was standing up tall ar the back round was a flat lair of snow in the back yard ther was bumpy snow

In Michelle Pena's first-grade classroom in Tenafly, New Jersey, children were introduced to notebooks as part of their thematic study on winter. The children built a bird feeder outside their classroom and studied the birds together. They took winter hikes, and each adopted a tiny patch of winterland. They followed footsteps and listened to winter sounds, and always, always, lived with their writer's notebook at their side. These are a few entries from Hannah Miller's notebook (Figure 7–7):

> I saw snow and ice and I heard soft sounds of brown leaves crackling through the snow. I felt the wind blow directly in my face. I saw a fallen down tree. I smelled fresh air.
>
> I heard the wind blowing like a monster. I saw footprints from a stick in the snow. I saw my bamboo leaning over to the snow as if it was eating it. I saw a tree that was standing up tall and the background was a flat layer of snow. In the back yard there was bumpy snow.

Revision in the Primary Grades

Five-year-old Mellisa had been in kindergarten for only a few days. On a sheet of construction paper she'd written a line of letters and from them she read, "Dear Daddy, I love you. Love, Mellisa." Crouching alongside Mellisa, my arm around her, I listened to the story. "You really love him, don't you?" I said, confirming what I'd heard.

"Yes, I love him because he lives with me," she solemnly answered.

I nodded, thinking to myself that having a father who lives with you is becoming a big thing. Turning the paper from one side to the other, I asked Mellisa, "Where did you put that, Mellisa?" as if I was surprised that such important information hadn't been included. Mellisa told me there wasn't enough room, so I took her hand and we headed to the writing corner, where I stapled two more pieces of construction paper onto the first. "Now you have a lot of space," I said, and the little girl returned to the patch of floor that served as her desk. From across the room, I watched as she counted the blank pages in her newly formed book, shrugged, and began filling them up. The cardinal rule in kindergarten and first grade seems to be, "Thou shalt fill up the space."

Adding on is a very natural part of young children's writing. It can be regarded as an early form of revision or as part of drafting, for there is no clear division between the two. Children write, and if given the chance to share their pieces with a responsive listener, they often realize they have more to tell and someone who hopes they will tell it. Before long, children are "making stories grow" on their own: one page becomes three, a six-inch text is extended into a giant scroll. Children enjoy stapling and taping, and they quickly learn to add on.

They are less quick to reread their own emerging texts, to shift from being writers to being readers, from pushing ahead to looking back. This is not unique to writing. In all they do, many young children seem to be always moving on. They finish a drawing and stuff it into their desk without a second glance. They finish a painting and immediately their attention shifts to whatever is next on their schedule. In writing, adding on without looking back leads to stories that are a collage of pieces held together with staples and tape. One way to support young children's growth in writing, then, is to encourage them to read what they have written to the children working alongside them and, most of all, to themselves.

Realizing this, many primary-grade teachers encourage children to work at tables or on the floor so they will interact with one another (and with their texts) throughout the workshop. Sometimes teachers also set aside areas for more extensive peer conferences. Some primary teachers begin or end the writing workshop by asking each student to find a conference partner and to have a brief conference.

"But are five- and six-year-olds really capable of holding effective peer conferences?" teachers ask. The question calls to mind a conference I recently observed involving two first graders. The youngsters pulled chairs close together, then each girl took hold of her story and, in unison, they read their stories to each other. Neither child listened and neither child was listened to, but both girls seemed pleased with their conference. They happily trotted back to the writing table and tackled writing with renewed vigor. Even when neither child really listens to the other, these interactions serve a purpose. This does not mean, however, that children cannot really listen to each other's stories. With help, children can learn not only to listen, but also to help their classmates rethink what they have done.

Children learn to confer with each other in these ways when their teacher confers with them. Six-year-old Dana read her recipe to Mary Ellen Giacobbe:

> Put the macaroni in the water and stir it on and off. After ten minutes
> it is done and you put the cheese in. Then you eat it all up.

Before Mary Ellen could respond, Dana added another bit of information—orally. "It'll get nice and bubbly, the tip-top will get all bubbly, and that's how you know it's done."

"Oh, I see!" Mary Ellen said. "I'll know if it's done because it gets all bubbly. Are you going to include that in the recipe, Dana? Because I didn't know about that."

"No," Dana shook her head. "People should know that. If they don't, then I'll invite them to my birthday and I'll *show* them how."

Mary Ellen tried again. "Dana," she said, "what if Chris takes this book home and his mother is going to follow your recipe? How will she know about how it gets nice and bubbly?"

"Okay, okay," Dana said and began inserting the missing information into her text.

When Dana adds missing information to her text, she is using a revision strategy that is very common in the early grades. When writers have readers who really try to understand and learn from them, writers soon internalize these readers.

When six-year-old Scott reread his homemade book, he scowled. "This story should go in the trash can," he muttered. "See, the kids will have so many questions." This is what Scott had written:

> I saw my father's collections. Then we left.

"I go through it wicked fast. The kids will say, 'What were the collections? What'd ya see?' " Scott's voice trails off as he begins to wind words up the margin of his page:

> We saw buttons, coins, stamps and other stuff.

"The kids will have questions still," Scott says, "but at least I got rid of some of them."

Two classmates listened as six-year-old Greg read the beginning of his story out loud:

> We got on a big bus. It took us to the game. The Patriots and the Jets played. The score was 55 to 21. We saw two men in long underwear at the game.

Then the story shifted back to the bus:

> There was a bathroom on the bus. There was a lot of people on the bus.

Once again, the story shifted:

> The policeman at the game made us throw our Coke in the garbage.

At this point, Sharon interrupted. "Greg," she said, "it isn't about one thing. It goes hippety-hop from one thing to the next. It's like you had a crazy dream. It's all mixed up." Seeing Greg's worried look, Sharon hurried to reassure him that with Jaws, the class staple remover, he could take his book apart and put the pages back together in a more logical order.

The revision strategy Greg used after discovering that his story went hippety-hop from one thing to another is a common one. With advice from his teacher and from Sharon, Greg took his book apart, spread the pages in front of him, and then reordered them. Similarly, when Shanti's friends heard her birthday party book, they protested because in her story she told about roller-skating *before* the cake, whereas in fact the cake came first. Shanti later rearranged the paper (and the events) sequentially.

It is common for first-grade children to jumble several stories into one, in which case revision may involve dividing their books into smaller pieces. One child proudly showed me her four-page book. Although the story was entitled "My Hamster," it was only partially about the hamster. There were also large sections about her father, and others about her school. After admiring the length of her masterpiece, I said, "What I'm wondering about is why the title is 'My Hamster' when parts are about your father, school, and other things." The youngster was quiet, her eyes scanning the story. Then she said, "I know," and jumping up, she ran to the writing corner. I expected her to return with scissors, in recognition of the fact that there were three stories in one. When she returned, however, she had instead brought a pen. Beside the title "My Hamster" she added, in her own spelling, "And My Father and School and Other Stuff."

My favorite revision story, however, involves not the title of a story but the ending. Six-year-old Lori had written a sad tale about a princess who was attacked by a witch, and when the princess ran away, the witch followed. The tale ended abruptly with the words "The End."

"What happened next?" Mary Ellen asked, as if she couldn't stand the suspense. Lori answered slowly, and it seemed clear she was making up the ending as she spoke. Mary Ellen listened intently to the conclusion of the tale. Then she said, "You know, Lori, I think maybe you should change the end—because I didn't know what happened next."

Lori nodded and, pulling the book close to her, she opened it to the last page where she had penciled:

The
n
d

This time, she set to work with bright colored crayons, revising the ending until it read:

THE
E
N
D

It would be easy to look at this incident and say, "The intervention didn't work." But although Lori did not change the ending of her tale, she did reread her draft, and perhaps she even saw her writing through the eyes of a reader. Revision means, quite literally, to see again, and it needs to be interpreted in the broadest sense. Sometimes revision involves reseeing our subject, sometimes it involves pulling back to take a look at our emerging text, sometimes it involves changing

The
n
d

to

THE
E
N
D

What a reminder this is that children are children, that "fixing up the end" will mean something very different to a six-year-old than it means to an adult. We may try again to convey our intentions, or we may not. It doesn't really matter. What does matter is that we enjoy Lori's revisions, that we give her a hug, that we take her wonderful story with us to the staff room to share with our colleagues. The important thing is that we are dazzled and delighted by what children do.

Literature to Read to Children

Baum, Frank. *Wizard of Oz*. New York: Scholastic, 1989.

Conrad, Pam. *The tub people*. New York: HarperCollins Children's Books, 1989.

Dahl, Roald. *James and the giant peach*. New York: Buccaneer Books, 1990.

————. *Matilda*. New York: Viking, 1988.

————. *Mr. Fantastic Fox*. New York: Penguin, 1970.

de Paola, Tomie. *Now one foot, now the other*. New York: Putnam Publishing Group, 1992.

De Veaux, Alexis. *An enchanted hair tale*. New York: HarperCollins Children's Books, 1987.

Dorros, Arthur. *Abuela*. New York: Dutton Children's Books, 1991.

Ehrlich, Amy, adapter. *The Random House book of fairy tales*. New York: Random Books for Young Readers, 1985.

Fleichman, Sid. *The whipping boy*. New York: Greenwillow Books, 1986.

Fleming, Denise. *In the tall, tall grass*. New York: Henry Holt & Co., 1991.

Gag, Wanda. *Millions of cats*. New York: Putnam Publishing Group, 1977.

Gardiner, John Reynolds. *Stone fox*. New York: Thomas Y. Crowell, 1980.

Gordon, Gaelyn. *Duckat*. New York: Scholastic, 1992.

Greenfield, Eloise. *Honey, I love and other love poems*. New York: HarperCollins Children's Books, 1978.

Hoffman, Mary. *Amazing grace.* New York: Dial Books, 1991.

Huck, Charlotte. *Princess Furball.* New York: Greenwillow, 1989.

Hughes, Ted. *The iron man: A story in five nights.* Illustrations by Dirk Zimmer. New York: HarperCollins, 1968.

Hunter, Mollie. *The knight of the golden plain.* New York: HarperCollins Children's Books, 1983.

Jonas, Ann. *The quilt.* New York: Greenwillow, 1984.

King-Smith, Dick. *Martin's mice.* New York: Dell Publishing, 1988.

Marshall, James. *Rats on the roof and other stories.* New York: Dial Books, 1991.

Milne, A. A. *Winnie the pooh.* New York: NAL-Dutton, 1961.

Naidoo, Beverly. *Journey to Jo'burg: A South African story.* New York: HarperCollins Children's Books, 1988.

Naylor, Phyllis R. *Shiloh.* New York: Dell, 1992.

Parish, Peggy. *Amelia Bedelia helps out.* New York: Greenwillow Books, 1979.

Paterson, Katherine. *The king's equal.* Illustrations by Vladimir Vogin. New York: HarperCollins, 1992.

Peterson, John. *Littles.* New York: Scholastic, 1986.

Rodanas, Kristina. *Dragonfly's tale.* New York: Clarion Books, 1991.

Ryder, Joanne. *The bear on the mountain.* Illustrated by Carol Lacey. New York: Morrow, 1991.

Say, Allen. *El Chino.* Boston: Houghton Mifflin, 1990.

Selden, George. *The cricket in Times Square.* New York: Dell, 1970.

Sendak, Maurice. *Where the wild things are.* New York: Harper & Row, 1963.

Steig, William. *Abel's island.* New York: Farrar, Straus & Giroux, 1976.

———. *Amos and Boris.* New York: Farrar, Straus & Giroux, 1971.

Tejima, Keizaburo. *Owl lake.* New York: Philomel Books, 1987.

Warner, Gertrude C. *Boxcar children.* New York: Buccaneer Books, 1992.

Wells, Rosemary. *First tomato / The island light / Moss pillows.* New York: Dial Books, 1992.

White, E. B. *Charlotte's web.* New York: Harper & Row, 1952.

———. *Stuart Little.* New York: HarperCollins Children's Books, 1974.

Wilder, Laura Ingalls. *Little house in the big woods.* New York: Harper & Row, 1981.

Williams, Vera B. *Music, music for everyone!* New York: Greenwillow, 1984.

Winter, Jeanette. *Follow the drinking gourd.* New York: Alfred A. Knopf, 1988.

Literature for Children to Read Independently or Collaboratively

Ahlberg, Janet, and Allan Ahlberg. *Each peach pear plum: An "I spy" story.* New York: Viking, 1979.

Bemmelmans, Ludwig. *Madeline.* New York: Viking, 1958.

Brown, Margaret Wise. *Goodnight moon.* New York: HarperCollins Children's Books, 1991.

———. *The runaway bunny.* New York: HarperCollins Children's Books, 1991.

Bulla, Clyde Robert. *The chalk-box kid.* New York: Random Books for Young Readers, 1987.

Bunting, Eve. *How many days to America? A Thanksgiving story.* New York: Clarion Books, 1988.

Burton, Virginia Lee. *Mike Mulligan and his steam shovel.* New York: Houghton Mifflin, 1987.

Cameron, Ann. *The stories Julian tells.* New York: Pantheon Books, 1981.

Carle, Eric. *The very hungry caterpillar.* New York: Putnam Publishing Group, 1981.

Clearly, Beverly. *Ramona and her father.* New York: Morrow, 1977.

Degen, Bruce. *Jamberry.* New York: HarperCollins Children's Books, 1983.

Freeman, Don. *Corduroy.* New York: Viking Press, 1968.

Galdone, Paul. *Three billy goats gruff.* New York: Houghton Mifflin, 1981.

Gannett, Ruth Stiles. *My father's dragon.* New York: Buccaneer Books, 1990.

Hutchins, Pat. *Tidy Titch.* New York: Greenwillow Books, 1991.

Kellogg, Steven. *Can I keep him?* New York: Dial Books, 1976.

Leaf, Munro. *The story of Ferdinand.* New York: Puffin Books, 1988.

Lobel, Arnold. *Frog and toad.* New York: Harper & Row, 1970.

Mahy, Margaret. *The boy who was followed home.* New York: Dial Books, 1986.

Martin, Bill, Jr. *Brown bear, brown bear, what do you see?* New York: Holt, Rinehart & Winston, 1983.

——. *Chicka chicka boom boom.* New York: Simon & Schuster, 1989.

Minarik, Else Holmelund. *Little bear's friend.* New York: HarperCollins Children's Books, 1960.

Numeroff, Laura Joffe. *If you give a mouse a cookie.* New York: HarperCollins Children's Books, 1985.

Peterson, John. *Littles.* New York: Scholastic, 1986.

Seeger, Pete. *Abiyoyo: Based on a South African lullaby and folk story.* New York: Macmillan Children's Book Group, 1985.

Sharmat, Marjorie. *Nate, the great.* New York: Putnam, 1986.

Shaw, Nancy. *Sheep in a jeep.* New York: Houghton Mifflin, 1991.

Slobodkina, Esphyr. *Caps for sale.* New York: Scholastic, 1989.

Steptoe, John. *Stevie.* New York: HarperCollins Children's Books, 1986.

Stevenson, James. *Rolling rose.* New York: Greenwillow Books, 1992.

Viorst, Judith. *Alexander and the terrible, horrible, no good, very bad day.* New York: Antheneum, 1972.

Zolotow, Charlotte. *The hating book.* New York: HarperCollins Children's Books, 1989.

The books listed in Chapters 6 and 8 are also recommended.

Recommended Professional Literature

Avery, Carol. *And with a light touch: Learning about reading, writing, and teaching from first graders.* Portsmouth, NH: Heinemann, 1993.

Bissex, Glenda. GNYS AT WRK: *A child learns to write and read.* Cambridge, MA: Harvard University Press, 1980.

Cambourne, Brian. *The whole story: Natural learning and the acquisition of literacy in the classroom.* New York: Scholastic, 1988.

Dyson, Amme Haas. *The multiple worlds of child writers: Friends learning to write.* New York: Teachers College Press, 1989.

Harste, Jerome, Virginia Woodward, and Carolyn Burke. *Language stories and literacy lessons.* Portsmouth, NH: Heinemann, 1984.

Holdaway, Donald. *The foundations of literacy.* Portsmouth, NH: Heinemann, 1979.

Karelitz, Ellen Blackburn. *The author's chair and beyond.* Portsmouth, NH: Heinemann, 1993.

Mills, Heidi, Timothy O'Keefe, and Diane Stephens. *Looking closely: Exploring the role of phonics in one whole language classroom.* Urbana, IL: National Council of Teachers of English, 1992.

Newkirk, Thomas. *More than stories: The range of children's writing.* Portsmouth, NH: Heinemann, 1989.

Newman, Judith, *The craft of children's writing.* Portsmouth, NH: Heinemann, 1985.

Routman, Regie. *Transitions: From literature to literacy.* Portsmouth, NH: Heinemann, 1988.

Temple, Charles, Ruth Nathan, Nancy Burris, and Frances Temple. *The beginnings of writing.* Boston: Allyn and Bacon, 1982.

8

In Between
Grades 2 and 3

When Nancie Atwell wrote her book about reading and writing in the junior high school years, she titled it *In the Middle*. Atwell described the early adolescent years by saying, "Twelve-, thirteen-, and fourteen-year-olds, in the middle of everything, are especially in the middle of changes—emotional, physical, psychological, and intellectual." Her words resonate for those of us who teach seven-, eight-, and nine-year-olds, for they, too, are in the middle of changes—emotional, physical, psychological, and intellectual—and all we can predict about a class of second or third graders is (as Atwell said of the junior high years) that within our classes there will be children with an enormously wide range of abilities and interests.

Within our classes there will be kids who can't tie their shoes and kids who can build electrical motors, kids who can't tell time and kids who can do double-digit division in their heads. These contrasts will be particularly dramatic in our reading and writing workshops. Many second graders can just barely read their names; others are devouring the entire works of Roald Dahl and Patricia MacLachlan. Some write only captions underneath drawings; others write long chapter books and research reports. Some children write with big, wobbly letters; others write with tiny, neat rows of cursive.

When I began to prepare to write this chapter, I couldn't help but wonder, "In the midst of all these differences, is it productive to try to say things in general about second and third graders?" In order to explore this question, I talked with my colleague Lydia Bellino, of Manhasset, New York, and gathered together a think tank of second- and third-grade teachers, each with years of experience in leading a writing workshop.* We wrote

---

* The teachers in the think tank included: Terry Moore, Tenafly, NJ; Charlotte Wolitz, Sue Frankel, and Susan Fox, Oceanside, NJ; Pat Mayher and Edith Giosetti, Closter, NJ; Susan Boyd, Leonia, NJ; and Jane Fraser, Westport, CT. Lydia Bellino, Manhasset, NY, was a particularly helpful advisor.

portraits of particular students, jotted generalizations about seven- and eight-year-olds, and talked and talked and talked. As we did this, the surprising things were the gasps. One of us would say something very particular about our kids' quirks, and the room would fill with gasps of recognition, with "yes, yes." Jane Fraser, for example, spoke of her second and third graders, who are so literal in their understanding of language that they are "like little Amelia Bedelias," and instantly, examples spilled out.

"When I told my kids, 'You're so loud, folks can hear you in Boston,' Joel asked whether his aunt, outside of Boston, could hear them."

"I told one fellow, 'You're writing so much, your arm's gonna fall off,' and he reached over to hold his arm, making sure it stayed in place."

The gasps of recognition felt good. Talking about them, we realized how rare it was for us to be in a conversation that focused on the middle years. At least in our community of educators, those of us who teach second and third graders have usually read and heard about the teaching of writing as it exists in kindergarten and first-grade rooms and in fifth- and sixth-grade rooms. We've had to translate those ideas as best we can so they apply to our second- and third-grade classrooms.

The think tank also felt good because we looked at what teachers face every day: the whole thing. Instead of looking at a self-contained issue such as portfolio assessment or trade books in the social studies classroom, we mused about questions as fundamental as "What might it mean to have a developmentally appropriate second/third-grade classroom?"

What Might It Mean to Have a Developmentally Appropriate Second/Third-Grade Classroom?

As we thought together about second- and third-grade youngsters, time and again we found ourselves asking, "If this is true of many second and third graders, does it reflect their developmental needs or our curriculum?" For example, many of us sensed that second graders are often concerned with doing things "the correct way." Is this a function of our children's developmental levels or of our classrooms? There are, of course, no definitive answers to these musings, but from the start we found ourselves talking not only about children, but also about curriculum. We talked especially about Lydia Bellino's observation that in many schools, it's as if there's a boundary line (it may come between kindergarten and first grade, first and second grades, or second and third grades). When kids cross that line, it's as if someone blows the whistle and calls, "Play time is over." As a result, second and third graders who want and need to build worlds out of blocks, to turn wooden spools and planks into spaceships and post offices, to record on bar graphs how many bluejays and cardinals come to their bird feeders, are often instead doing exclusively paper-and-pencil tasks. Oftentimes, the blocks get relegated to indoor recess, dramatic play gets moved to the playground, and a new sense of "hurry up" and "stay in line" comes into the school day. So often, all of the activity and energy, the interaction and initiative one sees in a kindergarten classroom get put on hold in the middle grades so that every student can be inducted into the world of doing things correctly, into cursive writing, times-tables, conventional spelling, book reports, and homework. One of the most important things to remember is that, in the words of Susan Fox, a third-grade teacher from Oceanside, New York, "second and third graders are *still so young.* " Susan explained, "If I can only remember that half my students still believe a tooth fairy exists, how much wiser my teaching would be!" How true. If we can only remember that second and third graders still need to move about, talk, climb, build, sing, perform, paint, plan, construct, design, and draw, our classrooms will be far better off!

"Oh, but we have very capable students in our school," teachers sometimes say, as if suggesting that project-oriented classrooms "hold kids back." The irony is that when project learning does return to a sanctioned place in the school day it is in talented and gifted programs and in doctoral programs for Ph.D. students.

My point is that when there is a Continental Divide separating "child-centered" from "curriculum-centered" grade levels, then what is lost is not only the dramatic play, artistic explorations, and real-world investigations of the early primary years but also the invitation to extend this sort of work into probing, original, intellectual work. What a loss! How sad it is that just as children are growing competent enough to use David Macaulay's *Cathedrals* as a reference in building their block structures, just as they are growing old enough to make architectural drawings of what they have done and to write local architects in order to learn more about designing weight-bearing arches, blocks are relegated to indoor recess. How sad it is that just when children could use their paints to depict the craters on Mars or to apprentice themselves to great illustrators, easels, paint, and clay are relegated to the weekly art class or to Friday afternoon play time. All of this is a loss for so many reasons.

One of the puzzling things about our schools is that although most kindergarten and first-grade teachers talk and think about developmentally appropriate education, in second and third grades these considerations often come to an abrupt halt. By second (or third) grade, the entire orientation of teachers (or, more precisely, of the system) changes. For example, although teachers in the early primary grades anticipate a wide developmental span and ask, "How can we design a curriculum that is right for *all* these kids?" by third grade the idea that some children need to "catch up" has often come crashing in on us—and on children. Seven- and eight-year-old children will often tell us, "I'm in the slow reading group" or "I have a spelling problem."

This concern with "falling behind" haunts many teachers, many parents, and many children. Second- and third-grade teachers, more than any other, are apt to come to me with questions about children "who aren't staying up with things." One third-grade boy found words to describe the entirely different orientation that often exists in third-grade as opposed to first-grade classrooms:

> When I first came to this school, when I started kindergarden, I was very nervous. But the next day I got to know some of the children and we sang songs together. It was a lot of fun. Oh—those were the good old days. We did not have so much work then, but now I am growing big and I am jammed full with work. But I am still thinking about kindergarden and first grade and all the fun that I had. Sometimes I wish that time flies back to the kindergarden. I was so smart back then. You know what? Some day I'll be a kindergarden or first grade teacher myself.
>
> The End.

Why must third graders remember, nostalgically, the "good old days" in kindergarten? Why must they look back and say, "I was so smart back then"? Why is the concern with "falling behind" so dramatic in these middle grades? Lydia Bellino recently helped me to realize that this concern may be so dramatic in second and third grades because students begin those years as unlabeled individuals, and, all too often, they end the year with labels attached. By fifth grade, the labels have become so affixed to children that alas, they seem somehow preordained and justified. By fifth grade, when we see a struggling student, we may think, "Yes, of course, she's not up with the others." But in second and third grades, many of us witness this process as it happens and know that it cannot be okay that seven- and eight-year-olds learn, in school, that they are slow, that they can't read, that they don't belong with certain kids. I am reminded of Susan Fox's wisdom. Second and third graders are, indeed, *still so young.* If we can only remember that half of them still believe in the tooth fairy, if we can only remember that they need to move about, talk, climb, build, sing—to grow—how much wiser our teaching will be!

The wonderful thing is that a classroom filled with building, singing, talking, observing, and planning is also a splendid environment for literacy. In such a classroom, writing can serve many purposes. In Pat Mayer's second-grade classroom, a few children recently wrote letters to the superintendent of the Closter, New Jersey, schools protesting the size of their coat closet. Soon they had written to board members, enclosing photographs, and to administrators, arranging for them to survey the area. Other children joined in the effort, sketching designs for a new coatroom and writing lumber yards for supplies. Meanwhile, other children in the classroom were using writing to enlist parents and neighbors in an effort to improve their classroom library. They made detailed plans for the new library, wrote job descriptions, scheduled author studies and book talks, and invited other classes to participate. How perfect such a classroom is for literacy learning—and for young children!

But I think a whole-class, hour-long writing workshop is also a perfect environment for literacy and for young children. One of the special advantages of a writing workshop is that in it, as in an art studio, children with very different levels of proficiency can work side by side. Both the child who has drawn a series of unrelated pictures and the child whose chapter book rambles will need to think about the issue of focus. Each of these children will need to reread and rethink the work, each will need an interested audience, each will benefit from questions like "How did you decide to do it this way?" "What will you do next?" "Are there parts you are uneasy about?" "How can we help you?"

The Writing Workshop: Strategies for Helping Writing and Writers to Grow

What our students do as writers will largely depend on what we expect them to do and on what they've done in the past. Sometimes people ask, "Do second graders keep notebooks? Do second graders revise? Do second graders write in particular genres?" and the answer is always, "It depends. It depends on our teaching."

I could almost say, "It depends on the paper they're given," because to a surprising extent, our medium is our message. I visit many second-grade classrooms in which most of the children are filling five- or six-page books with drawings and brief stories or lists of facts written in captionlike blurbs under the drawings. I visit many other second-grade classrooms in which each day, each child fills one (and only one) single sheet of "second grade" paper (often the newsprint-quality paper on which dotted lines alternate with darker ones). I visit still other second grades in which children construct books by folding and cutting notebook paper and stapling the pages together. Sometimes children construct scroll-like stories by taping one paper onto the end of another.

In some of the rooms, particularly those in which children write on scrolls or books, the written texts tend to be longwinded ramblings often consisting of several narratives strung together. In other rooms, the written texts tend to be formalized and wooden. They frequently begin, "Once upon a time," or sometimes, "On Saturday I went. . . . " In yet other rooms, children write in a wide range of genres, perhaps including riddle books and newspaper articles, stories and poems.

The interesting thing to me is that in each of these classrooms, the teacher may say to me, "I leave it totally up to the children to decide what they write," and yet of course, what our children choose to do will be affected by what we expect them to do and by all the subtle ways in which we convey our expectations.

My first suggestion is that at every grade level, we look for opportunities such as those Pat Mayer found to nudge individual children to write for functional, real-world reasons (letters, surveys, posters, songs, complaints, lists). For children, as for adults, much of this writing will not be drafted or revised, although it may need to be edited. My next suggestion is that we encourage second-grade children to move toward writing texts that do not depend on drawings. The easiest way to encourage young writers to make this move is to put away the paper with spaces for pictures and to put out instead small pieces of lined paper, perhaps stapled into little books.

As children first move from pages filled with drawings toward pages filled exclusively with written texts, their writing episodes often don't last very long. When I first launch second graders in notebooks, for example, after a few blissful moments when everyone is busily working (mostly, alas, on their penmanship and margins), one child will jump up from his seat. "I'm done," he says. "What do I do now?" Another jumps up. "I'm done." Then from all corners of the room, children jump up, one after another, saying, "I'm done." In no other elementary grade will so many children believe they are finished so soon after they begin writing. In first grade, children often continue working longer because they work on their drawings, and this occupies much of their writing time. Then, too, first graders sometimes sustain their composing longer because if they alternate between drawing and writing, their pictures will fuel the text. When they write in books filled with pictures and captions, the sequence of pages lures them on. If, in second grade, children begin instead to write on pages in a notebook or on single sheets of draft paper, they will need ways to nudge themselves to say more. By third and fourth grade, many children will be able to sustain their writing longer and move independently from one entry to another, but now they often approach writing expecting to write just a few lines. Perhaps a few sentences sufficed in first grade, but since then, the children's fluency in writing has grown while their expectations have not. Their expectations reveal themselves in the products the children produce. Often a second grader's first line of writing conveys the entire message: "For my birthday, I got a lot of presents and then I came home and went to bed." No wonder it is like popcorn in the classroom: "I'm done," "I'm done," "I'm done."

The most important thing I can suggest is that we do *not* abbreviate the writing workshop so that it lasts only as long as our children's attention for writing lasts. One of our major goals at this point is to encourage children to say more, to sustain their work longer, to approach a text expecting it to be more detailed, and all of this means that we need to give children more time for writing than they know what to do with. Once we've given them this time, we will also need to help them grow into it. We need to expect that for a while, they'll all be finishing their writing before we want them to be done. If half the class is saying "I'm done" at the same time, I'm apt to ask all the members of the class to look up from their work. "Writers," I say, "many of you are coming to me saying, 'I'm done, what do I do next?' When you finish writing one entry and don't know what else to say, I suggest you find a writing teacher and have a conference." Then I add, "But there is not *one* writing teacher in this classroom. There are *thirty-two* of you."

As I said in Chapter 7, these first conferences are invariably happy disasters. Sometimes I demonstrate conferring skills by publicly conferring with one child and asking the others to note what I do, or by letting children confer with me and varying the tone of voice in my responses to them in order to illustrate the wonderful effect of open-ended questions. As the year goes on, I might talk to the children about the importance of letting writers lead us to the subjects they care about or the need for asking follow-up questions. But I think it is easy to put too much emphasis on teaching the skills of peer conferences. When children have the opportunity to chat with each other about their topics and their writing, writing becomes less lonely.

Often in these conferences, once a child has told his or her vignette to a friend it is hard for that child to cycle back to the beginning of the episode in order to write it down. Instead, they write a sequel to what they have said or even an entirely different piece. It may help if conferences end with the listeners asking the writer how he or she might begin the piece. But this isn't essential. What I find is that young children's talk almost always moves their writing forward. At every grade level, there is always more to include, more to tell, but this is especially true for the second and third graders who finish their work a few minutes after they begin it. Often, talk will not only lead to longer and more fleshed-out texts, but it will also help the lilting sound of oral language to appear on the page. If we teach children the rhythm of writing, then conferring, and then adding on, their texts will get longer. I'm not promising these peer conferences will lead our children to write *better* texts, but they will lead them to write *longer* texts. (Their drafts may tend to be chaotic and to have additions at the end that should instead have been inserted in early sections, but I have learned to regard this as the price of progress.)

When teachers and parents ask me, "What if the revisions make the writing worse?" my response is that I wouldn't worry much about it. What I *do* care about is that the next time children write they add onto texts on their own and, better still, that they approach the texts already anticipating their audiences' interests and so write with more detail. When this happens, I make a very big deal about it.

What I am saying is that yes, we will show our students ways to structure their longer prose (and I'll discuss this in a moment), but it is important to remember that when our students seem to tape details and explanations onto the ends of their drafts, we need to have patience. Later, they will learn to incorporate these extensions into the body of their writing.

developmental process

It's interesting to realize that the growth spurts so evident in our students' bodies are also evident in their texts. In both instances, growth spurts sometimes lead to a leggy, long-limbed gangliness. When the child who begins his story with a summary encapsulating the entire sequence of events ("For my birthday, I got a lot of presents and then I came home and went to bed") decides that he can work longer and tell more, the added-on sections (perhaps about the presents or the cake) aren't apt to be well integrated into the original text. In the following entry, Andre probably planned initially to end with "I love my cousin." Then, after anticipating that his reader would ask, "Why do you call your dog your cousin?" he added his final two lines:

MY COUSIN
by Andre

I play with my cousin. When someone rings the bell, he jumps up. Do you know what? He is a dog. His name is Alfee. He lives in Long Island.

FIGURE 8–1 Marianna's draft

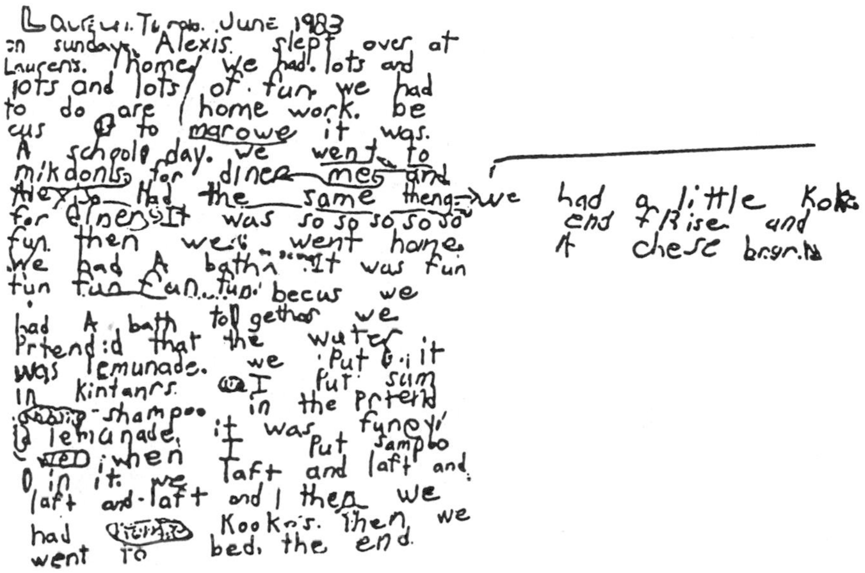
Lauren Tarpo. June 1983
on sunday, Alexis slept over at Laurens. home we had. lots and lots and lots of fun we had to do are home work. becus to marowe it was. A schoold day. we went to mikdonls for diner me and Alexis had the same theng we had a little koke and frise and A chese brgr. It was so so so so so fun. then we went home. We had A bath It was fun fun fun fun fun becus we had A bath toogethr we Prtend that the water was lemunade. we put it in kintanrs. I put sum shampoo in the prtend lemunade it was funey. when we put sampo in it we laft and laft and laft and laft and then we had kooks. then we went to bed. the end.

He is a golden color. He is tall. He is skinny. Sometimes he knocks me down. I love my cousin. Do you know why I call him my cousin? Because my Aunt and Uncle have no children.

In a similar way, Marianna has added an extraneous bit of information onto the bottom of her draft, but she has also used scissors and tape to add explanations to the middle of her text (see Figure 8–1).

Notebooks in the Middle Grades

Revision—adding on—is much simpler when youngsters keep notebooks, and my second main suggestion for helping second and third graders extend their writing is just this: I encourage notebooks in the second and third grades as long as children are not only gathering entries but also shaping them into specific genres, which are then published. But if notebooks are used like journals—as places for dead-end collections of first-draft writing—then I would prefer to have second- and third-grade children write first drafts of a wide range of genres and revise them for publication.

Keeping a notebook has a number of advantages. Children in second and third grades naturally write a little, then take a breather, then (with luck) dip back into more writing, so it makes a lot of sense that our nudges to "say more" are embodied in the material itself, the sequence of pages in the notebook. Similarly, because the medium is the message in these grades, it makes sense that the materials encourage young writers to stay with and to write more about a particular subject. If they divide their notebooks into sections and say, "This section is for writing about, around, and off of this entry," or if they make themselves small subject-specific notebooks (comprising five or six sheets of paper stapled together), either way, the shape of paper and the number of pages will encourage them to gather more about their topic.

I also find notebooks helpful in the second and third grades because when young writers collect a hodgepodge of vaguely related stuff as they try to "say more" about a subject, the stuff will be divided into separate entries rather than piled together onto a single, chaotic page. It is easier to reorder and select between separate entries than it is to divide a solid page of text into separate components.

Most of all, I find notebooks helpful in these grades because they encourage children to deal constructively with their growing ability to anticipate an audience's response to their writing. Let me explain. Before she learned about notebooks, Jenn, a second grader, tried to write stories that were instantly declared "great." In school, she began six stories in three days—and discarded each one. Her writing folder was a jumble of false starts, of stories that trailed off after a few lines.

doesn't have to be great in a notebook

"I'm broke," Greg said, pushing his chair away from the desk. "I'm clear out of stories. I'm out of space stories, I'm out of car stories. I'm broke."

Greg and Jenn are only a few months older and a few inches taller than they were near the end of late first grade, but their writing habits have changed markedly. Gone is their easy confidence. "It is as if the protective cloak of egocentricity has been taken from them," Don Graves has said in describing their new awareness. Jenn and Greg are aware of an audience. With audience awareness comes worry. "Will the kids like my story? It's messy. It's stupid. It's dumb." For the first time, they suffer writer's block.

Ironically, their worries—so common in second-grade children—are a sign of growth. Kindergartners and first graders rarely agonize over topic choice or fret about whether their stories will be good enough. As we saw in Chapter 7, first graders often write as they play blocks: for the sheer fun of the activity rather than for an eventual product, for themselves rather than for an audience. As these children become older, they are more able to distance themselves and to see their work through the eyes of another. They look back to assess what they have done, and they look forward toward an eventual audience. These emerging abilities bring new concerns.

The developmental psychologist Howard Gardner characterizes seven- and eight-year-olds by noting that now, for the first time, the child in the middle of singing or dancing will stop and anxiously ask, "Is this right?" Gardner claims that because seven-year-old children want to use words "right," their use of figurative language often declines. In their drawings, they replace expressive, dynamic pictures with spiked suns and rows of tulips. "How do I draw a spaceship?" they ask. "How do I make a person?" The seven- or eight-year-old's concern with the right way to do things can lead these students to spend longer on their table of contents and on making vines come out of the O in "Once upon a time" than on their entire stories. A concern for rightness can also lead second and third graders to erase so much that they rub holes in their pages. It can lead them to write exclusively about Ninjas and Spiderman, about topics someone else has already invented.

Interestingly enough, we learned from Jenn's mother that while Jenn was starting and discarding story after story in school, she often sneaked a flashlight into bed late at night and, safely hidden from the eyes of others, wrote story after story, filling books with the large, carefree letters that had been the trademark of her first-grade books. Notebooks can give Jenn that same under-the-covers safety.

I find that notebooks in the middle grades can also encourage children to continue (figuratively speaking) filling their pockets with shiny stones, acorns, noticings. So often, by the time children are in second and third grade, they have begun to value the fashionable toys, the designer labels, the peer-sanctioned jokes that are supported by the culture around them. It's during these grades that some children begin to lose the ability to watch in awe as a cicada bug sheds its skin. Unless we intervene, when second and third graders are asked to "write a story," many of the boys retell the comic-book scripts of currently popular superheroes, and girls do their own variations of this. If we instead ask children to write out their lives, they often tend to write about a trip to an amusement park, a weird and disgusting television show. In each of these instances, they choose topics that are peer-sanctioned, that feel "big enough" to be stories, and then they record the story as it already exists in their minds. When youngsters begin with topics in which the significance is already established, the writer need not *grow* the story's meaning. In the eyes of the writer, the topic is already a big deal. By implication, the writer doesn't have to write in order to bring significance to the topic.

I want children to experience what it is to find meaning in the moments of their lives, and so I want to help them to write about moments that do not come already packaged with ready-made significance.

When I introduce notebooks to second and third graders, I try to give the protective cloak of egocentricity back to children. I want children to know that this is a place to write, free from the eyes of a critical audience. I want the notebooks to encourage children to write about small, unimportant things, to explore a silly obsession, to carry on about their special interests, to explore private questions, to tell the truth. I want children to realize that when they begin poking around in search of something to write about, it is not wise to worry, "Will the kids like this?" or "Is this *right*?" Early on in the writing process, I want youngsters to be playful and explorative and quizzical as they write—and as they live.

Figure 8–2 outlines what notebooks usually look like in grades K–2, in grades 2–3, and in grades 3–6. (It's not an accident that second and third grades are included in two categories.)

Using Children's Concern with "the Right Way to Do Things" to Broaden Their Repertoire of Strategies

During their playtime, second and third graders will often spend more time inventing, reinventing, and arguing over the rules of a game than they spend actually playing it. Donna Skolnick's second graders in Westport, Connecticut, for example, have built a whole regimen of rules around trading stickers. Last week, one girl traded a sticker and then wanted the sticker back; soon five youngsters were deep in a discussion of whether the rules say you can or cannot change your mind when trading stickers. Once they'd agreed upon a rule, they hurried to their teacher. "Is this rule *fair*?" they asked, a question asked over and over again in second-grade classrooms. The habits of thought that led Donna's students to construct such complicated rules around trading stickers—and lead many students to obsess about the rules for their games and clubs—are evident throughout the school day in many second- and third-grade classrooms.

Terry Moore's third graders in Tenafly, New Jersey, have formed small reading/writing response groups they call "clubs." The clubs have names, mascots, meeting places, and rites of passage. The members of a club decide together on their club's procedures; they've invented methods of responding to texts, and they choose from among these each day; they have timekeepers and note-takers, rules and penalties. "My kids need a lot of structure," Terry says, "but they are very good at creating those structures themselves."

I suspect that just as it's very common for second and third graders to focus a lot of their attention on "the right way to do things," it's also very

FIGURE 8–2 Notebooks at different grade levels

Notebooks in grades K–2	Notebooks in grades 2–3	Notebooks in grades 3–6
Notebooks may first be introduced as tools to gather more around a particular subject. For example, the class may gather entries in individual notebooks about a topic for a thematic study. Alternatively, there may be a single class notebook in which each child writes observations and musings about the class pet.	Sometimes notebooks are introduced in conjunction with a class theme (i.e., grandparents, winter) or a whole-class genre ("Notebooks are a way to generate ideas for picture books"). Sometimes notebooks are introduced as the way to live with a writer's wide-awakeness.	Same as grades 2–3.
Children are encouraged to look, listen, notice, wonder, question—and to record all this in drawings, lists, and entries in their notebooks. If they have a notebook that is about all they see and think, they may also select a topic from this notebook and make another, smaller notebook for entries on that one topic.	Same as K–2, with less emphasis on drawing and more on writing.	Same as grades 2–3, usually with less emphasis on drawings and more emphasis on variety within the entries (observations, wonderings, imaginings, memories, lists of words, images).
Children do not usually make a single piece of writing out of their collected entries.	Children may return to their collected entries in order to find in them the stuff for a poem, a letter, even a photo essay or a picture book. (Other genres may tend to be more difficult.) The whole class may *all* look for the material for one genre together, as when each writer gathers images, words, and details in order to write poems.	Children reread their notebooks to find an idea to develop. Rather than make a new five-page notebook for gathering entries on the focused topic, they generally section off the notebook and devote a number of pages to developing one subject.
	Parts of the notebook are underlined or starred. These become starters for rough drafts that are written on white paper. These drafts are minimally revised and then edited.	Writers have a variety of strategies for not only collecting more but also learning more about the subject. Often, as entries accumulate, the topic changes. Children may collect entries with a genre in mind, or may reread their collections to see the possibility of different genres.
		Children usually begin drafting by writing several lead sentences or several rough outlines; then they write a draft (copying favorite sections from the notebook). Rewriting often involves bringing more bits from the notebook into the draft. It also often involves reading work they admire that is similar to what they hope to write.

common for them to focus on the *ways* to do things, on the procedures themselves. Young writers often pay more attention to procedures in the writing workshop than to the purposes behind those procedures. The procedures often become ends in and of themselves.

Recently, I worked with eight-year-old Renee, urging her to insert selected passages from her notebook entries into her draft. I showed Renee how she could write the passages she wanted to insert into the draft on little slips of paper and tape them on the edges of the draft at the appropriate spots.

Renee liked the procedure so much that for the next few weeks, whenever she sat down to write a draft, she first got out the tape and scissors and began hanging empty "spider legs" off the edges of her paper. Then she'd write her story, putting every third or fourth sentence onto a dangling "spider leg" rather than into the body of the story itself.

Among second- and third-grade teachers, there are countless similar stories. Once I showed Bradley how to cut apart his draft in order to insert a new section into it. The next time, immediately after he finished his draft he took out his scissors and cut the entire draft apart until it was, quite literally, a puzzle of sentence fragments. "I'm revising," he explained. Still another student heard she could use carets as codes for inserting information into her text. Interpreting this literally, Wendy used careful drawings of carrots—and celery, pumpkins, tomatoes, bananas—as codes signifying "Find a similar picture in the space at the end of my draft. Beside it, there will be words to insert into this spot." Wendy took such pleasure in this work that she even used a tiny vegetable to signify "Add a comma" or "Add a missing letter." Although she never admitted this to me, I suspect she deliberately left out punctuation marks in her drafts so she'd have the fun of adding codes to her pages.

These examples are, I think, extreme cases of something that happens a great deal, and for good reason, in these middle years. I see the same phenomenon happening when Wendy uses an exclamation mark once, receives positive feedback for having done so, and from that time on fills every page with strings of exclamation marks. Or when Anthony, in the share meeting at the end of a writing workshop, asks his friend what is proclaimed to be a good question, and thereafter this question becomes fixed like cement at the beginning of every share meeting. Or when one child writes a story starring another friend, and soon every writer has become a casting director for his or her own story, and children's concern about whether they are in a classmate's story (and about what role they are given) looms even larger than concern about whether they are invited to a peer's birthday party.

I suspect there are lots of lessons to be learned from these situations. One is that we need to recognize the power of our compliments and of the deliberate and unconscious ways in which we and others provide models. Second and third graders are still eager to please adults as well as their peers, and they are also very able to reproduce at will the behaviors that receive support.

Because we do not want pages filled with rows of exclamation marks or rote, mechanical questions asked over and over in share meetings, we may want to deliberately broaden the behaviors we support. Instead of congratulating Wendy on her use of exclamation marks, we might tell her that it's great to see her exploring the uses of punctuation and that we can't wait to see which other punctuation marks she uses. Instead of telling Anthony that he asked a "good question," we might tell him we loved the way he asked an honest question, something he was really truly wondering about.

Yet, even if we try to support the broad attitudes rather than the particular behaviors, I'm not convinced that Wendy or Anthony (or the children who overhear our support) will comprehend that what we support is not the use of an exclamation mark but the willingness to take a risk, not the particular question but the inquisitive stance. Children may well repeat the one behavior we have praised, but at least we can do whatever possible to help them understand that we support risk-taking, honesty, inquiry, and so on rather than rote recitations.

I think as teachers we are wise not only to learn the positive and problematic power of compliments and models, but also to notice how much many seven- and eight-year-olds focus on procedures. If we recognize that many children love to learn the conventional tools of the trade, we may want to regard these years as a time for sharing lots and lots of writing strategies. We may also find that when we try to teach flexible, intuitive strategies, children turn them into very concrete, step-by-step operations. I'm not sure that it's possible for some children to do otherwise. As I'll demonstrate soon, when I've tried to teach children to "play around with" the idea of different lead sentences, they turn this strategy into a rigid formula for finding the beginning of a draft. I've come to believe that this isn't necessarily a problem as long as children eventually internalize the concrete, spelled out, formulaic strategies they develop, making these into habits of mind.

Let me give some examples. When Don Graves and I studied third-grade writers at Atkinson Elementary School, one of the most common and effective revision strategies the children used was, as I've mentioned, to list several different lead sentences or paragraphs and then select one. When I toy with different leads for a piece, my jotted notes may begin like this:

Until recently ~~more few~~
~~The group was~~ I wanted until the
~~the~~ Last march, several hundred
educators gathered in Cedar Rapids, Iowa,
for a ...

My discarded fragments represent whole chains of ideas that I've tested and put aside. The third graders at Atkinson Elementary School, however, tended to toy with leads in a much more concrete and deliberate fashion. They wrote everything out in full. Typically, for example, they'd divide their page into four parts, and within each part they'd write out a possible lead. Only after they had filled each of their four parts did they look back, reread each alternative, and chose one. Watching them, I wondered if these children saw their goal less as exploring lots of possible leads in order to find the best way into their text than as listing and selecting from among four leads. This seemed to be an end in and of itself. Over time, however, many of the children at Atkinson began to internalize the strategy of lead writing and to use it more flexibly. I saw this begin to happen when Diane underlined a key sentence in the middle of her draft. Then, on another sheet of paper, she listed numbers 1 to 5 and proceeded to rewrite the problematic sentence five different ways. Although Diane was still working in an overly deliberate, stylized fashion, writing each version out in full and separating it from the others with a careful line, she was using the strategy of listing possible leads for a new purpose. Not long after that, Susie reread her first draft of "The Big Fish" and said, "I want to make the section where I catch the fish shorter, and it should be quicker." On a separate bit of paper, she listed numbers 1 to 3, as if she were about to write three different lead sentences, only this was to be three different ways to say a particular part of her narrative. Beside each of the first two numbers, Susie tried a different way of writing the section. Then she circled number 3 and put her pencil to the page, then pulled it away.

"What did you almost write?" I asked.

Susie was embarrassed, I think, that I'd read her mind. "I was going to say, 'Just then a quick jerk awakened me, and I saw my pole bending,' she said, "but it was too long." Now she was quiet again, her pencil dabbing at number 3, her lips moving as she whispered other alternatives to herself. The number 3 on her page seemed to scaffold her now internalized process of generating, weighing, and choosing among different ways of saying something.

Over the course of the next few months, I watched Susie using her lead writing strategy to accomplish many tasks. Often much of what she did was invisible, but it was clear to me that her mental operations were based on the same scaffolding of concrete options to which she'd once clung.

It shouldn't surprise us that in a child's writing as in a child's math, operations that are at one point done in a very sequential, concrete fashion later become more internalized and flexible. If we keep this in mind, we can deliberately give our students concrete structures with which to scaffold their writing process and help these structures become internal.

When children gather together entries about a particular topic, I want them to realize that the topic often changes as they think about it and look through their notebooks. In writing this chapter, for example, I began by noting that third graders make up rules for trading stickers and have ended up realizing that many seven- and eight-year-olds also delight in inventing rules and conventions for their writing. In order to encourage young writers to follow changing topics as they write, I might suggest that when they say, "Now I'm going to live with such and such a topic," they might actually write, on a folded-over page of their notebook or on the cover of their five-page, subject-specific notebook:

First working topic: _____
Second working topic: _____

I wouldn't want this to become as mechanical as a fill-in-the-blank ditto sheet, so I'd mention it lightly to a handful of children rather than assigning it to the entire class, and I'd soon say to children in conferences, "If you *were* to write down your first working topic and then write down what new topic seems to be growing out of that topic, what might you write?"

Because children sometimes can't imagine multiple ways of writing about a particular subject, I might ask them to join me in making a chart showing various ways to live with a topic. Such a chart might look like the one in Figure 8–3. I wouldn't display the chart in the classroom for very long, however, because I wouldn't want children merely to proceed in a mechanical fashion through a list of preset procedures, but when the chart had been taken down, I would probably say to individual children in a conference, "Let's look over the entries you've gathered on your subject and see, just for a moment, which of the strategies in the chart you've used so far."

FIGURE 8–3 Ways to develop a seed idea for writing

	Free write	What do you see?	Ask questions	Close-in camera	Write external and internal story	From then to now, from now to then	Take one question and think about it	Write to someone	Why is this on my mind now?	Search for related entries	Read a related book	Interview someone
Sarah	X	X	X						X			
Danielle	X		X					X			X	
Raymond			X									
Jerome	X		X									X
Diana			X		X			X				
Angelica			X			X						
Anabelle		X	X	X								
Daniel		X	X						X			
Andrew			X				X				X	

Then, too, there are structures I've already mentioned that I'd use in these middle grades. One is the author's chair. I would want to help children imagine themselves sitting in the author's chair, reading their own writing, sharing their draft with their classmates. "If you were sitting in the author's chair and you'd just read this aloud," I'd ask, "what questions do you think the kids might have?"

Even if a child sitting at his desk can imagine he's in the author's chair and can generate both the questions kids might ask and the ways he might respond, there's no guarantee that the child's written products won't become worse rather than better. Some youngsters quite literally add lines like "Yes, it was fun" at the end of their drafts! Yet whether or not their texts improve, these writers have learned a habit of thought that will eventually bring new flexibility and awareness to their writing process. In the end, the strategy of anticipating and responding to readers' questions will be helpful if it is used in conjunction with other strategies. The magic and power of effective writing results from trying to do different, almost conflicting things at the same time—such as clearly answering readers' questions while also writing in graceful, vibrant prose.

It is no small matter, then, that second and third graders tend to be one-track thinkers. If they are using metaphor in their writing, they tend not to worry also about answering their readers' questions. If they are writing with sound effects, their entire piece—as in Philip's waterfall story on the next page—begins to sound like the soundtrack to a film. If a child is answering her readers' questions, she tends not to balance this with an effort to maintain the song of her story.

I often joke that third graders can do anything except do something in moderation. They can use exclamation marks—but they will use tons of them, developing a hierarchy of fat ones and thin ones to show gradations in excitement. They can write with dialogue—but often the entire piece becomes a stream of chatter. They can write with detail—but they are less able to select where to expand the text with detailed information and where to summarize things in passing.

Because those of us who teach writing often encourage children to include details and to tell more about their subject, second and third graders often end up trying to tell *everything*. The resulting stories, so typical of second and third graders, often begin "I woke up and had breakfast" and end "I went to bed." Don Graves and I refer to these as "bed-to-bed" stories. The pieces, of course, may not begin and end in bed, but if the first line is "We got on the bus to go shopping," the last line will be something like "Finally, we got home." It is easy to be exasperated by the way third graders overdo whatever they do, but it is more helpful to be fascinated by this phenomenon.

In the draft below Philip uses dialogue and sound effects, but he seems unable to make the transition back to narration. Transitions, which require distance, control, and an ability to shift gears, seem hard for these children.

> Kersplash! "Oh boy I'm as wet as a . . . Oh no!" "A waterfall!" I said to my brother . . . "Uh bye." "Oh no!" I forgot! "I'm seatbelted! I'd better cover my head!" Ninety seconds later . . . "Whew." "We are lucky we missed that waterfall." Kerplunk! "We hit a rock." "We kept on going until . . ." Shlunk! "We hit the side of a cliff. "Awww it's over." "Now I know why they call it the Roaring Rapids." I said to my brother, "I'm soaked to the bone."

The developmental psychologist Jerome Bruner comments on the one-tracked nature of children's thinking, saying:

> There is a great distance between the one-tracked mind of the young child and the ten-year-old's ability to deal with an extraordinarily complex world.
>
> Intellectual development is marked by an increasing capacity to deal with several alternatives simultaneously, to tend to several sequences during the same period of time, and to allocate time and attention in a manner appropriate to these multiple demands. (1966, p. 6)

I suspect that Bruner's remarks pertain not only to the written products but also to the writing processes of second and third graders. During my research at Atkinson Academy, I observed Pat Howard's third graders and found that most of them wrote without stopping to reread and reconsider what they had written. They rarely interrupted themselves to reflect on their subject or their text, to plan ahead, or to consider alternative paths. For most of them, writing was a continual process of adding on. Their *process* as well as their *products* resembled a chain:

$$X \rightarrow X \rightarrow X \rightarrow X$$

Susie, for example, began the year by writing a long tale about a Chinese girl. It took many days to write the story, and every day Susie's method was the same. She'd reread the last few lines from the preceding day and begin adding on. Other children worked on shorter pieces but, like Susie, they spent very little time looking back, toying with options, or reconsidering. What many of these children lacked, it seemed, was what Carl Bereiter (1982) refers to as a "central executive function" that would allow them to shift attention back and forth between reading and writing, talking and writing, thinking and writing. In oral conversation, conversation partners provide the switchboard that allows participants to oscillate between talking and listening. But these oscillations are not built into the act of writing; the writer must learn how to disengage from one process in order to engage in another. Although these third graders were competent readers, writers, questioners, talkers, planners, and so forth, they were less able to shuttle from one activity to another and back again.

The unfortunate thing was that because Pat Howard's children were always moving forward as writers, they didn't learn from their writing. The importance of _revision_ is not the succession of drafts but the act of "revision," of using words as a lens for reseeing the emerging subject. When children merely add on and on and on, when they do not stop to hear and see what their writing is saying, they don't experience the potential power of revision.

Of course, one reason that Pat's children weren't rereading their drafts at the start of the year, or even reconsidering them, was that no one had ever encouraged them to do so. In time, Pat did begin encouraging peer conferences and revision, and many of the children started to write successive drafts. As we have seen, they often tried three or four possible leads before selecting one to begin a story. At first, I assumed this meant that they were no longer locked into merely adding on. But when I looked more closely and more honestly at the children's early revisions, I found that a pile of drafts and entries didn't necessarily mean they were engaged in a new kind of thinking. In fact, I found that, for many third graders, their chainlike thinking persisted even during revision.

When _I_ draft and revise a text, what is going on inside my head can be likened to a taffy pull. Different versions of my text—some written and some only sensed—exist simultaneously. Different ideas, voices, and forms (some written and some only imagined) interact. This creative tension in writing can be illustrated by this diagram, first drawn by Donald Murray:

For most second and third graders, revision seems to mean something very different. Their revisions tend to be either new versions of writing or corrections. Often their purpose is to be sure their text matches their subject. If a draft doesn't match "what really happened," they insert information or write a new draft or entry, which is meant as a more accurate, more complete version. Most of Pat's third graders, for example, spoke of revision as a form of correcting:

"The ending is boring so I will cross it out and try three others."

"I put this word two times in a sentence so I'm going to change it."

"How will they know where I am? I gotta fix it so they don't get confused."

Pat Howard's third graders did not know about the concept of writing entries, but what I find is that when children do write multiple entries about a particular subject, these entries often tend to be remarkably self-contained, as if each was an entirely separate piece. Even the draft the child eventually makes, supposedly "out of the entries," often does not incorporate anything at all but is, instead, yet another "take" on the subject. It is as if, for these children, time marches on, and they proceed to write one entry and then another, one draft and then another. Because they often do not turn around to rethink, these children tend not to understand that the purpose of revision is not to correct but to discover. They do not understand that by attending to what is said and unsaid in one entry, they can discover new meanings.

Sari, a struggling third-grade writer, reread her notebook and decided this sad and poignant entry was the one that mattered most to her:

> On Thursday my father brought me a costume. I slept over. I find that I'm a nobody. I find that my family is not together. Over the summer my mom stayed in a hospital. All I want is to be a family and everything to be good and to get good scores.

Sari's teacher, Laurie Pessah, responded personally to Sari's entry and then asked her what, in particular, she would develop out of it. Sari answered that she wanted to write more about her father leaving the family. (Like many third graders, she tends to broaden the subject as she writes, probably because she's afraid that otherwise, she won't have much to say.) These are some of Sari's entries:

FAMILY

I've spent lots of special moments with my family, with my father, mother, sisters and brother. It's all been fun but now I don't have none of this fun.

POEM

Everytime I ask him if I could
stay with him forever. He says I'll

try to. I believe him what he says every
word of it. I tell him how it is where
I live. Now I ask him if I could live
with him. I know he's trying.

I guess I love a lot of people but the one I most admire is my Dad. There
are a lot of things I love about him, like when he takes me places or
when he buys me stuff or when he's just around me. Things I like about
my dad is when he takes me to Penn State or to the beach or when he
takes me to a theater to see a play or when he takes me ice skating or
when he takes me to Central Park or Flushing Park.

I remember the time when I and my father went bicycle riding on
Monday. I had a lot of fun that time. We went in circles and then we
took a rest called a butt rest. Then we went home and went back out.
I got a chalkboard that day and my father went to play with my brother
(basketball) while I was eating pizza with a cherry coke. Then I went
somewhere that my brother had to go. Because some things only work
once, I spent that whole day with my Father.

I would feel real bad if my father died.

I don't think anybody would like to meet the person who invented
Divorces.

By now Sari's notebook contained all the ingredients for a very powerful
piece of writing. When I read over what she had written, it was easy for me
to imagine combining the passages in which she recalls ice skating and
bicycling with her father (and taking a "butt rest") with passages in which
she struggled with the fact that her father has left and she doesn't have this
fun anymore, and with her conclusions about divorce and her hopes that
someday she'll be able to stay with her father. *I* could see ways to combine
these entries, but this doesn't mean Sari could. I am not even sure she reread
her entries before writing the first draft of her final piece. When Sari was
asked to make something out of all these entries, she produced this poem:

> His skin is clear like a new day
> His Eyes are blue like the nice blue sea
> His Face is shiny like shiny glass
> He's my dad!

Reading this, I asked myself, "Where did this poem come from?" It
seemed at first glance that it came out of nowhere, but I think where it truly
came from was Sari's sense of what it means to write a poem. When Laurie
Pessah conferred with Sari, she suggested that Sari reread her collection of

entries and write another poem using bits from them. This time Sari wrote with a few more concrete details about her dad, but she still left her wonderful entries behind:

> He's there when you're born
> He's there to tuck you in
> He's there to spoil you with
> lots of toys and gifts
> He's the one person you'll always cherish
> your Dad.

If I'd conferred with Sari, I would probably have shown her how she could merge many of her entries together into a piece about all the ways she misses her father. In an instance such as this, I'd want to remember Vygotsky's comment, "What a child can do in cooperation today, he can do independently tomorrow." It seems to me that we may <u>have to demonstrate to children what it means to bring parts of several entries together</u>. But at this point, Sari was not working with direct guidance from a teacher. Knowing what I know about third graders, it's not surprising that when Sari revises this draft, what she produces is yet another piece, and again, looking at it, I wonder, "Where did this come from?"

> SADNESS
>
> I'm as sad as a funeral on a dark
> Friday afternoon.
>
> I'm as sad as a wolf howling in the night
>
> I'm as sad as a crying baby
>
> But when I'm with you I feel
> like every new day is going to be better
> then it was yesterday.

Later, Sari returned to the subject of her dad and wrote this letter:

> Dear Daddy,
> All the time I feel hurt because you're not with me. Every time I think back in the summer I think about you, Joanne, and John. Every time I think of you I always look at the phone to call you but I just can't. Every time I hear your voice I cry or laugh or smile. I think of you all the time.
>
> Love your little girl

It is puzzling to look closely at Sari's work. The final work certainly doesn't encompass the entries and lift them to another level. One could say, in fact, that the final product is disappointing as a piece of writing. This sometimes happens for writers at all grade levels, and perhaps it happens especially in second and third grades. Still, I can't help but sense that through the process of living with and writing about her topic, Sari has been on an important journey. In the end, she does two things. In her poem "Sadness" she makes art out of her pain. In her letter, she uses writing as a way to reach out to someone she loves and has lost. She can't talk to her father about her feelings, but she's learned that writing can be a way to reach out, from the depths of yourself, to another person.

I'm not trying to suggest that second and third graders will always follow in Sari's footsteps as they write, but I think it is helpful to anticipate that many children may, like Sari, approach each new entry and each new draft as if it is a new piece of first-draft-only writing. If we anticipate that this may happen, we'll be sure to show children how we write new entries that extend and deepen earlier entries. We'll teach children the strategy of underlining a key sentence in an entry, and then writing more entries just about it. Geirthrudur Finnbogadottir, for example, underlined this sentence in an entry: "I've never known anything but childhood and one day it will all be gone." She put it at the top of a page and wrote more entries exploring this feeling of missing her childhood. For example, she wrote this entry (also see Figure 8–4):

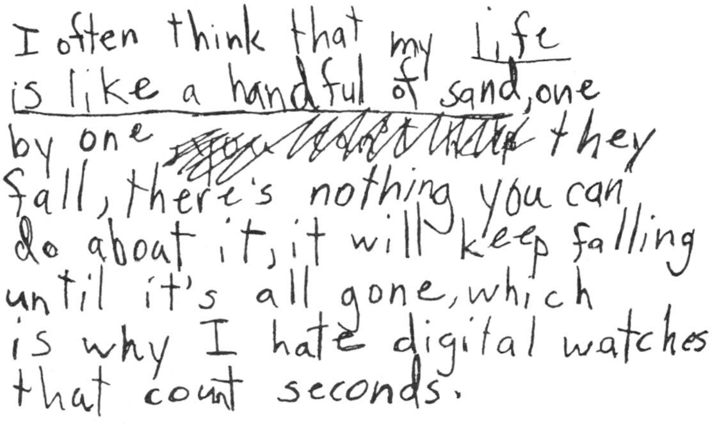

> I often think that my life is like a handful of sand, one by one they fall. There's nothing you can do about it. It will keep falling until it's all gone, which is why I hate digital watches that count seconds.

FIGURE 8–4   Geirthrudur's entry

FIGURE 8–5 Another of Geirthrudur's entries

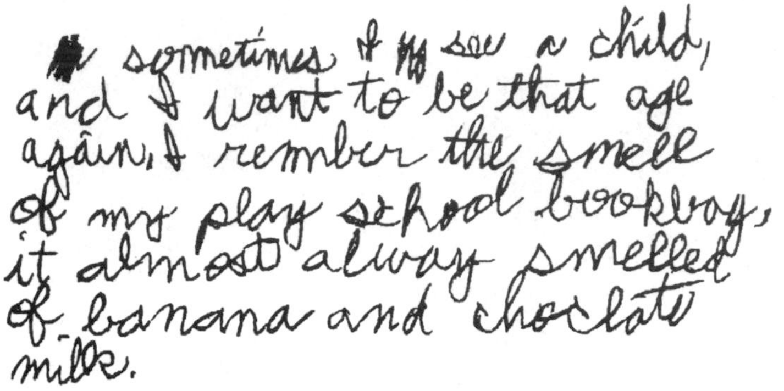
sometimes I see a child,
and I want to be that age
again, I rember the smell
of my play school bookbag,
it almost alway smelled
of banana and choclate
milk.

She also wrote, among other things, this entry (Figure 8–5):

> Sometimes I see a child, and I want to be that age again. I remember the smell of my Playschool bookbag, it almost always smelled of banana and chocolate milk.

We'll want to teach these children, too, to ask big, honest questions of their entries and to explore these questions. We'll want to teach them to write in the white spaces between two seemingly unconnected entries. Sometimes links can be built between different parts of ourselves, and in exploring these links, we can come to new realizations about ourselves. We'll want to encourage children to reread their entries and to "write off" from them, just as they might write off from a section of the novel we're reading aloud to the class. We'll want to tell children that writers reread and mark up their early entries and drafts, and we'll want to show them examples. In Chapter 4 I wrote about Jennifer, who wrote poems about her little brother, the pest. Readers will recall that as Jennifer reread her entries, Laurie Pessah suggested that she think of all those pages about her brother as cookie dough rolled out on the table in front of her. "Reread it and find the parts that feel like a poem," Laurie Pessah said, "and you'll lift these out as if you've got poetry-shaped cookie cutters and a spatula."

The wonderful thing that happens when we think about how third graders grow as writers is that we, too, can find bits to lift out and celebrate. We needn't wait to celebrate only the finished drafts. We can, instead, learn to celebrate a child who rereads an entry and stars part of it, or a child who stops in the midst of writing to say, "Wait, wait, I'm not sure this is what I wanted to say." We can learn to celebrate the child who writes, "I went on a vacation," and who only then refrains from trying to tell the whole story. We can learn to celebrate the small steps, and to extend them.

Literature for Children to Read Independently or Collaboratively

Blume, Judy. *Freckle juice.* New York: Dell, 1971.

Brown, Jeffrey. *Flat Stanley.* New York: HarperCollins Children's Books, 1989.

Bulla, Clyde Robert. *The chalk-box kid.* New York: Random Books for Young Readers, 1987.

———. *A lion to guard us.* New York: HarperCollins Children's Books, 1989.

———. *White bird.* New York: Random Books for Young Readers, 1990.

Cameron, Ann. *The stories Julian tells.* New York: Pantheon Books, 1981.

———. *Julian's glorious summer.* New York: Random House, 1987.

———. *Julian, secret agent.* New York: Random House, 1988.

———. *The most beautiful place in the world.* New York: Alfred A. Knopf, 1988.

Christopher, Matt. *The kid who only hit homers.* Boston: Little, Brown, 1986.

Cleary, Beverly. *Henry Huggins.* (4 vols.) New York: Dell, 1990.

———. *Ramona Quimby.* (5 vols.) New York: Dell, 1990.

Coerr, Eleanor. *Sadako and the thousand paper cranes.* New York: Putnam, 1977.

Dahl, Roald. *Mr. Fantastic Fox.* New York: Penguin Books, 1970.

Delton, Judy. *Pee Wee scout back pack.* (6 vols.) New York: Dell, 1990.

Fox, Paula. *Maurice's room.* Macmillan Children's Book Group, 1988.

Gannett, Ruth Stiles. *My father's dragon.* (3 vols.) New York: Buccaneer Books, 1990.

Gardiner, John Reynolds. *Stone fox.* New York: Thomas Y. Crowell, 1980.

Giff, Patricia R. *The kids of the Polk Street school.* (6 vols.) New York: Dell, 1988.

Hopkinson, Deborah. *Sweet Clara and the freedom quilt.* New York: Alfred A. Knopf, 1993.

Hurwitz, Johanna. *Russell and Elisa.* New York: Morrow Junior Books, 1989.

Kimmel-Smith, Robert. *Chocolate fever.* New York: Dell, 1972.

Levy, Elizabeth. *Something's queer.* (Series.) New York: Delacorte Press (various dates).

MacLachlan, Patricia. *Sarah, plain and tall.* New York: Harper & Row, 1985.

Naylor, Phyllis R. *Shiloh.* New York: Dell, 1992.

Peterson, John. *Littles.* (Series.) New York: Scholastic, 1986.

Ross, Pat. *M & M and the haunted house game.* (Various publishers.)

Rylant, Cynthia. *Every living thing.* New York: Macmillan, 1985.

———. *Henry and Mudge.* Vols. 1–13. New York: Macmillan Children's Book Group, 1987–1993.

Sharmat, Marjorie. *Nate, the great.* New York: Putnam, 1986.

Smith, Doris Buchanan. *A taste of blackberries.* New York: Scholastic. 1983.

Sobol, Donald J. *Encyclopedia Brown.* (Series.) (Various publishers.)

Warner, Gertrude C. *Boxcar children.* (Series.) New York: Buccaneer Books, 1992.

Whelan, Gloria. *Next spring an oriole.* New York: Random House, 1987.

White, E. B. *Stuart Little.* New York: HarperCollins Children's Books, 1974.

Wilder, Laura Ingalls. *Little house in the big woods.* New York: Harper & Row, 1981.

Winter, Jeanette. *Follow the drinking gourd.* New York: Alfred A. Knopf, 1988.

The books listed in Chapters 7 and 9 are also recommended.

Literature to Read to Children

The first books in the series included in the previous list are also recommended.

Banks, Lynne Reid. *The Indian in the cupboard.* New York: Avon Books, 1980.

Baum, Frank. *Wizard of Oz.* New York: Scholastic, 1989.

Bedford, Michael. *Emily.* New York: Doubleday, 1992.

Blume, Judy. *Superfudge.* New York: Dell, 1981.

———. *Tales of a fourth grade nothing.* New York: Dell, 1976.

Bunting, Eve. *Fly away home.* New York: Clarion Books, 1991.

———. *Summer wheels.* San Diego: Harcourt Brace Jovanovich, 1992.

Burnett, Frances H. *The secret garden.* New York: Bantam, 1987.

Conrad, Pam. *Staying nine.* New York: HarperCollins Children's Books, 1990.

Crews, Donald. *Big Mama's.* Greenwillow Books, 1991.

———. *Shortcut.* New York: Greenwillow Books, 1992.

Dahl, Roald. *George's marvelous medicine.* New York: Bantam, 1987.

———. *James and the giant peach.* New York: Buccaneer Books, 1990.

———. *Matilda.* New York: Viking, 1988.

Estes, Eleanor. *The hundred dresses.* San Diego: Harcourt Brace Jovanovich, 1974.

Facklam, Margery. *And then there was one: The mysteries of extinction.* Boston: Little, Brown, 1990.

Fleichman, Sid. *The whipping boy.* New York: Greenwillow Books, 1986.

Fleischman, Paul. *The half-a-moon inn.* New York: HarperCollins Children's Books, 1980.

Howe, James. *Bunnicula: The vampire bunny and his friends.* (4 vols.) New York: Avon Books, 1986.

Kimmel-Smith, Robert. *The war with Grandpa.* New York: Dell, 1971.

Konigsburg, E. L. *From the mixed-up files of Mrs. Basil E. Frankweiler.* New York: Macmillan Children's Book Group, 1987.

Little, Jean. *From Anna.* New York: HarperCollins Children's Books, 1973.
———. *Mama's going to buy you a mockingbird.* New York: Viking Children's Books, 1985.

Naidoo, Beverly. *Journey to Jo'burg: A South African Story.* New York: HarperCollins Children's Books, 1988.

Paterson, Katherine. *The great Gilly Hopkins.* New York: Dell, 1978.

Paterson, Katherine, and Vladimir Vagin. *The king's equal.* New York: HarperCollins Children's Books, 1992.

Phelps, Ethel Johnston. *Tatterhood and other tales: Stories of magic and adventure.* Old Westbury, NY: Feminist Press, 1978.

Radin, Ruth Y. *All Joseph wanted.* New York: Macmillan Children's Book Group, 1991.

Robinson, Barbara. *The best Christmas pageant ever.* New York: HarperCollins Children's Books, 1988.

Rylant, Cynthia. *Children of Christmas.* New York: Orchard Books, 1987.

Say, Allen. *Tree of cranes.* New York: Houghton Mifflin, 1991.

Sis, Peter. *Komodo!* New York: Greenwillow Books, 1993.
———. *Mississippi bridge.* New York: Dial Books, 1990.

Smith, Doris Buchanan. *A taste of blackberries.* New York: Thomas Y. Crowell, 1973.

Spinelli, Jerry. *Maniac Magee: A novel.* Boston: Little, Brown, 1990.

Steig, William. *Abel's island.* New York: Farrar, Straus & Giroux, 1985.

Taylor, Mildred D. *The friendship.* New York: Dial Books, 1987.

White, E. B. *Charlotte's web.* New York: Harper & Row, 1952.

The books listed in Chapters 7 and 9 are also recommended.

9

Developing Learning Communities in the Upper Elementary Grades

On the last day of fifth grade, David Tobias and his classmates reread the writing portfolios that had traveled with them through elementary school. David was intrigued to notice that in both fourth and fifth grade, the writing he'd selected as his best had been about his friends. In fourth grade, his rather quirky selection began like this:

> For this story I am writing about friends. There are many different kinds of friends (which I probably have all).
>
> This section of friends is: CRAZY.
> *Matthew Aronoff:* Let's flush our heads down the toilet!
> *Andrew:* Let's dance with tattoos on!!!!!!!
> *Ian:* What happened when the chicken laid an egg??? The chicken house started smelling!!!!!!!
> *Joe:* What happens when you put your hand in the blender?
> *Danny R.:* Can you fold your nose inside out?

David's fifth-grade selection, a picture book about saying goodbye to the neighborhood in which he had lived his entire life, has an entirely different tone (see Figure 9–1):

> I did not want to rush the morning. I wanted to keep every little thing tucked away in my head. I got on a pair of clothes and tiptoed down-stairs, out of my house and to my friend's front door. We ran down the road to the park. When we got there we heard nothing. Silentness.
>   It was like the silent country in the middle of a hustled, fast-paced world. Everything bundled into my head. Out of all that remembering one thing shot out of my mind:

I want to thank Kathy Doyle and Deeny Bennett for their assistance with this chapter.

FIGURE 9-1 David's fifth-grade selection

I did not want to rush the morning. I wanted to keep every little thing tucked away in my head. I got on a pair of clothes and tiptoed downstairs, out of my house and to my friend's front door. We ran down the road to the park. When we got there we heard nothing. Silentness.

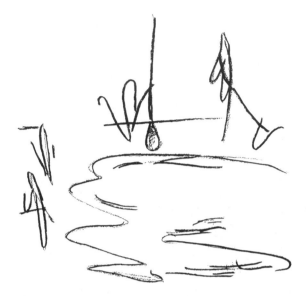

It was like the silent country in the middle of a hustled, fast-paced world. Everything bundled into my head. Out of all that remembering one thing shot out of my mind:

I was moving.

The water from a swing dripped into a puddle below. That's how I felt; my house, my things, my friends, all oozing out of me into a puddle.

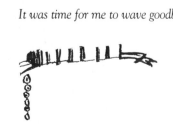

It was time for me to wave goodbye.

But the swing kept on swinging.

We walked to the kickball field. I could see the vision of kids, all different ages, playing kickball in the street. Parents were watching, and even the ice cream man was watching. Quickly that disappeared. Gone, like the bases of the baseball field, in which chalk had been running from the rain.

I was moving.

The water from a swing dripped into a puddle below. That's how I felt; my house, my things, my friends, all oozing out of me into a puddle.

But the swing kept on swinging.

We walked to the kickball field. I could see the vision of kids, all different ages, playing kickball in the street. Parents were watching, and even the ice cream man was watching. Quickly that disappeared. Gone, like the bases of the baseball field, in which chalk had been running from the rain.

It was time for me to wave goodbye.

Those of us who teach in the upper elementary grades will, I suspect, agree that David's two texts represent some of the problems and possibilities of these years. I'm not trying to suggest that fourth graders the world over will describe friends by writing about smelly farts, folding noses inside out, and flushing someone's head down the toilet, or that fifth graders the world over become more sensitive, melancholy, and self-aware. But I do think that as a child moves from one grade to another, from one classroom to another, it is not unusual for that child to move from writing about farts to writing about memories melting away like chalk baseball bases on wet pavement. I'm convinced that teachers in the upper elementary grades need to realize that the changes in David's writing between fourth and fifth grade were not random, idiosyncratic, or developmental. They were instead the result of changes in the tone, value, and relationships between the two classrooms.

In fourth grade David was hiding. I do not know why, but I do know that in the fourth-grade litany about his crazy friends and in other pieces he wrote that year, David hid behind feigned, back-slapping camaraderie and forced laughter. And David was not alone. When I first worked with David and his classmates at the start of their fifth-grade year, I remember finding it hard to fall in love with this class of children. "Their writing is actually *dull,*" I thought once, before rebuking myself for having such a thought. I tried to fake a responsiveness and interest in their drafts, but it didn't work. I blamed myself. "It must be me," I thought. "Have I lost my touch? What's happened to my ability to listen and to care?" Finally, I stopped faking things and began figuring them out. It dawned on me that I'd been faking responses to writing that was itself faked. No wonder I'd found very little to care about in these children's drafts. Their writing was a veneer; a hard, glossy, impenetrable surface they had constructed in order to protect their soft undersides.

The veneer I saw at the beginning of that fifth-grade year, like those I have seen in many other upper elementary-level classrooms, came in a great variety of forms. Many of David's classmates wrote in chirpy, ever-so-casual scrawls that glossed merrily over the comings and goings of their lives. Others glibly summarized their dreams and ambitions and decorated their pages with marginal rainbows and falling stars. Some retold or imitated cartoons. Others cited the socially acceptable adventures of their lives as if they were credentials. Although the veneer came in different forms, as I came to realize, this didn't mean that one child needed to learn about detail, another about topic choice, and still another about character development. Instead, they all needed a socially safe environment.

Establishing a Place for Writing in the Upper Elementary Grades

Over the course of that first month in their fifth-grade classroom, David and many of his classmates came out of hiding, and as this happened their writing changed radically. It became real and alive. The changes in their writing happened not as these children learned new techniques but as they learned new trust. And I was reminded that the quality of writing in our classrooms grows more from the tone, values, and relationships of our classroom communities than from anything else.

This is true for writers of any age, and yet it is also, I believe, *the* issue for those of us who teach writing in the upper elementary grades. Children in these grades can be unbelievably wonderful to each other or they can destroy each other. This is true for adolescents as well, but in fourth, fifth, and sixth grades, we are still the one deciding factor. To a very large extent, we create the social climate in these classrooms. What a responsibility!

I am not trying to suggest that our warmth and concern for children determine whether or not our classrooms are socially safe. We all care about our students. We all wish they would be respectful and nice to each other. But I think some of us try to ignore the peer subculture that exists under and around our teaching. We know that a certain amount of name-calling happens behind our backs, and we know that a few students are tormented on the playground and the bus, but we have resigned ourselves to it. We tell ourselves, "Ignore it." We think, "It's not my business" and "Kids will be kids." We try to stay on top of what directly involves our instruction and to overlook what happens in other provinces.

But of course, ignoring the problem doesn't work. We hear Anthony's pseudo-sophisticated classmates taunting him. "Slug," they say. "Pervert." When Anthony brings notes from his mother asking that he be excused from gym and recess, we know kids are jeering when he misses the ball, groaning when he joins their team, snapping towels at him in the locker room. One winter day, we learn that Anthony has smashed a window—the one beside the door into the gym locker room—and has been suspended. We hear later that his classmates had locked him outside on the snow-covered playground in his gym shorts. Apparently, that had been the final straw, and he'd exploded.

When Anthony returns to school a few days later, we will tell the class, "Write what you care about. Later, we'll read what we wrote to our classmates." Is it any surprise that Anthony will retell the plots of television programs and hide behind macho language?

What are we to do? The truth is, we don't ignore the peer subculture because we think it's unimportant, we ignore it because we feel helpless. It is difficult enough to do something about the major injustices we see; how can we get involved in the minor ones? What do we say when three girls tell a fourth, "We don't want to play with you anymore"? What are we to do about the fact that whenever a certain child speaks earnestly in our whole-class meetings, other children whisper wisecracks and perfectly timed put-downs?

The first answer is that we must *care*. If we are going to teach writing in the upper elementary grades, we need to know that the subculture in and around our classrooms matters, that it deeply affects our teaching. We must hear the whispered asides, see the rolled eyes. We must listen to the reports and repercussions from recess and lunch hour. And we must remember that the quality of writing and learning in our classrooms is absolutely determined by what happens on the playground, on the bus, and in the cafeteria. We cannot write well if we are afraid to put ourselves on the page. We cannot write well if we are afraid to let our individual voice stand out from other voices.

But we also need to know that children in the upper elementary grades can be unbelievably good to each other, and that when this happens, it's not random or idiosyncratic or developmental. Children are likely to be respectful and supportive of each other when we mentor this kind of behavior and when our classrooms are warm, safe communities.

After Anthony was locked out of the gym locker room, one of his classmates decided that he would not, could not, continue to overlook what was happening. In what I regard as an act of moral courage, Jonathan Bennett consciously and deliberately decided he would become Anthony's friend and protector. In time, Jonathan rounded up several other boys to join in the cause, and the five became fast friends. This vignette is as characteristic of the upper elementary grades as are the other, sadder ones. Jonathan didn't have a hard time convincing his friends to join him in protecting what is right. Children in the upper elementary grades are, for the most part, as willing to be swung toward the good as toward the bad. In the upper elementary classrooms in which writing flourishes, when one child whispers a hurtful aside, another child says, "You shouldn't say that" or "I don't think that's fair." This happens because from the start the teacher makes it clear that this year and this place will be different. "In this community, we are going to care about each other, we are going to respect each other and feel safe and supported." This is not just *a* priority for these teachers, it is *the* priority.

But how do we convey this sense of community? This is the question I asked of teacher after teacher.

"Truthfully, I think that this year the class became a community when I told my children about Shannon, my daughter," Kathy Doyle said. "I told them she is half black, and I told them about the hurtful things she's had to live through because she is different." Kathy was quiet for a moment. "It was a very serious moment, this talk, and my students felt it. They knew that if they were mean to each other, I'd take it very personally. They knew I meant it when I spoke about respect and trust."

For Judy Davis, a fifth-grade teacher at P.S. 183, it began when she shared her memoir with her students. Her voice was strong and clear, cracking only once, when she stood to read:

> My memories are shattered by a father who frightened me. I could never do things right in his eyes. I could never please him. My birthdays were always celebrated in the Catskill Mountain bungalow colony in which we spent our summers. My father brought a cake from the City, and this year as always, when I wanted to carry the cake to the casino by myself, he warned me that I wouldn't be able to do it.
>
> I was determined. I had to. Carefully I balanced the cake on my outstretched arm. It was heavier than I had imagined and I concentrated intently on holding it. Suddenly, I lost my footing in a muddy area, and the cake flew face down into the mud. I ran, muddy, crying, into the woods to hide from my father and his certain wrath, and now I hear myself telling my daughter she's not doing well enough . . . and I wonder if I hear my father.

For Kathy, Judy, and many other teachers, it was the moment in which they risked being real and vulnerable that changed the "name of the game" in their classrooms. It was as if in that moment of relationship, the class suddenly changed from being a place that operates through dominance, control, acting out, rules, and subterfuge to a place that operates through relationships, alliances, invitations, demonstrations, and encouragement.

To be sure, there are other factors that contribute to the construction of tolerant, respectful classroom communities, but I cannot overemphasize how important it is that we be authentic, real, vulnerable people in our classrooms, influencing the community by our demonstrations. When researchers Carol Edelsky and Kelly Draper (1983) studied Karen Smith, a brilliant sixth-grade teacher, in order to see how she inducted her difficult urban students into her whole-language classroom, they discovered that one of Karen's explicit goals was to get students to relate to and identify with her, because she knew that through respect, trust, and identification, her sixth graders would take on some of her values. At the beginning of the year Karen deliberately fostered the same sense of camaraderie, of "we're in this together," that was also crucial in Kathy Doyle's and Judy Davis's classrooms.

Like the other extraordinary upper elementary teachers I know best, Karen makes it clear that one of her most important goals is to help her students get along with and appreciate each other. Explaining this goal, she said she hoped "her students would see that you can get along with all kinds" and that they'd "look at the good in everybody." At the start of the school year, Karen frequently took on a role like that of a preacher in order to emphasize the importance of cooperation and mutual respect. On the second day of school, for example, in what Edelsky and Draper describe as evangelistic overtones, she said, "I want to talk to you for a minute about expectations in this classroom. We are human beings." Then she explained that, unlike animals, human beings have minds and mouths to talk. "In here, we talk our problems out."

I expect that in a great many other upper elementary-level classrooms, similar conversations are initiated, with similar overtones, on the first few days of school. It is worth noticing that these teachers make their concern for community-building explicit and mention it up front. They do not wait for interpersonal problems to develop before they try to make their classrooms into socially safe places.

When Edelsky and Draper studied Karen Smith's classroom, they recorded another crucially important dynamic that I believe develops in effective upper elementary-level writing workshops. Although they planned to spend six weeks watching the slow evolution in Karen's classroom as she gradually coerced her twenty-five city students, many with reputations as "bad kids," into functioning within an independent, caring community, they found that during the first day, Karen acted as if the desired behavior were actual. From the start she behaved as if her students *were* competent, sensible, and well-intentioned. On the first day Karen gave two boys a camera to photograph classmates and other students clipboards to record their classmates' ideas. She suggested that students organize themselves to work at the sink, five at a time, planting beans in milk cartons. "If there are five people at the sink already, use your judgment about what else to do. Work in your journals, or decorate your folders, or choose something else to do." If students misbehaved, she didn't interrupt the desired behavior to focus on the problem. Instead, she gave all the more attention to the desired behavior, perhaps giving a nod or an "evil eye" to signal the students to stop misbehaving. As a result, "by that afternoon, they [students] were cleaning up without being asked, helping one another, and taking responsibility for making decisions and completing assignments." On the first day, "the students were already becoming what the teacher wanted them to be" (p. 262).

Kathy Doyle also begins her year by acting as if her students are already responsible, caring, self-initiated learners. Last year, on the first day of school, instead of talking about homework policies, disciplinary proceedings, and so forth, Kathy and her students worked together in a garden students from the previous year had planted. They weeded and watered together, carefully labeled various plants, and then began to investigate which bulbs they would plant. Several months later, visitors to Kathy's classroom asked, "How did you get your students to act in such responsible, independent ways?" Kathy shrugged, gave a little laugh, and said, "I don't know, I guess I'm lucky. They came to me as great kids." Of course, her students always come to Kathy as "great kids" because Kathy expects this of them. Those of us who watch Kathy's teaching know that to a surprising degree, her kids act according to her expectations.

A sense of community begins during the earliest days of the school year, but wise teachers in the upper elementary grades find lots of ways to foster it throughout the year. Many teachers introduce rites, rituals, and celebrations to keep the values of their community alive. Some classrooms end each Friday with a sacred circle within which children read aloud from literature that moves them and reminds them of what matters most. Some classrooms use shared songs to support the sense of "we're in this together," and some have class chants, mascots, or banners. Others borrow rituals from sleep-over camps, using, for example, a variation of the "Secret Sisters" ritual in which each child has a secret buddy who leaves surprising little gifts. All this is important, but none of it takes the place of conversation. The most important thing these teachers do is that often throughout the year they call youngsters together to talk about the issues of their lives. If a few children taunt another child, these teachers are not apt to pull the offenders into the hall for a brief lecture and then carry on with the curriculum. Instead, the entire class gathers together. The room is filled with an air of great seriousness. "A crisis has occurred in our community," the teacher says, speaking very solemnly and softly. "What a concern this is; that it happened *here*. Let's talk about it."

Our Role as Mentors: Demonstrating a Love of Literacy

Teachers who stop everything in order to let students talk about what it means to care for each other will worry, "What about the curriculum? What about reading and writing?" I've had the same worries. But I know that nothing could be more important to our upper elementary classrooms than their tone. When children bond together, the entire group rallies around the value system of the newly formed community. "In this room," they say, "we believe. . . ." So often, what the children say they believe is very similar indeed to what we believe. I've smiled often to hear children claiming their teacher's values, even her evangelical tone, as their own.

How my colleagues and I laughed when Diana Lee, who seemed to us to be a timid, soft-spoken girl, decided that she needed to give her high school sister some writing help. "Do you do a lot of writing in high school?" Diana asked her sister in an interview she tape-recorded for us.

Diana's sister answered, in a rather haughty tone, "I write *essays*. They are a very important kind of writing."

Pausing for a long while, Diana said, "Is that *all* the kinds of writing you do? Other kinds of writing are important, too, you know. Like poetry. It is important to how you live your life. And memoir, too. If you want to become a writer someday . . ."

Diana's sister interrupted her. "No, I don't." Then she added, "I'd do it in my spare time."

Undaunted, Diana continued. "Well, I think you should really work hard on your writing because I learned a lot about really working on a piece of writing this year, and when you really work at it, you can publish it."

Diana has taken on her teacher's values. We can't tell children to do this. We can't assign it. But what a powerful thing it is within these communities when we model what it means for reading and writing to be at the heart of our lives! Children listen when we talk about the reading clubs we have with our friends. They look when we bring our notebooks with us to the classroom and, turning the pages, show them what we wrote while at a concert or a horse show. They notice when we cross out sections in our drafts.

When I was about this age I fell in love with the theater. On weekends, I rounded up all the neighborhood kids for my own playhouse. We wrote scripts, made scenery, sold tickets, and produced plays. My zeal for drama was inextricably linked with my devotion to Miss Armstrong, my seventh-grade English teacher. In a spiral notebook I listed everything I knew about her, and at the end of the year I presented it to her. I suspect many of us remember powerful mentors in these years.

Shirley Brice Heath has gone so far as to suggest that the single most important condition for literary learning is the presence of mentors who are joyfully literate people. Although this is true for all grades, I suspect that it may be particularly true during the upper elementary years. If we demonstrate a love for reading and writing and invite our children in, how glorious the writing and the learning and the loving can be in our classrooms!

Changes in Children's Writing and Their Thoughts About Writing

I think of David Tobias, the child who wrote about one friend with his head in the toilet and another with his nose inside out, who also wrote about his last melancholy walk to say goodbye to his neighborhood playground before he moved to a new house. David spent hours trying to develop the idea for the second story. "I want it to be something big," he said to me. "I don't want it to be just another little story." While he waited and worked toward inspiration, David wrote about his writing process in his notebook.

> When I got home, I could not wait to start the plan. I cracked my knuckles and got ready on the computer. "Okay, this time," I thought, "I'm going to try not to think so much. I'm going to forget about thinking so hard and getting headaches."
>
> I wrote one thing, but then I noticed I didn't feel stupendic about my draft. Any other normal human being could have done what I'd done. I wrote some more and finished. The draft was in front of me. It seemed like something was missing.
>
> I remembered about all those thoughts. I tried and tried to get them back, but I could not. My face looked like an apple from holding my breath. I realized that I'd lost some ideas that would only come to me once. I had liked the ideas, but it would not work. My thoughts had been something special, and I could not get them anymore. I worked and worked and wrote for a whole hour but nothing happened. I went downstairs to get a glass of milk to drink while I was doing the rest of my homework.
>
> "Maybe the homework will bring my thoughts back." I worked and worked, wrote and wondered.

The next day at school I did not try so hard to think. I tried hard but not pushing it. After a while, Mrs. Doyle said, "Now we're going to rearrange the room." BOOM. At that very moment, thoughts came zooming into my head like cars on the highway.

"Mrs. Doyle, can I go to the computer room to put some of my ideas on the computer?" I asked, and ran off.

It is not an accident that the moment I am using to illustrate fifth graders as writers is a moment of planning for writing and reflecting on writing. In the upper elementary grades many children can develop David's ability to coach, admonish, and advise themselves as they write. André Malraux has suggested that it is this new self-consciousness, this deliberateness, that separates the work of an adult from that of a young child. "Though a child is often artistic, he is not an artist. For his gift controls him; not he, his gift." Malraux feels we can expect anything of the very young child except awareness and, with it, mastery. The two are intrinsically connected because it is awareness that gives a child control, allowing the child to replicate what works, to strive toward particular effects, to avoid what doesn't work. Unless children are aware and deliberate, their artfulness can almost be thought of as a happy accident.

David's reflections on his own writing process demonstrate the new kinds of awareness one sometimes sees in upper elementary classrooms. But awareness such as David's isn't a given. It doesn't emerge *ex nihilo* in a child of this age. In fact, when David and his classmates were first asked to articulate what they did when they wrote, they answered, "I just wrote" or "I just sat and thought." But in David's classroom, when he and his friends gave their teacher brief three-word descriptions of their writing process, she valued whatever they said and in this way drew them out. "So, you *sat* and *thought!* That's *so* interesting; you spent some time *thinking* before you wrote. What, exactly, were you thinking about?"

If we give upper elementary children the chance to talk about their thinking, writing, and reading processes, many of them will become astonishingly articulate about their fleeting, intangible mental activities. And when children can describe what they are doing as they write, it adds enormously to their dawning sense of deliberateness and their control over their writing.

During her fourth-grade year, Susie Sible, the heroine of my first book, *Lessons from a Child,* decided, as she explained it, "to circle important sections of a piece about meeting my grandparents at the airport, and then, on another piece of paper, to stretch each of these small sections out into a detailed paragraph":

CIRCLED SECTIONS OF DRAFT 1	FINAL DRAFT
I started walking up to the airport from the plane. We had to go through a tunnel. I squeezed my mother's hand. I couldn't wait to see my grandparents.	My mother and I started to get off the plane. My sister, Jill, was right behind us. I looked at Jill. Her face was red from excitement. She smiled at me. I giggled. I could tell she was just as excited as I was.

By pulling my mother's hand, I hurried her to the entrance of the airport. As we got nearer, I heard the crowd inside, laughing and talking. I saw a lot of people. They were looking for the person they came to meet. They stretched their necks, searching through the crowd. Everyone was smiling, everyone was happy. |
| We were almost in the end. I saw my grandparents. | My grandmother's face was tanned. It made her look so healthy. My grandfather looked pretty much the same except he was tanned too. Somebody stepped in front of me. I lost sight of my grandparents. The crowd was moving very slowly so I wiggled past everybody. I ran straight to my grandparents. First I went to my grandmother. I threw my arms around her. |

As children get older, their work can become more intentional and deliberate. When Susie reread her final draft, she said, "It didn't really happen [that I could tell by looking at Jill that she was just as excited as me]. It didn't really happen, but I know she *was* excited and I wanted to put that in. . . . It's much better now!"

Because Susie can name and describe the strategy of circling sections of her draft that she hopes to expand, it is part of her repertoire, available for future use. Another time she can—and will—say to herself, "I should do as I did before, circling one part and then stretching it out. . . . I might not tell what *did* happen; I might imagine what *could have* happened."

Other children will invent, articulate, and use other strategies. As we saw earlier, Geirthruder decided to reread her entries, underlining the sentences that mattered most to her and then turning to a fresh page in her notebook in order to elaborate on her chosen sentence.

Clearly, these children have developed the ability to control their own writing processes, to be strategic writers. When Linda Flower studied the differences between novice and skilled writers, she found that skilled adult writers can plan not only what they will say in a piece, but also how they will proceed. They can say, "I'll just rush out a quick draft for now, and then I'll reread it. . . ." These fifth graders are well on their way toward planning their writing in ways similar to those we see in the adult writers Linda Flower studied.

Self-consciousness, however, doesn't always yield significance and vitality in writing—or in drawing. The older child's deliberateness and control can interfere with the spontaneous charm that is often evident in the work of younger writers and artists. Howard Gardner finds, for example, that as children grow older, their flavorful drawings are often replaced by a new realism, a new focus on getting every detail correct, and as a result, their pictures often lose some of their expressiveness. How true this is for children's writing as well! But Gardner is adamant that although the drawings of an older, more deliberate child may no longer have some of the magical aspects of early drawings, this does not mean that the period of middle childhood is a time of stagnation in the arts. "It is then," he says, during what he calls "the age of competence," that the child "develops particular technical skills; . . . it is then that he becomes able to plan his work with some thoroughness and accuracy; it is then that he can intentionally place in his own work . . . features . . . such as telltale details, subtle variations of color, and expressiveness of line" (1980, p. 261).

As children become more planful and more aware of what they do when they write, they also become more open to instruction. These years are a golden age for conferring and mini-lessons. When we say to students, "One thing you might try in your writing is . . ." they usually want to take our suggestions, because they want to be like us. They also take our suggestions because they want to do work that is big and important.

Children Learn to Expect Writing to Yield Insight

How often I've heard children say, "I don't want to write just another story! I want *this one* to be really important." For some children, writing something significant means entering one's text in a contest, mailing it to readers, rewriting it into a play script, or submitting it for publication to a newspaper. For others, as for Anna, a fourth grader at P.S. 87, writing something big and significant happens when you "write like Shakespeare" and spend a very long time doing so. One can almost feel the passion and intensity and ambition as they well up inside young Anna:

> I decided to write a long lasting story, like Romeo and Juliet. I changed my mind about being an FBI. I want to be a great writer like Shakespear. The book I'm going to write is called Twilight for Destiny. It is going to be about this girl treated like nobody, but one day she shows her deepness inside of her. I got this idea from a song called "One Moment in Time." I thought the main idea could encourage people to do something, or be somebody. If it's made into a movie, I want it to be rated G.
>
> All through my life people was encouraging me. Now I want to say I'm grateful so I'm writing this book and it is dedicated to every living thing.
>
> I'm going to spend the next five years, maybe next ten years, maybe the rest of my life.

Youngsters who've lived and worked in writing workshops can learn that a piece of writing becomes big and significant not only when it is published, but also when it is insightful and deeply true. "I worked and worked and wrote and wrote," David Tobias says. "I realized I'd lost an idea, and I liked the idea I'd lost." He adds, "I tried and tried to get it back, but it would not work. It was something special and I could not get it anymore." David was working not to spell or punctuate but to think; to catch a fleeting insight, to hold onto a thought.

David isn't alone in expecting his words to carry a big cargo of meaning. This is something he has learned from his experiences with reading and writing. Andrew Lindner, one of David's classmates, has a similar yearning to reach toward meaning. He described his process of writing poems by saying, "There's something in my mind, and I have to dig through my mind and then it comes toward me, and when it's on my fingers, my fingers move, and they write a poem."

Brian Jacobs says something similar. Reflecting on his experiences creating a memoir, he writes, "For me, I learned a lot. Mostly that you can take a very little idea in your mind and turn it into a big, long piece of literature."

Kathryn Kohlburg adds, "I've learned to go much deeper in my writing. It would be a boring story if I wrote just the facts of my life, so I have learned to write what they mean to me." Then she adds, "Before we wrote memoir, I didn't know how to get deep in my writing. I always skimmed the surface."

Ja-keeya has a similar expectation. She, too, believes that, as she writes, she can find a way to go beneath the surface and to say something deeply true. "When I take my writing out of the notebook," she explains, "I look at the paper with my eyes real hard and I say, 'Ja-keeya, this isn't the real part; it's a fake part,' and so I start on a scrap and change it . . . it's like magic, because I can make it real and true."

I suspect that these children have learned to reach toward meaning when they write independently because their teachers have helped them experience how writing can take them on trails of thought, how it can lead them to realizations and ideas. Because they have teachers who help them probe their topics and explore the mysteries of their subject to confront the questions that have always been there, to explore links between one facet of experience and another, they expect writing to be a time for thinking. Because it is tremendously important for our children to expect that their writing will yield insights, in share sessions and mini-lessons we may want to ask questions such as, "Did any of us feel a new idea growing in us as we wrote? Can you describe that?" As teachers, we need to remember that when we see light bulbs flashing, ideas dawning in our students' minds as they write, we'll want to name what we see. "Are you coming to a new idea?" we may ask. If the answer is yes, if the writer confirms that this has happened, what a cause for celebration!

Reading-Writing Connections in the Upper Elementary Grades

These years are a golden age for conferring and mini-lessons, but they are also a golden age for reading-writing connections. The same things that can make these children so open to instruction from their teachers also make them open to instruction from the authors of the texts they read. I think of what happened when I gathered David and his classmates together for a mini-lesson. I told them a story:

> Yesterday, I brought my four-year-old son to his swimming class, and for the first time I stayed to watch. Evan can't swim; I knew that, so I wondered what would happen. I figured he'd hold onto the pool's edge and kick a bit. Instead, his teacher dove into the pool and surfaced near the edge where Evan and his friends stood. Then she looked up at my skinny little waif of a son and said, "Okay, Evan, *jump*. Jump, Evan." Evan stood, his toes curled over the edge for a moment, looking down into the deep water. "Jump," she said, and he did, surfacing a moment later. He looked for her, but she was out of reach. "*Turn on your back, Evan*," she said. "*Turn . . . ,*" and he did.

I ended that mini-lesson by looking at the children who sat around me and saying,

You and I, as writers, need to have writing teachers who go into the deep water and who say, "Lucy, jump. Jump." In the books we're reading we've got those teachers. Let's all of us find, in the books we're reading, a section we love. Let's let the author of that section be our writing teacher, calling us to plunge in to do something deeper than we've ever done as writers.

David Tobias, the hero of this chapter, turned to a section in Patricia MacLachlan's *Journey* in which the boy, Journey, holds onto a photograph of his long-gone father. Journey turns the photograph one way, then another. He notices his father's youth, and remembers carrying the photograph with him everywhere when his father first left. He turns the photograph another way, notices his father's faraway look, and remembers searching for a way to meet his father's eyes.

Rereading that section, David tried to use the same technique in his writing. He tells of standing in an almost empty house trying to comprehend that he is really moving. He writes,

> I walked into the dusty white room. It seemed somehow different. It was huge, and there was no carpet, no chairs, no tables, nothing except boxes. One box was labeled albums.
>
> I sat on the cold wood floor and saw my old house in a colored fall picture, almost hidden. I turned the page. There was a small trimmed picture of me at my fifth birthday. I turned more pages: Cousins, places visited, people, birthdays. . . .

Rereading what he has written, David says, "After I step back and see what I've just done, it feels so, so immortal. My head. I start getting this big head full of thoughts. I can remember being in that empty room and the photo albums and looking at them and at my life from different angles. Like, I looked at the desk, ready to be moved, and I thought of leaving school. I turned my head, saw something else, thought something else. I looked at one photograph and thought about a whole year of my life. Then I turned to another photograph." David paused and then added, "Nothing has to happen in a whole piece of writing; it can just be me, turning my head to see something differently." Then he added, "It's like a marble game. There's a pile of thoughts in my head and a little hole. If you turn your head, one thought goes into the hole. If you turn it again, a different one comes rolling out . . . and you can go on forever!"

Literature for Read-Alouds and Independent Reading

Alexander, Lloyd. *The fortune-tellers.* New York: Dutton, 1992.

Babbitt, Natalie. *Tuck everlasting.* New York: Farrar, Straus & Giroux, 1985.

Barron, T. A. *The ancient one.* New York: Putnam Publishing Group, 1992.

Cassedy, Sylvia. *Lucie Babbidge's house.* New York: HarperCollins Children's Books, 1989.

———. *Sadako and the thousand paper cranes.* New York: Putnam Publishing Group, 1977.

Cole, Brock. *Goats.* New York: Farrar, Straus & Girioux, 1990.

Fox, Paula. *Monkey island.* New York: Orchard Books, 1991.

Henkes, Kevin. *Words of stone.* New York: Greenwillow Books, 1992.

Little, Jean. *Hey world, here I am!* New York: HarperCollins Children's Books, 1989.

Lord, Bette Bao. *In the year of the boar and Jackie Robinson.* New York: Harper & Row, 1984.

Lowry, Lois. *Number the stars.* New York: Dell, 1992.

MacLachlan, Patricia. *Arthur for the very first time.* New York: HarperCollins Children's Books, 1989.

———. *Journey.* New York: Doubleday, 1991.

Naidoo, Beverly. *Journey to Jo'burg: A South African story.* New York: HarperCollins Children's Books, 1988.

Naylor, Phyllis R. *Shiloh.* New York: Dell, 1992.

Paterson, Katherine. *Bridge to Terabithia.* New York: Thomas Y. Crowell, 1977.

———. *The great Gilly Hopkins.* New York: Thomas Y. Crowell, 1978.

Paulsen, Gary. *The monument.* New York: Delacorte, 1991.

Rawls, Wilson. *Where the red fern grows.* New York: Bantam, 1974.

Shelton, Rick. *Hoggle's Christmas.* New York: Cobblehill, 1993.

Spinelli, Jerry. *Maniac Magee: A novel.* Boston: Little, Brown, 1990.

Taylor, Mildred D. *Roll of thunder, hear my cry.* New York: Dial Press, 1976.

Taylor, Theodore. *The cay.* New York: Doubleday, 1987.

Wallace, Bill. *Trapped in death cave.* New York: Holiday House, 1984.

Yarborough, Camille. *The shimmershine queens.* New York: Putnam, 1989.

Yep, Laurence. *The star fisher.* New York: Morrow Junior Books, 1991.

Yolen, Jane. *Letting swift river go.* Boston: Little, Brown, 1992.

10
Teaching Adolescents
Improvisation and Commitment

"I think adolescence is like the flame in the ornery burner of a gas stove; the one that leaps ferociously one minute and then hardly makes a blue ring the next," Janet Goodson, a middle-school teacher, wrote. Janet was one of my students in Teaching of Secondary School English, and we began the course by thinking not about our teaching but about our students. "Adolescence is a time of struggling between extremes: fast and slow, blissful and tortured, seeking and shunning," she continued. "Perhaps *crucial* is the only word that applies unquestionably, because it is in adolescence that we begin to take responsibility for who we are."

Crucial. Kay Brigham, another middle-school teacher in that class, would agree. Recalling her own adolescence, she wrote, "It was a time of joy . . . coming out of the movies after seeing *Singing in the Rain* to find it pouring. Joining hands and swinging them fiercely as we preempted the sidewalk we strode, soaking wet, bellowing, 'It's a glorious feeling, I'm happy again, just singing, singing in the rain.'"

Tom Newkirk remembers a different side of adolescence:

> In eighth grade I worried constantly about my hands—worried about how they looked. Were the veins on the backs of my hands too prominent? Were my fingernails clean? too obviously bitten? In the winter my fingers looked bluish at the beginning of the day. I could, and sometimes did, put my hands in my pockets, but that looked, well, "strange" and anything was better than looking "strange." I was even sensitive about appearing sensitive.
>
> I had become *self-conscious*. Say it quickly and it is a weakness, implying unnecessary nervousness. But say it slowly—self . . .

I would like to thank Randy Bomer, Lucretia Pannozzo, and Margaret Queenan for their assistance with this chapter.

consciousness—and it's something more positive, perhaps the major achievement of the adolescent years. . . . In these years a kind of awareness emerges, a kind of personal intelligence, that can become a focus of language education. (1985, p. 111)

Randy Bomer, Co-Director of the Teachers College Writing Project and a former secondary-school teacher, finds that these two entries, written by one of his students on two consecutive days, capture something important about adolescence:

I think I've made up my decision about the world. I think it depends on the way you make the world. If you hate and despise the world and everybody in it, you're going to have a very hard life. I think I'm going to try to like most people.

Today we had no school, but I was sort of disappointed because it seems whenever there's no school because of snow or ice, my hair looks good and I have the perfect outfit. It never fails.

Throughout this book I claim that as human beings, we need to write, because writing allows us to understand our lives. But I think that during adolescence we have a special need to understand our lives, to find a plot line in the complexity of events, to see coordinates of continuity amid the discontinuity. During adolescence, youngsters construct a sense of personal identity. It is a time for trying on selves, for reflection, self-awareness, and self-definition. The adolescent learns to say, "This is my story" and "This is who I am."

It's no surprise that some adolescents turn to writing with a particular fervor, filling endless pages of diaries, writing deep, meaningful poems, long, heartfelt letters, editorials, petitions, and posters. As Steven Zemelman and Harvey Daniels say in *A Community of Writers*, "Writing comes closer to these kids' urgent personal concerns than any other school subject. After all, in learning to write, students are invited—compelled, really—to make sense of the world, to weigh ideas, to explore values, to find their own conventions, to invent voices, styles, personae on a page—and then to test everything out by communicating with others, sharing writing, and exchanging responses" (1988, p. 3).

At first, when fourteen-year-old Jose wrote in his notebook he didn't muse over the weightiest concerns of his life. In one of his first entries he reported on a substitute teacher he'd seen crying in the halls. "I've seen kids walk all over a sub before," Jose wrote, "but this was unbelievable. I looked at the sub. Her back was to the class. She had her head down. She had tears going down her face. She was crying. Those kids made her cry!"

The next day, Jose's teacher encouraged him to reread this first entry and think more about it. Jose wrote, "That sub must have tried hard not to cry." Then he began writing about a time when he'd hurt his leg and tried desperately to hold back the tears. The entry ends:

"OH GOD!" Pain like I never felt before.

I thought I would throw up all over the place. I broke into a sweat. Not from the summer heat but from pure unquestionable pain! Agony!

"Don't scream. Don't cry." That's all I told myself. People were around me asking me questions. I was aware that I was nodding my head in answers but I don't think the questions ever registered in my brain.

"Don't scream. Don't cry." That was all that was running through my head. My voice. My very own pain ridden voice in my mind, repeating over and over and over again, "Don't scream."

The following day, after Jose had reread his entry about the substitute teacher blinking back her tears and about himself doing the same thing, he began to consider why he'd tried so desperately to avoid crying:

Here I am lying on the ground dying of agony and I didn't worry about the pain or if I was terribly hurt or how I was going to get home or anything else except not embarassing myself in front of my buddies. Don't scream. Don't cry. Looking back I still can't believe that that's all I worried about.

If I was a girl I could have screamed and cried. But I am a guy. Guys can't cry. It sure is easier to be a girl. It was easier being a guy when I was 10 or 12 but now being a guy at 14 is rough.

It's turned into a game with too many rules to follow. When you break a rule you are out. There are no second chances. You have to be careful when you are playing for friends, chances, respect . . . you have to be careful when you are playing for life.

Sometimes when I'm preparing to supervise student teachers in secondary-level English classrooms, I find myself returning to Jose's work or to that of other adolescents. I do this, I think, because these texts remind me of how crucial writing can be in young people's lives, and that's something I need to remember if I'm going to lead a successful writing workshop. I need to *believe* that the writing workshop—and all it represents—matters enormously.

Of course we need to believe our methods of teaching matter. Isn't that obvious? But my hunch is that in the early grades, teachers often launch writing workshops feeling unsure about the ideas but willing to give them a try, and the success of the workshop lures them into a deeper commitment.

The opposite is true at the secondary level, where the more common scenario is that a teacher decides, with some ambivalence, to experiment with a writing workshop for a week or two. With mixed feelings, he tells students they are to choose their own topics and so forth, but then as he feared, problems emerge, and he decides the writing workshop "doesn't work" for his students.

I do not think we can talk about teaching in secondary schools without talking about how we respond to our students' resistance. One of the first-year teachers in our graduate program in secondary English recently told me that he'd tried asking his students to choose their own topics for writing, but, he said, "It didn't work." For two or three days he fielded student resistance to the writing workshop, and then, as students entered his room on the fourth day, he had a flash of inspiration. Tearing a few pages of paper into strips, he'd scrawled directions onto each slip. "Describe the worst meal you've ever eaten." "Tell us about your friends' farts." Students had fifteen minutes in which to do the assigned task, and then, with great hilarity, they listened to each other's writing. "It worked!" that first-year teacher told me, and he began trying to invent a similar activity for the next day, and the next.

Perhaps his students would do crossword puzzles the next day, or perhaps they'd pass stories around a circle, with each person adding another increment onto each story. I do not know. What I do know is that this first-year teacher's response to his students' resistance was not an unusual one. I empathize with his elation over surviving one day in good style, but I think it is very problematic if our goal as teachers becomes simply to have our classes "work." Toward what end are they working? We need to evaluate our teaching not only by asking, "Did the class go smoothly?" but also by asking, "Did we progress toward the principles that matter most to me in literacy education?" For me, those principles do not change depending on the age of my students. In every grade level and in every teaching situation I want my students to be engaged in their own ongoing, rigorous literacy projects. I want my students to be making plans and decisions, having intentions and concerns. I want to teach into their intentions, to teach in response to their concerns. Because I believe literacy must be purposeful and authentic, I wouldn't rip paper into little bits and ask each student to write a paper on my hilarious topics, even if I knew such an activity would "work." Randy Bomer addresses this in *A Time for Meaning,* his important new book about teaching secondary English. He writes, "I jealously, obsessively protect the regularity of workshop structures in my class, wherein we are writing every day of the week or reading every day of the week. I don't break up my class period into different agendas, nor do I break up my week."

This doesn't mean I'd expect that by jealously protecting the regularity of the workshop structures, I'd ensure that my writing workshop would progress smoothly in each of my classes. In fact, I think that when we teach at the secondary level, we can be almost certain that many of our adolescent students will be resistant to the workshop, if for no other reason than that, as adolescents, their job in life is to resist, to define themselves in opposition to parents and other authority figures. If we say, "I want to read one of the most beautiful stories in the world to you," some adolescents will say, "I think it's boring." If we say, "I know some of you are scared about reading your work aloud," a few of them will turn the occasion into a joke session with a dramatic rendition of the knee-knocking, teeth-chattering fear they are surely feeling. If we tell them they'll have a chance to write before long, some adolescents will groan and whine. The fact that we will encounter resistance when we teach secondary-school students is probably irrefutable.

What I can't help wondering is, when a teacher teaches Shakespeare, or prefixes and suffixes, and finds problems emerging, does that teacher then decide that "Shakespeare doesn't work for these kids" or "prefixes aren't feasible"? I doubt it. Because he *believes* in Shakespeare and in prefixes and suffixes, he holds onto these goals and invents or improvises new approaches to them.

Similarly, for me it would not be an option to give up on the idea that during my English class, my students will write in their notebooks, draft and revise pieces, confer with each other and with me. If they all said, "I have nothing to write about," I might invent and discard a whole range of ways to help them know they have stories to tell and ideas to develop, but I wouldn't give up on the central principles behind my teaching.

If we are going to be successful teachers in secondary-level writing workshops, we need to hold on with dogged persistence to the things we value most. While holding onto our beliefs, we also need to teach with enormous flexibility and spontaneity, responding and building off of our students' energies and intentions.

When my sons were two and three they went through a phase of needing to exert their control over me and our shared lives. People advised me, "You've got to set very clear boundaries, but you also need to let them have their victories." Secondary-school students need the same combination of clear structures and endless flexibility. It was sometimes enough to give my sons the illusion of control: "Do you want to go to bed in *five* minutes or in ten minutes?" I'd ask. "It's *totally* up to you." But with secondary-school students, small victories are not enough. We need them to join us in building a community, a place, a sense of we-ness, and an agenda that grows out of their intentions. Unless we do this, we will not be able to create alive, vital writing workshops.

Teaching writing at the secondary-school level is not unlike jazz improvisation. A trumpet plays up the scale, and the other instruments work off that melody. We and our students work off each other in the same way to invent the fabric of life in their workshops.

It would probably not be helpful to describe how one or even several teachers have organized their writing workshops. If we approach secondary-school teaching with only one or two fixed models in our minds, we may not be ready to think on our feet, to reinvent the workshop as we go. But it may be helpful to reflect on some of the questions all of us wrestle with as we improvise our way toward our own versions of a writing workshop.

- How can we adapt the writing workshop to fit the norms of secondary schools?
- What might our role as teachers be in a secondary-level writing workshop?
- How can we make peer conferring and response groups more viable in the writing workshop?
- How might we lure our students to care about writing?
- How do we maintain our students' energy for writing?

It is not hard to understand why secondary-school teachers have questioned whether the writing workshop is really suited for their age-level students. For the past decade, most of the literature on teaching writing has grown out of elementary school (or college) classrooms. But this is changing. Nancie Atwell's *In the Middle* and Tom Romano's *Clearing the Way* were among the first books to portray life in secondary-level writing classrooms. Linda Rief's *Seeking Diversity* echoes and extends Nancie Atwell's message and stands as further testimony that, yes indeed, secondary-school youngsters can thrive when they are invited into reading/writing workshops. More recently, Randy Bomer has written *A Time for Meaning*, the story of his high-school English classroom and of the classrooms he's come to know in his work as a teacher-educator throughout North America. Clearly, we need more middle- and high-school teachers to tell the stories of their teaching and to add to our repertoire of images for successful writing workshops at the secondary school level.

We need the voices and perspectives of secondary-school teachers because when we try to bring the writing workshop to the secondary level we face a host of very particular challenges. There are the overt, obvious challenges. Most middle-school teachers, for example, have well over a hundred students a day. This means that a secondary-school teacher must establish relationships with her students and a sense of community in her classroom not only once, but, because of the class load, sometimes five times over. On top of that, this teacher needs to do all this within forty-five-minute periods.

When people ask me, "How can I teach writing well when I have one hundred and twenty students?" I admit to myself, "It can't be done." My husband, who is a psychotherapist, limits the number of patients he sees to twenty-eight a week. He does this not because he wants to limit his hours in the office, but because he knows he cannot hold the details of more than twenty-eight lives in his head. We teachers cannot hold the details of one hundred and twenty lives in our minds at once. The answer lies in restructuring secondary schools so that we don't have to ask, "How do I teach writing well when I have one hundred and twenty students?"

More and more educators are calling for longer blocks of time each day with each class of students. When one teacher, for example, teaches both English and social studies to the same group of youngsters, the school year can contain seasons of deep involvement (and double periods) in reading and writing literature as well as seasons of deep involvement (and double periods) in historical inquiry and research.

When it isn't possible to extend the length of time we spend with a class of students (which implicitly limits the total number of classes with whom we can work), teachers can at least take their forty-five-minute English class and say, "For the next six weeks, our entire class time (short as it is) will be devoted to the writing workshop." And because each class session is so short, instead of adhering to the structure of mini-lesson / workshop / response groups, many middle-school writing workshops have a mini-lesson several times a week and response groups on alternate days.

I could continue in this mode, making suggestions about how to adapt the writing workshop to fit into a secondary-school framework, but I sometimes think all these suggestions miss the real point. The real point is that yes, it is hard to lead a writing workshop at the secondary level. The schedule makes it hard, the crowded curriculum makes it hard, and, I think, sometimes the *kids* make it hard.

We need to realize that there are a lot of new forces in the secondary school that complicate the teaching of writing, and one of them is our students. Randy Bomer helped me realize this when he said to me, "The first time I worked with fifth and sixth graders, all I could think was, 'These kids are a lot *smarter* than seventh and eighth graders.' " He added, "Of course, they're not, but as a secondary-school teacher you can't get over how accommodating sixth graders are compared to older students. They are *so* willing to please, so forthcoming." Randy's point was not to bemoan the difficulty of the secondary school teacher's job, it was to point out that if these teachers buy into the "standards of success" for writing workshops that have been set by teachers of younger students, they may end up feeling discouraged.

Of course, the boundaries between the upper elementary grades and the junior high years are not as dramatic as I'm suggesting. Young adolescents swing back and forth. Sometimes they want to adopt our values and receive our approval. Sometimes they want, even need, to define themselves in opposition to us. "It's important to remember, when kids don't take our suggestions or fall in line behind our examples," Randy points out, "that their job as adolescents is to build an identity for themselves in separation from the parent figures, the authority figures, of their lives. We shouldn't get discouraged and decide the workshop doesn't work because they groan and whine when we ask them to write."

More important, if the writing workshop doesn't meet with instant success, we shouldn't totally revamp the workshop to fit the givens of secondary schools. Yes, the secondary-school workshop will probably be different than the elementary school workshop. But let me stress from the start that it is one thing to say that the workshop will be different in the secondary school than it is in the elementary school, and it's another thing entirely to suggest that the writing workshop should be altered so that it fits into the norms of secondary education. The writing workshop is meant to run *against* the norms of secondary classrooms. It isn't meant to be "business as usual" at the secondary school level because "business as usual" hasn't worked very well. As John Goodlad reports, English is students' least favorite subject. The longer our students are in school, the less they like to read. Other studies have shown that of all the countries in the United Nations, the United States is only forty-ninth in literacy.

Too often, when secondary-level teachers try to alter the writing work-shop as they imagine it exists in elementary schools to fit the norms of secondary schools, they inadvertently take the heart out of the writing workshop. A middle-school teacher recently told me he wanted to adapt the writing workshop to fit into secondary schools, so he launched a "writing workshop" (complete with peer response groups and revision) in which his students each wrote five-paragraph compare-and-contrast essays on two plays. "It's not working," the teacher told me, so I volunteered to visit the class. When I entered the classroom I understood why. The teacher had written three "themes" on the chalkboard (The American Dream, Relationships, Truth). "For the next ten minutes, what I want you to do," the teacher said as he began the class, "is to pick one theme from the three we discussed yesterday and write down everything you know from *All My Sons* and *Death of a Salesman* that applies to that theme." Then, to help, the teacher passed out copies of this worksheet:

TOPIC SHEET   American Literature

Directions: Choose one of the major themes from the two plays that you
think you may want to write about and LIST everything you
can think of about that theme under each play. Don't worry
if it doesn't make sense, just write anything that comes to
mind.

THEME: _____

Death of a Salesman: *All My Sons:*

As students began to fill in the "writing process" ditto, the teacher interjected, "Remember, when you write *any* line about one play, you need to go immediately to the other column and write something corresponding about the second play."

After ten minutes, the teacher said, "It's time for revision. Go back to your list now and circle the ideas on which you want to write more." Turning to the chalkboard, he said, "Be sure you flesh out the idea by asking *who*, and then *how* and *why* questions." As he said each word (*who, how, why*), he wrote it on the chalkboard, and not surprisingly, students dragged themselves along as if they were doing grammar exercises on punctuation ditto sheets. When the bell rang and the classroom emptied, the teacher confided in me, "You see, they really don't get that turned on by the writing process at this age."

In thinking about the class later, I was struck by the fact that, intending to "adapt" the writing workshop to fit secondary-level classrooms, the teacher had in fact done what many of us do with radical new ideas: we stretch, chop, slice, and twist them so that they fit into the norms of American education. For example, in studying English classrooms throughout America, John Goodlad (1984) found that, especially as one goes up the grades, there is very little room for student choice, and that was certainly true of the class I observed. Goodlad also found that we tend to divide our class time into little segments—ten minutes on punctuation, twelve minutes on a comprehension activity, five minutes for a class discussion. The lesson on comparing and contrasting essays was, of course, similarly segmented, with the entire class moving through ten minutes of one activity and five minutes of another.

The problem here is that under the auspices of "adapting the writing workshop to fit the secondary-school student," the teacher has abandoned the writing workshop. He is putting his students through "writing process exercises" rather than helping them to write with purpose and self-investment.

I have seen many, many secondary-school teachers adapting the writing workshop to the secondary-school level by turning it into a series of small, whole-class, teacher-designed activities—brainstorming topics, circling one, writing ten related words, and so on. When Nancie Atwell first heard about the idea of a writing workshop, she also said that she tried to turn it into a series of whole-class activities. She describes this in *In the Middle* in a scene in which she argues with one of my colleagues, Susan Sowers, about the writing workshop:

> "But Susan, what if I have my class come up with a chain of memories, talk about them, choose one, and write it?"
> "Well, that sounds very nice," she answered. "But that's really an exercise."
> "Okay . . . but what if I give them a choice of four really funny dramatic monologues, and they get to role-play these, then choose one to write up?"
> "Ummm, I guess I'd call that an exercise, too."
> "Wait, wait. I haven't told you my best . . ."
> It was an exercise. They were all exercises. (1987, p. 11)

Susan Sowers was right. As long as the whole class moves in unison through a series of prescribed, teacher-assigned steps, the classroom is probably not significantly different from classes in which students spend most of their time on ditto sheets of drill-and-skill exercises.

What Might Our Role as Teachers Be in a Secondary-Level Writing Workshop?

When I wrote about working with adolescents in the first edition of this book, I argued that although the connection between teachers and students is crucial at every grade level, this is nowhere more true than during the middle-school years. To illustrate my point, I recalled the influence of Miss Armstrong when I was in seventh grade and reported that, as Nancie Atwell points out, David Halberstam (author and Pulitzer Prize-winning journalist), John Bushnell (Chief of Mission at the American Embassy in Buenos Aires), and Ralph Nader (consumer advocate) were all in the same seventh-grade social studies class. Halberstam has written about their teacher, Miss Thompson: "She taught with genuine passion, encouraging young people at a delicate moment to think they could be anything they wanted." Adolescents, I concluded, need mentors like Halberstam's Miss Thompson and my Miss Armstrong.

Looking back on that original chapter, I now suspect it was no accident that I illustrated the connectedness between middle-school teachers and their students by reminiscing about the effect junior high teachers had on me and my contemporaries when we were adolescents—thirty years ago! I have since moved my stories of Miss Armstrong's influence on me into my chapter on fourth, fifth, and sixth graders, which is, I believe, where those stories now belong. These days it tends to be in the upper-elementary grades that many youngsters model themselves after their teachers, who are their heroes. Today, most (but not all) middle-school teachers would probably agree with Lucretia Pannozzo, curriculum leader at John Jay Middle School in Cross River, New York, who says, "Most of my kids are glad when school starts in September. They want to be there. As one bold student put it, 'Summer sucks.' But they want to be at school because their *friends* are there. Many of them would prefer we teachers weren't there at all. For them, teachers and instruction interrupt the purpose of school."

Lucretia and her colleagues at John Jay Middle School often laugh about how fifth- and sixth-grade teachers leave school on the last day before the Christmas holiday loaded down with shopping bags full of gifts. "Those guys get memo pads, perfume, gloves, decorated clipboards . . . and we in eighth grade get, at the most, a card slipped onto our desks when we're not watching," Lucretia says. In the secondary school, we learn to be grateful for the small ways in which students thank us. Lucretia saved the letter she got from a student last Christmas. Peggy Stevens has saved a check she wrote to a student ten years ago, because when the student cashed the check, he not only signed it but also wrote a note to Peggy. The note was small—"with thanks"—but those of us who live and work in secondary schools realize how much cargo two or three small words (or a glance, a smile, a wink) can carry. What a difference this is from the upper elementary grades, when children often try, in endearing and obvious ways, to emulate us.

Many of us approach the idea of teaching a writing workshop expecting that we can touch and move all our students by talking fervently and openly about our love of reading and writing. "I used to think I could get in front of them and be this person who spoke in heartfelt ways to them, and they'd *really* listen and be transformed," one teacher remembers. "But when I start talking, I know that many of my students tune out. I can't always even tell if they are with me, because many are used to putting masks on for teachers; they are good at pretending to listen. If I talk away about how much I love writing and so forth, they look at me politely, pretending to be the person I want them to be, but I know many of them are miles away."

Of course, sometimes when we talk or read in front of our classes, we do feel that the kids are with us. Sometimes we sense them emulating us, saying, "I want to do that, too." But I think that when we expect secondary-school youngsters to fall in line behind our exciting, wonderful ideas, we need to understand how common it is to meet with mixed success. The truth is that even if our adolescent students *are* moved by our writing and our example, many will do everything possible to feign detachment.

The answer is not to give up on establishing relationships with students. Instead, it requires trusting in the power of small, individual encounters. When I asked Lucretia, "How do you build relationships with your classes?" she answered with the same answer countless other writing workshop teachers have given: "I build relationships one by one. One by one, that's how." Lucretia establishes a relationship by pausing to talk with Monica about Avi's *Nothing but the Truth* and bringing in another similar book for her a few days later. She establishes relationships by noticing that one of her girls has red, puffy eyes, pausing to ask if she's okay, and then giving that girl and three friends a pass to go together to the guidance counselor. She establishes relationships by spending hours and hours during these first weeks of school writing long, personal, not-patronizing, not-teacherly letters to her students about their responses to literature. When Tara wrote, "In my opinion, my book is the best book ever written. I know that sounds dumb, but I get so enthralled reading it, I forget everything," Lucretia responded by telling Tara about times when she, too, has gotten lost in a book. Lucretia also establishes one-to-one relationships as she moves about the room, responding to her students' writing. She establishes personal relationships by teaching on her toes, by being ready to make a big deal about whatever feels alive and real in the classroom. These gestures may seem small, but they are not. When Mihalyi Csikszentmihalyi and Reed Larson (1984) studied how American adolescents actually spend their time, they attached beepers to them and beeped them at random intervals. The adolescents then filled out a self-report. Out of 2,700 reports, there were only five occasions when the adolescents reported that they were or had just been speaking on a one-on-one basis with their teacher. The connections that are so essential in Lucretia's teaching are indeed rare in most secondary-school classrooms.

How Can We Make Peer Conferring and Response Groups More Viable in the Writing Workshop?

If in the first edition of this book I overemphasized our students' willingness to emulate us as teachers and to seek our approval, I did so because I underestimated the role played by the peer group. The topics our students write about in our workshop, the tone they adopt in writing, the genres they enjoy, the time they invest in their work, the revisions they make, will all, to a great degree, depend on what happens interpersonally. The peer group is a powerful enough force in our classrooms that it can damage as well as support our students' engagement in writing. If a student reads aloud a draft in which he writes about an authentic, important issue in his life and his peers respond by rolling their eyes, looking bored, or criticizing a passage, the writer will probably pull into his protective shell, refusing to emerge for months.

The question, then, is how do we tap into the advantages of peer response groups and avoid the disadvantages? In *A Time for Meaning* Randy Bomer suggests that some of the structures basic to the elementary-level writing workshop may need to be altered because of the self-consciousness of many adolescents. For example, he writes:

> When I first started teaching through a writing workshop, I usually tried to have a time at the end of every period when one or two students would read their piece to the class. I did this because I thought I had to: Calkins, Graves, and Atwell said so. Unfortunately, my students had not read any of those people's books, and they, for the most part, didn't

want to read their heartfelt pieces in front of 30 other 15-year-olds. . . . I began to think that, in spite of all my efforts to build community, it might just be too socially dangerous for many adolescents to risk looking stupid in front of their peers. . . . For the writer, it was like castor oil, still unpleasant no matter how much I protested it was good for her. For the listeners, listening to mediocre drafts badly read was usually boring. Guiltily, secretively, I gave "the share" up.

After a while, when I would have an interesting conference with a student, where we discussed something I thought might benefit the whole class, I would ask whether in the last few minutes, she would tell the others about what had been going on in her writing, perhaps what the problem had been, and what she and I had figured out as a solution. She might read relevant sections aloud. . . . Usually, I would pitch in to help the rest of the class see how this strategy might apply to other situations as well.

Neither Randy Bomer nor most of the other secondary-level writing workshop teachers with whom I work have abandoned the idea of peer conferring, but some people question whether it is realistic or necessary to expect adolescent students to critique one another's work or to raise questions that lead to revision. Randy discusses this issue in A *Time for Meaning:*

> In my experience, adolescents almost always respond to each other's writing with "It's good. I like it." Maybe, once they have internalized one or two of my values about writing, they might say something like "Add details and correct the spelling." At their stage of life, when their main job is to define themselves in relation to [their] peers, it's just too socially dangerous to say anything, even a question, that might be interpreted as criticism. I have tried to work with them on this, but to be honest, I've never been satisfied. A few other teachers tell me I'm wrong about this, but I can't lie and say I've ever seen one-on-one peer conferring among adolescents be rigorous inquiry that results in significant revision.

Randy goes on to say, however, that this does not mean peer conferring time is worthless or wasted.

> It is crucial to have cheerleaders in the lonely business of writing. Often in the writing of this book I have given drafts of chapters to friends, hoping they would just say, "It's good. I like it." Moreover, any time a student has a peer read what he has written, his sense of audience is strengthened, regardless of whether the feedback is helpful. Sometimes just a vote of confidence is all that's needed to keep a writer writing. The more rigorous collaborative inquiry into writing, I think, can occur in response groups.

Margaret Queenan, English department chair in Stamford, Connecticut, agrees with Randy. "Only when my kids and I develop very clear guidelines for peer conferring do I expect them to give each other critical feedback," she says. In Margaret's writing workshop, students may as a group list the characteristics they see and like in the short fiction they read and then use that list as a guideline for conferences. If one item on the list is "Can the reader picture the character?" students in Margaret's classroom can use such a question as a guideline for responding to one another's work. Margaret also agrees with Randy in his view that peer conferring and response groups are crucially important even when students simply act as cheerleaders for one another.

Margaret's students are in response groups that last throughout the semester, and the groups begin with exercises designed to help them develop a sense of trust. "I can't tell you what a difference it makes that my students know they'll be meeting to share their work in little supportive response groups," Margaret tells me. Her students write silently together for about half an hour. "During that time, I can actually see kids anticipating the immediate upcoming audience. I'll see a kid chuckle to himself over an image he's written, and as he does so, he'll glance around the room to find the members of his response group with eyes that seem to be saying, 'Just wait! I've got something great to show you!' "

How Might We Lure Our Students to Care About Writing?

As part of his beautiful book about what it means to live caught in a self-perpetuating cycle of despair and defeat, Mike Rose recalls his own adolescence in a Los Angeles ghetto. His words are some of the most important I've ever read.

> It is popular these days to claim you grew up on the streets. Men tell violent tales and romanticize the lessons violence brings. But, though it was occasionally violent, it wasn't the violence in South L.A. that marked me . . . what finally affected me was subtler, but more pervasive: I cannot recall a young person who was crazy in love or lost in work or one old person who was passionate about a cause or an idea. (1989, p. 17)

Rose goes on to say,

> I developed a picture of human existence that rendered it short and brutish or sad and aimless or long and quiet with rewards like afternoon naps, the evening newspaper, walks around the block, occasional letters

> from children in other states. When, years later, I was introduced to humanistic psychologists . . . with their visions of self-actualization . . . it all sounded like a glorious fairy tale, . . . full of hope and empowerment. Sinbad and Cinderella couldn't have been more fanciful. (p. 18)

Some of the young people in my town have bumper stickers that say, "Give up. It hurts less." When I think of those bumper stickers, when I think of Mike Rose saying that as an adolescent he didn't know a single person who was "crazy in love or lost in work or . . . passionate about a cause or an idea," I begin to believe that my goal in life isn't to lure young people to care about writing; it's to lure them to care about something. It is during adolescence that children, so full of passion and promise, become either disillusioned and bitter or productive and committed. When we help our students find and pursue their own projects and goals, we make it more likely that they will turn toward becoming productive and committed rather than disillusioned and bitter.

Mike Rose was able to escape the lethargy he saw around him when he was given a small chemistry set for Christmas: "The set came equipped with chemicals, minerals, and various treated paper—all in little square bottles. You could send away to someplace in Maryland for more, and I did, saving pennies and nickels to get the substances" (p. 19). Later, in the public library, Rose discovered star maps, maps of lunar seas, charts upon charts of the solar system. "My rhapsodic and prescientific astronomy carried me into my teens, consumed me right up 'til high school, losing out finally and only to the siren call of pubescence."

Many of our students have interests, and circles of friends who share those interests, but often they believe all of this must be kept on hold until the school day ends, the bell rings, and *their* time begins. Yet our students will not learn to write unless they are involved in our class. Our writing workshop will not feel alive and significant if our students sit through it bored and uninvolved, waiting for the bell to ring and life to begin. Adolescents can be energetic, enthusiastic, involved, imaginative young people. But too often, we see their energy only in the hall and cafeteria, before and after our classes, and especially after school, when they are out from under our control and can pursue their own projects. Too often in our classrooms they sit glassy-eyed, waiting for the bell to ring.

When Czikszentmihalyi and Larson (1984) studied adolescents by beeping them at various random times in a day and asking them to fill out a self-report at each beep, one of the questions they asked was "Do you wish you had been doing something else?" The adolescents reported that they liked what they were doing only 25 percent of the time. The adults who were studied, most of whom held blue-collar or secretarial jobs, reported liking what they were doing 40 percent of the time. Czikszentmihalyi and Larson summarized their findings by saying, "Day in and day out, teenagers appear to be more alienated from what they are doing [than blue-collar workers]; their personal goals are not in harmony with their actual behavior. . . . They appear less willing and able to mobilize their psychic energy. . . . They do not use their mental capacities to the fullest because they are less involved in what they are doing" (pp. 88–89). These researchers went on to find that the most intrinsically rewarding activities for adolescents were not the leisure activities one might expect (television, hanging around with friends) but were instead the structured activities, like sports, art, music, and hobbies, in which they used their skills to pursue definite goals.

What can we, as teachers, do with this information? I think that first, we need to recognize that despite the apathy we sometimes see in our classrooms, our students often do have hobbies and interests. In our classrooms, circles of friends have often formed around sports, music, parties, mathematics, cars, hunting and camping, horses, comics, and baseball cards, and if we're going to lure adolescents to care about writing, one way to do this is to encourage them to write about these projects, intentions, and purposes. If our students care about the environment, we need to encourage them to voice their concerns through petitions and speeches and letters to the editor. If they are angry about unfair policies at school, we need to help them see that writing can give them a voice to protest against authority. If they want more spending money, they can write for the reward in a writing contest. If they belong to an after-school band, they can compose their own songs. If they are worried about getting into the right colleges, they can write college entrance essays. If they love mopeds or the Rolling Stones or their church youth group . . . they can write *about* or *for* these things.

We will tap into an enormous energy source when we bring students' interests into the classroom. Part of this effort means encouraging students to write about their interests, but it is equally important that we simply find ways to bring their passions into the classroom. In one of Lucretia Pannozzo's classes last year, several of her boys, who'd formed themselves into an after-school band, brought their guitars to class, which was the last period of the day. When Lucretia arrived in her classroom, she'd often find one of the boys strumming his guitar in the corner. "You learn to use this sort of thing," Lucretia says. When her interdisciplinary team had a team party, Lucretia asked the boys if their band might provide the music. "I think they had a repertoire of only three songs, which they played over and over all afternoon," Lucretia said, "but it was worth whatever headaches we got. That party made those kids famous; it gave them an identity."

How Do We Maintain Our Students' Energy for Writing?

Although I've touched on the importance of inviting our students to write about their issues and interests, I do not mean that adolescents write about their "hobbies" instead of writing about their personal lives. Earlier I said that I believe too strongly in the importance of collaboration and conversation ever to give up on the goal of having students work in small groups or pairs. I also believe too much in the value of turning our life experiences into art and imbuing them with meaning to give up on the idea of having adolescent students writing about the stuff of their lives.

In a secondary-school writing workshop, I expect that many students will be writing about topics such as wanting a parent's approval, wishing for bigger muscles, feeling isolated, being afraid of next year, valuing the teamwork in their after-school basketball games, feeling pressured to get good grades, hating their haircut, being afraid to cry in front of a friend, feeling jealous toward an older sibling, worrying about a sick grandparent. Some of my colleagues argue with me: "They don't want to write about their love lives, their fears, their personal experiences." But I believe that adolescents very much need to write about the poignant, turbulent events of their lives.

When our students do write about these events, we need to take their lives seriously. Sometimes, when an adolescent writes as if her life is ending because so-and-so didn't phone last night, we adults find ourselves feeling impatient over how young people overdramatize their little ups and downs. "Their lives are soap operas," we think. Sometimes, from our adult perspective, we shrug at their adolescent anguish knowing "this, too, shall pass." We want to tell them, "Come on, come on, life will go on. You'll forget all this in a few days." But we should not do this. We need to remember that emotionally, we and our students are not all that different. The tragedies of their lives are as real as those in our lives. Their heartaches are every bit as deep and serious and real as are the heartaches we experience.

Earlier I raised the question, "How do we, as teachers, connect with our students?" and my answer was "one by one." As I write this chapter, I see that, in a sense, I've raised a second question: "How do we help our students to connect with writing?" and my answer has again been "one by one." As we find out what matters to each particular student, we can help that student bring the concerns of his or her life to the page.

I've argued that we build relationships between adolescents and ourselves, between adolescents and the page, on a one-to-one basis. Yet, ironically, adolescence is the stage of life in which peer interaction matters more than anything. And I think that when the writing workshop really works in a secondary-school classroom, the energy and life force for the workshop is rooted in the sense of we-ness, of community I described in Chapter 9.

When I asked secondary-school teachers to tell me about how they developed a community spirit within their classrooms, Randy Bomer said that every year, he begins his writing workshop with improvisational drama and trust games, which signify in a dramatic way that "this year is going to be different." I'm not sure I'd have the confidence or the aplomb to pull this off (Randy can start the year this way because he was once a professional actor), but I think he is wise to put community-building up front on his agenda as a teacher. In addition to the trust games and improvisational drama, Randy builds a community in the classroom by reading aloud the most intense and powerful literature he can find. "The content of the books," he says, "has to be *so compelling* that we end up feeling something together, living through something together."

In *A Time for Meaning* Randy writes:

> I choose stories, poems, memoirs, and picture books that I hope (though you never know for sure) will make us cry (or almost), laugh, or lift us with inspiration. I've chosen stories like Robert Cormier's "Guess What: I Almost Kissed My Father Goodnight," Ouida Sebestyen's "Welcome," poems like Edward Hirsch's "A Photograph Ripped in Half" and Daniel Mark Epstein's "Miami," memoirs such as sections of Maya Angelou's *I Know Why the Caged Bird Sings* and Donald Murray's "I Still Wait for the Sheets to Move." Some of the most effective pieces I have ever used early on in the year have been those written by students, either my own in previous years, or students from friends' classrooms, or sometimes the more powerful examples from professional literature.

Margaret Queenan tells me, "What I've learned is that if I'm going to pull a class together into a communitiy, I do this by letting something grow out of the energy that is in that class. For months I tried to keep my third-period ninth graders from writing television-style adventure stories. But finally, I realized that was where their energy was, and I had to go with their energy. And once I said yes, we'll go with *your* energy, their willingness to work and their cohesiveness as a group was amazing. There was no stopping them."

In *Seeking Diversity* Linda Rief tells about one year in which she and the art teacher worked together with their students on the Holocaust, writing and making amazing murals. One of my colleagues, Perdita Finn, found that it was the challenge to write picture books that pulled her class together as a team and captured her students' imagination. In each instance, these teachers followed the energy they sensed in their classrooms.

Time after time, when I speak with secondary-school teachers about how they create a sense of we-ness in their classrooms, they stress the importance of following and building upon the energy in the classroom, and of working together on a project that becomes bigger than anyone dreamed it would be. "My kids last year had been in successful writing workshops for years and years," Lucretia told me, "but they seemed reluctant now to write about their lives. We needed something new that would capture their imaginations, so I decided to work with a colleague to create a unit on writing historical fiction. I didn't know that historical fiction would catch on, but it did, and the energy was incredible." When Lucretia saw that her students cared about their historical fiction, she knew she needed to stay with their energy in the same way that when she finds a student who loves Stephen King's books she stays with that passion. "We decided to turn our work into a museum," she said, "so we learned about the roles people hold in museums, and we became curators, archivists, docents, conservators of collections. . . . The kids worked in groups to make huge three-dimensional exhibits. The students who'd written historical fiction about Ellis Island made an exhibit in which two people, each made with a balloon as a head and clothes draped on a chair for the body, were having a conversation."

Lucretia continued talking in great detail about each of the booths—about how students had used a pulley to make a model of the *Titanic* sink, and created a fake fire to depict the famous fire in a shirtwaist factory. It was clear, listening to her, that she and the class had become one big community as they invented this project together. It wasn't the project itself that had captured their imagination—there is nothing magical about turning one's writing into a museum—but there is something magical, indeed, about saying, "This is good work we're doing. How can we build on it? How can we take it even further?"

This may be the most important thing that can be said about teaching in secondary-level classrooms: We need to seize the moment. We need to see where the energy in our classrooms is and go with it.

Literature That Helps Us Teach at the Secondary-School Level

Avi. *Nothing but the truth: A documentary novel.* New York: Orchard Books, 1991.

————. *The true confessions of Charlotte Doyle.* New York: Orchard Books, 1987.

Barron, T. A. *Heartlight.* New York: Philomel Books, 1990.

Berry, James. *Ajeemah and his son.* New York: HarperCollins, 1992.

Bridgers, Sue Ellen. *Permanent connections.* New York: Harper & Row, 1987.

Brooks, Bruce. *The moves make the man.* New York: Harper & Row, 1984.

————. *What hearts?* New York: HarperCollins, 1992.

Cole, Brock. *The goats.* New York: Farrar, Straus & Giroux, 1990.

Cooper, Susan. *The dark is rising.* New York: Atheneum, 1973.

Cormier, Robert. *The chocolate war.* New York: Dell Publishing Co., 1986.

Doherty, Berlie. *Granny was a buffer girl.* New York: Orchard Books, 1988.

————. *White peak farm.* New York: Orchard Books, 1990.

Frank, Anne. *The diary of a young girl.* New York: Pocket Books, 1972.

Hesse, Karen. *Letters from Rifka.* New York: Henry Holt & Co., 1992.

Hinton, S. E. *The outsiders.* New York: Dell Publishing Co., 1968.

Knowles, John. *A separate peace.* New York: Macmillan Children's Book Group, 1987.

Lasky, Kathryn. *The bone wars.* New York: Morrow, 1988.

Lee, Marie. *Finding my voice.* New York: Houghton Mifflin Company, 1992.

Le Guin, Ursula K. *Wizard of Earthsea.* New York: Macmillan, 1991.

Levitin, Sonia. *The return.* New York: Atheneum, 1987.

Lipsyte, Robert. *The contender.* New York: Harper & Row, 1967.

Lowry, Lois. *Autumn Street.* New York: Dell Publishing Co., 1980.

Lyons, Mary E. *Letters from a slave girl.* New York: Charles Scribner's Sons, 1992.

Myers, Walter Dean. *Fallen angels.* New York: Scholastic, 1988.

————. *Hoops.* New York: Dell Publishing Co., 1983.

————. *Scorpions.* New York: Harper & Row, 1988.

Naidoo, Beverly. *Chain of fire.* New York: Lippincott, 1990.

Paterson, Katherine. *Jacob have I loved.* New York: HarperCollins Children's Books, 1990.

————. *Lyddie.* New York: Dutton Children's Books, 1991.

Paulsen, Gary. *Dogsong.* New York: Bradbury Press, 1985.

Price, Susan. *Ghost drum.* New York: Farrar, Straus & Giroux, 1992.

Salinger, J. D. *The catcher in the rye.* New York: Buccaneer Books, 1991.

Shakespeare, William. *Romeo and Juliet.* New York: Bantam Classics, 1988.

Soto, Gary. *Baseball in April and other stories.* San Diego: Harcourt Brace Jovanovich, 1990.

Spinelli, Jerry. *Maniac Magee: A novel.* Boston: Little, Brown, 1990.

Taylor, Mildred D. *The road to Memphis.* New York: Dial Books, 1990.

Temple, Francis. *A taste of salt.* New York: Orchard Books, 1992.

Tolkien, J. R. R. *The hobbit.* New York: Ballantine Books, 1988.

————. *Lord of the rings.* Boston: Houghton Mifflin, 1988.

Twain, Mark. *The adventures of Huckleberry Finn.* New York: Viking Children's Books, 1986.

————. *The adventures of Tom Sawyer.* New York: Viking Penguin, 1986.

Voigt, Cynthia. *Dicey's song.* New York: Ballantine Books, 1982.

Wilson, Budge. *The leaving.* New York: Philomel Books, 1992.

Yolen, Jane. *The devil's arithmetic.* New York: Puffin Books, 1988.

Zindel, Paul. *The pigman: A novel.* New York: Harper & Row, 1968.

Professional Literature

Atwell, Nancie. *In the middle: Writing, reading, and learning with adolescents.* Portsmouth, NH: Boynton/Cook–Heinemann, 1987.

Bartholomae, David, and Anthony Petrosky, eds. *Facts, artifacts, and counterfacts: Theory and method for a reading and writing course.* Portsmouth, NH: Boynton/Cook–Heinemann, 1986.

Bomer, Randy. *A time for meaning: Learning literacy with people aged 10–20.* Portsmouth, NH: Heinemann, in press.

Elbow, Peter. *What is English?* New York: Modern Language Association, 1990.

Kutz, Eleanor, and Hephzibah Roskelly. *An unquiet pedagogy: Transforming practice in the English classroom.* Portsmouth, NH: Boynton/Cook–Heinemann, 1991.

Mayher, John. *Uncommon sense: Theoretical practice in language education.* Portsmouth, NH: Boynton/Cook–Heinemann, 1990.

Rief, Linda. *Seeking diversity: Language arts with adolescents.* Portsmouth, NH: Heinemann, 1991.

Romano, Tom. *Clearing the way: Working with teenage writers.* Portsmouth, NH: Heinemann, 1987.

Zemelman, Steven, and Harvey Daniels. *A community of writers: Teaching writing in the junior and senior high school.* Portsmouth, NH: Heinemann, 1988.

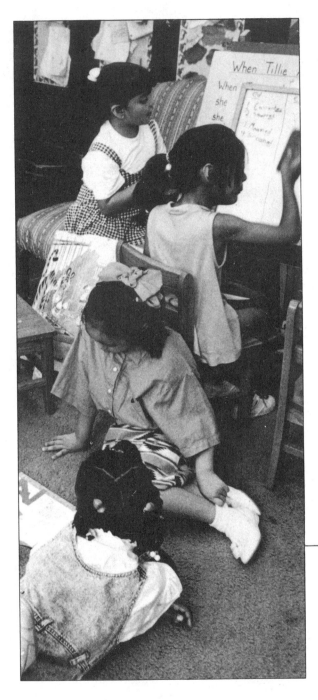

III

Ongoing Structures in the Writing Workshop

11
Establish a Predictable Workshop Environment

I used to think that in order to teach creative writing I needed to have a creative lesson plan. I thought creative environments, by definition, were ever-changing, complex, and stimulating. Every day my classroom was different: one day we wrote for ten minutes, another day, not at all; sometimes youngsters published their writing, sometimes they didn't. The classroom was a whirlwind, a kaleidoscope, and I felt very creative. Rightly so. My days were full of planning, scheming, experimenting, replanning. Meanwhile, my children waited on my changing agendas. They could not develop their own rhythms and strategies because they were controlled by mine. They could not plan because they never knew what tomorrow would hold. They could only wait.

I have finally realized that the most creative environments in our society are not the kaleidoscopic environments in which everything is always changing and complex. They are, instead, the predictable and consistent ones—the scholar's library, the researcher's laboratory, the artist's studio. Each of these environments is deliberately kept *predictable* and *simple* because the work at hand and the changing interactions around that work are so unpredictable and complex (Calkins 1983, p. 32).

Our teaching changes when we turn our classrooms into writing workshops. Instead of planning each day's new activities and assignments, we need to anticipate how we will initiate, scaffold, and guide the classroom community toward an ever-deepening involvement, and we need to select rituals, arrangements, and classroom structures. This is no small challenge.

Janet Emig, a researcher in the field of writing, tells the story of an elementary school principal who went into a writing workshop to observe the teacher. For a moment, he stood in the doorway, glancing around the room. There was no sign of the teacher. Two youngsters worked at the chalkboard, one of them drawing a crude diagram depicting the sections of his volcano report. Nearby, three children clustered closely together on the floor listening to Act 2 of Jorge's play, "The Missing Egyptian Pearl." Other children worked at their desks, some scrawling furiously—or doodling idly—in their writers' notebooks. Some carefully copied rough drafts of their work onto white paper. Occasionally a child would turn around in his or her chair to read a line or discuss a point with a classmate. On the edges of the classroom, children listen in twos to each other's pieces. In the far corner, three or four children worked at a table full of dictionaries and editing checklists. The principal finally spotted the teacher, who was sitting alongside one student in the midst of the workshop. Making his way across the room to where the teacher sat, the principal leaned down and said in a stage whisper, "I'll come back when you are teaching."

How little he knows! How little he knows about the amount of forethought, wisdom, and skill that goes into establishing a workshop in which youngsters can "carry on." How little he knows about the challenge of teaching writing well. Instead of asking, "What should I say and do tomorrow?" the teacher of writing must ask, "How will we organize time and materials?" "What will be the rhythms of talk and silence?" "How can I establish a classroom environment that supports growth in writing?"

The environment for writing is created with a library corner, with clusters of desks or tables, with a carpet on which the class gathers together. The environment for writing is created with areas for displaying children's collections, with poems that hang alongside the aquarium, math manipulatives, and the science table, with magnifying lenses and cameras. But mostly, the classroom environment is created with relationships and the structures that support them.

One of my favorite anecdotes about teaching writing is the story Nancie Atwell tells at the start of her book *In the Middle* (1987). She describes the hubbub of excitement in her school on the day researchers Don Graves and Mary Ellen Giacobbe came to visit. Bert, who happened to be passing through the front lobby when they arrived, took the stairs to the junior high wing three at a time, Atwell says, "and then whipped down our corridor like some eighth-grade Paul Revere, shouting as he passed each room, 'The world's most famous writing teachers are here! The world's most famous writing teachers are here!' "

Nancie learned an important lesson that day. She writes:

> At the end of the day, Don came and stood in my doorway with his coat on, smiling. "What are you smiling about?" I asked.
>
> "I'm smiling at you," he said. "You know what makes you such a good writing teacher?"
>
> Oh God, I thought. Here it comes: validation, from one of the world's greatest writing teachers. In a split second, I flipped through the best possibilities. Was he going to remark on my intelligence? My commitment? My sensitivity?
>
> "What?" I asked.
>
> And he answered, "You're so damned organized." (pp. 53–54)

Nancie goes on to say that her face crumpled, and so Don explained. "Look," he said. "You can't teach writing this way if you're not organized. This isn't an open classroom approach, and you know it."

Don Graves was right. The best workshop teachers value structure and organization.

Time for Writing

Setting aside *predictable* time for writing is important. If children know that every morning will begin with an hour for writing, or that Tuesday, Wednesday, and Friday afternoons will be for writing, then they can anticipate and plan for their own writing. They can use time away from the desk to gain distance on a draft, to reconsider their choices, to mull over their possibilities. "Last night in bed, I thought of a better lead to my story," they tell us. "When I was at the movies, I figured out how to end my book," they say. Then, too, when children know the parameters within which they are working, they can be more strategic, deliberate writers. If they know they'll be writing tomorrow, they are more apt to say, "I'll just write a sketchy draft for now, and tomorrow I'll redo the sections that are weak." They can make plans to confer with a friend or to put aside a piece of writing. But if the writing workshop is always changing, always haphazard, children remain pawns, waiting for their teacher's agenda.

In each of the examples above, teachers not only structured in *predictable* time for writing, they also gave a *lot* of time to writing. This is essential. The writing process requires a radically different pace than we are used to in schools and in society.

If students are going to become deeply invested in their writing, and if they are going to live toward a piece of writing and let their ideas grow and gather momentum, if they are going to draft and revise, sharing their texts with one another as they write, they need the luxury of time. If our students are going to have the chance to do their best and then to make their best better, they need long blocks of time. Sustained effort and craftsmanship are essential in writing well, yet they run contrary to the modern American way. We live in a one-draft-only society, a land of disposable cameras, flashlights, and razors, a land of instant diets and frozen waffles. Our society allows little time for sustained effort, for knowing what it is to do one's best and then make one's best better. When my stepdaughter was a teenager, she and her friends vacuumed by standing in the middle of the room and pushing the vacuum as they turned around in a circle. They scrubbed the bathtub by turning on the shower. Sometimes it seemed that the only area in which they really knew the meaning of craftsmanship and revision was their hairstyles.

Like our society, our schools have adopted a one-draft-only mentality. Their motto seems to be "get it done" and "move along." It is a sign of the times that "silent, sustained reading" often lasts for only twelve minutes. The entire school day is fragmented: ten minutes on spelling, six minutes on a ditto, fifteen minutes for a class discussion, three minutes to copy off the board. Don Graves calls this the "cha-cha-cha" curriculum. Many researchers emphasize that because the school day is so segmented, teachers spend an average of forty percent of their time on choreography. We move the class from one thing to another: "sit there," "come here," "open this book," "close that one," "get such and such out," "put it away," "line up," "sit down," "do this," "do that. . . ."

Interruptions shatter the school day, making absorption in one's work almost impossible. Children are shuttled in and out of classrooms for music instruction, remedial reading, testing, and computer classes. Then, too, there is the PA system: "Mrs. Jones, you have a package in the office. It's nothing important." "Buses 16 and 9 will be late." "The game at Frontier has been canceled." Added to this, there is the problem of "specials." I am not against police officers, grandparents, trees, or international relations, but "specials" such as "Love Your Grandparents" days, "Honor the Police" ceremonies, and "Draw a Tree" contests are keeping young people from knowing what it is to work in a sustained way on projects of great importance.

In addition, the myth of "coverage" also contributes to the frenzied pace of the school day. "Have I *covered* the sixteen causes of the Civil War?"

"Have I *covered* the thirteen uses of the comma?" We don't stop to realize that we are rushing to "cover" the thirteen uses of commas in third grade, and again in fourth, fifth, sixth, seventh, eighth, ninth . . . and still students don't use commas correctly.

Eve Merriam has a poem that describes the pace of our lives:

A LAZY THOUGHT

There go the grownups
To the office,
To the store.
Subway rush,
Traffic crush;
Hurry, scurry,
Worry, flurry.

No wonder
Grown ups
Don't grow up
Any more.
It takes a lot
Of slow
To grow.

Where in the helter-skelter pace of the school day is there time for the probing, experimentation, dialogue, and reflection that contribute to genuine learning? We now have courses in philosophy, critical thinking, health, housing, decision-making, career education, and law. We have layers and layers of pullout programs. When is someone going to be an activist and speak out against what Don Graves calls the rampant inflation of curriculum?

The writing process approach requires a radically different pace than we are used to in our schools. But time is our scarcest resource. Teachers often ask me, "How do I squeeze writing in on top of everything else?" My suggestion is simple: Don't. Instead of shoehorning one more thing into the crowded curriculum, I suggest that we each take a good, hard look at our school day to determine what is no longer needed there. My husband and I recently moved from one Connecticut town to another, and the thing that surprised me most about the move was the amount of junk we had accumulated. We took fifteen *carloads* of trash to the dump. Sometimes I think that if we, as teachers, want to move on, we need to take carloads of curricula to the dump. It is only by cleaning out some old things that we can give time and space to new ones.

I urge teachers to begin by <u>setting aside an hour a day, every day, for the writing workshop.</u> Once the year is under way, there may be a month or two when this workshop time is used for theme studies. Some of the writing workshop may be spent reviewing short or familiar pieces of literature with a writer's eye. Still, the place to begin is probably with a clearly defined, self-standing workshop each day.

Sometimes this isn't possible. Kindergarten teachers may have their children for only a half-day. Secondary-school English often lasts for only forty minutes a day, and this time must be divided among literature, writing, and language. (In Chapter 10, I suggest some ways of working within these unfortunate constraints.) My suggestion in situations such as these is that we take whatever time there is and clump it together. Instead of writing one day a week for a year, I'd advise writing three days a week for half a year or five days a week for several months.

It is almost impossible to create an effective writing workshop if students write only once or twice a week. If Emmanuel begins a piece on Monday and he doesn't see that piece again until Friday, he will find it hard to sustain an interest in it, and harder still to remember the questions his friends asked during a conference. It is like any sport. If we jog once a week, it is hard to break the inertia brought on by six days of not jogging. But if we jog every day, it becomes easier and easier; we get into a rhythm, we find our stride. The same is true of writing.

Components of the Writing Workshop

Not only is it important that writing have a predictable place in the schedule so that children can anticipate and plan for it, it is also important that the writing workshop itself have a simple structure. Children should know what to expect. This allows them to carry on; it frees us as teachers from choreographing activities and allows us to listen and respond to individual students.

How we structure the workshop is less important than *that* we structure it. My friend Pat Wilk suggests that one way to think about the process of designing a writing workshop is to imagine that you have some modular furniture—some components of the writing workshop—that can be arranged in a variety of different ways. (These will be described briefly in this chapter and in more detail in the chapters that follow.)

Mini-Lessons

Some teachers begin (or end) every workshop with the ritual of a mini-lesson. Students usually gather in a close circle, often sitting on a carpet. The teacher (or eventually, a student) offers something to the group that is meant to inspire and instruct. The teacher may begin by saying, "I want to read something I found that is lovely. In the silence after I read, let's all go back to our desks—absolutely quietly—and begin to write." Or the teacher may begin, "Last night, I was looking through your writing and realized that many of you are struggling with something that is difficult for me as well. . . ." When the mini-lesson is about something every writer needs to do often, such as rereading one's work or keeping an image of one's topic in mind, the mini-lesson may end with the teacher suggesting that each writer spend some time that day (or even right then and there) doing a particular thing. Often, the teacher introduces a strategy that may go onto a class chart or into student notebooks for future reference, but that is only timely for a handful of students. Those writers may work together after the mini-lesson while the rest of the class disperses.

Work Time (Writing and Conferring)

Work time is the only indispensable part of the writing workshop. During work time, students go to their desks, tables, or patches of floor space as artists in a studio go to their stations, and they work on their ongoing projects. Unless the class is doing a genre study (such as reading and writing poetry), students will probably be writing very different things, with one student writing an essay, another, a poem. At the beginning of the year, students may move along somewhat in unison, while teachers suggest that everyone might try this strategy or that one. Later in the year, it's much more likely that a handful of students will be gathering entries toward finding a topic, while others are editing finished work. Once the year is under way, students tend to take different lengths of time on their pieces, with one spending a week on a piece, another, two weeks. Generally, the rule is that during the writing workshop, everyone writes. When you finish one piece, you move on to another. Some teachers write alongside students for a few minutes of silent work time, then, generally, the teacher moves among individuals, conferring with them. These conferences are at the heart of our teaching.

Peer Conferring and/or Response Groups

Response groups meet almost daily for at least twenty minutes. Frequently, the response group begins with the "status of the group" reports in which each member of the group says, in a single sentence, what he or she needs that day. Out of these summaries and requests, the child who is acting as the facilitator of the response group sets up an agenda. "We'll help Ben with his ending and then help Jerome with getting an idea and then help Sarah with her 'Is it done?' question," the facilitator may say. When it is a student's turn for help, he or she talks about the writing, reads relevant sections aloud, answers the group's questions, and thinks aloud about the writing. Most of the talk about a piece is done by the writer. The group acts mostly as a sounding board. Often response groups end with each member saying in one sentence what he or she will do before the group meets again. As writers, we need to be able to see what is almost there in a draft; we need to be able to see possibilities. We need to be able to imagine a draft written differently. People learn this special kind of reading by reading work in progress and talking about it. Peer conferences and response groups provide a forum for this. Peer conferences are usually student-initiated, five-minute-long talks about works in progress. Response groups are usually formed by students at the teacher's suggestion, and there are usually four or five members in a response group.

Share Sessions

Share sessions generally begin after the entire class has gathered on a corner carpet or in a circle of chairs. The overt purpose of these sessions is to share and support work in progress, but there is also another purpose. Share sessions function as public, teacher-supported conferences. By participating in them, students learn how to confer with each other in one-to-one peer conferences. One format for a share session is that each of three or four children take a turn sitting in the author's chair at the front of the circle reading notebook entries or a draft aloud and soliciting responses from listeners. Another format is that the group shares their *process* of writing, perhaps talking about how they feel about silent writing time or about an upcoming deadline, or brainstorming together on what individual writers can do when they are stuck. These formats provide models for what students can do in their response groups and peer conferences.

Publication Celebrations

At regular intervals throughout the year writers come together to publish and celebrate their finished work. Some teachers set up a schedule so that four students publish every Friday, and before their day these students work on final revisions and hold editing conferences. Other teachers use celebrations as a way to punctuate the year for the entire class. These teachers may think of the year as divided into six- or eight-week units, with a celebration climaxing each unit. For example, a class of sixth graders may publish writing in a genre of their choice in mid-October. They may then all work on a poetry course of study, which ends with a second celebration, this one focused on poetry. Most teachers do different things in different celebrations. They may invite parents and grandparents into the classroom for one celebration, another time help each writer make an audiotape of his or her best work, and another time publish and toast a literary anthology.

12

Don't Be Afraid to Teach
Tools to Help Us Create Mini-Lessons

Just as the art instructor sometimes pulls students who are working at their separate places in the studio together in order to demonstrate a new technique, so too, writing teachers often gather their students for brief whole-class meetings. I call these gatherings *mini-lessons*. The mini-lesson can serve as a forum for planning the day's work, as a time to call writers together (like the huddle at the start of a football game), or as a time for demonstrating a new method. In many classrooms, the mini-lesson occurs during the first five minutes of the writing workshop. Sometimes, however, it is more helpful to schedule a mini-lesson in the midst of the workshop. Children in one classroom, for example, may know that at approximately ten o'clock they should shift from independent reading to working on their own writing. The teacher in this classroom may begin each workshop by moving among his students for a while as they work on their various writing projects, noticing the range of problems and possibilities in the room. Then, at some point, he will probably ask writers to gather for a few minutes. In other classrooms, each day's workshop begins with peer conferring or response groups and ends with a mini-lesson.

The Purposes of Mini-Lessons

The mini-lesson is our forum for making a suggestion to the whole class—raising a concern, exploring an issue, modeling a technique, reinforcing a strategy. Although mini-lessons may often look like miniature speeches, like brief lectures, they are entirely different from the lectures that were such a part of my own schooling. The difference can be summed up in a single word: *context*. In mini-lessons, we teach *into* our students' intentions. Our students are first deeply engaged in their self-sponsored work, and then we bring them together to learn what they need to know in order to do that work. This way, they stand a chance of being active meaning-makers, even during this bit of formal instruction. First our students are engaged in their own important work. Then we ask ourselves, "What is the one thing I can suggest or demonstrate that might help the most?"

Sometimes the mini-lesson will be designed to create a warm glow around the workshop. The easiest way to do this is to read aloud from wonderful literature—a story, a poem—and to do so *without* turning the reading into a lesson. If we are reading a work of literature aloud in order to cast a spell on the writing workshop, I think it is crucial that we avoid previewing vocabulary words, asking "What will happen next?" or giving admonitions such as "Listen to the adjectives." Instead, we simply read aloud . . . and then immediately, and with no discussion, we write and write and write.

Mini-lessons can also be designed to provide occasions for writerly conversations. These discussions can focus on such things as

- Where do you write? When? How is your home-writing different from your school-writing?
- Have you ever found when you were writing that you were being influenced by another author? How? If we want to make it more likely that authors will affect us, what might we do?
- What do you do when you're stuck? What do you think other writers do? What do you find helpful/not helpful?
- Have you ever found yourself writing about one idea and then in the middle of writing getting another idea?

Mini-lessons can also be a time for talking about procedural issues in the writing workshop. In mini-lessons, we may address such issues as

- How can we devise a system for gathering into a meeting area without pushing and arguing and feeling perturbed with each other?
- If some of us are conferring while others write, how can we keep from disturbing one another?
- How can we plan for a wonderful author's celebration?
- Where can we keep our tools—our stapler and staple remover, white-out, date stamp, paper clips, envelopes, and stationery—so that we always know where they are?

Mini-lessons can also be a forum for demonstrating writing strategies. Using an overhead projector, we can display our own pages and show our students how we reread an entry, starring and circling special parts. Using a blank transparency and a marker pen, we can show students how we copy a favorite part of the entry to use as starter dough for the first draft of a poem or a letter. Alternatively, we may read the entry aloud to see if we find a line or a word that feels saturated with meaning. On the chalkboard, we write that line or word and then begin to open it up by writing a whole lot more about it. "Maybe I'll first try to picture it," we say . . . and we're off.

Mini-lessons will not always consist of a talk or a demonstration. They can also become a time for *very brief* experimentation. Sometimes the best way to introduce a strategy to a writer is to ask everyone to try it for a moment. For example, we may suggest that students write in the white space between two entries, exploring ways in which these separate entries may in fact speak to each other. Or we may suggest that writers take one sentence of their draft, put it at the top of a clean piece of paper, and write and write about that one sentence.

In the instances above, students are asked to take a moment or two during the mini-lesson to try out a strategy. This does *not* mean they are necessarily expected to use that strategy later that day when they resume their writing. If students had to jump through our hoops every day, they couldn't follow where their work led them. On the other hand, if we never nudge students to experiment, they will probably never know the power these strategies can have.

The Format of Mini-Lessons

Although the purpose of our mini-lessons will vary, the procedures will probably be quite consistent. Each of us, working with our students, will develop our own routines. Whatever ones we choose, we'll probably stay with them, at least for a time. If the routines of our mini-lessons are different every day, our focus, and our students' focus, will tend to be on the changing *frame* of mini-lessons, rather than on their actual content.

In an effort to reduce the amount of time we spend choreographing our students' movements many of us will develop consistent procedures for gathering students together. First-grade teacher Bobbi Fisher gathers her students together by sitting on the meeting-area carpet and beginning to sing a song. The children who are near enter in and this signals to the others, "Finish up what you are doing and join us." Soon the entire class is singing together. Under Bobbi's direction, the song becomes quieter and quieter . . . then, in the silence, she speaks to her children as authors. Other teachers take a seat in the author's chair at the front of the meeting area as a way of signaling "Let's gather." In Holly Zuber's fifth-grade classroom in the Bronx, Holly quietly asks one child, "Will you ask people to gather?" and then that child moves among the other children. Soon Holly's thirty-eight youngsters have taken their seats, some on the floor, others on nearby chairs and desktops. In Brenda Story's classroom, each child is assigned a place on the rug, and the whole class practices coming to—and going from—the meeting area even before the first meeting is held. Each of these transitions happened smoothly because the classroom teacher paid attention to it. Among writers there is a saying, "Our greatest challenge is getting a character from here to there." Isn't this also true for teaching?

Paying attention to transitions doesn't necessarily mean that we approach our teaching with predesigned procedures like the ones I've described. It is never possible to steer clear of all potential problems. Sometimes teachers decide, "I don't want to legislate comings and goings unless I must, and then *we*, as a community, can invent our own unique solutions to the problems." We *do* need to be aware, however, that getting twenty or thirty characters from here to there can be a major challenge indeed!

In the same way that we think through the logistics of gathering students together for a mini-lesson, we'll want to think about a number of other possible structures for a mini-lesson. In order to do so, it's helpful to consider some of the following questions:

- Where will we gather? Will we gather together as a group on a carpet (which is what I usually advise for elementary-school students), in a circle or hodgepodge of desktops and chairs (which only works if very little furniture is moved)? Is there a way for us to sit so that we can all see one another, as in a circle, or must we cluster like grapes? If we don't physically gather together but instead remain at our desks or tables, is there another way I can signal that this is a whole-class meeting, a huddling together, rather than an instance of traditional frontal teaching? Can *I* stand in a predictable unteacherly place, such as the center of the classroom, with desks on all sides of me?

- Will we want to bring our writer's notebooks and/or drafts, pencils, and so on to the meeting, and if so, how will they be used? Will we hope that students jot notes on the mini-lesson in their notebooks? Will there be a special section for such notes or not? Will students all bring their notebooks and drafts so that we can refer to them, or would we rather they clear their desks off in order to really listen? If we bring pens and work to the meeting area, is there a rule that can quiet the ruffling papers and tapping pens . . . a rule such as, "Put everything on the floor in front of you until you are using it"?
- Will there be specific procedures for coming to the meeting area? ("Table one can come, table two . . .") If so, will I want to be in charge, or will I want a student facilitator? Will there be specific procedures for going from the meeting area to their tables or desks? ("The authors in the back of the group can begin work. The rest of us, let's watch them as they get going," or, "As I reach your writing folder in my pile and call your name, please come and tell me in one sentence what you'll be working on, and you can get going.")
- Will we make public records of our mini-lessons? Will we regularly make charts or lists ("What to Do When I'm Stuck," "Ideas for Generating More Entries about a Single Topic," "What We Know About Memoir")? If so, will these be on chart paper? a chalkboard? Will one student enter the mini-lesson proceedings into a class log?
- Will there be any predictable rhythm to the content of our mini-lessons? If we take the writing of one cluster of students home every Monday night, will we want it to become a tradition that on Tuesday we begin, "Last night, as I read through your writing . . ."? Will we want to have one day—Fridays—be for student-led mini-lessons? A student could share a strategy that has worked, recommend a technique, describe a reading-writing connection.

When I suggest that we consider such questions, I most certainly do *not* mean that we need to answer them before the year begins. Clearly, the format and traditions of our mini-lessons will evolve. But this doesn't happen by accident; it happens because of forethought and design, because of a readiness to imagine possibilities.

Predictable Problems with Mini-Lessons

In theory, mini-lessons are wonderful. The ritual of beginning every writing workshop with a whole-group gathering can bring form and unity to the workshop, and it's wonderful, when writers are deeply absorbed in their writing, to see the effect of a few carefully chosen tips from experts. Yet in practice I have found that mini-lessons often represent the worst part of a writing workshop. When I bring visitors in to observe writing workshops, I often deliberately time our visits so we avoid the mini-lesson. I think mini-lessons become particularly problematic because they are the one part of the writing workshop that most resembles our old ways of teaching. In mini-lessons, we often slip back into an old persona, into old habits. It's an interesting challenge to ask, "How does frontal teaching change when our classrooms are structured as workshops? What are *new* ways of teaching from the front of the room?"

A colleague recently suggested that it might help to change the title "mini-lessons" to something with less traditional overtones. "As soon as we teachers hear 'mini-*lessons,*'" she explained, "we think of the rhetorical questions that elicit little bits of input from children, of a particular tone of voice." What title would be more accurate? Writing workshop huddles? I would want the new title to convey the simplicity, brevity, and directness of a good mini-lesson.

Once, after I had observed Shelley Harwayne teaching a writing workshop, I commented to her that her mini-lesson had been fabulous. Apparently this comment perplexed her because as far as she knew, she hadn't given a mini-lesson that day. At the time, Shelley said nothing to me about her confusion. At home that night she reread her notes. "What could Lucy have meant?" Then she realized that instead of what she perceived as a mini-lesson, she had begun the workshop with a quick tip. She had said to the children, "Can I ask just one thing of you before you begin your writing? When you open your folders today, and every day, would you reread what you have written? Before you add to it, have a little conference with yourself. Ask yourself how you feel about the piece, whether there are ways you could make it better." Then she said, "All right, take out your folders and, first, read them to yourselves." To my way of thinking, this was a perfect mini-lesson. Shelley had given students a strategy they could use often. She had not interrupted their ongoing commitment to writing with an elaborate assignment. Best of all, instead of a long whole-class discussion in which she'd asked leading questions and tried to elicit comments from students on rereading, she simply told them about this strategy. The mini-lesson had not become a maxi-lesson.

Our mini-lessons become maxi-lessons in part because we have been taught that there is something wrong with "lecturing" to students. We therefore turn every little speech into a fill-in-the-blank exercise by using a question-and-answer format. In one study, Hoetker (1982) found that English teachers ask questions at the average rate of one every 11.8 seconds. But mini-lessons become diffuse and clumsy when we teachers persist in the question-and-answer mode that is so pervasive in our schools. To illustrate my point, let me describe an effective mini-lesson on how to write good titles, and then show how that same lesson might have looked if it had been taught through a more traditional reliance on recitation.

In the first (and recommended) version, the teacher might say something like this:

> Last night I was thinking about the titles you are using for your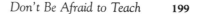
> drafts and it occurred to me that if your draft was about your dog, many of you—without thinking twice—are putting the label "My Dog" on the top of the page. You might want to stop and think about how to change that *label* into a *title* that might catch the reader's eye.
>
> To do this, it may help you to think about the titles other authors have used. Jerome is reading a book about two dogs but instead of calling it "Two Dogs," the author, Wilson Rawls, has named it *Where the Red Fern Grows*. It is a curious title, isn't it, but if you read the book you will understand why he selected it. Cynthia's book is about a journey taken by three children, but instead of being called "The Trip" it is called *The Lion, the Witch, and the Wardrobe*.
>
> When it comes time for you to work on titles, and that won't be today for most of you, you may want to go to the library and look at the titles there, or you may want to brainstorm a list of possibilities before selecting one.
>
> If there are any of us who do want to work on titles today, why don't we gather after the mini-lesson and have a think-tank on titles. The rest of you, off you go, and let's have a good day.

The same lesson taught through recitation might begin like this:

> The teacher has a book with her. She holds the cover up toward the class as she says, "Last night I was thinking about a part of your writing we haven't talked about." Pointing to the title of the book in her hand, she says, "The what, class?"

The children respond in chorus, "The name."

"Title, we call it," and the teacher writes *title* on the chalkboard. "It occurred to me that instead of giving your pieces catchy titles, you do what?"

"Hand it in," Robert guessed.

"Yes, you do hand it in and class, I am glad you're now remembering to put your pieces in the box called 'Final Editing,' but before you hand it in, what do you write? (Pause) Not titles, but labels. You are labeling your stories, telling what they are about. If your piece is about dogs, what would you probably call it, Sarah?"

Sarah has evidently not been following the discussion. She fumbles for an answer, and so the teacher calls on two more children. The second one guesses correctly, "Dogs."

Another common problem occurs when we expect that every student will use the content of a mini-lesson on the day of that mini-lesson. In some classes, on the day titles are the subject of the mini-lesson, every child is expected to list ten possible titles for his or her piece. Although there are certainly many occasions when it makes sense to ask every child to do something—as when we suggest that every child take a moment to reread his or her draft—often, a mini-lesson will only pertain to what several children are doing that day. We need to think of mini-lessons, then, as ways of adding information to the class pot. If five children use an idea when it is presented and others merely jot it in a list of possible strategies at the back of their writer's notebook, that idea is nevertheless in the room. When those five children share their work, the idea will be recirculated. Meanwhile, other children have tucked the idea into the back of their minds, and they may draw upon it when they need it.

But all of this avoids the basic question, What does one teach in a mini-lesson? Clearly, this is one that all of us as teachers will need to answer for ourselves. Perhaps, however, if I describe an array of mini-lessons, it will be easier for readers to invent your own.

Mini-Lessons That Are Particularly Helpful to Young Writers

Mini-lessons can help young children understand the functions and the power of print. I sometimes gather together a class of kindergarten children and, showing them examples of environmental print, I ask them to read what the print probably says. The letters on the milk carton probably say "milk" and the letters on the can of peas probably say "peas." Usually I end the lesson by switching from reading environmental print to writing it. I ask children what word I should write on a tagboard label hanging on the door, and soon the children and I have labeled the library area, the hamster, the coat hooks, and the math manipulatives. At the end of the mini-lesson I might ask whether some children want to write more labels during the writing workshop while the others go off to their drawing and writing.

A natural follow-up for this mini-lesson might be for me to draw a picture and then, sounding out words, label different parts of the picture. Then I could encourage children to label parts of their own pictures. Alternately, if two or three children had made the breakthrough and were writing words to accompany their pictures (even if these words were written with initial consonants only), I might celebrate and share these in a mini-lesson. Still another mini-lesson might involve the children in brainstorming the sorts of writing they might do in the block area (road signs, maps, billboards, store names) or the playhouse area (phone messages, grocery lists, labels for each child's room) and so forth. Although I'd want to demonstrate a wide range of writing, the type I would model most often would be stories. Standing at the easel or chalkboard, I would begin to draw a picture. As I worked, I'd let my ideas change and develop because I'd want my students to see that drawing (like notebook writing, for older students) is a vehicle for thinking about my subject. Eventually, I'd shift from drawing to writing. Each time I did this mini-lesson I might emphasize a different point. One time I might want to demonstrate how I think of a good beginning for my story. Another time I might emphasize how I close my eyes and picture my subject in exact detail.

Although many young writers will need very little help with spelling, some will need to learn how to listen for sounds. In mini-lessons I sometimes encourage children to stretch out a word, listening slowly to the component sounds. After gathering together a group of five-year-olds, Martha Horn, who was at the time a staff member in the Writing Project, brought out a miniature chalkboard and told the class they were going to be spellers. "Does anyone have a special word we could spell together?" she asked. The children suggested *spaghetti*, *Tyrannosaurus rex*, and *hippopotamus*, and after each suggestion, the class worked together to say the word slowly. "Watch my hand and see if you can say it as slowly as my hand goes," Martha said, stretching out the word with her hand. "Stretch it like a rubber band," she urged, "and listen to the sounds." Then she asked, "What sounds do you hear?" and transcribed the children's guesses on the chalkboard. Her purpose was not to arrive at correct spellings, of course, but to model one way of spelling words. For this reason, if a child called out an incorrect letter, Martha did not correct the youngster.

If many children are uneasy about invented spelling, I sometimes begin a mini-lesson by asking children, "Who is the boss of your book? Who makes the decisions?" Once we establish that each child is the boss of his or her writing, I ask, "Who decides whether you will write with pencil or with marker?"

"We do!"

"Who decides whether you are going to write a big, big book or a very little book?"

"We do!"

After a series of such questions, I come to the crucial question: "Who decides how you will spell a word? If you come to the word *rattlesnake*, who decides how to spell it?"

"You do!" the children will often answer, which gives me the chance to tell them that no, *they* are the boss of their spelling. "Just do the best you can and don't worry. An editor can help you fix up spelling later if you want to publish your book. The main thing to remember as you write is that you are the boss of your writing." Soon many children will write whole sentences and use these sentences to tell stories, write recipes, compose poetry, and so forth. Mini-lessons can provide a forum for sharing those breakthroughs.

Ideally, mini-lessons should support the less able youngsters while also celebrating and raising the upper level of what children are doing. I particularly liked the way Shelley Harwayne did this on her third day with kindergartners at P.S. 10. Once the children had quieted down, Shelley said, "This morning I looked on my bookshelf and saw some books. I thought to myself, 'These authors are doing just the same things as the children at P.S. 10.'" Then, holding up a picturebook she said, "In Tana Hoban's book, she put a picture on each page and one word to tell about the picture." Then Shelley held up a child's writing. "Here is a piece by Sylvia and see, she too has written one word to tell about her picture. She has written 'family'" (spelled FME). In the same way, Shelley showed the class that Marigold had written like Richard Scarey, whose books have lots of labeled pictures on every page, and that Alex was writing like Dick Bruna, who'd written *The Little Bird*. Shelley said, "After Dick draws a picture, he puts down a sentence that tells what is happening in the picture. On one page, he wrote, 'A little yellow bird flies in the air looking for a place to build a nest.'" Then Shelley likened this to Alex's work, showing that he, too, had written a sentence to tell what was happening in his picture. The mini-lesson ended with Shelley congratulating the children on being authors and sending them on their way.

Recently I watched a simple lesson in a kindergarten classroom. The teacher, Carol Seltzer, told the class that she was excited by their topics. Then she simply asked youngsters to tell their classmates, in one sentence, what they were writing about. The lesson was particularly effective because each child stood to announce his or her topic. One by one, these youngsters jumped to their feet and, sticking their chests out proudly, said, "This is a make-believe story and I'm writing about how a puppy drowned," "I'm writing about when I had a bad dream and I was all alone on the ocean," "I have a three-months cat," or "I went on a house tour." Of course, children who did not have ideas for their writing got ideas from those who did, and the class as a whole enjoyed knowing what others were doing.

I have also seen effective mini-lessons in which the teacher begins by telling her children about a visit she took to another writing classroom. By showing samples of what the writers in that room were doing (notebooks, books with chapters, tiny three-inch-square books, poetry, class newspapers), the teacher encouraged her youngsters to move in new directions.

Literature can be the source of countless other mini-lessons. The teacher might bring in many different kinds of books, ranging from Kunhardt's *Pat the Bunny* to wordless books, from listing books to collections of riddles, and the teacher may use these to encourage youngsters to expand their ranges as writers. Primary-school teachers will also find that most of the mini-lessons described in the following sections can be adapted to the needs of very young children.

Mini-Lessons That Use Literature to Generate Good Writing

Often, when I help teachers launch upper-grade writing workshops, I tell them, "You will do everything just right. Then you'll move about from one student to the next, and their writing will be *all wrong*. If you're not careful, your forehead will furrow and you'll get more and more frazzled." I tell them, "Give yourself a forehead massage before you look at their writing. When kids record every boring detail about their days, practice saying, 'That's an interesting thing to do,' or 'Oh, so you recorded the exact facts of the day! Hmm . . . that's *one* thing to do.'" It doesn't help to get angry at your students or at yourself. But it *does* help to gather up your students' notebooks, to take them to a colleague, and to pore over them, asking, "What is it that my students are trying to do in these notebooks? What is their image of good writing? What can I do in my mini-lessons that might help?"

My sense is that each of us will find a handful of problems unique to our students but that we'll also find almost universal problems. And I believe that the wise use of literature in our writing workshops can help us address many of those universal problems.

If more than a few students are sitting in front of the blank page saying, "Nothing happens in my life," or "I don't have anything to write about," it sometimes helps to "prime the pumps" for writing by reading aloud books that spark shared stories. In *Aunt Flossie's Hats*, for example, Elizabeth Fitzgerald Howard tells of children rummaging through their great-great-aunt Flossie's collection of hats. Each hat leads Aunt Flossie to another memory.

> We pick out hats and try them on. Aunt Flossie says they are her memories, and each hat has its story . . .
> One Sunday afternoon, I picked out a wooly winter hat, sort of green. Maybe Aunt Flossie thought a minute. Aunt Flossie almost always thinks a minute before she starts a hat story. Then she sniffed the wooly hat. "Just a little smoky smell now," she said. . . .

Soon Aunt Flossie launched into a story about the great fire in Baltimore.

After reading *Aunt Flossie's Hats* aloud, I said to the children, "I suppose we each have things in *our* houses, in *our* families, that hold stories." I added, "I'm thinking of the dusty old animal cages my family has in our basement: a rusty bird cage from the time I wanted a baby crow, a rabbit hutch from all these litters of Dutch rabbits. . . ."

Children will have their own treasures, and in the circle of their classmates, one child after another may tell the story of a rock, old clothes, a badge, a photograph. Elizabeth Fitzgerald Howard's writing may nudge students not only to realize that their lives hold stories, but also to tell their stories well. When Howard, for example, told of a wooly winter hat, she said it was sort of green with just a little smoky smell, as if she were savoring and recalling the color and the smell of the hat. In our mini-lesson, we may remind students of this and encourage them to linger in similar ways over the particulars of their stories.

Another day, we may read Montzalee Miller's *My Grandmother's Cookie Jar*, in which a little girl sits with her grandmother eating cookies, and each cookie calls forth another memory, another family story. Margaret Reid's

The Button Box shows that buttons, like hats and cookies, can also hold stories. There are countless other books that can be used in the same way. Ruth Heller's *The Front Hall Carpet* (in which a child makes believe the blue carpet in her parents' bedroom is the sea and the checkered carpet in her bedroom is a game board) can lead to wonderful talk about the pretend play that happens around soap bubbles in the bathtub, raindrops on the window-panes, and patchwork squares in the bed quilt. The important thing is not that these specific books have particular powers but that books in general can create circles of storytelling, and that these circles will help children who continue to sit before the empty page saying, "Nothing happens in my life."

The problem with using books to prime the pump for writing is that this strategy works almost *too* well, and it's easy for our children to get into the habit of needing a daily jump-start for their entries. This becomes very problematic because in the end, all of us need to realize that life itself can jump-start writing. If our students wait for us to read aloud, they won't write often throughout every day, all their lives long. So we will want to deliberately wean students from relying on a read-aloud selection to jump-start their writing. We take small steps toward this when we encourage students to have their notebooks beside them as they read their independent books, and we do it when we read a book aloud to the whole class, and give each of our students (and ourselves) a few stick-on notes. "I know, as we listen, we're always filled with our own stories. Today (and every day after this) let's keep in mind that we may want to jot a few words onto a stick-on note just to remind us of what comes to mind. Later, we can stick the notes into our notebooks and use them as starters for new entries."

Mini-Lessons That Help Students Learn Peer Conferring

When I'm introducing peer conferring into a classroom, I'm apt to say, "There are thirty-two writing teachers in this room. Every one of you must be a writing teacher." As I suggested in Chapter 8, in order to show what this entails, I might ask the entire class to act as teachers for one child. After the youngster reads a draft out loud, I might lead the class to respond to the draft, asking questions of the writer and perhaps making tentative suggestions. If the students and I then review what we had done together, this would provide us with a list of the steps involved in peer conferences.

This mini-lesson, like most, could be repeated many times during the year. Each time, I might add a new point of emphasis. For example, children often ask trivial questions. If a writer's draft is about falling down while roller-skating, it would not be unusual for a child to respond, "What color were your roller skates?" Mini-lessons can highlight the need to ask impor- *conferencing* tant questions. I might suggest that children think of the single most important question they could ask to respond to a particular draft, and for just this one time, we might gather those questions in order to reflect on why some seem particularly effective. Or I might confer publicly with a child, asking the class to notice and record the ways I invite the child to tell me about her writing process. Later we might talk about how questions about what one has done and hopes to do—about process—can be even more helpful than questions about content. Another time, I might give each child a slip of paper. "Imagine you're sitting in the author's chair. Write down what you'd *most* want a friend to ask about," I might say.

Children not only have a hard time asking important questions, they also have difficulty following a line of questioning. It would not be unusual for a discussion to go like this:

FIRST CHILD: Where were you when you caught the fish?

WRITER: Near a lake.

SECOND CHILD: What did the bite feel like on your fishing line?

WRITER: It was a gentle pull. It surprised me because it wasn't a jerk.

THIRD CHILD: What kind of boat do you have?

In a mini-lesson, I might talk about the importance of pursuing one line of thought. "Keep the idea going," I might say, "keep it going back and forth between you and the writer just as if you were keeping a ball going over a net." To illustrate, I could take a segment of the class discussion and role-play how it could have been done differently:

FIRST CHILD: Where were you when you caught the fish?

WRITER: Near a lake.

SECOND CHILD: Can you tell us a little more about where you were, can you set the scene so we can picture it?

WRITER: Well, it was early morning, and the mist was still on this lake near my aunt's house. I had planned to fish in the brook, but it was so pretty at the lake, I just put my stuff down and sat on a soggy stump near the edge of the water.

FIRST CHILD: Do you think you should write an entry about that, because when you told me, I could feel like I was there. Then you could try adding it to the draft.

WRITER: Tell all of it? My story would get pretty long!

CLASS: So?

One word of caution: We must avoid turning conferences into recitations of preset questions. Too much attention to conferences can make children overly self-conscious. This is probably less apt to happen if we avoid laying down rules and preaching the "right way" to respond and instead use mini-lessons to create a predictable structure, to show our concern about conferences, and to gently coach children to become more responsive and more helpful listeners.

Mini-Lessons That Help Children Learn Workshop Procedures

If we are going to have the luxury of responding well to individual students, the class as a whole should be able to carry on without us. For this reason, we need a simple, clear, reasonable management system and we need to teach it to our children. Many writing workshops flounder because the workshop context requires new expectations, rules, and rituals, and teachers are too intent upon listening and responding to individuals to establish the new order.

The simplest mini-lesson on classroom management I know of involves simply reviewing the predictable structure of the writing workshop. After I have worked with children (of any age) for about a week, I sometimes say, "Writers, you may have noticed that we have been writing from ten o'clock to eleven o'clock every morning. You can count on this time. This will be our special time set aside for writing. And the writing workshop will always begin with our gathering here on the floor for a mini-lesson, as we are doing right now. During the mini-lesson, I may give you a tip about good writing or I may read some literature aloud. What we do each day will be a little different, but you can count on our meeting together. After the mini-lesson, you can count on having the chance to work on your notebooks and drafts. You can count on time to work silently and time to share your writing with one another or with me. Every day the workshop will end with our meeting again. During this meeting, several children will read their work in progress and we will talk about it as we did with Miguel and Marissa yesterday."

This mini-lesson paves the way for others. Another day we may want to focus specifically on the procedures for coming to a mini-lesson. This may entail having the children actually practice pushing in their chairs and walking quietly to the meeting area. We may suggest that they bring their writer's notebooks with them, putting these on the floor in front of them. This may sound very mundane, but an extraordinary amount of classroom time is wasted on transitions. If children know when and how to come to the meeting area, it will save time and spare everyone irritation.

Children also need to learn that they must return the stapler to the writing area and put caps on marker pens. They need to know that once they complete their final drafts, they must staple all the rough drafts together in order and file them in their cumulative folders. All of these expectations can be subjects for mini-lessons.

Mini-Lessons That Help Students Learn Revision Strategies

Several years ago I watched a youngster alternate between writing and crumpling up her paper. She leaned low over her paper and carefully wrote her draft. Then she took the paper in both hands and scrunched it this way and that. I was astonished and bewildered by what I saw. When I asked her what she was doing, she answered, "Revising," and proudly patted the crumpled page. "See, it's all loved up."

We may laugh at this story, but I have found that this youngster is not as unusual as we might think. When they sense that their teachers value messy rough drafts and endless revisions, many children will write and revise up a storm. Yet a closer look shows that these children often do not know what revision is. Often they write successive drafts, each with only a peripheral connection to the one before it or to their notebook entries. Equally often they write successive entries and drafts, each almost identical to the next save for a few insertions, deletions, or corrections.

If we are going to help our students understand revision, I think we need to help them understand that drafting and revision are of a piece. I have come to believe that, just as in my family, the anticipation of Christmas is more fun than the holiday itself, so too, the expectation of revision is probably more important than the alterations themselves. If we can help our students anticipate revision, then we can help them take risks as writers. This is unbelievably important, because oftentimes when we let words lead us, we find ourselves saying things we never knew were true, feeling things we never imagined we felt. Randy Bomer, in his book *A Time for Meaning*, writes:

William Faulkner said that writing a first draft is like trying to build a house in a strong wind. That is the feeling I try to instill in my students as they work on their first drafts, a sense of urgency in getting it quickly hammered down, whether it's from beginning to end, or middle to end to beginning. This is just one of many possible guesses at how their piece should go, and I push them to fly through it in one or two sittings so that they can then go back to the notebook and see what they need to add or rethink in the draft. . . . Many students do feel that I'm rushing them, and I am. I'm rushing them past trying to feel they must solve all the problems of their piece in the first draft. I want them to be unsatisfied with what they can do in one draft so that the possibility of revision remains open, so that they don't think the making of a piece of writing begins at the top of page one and ends at the bottom of the final page. I am trying to hold open spaces of possibility by pushing them through the first draft.

In mini-lessons on revision, then, I'd want to encourage writers to read over all their entries on a topic, and then, after perhaps copying a passage or two onto draft paper, to put their notebooks aside. "Think about what you want this to be in the end," I'd tell them. "Imagine what you want your readers to experience," I'd suggest. "Write toward what you imagine for your piece," I'd say. "Later you can reread your notebook and add sections into your draft."

Of course, I could convey this idea by writing publicly, by telling the story of having done this, by showing a student who has written this way. In mini-lessons on revision, I could use similar methods to demonstrate any of the revision strategies that I find in Donald Murray's book *Write to Learn* and Peter Elbow's *Writing with Power* or in my *Living Between the Lines.* These are some recommended strategies:

revision strategies

- Write about the subject in a different genre, changing from a personal narrative to a poem, for example.
- Rework a confused section—the ending, the title, the lead, part of the text. This is often done in the notebook.
- Reconsider tone or voice. Try a different voice and see if it is preferable. This exploration often happens in notebooks.
- Take a long draft and make it shorter.
- Take a short entry or section of a draft and expand it.
- Experiment with different leads.
- Imagine a purpose and an audience for the draft and then reorient the writing so that it accomplishes the task.

- Predict a reader's questions, then revise in order to be sure the important ones are answered, ideally in the order in which they are asked.
- Reread the draft evaluating what works and what does not work. After selecting what works, write another draft or portion of a draft building on that strength. Decide whether to delete, repair, or ignore what does not work.
- Reread one's entries or draft and think, "Where's the mystery here?" "What do I wonder about?" Write to explore these mysteries, these questions.
- Read the entries and/or the draft over, listening to how it sounds.
- Put the draft aside and return to it another day.
- Talk with someone about the topic, then rewrite the draft without looking back at the previous versions.
- Take a jumbled piece and rewrite it in sections or chapters.
- Find a single word or a phrase that matters especially in an entry. Put it at the top of a blank page and write and write and write off this word, these words.

Each of these and countless other strategies can be the topic for a mini-lesson. Sometimes during the workshop I deliberately encourage one or two children to try a new strategy. Then the story of what they do becomes a mini-lesson. For example, when Pat Howard sensed that many of her students were restricted to small-scale revisions, inserting clarifying phrases and omitting needless details but rarely approaching a second draft with a spirit of openness and adventure, she conferred with one child, suggesting a larger-scale revision for her. "Susie," she said, "do you notice that all of your stories seem to be about the same length?" It was a wise observation, for Susie seemed to have developed a scheme for writing two-page stories, and each story was similar to the last. In the discussion that ensued, Mrs. Howard suggested that Susie challenge herself by taking the two-page draft of "Seeing My Grandparents" and extending it into the much longer draft that we saw in Chapter 9. In that chapter we saw Susie circling sections of the original draft, which she felt could be expanded with more detail and then rewritten, turning sentences into paragraphs.

During the next day's mini-lesson Susie told the class what she had done and, using the overhead projector, showed them her first and second drafts. As a result, one or two children used that revision strategy the next day, and this meant a new strategy was in the air in that classroom.

There are other ways to introduce revision strategies. Sometimes it may be more helpful to survey several options than to discuss one in detail. I could begin a mini-lesson by saying, "I thought it might help you to hear the revision strategies I saw you using yesterday as I went from writer to writer. Several of you, Mohammed, Allison, and perhaps others, are working on different leads. You are finding in your notebooks several possible ways to start your draft, and you are trying to select the best beginning from among them. This is exactly what some writers do—they call it experimenting with leads—and I think it is a strategy we could add to our 'Revision Strategies' chart. Marigold has invented her own revision strategy. She read her memoir over and decided she could hear a song in it, and so she is making up a tune and changing the words to match the mood and beat of her song. Not everyone will want to write songs, but the idea of taking your entries and writing them in several different genres is an important strategy; we can take a narrative and turn it into a song, take a letter and make it into a picture book, and so forth. So let's add that strategy to our list."

Mini-lessons on revision strategies will not always emerge from what the children are already doing. So I might, for example, encourage children to revise for the sound of their language by reading them Katherine Mansfield's description of how she wrote "Miss Brill." "I chose not only the length of each sentence," she said, "but the sound of every sentence. I chose the rise and fall of every paragraph to fit her, to fit her on that day on that very moment. After I'd written it I read it aloud—numbers of times—just as one would play over a musical composition—trying to get it nearer and nearer to the expression of Miss Brill—until it fitted her."

I would *not* end by suggesting that every child stop what he or she is doing and listen to their texts. No *one* revision strategy is right for every child, and certainly no strategy could be right for every child on any given day. The purpose of the mini-lesson is to suggest options, to add to the class pot, to give children a repertoire of strategies from which they can draw.

Mini-Lessons That Help Students Learn the Qualities of Good Writing

I grew up believing that good writers insert as many adjectives and adverbs as they possibly can into their writing. I remember, in my story about wading around lily ponds in hopes of catching turtles, how proud I was of the way I described the mud. It was cement-thick, charcoal-black, smelly, wet, granular mud. I counted my adjectives—five—and basked in my success as a writer.

Then, long after I graduated from school, I read E. B. White's *Elements of Style* and William Zinsser's *On Writing Well* and learned, to my amazement, that good writers often regard adjectives and adverbs as signs of *weak* sentences. Rather than use adjectives and adverbs to prop up weak nouns and verbs, writers try to write with precise, strong nouns and verbs. Rather than say "the young dog," the writer says "the puppy"; rather than say "I walked quietly," the writer says "I tiptoed." Two decades after I wrote my lily pond story, I learned that I would have had more success in describing the lily pond if I'd used precise verbs rather than adjectives and adverbs, if I'd written about oozing into the mud, sinking up to my ankles, my knees, my thighs, and about how the mud slurped and sucked as I tried to pull one foot from it, then another.

My teachers didn't teach me to value precise nouns and verbs because no one had taught them. Today's teachers have a new access to insights on effective writing. It is only natural, then, that we spend time during mini-lessons helping children deepen their understanding of good writing. During these mini-lessons we will want to tell children about the qualities of good writing we ourselves strive toward as we write, but we'll also want to give them opportunities to articulate *their* images of good writing.

"My story is good because it starts exciting, ends exciting, and the excitement keeps on going," eight-year-old Birger told me. Birger often put ten or fifteen exclamation marks on each page of his writing, and he revised even his social studies report on squirrels to add more excitement to it. Birger's understanding of good writing influences everything he does when he writes.

Jen is seven, and she wants very much to be grown-up. She carries a purse now and envies her friend Melissa for her thin legs. Jen thinks her stories are terrible, "babyish" she calls them. She toils over the shape of each letter and often crumples up her paper in disgust. For Jen as for Birger, a sense of what makes good writing influences everything she does when she writes.

In order to learn about our students' images of good writing, we might ask each child to think of the *best* book he or she has ever read, and then to tell a friend what made that book so wonderful. If we were to move among the pairs of children, taking note of what they were saying, we could end the meeting with a brief summary of what we heard and then remind children that those same qualities will be important in their own writing. Another day, we might ask children to select the best passage. Later, they could reread the passage, asking, "What could I learn from the way this is written?" These same mini-lessons could be applied to a particular mode of writing. If the class was working on literary non-fiction, the children could bring examples of good nonfiction writing to class to read and discuss with a partner. If the class was working on poetry, each child could select the best poem he or she had ever read, and then in pairs children could discuss their selections. Similarly, these mini-lessons could use the children's own writing. Which is their best passage? Their best piece? Their best poem? Why? These mini-lessons may sound simple, almost mundane, and yet we can imagine what fun it would be to search for our own favorite poem and then to meet with colleagues to share our choices and discuss what drew us to this poem and not to others.

The children's values will differ from ours. Many children especially value good pictures, action, excitement, and funny topics. We will want to share our criteria for evaluating writing with children, and this will probably mean telling them we value information. Readers thrive on the concrete and the specific, on the anecdote, statistic, quotation, or example. As Murray (1968) points out, "The amateur thinks that the writer has an idea, perhaps a vague thought and a few facts. He doesn't. He has shelves of reports, miles of tape-recorded interviews, notebooks of quotations and facts and ideas and possible constructions. It takes thirty gallons of sap to make a gallon of maple syrup; it takes hundreds of pages of notes to make one *Reader's Digest* article" (p. 6).

In their notebooks, children will collect a wealth of concrete information. Too often when they go to write a draft from their notebook entries, they assume that no one cares about their little details. They are accustomed to adults who want only cursory answers to their questions. An adult asks, "Did you have a good time at the beach?" and children nod yes. Most children don't bother to tell adults that they draped themselves with seaweed and pretended they were brides. Yet this is a detail that could make their writing powerful.

I might show children the importance of detail by showing them the example of a child who wrote a draft and then rewrote it, adding details from her notebook. These are Susie's two drafts:

DRAFT 1

I was at a beach in Florida. I pressed my toes into the hot sand. I saw my sister jumping out in the waves with my Aunt. She was jumping around as the waves hit her, she was out deep . . . I wanted to go and play in the big waves but I was nervous to.

DRAFT 2

I pressed my toes in the hot sand. I wiggled them around. The gritty sand felt good on my sunburnt toes. I looked out over the ocean. My sister was out deep, jumping over waves with my Aunt. Sometimes the waves got too big and they would knock her over, then my Aunt would pull her up and she'd be dripping wet and they'd start laughing. My shoulders were hot from the burning sun. I would have loved to be out there in the waves but I was too scared.

Hindy List recently gave a similar mini-lesson. She told a group of fifth graders, "I want to give you a tip about good writing today, so listen closely. I have been going around to classes and often see entries like this one: 'I had so much fun at the party. I got a lot of presents and I ate a lot and the food was delicious.' When I read this, I have a hard time picturing exactly what the author meant. I would love it if the author told me more specifics. I want to hear about the sextuplet dolls she received, with blankets and beds and carriages for each. I'd love to hear about the walkie-talkie that only conveyed static. And instead of telling us she ate delicious food, I would have liked to see the seven-layered cake and the four glasses of coke. So when you are writing, remember to add details."

Hindy turned to the entry she had written on the chalkboard. With chalk in hand, she continued, "If I had written this entry, I might reread it afterward and think, 'Can I tell more? Can I help the reader see?' Rereading it, I notice that I haven't told specifically about the presents, and so I put a little asterisk here" (and she inserts a star into the appropriate place in her entry) "and then, turning the paper over, I put the same code on the back and beside it, I explain the entry more specifically. Whenever I get to spots where I could have been more specific, I insert a code, and then in a different place I write what belongs there." Hindy ended the mini-lesson by asking, "Do any of you want to reread your entries today searching for places where you could be more specific?" Many children nodded, and Hindy told them she would be coming around to help and sent them off to work.

Readers may notice several things. Hindy used a hypothetical entry rather than a real one as her negative example. The only time I would use a child's writing as a negative example is when I want to show how the youngster improved his or her own draft, as in the earlier example of Susie's writing. Also, Hindy did not label the component of writing she was trying to teach. She did not write "Telling Details" or "Show, Not Tell" on the chalkboard and ask the children to recite the phrase and record it in their notebooks. Hindy learned not to do this the hard way. For a number of years, my colleagues and I would tell children that writers have a saying: "Show, not tell." We'd illustrate the motto with mini-lessons like this one of Hindy's on details. But after a while, whenever I'd visit classrooms, I'd hear children parroting "show, not tell." It became clear to my colleagues and me that *labeling* a quality of good writing creates a cliché. Clichés are too easy. They allow people to recite easy dictums rather than respond honestly and freshly to written work.

Readers may also have noticed that Hindy ended the mini-lesson by talking about how the children might go about adding more specific details to their entries or drafts. Had she not ended the mini-lesson this way, few children would have incorporated the lesson on specifics in their work in progress. Almost every mini-lesson ought to end with a specific, concrete discussion of what the children can do next with their writing.

There are countless other qualities that make writing good. I find it helpful, for example, to talk about honesty in writing. It is easy to say "White snow covered the world," but was the snow really white? It is easy to say "I had a terrific time," but weren't there moments that shadowed the happiness? Donald Hall emphasizes that honesty is one of the most important qualities of good writing. "Concentration upon honesty is the only way to exclude the sounds of the bad style that assault us all," he writes, and I would tell children this.

The Tools for Developing Our Own Mini-Lessons

In the preceding pages, I have suggested about two dozen mini-lessons, but these could easily be multiplied exponentially into many, many more. It helps to realize that any one particular bit of information can and should be conveyed to students many different ways. If I want to show students that writers often take the time to consider alternate beginnings—or leads—for their drafts, I could do so in a whole range of ways:

- I could *write publicly* in front of my students. Standing at the chalkboard or the overhead projector, I might say to students,

"Now that I've decided I'm writing a memoir, now that I know I'll be working off the entries about how my writing is rooted in my childhood adventures alongside the creek, I might begin by copying my favorite section from that entry. So I could start like this:

> Under the roots of Old Lean Over tree, I created a nature center . . .

"Then again, I might want to put all of that in a bigger context, so I may want to start with my writing history. I've got entries on that, too. I might start:

> I remember writing book reports and thank-you letters as a child, but I don't remember any other writing, and I don't remember liking to write . . .

"Or, now that I think about it, I might begin in the present, and talk about the role writing plays in my life:

> When my sister gave my husband, John, and me the most supreme gift of all—a weekend's worth of babysitting—my husband's eyes lit up. "A weekend of skiing," he said. My eyes lit up. "A weekend of writing!" I said, and then added, "Will you take John, too?"

- I could *read excerpts* from the writing I've done at home and *talk about it*. "Sometimes people think that writers just pick up their pens and produce wonderful drafts. For me, and for most writers I know, it's not like that at all. When I was working on. . . ."
- *A student could tell* about how he or she began writing a piece.
- I could *tell the story of a conference* I'd had with a student. "Yesterday, when I came to Bradley, he'd just begun his article about the litter outside our school. I read what he'd written and then surprised Bradley by drawing a line under his sentences and saying, 'That's *one* way to begin an article. How *else* might you begin it?' Bradley was a bit dumbfounded, but he proceeded to write a second, very different lead. He wrote . . . [and I'd read it]. Then he was *really* dumbfounded to have me draw yet another line under this second lead and say, 'Hmmm, Bradley, how *else* could you start your article?' This time he wrote . . . [and I'd again read it]. Class, what Bradley has done in writing three different leads is that he has imagined three different versions of his article. He has weighed three different drafts in his mind's eye. . . ."
- I could tell students that writers often spend lots and lots of time considering different ways in which they *could* begin their pieces . . . and then we could each look at our last few pieces asking,

"How do I tend to begin my writing?" Just for fun, we could look back at one of our drafts and ask, "How else *might* I have begun this piece?" In this way, we could *practice conceiving of different beginnings.*

- Each member of the class could *bring a few dearly loved books* to the mini-lesson, and after talking for a moment about the importance of leads, we could rummage through familiar books noticing what the writers we love most have done in their leads. Then we could talk about what we learn from these authors.
- I could *read aloud an excerpt* about leads from the books on good writing. I particularly like Zinsser's discussion in *On Writing Well.*
- I may give students a chapter about writing to read at home, and then we could discuss what they learned as our mini-lesson.

My point is not that all teachers should teach their students about lead writing, and it is certainly not that we should have twenty mini-lessons on this one topic. Instead, my point is that there are many ways to teach anything we choose to teach. The grid shown in Figure 12–1 may help remind us of our options.

There are countless other ways to teach children the qualities that make writing good. Readers who want further information about good writing may want to read writers such as Annie Dillard, Ralph Fletcher, Donald Hall, William Zinsser, and especially Donald Murray. The ideas expressed in their books can be invaluable resources for us and for our students.

Perhaps the challenge is not to dream up new possibilities for mini-lessons but to select the ones that will help children the most today. When we have selected a mini-lesson for important reasons and after considering a range of options, our voice, our tone, will convey, "Come close, let's *really listen.* I've been thinking a lot about you, and the one thing I most want to say today is this. . . ."

FIGURE 12–1 Ways to multiply one's mini-lessons

Ways to convey information

Possible topics for mini-lessons:	We can write publicly.	We can tell students about our writing and show our drafts.	We can ask a student to tell his or her peers about his or her writing.	We can tell about a conference with a student.	We can reread old writing from our notebooks and folders looking for the patterns we see in our writing.	We can read (or discuss) what someone has written about good writing.	Etc.
Lead writing.							
Writers are like photographers. We have to ask, "Of all that I see, what's the one thing I want to focus on?"							
Writers live with their topics, gathering entries on them.							
Writers know the value of closing one's eyes and making a mental picture of one's subject, then writing down what one sees.							
Etc.							

Resources for Creating Mini-Lessons

Atwell, Nancie. *In the middle: Writing, reading and learning with adolescents.* Portsmouth, NH: Boynton/Cook–Heinemann, 1987.

Bomer, Randy. *A time for meaning: Learning literacy with people aged 10–20.* Portsmouth, NH: Heinemann, in press.

Calkins, Lucy McCormick, with Shelley Harwayne. *Living between the lines.* Portsmouth, NH: Heinemann, 1991.

Fletcher, Ralph. *What a writer needs.* Portsmouth, NH: Heinemann, 1992.

Harwayne, Shelley. *Lasting impressions: Weaving literature into the writing workshop.* Portsmouth, NH: Heinemann, 1992.

Murray, Donald. *Shoptalk: Learning to write with writers.* Portsmouth, NH: Boynton/Cook–Heinemann, 1990.

———. *Write to learn.* Chicago: Holt, Rinehart and Winston, 1984.

———. *A writer teaches writing.* 2nd ed. Boston: Houghton Mifflin, 1985.

Zinsser, William. *On writing well: An informal guide to writing nonfiction.* New York: Harper & Row, 1990.

13
Conferring
Writing Becomes a Tool for Thought

"I can confer with myself," nine-year-old Becky said to me one morning. "I just read my writing over to myself and it's like there is another person there. I think thoughts to myself. I say things other kids might ask me." The brown-eyed youngster paused. "I talk it over with myself. I ask myself questions."

Similarly, seven-year-old Heather reread each page of her homemade book. "I'm having an individual writing conference with myself," she said in a prim, matter-of-fact voice. "On each page I ask myself the questions the other kids would ask me." Then Heather opened her book. "Here I wrote,

> I have a horse.

"The kids will ask me if I ride it, so I'm going to add,

> I ride my horse every day unless it's raining."

During the writing workshop, Maria sits in the author's chair. It is not yet time for the children to gather for a sharing session, so there is no one on the rug in front of her. Maria's teacher, Aida Montero, sees the youngster and asks, "What are you doing in the share area now?"

"I'm pretend-sharing," Maria answers.

Puzzled, Ms. Montero asks, "What do you mean?"

"I'm thinking, if I get to share this piece with the kids, what will they ask me?" Maria reads the story to her teacher:

> I hav fun wif my ubwala. I go evry satrda.
> (*Abuela* is Spanish for grandmother.)

Then Maria says, "I think they'll ask me, 'What ya' do with her?' so now I'm going to make a page two." Maria returned to her desk and wrote:

> We wach Tom an Jerry an eat Fetos an pla Trabl.
> (We watch Tom and Jerry and eat Fritos and play Trouble.)

Throughout the country there are now thousands of classrooms in which young writers of all ages pull back from their pages in order to ask themselves the questions that have been asked of them. "What else can I say?" "What can I add here?" "Will this make sense?" "Is this *really* what happened?" "What will the kids ask me?"

Often I tell young children that making a piece of writing is not very different from making a clay rabbit. You pull in to sculpt the ears, then pull back to ask, "How do these look?" You pull in to reshape one ear, to bend over the other. You pull back to ask, "Is it better?" Creation and criticism—these are central to our work with clay and blocks, and they are also central to our work with words.

The powerful thing about working with words is that we are really working with thoughts. Writing allows us to put our thoughts on the page and in our pockets; writing allows us to pull back and ask questions of our thoughts. It is this dynamic of creation and criticism, of pulling in to put thoughts on the page and pulling back to question, wonder, remember more, organize, and rethink that makes writing such a powerful tool for learning.

In his important article "Teaching the Other Self: The Writer's First Reader," Don Murray (1982) likens writing to a conversation between two workers muttering to each other at the bench. "The self speaks, the other self listens and considers. The self proposes, the other self considers. The self makes, the other self evaluates. The two selves collaborate" (p. 165).

Writing helps us develop our thinking because it allows us to revisit our first thoughts. Spoken words fade away, but print fastens our thoughts onto paper. We can hold our ideas in our hands. We can carry them in our knapsacks. We can think about our thinking and use writing as a way to outgrow ourselves. Through writing, we can "re-see," reshape, and refine our thoughts. Frank Smith explains, "Writing separates our ideas from ourselves in a way that it is easiest for us to examine, explore, and develop them" (1982, p. 15).

When writing is thought of as a process of dialogue between the writer and the emerging text, it means that we shift from being writers to being readers of our own drafts. As readers, we ask a question or two of our own draft, and we ask these same questions over and over as we continue through our writing lives. We ask these questions whether we are four or ninety-four years old, and we ask them whether we are writing a poem or a nonfiction book.

- What have I said so far? What am I trying to say?
- How do I like it? What is good here that I can build on? What is not so good that I can fix?

- How does it sound? How does it look!
- How else could I have done this?
- What will my readers think as they read this? What questions will they ask? What will they notice? Feel? Think?
- What am I going to do next?

In order for young writers to learn to ask such questions of themselves, teachers and peers need to ask them of young writers. Teacher-student and peer conferences, then, are at the heart of teaching writing. Through them students learn to interact with their own writing.

When a Student Says, "I'm Done," What Can We Say?

We may think of writing as a process of engaging in dialogue with our emerging drafts, but our students usually come to us thinking of writing quite differently. As I said in discussing the second- and third-grade writing workshop in Chapter 8, all too often our classrooms no sooner settle into that blessed hush, that heavenly moment when one can hear the scratch of pencils and the creak of chairs, when suddenly one child says, "I'm done." Then it's like popcorn. From all corners of the room, one writer after another pops up saying, "I'm done." "I'm done." "I'm done."

What are we to do? A dozen children think they are finished and we are supposed to show each one that "writing is a process of engaging in dialogue with one's emerging draft"?

Many of us try valiantly to rush to each of the writers who has popped up from the desk. "What else happened on your trip?" we say to one. "Why don't you add that?" Then we rush to the next and the next, like circus performers who run about trying to keep plates spinning on the ends of sticks. "Keep going," we say to one writer. "Write some more entries," we extoll another. "Add on," we say to yet a third. If we're lucky, each writer does as we suggest, adding a line, inserting a detail . . . but a moment later the writers begin popping up again. "We're done." "We're done." We collapse into the author's chair, certain that the idea of having one-to-one conferences was invented in some ivory tower.

I've seen good teachers give up on the notion of conferring individually with their students, and this is understandable—but not acceptable. In the teaching of writing, there could be no compromise that costs so much. It is for good reason that the writing process approach to teaching writing is also known as "the conference approach." Conferring is at the heart of the writing workshop. It's difficult to learn to confer well, and it's difficult to learn to manage the workshop so that frequent, effective conferring is possible, but it's worth the struggle.

The Components of Effective Conferences: Research, Decide, Teach

I remember, fifteen years ago, when I was teaching third grade at the Center School, the first time I arrived at the University of New Hampshire for a conference with Don Murray. I entered his office saying, "I'm done." I can recall reaching out to hand him my draft, and I can recall the awkwardness and surprise when he neither took the draft from me nor glanced at it. I found a seat and met his eyes with my own.

"How's it going?" he asked, or so I recall. Perhaps instead he asked, "What's been happening?" or "What are you up to?" "How's the writing?" or "Have you met any new problems lately?"

Years later, I can still recall how odd the entire interaction felt, how entirely different. It was odd, in the first place, to have my writing teacher look past my writing to me. It was odd to come with my draft in hand and have my writing teacher not even glance at it, let alone take it into his hands. I'll never forget sitting in Murray's office holding my writing and my writing life in my hands and telling him how things were going.

Before long, during my long drives to the University of New Hampshire, I'd rehearse for his questions. "How *is* my writing going?" I'd ask myself. "What *do* I need help on?" Although I didn't realize it at the time, if Murray regarded his job as putting himself out of a job, if he saw his job as interacting with me in ways that taught me how to interact with my writing, he accomplished a large part of it simply by insisting that our conferences begin with my taking responsibility for their direction. Because his very simple and yet wonderful question, "How's it going?" was predictable, I internalized it and asked it of myself. I was on my way toward learning to confer with myself, toward developing that internalized "other" self. In retrospect, I think that during the first moments of each conference, Murray worked from all he already knew about me and whatever I said to him to construct a theory about who I was on that day as a writer and what help I most needed.

If I opened the conference by saying I liked everything about my draft except the last paragraph, for example, then Murray might respond, "Could you walk me through the life of this piece? When did you start writing it, how'd it proceed?" Instead of necessarily taking my stated problem—the ending—at face value, Murray was clearly trying to figure out what was going on. If he responded to my concern about my ending by asking, "Could you walk me through the life of the piece?" he was probably wondering, "Is Lucy trying to conclude this draft prematurely, or has she taken it as far as it can go?" Of course, Murray might have ruminated in a different way about my concern over the ending. He might have wondered why I didn't like the ending ("Lucy, what do you aim toward in your endings?"). He might have wondered what I imagined doing with the ending and how I tended to go about revising my drafts in general ("So what are you thinking you might do with the ending?" "Is that the sort of thing you often do to improve your pieces?").

The important thing to realize is that our job, as teachers, is to listen to everything we see and know and hear about a child in order to develop a theory about this particular writer. During this first phase of conferences, which I'll call the *research* phase, writing teachers often ask questions of the writer, but we're not firing out a random barrage. Instead, our questions are intended to develop and test the hypothesis we are forming about this writer. Our job during this first phase of a conference is not simply to ask a stream of questions; it is to understand the writer. The questions will come, of course, but they are not the goal. They are the by-products of our efforts to understand our students. I am stressing this point not to devalue the questions we ask but to empower them. When our questions grow out of our emerging understanding of the writer, they are alive and fresh and powerful. When the same questions grow only out of a chapter on good questions to ask in writing conferences, they quickly become canned and mechanical.

It's not easy to learn to be a researcher of one's students. When I work with teachers in staff development sessions, I sometimes role-play the part of a student. "Can I publish this?" I say, mimicking the students we know so well. "I wrote it yesterday and it's done. What should I do next?"

Almost invariably, teachers ask about my *subject*, not my writing *process*. This is a perfectly acceptable thing to do in a conference if it seems that this is what a writer needs most from us, but talking with a writer about his or her subject usually will not help a teacher decide on the direction of a conference. When I urge teachers to postpone looking at the draft or talking about the subject and to look instead at me as a writer, they don't know what to say. Usually they end up asking questions that lead me to summarize the draft. "What did you write about?" they ask, or "What's your piece called?" or "Where did you get the idea for your piece?" As soon as part of my subject emerges into the conversational horizon, all the hesitations over what to say disappear and they begin interviewing me with ease—but again, they are asking me about my subject rather than my writing process. "When did you get your guinea pig?" they ask. "What's he look like?" "What does he eat?" Earlier in this chapter and again in Chapter 14, I show the potential power of questions that elicit more talk about the writer's content, but let me warn again that these questions are *not* the most helpful way to decide what tack to take in a conference. Information about the writer's guinea pig will probably not steer the conference in a helpful direction; it's not what we need most in order to develop a theory of our students as writers and what they need next. The lines of discussion that can guide us the most, early in the conferences, are those that focus on the *writing process,* on the writer's assessments and hopes and concerns, rather than on details about the guinea pig.

What a difference it makes when we shift from saying, "Tell me about your guinea pig" to

- Can you tell me about how you wrote this?
- How's it going?
- What problems have you encountered while writing this?
- When you read over your text, how do you feel about it? If you were to lay out all your finished drafts and then sort them into piles of "very best," "good," and "less good," which pile would this be in? Why?
- What are you planning to do next? If you *were* going to do more with this piece, what *might* you do?
- What kind of writing are you trying to do? Do you have a sense of how you want your writing to be in the end?
- How long have you been working on this draft?

Often during this research portion of a conference, we will look at the writer's notebook or draft. Our perspective on what we read will be shaped by what the writer has said to us. For example, if Diana has said, "I've got six entries about coming to this country, but now I don't know how to put them together into anything," we may glance at her entries to learn more about the dilemma she faces. At least two things will happen when we read over her entries. First, our emerging theory about Diana will be extended. If we see that the six entries are restatements of each other, and that all of them are general, sweeping comments about how hard it was to come to America, we store in our heads the fact that Diana needs help going past generalities into details, and she needs help angling her entries so that some of them pursue different aspects of her topic.

But something else happens when we skim over Diana's entries: We become her first reader. At this moment we need to set aside our teaching agenda and hear what Diana the writer has said, whether it's about her guinea pig or her trip to America. And so we look Diana in the eye and tell her, "It sounds like it was hard." We need to tell her that we can't imagine doing such a brave, scary thing. We are looking beyond her entries and seeing the writer. When we are trying to be good teachers of writing, when we are trying to crack the puzzle of this particular writer, we must not forget to listen.

Our first job, then, whenever we read a writer's entries or drafts, is to be fully present as a listener. Our job for that moment is to enjoy, to care, to be reminded of our own lives, and to respond. We cry, laugh, nod, and sigh. We let the writer know she has been heard.

The Decision and Teaching Components of a Conference

Usually the force of this listening is so powerful that it energizes whatever we decide to teach in the conference. Because we listen to Diana's sadness over her move to America, she begins to tell us the details that were absent from her entries. She starts to talk about the warm sunshine on her back in Haiti, and about the smell of flowers everywhere. After we hear these wonderful details about her subject, we still need to move from the research component of the conference to the decision stage. We think, "Of all that we could say to Diana, how can we best help her?" Diana has told us wonderful details about her country, and our instinct may be to assume that the only possible response is to say, "Diana, why don't you write about that?" But we need to pause for a moment and realize that there are other ways we could proceed. One of the most important things to remember is that we do have a decision to make.

There are options before us. We need to think, "Of all that I might say now to Diana, what is it she most needs to hear?" We may wish she'd add those details to her entries and yet decide to save this suggestion for another day. Perhaps, for now, we decide it's more important to tell Diana we are delighted to see that she's begun writing often during the day and that we hope she continues doing so. Then again, we might say, "What I notice about your entries, Diana, is that you say the big, general thing about how moving was hard over and over. When you told me the details about the sun on your back in Haiti and the flowers, that is when I began to imagine how you must feel." We might tell her, "When you write big, sweeping things after this, you may want to think, '*Exactly* how did I feel?'" Then again, perhaps we tell Diana that she has said an amazing amount about her subject as she has talked to us, and we may want to suggest that whenever she writes, she may want to talk to a listener.

In this discussion, I have already shifted from the decision component of a conference to the teaching component. The two become indistinguishable. The important thing to remember when we decide what we will teach is that it's far better to suggest a strategy a student might add to her repertoire than a one-shot solution. It's far better to suggest, "Maybe you can take the things you say to me, when we're just chatting about your subject, and try to add them to your to your draft," than to say, "Why don't you add the part about the sunshine and flowers to your draft?" We need to give the writer something that will help not only today, with this piece of writing, but also tomorrow, with other pieces of writing.

As we read a student's writing we also have to be aware of how tempting it is to think, "What would I do if this piece were mine?" I find that my own writing block vanishes the instant I see someone else's text. My fingers begin to itch. I envision my ideal version of it, and I know exactly what changes I would make. Buried three lines into a notebook entry I spot a much better lead sentence. I notice where the pace breaks down in the existing draft and envision just how I would remedy the problem. I see a passage in another entry I'd move into the draft. But it is *not* my piece of writing. It belongs to somebody else. If I ask questions and make suggestions so that a student's text ends up matching what I had in mind, what have I accomplished? Better bulletin boards, perhaps, and probably also longer lines during the writing workshop, since I've mistakenly taught students to be dependent on my evaluation and advice.

If we can keep only one thing in mind—and I fail at this half the time—it is that we are teaching the writer and not the writing. Our decisions must be guided by "what might help this *writer*" rather than "what might help this *writing*." If the piece of writing gets better but the writer has learned nothing that will help him or her another day on another piece, then the conference was a waste of everyone's time. It may even have done more harm than good, for such conferences teach students not to trust their own reactions.

There are many ways in which, without meaning to do so, we convey to students that we, rather than they, are the critics of their rough drafts. The most common and most hidden way in which we often take over the students' job is with our compliments. "I love the first part," we say, and all too often, students assume that we mean their beginning should remain as it is. How much better it is if we show that we're affected by the piece by responding to it as a whole but then ask the writer to think about what works and what doesn't work. We may agree or disagree, but our assessment shouldn't take the place of the writer's own assessment.

Sometimes we take control of a student's draft in coy ways. "I'm wondering if you see a different way to start your narrative?" I've asked. Then, pointing vaguely to a middle section of the draft, I ask, "Is there a different sentence, maybe down around here, that might work better as a lead?" If the youngster doesn't catch my hint, I may even read the draft aloud, saying, "Listen and see if you hear where the action picks up." Then, of course, I use my voice to signal the "right" answer, and pretty soon the student's text has become my own.

Then, too, we take control by asking specific content questions that pull the writer toward things in which we are interested. "Oh, tell me about your dog," I ask. "What kind of dog is he?" "Does he like to play fetch?" We pump for specific bits of information that the writer will then, we hope, add to the text. Yet who is to say that the writer wants to expand upon these things? We may want the writer to add this information, but it would be far better to help *the writer* choose what's important by asking, "What are you getting at in this story? What's the main thing?" These questions will be better still if we tell the writer what we've sensed. "It seems to me you've told about a lot of things. Sometimes I find it helpful, when I've done this in my writing, to reread it and ask, 'Of all that I've mentioned, are there one or two things I'm particularly interested in exploring?'" When we let writers in on what we notice about their writing process, then they can learn something that applies not only to this draft but to future drafts as well.

As teachers, we need to remember that we will not always be there when our students write. Students need to become critical readers of their own texts. Our job in a writing conference is to put ourselves out of a job, to interact with students in such a way that they learn how to interact with their own developing drafts.

14
Learning to Confer

I'll never forget, at a staff development workshop, how I played the role of a student. "Here is my story. I'm done," I announced and on an overhead projector I displayed the draft (Figure 14–1):

> One time my grandfather was in the hospital. He didn't get any better.
> So he went to God. I miss my grandfather.

Hands went up as members of the audience took the part of the teacher. "What did the hospital look like?" one woman asked. Still others wanted to know what it had been like when my grandfather was alive. A woman said no, she would ask if the draft was done, did I plan to revise it? After many such responses, someone timidly said, "This probably isn't the right re-

FIGURE 14–1   A draft story

One tim my gan Fath
Was in The Hbtl
He dinH. git badr.
So He wet to God
I Mid my gan Fath

sponse, but to tell the truth, I'd hug the child and say I was sorry her grandfather died."

Why is it so difficult to give a simple human response? I think it is because we try so hard to be helpful we forget to be real. Especially when we first learn to confer we often worry so much about asking the right questions that we forget to listen. We focus on asking the questions that will draw out more information, not realizing that it is listening that creates a magnetic force between writer and audience. The force of listening will draw words out. Writers will find themselves saying things they didn't know they knew. And so we let the writer know she has been heard. We tell the youngster we are sorry about her grandfather. Sometimes that is enough. Sometimes the purpose of a conference is simply to respond. Other times, if the moment seems right, we try to extend what the youngster can do as a writer.

It is with some trepidation that I now move into a chapter in which I give guidelines for thinking about conferring.

I've seen teachers who become so intent about following someone else's guidelines for conferring well, they forget that conferring is another word for discussing and that it is something they've done throughout their professional lives. I hope, therefore, that readers will use what I say in the following pages merely as lenses through which to think about conferring and not as scripts to follow.

I've found it helpful to divide conferences almost arbitrarily into categories. Sometimes we and our students talk mainly about the writer's *content*. Sometimes we talk mainly about the *design* or genre of the text, sometimes about the writer's *processes*, sometimes about the writer's *evaluations* of the draft. And sometimes we talk about *editorial* issues such as word choice, spelling, and punctuation. I'll discuss editorial conferences in Chapter 18, but let me briefly discuss the others now.

Content Conferences

Every morning when our children pile off the school bus and gather around us, we confer. We hear that Ming fell and scraped her face over the weekend and we examine her wounds. Gordon tells us about a store that sells comic books worth *twenty dollars* each. We share Mary Ann's dismay over the fact that squirrels have chased all the birds away from her feeder. We ask questions to learn more about another student's guinea pig; what does it eat, where do you keep it, how do you like it? Each of these interactions contains most of the features of a good content conference.

A friend listening to these conferences comments, "But they are just conversations." And, of course, that is the point. Content conferences are just interested conversations about the content of writing or even about the content of our students' lives. In a writing classroom, children's lives and areas of expertise fill the room. Don Graves once said, "You can tell a good writing classroom by the presence of the children's own interests in the room." Graves is wise to suggest that it's essential for us to know what our students know.

Eric tore a sheet of paper from his notebook and added it to the discarded pages that already littered the floor around him. "I've got nuthin'. I'm out of entries."

"I'll tell you what," Eric's teacher, Joan Gerwin, said, crouching next to his desk. "Why don't you and I make a list of things you know a lot about, things you're an expert in." In making this suggestion, the teacher has essentially bypassed the research component of her conference and made an instant decision based on the situation as she sees it. This will happen to all of us as we teach. She wants to mobilize Eric by helping him know what he knows.

"I'm not an expert on anything," Eric answered. "TV, that's all," he said, "and baseball. That's all."

"Oh, that's right, you play baseball!" Mrs. Gerwin said, her voice filled with interest.

Eric nodded. "Almost made a home run last night," he muttered. "Got to third."

"In one hit? Tell me about it, what happened?"

"When I stood up to bat, I had the feeling it'd be a lucky one," Eric said, his resistance melting. "I took hold of the bat and I said to myself, 'Stay cool.' "

Turning Eric's notebook to a clean page, Mrs. Gerwin interrupted to say, "Eric, would you put that down—just how you said it to me," and she repeated his words, looking expectantly at his paper until he started writing. Then she moved on to another child. Another time, perhaps another day, Mrs. Gerwin will try to show Eric that what they did together that day can be something he does with other students and with himself. But for today, she wanted simply to mobilize him.

Eleven-year-old Sumi paused in the midst of writing and stared into space. Drawing her chair alongside Sumi's desk, Mrs. Thornton asked if she could interrupt. "How's it going?"

Sumi slid her notebook toward her teacher and looked down at her hands as Mrs. Thornton quietly read the entry.

My father died when I was three but my sister was twelve and my brother, ten. When I see pictures of him holding me, it's like he is a stranger. In the same picture is my brother and sister only they knew him well. They never talk about him except to say, "You would have liked him." When I see other kids with their fathers, I wonder what it would be like to be his daughter.

"Sumi," Mrs. Thornton said, pushing a strand of hair from the girl's face, "I'm glad you are writing about this. I can tell how special your father is to you, even though you never got the chance to know him."

Sumi nodded. There was a long pause before she began to talk. "When people ask me how it feels not to have a father, I tell them it doesn't matter because I never knew him. But when I see my sister and brother with him in pictures, I feel sorry for myself because I didn't get to know him like they did. I sort of feel cheated."

"I'd feel the same way, Sumi," Mrs. Thornton said. They were quiet for a moment and then, touching Sumi lightly on the shoulder, Mrs. Thornton said, "I'm going to leave you now because I don't want to get in the way of what you are doing. It is so important, the things you have been saying. I'll be back, my friend."

Although Eric and Sumi were each in different places—Eric facing the blank page and Sumi working her way into an entry—their conferences were similar. I call these content conferences because in both, the teachers focused on the subject. They did not focus on the writer's processes (How was it to write this entry? What are you going to do next?) or on encouraging writers to evaluate the text (What do you like best about it?). Instead, they responded to and asked questions about the content and in this way helped the youngsters add to (or begin) their entries. Because this is a common pattern in teacher-student and peer conferences, it is important to consider why some of these conferences are more successful than others.

If a conference is going well, the child's energy for writing increases. The child should leave the conference wanting to write. Eric and Sumi's energy increased, I believe, because their teachers focused on what they *did* say. Their energy level would have been very different had the teachers' focus been instead on what they *did not* say, on eliciting more information. Many of us, well-intended writing teachers, might have responded to Sumi's draft differently.

MRS. THORNTON'S RESPONSE

"Sumi," Mrs. Thornton said, pushing a strand of hair from the girl's face, "I'm glad you are writing about this. I can tell how special your father is to you, even though you never got the chance to know him." Sumi nodded. There was a long pause before she began to talk. "When people ask me how it feels not to have a father, I tell them it doesn't matter because I never knew him. But when I see my sister and brother with him in pictures, I feel sorry for myself because I didn't get to know him like they did. I sort of feel cheated." "I'd feel the same way, Sumi," Mrs. Thornton said. They were quiet for a moment, and then, touching Sumi lightly on the shoulder, Mrs. Thornton said, "I'm going to leave you now because I don't want to get in the way of what you are doing. It is so important. . . ."

MANY OF OUR RESPONSES

"It is too bad about your father, Sumi," the teacher said, her eyes flickering over the entry as she searched for places where more details were needed. "Um, Sumi, you told about seeing photographs of your father. What did he look like in the photographs?" After Sumi answered, the teacher said, "Do you think you should add that? When I read your piece, I didn't know about it." Sumi nodded dutifully, and the teacher again scanned the page. "Another thing, you never told your brother's and sister's names. Don't you think that might help? . . ."

Is it any surprise that some content conferences empower youngsters, making them feel like experts, while others pull them down, making them feel that their drafts aren't good enough?

It is common for children to summarize their content, as Eric did when he said, "I almost made a home run . . . made it to third." Usually I respond by circling back to what the child has said, encouraging the youngster to include more detail. "You made it to third base!" I might say. "What happened?" If the youngster still responds with broad generalities ("I just hit it,") I try again. "It is hard for me to really picture it when you tell about it so fast, in one sentence. What was it like for you?"

When content conferences such as these work well, writers learn that just as it is important in tennis to keep one's eye on the ball, and just as in piano playing it's important to focus on the melody rather than on the fingering, so too, writers need to keep their eyes on their subject. Through content conferences, writers can also learn to anticipate their audience's hunger for information and to anticipate places where their readers may be confused and need clarification. Writers will learn to do this if we, as readers, let students know when we have *real* questions, when we cannot respond to their writing because we do not understand it.

The cluster of first graders listened as Charles, a stout youngster with dark curls framing his face, read his entry to them.

Me and my friends ran in the football field. Then we went to the Hornell's house. When we got to the Hornell's house we ate dead pig. Then we went to our house. I watched TV with my dog. Then I went to sleep. The End.

"Ate dead pig!" Scott repeated. "Yucky, yucky." The children laughed and Charles beamed, proud at his unexpected luck. Charles was a solemn fellow and it was rare for children to laugh at his stories. "What *is* dead pig?" Scott wanted to know. "On your plate did you have a pig with ears and a nose and a curly tail? Did it say *oink*?"

"It was a big ugly thing and it was cooked and it was brownish. There was a nose but Mr. Hornell cut it off. It was like a different kind of ham."

"That's important information, Charles," Dave Osborne said. "Some of us were a bit confused about that part." Charles nodded and with Mr. Osborne's nudging said he'd add the part about the dead pig. When Mr. Osborne asked how he might go about adding this information, the class talked about ways Charles could use arrows or carets to insert the information in his entry.

It is worth noting that Charles's content conference ended with a discussion of ways in which he could add information to the entry just as Eric's conference ended with his teacher opening Eric's notebook to a clean page and saying, "Would you put that down." Other content conferences may end with the child compiling a list of topics for future entries, or taping a second sheet onto the bottom of the first, or stapling paper together to make a book with chapters. As each of these content conferences concludes, the focus tends to shift from content to process, from "What do you have to say?" to "How will you go about saying it?"

It is also important to notice how Mr. Osborne scaffolds this whole-class share session so that all the children act as teachers—or conferrers—for Charles. It wasn't hard for his classmates to take on the role of being very effective conference partners. They listened, responded, and asked an honest question in order to clarify something they didn't understand. This in and of itself may not lead to improved writing, however, and these first graders probably do not yet know how to turn a conversation about dead pigs into a conversation about writing. It was wise of Mr. Osborne to step in to help the conversation "turn a bend" back toward the writing process by suggesting that Charles might want to add the clarifying information to his draft and encouraging the class to muse over how he might do this.

Soon children will learn to conduct these content conferences on their own. If they can hold content conferences with one another, they are well on their way toward holding content conferences with themselves, and clearly this marks important growth in a child's abilities as a writer. We have already seen many examples of children holding content conferences with themselves. In Chapter 7, when six-year-old Scott reread his homemade book about his father's collections, realized that the kids would say, "What were the collections?" and proceeded to add details to his text, he was holding a content conference with himself. And in Chapter 13 when Becky said, "I can confer with myself," what she was doing was holding a content conference with herself about her horse. When Maria sat in the author's chair and pretended the kids were asking her questions, the questions she imagined lead her to add to her content.

In each of these content conferences, what happened was that the writer taught the listener about the subject and then added more information to the page.

In the content conferences we've examined thus far, the texts have not been used as ways to "re-see" the subject. The subject hasn't changed during the writing process. The purpose of these conferences was simply to elicit what the writer *already* knew rather than to engage the writer in further exploration.

But the wonderful, powerful thing about writing is that we can read through our early words and gain a new vision of our subject. As we write, we can deepen our understanding of our subjects. It's important to realize that we can focus not only on what we already know about a subject, but also on what we wonder. In *One Writer's Beginnings*, Eudora Welty says, "Write what you don't know about what you know."

At a recent workshop, Don Murray said to my colleagues and me, "As writers, we usually have a few topics we return to again and again." Don's list, he told us, included his daughter's death, the war, his writing. Then Murray said, "Jot down the topics you return to again and again."

I listed, "My childhood, the teaching of reading and writing, my sons."

Then Murray said, "When we look at the list, we need to ask not 'What do I know?' but 'What do I wonder? Where's the mystery here?' " And then he said, "Pick one of your topics and write to explore the mystery that is there."

I began exploring whether or not my life as a writer is rooted in my childhood. My memories of writing are not good ones. I wrote dreaded thank-you letters and book reports. How did I grow up to love writing? As I explored this mystery, I realized that as a child I invented worlds under the huge oak tree that leaned out over our creek. When I played in the swamp behind our house, I turned clumps of trees into islands and named each one of them. I was authoring a world. These are the roots of my writing.

My point here is that during content conferences, it's not only the listener who can learn about a subject, but the writer as well. Instead of saying to children, "Tell me what you know," we can say, "Tell me what you wonder." We can ask our students, "What questions do you have about this entry?" "Where's the mystery here, for you?"

Megan reread an entry in which she told about how she accidentally shaved off one of her eyebrows. Her sister offered to help and did so by shaving off the *other* eyebrow. In the margin alongside this entry, Megan wrote, "Why did I always do weird things like this? Am I the only person in my family who does such weird things? When my mother was little, did *she* used to do weird things?"

Megan's wonderings changed her entry from a funny little anecdote into an exploration of what it means to be herself and the ways in which she is like, and unlike, her family.

Design Conferences

Earlier, I described how Sharon interrupted six-year-old Greg as he read his jumbled account of his bus trip to the Patriots game (see Chapter 7).

"It goes hippety-hop from one thing to the next," she said. "It's like you had a crazy dream. It's all mixed up."

In this episode, Sharon is conducting a simple form of a design conference with her classmate. Even very young children can learn to read their writing, or a classmate's writing, and think about the sequence of events. Perhaps the simplest question for a writer to ask is, "Did it really happen this way?" Rereading their writing, writers can realize, "Wait, this is out of order," or "Oh no, I got this mixed up."

It's one thing to recognize that a text "goes hippety-hop" and another to repair the problem, but if we give youngsters staple removers and scissors and encourage them to disassemble the original draft, piecing it back together in a corrected fashion, *most* of them can learn to do it.

Questions of design become slightly more complicated when youngsters have written "all-about books" rather than chronological narratives. Often a first grader, for example, will fill a book with attributes about his or her dog, family, or trip. These books—like the all-about books on distant topics such as the planets or dinosaurs—tend to have predictable structural problems. As Sharon says, "It's like you had a crazy dream. It's all mixed up." Information about what a dinosaur eats will be interspersed before, during, and after information about hunting for fossils. In instances such as this, the question is not "How do I make my text match the sequence of events?" nor is it "Did I tell it like it happened?" In these instances, the sequence of the text isn't determined by sequence but by the writer's mind. The writer must ask, "What do I want to tell about first? Second?"

Very young children can learn that just as they put all their blue beads in one pile and their brown beads in another pile, they can put all the facts about what dinosaurs eat in one pile and the facts about hunting for fossils in another pile. They may need to cut apart the bits of their writing so they can quite literally sort each bit into its proper category, but this isn't tremendously difficult.

In some instances, I find that rather than encouraging children to scissor their draft into bits and then categorize those bits, it works better if they use their early draft to give them ideas for a whole new draft. The young author of a chaotic page about dinosaurs may find it helpful to try writing a whole book on the subject and to begin the book by listing chapters in a table of contents. This way, there can be a chapter titled "Hunting for Fossils" and one titled "What Did Dinosaurs Eat?" This structure encourages youngsters not only to sort out the separate subjects within their writing, but also to say more about each one. If a child who has written a page with one or two lines about each family member is encouraged to write a chapter book, soon the child is engrossed in an entire chapter devoted to Mom and another chapter about Grandma.

It takes a whole different level of maturity for a writer to realize that the boundaries of one's writing aren't determined by the boundaries of one's subject. Time and again, when young writers bring me their drafts, I've asked, "Why did you decide to start your draft this way?" Children look at me as if I've asked the dumbest question imaginable and answer, "Because that's how swimming class [or camp, or my life with Gismo, or the birthday] started!" As writers get older, they come to learn that a story about a great day needn't begin with waking up, nor must it end with going to bed. A story about a trip needn't begin with packing and end with unpacking. Once writers *can* tell an event as it happened, they must learn that they need not follow the sequence of the event, nor do they need to show the whole scene. "Writers are like photographers," Donald Murray reminds us. The photographer doesn't snap a picture while scanning an entire scene. Instead, he selects a single focus. We can help our students do the same thing. Our students need to know that a writer, like a photographer, can pull in very close to a subject or back away from it. When all Monica's entries about coming to America seemed the same, it was partly because she hadn't varied her perspective on the subject.

When I'm trying to help children realize that the design of their writing need not be determined by the design of their subject, I sometimes write on chart paper or on the blackboard in order to show them how I consider a range of options for my writing. For example, I once made a timeline of my day on the chalkboard:

MY MOUNTAIN CLIMB

- Waking up on the day we were going to climb the mountain.
- Having breakfast.
- Driving to the mountain.
- Climbing up it.
- Reaching the top.
- Climbing down.
- Getting home.

"Where do you think I could begin my story?" I asked the class. The response was unanimous: I could begin with waking up. "Anywhere else?" I questioned, and soon the children realized that the piece could begin anywhere, and that if it began with returning home, it might become a flashback.

Sometimes students and I talk together about how they tend to write what I call "A through Z" pieces. I tell them that if they write "M through P" drafts instead, the drafts will probably be much better, because they'll tend to be more detailed and to contain internal as well as external action.

When a child decides to write an "M through P" piece rather than tell "the whole story," that child is learning to focus as a writer. I find that the easiest kind of focus involves selecting a smaller subject. I often describe this kind of focus by likening writers to photographers. In the darkroom the photographer decides that instead of printing the whole negative he will focus on the bird in the left-hand corner, enlarging it. In the writing workshop, writers also select and then enlarge what they select.

It is more difficult, but very important, for writers to learn that their writing can also have a *thematic* focus. For example, although Carmen might try to focus her writing about her grandmother by selecting just one vignette from their life together, in time, she will need to learn that she could also write about several vignettes, all of which illustrate the secret ways her grandmother finds to boost her spirits.

Let me say again that I think we do children a disservice if we teach them that a focused piece of writing necessarily stays with one small incident. If they attempt to stitch together several incidents or to write with a unifying theme, they may struggle and even fail. But, as Faulkner says, "You have to write badly in order to write well." Although he was talking about the need to write terrible rough drafts in order to write good ones, I think we sometimes need to write badly within our lives as writers. Children need to be learners-of-writing more than they need to be producers-of-good-writing.

Another angle on design conferences, one that is also appropriate at all grade levels, centers on the question "What kind of thing are you making?" Let me explain. Often, when we and our students first begin writing, what we do is to gather our material. If we have a notebook, we are apt to collect material handily in the notebook. If we don't have a notebook, we may stitch together a bunch of related stuff into a very loose, shapeless first draft. Either way, once we've recalled our trip or gathered our ideas or relived our experiences, we need to pull back and ask, "What kind of thing will I make out of this?"

In our design conferences we help writers to ask, "Do I want to write a poem, or several poems? A picture book? A letter? A short story? A memoir? Journalism?" Oftentimes, youngsters don't realize that what they have in their notebooks or in their early drafts is like a block of marble; it is material that can be sculpted into many different shapes.

Dori, for example, wrote an entry comparing her cat Gismo with another cat and one about her thoughts as she walked away from the veterinarian's knowing that Gismo was being put to sleep. She also wrote entries in which she used a wide-angle lens to tell general things about Gismo; in one, for example, she wrote about all the ways she loved him, and in another, about why he was the perfect friend. Having written entries with these different designs, Dori now wanted to sculpt a single shape out of her material. It's almost impossible *not* to have a design conference when a writer like Dori wants to create a single piece of writing and has entries about getting her cat Gismo, about loving Gismo, about Gismo's odd antics, about how Gismo compared to her other cat, about Gismo's death, about her quandary over whether to try to replace Gismo.

Whatever decision Dori makes, she'll also need to ask, "How shall I design my picture book . . . my letter . . . my memoir?" Even just the fact that Dori *asks* this question is worth celebrating.

Process Conferences

We teachers of writing are coaches, watching how our students go about writing, giving them pointers and support, nudging them forward. Our coaching, like the coaching that my tennis teacher does, usually follows the format of research, decide, teach. The research phase of a process conference is particularly important.

When we act as coaches, much of our teaching is guided by the fact that we study our students. This is true in teaching tennis, and it is true in teaching writing. We need to understand *how* a student has gone about trying to hit the tennis ball, *how* a student has gone about writing a poem, if we're going to be helpful. If my tennis coach simply watched where my ball (my product) went, calling "Against the net!" or "Out," this would not be helpful. If I am going to improve my game, I need help with the process rather than simply evaluations of the products. So my coach watches *how* I play the game, noticing what works and what does not work for me. "You are stepping away from the ball," she says. "Try stepping into it." In a similar way, the writing teacher asks, "What is this youngster doing that works well? What problems is she encountering? How is she trying to meet those problems?"

If we, as writing teachers, watch how our students go about writing and talk with them about their strategies, we can help them develop more effective strategies for writing. In a process conference we give children the chance to teach us about what they do when they write. "I have heaps and heaps of drafts," Diane tells me, "because every time I start anything I botch it up and have to copy it over. Then I end up botching up the next draft, too, and so it goes." Diane has given me a glimpse of her writing, and by following up on her casual comment I will learn a great deal more. "What do you mean, you botch it up?" I might ask, or "Have you always written heaps of drafts, or is this a new thing for you?"

As a researcher, I often ask children to teach me about their writing processes. I ask questions such as:

- How did you go about writing this? Did you just pick up your pencil and write straight through, or did you stop and think, or did you reread? What made you stop?

- What problems did you run into while you were gathering entries?
- How did you go about choosing the seed idea for your piece? Once you found the seed idea, was it easy to gather entries about it?
- How is your writing process changing?
- I notice you made some cross-outs here. What led you to do that?

In a writing process classroom, it's the students, more than the teacher, who put writing processes into words. Our students describe the strategies they have used, and with our help, they speculate about strategies they might someday use.

Once we understand what our children do as writers, it's not difficult to extend these processes by teaching them a new strategy they can use often. If a child does a lot of sitting in front of a blank page, we'll want to help that child know ways to jump-start his or her writing. If a child keeps writing and writing and writing without ever pausing to reread and to judge what he or she has done, we'll want to teach that youngster ways to shift from being a writer to being a reader, from being a creator to being a critic. If a youngster seems to tape every related entry together into a big, shapeless piece of writing, we may want to teach the youngster how to mine several small, well-shaped pieces from the quarry of entries in that child's notebook.

As I listen to a student describe how he or she has gone about writing, I make a great point of telling that writer what I notice about his or her process, because I know that although it's helpful to give a writer a new strategy, it's even more helpful to make writers conscious of what they tend to do over and over as they write.

In her research on the differences between skilled and unskilled writers, Linda Flower claims that skilled writers approach writing by planning not only what they will say, but also what they will do. These plans allow a writer to set priorities and to organize ways of solving a problem. The writer might say, "I'm not going to worry about being precise right now, I just want to get down the gist of things." Or the writer might say, "I want to be certain each word is right; then I can build up from a strong base. I'm going to spend today just working on the beginning."

Children gain this sort of awareness of the processes of writing—and the accompanying control that comes with awareness—when we tell them what we notice about their ways of approaching writing. They also gain awareness simply by having the chance to articulate what they do when they write. Because they grow to expect that we will ask, "What problems did you run into as you wrote this?" and "What did you do to wrestle with that problem?"

writers begin to rehearse for these questions. They notice and name the problems they encounter, they watch themselves inventing and choosing from among several ways of wrestling with their problems. Then, too, students who talk about and choose their writing strategies can look back on them and reflect on those that did or didn't work. "Was that a wise choice?" the student asks. "Have I done something new as a writer?"

Sometimes our one-to-one conferences with students make us realize that we need to do more whole-class or small-group activities. The following activities help focus attention on the processes of writing:

- Students can conduct surveys to learn how their peers go about writing. They can ask classmates, for example, when they write in their notebooks, how they choose seed ideas to develop, how their entries change once they have a topic, what they do to build a major story from their entries, whether they try different leads, what revisions they do on their drafts.

- For many of us, recent books and articles on the writing process have heightened our awareness of the components of writing. Upper elementary school and junior high children could read these sources. In some classrooms, children have gone so far as to write their own articles.

- One fifth-grade class was studying flow charts in science and decided to make flow charts of how they go about writing. Later, in response groups, the diagrams became a starting place for discussion.

- In *Writing with Power*, Peter Elbow portrays different kinds of writers. Students (and teachers) will see themselves in his portraits. These sections of the book can be read aloud in mini-lessons or used as the basis for discussion in response groups. Children may want to write their own portraits of themselves as writers. If they want to show how their writing strategies have changed over time, they may want to write autobiographies of themselves as writers.

- The class can compile a list of process questions for students to mull over in peer-response groups: What problems do you run into when you were writing? How did you go about solving those problems? How has your writing changed over time? What kind of revision do you usually do?

- It will always be best to *entertain* only one question at a time rather than attempting to rush along, *answering* a list of questions.

Teachers or students might compose aloud while they write on the chalkboard. Later the class can reconstruct what the writer did during writing and reflect on what worked and what did not.

- The teacher can show the class a strategy he or she uses during writing (shaping entries into one genre, then another, and another; taking a key line from an entry and putting it on top of a blank page, then writing and writing and writing off that one entry; reading an entry aloud to hear how it sounds; etc.). Over the rest of the school year, students might take turns sharing strategies that have been particularly helpful to them.

- Class members might have a section of their notebooks set aside for recording how they go about writing and how their processes are changing.

- When they finish a piece of writing, students could be asked to write an entry for their portfolio on a cover sheet in which they ponder what they learned from the writing and what they plan to do differently another time. Alternatively, this could be done once a month, or before an Authors' Day, in which case the students would look back on all the pieces of writing they had done in the recent past.

Any of these activities could be a helpful tool for learning about students' writing processes, but let me caution against using *all* of them. If the activities are to be a forum for thinking about one's writing process, they must become part of the backdrop of the workshop. If they are always changing, always new, they themselves become the focus of attention rather than tools for focusing on something else. I urge teachers to use one or two of these activities often, over and over, rather than attempt to do a little of everything.

Evaluation Conferences

We can also hold evaluation conferences with our students. Earlier, in Chapter 13, I drew a comparison between a writer and a person making a clay rabbit. We shape the rabbit's ears, pull back to look at our creature, then we pull in again to reshape an ear. In a similar way, writers shift between being passionate hot and critic cold, between being a writer and being a reader.

Often, students come to us with their drafts in hand asking, "Is this good?" They write and write and write and then, without so much as a glance back over what they have written, they gather around us to ask, "Am I done?" How important it is, then, for us to refrain from being the child's first evaluator.

"What do you think?" we ask.

"It's okay," the writer will respond, without pausing for a moment to reread the text. Then, not missing a beat, the writer will ask, "Can I edit and copy it over?" or "Can I put it in your box?"

We can predict that children will assume we aren't serious when we ask "What do you think?" We can anticipate that our students don't expect that their assessments matter. If our students are going to become truly critical readers of their writing, we need to show them that we *really mean it* when we ask "What do you think?"

If a child answers in a perfunctory fashion, dismissing our question, we need to take the child by both shoulders, look her in the eye and say, "I mean it. I *really* need to know what you think."

We can give one child a special pen and ask him to reread the draft, starring and marking parts that work especially well, and making X's beside the troublesome sections. What a simple task, and yet what profound discussions ensue.

It is equally simple to suggest that a child lay all the work he or she has done out on the table and to do some research by asking questions, such as:

- What's my best work, less good work, worst work?
- How is my writing changing?
- What new things am I attempting to do?
- What patterns do I see across much of my writing?

In this instance and in other similar instances it will be important to ask only *one* of these questions, and to ask it like it's the biggest in the world. If we race through a list of questions, we belittle them and lead children to rattle off short answers to each.

Assessment conferences can also be called reading-writing conferences. This is true first because writers are ready to become readers, and second because inevitably an assessment conference ends up as a discussion about the kind of texts writers work toward when they write. "It's good because it starts exciting, ends exciting, and the excitement keeps on going," Birger told me. This led to a discussion of how we, as writers, can create intensity when we write. "It's good because it has a surprise ending" can lead to a look at how other authors end their texts.

These categories of conferring (editing conferences are discussed in Chapter 18) aren't intended as scripts to follow, but as lenses for thinking about conferring. It may help, for example, to tape-record one's conferences for a day and then look back, asking, "What kinds of conferring did I do—and not do?" We will want to ask also, "What works well in my conferring?" If we answer carelessly, we'll need to take ourselves by the shoulders, look ourselves in the eye and say, "Really, I mean it. What works well?" In the end, conferring is useful not only when rethinking writing, but also when rethinking our clay rabbits . . . and our teaching.

15

Writing Literature Under the Influence of Literature

We were snowed in that December morning. My husband lingered in bed with coffee, *The New York Times,* and our son, Miles, who pulls close whenever John or I read the newspaper. I worked for a while in my study, then emerged with this edition of *The Art of Teaching Writing* in hand. "It's getting there," I said. John and I took turns holding the manuscript, feeling its weight, stroking its cover page. Miles, pulling against me now instead of his father, asked, "Am I in it?" and then snuggled into the crook of my arm as I read to him. He listened, absolutely motionless, spellbound as I read.

> My son entered nursery school in the middle of the year, so neither he nor I received a proper introduction to the school's rituals. In particular, we didn't realize that Fridays were for show-and-tell. Apparently, on Miles's first Friday, everyone gathered in a circle. One child had a robot, another a dog that walked and barked, another a Spiderman figure. Only Miles was empty-handed. Each child, in turn, sat in a special chair and showed an item to the admiring circle. Miles's turn came. He took his seat in the special chair. The group looked at him expectantly. "Ummm . . ." Miles said slowly, looking out at the circle. Then he fished around in his pocket. With great seriousness, he produced a little yellow thread from his blanket. "I brought this thread," he said, turning ceremoniously so everyone could see it. Then he began rolling the thread on his hand like a miniature snowball. "If you roll it like this and like this," he said, "you can make a love ball." And Miles gave the love ball to Jonathan, who was becoming his friend.

Pages and pages and pages went by, and when I put down the manuscript, Miles was still motionless, still silent. I sat, letting the cadence of my words and the early morning snowflakes settle around me. Miles shifted his weight. I looked down, half expecting him to tell me what he liked, what he wondered, what he wanted me to revise. But no, he was getting up, and then like a bolt he was gone. "Off to his Legos, his brother, his projects," I thought, and smiled to myself, entertained to think that for a moment I'd expected a writing conference from my five-year-old son.

Minutes later, Miles was at the door of our bedroom, paper in hand. "I wrote a poem," he said. On the bed Miles sat straight and tall like a choirboy. He held his poem high, raised his eyes to it, and in an angelic voice, brimming with tenderness, he read his very first poem (Figure 15–1):

> Loving books
> is what's for you.
> The sun
> hits your back
> and hits your book
> and you take a trip
> into your
> memory.

My son's poem was a miracle. I knew that. Everything he'd written until then had been of an entirely different sort. He'd written captions and labels, lists and announcements, letters and posters, but this was literature, and it had emerged *ex nihilo.* A miracle.

Miles knew his poem was a miracle. He read it again to his father and then to his babysitter, his kindergarten teacher, his friend. He read it with

FIGURE 15–1 Miles's poem

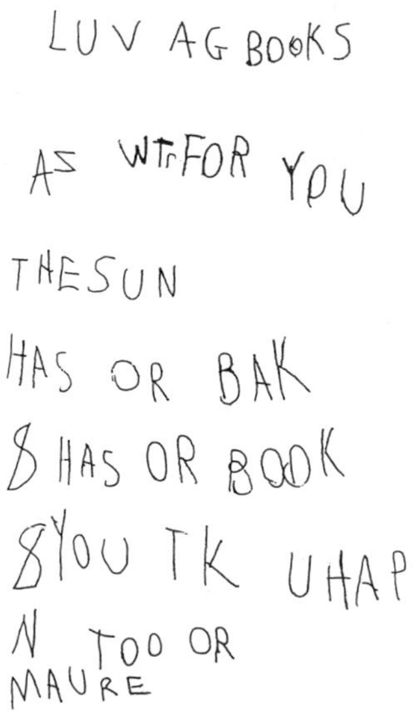
LUV AG BOOKS
AS WTFOR YOU
THESUN
HAS OR BAK
8 HAS OR BOOK
8YOU TK UHAP
N TOO OR
MAURE

a quiet reverence, as if awed that he'd written something so fine. And the poem became even more of a miracle because my son grew into it. "I am one who writes poems," he seemed to say, and then, over the next few days, he recreated himself according to this new image, writing more and more poems (see Figure 15–2).

It is not only through conferring and mini-lessons, coaching and instruction that our children grow as writers. It's also through miracles. We cannot require our children to write beyond their capacity. We cannot assign them to be brilliant and original and deeply true. But we can create conditions in which this will happen, and those conditions were all present on that snowy morning when my son wrote his first poem.

"Loving Books" didn't emerge *ex nihilo* after all. It emerged out of an extraordinary, passionate, intimate moment between a child and a story. On that snowy morning Miles was invited inside literature. He quite literally lived in the pages I read to him. They were about him, about how he made love balls from his blanket, and a Sons of Liberty club from his neighborhood. But isn't aesthetic reading always about finding oneself in the pages of a book? Haven't we all found our friendships and our hopes tucked into those little black words on the page? When Cynthia Rylant was asked how to teach writing to children, she answered, "Read to them. Read them *Ox-Cart Man*, *The Animal Farm*, and *The Birds and the Beasts and the*

FIGURE 15–2   More poems by Miles

Third Thing. Take their breath away. Read with the same feeling in your throat as when you first see the ocean after driving hours and hours to get there. Close the final page of the book with the same reverence you feel when you kiss your sleeping child at night. Be quiet. Don't talk the experience to death. Shut up and let these kids feel and think. Teach your children to be moved and you will be preparing them to move others."

If we are going to design writing workshops in which there are places not only for editing conferences and response groups but also for miracles, we need to bring powerful literature into those classrooms and to do everything possible to invite children to live and write inside that literature.

It begins, I think, with believing that the books we read aloud will change everything in the classroom community. And they do. When our children pull close around a shared text, when we read until our eyes shine with tears and we are silenced in the presence of the deepest parts of our lives, it shakes the ground that we and our students stand on as writers and as people. Realizing this, we begin to choose books differently. "I'm picking different kinds of books. I used to look at the deeper, more layered books, like Paula Fox's and Larry Yep's, and think, 'My kids won't sit still for those,' so I'd go to books that didn't ask so much of us, sillier, shorter books," a teacher recently told my colleague, Shirley McPhillips. "Now I find the richest, most important books, and I say, 'This book is going to really matter. It's gonna be huge.'" The poet Georgia Heard says something similar when she chooses poems for reading aloud.

> I look for poems as varied as trees or flowers or the many different faces on city streets—poems that tell the truth about the world, poems that will move my students. . . . I read poems whose inner life and language will permeate my students' world. I can see it in their faces when they are gathered around us, listening, taking in the cadences and the words, sometimes without even knowing it at first, the way a child hears a lullaby as she drifts into sleep. I read poems that will act as a key to open the doors to their feelings, their imaginations, and their voices. (1989, pp. 3–4)

Georgia reads poems that say to children, "Come out, come out, wherever you are." When I was little and used to play Hide and Go Seek I remember hiding in the raspberry patch and the hayloft, and hearing my older brother's voice ring out with "Come out, come out, wherever you are." Sometimes, in writing workshops, I remember that call. So often children—particularly, I find, suburban children—seem to be hiding. They hide behind conventional clothes and roles and hairstyles and ways of being and life stories. At a local concert I looked up at all the girls in their look-alike clothes and hairstyles and whispered to my husband, "Circle the one that's different."

Sometimes when I'm in the writing workshop in September, I find myself reading through look-alike pieces of writing and I want to call, "Come out, come out, wherever you are." And so I read books that bring us out, as people, to tell the stories of our lives in all their specificity. I read books that say, "Come out, come out, wherever you are."

It's not texts alone that call us out of hiding. It's texts and the white space around them. "Creativity," a writer once said, "requires the illusion of infinite time." It was no accident that Miles wrote his first poem on the day we were all snowed in, while his father lingered over his reading and I, over my writing. The question we as teachers face is, how can we create that lovely snowed-in feeling in a day that looks like one of these?

All days except Wednesday		Wednesday
7:45	Warning Bell	7:45
7:50–7:55	AG	7:50–8:15
8:00–8:42	Period 1	8:20–9:00
8:47–9:29	Period 2	9:05–9:45
9:34–10:16	Period 3	9:50–10:30
10:21–11:03	Period 4	10:35–11:15
11:08–11:50	Period 5	11:20–12:00
11:55–12:37	Period 6	12:05–12:45
12:42–1:24	Period 7	12:50–1:30
1:29–2:11	Period 8	1:35–2:15
2:11–Announcements		

We do it, I think, through ritual and ceremony. In *Life in a Crowded Place,* Ralph Peterson tells of a classroom in which, after the children gather on the story carpet, one child goes to the cupboard and ever so carefully brings forth the Story Candle and sets it in the center of a small table. The candle is lit and the room grows silent. Out of that silence the story begins.

In other classrooms, the sharing of a story begins with the class coming together around a shared incantation. Sometimes the children make quiet fingertaps on the floor while joining in to say a Native American chant:

Spirits above the ground
Spirits below the ground

Spirits gather around
Spirits gather around.

In a first-grade classroom in my hometown, the children and I created a chant by adapting a Gaelic verse from one of Gail Haley's books. Our variation went like this:

I do not mean
I do not mean that what I'm about to say is true
A story, a story
Let it come, let it go.

My colleague Isoke Nia wrote a verse for her students to use as their ritualized invitation to shared books:

Listen, my friends, and listen well
to the story I am about to tell.
Listen, my friends, and take heed
to the story I am about to read.

Other classrooms join together to recite a familiar Silverstein poem as the opening to their reading-aloud times. The poem begins

If you are a dreamer, come in
If you are a dreamer, a wisher, a liar

and ends

Come in
Come in

It will not always be the dancing flame of a candle or a shared chorus that creates the space for a story. Sometimes a tape-recorded song will signal that it's time to gather, as in a fireside circle. Sometimes a child will move among the clusters of children whispering, "Story time." Whatever the ritual, the community will gather, the circle will grow silent, and in that silence we will sometimes say, "Today, in the silence after the story, in the silence *of* the story, let's write."

My colleague Kathy Bearden recently said, "When I read this poem, let's let the words flow over us like a waterfall," and then she read the following poem aloud:

HARRIET TUBMAN
by Eloise Greenfield

Harriet Tubman didn't take no stuff
Wasn't scared of nothing neither

Didn't come in this world to be no slave
And wasn't going to stay one either

"Farewell!" she sang to her friends one night
She was mighty sad to leave 'em
But she ran away that dark, hot night
Ran looking for her freedom

She ran to the woods and she ran through the woods
With the slave catchers right behind her
And she kept on going till she got to the North
Where those mean men couldn't find her

Nineteen times she went back South
To get three hundred others
She ran for her freedom nineteen times
To save Black sisters and brothers

Harriet Tubman didn't take no stuff
Wasn't scared of nothing neither
Didn't come in this world to be no slave
And didn't stay one either

And didn't stay one either

Quietly, Kathy added, "Let's remember the words. Hear them in our minds. Now let's take one word, just one word, that matters to us. Ever so quietly, let's hold that word in our hands, take it to our desks, put it on the page, and write and write and write off that one word."

Doris's one word became a word list that sang out from the page and then an entry. This is what she wrote:

Alone. To be afraid of going on a bus with white in the front and black in the back, to be scared to walk in the street so alone you don't have anything to do but just think about what's next in the world, to see what's going to do in the next days. You can't go out, you're surrounded by white who kill just because of color. You just feel, "what? where? why do they do such a thing?" I mean there's no reason for it. It's so cruel you get tired of it. You can't stand it. You get so tired of it you can faint. Hey, I don't know, I'm just a kid. I really have no idea. That's what I think. Now what do you think?

This is a miracle, one that did not come *ex nihilo* but instead came from an intimate moment between a child and a poem. It came because Kathy didn't let talk about vocabulary words and prior knowledge and prediction, or comments such as "Does everyone have a pencil?" or "Remember, we're going to write SILENTLY" break the spell of the poem.

The miracle also came because Kathy read aloud with the intimacy of a mother reading to her child on a snowy winter's evening. So often, we read aloud with the strained hype that comes from trying frantically to round up the attention of our thirty distracted students. This time, when a child on the fringes of the class began wandering off, Kathy did not sheep-dog that student with her voice, her eyes didn't dart and nip at the wanderer. Instead, she responded to the child's wandering attention by focusing her own attention all the more raptly on the poem. Kathy's intent focus on the poem drew children into it. They listened not *to* but *through* her to the voice of the poem. Eudora Welty describes the voice:

> Ever since I was first read to, then started reading myself, there has never been a line read that I didn't *hear*. As my eyes followed the sentence, a voice was saying it silently to me. It isn't my mother's voice, or the voice of any person I can identify, certainly not my own. It is human, but inward, and it is inwardly that I listen to it. It is to me the voice of the story or the poem itself. The cadence, whatever it is that asks you to believe, the feeling that resides in the printed word, reaches me through the reader-voice. (1984, pp. 12–13)

When youngsters learn to listen through an author's words to the story, they learn a way of listening that is essential to writing. Eudora Welty describes that listening when she speaks of how, ever since she was first read to, "there has never been a line . . . I didn't *hear*. It is to me the voice of the story or the poem itself." She describes this voice, this cadence, as "whatever it is that asks you to believe."

I believe Miles read his poem "Loving Books" in a tender, heartfelt voice because he first wrote it listening to the voice of the poem, listening to "whatever it is that asks you to believe." The poem was utterly unlike anything he'd ever written before, because in order to *write* as well as to *read* his poem, he, at least in a figurative way, sat up tall, like a choirboy, and took on an angelic voice. We needn't take on that particular pose in order to write literature. We can write finger-snapping, foot-stomping prose or penetrating, complex texts. But either way, I think that part of what we learn to do as writers is to position ourselves in relation to the page. Just as skiers adjust their position at the top of a hill, so too, writers set ourselves up for that whoosh of words, that descent into meaning. Sometimes what we do *externally* is to tidy our desk, sharpen our pencils, reread our words. What we do *internally*, I think, is imagine our readers and imagine ourselves to be the kind of person who can ask those readers to believe. Reading matters in a writing workshop because when we let the work of other authors matter to us in significant ways, we can expect our texts to matter as well.

Sophie had been researching the homeless for a while before her teacher, Judy Davis, read aloud from Jonathan Kozol's devastating book, *Rachel and Her Children.* "It changed me," Sophie said. She tried to explain, then paused, then tried again. Finally, Sophie said, "Before, I just wrote anything. I didn't really think about it. But now, when I write, I have to think and think and think and feel depressed and then I can write *serious.* Hearing the reading, sitting there, you remember a homeless person you saw and how his feet were blistered and his hair matted, and then you keep that picture and that discouragement in you, and you write. . . . You feel all those discouraged feelings and then you can write serious."

Because Sophie has recognized and named the effect a book has had on her writing, another time when she sits at her desk yearning to write something important, she may remember that sometimes, by reading a powerful book to ourselves, we position ourselves to "write *serious.*" When Zanve, another fifth grader, wanted to grow a story out of the image of three homeless kittens sitting on her doorstep, she spent a few minutes rereading Paterson's beloved *The Bridge to Terabithia.* Although the book has nothing to do with cats, it nevertheless brought Zanve to a place from which she could write with a new depth. In the midst of her entries about cats, she wrote:

> I can relate to a book called *Bridge to Terabithia.* Jess, the boy in the book, loses his best friend. That is how I am with cats. One minute, they are with you and another, they are gone. And sometimes I feel like I have nobody to talk to. I talk to the kittens just like Jess talked to Leslie. I just love when the kittens are just sometimes asleep. They look so peaceful, like nothing could bother them.
>
> Sometimes I talk to the kittens and I say, "I will reward you for listening to me when nobody else would." Then for their reward, I read to them. I think they like that.

Like Zanve, many of our students will stumble accidentally into writing in miraculous ways. As teachers, our job is to spot those miracles and to be moved by them. The poet William Stafford describes these small miracles as poems and reminds us that in order to find these poems, we "must kneel down and explore for them. They seep into the world all the time and lodge in odd corners almost anywhere, in your talk, in the conversations around you." As teachers, our job is to spot those places where language "lucks into poetry."

> Those lucky places—everyone stumbles upon them; they are homogenized into our lives. And in class I try to recognize what comes at me, not to commend or admire it . . . but simply to feel it myself. The signals I give off when someone says or writes something that lucks into poetry will come naturally—in my eyes, in the way I lean forward, maybe even in my sudden look of envy. (1986, pp. 97–98)

If Zanve has seen her own words matter to a reader, if she's seen her reader lean forward, she can begin to write with the expectation that her words do matter. And this yearning to write in ways that matter can become the life force and direction behind all that our students do as writers.

As I wrote in Chapter 9, David reread his draft and then, in an entry about the draft, he mused,

> I wrote one thing, but then I noticed I didn't feel stupendic about my draft. Any other normal human being could have done what I'd done.

David goes on:

> My thoughts had been something special, and I could not get them anymore. I worked and worked and wrote for a whole hour but nothing happened.

Eventually, when David let his mind wander onto something else entirely, he suddenly had a brainstorm. "Thoughts came zooming into my head like cars on the highway," he said, and he raced off to write.

Angelica, like David, expects her writing to be huge. She listened to her teacher, Judy Davis, reading aloud *The Dakota Dug Out,* and then, in the wake of the story, she began to write. Whereas David looked critically at his writing and thought, "I did not feel stupendic," Angelica reread her writing and thought, "If I write it like this, it will be the dullest thing. Just blah, blah, blah." When David felt his written version didn't do justice to his earlier idea, he turned back inside himself and listened again to his subject. Angelica did the same:

> I kept thinking about the farm and the diner . . . I look at what I am writing about from all angles so I can think of the perfect thing to say, so someone will think, "Oh, wow, this has something *so* beautiful in it!" I keep thinking until there's this feeling I get that tells me it's time to write.

When writers learn to listen for the voice of a story, to look for language with a little luck in it, we approach writing with a different sort of expectation. Instead of expecting ourselves to write silly, short texts, we hold our subject in our hands and say, "This is going to be huge." We expect to layer our writing with the deepest, richest parts of our lives.

"When I think about how to write something," ten-year-old Angelica explained to me, "I don't have the same tone as when I'm on the playground and call, 'Hey, yo, wanna get something to eat?' I have this whole different feel of me. I like to be alone then and I get the intellectual feel of me. I get to be the kind of person who comes up with all these things that are so special. And then, when I'm finished writing, I'm back to my normal self."

Only, of course, she isn't.

16
Publication
The Beginning of the Writerly Life

I remember when my first book, *Lessons from a Child,* was published. I knew approximately when it would be out, and for a month in advance I'd rush home to see if it had arrived. Driving home, I'd construct images of the book. In my mind's eye, I'd retrace the cover photograph and recall the carefully worded dedication. I even bought wrapping paper and mailing envelopes, and day after day, I hurried home.

Then one day the book was there. My husband had opened the box. There were dirty coffee cups on the kitchen table and copies of my book strewn this way and that. I stared. They looked so casual, so small, so insignificant. I took one copy into the living room and, looking at it, began to cry. All those years of work . . . it looked so small.

I think I expected that a truck would arrive at the house and three men would stagger in with The Book. Gazing at my monument, I would feel Authorship. All the years of work would culminate in that moment of publication.

Now, years later, I have learned that publication has little to do with creating a monument and more to do with gaining a new consciousness. Although I touch, look at, and hold *Lessons from a Child* with affection, that book, and the others since, are still relatively inconsequential in my life. It is the experience of writing and of having been published that has changed everything for me. I knew that composing would be a process more than a product, but I thought once the book was published, the process would be over. Publication, by definition, would mean having and holding the product. But I have found that authorship is also a process, and that it has less to do with looking back on a monument than with looking forward with new insight into what I read, finding new layers of meaning in the work of other authors. I have become an insider in reading. My perception of myself has changed, and this affects my entire experience as a reader. I now feel part of the inner circle.

The change is rather like the difference between my first National Council of Teachers of English conference and the ones I now attend. Because I am an insider, everything at the conference now takes on extra significance. Even a disappointing session is worth thinking about (Who spoke? Where is he from? With whom does he work? Who was that fellow up in the front row, the one who kept nodding?) I look for the meaning behind the events. I do the same when I read.

In writing, too, everything takes on extra significance because I am an insider. Why did the author decide to start this way? Where did the information come from? How else could the book have been organized? What an unusual chapter heading! What a difference this powerful image makes in the chapter! I read with admiration, with envy, and above all, with an eagerness to learn from my colleagues.

I also read critically. Because I know, as no one else could, the gaps in my own published books, the compromises I have made, the goals I haven't met, I view the books and journals on my shelves a little differently. They are less imposing to me, they seem less final and complete. Because I know that behind my own books there is an emperor with no clothes on, the books I read have taken on a more human dimension. I can see writers behind the texts, and I can learn vicariously from their successes and struggles.

Lessons from a Child was published when I was thirty-one. It was only then, as an adult, that I began to discover the ways in which being a published author can change how I read.

Noah has just turned five. His legs don't quite reach the floor when he sits on the little red chairs in his kindergarten, and he doesn't sit for long. But Noah has written a ten-page book, with words and a picture on each page.

"Would you read it to me?" his teacher asked. Leaning against her, Noah began to read. He told the story of each picture, and then he decoded the words he'd written underneath it. It was a book about his father's cooking, and Noah was proud. "There," he said, when he came to the last page. "That's all. The end." He closed the book and looked up expectantly.

But the teacher wasn't looking at Noah. Instead she peered down at the book. Centered on the back cover were four letters:

"What's this?" she said. "You forgot to read this page."

"Naw, that's nuthin," Noah answered, and waving his hand, he dismissed the letters.

More curious than ever, his teacher asked again. "What's it say?"

"Oh, it's just sumfin for the library," Noah told her. Pointing to the letters he read:

BP (Big Picturebook)
NM (Noah Mystand)

We can laugh at this story, enjoy it for a moment, and dismiss it. Or we can pause and consider its significance. Noah is only five, yet already he views himself as an insider, as a member of the circle of authors. His teacher has not only helped him develop skills, she has also helped him develop a self-concept as an author. She believes that, rather than simply instructing children in a piecemeal fashion in the components of reading and writing, she must also give them a gestalt, a sense that "I am an author." Because her children perceive themselves as authors, they will make connections with the books they read. They'll notice the way a word is spelled, the use of the table of contents, the presence of exclamation points. For these five-year-olds as for me, reading provides an opportunity to learn from other authors.

Some kindergarten children will notice the dedications in their reading books and soon their teacher—and the class pet—will have many books written in his or her honor. Other children will notice page numbers, chapter titles, or "about the author" blurbs on the back cover of books.

Recently, several of us watched Noah as he worked on a scary Halloween book. Every time he finished a page, Noah flipped to the back of the book and jotted something onto it. "What are you doing?" we asked, and then Noah showed us what he had written:

gosts   p. 1
wiches   p. 1
owls   p. 2
skeletn   p. 4

He was making an index for his own book to match the one in the back of his reading book.

Audrey entitled her story "The Three Pigs." It was a curious title because this story had nothing to do with pigs. "How did you happen to name this?" I asked her.

"It's like a book I read," she answered.

Mystified, I pressed further. "What book is it like?"

"*The Three Pigs,*" Audrey said. The scorn in her voice insinuated that I'd just asked a very silly question. I still didn't see the connection, and so I pressed further, asking how her story was like *The Three Pigs*. "Simple," she answered. "They begin the same and they end the same." Indeed they did. They both began "Once upon a time" and they both ended "They lived happily ever after."

In a crowded kindergarten in Brooklyn, Kendra took her turn, sitting in the author's chair with her friends gathered around her. She read her story (see Figure 16–1):

> THE CIRCUS
> *by Kendra*
>
> This is a circus.
> The man is training the lion.
> The man said to the lion,
> "You roar."
> He did.

FIGURE 16–1   "The Circus" by Kendra

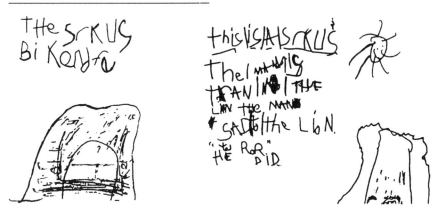

When Kendra finished reading, Brad's hand was already up. "Why is the man training the lion?" he asked.

"Because he's gonna work at the zoo. This is a zoo lion."

"So why do you have to train the lion?" Brad wondered.

"So, 'cause, children will pet him and he has to be trained," Kendra answered, and then she called on Rachel.

"How come you call your book '*The Circus*' if it is gonna be about the zoo?" The teacher and I exchanged glances, amazed that even these five-year-olds were wrestling with the issue of the main idea. But Kendra was not stumped by the question. "I'm writing *another* book about the zoo. I'm taking the lion to the zoo in another book."

Harry wasn't pleased with her answer. "No, that's no fair. You can't have two books about the same people and the same animals." For a moment Kendra looked troubled.

Then Hanif got an idea. "Hey, wait. What about Curious George? *Curious George Goes to the Hospital, Curious George Gets a Medal.* That's two books and the same monkey."

Rachel agreed. "My sister reads lots of books and Laura is in every one. Laura and Pa and Mary." Because these children view themselves as authors, they notice and learn from the choices made by the authors of the books they read.

When Students Are Published Authors, They Make Reading-Writing Connections

As I mentioned earlier, when I work with teachers at our summer institutes on the teaching of writing, we often begin by reflecting on our own histories as readers and writers. "Let's take a few minutes," I suggest, "and make a timeline of our writing lives."

The room is silent, filled only with the scratch of pencils. Then I say, "Let's look back on our timelines for a moment, asking, 'What were the turning points for me as a writer?'"

Time and again, people say that for them, the turning points were the times they were published. Even our most famous literary figures remember, in vivid detail, what it first felt like to have their words read aloud, to see their texts in print. In *Growing Up,* Russell Baker describes what it means to see his words moving an audience:

"Now boys," he [Mr. Feagle] said, "I want to read you an essay. This is titled 'The Art of Eating Spaghetti.' "

And he started to read. My words! He was reading my words out loud to the entire class. . . . Then somebody laughed, then the entire class was laughing, and not in contempt and ridicule, but with open-hearted enjoyment. Even Mr. Feagle stopped two or three times to repress a small prim smile.

I did my best to avoid showing pleasure, but what I was feeling was pure ecstasy at this startling demonstration that my words had the power to make people laugh. . . . I had discovered a calling. It was the happiest moment of my entire school career. (1982, p. 239)

Mem Fox recalls the day her publishers personally delivered to her the first copy of *Possum Magic:* "I stroked it as if it were made of silk. This beautiful book was mine! I hugged it. I was a writer" (1990, p. 107).

For Mem Fox, Russell Baker, and me, the moment of publication made each of us feel like insiders in the world of authorship. What an important lesson this is for those of us who work with young people! Publication matters, and it matters because it inducts us into the writerly life. Publication, then, is the *beginning,* not the *culmination* of the writing process. Publication does not mean that the process is over, that children can now gaze at their monuments. Instead, publication inducts us as insiders into the world of authorship.

When Publication Happens Early and Predictably, We Tap Its Teaching Power

All too often in our classrooms, publication happens once, in the final months of the school year, in the form of a districtwide or statewide Young Authors' Celebration. There is nothing wrong with a Young Authors' Conference. In fact, occasions such as these become crucial parts of our memory maps, turning points on the timelines of our literary histories. But what a waste it is to postpone authors' celebrations until the end of the year, when it's too late to use the momentum these occasions create. "As soon as your workshop is under way," I often tell teachers, "it is time to help children view themselves as authors. Publish the pieces, put out bookbinding supplies, celebrate their finished work . . . and do it by mid-October."

"But the papers aren't any good yet," teachers protest. "They haven't done any revisions, their pieces are short and general and voiceless. Shouldn't we wait until they produce some reasonably good work?"

I don't think so. The first step toward improving our student's earliest efforts is, I believe, to attend to them. The first way to improve their initial skills is to give students a sense of authorship. I like Authors' Days best if they are scheduled not only frequently but predictably. Many teachers find it helpful to set aside, say, the first Wednesday of every month (for young children) or of every other month (for older children) for such a celebration. Some teachers make the day special by bringing in juice and fruit, or by having children meet in small sharing groups. A ritual I particularly like—one I use often when working with adults—is to have each writer read a short piece of his or her writing aloud. After each reading, there is a moment of silence while listeners jot down their responses on index cards. These are later given to the author. (I recently mentioned this strategy at a conference, cautioning that it would only work in the upper grades. Two weeks later a kindergarten teacher proved me wrong!) My brother used to have a quote on his bulletin board: "I can live two months on a good compliment," so I recommend doing this at least every two months.

Just as the ending of one semester and the beginning of another always provided my stepdaughter Kira with a chance to clean her looseleaf notebook, buy new spirals, and make new resolutions, so too, these Authors' Days can become part of the rhythm of a writing classroom. In preparation for Authors' Day, children complete whatever pieces they are working on, and make sure that their rough drafts are stapled with their final copies and that their work is filed into either cumulative folders or portfolios or else taken home. Authors' Days provide a deadline, an impetus to finish dangling pieces, a chance for students to look back over what they have done and learn from it before they move on. Students may perhaps spend some time ranking their pieces from best to worst and talking about their progress during the interval since the last Authors' Day (this, of course, is revision: looking back in order to look forward). But Authors' Days also provide a chance for new beginnings, for a fresh start with a new resolve.

What actually occurs on these Authors' Days is probably less important than the fact that they occur at all. In one third-grade room, children go into the hallway for Publishing Conferences. Each time, the ritual is the same. The author lays all his or her work out on the floor and says to the partner, "Guess which one I'm going to publish!" Then the friend must read *all* the pieces trying to second-guess the author's decision. "Wrong!" the author announced with great glee on the day I observed, and then proceeded to explain why he'd chosen a piece called "Lice, Fleas, Roaches and Flies."

One of my colleagues, Georgia Heard, often publishes children's final drafts by simply folding a piece of brightly colored binding tape around the outer edges of the page. The result is an eloquent frame—yet the process is so simple! The children love this ritual, and it works within their classroom. Ideally, however, our methods of publication should be as authentic as possible. Ideally, texts should be published in ways that match the author's intentions.

As Frank Smith has said, "Writing is for stories to be read, books to be published, poems to be recited, plays to be acted, cartoons to be labeled, instructions to be followed, designs to be made, recipes to be cooked, diaries to be collected. . . . Writing is for ideas, action, interaction, and experience" (1986, p. 179).

If we and our students write poems, we can learn these poems by heart, perform them as choral readings, set them to music on audiotape, give them as birthday gifts, read them aloud as toasts. We can celebrate winter's first snowfall by gathering before the classroom windows and doing an eloquent but totally informal reading of our own poems and some by other authors.

If our children write memoirs, we can read several memoirs as a text-set within our literature study groups, we can shelve them in the library alongside Mem Fox's *Mem's the Word* and Gary Paulsen's *Woodsong*. We can gather them in a single anthology, use them as examples in introducing another class of children to the genre, present a formal reading in the school auditorium, or gather our memoirs into a single published anthology. Our children will regard themselves in a dramatically new light if they are published authors. Because publication can provide such perspective and tap such energy, I believe it must be one of the first priorities in our classrooms.

Putting Publication into the Hands of Young Authors

Fifteen years ago, when I first learned about teaching writing, I think I assumed that teachers of writing spent hours and hours of their time at home "publishing" student drafts. I talked about the teacher of writing as a "two-bag teacher," because I, for one, lugged bags and bags full of student writing home and often spent my evenings selecting which of a child's many texts would be published. Then I spent yet more time typing these texts into little books with cardboard covers and call numbers or, when my students were adolescents, into literary magazines and anthologies. I've come to believe, however, that it is better to put publication in its place—that is, into the hands of youngsters as they write. Young writers need to ask themselves, "Who will my readers be? What shall I make of this?" Writers need to imagine the form their texts will take, and most of all, writers need to imagine readers, perhaps opening their books as picture books and turning the pages, perhaps hearing the words as a toast at a family gathering.

The writer needs to see these possibilities for publication early and then write toward these possibilities. When children begin to gather their entries around a seed idea, surely they'll want to be asking, "What might I make of this?" They will need to write their drafts with an internalized audience in mind. In *If You Want to Write*, Brenda Ueland talks about the importance of this internalized audience:

> Once I was playing the piano and a musician, overhearing it, said to me: "It isn't *going* anywhere. You must always play to someone—it may be to the river, or God, or to someone who is dead, or to someone in the room, but it must go somewhere."
> This is why it helps, often, to have an imaginary listener when you are writing, telling a story, so that you will be interesting and convincing throughout. . . . A listener helps to shape and create the story. Say that you are telling a story to children. You instinctively tell it, change it, adapt it, cut it, expand it, all under their large, listening eyes, so that they will be arrested and held by it throughout. (1938, pp. 163–64)

Although we'll want to put publication into the hands of young writers, this doesn't mean that we don't have a big role in helping our children regard themselves as insiders in the world of authorship. We will probably not want to devote most of our evenings to typing our students' texts, but we *will* need to plan for our students' publications. We'll need to supply our writing centers with binding tape, cardboard, wallpaper, and directions for bookbinding (and perhaps, with parent volunteers or older children to act as bookbinding mentors). We'll want to bring tape recorders and audiotapes into our classrooms along with poster paper and calligraphy pens. We'll want to bring in lots and lots of examples of what children might write: brochures, guides to the school, photo essays, field guides of wildlife, calendars with poems and paintings for each month and quotes to live by, audiotapes full of favorite poems, anthologies of rainy-day stories and poems. . . .

We'll want to weave talk of publication into many of our mini-lessons and conferences. As Becka gathers entries about the deer she sees in the early mornings, we'll want to ask, "What might you make of this?" We'll want to tell her we could imagine it as a photo essay or a collection of poems or a picture book. What does *she* imagine? We'll want to show her published texts that remind us of what she has done.

We'll also want to demonstrate, day in and day out, that we regard our children as authors. Just as I will never forget the silent, hidden thrill I felt when I was apprenticing with Don Murray and he said, in an aside to me, "Writers like you . . . ," so, too, our youngsters will not forget it when we call them together by saying, "Authors, can we meet. . . ." And if we say to a particular child, "Your writing reminds me of Cynthia Rylant's," or "You may want to read this book; it reminds me of the book you are writing." These words are so easy to say, and oh, the difference they must make to those who hear them!

We say these things through our actions as well as through our words. What a message we convey, for example, when during read-aloud times, we read aloud not only the work of grown-up authors, but also that of youngsters. Don Graves tells a story about Ellen Blackburn Karelitz. Her children wrote eagerly, published their stories, and frequently read them to each other. They called themselves authors. Yet when they were asked, "Which of these books does your teacher like best?" and shown three kinds of books—a work of literature, a basal reader, and their own writing—the youngsters all said their teacher liked the literature best, then the basal, then their writing. "What makes you say this?" Graves asked, puzzled by their answer. "When we have reading time on the rug, she reads *this* the most, and this the next most," they told him, pointing to the literature and then to the basal. Because Ellen did not, at the time, read the children's stories during reading time, they had decided that their own writing wasn't as valuable to their teacher.

Ellen now reads two kinds of books during her literature sharing time—one written by an author from the class and one by an adult author. In her classroom, as in many others, the writer sits in the author's chair during share meetings. In many classrooms, bulletin boards feature an "Author of the Week," with one child's photograph and a collection of his or her work. Visiting authors from upper-grade classrooms are sometimes interviewed by younger children (and vice versa). During silent reading time, children are encouraged to read each other's work as well as the work of more well-known writers. In these and other ways, we help youngsters view themselves as authors.

17
Apprenticeships in the Writing Workshop
Learning from Authors

When I think about reading-writing connections in the writing workshop, I think about five-year-old Noah writing call numbers on the back of his homemade book. I think of Kendra, deciding that if Curious George can reappear in a whole sequence of H. A. Rey's books, then her lion can reappear in her books as well. I think of children who take their cue from beautiful printed books and entwine vines and leaves around the first letters of their stories. I think of the youngsters who love knowing that author Joy Cowley lives in such a remote section of New Zealand that her ice cream is delivered by helicopter. I think of classroom libraries filled with displays of books by and about a favorite author. I think of the correspondence and classroom visits the children I know have received from Naomi Nye, Walter Dean Myers, Vera Williams, and so many others. I think of all this, and I feel like basking in the abundant connections children the world over are making with authors.

Those connections are happening because teachers are falling in love with children's literature. Some people collect baseball cards, comics, stamps, or coins, but those of us who teach, it seems, all become collectors of children's books. We collect author anecdotes and autographs, book posters, book bags . . . but above all, we collect books. How we love those books—the satiny feel of their covers, the glorious pictures, the words that make us want to break into song, into dance, into prayer. We love knowing our favorite author has a new book coming out; we wait and wait and then, yes, the book is out, and we have it. We read it to friends, to colleagues, to spouses, and then, finally, we're in school and our children can gather near and hear the long-awaited book.

It's no surprise that our love for books and authors is a contagious one. Soon our students refer to authors as if they belong to the classroom. Little children write authors: "You are our class mascot" and "You are our class pet." Students make murals and bookmarks and book jackets celebrating their favorite authors. They pester their parents for books, deluge beloved authors with fan mail, and flock to book signings.

The important thing, of course, is not the murals or the mail, but the love that inspires them. Dawn Harris Martime demonstrates that love when she washes her hands before opening a book to read aloud to her students. "Whenever she goes to the sink, we know what's coming!" her children tell us, and they know not only that a book is coming, but also that it is treasured. Kathy Doyle demonstrates her love for books when she lights a candle before reading aloud. Lydia Bellino demonstrates that love when her friend copies a poem for her in beautiful calligraphy, and she frames it and hangs it beside her office door. How important it is that we love literature, and that we love it so much we cannot possibly keep this love to ourselves.

When we, as writers, reread our writing, we often ask ourselves, "What's good that I can build upon?" Similarly, when we, as teachers, reconsider our writing workshops, we also need to ask ourselves, "What's good that I can build upon?" For many of us, the role literature plays in our writing workshop is one that deserves to be celebrated—and extended. In this chapter I want to discuss some of the ways in which good books can play an even stronger role in improving the quality of our writing workshops. If we are going to nurture reading-writing connections in our classrooms, we need to:

- Invite students to know a book or an author so well that the book or author stands a chance of affecting even their writing.
- Help students match their writing and their reading.
- Pay attention to the reading-writing connections our students are already making.
- Help students realize that the effects of literature are achieved because of an author's deliberate craftsmanship.

Knowing a Book or Author So Well That It Stands a Chance of Affecting Our Writing

Several years ago, my husband brought me to Colorado for the first time. We were driving through a mountain pass, with snow-capped peaks and blue, blue sky on all sides of us. "How do you like it?" he asked.

"It's *so beautiful,*" I answered. "It's like a postcard, a calendar."

Then, suddenly, for no accountable reason, we were stopping. John got out of the car. Befuddled, I wondered, "What's going on?"

"Let's go," John said, and began walking out onto the rocky plain that stretched before us. He didn't explain, he didn't wait, he just walked off.

I made my way after him thinking, "This is crazy." There was no mountaintop near, no meadow with wildflowers and cascading steams, just a flat stretch of rocky rubble. I walked and walked. Sitting down on a little boulder, I saw goat droppings, then a tiny Alpine flower. The sky was everywhere, a giant dome. The air, cold and wet, rose up from below. The world stretched out before me, a rolling sea of clouds and mountain peaks, on and on and on. I felt so small, like a little blip on the mountainside, with a giant forever sky on all sides of me.

So often, we look out at books the way I looked out at that mountaintop world. How badly we need someone to stop the car and say, "Let's go." Let's get out into the story. Let's read aloud, let's act out parts, let's set the story to music, let's perform, let's make believe . . . let's live our way into the story world. "If you love a poem," John Ciardi has said, "you never have to study it. You live your way into it."

Reading-writing connections begin when we help our children fall in love with a single poem, a book, an essay. This is a radical statement. I used to believe that I sponsored reading-writing connections when I selected an author such as Steven Kellogg to be Author of the Month and filled the chalkboard tray with his books, the bulletin board with photographs of him and jackets from his books, and mini-lessons and read-aloud times with anecdotes about his two Great Danes and his home in Sandy Hook, Connecticut.

I've come to believe, however, that when I conducted elaborate author studies, immersing my students in a sea of trivial details about my favorite authors, I was probably learning more than were my children. I was the one who had all the fun of choosing a favorite author, of beginning to make a collection of that author's work, of digging up information on the author. How much better it would have been had I invited each of my students to find a book that mattered enormously to him or her, and then to search for a second book by the same author, and finally, to put those two books together, asking, "What does this author tend to do?" and "Can I borrow any of these techniques in my own writing?"

This work needn't be done independently, with each child pursuing a favorite author. In every class of children there will be texts that end up touching the entire class. We can (and probably will) be matchmakers, reading aloud texts we've already chosen as our favorites in the hopes that children will fall in love as well. But reading-writing connections begin when sparks fly between a text and a reader, and for this reason it's hard for us to plan those connections.

Love works in mysterious ways. We need to watch for the sparks to fly and encourage them. As we read books and poems and articles aloud to our classes, we'll watch for the texts that have the potential to become touchstone texts. When we feel our children responding deeply to a text, we stand a chance of sponsoring connections between that text and our children's writing.

Although I used to select excerpts from books I love, using these to demonstrate particular qualities of writing I hoped my students would strive toward, now I wait and watch for their responses to books. If my children react with responsive laughter and enormous empathy to the section of Lois Lowry's *Autumn Street* (1980) in which she describes the warm, waxy taste of school milk, then (and only then) will I ask, "What did the author do to affect us this way? How has she made us feel so strongly about such a little thing as school milk?" Together we'd then reread and discuss the passage:

> "Why won't you drink your milk at school? You always drink it at home," my mother said.
>
> "It tastes different. I don't like it."
>
> She sighed and wrote a note back requesting that I not have to drink school milk. It was true that it tasted different. The paper container, the straw that collapsed and grew soggy, and the wax that peeled in flakes from the carton all conspired to give a strange papery taste to the warmish milk they placed in front of us at the little kindergarten tables. Even listening to the gurgling sounds that the other children made through their straws as they emptied the containers brought a feeling of gagging to the back of my throat. It was the milk at the very bottom that tasted the worst. By then it was mixed with spit. (pp. 10–11)

Often, before we talk about a book that affects us, I find ways to help students inhabit the book. Sometimes I simply suggest to the children that we each find the word or line that matters most to us. Then we gather in a circle for an eloquent ceremony. We sit silently until one person, speaking into the silence, reads his or her best-loved line aloud as if it were the most precious thing in the world. Then there is silence. No one breaks the silence with commentary, cajoling, wisecracks, discussion, apologies. Another person reads, then another, until from all sides of the circle, the text has been recreated. (I describe this ritual, which I call "reading into the circle," in more detail in Chapter 20.)

Often, instead, we cluster into tiny circles of performers and spend just a few minutes choreographing and then performing readers' theater renditions of a favorite passage. Sometimes, as an alternative, we each take the text home (in our hands or in our hearts) and invent our own ways to speak back to the text. The next day there is a ceremony in which each child rereads a section of the text and then performs or presents his or her response. For one child, the response may be a painting; for another, a poem; for another, a list of "I wonder" questions; for another, a letter to the author or a book review.

Sometimes we live our way into a book by having the book quite literally live in our classroom. Kathy Mason's first and second graders were touched by Byrd Baylor's *I'm in Charge of Celebrations*, particularly by the image of Baylor gazing up at the green clouds overhead. The children decided to fill the upper rim of their classroom with green clouds, and in the clouds, to put the miracles of their lives. Baylor has a calendar in which she commemorates special days—like the day she saw a green cloud—and Kathy Mason's children have a similar calendar, on which their own days for celebration are circled. Another class of children was so affected by Bill Martin, Jr.'s *Knots on a Counting Rope* that they now have their own counting rope, and they, too, add a knot each time a story is retold. Yet another class borrowed an idea from Charlotte, the spider in E. B. White's *Charlotte's Web*. Over their classroom door they have a spider web, and on it there are the words "SOME CLASS."

Whatever else we do with a touchstone book, we will most certainly reread it. When he was asked "How do you learn to write?" Hemingway answered, "Read *Anna Karenina*, read *Anna Karenina*, read *Anna Karenina*." It's a good answer. Only when we read and reread a dearly loved poem or story can the text affect us so much that it affects even our writing. Very young children and their teachers already know the value of rereading. In first grade, we're glad when children plead for us to read Margaret Wise Brown's *Goodnight Moon* or *The Important Book* again and again, until we all know these books by heart. But we are often less pleased when older students want to read beloved texts over and over. "You've read that already," we say, as if the youngster who returns to a familiar book is somehow cheating. What a mistake we're making! It's the books we've read and reread, savored and shared, that will affect us as writers. Of course, rereading doesn't always mean that we return to page one and progress page by page through the entire book, as if we'd never encountered it before. Instead, my friend Adrian Peetom suggests we reread a book as we revisit a park, hurrying to our favorite sections, spending time in those special spots. In our classrooms, we need to help students learn the power of rereading the books that might become touchstone texts.

When we find a text that has the potential to be a touchstone for a writing community, we need to keep that text beside the chair where we read other books aloud, so that we can refer back to it often as we continue on to new texts. Young writers need to keep copies of touchstone texts (or at least, of favorite sections) on their desks as well, so that when Eric wonders how to begin his memoir, he can reread the chapter leads in MacLachlan's *Journey*, and when Nate wonders how to describe his grandfather's farm, he can reread *Journey*'s descriptive passage. As teachers, we also need to carry a touchstone text with us as we move around the workshop conferring with young writers.

In my early staff development workshops on the reading-writing connection, I used to tell teachers that William Steig's books could help youngsters select words in playful, bold ways, that Bernard Waber's books could show youngsters the ways dialogue can reveal characters, that Emily Arnold McCully's books could demonstrate how to turn a life episode into a human drama, that Ted Hughes's books could show how the sounds of language can create effects. But I've come to believe that we needn't try to find the particular book that can best teach our students about this or that. Any single wonderful text can teach students about dialogue, language, drama, detail, and everything else there is to learn from literature.

This has a lot of practical advantages. It means that instead of bringing one text to a mini-lesson on metaphor and another to a mini-lesson on details, we can return over and over to books we have already experienced. If one text can be used as an exemplar of many qualities of good writing, we can take the time to read it together for all the wondrous ways in which it affects us, and only then return to it in order to examine the ways in which it embodies particular qualities of writing. What is most important is that we and our students be moved by a book. Only then do we return to the book to ask, "What did the author do to affect me in these ways?" If *Owl Moon* is a familiar book to our class, we might look at its lead sentence and those of several other touchstone books during a single mini-lesson. We won't be disembodying those leads or tearing them from their contexts, because if these are touchstone books, members of our classroom community will already know the book. As we discuss the lead, we will be able to talk about how it fits with the whole of the book. Another day, we may notice metaphor, or description, or the sounds of words, or dramatic scenes, or treatment of chronological time. As we return to the book again and again, we find ourselves understanding the author's message more deeply, the author's craft more completely.

Helping Students Match Their Writing and Their Reading

Often I find that among all the grade levels in a school, it's the kindergartners and first graders who make the most reading-writing connections. It's probably not an accident that almost all the anecdotes I've told about reading-writing connections happened in the primary grades. Little children believe they are pilots, doctors, kings, and queens . . . and we can easily help them believe they are writers as well.

How sad it is that when children grow up in our schools, they stop believing they are writing books and anthologies of poems and newspaper articles and begin to regard their efforts as school assignments. "I'm writing a composition for the teacher," they tell us. By the time students are in fifth grade, all too often they write with school headings and margins rather than with about-the-author pages and dedications.

I'm not surprised that fifth graders do not believe they are writing literature. In fact, it's hard to imagine trying to convince them that when they write their little stories, they are doing the same thing Wilson Rawls did when he wrote *Where the Red Fern Grows*, or Roald Dahl did when he wrote *Charlie and the Chocolate Factory*. Because there is often a world of difference between what fifth graders read and what they write, it's even more of a challenge to figure out how we can help them make reading-writing connections.

I'm not surprised that when our fourth graders write page-long personal narratives, stories, and reports and when they read book-length novels, they don't make a lot of connections between them. For first graders the gaps between what they write and what they read are more easily bridged. These youngsters often read simple, predictable books, stories with captions underneath the pictures, rhymes and recipes and signs. If they are encouraged to write in a range of genres, these are the genres in which they write. Is it any surprise, then, that it's very young children who tend to regard themselves as authors?

Imagine how different the possibilities for reading-writing connections would be if fourth graders were reading, studying, *and* writing alphabet books or about-the-author blurbs, poems, or Big Books for children. Imagine how different the landscape for reading-writing connections would be if eighth graders were reading and studying sports journalism, science fiction, or short-short stories and writing in a matching genre.

In Section IV I suggest that our students spend major chunks of the year immersed in whole-class "genre studies." In Chapter 23, for example, I suggest ways of immersing a classroom community in reading and writing poetry. In Chapter 24 I describe a genre study in memoir and in Chapter 25, literary nonfiction. In genre studies such as these, teachers may suggest that during independent reading time everyone select their reading from a shelf full of memoirs (or poetry or short stories). If the reading program involves reading shared books and meeting in response groups to discuss them, teachers can fill their bookshelves with multiple copies of books from within the genres. Sometimes each writer will pursue his or her own individual genre study, and in these instances, the writers will have to find the books that can be used as examples, the authors who can become mentors, for themselves.

Morat is an avid mystery reader, so his teacher, Rose Napoli, wisely encouraged him to try his hand at writing mysteries. After he'd written a page of his story, Morat explained to me that he was including "fake clues." He said, "I want to fool the readers, to give them the wrong ideas so the ending is a surprise." He added, "In the book I'm reading, that's what the guy did." Morat also decided not to put much description into his story because he figured the kids would skip it or get bored, just as he does with similar passages in his reading book. Once Morat looked up from his reading and said, "I'm better at titles than this author is. It is pretty stupid how he calls this book *Mystery of the Silent Friends* when they talk all the time."

Morat is able to apprentice himself to the author of *Mystery of the Silent Friends* not only because both he and his mentor are working within similar genres, but also and more primarily, because Morat believes that he is a writer of literature. In order for Morat to deliberately adopt the strategies he sees his mentor using, Morat first needs to know that he, like his mentor, is crafting a piece of real literature that will be read by real readers. When Morat moved from gathering entries toward crafting a mystery, one of his teacher's goals in her conferring was to help Morat imagine the literature he would be making. She did this by asking as she reread his collection of entries, "What do you think this will end up being? A short story? A play? A letter?" She helped Morat see himself as a writer of literature also by talking with him about his readers. "What do you want your readers to feel when they read this? How are you hoping to affect them?" Then, too, she nudged Morat to find texts that could act as models for him as he wrote. "What books have you read that are sort of similar to what you want to write?" she asked, and it was this that led Morat to make connections between his draft and *Mystery of the Silent Friends*.

It's entirely possible for us to ask all our children to keep books on their desks that represent "the kind of thing" they hope they will write. But having these books on their desks doesn't ensure that they will think about them as they craft their own texts. Oftentimes, unless we intervene, the reading-writing connections children make are only superficial ones. It is not accidental that when I listed examples of the wonderful ways in which young authors are modeling themselves after older authors, most of them revolved around the *trappings* of literature. Young children see that a beloved author's book has a foreword, a dedication page, an about-the-author section, or vines growing out of the O in "Once upon a time," and soon the child's work has the same. These reading-writing connections are not to be dismissed as trivial, for they demonstrate the writer's commitment "to writing like professional authors," and they are the youngster's way of saying to the world, "I am making literature." But clearly, our goal is to deepen these reading-writing connections.

In our conferences, we can encourage students to use books as resources for their writing problems. If a student can't seem to get started on a draft, we can suggest she read books that make her want to tell a story. If a student struggles over how to write transitions between one of her vignettes and another, we can suggest she examine how authors have handled similar transitions. If the student isn't sure of how to write a title, an ending, a lead, help on each of these is at hand.

Supporting Reading-Writing Connections by Paying Attention to Them

We can also support reading-writing connections by asking youngsters to pay attention to them in response groups and peer conferences. "Today, in your response groups, let's bring the books that are functioning as models for us," we can say. "When we struggle over our writing, let's ask each other, 'How would the author of your chosen book have written that?' " When the class gathers for a share session, rather than just listening to each other's drafts we might listen to each other's discussions about writing. These might be organized around the theme of reading-writing connections, and youngsters could bring not only their writing but also the texts that have informed their writing to the share session. Similarly, children could compile a class book about reading-writing connections in which they record the connections they make. The book would be valuable as they add to it and as they read and discuss it (even years later). They could reread their predecessors' records in order to categorize different kinds of reading-writing connections. Children may also decide to include the anecdotes they hear about how, for example, Charlotte Zolotow attributes much of what she knows as a writer to a single book, *The Secret Garden.*

If we want to encourage our children to model their own writing after the literature they love, we can also suggest that they add a marginal code—perhaps a small picture of a book—to their drafts whenever they find themselves standing on the shoulders of a great book. These codes will be useful as we interview young writers to learn about these connections in more detail, or as children share these connections during share meetings, mini-lessons, conferences, and response groups.

Author celebrations, too, can be organized around a theme such as reading-writing connections. We might suggest that youngsters draw from all the writing they've done in order to select a draft to which another author made important contributions. The children might bring the text they read as well as the one they wrote to this celebration and put into words the ways the one affected the other. If younger children were invited to such an occasion, what a lesson this would be for them!

The Effects of Literature Are Achieved by Deliberate Craftsmanship

Recently my research focus has shifted from writing to reading. Last year, when Kathy Doyle and I decided to explore together some new ideas on the teaching of reading, we put the writing workshop on the back burner for a few months in order to give reading and theme studies as much time and attention as possible. Kathy's fifth graders met in response groups, and we studied their talk about books.

They gossiped about the characters: "If Dicey ends up going to the hospital, I don't know *what* will happen," they'd say. They exclaimed over the characters' actions: "I don't know *how* she could do that!" They worried and watched over the characters as if they were real. It was wonderful book talk; it felt as if these readers truly lived in the worlds of the books they read, as if they inhabited those worlds. "I'm *so mad* at him," they'd say. "He'd better stop doing that."

As we studied these book talks, we discovered a curious thing: almost every comment Kathy's students made was something they might have said as they chatted together on the phone in the evening about the social system in their school. I began to realize that although there were a lot of reasons to celebrate how these children had become immersed in the world of their books, something was also missing from this book talk.

No child ever said, "Do you think Voight might make Dicey go to the hospital? Why would she do this?" It was as if the children in Kathy's room assumed that the characters—Dicey and her siblings—were truly alive. It was as if, in their book talk, no one took into account the fact that the story was written by an author in order to achieve an effect on readers. And if no one saw the book as an artifact, as different from reality, an entire level of discussion was out of the question. Kathy and I began to realize that we would never be able to study a wonderful reading workshop if that workshop didn't exist alongside an equally wonderful writing workshop.

Once the writing workshop was well under way, the book talk in Kathy's class changed. Soon many of the children, particularly the boys, were talking about the authors' intentions and techniques: "Why did he make the story jump around in time like this?" they'd ask. "Why did he end the book *here?*"

Unless children are conscious of an author's technique when they read, it is hard to imagine that they will deliberately borrow these techniques when they write. On the other hand, the child who says, "The author begins every chapter with a little mystery that lasts just one paragraph" will probably be tempted to do likewise.

Interestingly enough, when I recently asked the British educator Nigel Hall, "How do you encourage kids to make reading-writing connections?" he answered, "When they are affected by a book they read, I ask them, 'How did the author create that effect?'" Nigel's comment fits exactly into my own dawning sense that our children need help to become aware that authors use their craft in order to make readers laugh, cry, or question. When Nigel wants to help children make reading-writing connections, he typically reads a book aloud to the entire class and waits until they break into laughter. Then he asks, "What did the author do to make us laugh aloud?" and a discussion ensues.

As I mentioned earlier, these are seize-the-moment discussions. We can't plan for them. They happen when a text affects the class community, and we or our students turn around to ask, "Why do I feel like this?" It is only when Nigel reads a book to the class and they all get so wrapped up in the suspense of it that they cannot put it down, that they look back asking, "How did the author create this suspense?"

Of course, our students also need to think when they write, "What effect am I hoping to create in my readers?" This question can lead them to look at how other authors have created similar effects. This way of thinking about texts—that they are crafted by an author for a purpose—lies at the heart of reading-writing connections. So often, inexperienced readers and writers don't realize that the same material—the same subject—can be shaped to create different effects. In mini-lessons, we can help children see that if, for example, a child was writing about not wanting to get out of bed in the morning, she could write about it in ways that emphasize its comic aspects (the mother coming again and again to the foot of the stairs, the child crawling deeper and deeper into her quilt) or in ways that emphasize the violence of the moment (how the child's important thoughts, plans, and dreams were torn apart by a shrill, demanding voice from the bottom of the stairs).

But in the end, the reading-writing connections that matter most will not be sponsored by the teacher. Just as we cannot *plan* for our class to fall in love with a book, because love happens in mysterious ways, we cannot synchronize an entire class of children to make the ah-ha's that are the lifeblood of reading-writing connections.

In November, Brian Jacobs and three of his friends spent an hour a day for two weeks talking their way through Jean Little's memoir, *Little by Little*. Often, their discussion circled back to an opening scene in which she'd slowly, hand over hand, climbed to the top of a tree. Little by little, she'd made her way past the branches, the obstacles, to the top of the tree. As they talked, Brian and his friends realized that the title of Jean Little's memoir was not only a play on her last name, it was reminiscent of her making her way, little by little, up the tree.

Four months later, when Brian wanted to write a memoir, he chose to include an entry about playing in the sand at the beach. This is part of the entry:

> A sea gull flies by and lands. It leaves its tiny footprints in the damp sand. A beach patrol truck drives by and leaves its track in the damp sand. I walk over to the newly made tracks and press my finger into the zig zag line protruding out of the sand. I begin making little hand prints in the tracks. I love the feeling of the cool moist sand. I love putting my prints on the sand.

Looking over the entry, Brian says, "Remember how Jean Little explained about climbing the tree in big detail and then in the end, she made that a simile for her life? She sort of said, 'The tree is like my life.' The part about climbing the tree isn't really a *big* moment in her life, it doesn't have to be. But she says, 'This moment is about how my life is.' My beach story isn't a *big* thing, but I'm explaining it in detail, and I might make it a simile of my life."

Brian wasn't sure how to turn his beach scene into a simile for his life, so he began rereading his notebook, hoping for inspiration. He found it in an entry he'd written during his science class about a sensitive plant that reacts to the slightest touch. "I'm like the plant," he said. "I notice the littlest things, like tracks on the beach."

These are the ah-ha's we wait for and work toward when our children read and write literature. Brian's insight was, in some ways, a lightning bolt, a flash of genius. The insight came when neither I nor his teacher expected it, and it was totally his own. Yet it emerged out of many conversations about books, about how writing is made, about how authors affect readers. In the end, this is probably how most reading-writing connections happen. As teachers, we prepare for them, but they happen when we're looking the other way, and they catch us by surprise.

Recommended Literature

Barton, Bob, and David Booth. *Stories in the classroom.* Portsmouth, NH: Heinemann, 1990.

Booth, David, Larry Swartz, and Meguido Zola. *Choosing children's books.* Markham, Ontario: Pembroke Publishers, 1987.

Calkins, Lucy McCormick, with Kathy Bearden. *A writer's shelf: Literature in the writing workshop.* New York: HarperCollins, 1992.

Harste, Jerome, and Kathy Short, with Carolyn Burke. *Creating classrooms for authors: The reading-writing connection.* Portsmouth, NH: Heinemann, 1988.

Harwayne, Shelley. *Lasting impressions.* Portsmouth, NH: Heinemann, 1992.

The Horn Book magazine. Boston: Horn Book.

Landsberg, Michele. *Michele Landsberg's guide to children's books.* Toronto, Ontario: Penguin, 1985.

Meek, Margaret. *How texts teach what readers learn.* Stroud, Gloucester, England: The Thimble Press; Rozelle, N.S.W.: Primary English Teaching Association, 1989.

———. *Learning to read.* Portsmouth, NH: Heinemann, 1986.

Murray, Donald. *Read to write: A writing process reader.* Chicago: Holt, Rinehart and Winston, 1990.

Trelease, Jim. *The read-aloud handbook.* Toronto, Ontario: Penguin, 1984.

18
Editing
Learning the Conventions of Written Language

"A noun is a person, place, or thing."
"A verb is an action word or a state of being."
"An adjective modifies a noun or pronoun."

I remember copying these definitions when I was a kid, and I remember underlining the nouns and circling the verbs on my workbook pages. I remember, too, trying to memorize the sixteen uses for the comma and the nine reasons for capitalizing a word, though I don't remember them now. This, to me, was English. It was English to many of us who teach today.

It has been somewhat disorienting, then, for us to find that, as many research studies show, instruction in formal grammar has no effect on the quality of student writing. After an extensive review of all the studies they could find on grammar instruction, for example, Braddock, Lloyd-Jones, and Schoer conclude,

> In view of the widespread agreement of research studies based upon many types of students and teachers, the conclusion can be stated in strong and unqualified terms: the teaching of formal grammar has a negligible or, because it usually displaces some instruction and practice in actual composition, even a harmful effect on the improvement of writing. (1963)

In 1969, John Mellon, another respected researcher in English education, also did a lengthy review of the literature on teaching grammar and found no evidence of any enabling effect. Around the same time, the well-known linguist Roger Brown wrote:

> It is extremely improbable that communication skills should be affected at all by instruction in explicit grammar, whether that grammar be traditional or traditional circa 1958, or transformational circa 1965, or

the current transformational frontier. Study of the theory of language is probably completely irrelevant to the development of skill in the use of language. (1968, p. xi)

Courtney Cazden, a child language expert at Harvard University, puts it this way: "There is no evidence that learning to be aware of one's tacit grammatical knowledge makes any difference in verbal behavior" (1972, p. 240).

What do these findings mean? Could the research really be suggesting that it's a waste of time to teach children that a noun is a person, place, or thing? Are there truly no good reasons for students to learn that complete sentences must have a noun and a verb in them?

No one is suggesting that whether or not a student can write complete sentences is inconsequential. The question is only whether or not grammar drills help students to do so. As James Moffett once explained, although bike riders must all *use* the rules of physics when they lean into their curves, being well versed in the laws of physics doesn't make people into more competent bike riders. Similarly, although we all *use* prepositional phrases when we write, we apparently don't write more effectively when we can label our language in these ways. Writers don't think, "It's time for another gerund" or "I'm going to add some dependent clauses to this poem."

Although English education researchers conclude that exercises that drill students on parts of speech, punctuation, or capitalization rules do not make it more likely that students will show a command of the conventions of written language when they write, this does not mean that instruction in grammar has *no* benefits. Some teachers and some school district officials will decide that even though lessons on grammar don't affect students' ability to write grammatically, students need to be schooled in the structure of the English language. It is probably true that students who spend time on grammar exercises are more likely to do well on tests filled with similar exercises. And some people think it important that students who have studied the parts of speech may someday be able to carry on conversations about prepositional phrases and dangling participles. There are, therefore, some reasons why some people might want to support instruction in grammar. I would argue, however, that if we want students to understand how our language works, we should encourage them to select a concentrated, semester-long, advanced-level linguistics course in high school. I could imagine students in this course comparing English with other languages. Why in English do we say "the big blue ball" instead of "the blue big ball"? As the renowned linguist Noam Chomsky once wrote to an English teacher,

"There are questions that are, or should be, fascinating and puzzling: . . . Why do the sentences 'John is too stubborn to talk to Bill' and 'John is too stubborn to talk to' have different 'understood subjects' for 'talk to' . . . ?" Chomsky went on to suggest that by exploring questions such as these, students "might be introduced into the marvellous world of inquiry in which one learns to wonder about [language]."

Our first priority must be to establish reading and writing workshops in which students learn to use words, parts of speech, punctuation, and conventions effectively. Our first priority must be to encourage our students to regard themselves as people who have important reasons not only to write well, but also to spell and punctuate well and use precise, graceful language. Then we can encourage them to notice and explore and borrow and reflect on the conventions of written language they see around them.

Certainly, it does not make sense for instruction in grammar to dominate our language arts classes so that year after year, our children think of English as ditto sheets on the parts of speech and drills on the components of a complete sentence. It may be that when some of our students become interested in the structure of the English language, they'll want to study grammar in an intensive fashion. But our first priority must be for them to use the English language in important ways.

Separating a Concern for Content from a Concern for Mechanics

Figure 18–1 shows the beginning of Clara's essay as she turned it in to her teacher. Figure 18–2 shows Clara's essay as her teacher returned it to her, defaced with such criticisms as "much too general," "too many grammatical errors," "verb endings," "run-on sentences," "vague," "explain."

Mina Shaughnessy, who has studied writers like Clara, remarks that before long, writing for these students will be "but a line that moves haltingly across the page, exposing as it goes all that the writer does not know, then passing into the hands of a stranger who reads it with a lawyer's eyes, searching for flaws." These writers are all too aware of their vulnerability as writers. They are aware, Shaughnessy continues, that they leave behind what she calls "a trail of errors as they write," but they don't know what to do about it. "Writing puts them on the line, and they don't want to be there."

Many of us have young Claras entering our classroom, children who have been taught to regard writing as a display of spelling, penmanship, and punctuation. For some children, this means that they focus more on the

FIGURE 18–1   Clara's essay

For many years now Kim and I have been the best of friends. Even though she lived far away from me, her life has influnced mine, and has taught me a lot

When we were little kids I would go to her house and noticed that her mother was always bossy, making Kim and her sister do everything around the house. When she got older her mother was still trying to treat her like a baby, never trusting her. It wasn't long after that she rebel. She drank often and went around with a "bad" crowd. Then she became pregnant and had to get an abortion. Things just went down hill from there. Everyone at her school found out about it, thanks to her sister and her boyfriend left her.   Problems with her mother got worst, it went from yelling to hitting and thats when she decided to get out.

---

shapes of their letters than on the content of their texts. For others it means that they're ashamed of their words. They sit with a dictionary, a thesaurus, white-out, and an eraser, agonizing so much over each word that they never get caught up in the natural lilt of language. They sit before the empty page saying, "Nothing happens in my life," and what they mean is, "Nothing happens that I can spell."

The most important thing we can do for these students is to help them write freely and unselfconsciously. No one learns well while feeling afraid and ashamed. Our students need to realize that it's okay to make editorial errors as they write; all of us do, and then we correct them as we edit. Although it's important to teach our students to edit, probably the single most important thing we can do for their syntax, spelling, penmanship, and use of mechanics is to help them write often and with confidence.

FIGURE 18–2 Clara's essay, as marked by teacher

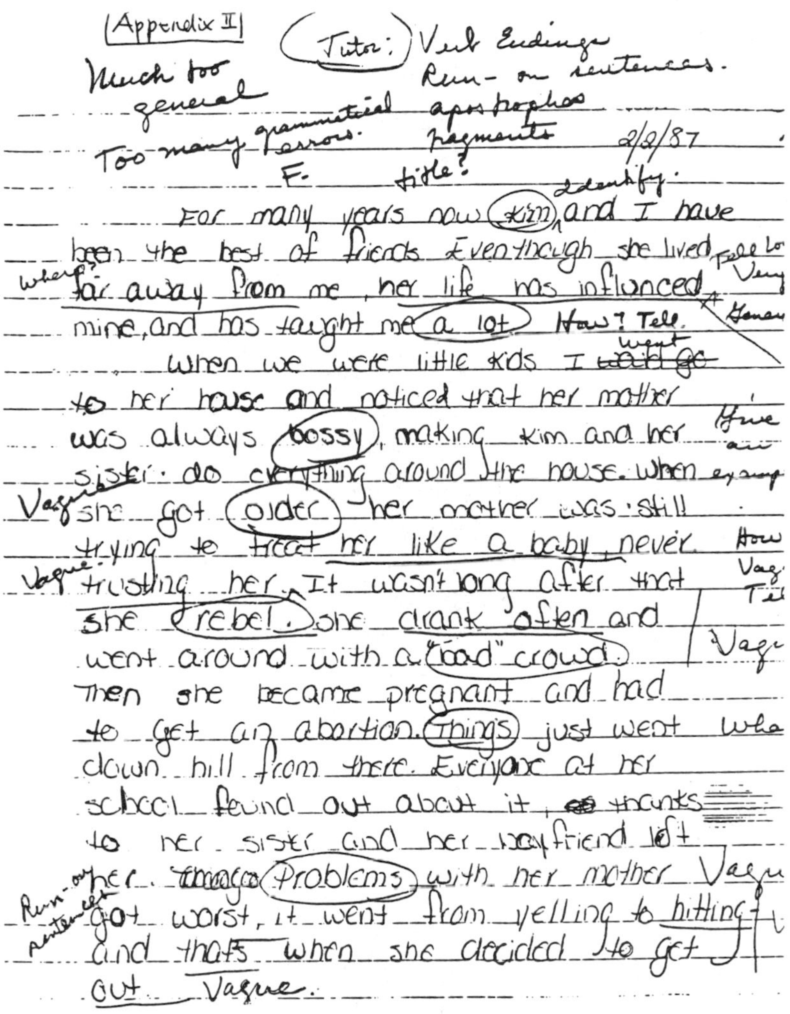

[Teacher's marginal notes at top:] Much too general / Too many grammatical errors. / Verb Endings / Run-on sentences. / apostrophes / fragments / 2/2/87 / F. / title? / (Tutor:) / [Appendix II] / identify

[Essay text, handwritten:]

For many years now Kim and I have been the best of friends. Even though she lived far away from me, her life has influenced mine, and has taught me a lot. When we were little kids I went to her house and noticed that her mother was always bossy, making Kim and her sister do everything around the house. When she got older her mother was still trying to treat her like a baby, never trusting her. It wasn't long after that she rebel. She drank often and went around with a "bad" crowd. Then she became pregnant and had to get an abortion. Things just went down hill from there. Everyone at her school found out about it, thanks to her sister and her boyfriend. Her Problems with her mother got worst, it went from yelling to hitting, and that's when she decided to get out.

[Teacher's marginal comments alongside essay:] Tell to / Very / Gener. / How? Tell. / went / Give ex. / Vague / example / How / Vague / Til / Vague / Vague / Run-on / Vague / Vague

---

When I launch children in the writing workshop, I tell them, "Your notebooks aren't meant to be displays of perfect spelling and handwriting. They're places for deep, thoughtful ideas and careful observations. Concentrate above all on what you are saying and let the spellings come out naturally, however they do. We'll look for them later."

"Do we use cursive or can we print?" the children often ask.

"Use whichever is most comfortable to you," I say. "This is rough draft writing. It's meant to be rough. There will be a time later for making it beautiful."

"Pen or pencil?" they ask.

I am apt to turn the question around. "What do you think?" I'll say.

"Whichever we want."

"Yes, use whatever will help you think."

I find that sometimes giving children permission to regard their work as a rough draft is not enough. By the time students are in second grade, many of them have been taught that good writers produce neat, correct texts. As I move about the workshop, I keep an eye out for the child who writes a letter, scrutinizes it to be certain it is perfectly rounded, then erases it and tries again. "It is important for you to worry about what you are saying now," I tell this youngster. "Let the penmanship go." Once in a while I have even said, "No erasing allowed. Just cross it out and keep going." Perhaps, to reassure a child, I might show him one of my drafts. "This is what writers do," I say, pointing out my cross-outs and false starts. As I move through the workshop, I also look for the youngster who composes with a dictionary on the desk. "I want to suggest something," I say. "Instead of interrupting yourself every three minutes to look up yet another word, why not put the dictionary away and for now, spell whichever way seems right, spell by instinct." Then, because of course dictionaries are important and will get attention eventually, I add, "Later, when you've written something for publication and it's done, you and I can look up the spellings and fix them up." Similarly, if a child often asks how a word is spelled as she writes, rather than giving her each of the spellings, I will say, "Take a guess, okay?" and then add, "If you worry too much about spelling at this stage, it can keep you from thinking about how to tell the truth in your writing."

"But my children keep asking for spelling help," teachers tell me.

"That's because you keep giving it," I respond. If we are clear and consistent, children quickly become independent spellers. But if we intermittently reinforce their dependence by giving correct spellings some of the time and not other times, the children will keep asking.

What I am suggesting is that we must help children separate composition from transcription. If children continually ask for spelling help as they draft, they are focusing on editing too early in the composing process. In *Writing and the Writer* Frank Smith explains why this is a problem:

> Composition and transcription can interfere with each other. . . . The problem is basically one of competition for attention. If we are struggling for ideas, or for particular words or constructions, or if our thoughts are coming too fast, then the quality of our handwriting or typing, spelling or punctuation is likely to decline. If we concentrate on

the transcription or appearance of what we write, on the other hand, then composition will be affected. (1982, p. 21)

Because spelling is second nature to us as adults, we can attend to spelling and content at the same time. But imagine if we were trying to produce a powerful piece of writing about something important—perhaps our relationship with our children—and were told to insert an exclamation point after every proper noun and to capitalize every *r*, *v*, *s*, and *b*. Such an assignment would be impossible. Our heads would soon be a swirl of mixed-up rules, and we certainly would not produce our best piece of writing. Yet this is the kind of exercise we ask of students.

No one has ever told my sons that spelling and punctuation are dreaded subjects. Miles, Evan, and I often sit snuggled together on the couch and talk about the little marks on a page in our book. We chat and laugh and fool around and wonder about apostrophes and commas and quotation marks and ellipses. We notice silent *e*'s at the ends of words, and final *y*'s that sound like *e*'s. We see parentheses in math problems and periods after the initials on my briefcase. These conventions come easily into our conversations and our life together. "I had a dream last night," Evan told me, "but no dots came out of my head." Evan wrote his initials: E. N. I was puzzled, because his last name, Skorpen, begins with an *S*. Then he explained: *E*van Skorpe*N*. Miles was delighted to use ditto marks (he called them elevens) when writing a song in which the lines repeat themselves ("Even rises up from the dead, Evan rises up from the dead . . ."). When Miles and Evan write, they use whatever knowledge of conventions comes to mind as they proceed. They think spelling and punctuation are complicated, fun, and curious, and they enjoy messing about with them.

All too often, this changes when children go to school. Spelling becomes a list of words copied on Monday, syllabicated on Tuesday, put into sentences on Wednesday. . . . Punctuation becomes yet another slot in the school day—one that is filled with exercises. During the writing workshop, spelling and punctuation can become a source of endless heartaches.

Inviting Writers to Explore Written Conventions

Although it is absolutely essential to help our students focus on what they are saying as they write, I think we make a mistake if we ban all talk of conventions from the writing workshop. In our effort to be sure that a concern about convention doesn't tyrannize our writers, we sometimes declare the entire subject off limits until the editing stage of writing.

"Spelling isn't important," we say. "Think about your *content,* not your punctuation." Or "Spell things any old way; the spelling doesn't count. That's for later," we say. But all too often, later never comes. Too often, when students *do* complete their drafts, there's not much time left for editing. We end up taking the assignments home, doing with them whatever we can, and then holding hurried editing conferences. . . .

How much better it is if we have a balanced relationship with the conventions of written language from the start! How much better it is if we invite our students as readers and writers to share our own fascination with and delight over words and the ways they are spelled, with sentences and paragraphs and tables of contents. Then editing can be a time to look again at our use of conventions, to polish our writing. But it should not be the one and only time for conversations about ellipses or quotation marks.

I recommend that we try to imagine ways to bring the intimate, playful explorations that Miles, Evan, and I have as we pore over a page of a book into our classrooms. Wonderful kindergarten teachers taught me to linger over the page of a book, asking, "What do you notice?" At P.S. 148 in Queens, teachers often pause over a big page of print propped on the easel and say, "What do you see?" Their students spill forth wonderful observations about rhymes and word endings and punctuation. When I first tried this myself with a class full of squirming little children, Melissa noticed an M on the page. I wasn't terribly impressed. I wanted to say, "Of course, there are *letters,* but what *else* do you notice?" but then I remembered how Isoke Nia responded with such delight when a child said, "I notice *words* in your notebook" (see Chapter 3).

"Yes, Melissa, you're right. There *is* an M here, isn't there? Good noticing!" I said. "There are other M's, too, aren't there?" Soon Melissa will notice rhymes and word endings and interesting spellings and quotation marks.

When Joanne Hindley taught a first- and second-grade class, she began every day during the first month of school by reading wonderful stories aloud. Many of these stories had been written by young authors from other classes during previous years. "Which of these words are you dying to know how the author spelled?" Joanne often asked, and the children would choose a word. If the word was *elephant,* they would work in pairs to invent their own best guesses about how the word might be spelled. Then, with great ceremony, Joanne would reveal the author's spelling. "What do you notice?" she'd ask as children puzzled over the correct spelling. "What surprises you?"

When Joanne first asked that question, her children probably didn't have much to contribute. But because she asked the question "What surprises you?" every day, her children grew into it. Soon they were conducting long, probing conversations about spelling. Now, as Joanne works with third graders, children put their best guesses onto tagboard cards and line them up along the chalk tray, explaining the rationale for these guesses to each other. Then, once all the "best guesses" have been shared, they are invited to have a second go at their spellings and revise them based on what they learned from one another. Finally, Joanne shares the way the author has, in fact, spelled the word, and again, the children talk about what they notice and about what surprises them.

Teachers need not adopt Joanne's particular methods for inviting good talk about spelling, but I do think we need to be certain that our young children do not grow up believing that being concerned about convention is an onerous chore. We'll want to focus in a very deliberate fashion on editing during the final phase of writing, but we'll also want to encourage our youngsters to notice the conventions of written language around them.

Writers See Punctuation Marks Everywhere

In his article "Reading Like a Writer," Frank Smith argues that the only way to account for how some children learn hundreds, even thousands of spellings a year is to recognize that they learn to spell by reading like a writer:

> The author is in effect writing on our behalf. . . . Everything the learner would want to spell the author spells. Every nuance of expression, every relevant syntactic device, every turn of phrase, the author and learner write together. Bit by bit, one at a time . . . the learner learns through reading like a writer, to write like a writer. (1983, p. 564)

My husband and I are going to buy a car soon. Whenever I drive now, I find myself noticing the differences between Toyotas and Subarus, Pintos and Saturns. The curious thing is that all my life I have been surrounded by cars, yet until now I have not taken note of the different makes. Because I now view myself as someone who needs to know about cars, I see them everywhere. Similarly, when children perceive themselves as insiders in written language, as what Smith calls members of the club, we can encourage them to notice the conventions of written language everywhere.

When I was new to composition research, I did a small study comparing two third-grade classrooms (Calkins 1980a). In Mrs. Howard's classroom, the children wrote every day and chatted, as writers do, about the conventions of written language. They also edited their rough drafts prior to publishing them. Across the hall, Mrs. West taught mechanics through daily drills and workbook exercises. "I start at the very beginning, teaching them simple sentences, periods, capitals," Mrs. West explained. "I do a whole lesson on it, everything in the book." Mrs. West wrote sentences on the chalkboard and asked her children to insert missing punctuation. She made dittos on question marks and gave pretests and post-tests on periods. Her children rarely wrote.

Both teachers said, "I begin at the very beginning." For Mrs. West, the beginning was the declarative sentence and the rules for using periods. For Mrs. Howard, the beginning was the child's information, the child's desire to be seen and heard.

When I met with each child in the two classrooms, I drew punctuation symbols and asked, "What is this for?" What I found was that the "writers" who had not had formal instruction in punctuation could explain an average of 8.66 kinds of punctuation, whereas the children who had studied punctuation every day through classwork and drills but had rarely written were only able to explain 3.85 kinds of punctuation. Even more important, the children in the writing classroom liked punctuation. Tracey explained, "Punctuation sounds good. I mean, it doesn't have a sound like a letter has a sound, but it makes all the letters sound better. If writing had no punctuation, it would sound dull" (Calkins 1980b, p. 87). Chip liked punctuation because his readers needed it. "It lets them know where the sentence ends, so otherwise one minute you'd be sledding down the hill and the next minute you're inside the house, without even stopping."

My sense is that when children view themselves as writers, they see punctuation everywhere—just as I now see makes of cars everywhere. Even when Mrs. Howard's children had never used a particular kind of punctuation, they were familiar with it. Shawn recognized the colon: "My dad uses them in his writing," he said. "But one thing: I can't read his writing." Melissa nods at the sight of an ellipsis. "Those three periods—people use them at the end of paragraphs. But I usually just use one period."

Melissa was not unusual among the writers. She had a sense of how one might use a punctuation mark even if she didn't know the correct name for it. One of the things children like these teach us is that it may not matter whether students can list the sixteen uses of a comma or define a prepositional phrase. What matters far more is that children get a feel for linking sentences and embedding phrases, for using symbols to encode the sounds of their voices. The use of the English language is a skill to be developed, not content to be taught, and it is best learned through active and purposeful experience with it.

Many writers at Atkinson Elementary School called punctuation marks "what-ja-ma-call-its." When six-year-old Jennice used quote marks in her story, I asked, "What's that?"

"Um, oh, that thing, you know . . ." was her response.

"Well, when do you use them?" I asked.

Jennice had a ready answer. "When they talk. You know, when they say things."

Exclamation points were called by all sorts of names. A first grader called them "happy marks," and many of the third graders called them "explanations." The students' ignorance of the proper names for these marks did not hinder them from using the symbols to improve their stories. "I like explanations," Diane said. "They change the way people read my words. They read them faster. They are like action words: run! quick!"

The nonwriters described punctuation by trying to remember the rules they'd been taught. Mrs. West's class knew that a period comes at the end of a sentence, but when I asked them how they knew when to end a sentence, they didn't know. "You can tell where a sentence ends by the period" was all they could say. One boy had mastered the punctuation worksheets, if not ways of punctuating real sentences. He suggested that the way to punctuate is to look and see if a capital letter comes next, and if so, insert the period.

Commas are for lists of people—Joe, Frank, Peter. "Anything else?" I asked. "Sometimes when you paint," Jack said. "Different colors—purple, green, blue." Many of the mechanics students defined commas by referring to one specific use only. "Put them between fruit." "Commas separate states."

Amy, a writer, explained commas quite differently: "If you have a long sentence and you want to keep it all there, you put a comma in to take a breath. If you were to make a new sentence, you'd change it. One example is my flying piece of writing. I said 'We got a little lower and over the beach, I saw tiny colored dots.' Before and after the comma, they are both parts of the same sentence. Like the first half of the sentence is one paragraph, and the other half is the second paragraph . . . like two edges of the same idea."

Amy does not know all the proper rules and definitions for language conventions, but she has developed an intuitive sense of the nuances of punctuation.

Help Students Edit

Editing has a very real place in the writing process, and with encouragement and guidance, even kindergarten children can engage in an early form of editing.

I once watched Shelley Harwayne as she introduced editing to five-year-olds. This was her third day as a staff developer in this classroom and her goal was, first, to avoid a bottleneck of children saying, "I am done, what should I do next?" by clearly telling children what to do when their pieces were finished. Her second goal was to introduce them to a rudimentary sort of editing and, in doing so, to set up a system for dealing with editing. Shelley began the mini-lesson by saying, "It is nice to see so many authors." She held a stack of folders in her lap, and turning to the children she said, "Your papers from yesterday are in beautiful writing folders now. You each have one with your name on it. I am going to hold up your folder and then you can look at your piece of writing and you will have a decision to make. You have to decide whether you are finished or whether you have more to put in your story. If you are finished, do you know what you will do?" The children, big-eyed and silent, shook their heads. Shelley continued, "When authors finished all the beautiful books in your library, do you know what they did? They started on the *next one!* When you finish one story and it is your best, the very best you can do, then you can begin to think about your next writing. And so when I show you your piece of writing, you decide if it is your best." Holding up one child's story, Shelley said, "Anthony, what about you? Is this your best?"

"Yes, I'm finished."

"Anthony, I have this big blue box and it says 'Finished Pieces.' you can put your story here, but first, do you see what else it says on the box? It says:

1. Name.
2. Date.
3. Page numbers.

"Before you put your story in the big blue box, you have to *edit* it. This is the editing list and it tells you to check that you have your name and the date, and that you have numbered your pages like authors do. What do you need to do before putting your story in the box, Anthony?"

"Page numbers and date," he said, and began to add these as Shelley moved on to the next child.

"Ricardo, is this your best, or do you have more to add?" she asked. He was done, and so Shelley reminded him to edit before he put the piece in the big blue box. Soon all the folders had been passed out, and a system had been established that told children what to do when they were done.

The editing chart changes as children become capable of new skills. In this particular classroom, some children were soon adding periods, rereading to be sure their pieces made sense, and capitalizing the first letter in their sentences. They could not define a period or list the uses for capitals, and they did not necessarily edit correctly, but they had learned that editing is a crucial part of the writing cycle. This may be a more important lesson than anything else.

Other teachers have found their own ways to guide their children into editing. When Mary Ellen Giacobbe went over finished stories with her first graders, she noticed and celebrated the conventions that each child had used independently. These conventions were then added to a list stapled to the front cover of the child's daily writing folder. This was Audrey's list in November:

THINGS AUDREY CAN DO:

1. Write her name on the book.
2. Write the title on the book.
3. Write the date on the book.
4. Begin each sentence with a capital letter.
5. Use quotation marks.
6. Use a question mark at the end of a sentence.
7. Use a period at the end of a sentence.

When Audrey completed her next piece, she was expected to reread the list and use it as a guide for editing. In a similar way, every child had his or her individualized checklist. This is a splendid system, but for crowded New York City classrooms it is too dependent on extensive teacher input, so teachers have devised notions such as hanging a chart over the "big blue box." Teachers need to be problem-solvers and to find ways to make general concepts work within their own classrooms.

By the time children are in second grade, most of the teachers with whom I work make editing checklists on rexograph sheets so that children can actually check off each item as they deal with it. The editing sheets vary depending on the teacher, the child, and the age; Figure 18–3 gives two examples.

FIGURE 18–3 Editing checklists

Name _____ Date _____

Editing Sheet

	Check ✓
1. Does it make sense?	
2. Does it have my name?	
the date?	
a title?	
periods?	
capitals?	
3. Did I check the spelling?	

Author: _____

Title: _____

Date began:_____ Date finished:_____

Editor:_____ Peer Editor:_____

Have you reread it carefully, trying to imagine places where readers might be confused?
_____

Have you underlined words that look as if they may not be spelled correctly and tried to get some help on those words? _____

Have you reread your piece aloud, paying attention to "the road signs" (the punctuation)?
_____

Have you tried to cut your piece, taking out the extra words that don't add much?
_____

What new risks have you taken with the conventions of written language? _____
_____

What questions do you have? What are the issues around which you want help?
_____

_____

It is important to remember, of course, that the items on the checklist change over the course of the year as children become more and more capable. When most children are using terminal punctuation correctly, this item can be deleted from the list and a new one added. The lists should change as the children do. Because there is always a wide range of abilities within a room, it makes sense to have several different checklists, each representing different levels of editing sophistication.

According to the system in some classrooms, once a child has revised his or her piece, the child takes it to an editing table. There, with a checklist as a guide, the child rereads and corrects the piece. In mini-lessons and editing conferences, teachers will have shown the child how to go about editing. The child might have learned, for example, that in order to check for spelling, she should read the draft with pencil in hand, touching each word and asking, "Is this right?" Alternatively, the child might have been taught to begin at the end of the piece and read up the page so that the words are seen out of context, which makes errors more obvious. Generally, we suggest that the child lightly underline words that look misspelled (circling it destroys the appearance of the draft). The key point here is that children, not teachers, are the ones to identify misspelled words. Although spelling correctly is nice, many brilliant people are lousy spellers. The bottom line is that it is especially important to recognize if a word is misspelled. Once a child has identified a word that looks misspelled, we have him try to spell the word several different ways and then ask himself, "Which *looks* right?" We want children to know that this is a strategy good spellers use, that good spellers rely a lot on how a word looks. We may also suggest that they ask themselves, "Is this word similar (in meaning) to other words I can spell?" If a child is struggling over the word *courageous*, it helps to remember the spelling of *courage*.

It is important that the editing system in our classrooms does not put extraordinary demands on writers who have severe problems. If these children know they must find every single misspelled word in a dictionary, they will write with safe words, choosing *big* when they wanted to say *enormous*.

Readers may have noticed that on these editing checklists, children reread looking not only for errors in their use of periods and capitals but also for sense and excess words. Children need to know that editing involves not only correcting errors but also tightening and linking, smoothing out language, ordering thoughts, and listening to the poetry of one's sentences.

In some classrooms, the editing checklists contain a column for peer editors. There are obvious advantages to this: children help each other, they talk about punctuation and spelling, they use each other's strengths, they need less input from teachers. The disadvantages of peer editing are less obvious until one introduces it in the classroom, when they become all too apparent. Children love to play teacher. In large scrawly letters, they mark all over a friend's piece. Major warfare often breaks out, especially when the writer protests that the peer editor is wrong (as is often the case). My suggestion, then, is that if children edit each other's papers, they must understand that the writer makes the final decision. One way to emphasize this is to say that peer editors can advise but they cannot write on a draft.

Once a child has edited his or her piece, it is time for the teacher to look it over. Ideally, the child brings the draft and the editing checklist to the teacher, and we have an editing conference with the child. Classrooms are rarely ideal, however, and I find that the class size is generally too large for this to work. We end up spending half of our time in editing conferences, and our youngsters spend too long waiting for editing conferences. They become restless, adding to the chaos in the room. The best way to avoid this bottleneck is for children to put their edited work into the teacher's box and to begin a new piece while they are waiting for a conference.

Editing Conferences

Often we say, "When you have edited your piece, show it to me, and if it looks as if you have done your best you can put it in my box." The question "Is this your best?" can be perfunctory, or it can be a two-hands-on-the-shoulders, look-in-a-child's-eyes question. *"Is this your best?"* we can ask, and we can say our question as if it matters more than anything in the world. The child who has dashed off a sloppy editing job will squirm, look at his or her feet, and say, "Wel-l-l . . . um. . . ."

We need to act as if we are dumbfounded. How could it *possibly* happen that a child would do less than his or her best? "What is the point in not doing your best?" we say, as if amazed and baffled at the notion of giving less than one hundred percent to a piece of writing.

I am reminded of a story Donald Murray tells about a senior editor who assigned a project to his team of writers. They turned in the work on the day it was due, and the senior editor took it home but did not read it. The next day he called the team together and, returning the paper to them, he barked, "Was this your best?"

The writers shuffled their feet, hemmed and hawed, and began to explain. "You see, sir, we would have done our best but this and that happened. . . ." The editor cut them off. "Turn it in on Wednesday." Wednesday came and again the editor took the paper home and again he did not read it. The next day he held it out to the team of writers, and shaking it in the air as he spoke, he said, "Was *this* your best?" Again there were apologies, and the editor said, "Bring it in on Monday."

Monday night, the editor once again took the paper home and did not read it. Tuesday he dropped it on the table in front of the writers and growled, "Was this your best?"

"Goddamn it, *yes,*" they answered.

"Then I shall read it," he said. I think we would do well to learn from this example.

When I read students' edited work, I find it helpful to skim the piece quickly first without a pen. This allows me to get a broader picture of what the child has and has not done. But a word of caution. The story may be a laundry list of everything the child did all summer, and I'm surprised that it's gotten to the editing stage without more substantive revisions. I'm tempted to ask the writer to back up and think about the focus of the piece. The problem is that if I use the editing conference as a gate, I'll have even more problems with a logjammed system, and I'll also be clearly conveying the message that I'm in charge of the student's piece.

When I read the piece in an editing conference then, I am *not* looking at whether I believe the piece deserves to be pronounced "done." I am looking instead at spelling, punctuation, paragraphs, logic, clarity, sentence length, language, syntax. I always try to look first at what the child *has* done, and especially at the risks the child has taken. I jot notes about what the child has done in the appropriate space on the editing checklist or in my records, because I know that when the writer and I meet for an editing conference, I will want to begin by celebrating these things.

What a difference this makes! When I was a child, editing meant error (bad, wrong, red pen, points off). It is important to reverse this negative learning and to help children be *learners of language conventions*. Children, like adults, learn best in a supportive context. Like all of us, children are more apt to remember kind words about their successes than harsh words about their failures. They will take risks if we reinforce risk-taking. The tendency instead is to reinforce correctness. In playing tennis, I spent a decade dropping the ball and then hitting it over the net rather than attempting a proper serve because my drop-serve was safe. I would never have learned to serve if I didn't take some risks. Children will only learn quotation marks and colons and the spelling of long and difficult words if they, too, are risk-takers.

I do look at errors, but instead of dealing with each one in isolation I try to see a pattern. Although at first glance the child's page may seem to be a chaos of errors, a closer look usually shows that, in fact, the child has made two or three errors over and over again. The crucial thing is that I must avoid being overwhelmed by all the errors on the child's page, because if *I* feel overwhelmed, I convey this to the child. Mina Shaughnessy is wise when she says, "Assume at the outset that the misspellings . . . can be brought under control. Nothing inhibits growth among Basic Writing students more than the conviction that their errors are both infinite and unpredictable" (1977, p. 160). If we can help students believe they can take control of written language, if we can change their self-perception from "I can't" to "I can," then they can live their lives as learners of written language.

In an editing conference, then, I begin by celebrating what the student *has* done, and then I teach one or two items. If I show the student how to add periods to his work, the student will probably return to his seat with the draft and add periods to it. Later, we go over it again, perhaps continuing to work on terminal punctuation, perhaps going on to a second issue. By then, I will probably decide that the student has learned enough from this one piece of writing and the draft is once again put into my box. This time I will correct it at home (with blue pen or pencil), and eventually the student will recopy it so that the final draft is perfect (well, almost).

Some people will disagree, claiming that by correcting students' writing I take away the child's ownership of the piece. I respect this opinion, but I disagree with it. There is a time when published writing leaves the writer's hands and becomes a public document. My books are edited professionally, and for this I am grateful. I don't want to "own" all my errors.

The exception, it seems to me, is the writing of youngsters in kindergarten and first grade. I am always sorry when I visit classrooms in which the children's invented spellings are kept hidden and only the teacher's spelling is evident. It is so much more exciting and interesting to see the children's own efforts! I recommend, therefore, that if teachers in these grades feel the need to have corrected final drafts, they might type children's writing themselves, but I hope the children's own spectacular spellings will be proudly displayed alongside the published versions.

But let me back up for a moment and talk about what I do when I read students' papers, searching for the one or two things that I'll talk about in an editing conference. My question, as I read through rough drafts, is "What seems to be the primary problem this student is having?" If I find twenty small problems, I will *not* talk to the student about each one. I know from my own experience in learning to play tennis that after hearing one or two suggestions I become overwhelmed and can't hear any more. And so the question I ask is, "What are the one or two most essential concepts I can teach today?"

The next thing that guides me as I prepare for an editing conference is this: I know that if I am to help students, I need to assume that their errors grow out of some logic, some understanding about conventions. If I am to help a particular writer, I need to understand her operating principles. For example, at first glance, the child who wrote the following (see also Figure 18–4) needs to be told about terminal punctuation:

> My life story once in my life I went away to see my grandmother. Once when I went to see my grandmother my family that lives with her was

FIGURE 18–4 "My Life Story"

so happy to see me. In the night my cousins and I went out to play we played monster my cousin was the monster. Our friends were playing with us then my grandmother called us me and my cousin was so excited when she called us my other cousins came for the vacation me and my cousin was so happy my grandmother was happy too. The End.

My first instinct might be to tell this writer that writers use periods at the ends of sentences, at the end of a complete thought. But if I assume that this writer is following some logic and look closely to try to understand the rationale for her errors, I begin to suspect that she is already putting a period at what she believes is the end of each complete thought. When she writes, "In the night my cousins and I went out to play we played monster my cousin was the monster," she probably puts all of this into a single sentence because it does, in fact, seem like one thought within her piece. How confusing it would be if I acted as if these efforts to use periods were *all wrong*. The truth is that deciding where a sentence ends is one of the more complicated decisions a writer makes, and this writer is on her way toward figuring it out. She needs to be supported, encouraged, and guided rather than corrected and reprimanded.

We can try to infer the logic behind a student's errors, but it's far more helpful to ask students to teach us what they are thinking as they write. Maria, a first grader, put a colon at the end of every page in her homemade book. This puzzled me, but talking with Maria helped me understand. Earlier in the year Maria had written "There are many kinds of dinosaurs," and her teacher had suggested that if she added a colon before the list of dinosaurs, the reader would know there was more to come. Therefore, Maria figured, it made sense to put the colon at the bottom of each page as a way to signify, "Read on, there is more to come!" A closer look showed that she had carefully and appropriately omitted the colon from her final page.

When we understand the intelligence behind students' errors, we can help in a way that truly extends their understanding.

Is There a Place for Language Instruction?

Once we've encouraged our students to write unselfconsciously, immersed the classroom in lots of informal exploratory talk about the conventions of written language, and begun to help students systematically and carefully edit their final drafts, we will have gone a long way toward developing a wise approach to the conventions of written language. But we may also want to have, for example, a carefully designed spelling program. My first suggestion for teachers who are interested in devising such a program is that they read Sandra Wilde's book, *You Kan Red This!*, a book that grows out of her doctoral research under Ken and Yetta Goodman, and Faye Bolton and Diane Snowball's *Teaching Spelling: A Practical Approach*. Here are some of the principles about spelling I have learned from these educators:

- When writing workshop teachers go from having a publisher dole out weekly lists of spelling words to having children gather their own lists or themselves devising lists of words based on the curriculum, this is, as Wilde says, "a step in the right direction," but the approach is still "locked into a list mentality." Spelling can never be learned through memorization. What is necessary is for children to develop the *strategies* and *concepts* of a speller. Spellers need to know, for example, that when they are struggling to spell a word (*courageous*), it's helpful to think of related words (*courage*). They need to know that one way to decide on how to spell a word is to write it several different ways and then to see which one *looks* right. Children need to know how to use resources to find spellings. In order to teach these strategies, we need to invite children to join together in puzzling over spellings, and we need to talk with them about what they do when they don't know how to spell a word. We especially need to be sure that students rely on more than just "sounding out."

- When we want to teach children a generalization about spelling, it's probably best to have children gather *particulars* and then speculate over the generalization that might best explain those particulars. For example, children may fill one page of chart paper with words that become plural by adding an *s* and another piece of chart paper with words that add *es*. What do the words on the one page have in common? On the other page? What rationale might there be for the different plural endings? In similar ways, children could gather instances of *able* versus *ible* endings, and ask, "Why is it '*workable*' and '*livable*'; why is it '*visible*' and '*legible*'?" That is to say, children will understand the generalizations that pertain to our language best if they *invent* them.

- Di Snowball helped me realize that when a child learns a single spelling, he or she can get a lot of mileage out of it. For example, once a child knows how to spell *sign*, the child can brainstorm a whole collection of related spellings (*signature, insignia, resign, assign, signal* . . .). This suggests that if we are going to give children lists of spelling words, we might give them a few words and invite them to gather related words around these. Of course, this also suggests that when a child is stumped by a spelling, one strategy is to think, "What similar words do I know that might help me spell this word?"

- We need to help students spell many words through visual memory. We can begin doing this when working with very young students. Instead of saying "sound it out" over and over to our five- and six-year-old writers, we can say, "You know how to spell *the* (or *-ing*). You remember *the,* don't you?" Instead of always saying, "What does the word *sound* like?" we can say, "Close your eyes and see if you can picture that word. What does it look like?" By the time children are in third and fourth grade, Wilde found that the same thirty-seven words accounted for half of what students write. There is no reason why we shouldn't help students spell these words automatically and fluently in all of their writing, including their first drafts.

My colleagues and I in the Teachers College Writing Project are excited about the ideas described in this chapter. We've had great fun reading Wilde's book together and trying some of the techniques she suggests. We even had fun sitting, as students, around Di Snowball and hearing her say, "Take out a piece of paper, number it from one to twenty. I'm going to give you a spelling test." Di did this with us so that we could relive and discuss the entire phenomenon, and what an eye-opener it was to see how resourceless many of us felt when it came to tackling unfamiliar spellings! We've also had fun gathering together the picture books that play with and problematize language. And as we've done this work, we've rediscovered how it feels to turn words over and over in our minds, wondering at how they are made, puzzling over categories of words, and finding patterns across words. How far we've come from when, in the early days of writing workshop, we used to say, "It's your ideas that count; don't worry too much about spelling." Now we say, "Let's not *worry* about spelling, punctuation, editing . . . but let's explore, enjoy, understand, and wonder about these things."

Resources on Language Conventions

Bolton, Faye, and Diane Snowball. *Teaching spelling: A practical approach.* Portsmouth, NH: Heinemann, 1993.

Chomsky, Carol. Reading, writing, and phonology. In *Thought and language, language and reading,* ed. Maryanne Wolf, Mark McQuillan, and Eugene Radwin. *Harvard Educational Review* Reprint Services No. 14 (1980): 51–71.

Shaughnessy, Mina P. *Errors and expectations.* New York: Oxford University Press, 1977.

Wilde, Sandra. *You kan red this! Spelling and punctuation for whole language classrooms, K–6.* Portsmouth, NH: Heinemann, 1991.

19

Assessment

A Minds-On Approach to Teaching

The first edition of *The Art of Teaching Writing* did not have even a page on assessment. When I wrote it I think I imagined the writing workshop as a sanctuary from assessment. I equated assessment with evaluation, and both with stanines and percentiles, testing and accountability. I was against assessment and all it had done to teachers and children. I wanted to create worlds that revolved around more lofty and humanistic concerns. Now, a decade later, it would be inconceivable not to address the issue of authentic assessment. It is no accident that Don Graves and Ken and Yetta Goodman, key figures in the teaching of writing, have edited books on the topic of assessment. Assessment is an issue whose time has come.

Summarizing the Current Scene in Assessment

I think it's fair to summarize the current scene in assessment this way. Some teachers still teach language arts (and everything else) by fractioning the curriculum into an array of little skills, which they teach in a frontal, teacher-led fashion with pretests, post-tests, short lectures, work on the chalkboard, exercises, and activities. This teaching is supported both by standardized tests and by the practice of accumulating lots of little scores in gradebooks. Yet meanwhile, more and more teachers no longer teach by fractioning the curriculum into an array of skills and then dealing with each skill in isolation. Instead, they lead reading and writing workshops and inquiries into shared themes, and these approaches to teaching are often not scaffolded by any official assessment measures. As more teachers begin to teach in these ways, and as official institutions put their support behind workshop teaching, it has become clear that workshops do need to be scaffolded by assessment measures. But what should these be? How can workshop teachers develop and use new assessment measures? And what is the relationship between new assessment measures and teachers who continue to teach through exercises and drills?

Another way to summarize the current scene in assessment is to say that there is a revolution in the field of assessment and that it exists because constructivist teachers have begun realizing that it doesn't work if our methods of instruction have changed while our schools' methods of assessment have remained the same. One of my colleagues, Shirley McPhillips, describes the resulting disequilibrium this way:

> You get all of this new stuff happening in your classroom, with students taking initiative, launching big projects, working collaboratively . . . then report card time comes and *Boom.* When you had a row of 82's and 96's to add up, you could fill in the squares on the report card, but now you stare at the report card and it looks so foreign and you think, "How can I convert all that we're doing into those little squares?" You try but you feel like a traitor, like you are betraying something. Then parents come in for conferences and you have to talk off scores you don't believe in anyway, and you get tangled up in double-talk and the whole thing becomes so distasteful.

We are angry about old methods of assessment. We resist and resent having to reduce our students to a score, to an 87 or a 92, a B— or an A. Then, too, we know that "standardized" tests are designed by people outside the classroom as instruments of control over those inside the classroom. We don't want exams filled with isolated reading passages and swarms of tiny questions to control our teaching. And we know that tests—even tests that happen only once a year—often *do* tyrannize the curriculum, filling each day with miniature tests in the form of worksheets, exercises, drills, and textbook questions. We are angry that, as James Britton says, in the name of education, teachers are told that after we plant little fragile seedlings, we are to uproot them every few hours to measure whether their roots have grown. We also question what the test scores show about our students. We do not believe that standardized test scores can be regarded as evidence of our students' learning or of our teaching. Do these tests convey a child's self-image as a reader and a writer, the child's purposes for reading and writing, the child's initiative and ambition and attitudes? No.

We are also angry that in the name of education, schools have labeled young children bluebirds and buzzards. If an institution wanted to punish and damage children deliberately, one could imagine it might invent such a system for dividing and labeling children, but it is inconceivable that anyone would impose this psychological damage on a child in the name of education. Ray Rist studied grouping in one kindergarten classroom and found that by the eighth day of the school year, children in this class were assigned to three reading groups, and these groups echoed the teacher's perceptions of the children's socioeconomic classes. The single-parent children, who were least well-dressed and came from welfare homes, were in the bottom group. This group received less of the teacher's attention and more instruction on the sounds of isolated words, letters, and other meaningless fragments. In the three years Rist followed these children, no child ever moved up a group. It is no wonder that, as Don Graves has said, no curricular change, not even the change from basal readers to trade books, is more significant than the change that occurs when a school system stops dividing children into "ability" groups.

When teachers look at the mismatch between old methods of assessment and current methods of teaching and say, "The whole thing becomes so distasteful," these teachers are accurately conveying the context for current reform on assessment. But the dissatisfaction, even rage, that has galvanized some teachers, parents, and administrators into exploring authentic assessment has led other educators to boycott assessment altogether. I was one such educator.

The Potential Benefits and Problems in the New Emphasis on Assessment

As I work with teachers across the country, I find that a surprising number of dedicated, knowledgeable teachers of writing do very little systematic or written assessment. A fair percentage of workshop teachers do not record conferences, save student writing, or observe the classroom in any systematic way. I feel as if I understand these teachers because for years I was one of them.

If someone during my first years of teaching writing had asked me about my methods of assessment, I would have interpreted their question as being about grades. I never dreamed of keeping assessment records for any reason other than grading. And I figured that because I was emphasizing the writing process rather than written products, it didn't make sense to give each piece of writing a grade. Instead, I graded my students every five weeks, looking in some general fashion at their effort, volume of writing, risk-taking, willingness to revise, ability to edit, helpfulness when peer conferring, and so forth. That was the sum total of my deliberate assessment.

What happens for many of us, I think, is that we get so consumed by all we must do as teachers, we end up feeling as if really keeping track of individual students is a luxury we can't afford. We have so much else to do—setting up a writing center, giving mini-lessons, conducting conferences, cajoling the nonwriters toward topics, supervising peer editing. But the problem with focusing only on the plot line of teaching is that what we do when we teach needs to grow out of what we notice, think, and remember. The *external* story must be based on the *internal* action that ultimately characterizes our teaching. Tom Newkirk, who likens teaching to basketball, says there is an "outer game" of teaching (and of basketball):

> This outer game can be diagrammed, specified in curricular manuals and methods textbooks. And that information is clearly useful. Nevertheless, it provides little insight into the moment-by-moment decision-making of the skilled teacher. (1992, p. 115)

Our ability to play the inner game of teaching depends on our ability to read the room, to read our students' ambitions and intentions and fears and strengths and habits of thought. Assessment is what the teacher of writing and reading does. Eleanor Duckworth, Jack Easley, David Hawkins, and Androula Henriques have written a book entitled *Science Education: A Minds-On Approach for the Elementary Years* (1990). Assessment allows us to have a "minds-on approach" to all our teaching.

It's all too easy to have only the trappings of a student-centered curriculum: the small-group discussions, the optional activities, the hands-on and interactive work. In the end, a classroom is student-centered if and only if our teaching happens in response to individual students. Assessment allows us to be truly student-centered in our teaching.

The most extraordinary benefit of assessment is that we are given the gift of our children. They are there always, of course, but it's easy not to see what they are showing us. I remember looking over the room, over all of those faces, over all those pieces of writing, and feeling a sort of throwing-my-hands-in-the-air sense of resignation. Was anyone *really* progressing? I felt somewhat at sea. Sometimes it seemed that half the class was slipping through the cracks. I secretly missed those columns of 82's and 96's, and the checkmarks, pluses, and minuses. I missed holding onto that gradebook and feeling somehow reassured that the columns of scores meant yes, indeed, my students were progressing.

If I felt that half my class was slipping through the cracks, it not a big surprise that district office personnel and parents and administrators also look at some writing workshops and have the same worry. "How do you know they're progressing?"

Into this context enters the idea of authentic assessment. Authentic assessment is an idea whose time has come. Everyone everywhere seems to be talking about it. Candidates for principalships, workshop leaders, curriculum committees at the state, local, and school level, and publishers of books and curricular materials—all of them talk about authentic assessment.

There are many reasons to applaud the new interest in authentic assessment. Above all, we can applaud because the current interest grows out of the fact that constructivist approaches to teaching are becoming more central, more mainstream, in our schools. State education departments, district offices, and administrators are developing new methods of assessment because they are now experiencing the same disequilibrium many constructivist teachers have felt for a long time. It's difficult to expound inquiry methods of learning science, collaborative groups, hands-on math, theme studies, reading and writing workshops, without feeling a new unease over whether standardized tests and rows of grades are really assessing the growth that matters.

Those of us who teach reading and writing workshops should be rejoicing at the current interest in authentic assessment, but many of us instead feel ambivalent, even deeply troubled, by what we see. As more and more school districts hurry to join the bandwagon of authentic assessment, strange things are happening. My colleagues and I often receive calls from school districts wanting to bring writing portfolios into their districts. When we ask about the district's involvement in writing workshops, we learn that often these same districts have not given their teachers help in turning their classrooms into writing workshops. How ironic it is to imagine a district investing in portfolios when it hasn't first invested in professional support for the teaching of writing. Then, too, I often hear of districts that are either purchasing a ready-made program for authentic assessment or adopting the authentic assessment program developed by another school district. And in far too many instances, good teachers tell me they can no longer teach according to their beliefs because they are controlled by the portfolio guidelines that someone else has developed. It's as if the old list of "skills to cover" has reappeared under the guise of authentic assessment.

Recently a teacher asked me whether I thought fairy tales would be a good genre for her students. When I looked a bit skeptical, she wondered about tall tales. Before I could say anything, she asked, "Or should they write fables? Or nursery rhymes?" Before she could list even more, I said, "These seem like such a curious bunch of genres. We don't usually sit down to write fairy tales, tall tales, fables. Where did you get the idea of using them in your writing workshop?"

"They are in our portfolio requirements," she said. "We're supposed to include ten different genres in each child's portfolio." Getting out a sheet of paper, she said, "Here's the list."

How disappointing it is to see what some people and some institutions have done in the name of authentic assessment. One would almost rather return to the days of standardized test scores than use this sort of "authentic assessment," since at least some teachers could keep the yearly tests from *necessarily* intruding into the day-to-day life of their classrooms.

Jane Hansen, Bonnie Sunstein, Don Graves, and their colleagues from the University of New Hampshire (Graves and Sunstein 1992) have wisely sounded the alarm against the ways in which some school districts and states are trying to standardize portfolios. It's crucial for districts to listen to this alarm.

Real assessment—the inner game of assessment—cannot happen merely by decree. Although the collection of artifacts and the completion of records can be legislated, in the end, minds-on teaching is something that happens deep within the self. If we teachers want to reform our methods of assessment (and even if we eventually want to establish new district policies), it's important to realize that the place to begin is within ourselves. But of course, we can go through the motions of assessment—we can play the external game—without really assessing at all. Assessment is an act of mind.

Systems for authentic assessment must, quite literally, be "fleshed out" in classrooms, for it is there they must live. Authentic assessment can never be effectively mandated. The truth is, "authentic assessment" cannot exist unless we, as teachers, inhabit and claim the process as our own. We can be required to fill our classrooms with the trappings of authentic assessment, but even if rooms are filled from floor to ceiling with portfolios, this doesn't mean assessment is alive in those classrooms. In the end, assessment happens in the minds and hearts, in the memories and plans, of those who are involved.

I am not arguing that we be given total autonomy around the issue of assessment. In the schools I know best, when writing workshop teachers have been given this autonomy on assessment, when we haven't had to answer to anyone about our record-keeping, there has sometimes been surprisingly little record-keeping and assessment going on. I don't think that people who support teachers need to wait patiently for us to devise our own measures of authentic assessment.

Randy Bomer and I tell the two hundred principals with whom we work most closely that we think it is appropriate and wise for them to ask teachers these two questions:

- What kinds of records are you keeping of your students' growth?
- How are you saving students' work?

Some people ask these questions indirectly. I recently heard, for example, that Bob Wortman, a principal in Arizona, evaluates his teachers by meeting in mid-October with each of them. He asks, "Would you jot down a list of your students?" Then (after noticing who is and is not included on the list) Bob chooses one child's name from the list and says, "Tell me about this child." I admire Bob's insistence on assessment, on our knowing our students.

A decade ago, Don Graves suggested a procedure that is rather similar to Bob Wortman's. "In order to teach writing," Graves said, "we need to know what our students know." He suggested that if we ever had competency tests for teachers of writing, the tests might involve listing children's names and then, beside each name, writing down that child's areas of expertise.

Both of these suggestions are particularly interesting to me in light of a story I heard recently. Jeff Smith at Rutgers University has been studying a large preschool involving seventy students, three teachers, and some teaching aides. The teachers and aides were each asked to list the name of every child they could think of, and after Smith examined the resulting lists, it became clear that the names of eight children didn't appear on anyone's list. This may be our greatest fear as teachers.

I like to believe that I'm too child-centered, too caring, to overlook a child, and I suspect that many of us hold this belief. Randy Bomer recently worked with a group of experienced writing workshop teachers who claimed they didn't need to record their writing conferences. "We *know* which kids we get to," they said. Randy convinced them nevertheless to try keeping some records, just for a little while, just as an experiment. The teachers came away from doing it saying, "I didn't realize how much I wasn't seeing." Of course, the problem is that the children we tend to overlook are the very ones who most need our attention.

Developing Our Own Systems of Assessment

I've come to believe that developing our own systems for authentic assessment begins by bringing a new mindfulness to the assessment measures we already have in place. And although when I first led a writing workshop I thought I had no assessment procedures in place, the truth was that they were there; I just didn't see them or use them as methods of assessment.

For example, I remember asking my children at the start of the year to make a personal coat of arms that would reveal who they were. I hung their work up, but I didn't study it and I certainly didn't use it as an invitation to interview my students and begin building a portrait of each one of them. What a loss! Often in our teaching we do not learn from what our students show us. We may ask students to cut out magazine pictures and combine them into collages that demonstrate their interests, but then we don't study the collages. We need to realize that our teaching will begin to work only when we look with great care at the coats of arms and collages, timelines and autobiographies, surveys and questionnaires our children give us. Sometimes we do "Getting to Know Our Students" procedures just because that's what other teachers do. Nancie Atwell surveyed her students, asking, "Are you a good writer? Are you a good reader? Who is your favorite author?" and so we do the same. Soon we have a bulging folder of thirty-two surveys, and we stash the folder away somewhere or dutifully file each child's survey in that child's folder, feeling pleased that we've conducted surveys. But the entire process is only valuable if we use the surveys to make meaning. We need to ask from the start, "How can I collect information that will *really* matter to me and to the child?" We need to ask, "What will I do with this information once it's collected?"

Once we begin expecting to develop portraits of our students from these early sources of information, our methods change. For me, for example, I find it's difficult to draw a lot of significance out of students' short answers to a list of questions. Granted, I would find it enormously significant to see my sons' answers to the question "Are you a good writer?" or "Who is your favorite author?" but this is because I know them so well, their answers would fit into or challenge assumptions I already have about them. But I'm less clear that I'd be able to find a lot of meaning in having thirty children, each new to me, telling me their favorite author, their favorite places for reading, and so forth. My goal at the start of the year is to connect with children, to learn their passions, fears, and preoccupations. I want to understand first what it is that makes each child tick, so I would probably *not* begin by conducting a survey filled with prepared, short-answer questions.

Instead of conducting surveys, then, many of the teachers with whom I work begin in August to form a portrait of each of the students in their incoming class. They often write to the parents of each child (or to the student, if he or she is in secondary school). I describe these letters in detail in Chapter 2 of *Living Between the Lines*.

Let me be clear. I am not trying to suggest that teachers the world over must write letters in August to the parents of their students. Some readers may want to try this, just as many of my colleagues and I tried Nancie Atwell's surveys. My point, however, is that if we do any one of those procedures merely because it's what writing workshop teachers do, it will lead us nowhere. The crucial thing about all these activities—surveys, letters to parents, personal coats of arms—is that they are intended as instruments of assessment. They are tools. A tool—an instrument—gets its identity from the fact that it is used for a purpose.

If our purpose is to know our students so well that our teaching responds to each one of them, we will undoubtedly alter and outgrow the tools others invent. One could almost say that one way we can assess whether we are truly using assessment procedures is that if we are, we will by definition be altering them.

Marilyn Berkowitz, in Tenafly, New Jersey, found that for her, what worked best at the start of the year was to send a survey rather than a letter to her children's parents. In it, she asked these questions:

1. Does your child ask to be read to?
2. Does your child offer to read to you?
3. Does your child choose to read/look at books independently at home?
4. Does your child show an interest in using markers, crayons, or pencils for writing and drawing at home?

She also invited additional comments.

Later, in the middle of the year, Marilyn wrote a letter home asking her children's parents for their input:

Dear Parents:

I am very pleased about how well the children are evolving as writers and readers. I hope you are enjoying seeing your child go through this process.

At the beginning of the school year, I sent home a questionnaire so I could learn more about your child. Your responses were very helpful. Most of you enjoyed the opportunity to write about your child. I would like to ask you again to write a letter telling how you have observed your child emerging as a reader and writer. It would be most helpful if you could give specific examples when you respond. Your responses will help me think about and evaluate the current program. Please consider these questions only as a guide.

Does your child enjoy writing and drawing pictures? Has there been a change in this activity since your child entered school?

Does your child tell you stories? Does your child write stories at home? Does your child write letters to you or other people?

Does your child show an interest in words while listening to a story? while shopping in a store? while riding in a car?

Does your child ever choose to read books for leisure time enjoyment? Does your child ask to take books on trips? Does your child ask to go to the library or a bookstore?

Does your child show an awareness of authors? Can your child name some authors?

Does your child generally have more of an interest in print and words? Does he/she use the pictures to help understand the story or figure out a word?

Thank you so much for your written observations. I would appreciate having your responses by Wednesday, February 24. If you have your response sooner, please send it in.

Sincerely,
Marilyn Berkowitz

When I work with teachers who want to write letters to the parents of their incoming students, I ask them, "What might you ask?" One teacher thought she would request the following:

- What books does your child have at home?
- Please tell me about your child's study habits.

- What are some books your child reads easily? With difficulty?
- What are your child's strengths and weaknesses as a reader and a writer?

Another thought she would ask,

- What is your youngster like? What are your child's interests?
- How does your child play and pretend?
- What are your child's passions? Areas of expertise? Dreams?

Then I suggested that the teachers look back over their questions and ask themselves, "What do these reveal about what *I* most value and need to know?"

Let me reemphasize that I am not recommending we all write letters to parents or conduct surveys of our young authors. Although I do believe we'll want to begin the year by getting to know our students, there are, of course, countless other ways to do so. Judy Davis uses yarn to divide her bulletin board into a grid of thirty squares. She and her children each take one square as their own. In this square, they put artifacts that are emblematic of themselves, things that, taken as a whole, combine to say, "This is who I am." Other teachers begin their year with share sessions, which are not intended as times to talk about writing, but rather, as times to talk about each child's literary history. On one day, the teacher and children chat together about the question "What is the most important writing I've ever done in my life?" On another day, they talk about "What are my fears as a writer?" or "Who are the people who have helped me most with my writing?" Some teachers suggest that instead of talking about these questions, the members of a class might take a few minutes to write on one of these issues and then read their writing to the circle or to the person on their right or left.

Is this assessment or is it instruction? The answer, of course, is that it is both. When we attend to the ways in which our children compose their lives as readers and writers, we help them claim who they are as readers and writers and invite them to become more deliberate about their choices, more conscious of what they are choosing for themselves.

I think it's a wise idea to invite everyone to join together in learning about one another as readers, writers, and learners, because nothing enriches a community more than awareness and respect. If we interview children individually about their reading and writing histories, we will want to talk about our discoveries with the whole class so that the other children can hear about the ways their classmates have composed their own literary lives. It is important for children, as for teachers, to notice and celebrate and muse over and question and learn from the different ways reading and writing fit into people's lives. When we hear that Sonya keeps a running list of recommended books, we wonder whether we'd like to do the same. When we learn that Jana gives her writing away as Christmas gifts, we wonder if anyone would want our writing. When we learn that Andrew has a desk drawer filled with things to inspire his writing—a photograph from the camp in Australia, a map of the world, a special pencil—we wonder what we would put in our inspiration drawer.

Of course, we needn't choose between conducting our own one-on-one interviews with children and involving the entire class in a shared inquiry into each other's reading and writing. If we conduct long interviews with some of our children, we may want to play the audiotape of parts of those interviews to the class, asking everyone to join us in jotting down what they notice and admire and wonder about in their friends' life stories. We could also jot notes about ways we are similar to and different from the interviewed writer. The challenge, always, will be to make meaning from what we learn.

I have talked at length about getting to know our students at the beginning of the year. I've done this partly because I have come to believe that each teacher must, in his or her own way, develop strategies for really seeing what it is our students do. But I have also tried to show that methods for gathering information get their life and direction from our purposes and values. Although I support the idea that as teachers, each of us should be expected to develop tools for learning about our students, I think it is essential that we be given a chance to devise and alter these tools. In September, along with developing ways to begin getting to know our students, we'll also want to

1. Develop a system for recording our conferences. Randy Bomer suggests that our record-keeping method should be portable (it will need to move about the room with us) and efficient, and that it should allow our notes on any given child to accumulate over time.
2. Devise a method for systematically saving the entries, rough drafts, editing checklists, and so on for at least representative pieces of writing.

Efficiency is one of the most important characteristics of a good system of record-keeping. Each of us needs to invent a system that is practical and suits our individual quirky habits and needs. For a start, we need to find an efficient way to jot notes on what a child says and does during our conferences. Some teachers carry notebooks with a section for each student around with them. Other teachers put the name of every student on a single sheet of paper, with a space beside each for comments.

Randy kept his own variation of such a record-keeping sheet, and when he began helping teachers at P.S. 183 rethink their methods of assessment, he brought along a copy. "I knew these teachers would need to develop their own assessment measures that were as close to the bone of their teaching as possible," Randy said. "I knew they would treat my form as a straw dog to take apart. But I brought it because I'd made it, so at least I could tell them how it had fit into the life of my classroom, into the moves of my room."

Some of the teachers made copies of Randy's form and for a week tried keeping their own notes on it. Not surprisingly, Randy later told me, every one of these teachers found that, for one reason or another, the form was all wrong. Each changed the form in different, often subtle ways. Musing about this, Randy suggested that we will *always* resist a form someone else has made. "When Nicole Martin felt an almost physical revulsion to the form—as if I'd been trying to put *her* inside those boxes—it reminded me that the decision about how we keep records is an intimate, individual thing," Randy said. "What we, as teachers, need to do is to invent methods of record-keeping that allow us to fit writing into the steps of our own work."

In the end, each of us as teachers will need to develop our own system for recording our writing conferences and our observations of our students. One way to begin inventing these is to adopt someone else's system, knowing that we'll end up rejecting and revising it as we learn what works and doesn't work for us.

We might, for example, try carrying a page full of large mailing labels on a clipboard, so that rather than spending time finding a particular child's name on a page, they can just put the name on a label, jot some notes beside it, and then later, after school, unpeel the labels and stick them onto the appropriate child's record sheet. We might, alternatively, follow the example of Ellen Blackburn Karelitz, a primary-level teacher in South Berwick, Maine, who keeps a composition book in every student's writing folder and records eclectic notes there. She also borrows an idea developed a decade ago by teachers Judy Eagen and Mary Ellen Giacobbe, and has her students each keep a running list entitled "Things I Can Do in My Writing."

Portfolios

The saying "A picture is worth a thousand words" is a wise one, and in a similar fashion, one piece of a child's writing carries more information than a great many anecdotal notes. I think it is wise, therefore, for teachers to insist that each student keep a portfolio.

A portfolio should not be confused with a collection of Best Work. It is meant, instead, as a record of the writer's journey. A portfolio should reflect the turning points, the low moments, the ruts, the breakthroughs, the mountain peaks. Portfolios will include not only the writing itself, but also some of the other records children keep. For example, in some classrooms, children keep a weekly or monthly calendar in which they jot their plans for a day (or a week) and then, later, their accomplishments. In some classrooms, children write a letter to the teacher each week reflecting on their work over the course of that week. In some classrooms, children keep a checklist of the strategies they've used to linger with and develop an entry, or of the genres they've written in, or of what they've learned in peer conferences. In most classrooms, writers have some form of an editing checklist. All these records belong in the writing portfolio. The portfolio provides a testimony and a record, but it is also a place from which to plan, to set goals. Learners look back on what they have done and forward to what they want to do. Collections exist in order to evoke this kind of reflection, planning, and goal-setting, so it is pointless for children to assemble their portfolio at the end of a year. Throughout the year, children will need to reflect on their portfolio in order to categorize the genres they have and haven't used, notice patterns in their writing, identify and learn from their turning points, and rank pieces from best to worst.

Of course, the important question is not so much what to collect but rather, how to make something of those collections. This is an important question not only for teachers, but also for children. Youngsters need to see that their portfolios have real purposes and real value. In East Williston, New Jersey, children turn their kindergarten, first-, and second-grade portfolios into a book entitled "On Becoming Eight," which they present to their parents at a ceremony held near their birthday. At Central Park East in New York City, graduating twelfth graders give an individual oral presentation of their portfolio to an audience of raters, which includes a teacher, an outside mentor, and an eleventh-grade student. At Shelter Rock School in Manhasset, Long Island, Lydia Bellino and her colleagues ask children, during their final days of school, to look through their portfolios and write a letter to their teacher for the next year. The letters accompany their portfolios. Teachers also have a final day together after the children have left in which they go through the same process of reviewing folders and writing to the following year's teacher. The folders and letters are then given to the teacher, who has an entire summer to begin knowing his or her incoming class.

Assessment, Like Writing, Is a Process of Developing Meaning

We can picture it. Mrs. Robertson carries a grid around with her on a clipboard and on it she records the main events of her conferring. Mrs. Strauss, meanwhile, keeps what looks like a recipe box with index cards full of her notes on particular children. In one classroom, at the end of each month, the teacher puts representative pieces in each child's portfolio. In another classroom, old notebooks and rough drafts go into the portfolio, as do final drafts when they're not mailed or posted or given as gifts.

All of this is necessary—but not sufficient. Keeping records such as these can be crucial—or trivial. It all depends on what we make of what we collect. Someone once pointed out that a sculptor chips away at a block of marble for days and days . . . and a horse or a man emerges. But an ordinary person could chip away at the same block of marble for months and nothing at all might emerge. The difference is the quality of attention. It's the intention.

I have heard people say, "The difference between a portfolio and a folder of student work is *purpose.*" I would go further and say, "The difference between assessment that is busywork and assessment that reflects the essence of our teaching is what we and our students make of what we collect."

In many of the districts I know best, teachers and administrators hope that authentic assessment procedures will release their districts from the bondage of standardized tests. These administrators believe that in order to overthrow standardized tests, authentic assessment procedures need to yield numbers, or rankings. *The Primary Language Record* and *The English Profiles Handbook* are among the more thoughtful published assessment programs that provide such rubrics, and when we see them, it's tempting to adopt them as our own.

These published rubrics can be helpful to us because they can be one of the starting points from which we make our own rubrics. I do not think, however, that our observations, our data, should be used in the service of someone else's rubrics. Just as writing is a meaning-making process, so, too, assessment is a meaning-making process. Just as we learn to gather fragments of our lives in our notebooks and grow them into major pieces of writing, so too, we will want to take our small observations about our children and grow these into big ideas. Each of us needs to be nudged to grow meaning from our own notes. We'll do so by talking with our colleagues about the fine-grained details of our teaching and our children's learning. In order to do this, we need time. No workshop on assessment, no consultants, no programs or materials, can take the place of time. We need time to reread our notes, to write about them, and to meet with each other—to talk, wonder, question, compare, reread, write, rethink. . . .

We need time to reflect and to make meaning from what we collect, and our students need it as well. The time has to come often, in the midst of the school year, not merely at the end. All of us need to look back in order to look ahead. In one school, Randy Bomer nudged children to look back on their portfolios by suggesting that in each response group, one writer spread his or her writing out on the desk and that the entire response group then spend a few minutes reading their friends' writing and making notes on it. After some silent time, Randy suggested that the groups talk and talk and talk. "What has this writer done?" Randy asked. "What do you notice about this writer's writing?"

The children were tongue-tied. It was as if they didn't know *how* to talk about texts. They could talk about the writer's subjects, but they didn't seem to have any idea of what it meant to talk about texts, and especially to talk in any words other than "You can picture it," a phrase that had been coined and sanctioned by the teacher.

This is why we assess: to learn. If these children can't talk easily about texts, they will have a hard time being critical readers of their own or anyone else's writing. They will have a hard time making deliberate improvements in their writing and writing reflective pieces to accompany their portfolios. The answer, of course, is not to stay away from an activity that proved difficult but to do far more of it.

Sometimes it will help if we regularly ask young writers to reread their collections of writing looking for one or two things. We might suggest, for example, that after they reread their portfolios, they write and later talk about any one of the following (focusing on one question is generally more productive than skimming through several):

- What surprises me in my portfolio?
- What new risks have I taken?
- How is my writing changing? Not changing?

- If I were to categorize my writing, what are some categories I might invent?
- What patterns do I see in my writing?

At first, our children may not know what to say in response to any one of these questions. Their answers will probably be wooden, stilted, and abbreviated. As teachers, we will be tempted to move on to a different question. But if we ask one question often and encourage children to share and develop and talk about their responses, they'll grow into the language they need to reflect on their writing.

Developing Systematic Methods of Assessment

Once we and our students begin rereading the data we are collecting, letting patterns and surprises and trends emerge, we may be in a position to develop both our own rubrics and some more directed forms of data collection. If we notice, for example, that some of our young spellers move from relying on phonics to also relying on their visual memory of words, two things may result:

- We may have the beginnings of a rubric—or a descriptive scale—on which we can plot our children's growth as spellers.
- We may have the seed idea behind a more systematic form of data collection. We may, for example, want to ask each child to spell ten words that are high-frequency words in that child's life (*school, home,* and so on), and then we may look to see whether the spellings appear to be purely phonetic or whether they are also sight-based.

My point is not to encourage someone to collect data about children's transition from phonetic to sight-based spellings. My point is that a system for assessment grows over time, out of the meanings we make from our early records. The place to begin is with the very essential process of taking notes on whatever seems significant in our children's writing lives and ensuring that children keep collections of their written work. In a sense, these early forms of collection parallel the early uses of a notebook. There is no particular "topic" yet. We record whatever bits and pieces we see and wonder about and notice. Then, when we reread our notes, things begin to emerge that strike us as worth pursuing in more focused ways. Just as we begin after a time to collect more entries about a particular subject, we may in our assessment begin to pursue something we've noticed or something that points to a particular concern.

I love it when I'm on the trail of a concern or an idea. The question is, how do we know what area to collect data around? How do we know what deserves to go on the front burner of our assessment work?

At a recent Writing Project meeting, Randy Bomer suggested that it is sometimes helpful to ask, "What are my students doing when they seem to me to be doing writing workshop well? What are they doing when they seem to be doing reading workshop well?" If we don't know the answers to these questions, we can write down whatever we see in the workshop. By paying closer, more systematic attention to what we notice in our classrooms, we can begin to gather a list of indicators—and values—that matter to us. A teacher, for example, may note the following:

- I notice when a writer keeps on writing past the lunch bell, past my invitations to gather for a class meeting. I notice when a writer says, "Let me finish this" or "Wait, one sec!"
- I notice when my kids clap when we announce writing time.
- I notice when the energy for writing goes up . . . or down.
- I notice when my kids move independently from finishing one piece of writing to initiating another.
- I notice when a writer brings her draft to a peer conference with specific questions in mind for her readers.
- I notice when kids respond to a piece of writing by talking not just about the subject but also about the text, about the way the writer has rendered the subject.

By naming what we are already using as informal indicators of an effective writing workshop, we can derive goals that are truly our own. Alternatively, we can begin by backing away from our classrooms and asking, "Why did I choose teaching and not banking?" "What ultimately matters more to me than anything else in my teaching?" The answers to these questions will help us to direct and focus some of our forms of data collection.

If a teacher or a group of teachers says, "What I want more than anything in the world is for my students to be lifelong readers and writers. I want them to read and write during their own lived lives—at home, with friends, for their own reasons," then it's important to think, "How can my methods of assessment encourage me to *value* and *evaluate* lifelong literacy? How can assessment help me teach toward that goal in more thoughtful and

FIGURE 19–1   Assessment measures for teachers who want students to become lifelong writers

Literary history	Collection of artifacts	Record keeping
May interview students about the reading and writing that happens in their homes. Who does it? When, where, why . . . ?	May ask students to save and later to categorize or reflect on *all* the writing they do in a week, including the functional writing.	It may seem important for students to record the context in which their reading and writing happen so that, for example, their notebook entries begin with a brief record of the setting and occasion for the writing episode. Students may later look back to analyze and reflect on how their writing changes based on its context.
May learn about students' passions, projects, and ambitions.	May ask students to take turns as "The Reader of the Week," and in that capacity, to bring in all the reading they like to do, creating a chalkboard library out of the collection of books, magazines, postcards, brochures.	Instead of keeping an index entitled "Books I Have Read," students may want to record "Texts I Have Read" or "Reading Occasions." Students could keep parallel lists of their writing.
May find out about the audiences students have had for their writing. When has their writing made someone feel something? When has their writing been useful? Important? Connected to their projects?	May ask students to bring drafts related to whatever their passions may be: collections, magazines, Lego sculptures, and so on.	

wise and responsive ways?" If another teacher or group of teachers says, "My dream is that my students will read like writers. I want them to read literature thinking, 'How can I write like this?'" that teacher will want to ask, "How can my students and I use assessment measures to help us as we work toward making more reading-writing connections?"

Likewise, if a group of teachers or even an entire staff is studying a particular subject (spelling, revision, children's ability to talk about good writing), they will want to ask, "How can we gather information from our students?" It is crucial for teachers and students to realize that specific assessment instruments grow out of values. As teachers, we must consider how we and our students can collect literary artifacts and samples, and do interventions and observations that support our goals and those of our students. Figures 19–1 and 19–2 provide some guidelines on how this may be accomplished.

FIGURE 19–2 Assessment measures for teachers who want to foster reading and writing connections

Literary history	Collection of artifacts	Record keeping	Intervention	Observation
Might interview students about times in their lives when they have tried to write like a particular author.	May ask students to bring in whatever they've read that is written by their favorite author and any texts that remind them of those by that author.	Students may, in the margins of their notebooks and drafts, note the times when their writing is affected by their reading.	Students may be asked to spend time every Friday writing or talking about an issue such as, "Have you found ways to attach reading and writing to the projects of your lives?"	Students may be asked to write with their books out on the table. The teacher may watch the class to record instances when a child moves between his or her writing and reading.
May learn which books have mattered so much to students that they have read and reread them.		Students may read with stick-ons in hand, and if something in the book makes them think, "I'd like to write like that," they put a stick-on in the book. These sections of text can later be talked or written about.	Students may be asked, on Fridays, to spend time talking together about the times and ways in which reading has affected their writing.	
May want to know if students have had mentor relationships in other aspects of their lives.			Students may be asked, when a piece of writing is completed, to write an accompanying process log about what they did in order to write the piece. They may be encouraged to address especially big questions about their reading-writing connections.	

Assessment is about values. In our classrooms, we build a world. That world is shaped by our carpet and our author's chair, by our rituals and procedures, but it is shaped even more by our values. Just as small towns are defined by the way some behavior is regarded as normal and other as deviant, so too, classrooms are shaped by what we reward and reprimand, by what we celebrate, by what we hold up as a model. By collecting evidence of a particular thing—say, of writing-reading connections—we embody our values and goals, we put flags into the ground that say, "*This* is my goal."

Developing Shared Systems for Assessment

Once individual teachers or clusters of teachers realize that through assessment practices we can invent and pursue our own important questions and goals, we can come together and begin to find assessment instruments that can work for all of us. For example, once a number of teachers have invented different ways of using portfolios in their classrooms, it makes sense for these teachers (and this may be the entire staff in a district or a team of people) to pool what they have learned and to begin to wonder whether there couldn't be some common threads to all of their portfolio work.

The important thing is that if a group of teachers are going to share ideas about how to use portfolios, the shared ideas need to emerge out of independent work in classrooms. The teachers who come together in this way will be intrigued to see what teachers in other states and countries have invented, but it's unlikely they would merely adopt someone else's portfolio procedures. Instead, they will ask questions like those the teachers in Tenafly, New Jersey, are already asking: What do we value in our students' literacy learning? What could we—all of us—observe that might give us indications of that? How might we gather these things within the flow of our everyday classroom life? How often might we collect it?

In the Manhasset school district on Long Island, the teachers who work with Lydia Bellino do their own individual record-keeping, but they all collect information about three items many of the district's teachers feel they especially value: revision strategies, the ability to choose topics, and competence with written conventions. These teachers also decided that it made sense, across the district, for all of them to learn about their students' attitudes toward reading and writing, and so they ask every child to complete a particular attitude survey they have developed. One item on the survey, for example, lists eight different genres and then asks the child, "Which of these do you like to read?" The Manhasset teachers also fill out a summary sheet about reading for each child. These sheets include scales such as this one:

Asks questions to clarify meaning:

| Not yet | Sometimes,
with support | Independently | Independently,
with strength |

Expresses interpretations and opinions in discussions and in writing:

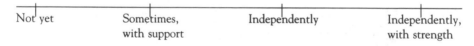

| Not yet | Sometimes,
with support | Independently | Independently,
with strength |

In Manhasset, the children spend a lot of time during the school year writing in response to literature, and the teachers spend a great deal of time with Lydia Bellino studying this subject. The teachers have therefore decided to gather some standardized information by asking, for example, that every fourth grader write a response to a particular entry from Jean Little's *Hey World, Here I Am*. Children also include responses they've written to other pieces of literature in their portfolios.

My hunch is that the *real* reason for asking all fourth graders to write in response to a piece of literature may be that the papers that result from such an activity can help these teachers see his or her teaching alongside that of colleagues. Then, too, this work nudges them to talk together about what they value and aim toward. The Manhasset teachers have spent hours trying to invent a rubric for assessing this year's stack of papers. "What is it that we regard as good work?" they've asked, and they have begun to build a rubric that fits into a scale such as this one:

Understanding of reading selection:

1	2	3	4	5
Appears to have minimal understanding of reading selection	Appears to have little understanding of reading selection	Appears to have partial understanding of issues	Appears to have adequate understanding of issues	Appears to have a well-considered understanding of key issues

Thoughtfulness:

1	2	3	4	5
Ideas or opinions are inappropriate; no supporting details or references to text	Ideas and opinions are not supported by details or references	Ideas or opinions are supported by details or references that are general in nature	Ideas and opinions are supported by appropriate details and/or references to text	Ideas and opinions are supported by specific details and references; support is precise and thoughtfully selected

Organization:

1	2	3	4	5
Lacks organization and/or includes digressions	Weak organization	Adequately organized	Focused and clearly organized	Expressive, focused, logically organized

For teachers who have invented the idea of having children write in response to a particular selection of literature and for those who spend hours looking at these responses and asking "What can I make of them?" this process is probably very worthwhile indeed. But five years from now, if teachers are still doing this, it will certainly have lost its value. It will have become just one more hoop to jump through. It is crucial, therefore, not only that teachers invent their own assessment procedures, but that these procedures self-destruct after a limited period of time. A system for gathering data will be interesting and helpful to the teachers who have chosen that system because it fits their needs and interests. The goal, then, is never to have an assessment system firmly in place. Instead, it is to be engaged in an ongoing process of inventing, piloting, rethinking, learning from, and revising measures of assessment.

If a district creates opportunities that encourage all teachers to value and think collaboratively about asking their students to write in response to literature, it may make sense to ask all children to do this in a standardized way for a time. After a while, the focus among these teachers will switch to something else. Perhaps teachers in the district will become interested in helping children become more strategic as spellers. If release time is made available for teachers to notice their students' spelling strategies and think about them, this can become a rewarding form of professional development.

Final Thoughts

In some districts, teachers have been steeped in assessment for a long time. In other districts, people are just now realizing that adjoining districts "are ahead," and so are scurrying to catch up. If I have a bit of advice, it is this: Slow down. Our goal, I think, should not be to have an assessment program in place, but to have forums for rethinking assessment in place. Process is everything in rethinking assessment. As Ted Chittendon for Educational Testing Services once said, "Assessment measures will almost always be valuable to those who authored them . . . and they will almost always be annoying to those who inherit them."

To me, all of this means that the teaching staff in each district (and indeed, each teacher) will need to invent these procedures. The process can be a collaborative one, and it certainly can involve learning from the observation forms and checklists others have invented, but in the end I believe the process must also be a very personal one.

If I have a second bit of advice, it is that we must do everything possible to be sure that our "authentic assessment" measures *are* authentic. Our measures of assessment will only be authentic if they

- Grow out of and reflect our values and plans, and our students' values and plans.
- Grow out of and are woven into the very fabric of the school day.
- Inform our teaching and our students' learning.

We *do* need ways to hold ourselves accountable for our students' growth. It's not enough to teach our hearts out and hope our students are growing. We *do* need ways to document and to attend to our students' progress. We *do* need to ask, "What will take the place of the grade book?" Assessment allows us to have "a minds-on approach" to all our teaching. Without it, we can't design mini-lessons that extend what our students do, nor can we intervene to lift up the level of our students' peer conferring. Assessment is not an optional add-on to our teaching; it is not an afterthought. Assessment is where the action lies. It is the main event.

Literature on Assessment

Arter, Judith A., and Vicki Spandel. Using portfolios of student work in instruction and assessment, *Northwest Regional Educational Laboratory*, pp. 1–21. Portland, OR: Northwest Regional Educational Laboratory, June 1991.

Cambourne, Brian, and Jan Turbill. Assessment in whole language classrooms: Theory into practice. *The Elementary School Journal*, vol. 90, no. 3 (1990): 337–49.

Cohen, Miriam. *First grade takes a test*. New York: Dell Young Yearling Book, 1980.

English profiles handbook: Assessing and reporting students' progress in English. Victoria, Australia: School Programs Division, Ministry of Education and Training, 1991.

Graves, Donald H., and Bonnie S. Sunstein, eds. *Portfolio portraits.* Portsmouth, NH: Heinemann, 1992.

Inner London Education Authority. *The primary language record: Handbook for teachers.* London: Centre for Language in Primary Education, 1988. (Distributed in the U.S. by Heinemann, Portsmouth, NH.)

20
Workshop Teaching Throughout the Day

I'll never forget Lonnie. For most of the school day Lonnie seemed to stand at the chalkboard, walk the aisles in her classroom, and work at her desk. For most of the school day, Lonnie's children filled in blanks, answered questions, competed with each other, lined up quietly. Then at eleven o'clock sharp each day, Lonnie would say, "It's time to write. Desk monitors, are you ready? Paper monitors, are you ready? Portfolio monitors? Tool monitors?" The monitors would respond in unison, "Re-e-e-a-d-y," and then, on signal, they'd all spring into action, racing to do their allotted tasks. Three children moved the desks from rows into clumps, three others spread carpet samples onto the floor to create a corner rug, three others brought out a variety of paper and created "a writing supply center" . . . and in a flash, Lonnie's classroom was transformed from a traditional one, filled with frontal teaching and student passivity, into an active, interactive writing workshop.

Lonnie's classroom is, in a sense, an extreme version of what I often see as I work with teachers who want to establish writing workshops. For many of us, the writing workshop has acted as a counterculture to the rest of our classroom life, a world apart.

This has always seemed right to me. Writing workshops belong within all kinds of classrooms. If a teacher teaches math, social studies, and reading with pre- and post-tests, exercises, and "motivating activities," then I think it is an extraordinary and brave thing for that teacher to establish a time and place—an hour a day—in which the classroom revolves around different norms and ways of being. Lonnie and all the other teachers who turn their traditional classrooms into workshops for one hour of every school day deserve to be celebrated.

But it is also true that no matter how many monitors Lonnie has to rearrange desks, carpets, and materials, she will never be able to blow a whistle and transform the culture of her room. We can rearrange desks on command, but we cannot do the same for the relationships, tone, and value system in our classrooms. We cannot expect, for example, that from eleven to twelve o'clock each day, our dutiful students will become independent, resourceful learners.

From John Goodlad's studies of American classrooms as well as from our own experiences, we know that for most of the day, in most classrooms, children make few significant choices. They work on teacher-assigned tasks for the teacher-as-evaluator. Is it any surprise, then, that when these classrooms are turned into writing workshops, children keep asking, over and over, "What should I do next?" and "Is this okay?" Is it any surprise that when these teachers ask, "How do you like your draft?" children look startled by the question, shrug and say, "It's fine, I guess. Can I copy it over?" Is it any surprise that when these teachers ask them, "What are you planning to do with your poem when it's done?" children shift from one foot to another nervously and say, "I don't know"?

Although there are ways of responding when children ask "What should I do next?" or "Is this okay?" and there are ways to nudge children to become self-critics, no remedial measures will ever take the place of establishing norms, values, relationships, and traditions that are consistent throughout the child's school day and school career. I recently visited the Mooney Pond School in Melbourne, Australia. I went first to a big hall outside eight classrooms where about five children from each of the eight classrooms were spending an hour working in dress-up areas, in an oversized sandbox, in the woodworking area, and in an area filled with large hollow wooden blocks. As I watched, a child went among the clusters of children, saying, "We'll gather in five minutes." Before long the children had gathered in a circle that seemed reminiscent of the "author's share" circle I know so well. The teacher (who was, I believe, what we would call a paraprofessional) opened the meeting by asking, "Is someone willing to share what they've been doing?"

Two very small boys raised their hands and began describing how they'd built wooden airplanes. "They might not fly," one of the boys explained.

"What do you think of that?" the teacher said, directing her question to the circle of listeners. "Do you think the planes look aerodynamic?" A discussion ensued about whether the giant jets at airports *look* aerodynamic, and about why those planes *can* stay up in the air. In the end, two older children agreed to help the creators of the airplanes think again about how to make them efficient.

"Who else has done something they'd be willing to share?" the teacher asked, and the sharing shifted to a cluster of children who'd been pretending they were in a hospital. "She had high blood pressure. She had eighty over forty," one child said.

Later that morning I visited a fifth/sixth grade classroom in which the children were involved in "personal maths." Again, the children sat in a circle on the floor, only this time the gathering was clearly a time to launch rather than to reflect upon the math workshop. "Who else will be tackling a new problem today?" the teacher asked. "Nigel and I will be trying to build an orienteering course," one boy answered.

"Have you done your planning sheet?" the teacher asked, and the boys nodded, motioning to a sheet on the floor in front of them that asked such questions as: What will you investigate? What will you need in order to pursue this investigation? When will you be done?

That day I watched two girls trying to find the average age of the girls in their classroom, and of the boys (the girls, they felt, seemed more mature, but they weren't sure if they were chronologically older), and I watched two others calculating how much Australian money another child would need to change into American currency for his trip. As the children worked, their teacher moved among them. When I listened in on her conversations, I heard her asking, "What problems are you running into? How do you think you could solve that? What else could you try?"

I also watched several writing workshops. I was struck by the sense that at Mooney Pond School, teachers don't appear to find it difficult to lead a writing workshop. And no wonder. All day long, children are working in response groups, peer conferring with one another, planning for their own work, and assessing what they have done. The writing workshop runs according to expectations and management structures that last throughout the day.

There is no question that across America, changes are taking place in the teaching of math, reading, social studies, and science that parallel one another. The move toward inquiry-based science, discovery-oriented math, thematic studies, and collaborative learning are all different avenues to accomplish the same thing. Obviously, the ideal thing would be for us to weave these various strands together into a classroom that supports not only writing across the curriculum, but also inquiry and curiosity, collaboration and personal investment across the curriculum. And yet what I often see is that rather than regarding all of these reforms as unified, we view them as competing. The teacher who builds her reputation on having a wonderful reading and writing workshop competes *against* the teacher who builds her reputation on having a wonderful LOGO computer workshop. And the teacher who focuses on the teaching of writing one year disassembles the writing workshop another year in order to refocus her priorities on theme studies.

What an obvious and wonderful thing it would be for all of our curricular specialties to come together so that our classrooms would become active interactive workshops all day long. If this were to happen, I suspect that each curricular area would contribute not only by functioning as one part of the whole but also by adding to the culture of the classroom.

I have seen the science curriculum, for example, bring life—and I mean this quite literally—into the classroom. The spirit and tone of a classroom change when children are custodians of small creatures, of geckos and crickets and horned toads. I've seen a rich science curriculum teach children a reverence and respect for living things. I have seen a social studies curriculum help children delight in and inquire about the rich diversity within their own communities. And I have seen writing workshops contribute to a workshop-oriented classroom by helping all of us know that meaning isn't found, it is grown.

We can reflect on our weekend adventures and say "It was okay," or we can find millions of small things to notice and wonder about. In the same way, we can look at a horned toad and learn almost nothing, or we can look at the same creature and surmise, explore, and investigate. In the writing workshop, we learn that the responsibility to make meaning lies in an individual's hands, and as I discuss in Chapter 27, this lesson can contribute to learning across our lives as well as across the curriculum. In this chapter I want to suggest that the writing workshop can also contribute something else to a unified day of workshop teaching. Those of us who think often about the teaching of writing have developed, I believe, an array of management structures and teaching methods that can be used in workshops throughout the day.

Conferring

A teacher pulled her chair alongside Lila. "What are you reading?" the teacher asked.

"*Number the Stars,*" Lila answered, showing her the book cover.

"How did you happen to pick this book?" the teacher responded.

"I like books about the Holocaust," Lila answered. "And Becca suggested this one."

"Oh, you've read others about the Holocaust?"

"Yeah."

"How does this one compare?"

"I like it because it's not too gory; it's a gory *subject*, but it's not written too gorylike."

"Oh . . ." the teacher responded, "it's not too gory?" Then, seeming unsure of what to say next, she asked, "Are you having any problems?"

"No, it's off to a good start. I'm into it," Lila answered and, seeing that her teacher was moving on, she returned to the text.

Again and again, I've watched effective writing workshop teachers conduct less than effective reading conferences during independent reading time. Watching these conferences, I can't help but ask the same questions of these reading conferences that I ask of writing conferences.

- Was there a research phase in which you developed a theory about this reader and about how you might extend her reading?
- What—if any—hypotheses about this reader guided your questions to her and the teaching you did in the conference?
- What are the possible things you could have decided to teach within this conference? Which did you select?
- What have you taught the reader that will help another day with another text?

How different the reading conference would have been had the teacher followed the research-decide-teach pattern that is so fundamental to writing conferences. One might imagine that the conference would have begun similarly, but once the teacher learned that Lila had chosen this book because it was about the Holocaust, and that Becca had recommended it, one might imagine that the teacher could at this point have begun pursuing an emerging theory about this reader. For example, the teacher might have asked, "Do you tend to choose fictional books by subject, as you chose this book on the Holocaust? Do you have other subjects you like to read about?" Then, too, she might have said, "It's interesting to see that your friend knows you like to read on the Holocaust. How does she happen to know this? What kinds of conversations do you and your friends have about books? Do you talk with friends as you read a book? Have you and Becca been comparing notes?" A number of theories might emerge from all of this, and each would suggest different ways of intervening. Perhaps the teacher might suggest that Lila look back over all of her books on the Holocaust, wondering why some authors are able to avoid being gory when they write. Perhaps the teacher might suggest that Lila consider writing as well as reading historical fiction. Perhaps Lila might be encouraged to talk to friends not only when she needs book recommendations but also in the midst of her reading.

My point is not to launch into a chapter on reading conferences but to suggest that what we know about conferring in writing can inform us as we confer in reading and across the curriculum.

"Status of the Class" Reports

In her book *In the Middle,* Nancie Atwell suggests that "status of the class" reports provide one way for a teacher to quickly survey what her children are doing. "Before we get going today," the teacher of writing says to her students, who are gathered in a meeting area, "Can we zip around the circle, and each of you tell me, in one sentence, what you'll do today?"

When we first ask our students to update us on what they are doing, this procedure hardly feels like "zipping" around the room. Children aren't sure *what* they are doing. "Ummm," one says, "I *could* do this or I *might* do that." Another says, "Do you think I should . . ." or "You wanna hear what I wrote so far? See, yesterday I started. . . ."

The wonderful thing is that if we are using "status of the class" reports throughout the day in many different subject areas, it's worthwhile for us to take the time to intervene, increasing the efficiency of this procedure. It's worth it to say, "I'll give you three minutes of silent time to look over what you've been doing and to decide, 'What will I do next?'" and then, three minutes later, to say, "Now, think of one sentence that *best* explains your next steps."

Of course, when we ask readers or math students what they will be doing, we are going beyond inventing a way to record what people are doing. We're also creating a forum for our children to be planful, strategic, deliberate learners.

"I'm just doing math," children will say when we first ask them this question. "That's all."

"But will you try to do today's math problems any differently than you did yesterday's problems?" we might ask, and this might lead us to discuss the different ways one might work with a page of multiplication problems. It's possible to do the problems first by approximating, then by calculating, checking them only when there's a gap between the expected and the actual answer. It's possible to do the page very quickly and then return to check each one. It's possible to do a few problems and then to stop and wonder whether there's a pattern to the whole page. It's possible to work alone or with a friend, to use or not use manipulatives, to time oneself for speed or to work in a more leisurely way.

Is it important to choose one's stance toward a page of math problems? I think so. Surely this ability to be planful and flexible is one of the supreme abilities readers and writers need, and my hunch is that it's important across the curriculum.

Share Meetings

At the Mooney Pond School in Melbourne, Australia, what I watched in the big hall was children sharing their play just as I've seen children throughout the United States sharing their writing. When a child says to a circle of classmates, "Today I decided to do this . . . and it's turned out in such and such a way . . . and I need help on that," the amazing thing is not that the child has a chance to share, but the amount of intention and personal ownership that are reflected in the shared accomplishments. In Australia, it was wonderful indeed to see this sense of purpose and intention and reflectiveness when children were "playing," and to see that all of this also exists within children's "personal maths" and within their reading.

Of course, share sessions don't always work well. One of the first challenges is to help the child who is sharing to speak clearly and to share not only the work—the painting, poem, or math problem itself—but the story behind it. Sometimes we do this by having the person who'll be sharing warm up by talking first with one friend. Sometimes we divide the class into smaller sharing circles so that each child shares with only two or three classmates. Sometimes we help children to share by seating them in a special chair or stool to create a sense of occasion, while we sit among the listeners. "Wait until you can tell we're all listening," we say to the child. "Okay now, make us really understand what you've been doing."

The more difficult challenge is to be sure that these share sessions help not only the three or four children who have an opportunity to share but also the others who are listening. What I try to remember is that most instruction can happen through particular cases. If a child tells a circle of classmates that the math problem she tackled turned out to be too difficult for her, we can use this as an occasion for talking about what we can do when our math seems difficult. When a child says that she got some facts about frogs out of the encyclopedia, we can talk with children about ways of using our notebooks to *record* what we learn about frogs as well as to ask questions, to explore connections with what we already know, and so forth.

In the writing workshops I know best, the format of one child sharing work in progress, then asking, "Any questions or comments?" is only one of several ways to organize share sessions. Often, instead of responding to one child after another, share sessions become conversation circles. I might begin one by asking, "What's it been like, carrying your notebook with you throughout the day and writing in it often?"

The trick, I find, is to *expect* that some children will say "Boring" or "I hate it." If these conversation circles are going to be authentic and honest, then it's far better for children to say "Boring" than for them to posture for us and say what they know we want to hear. We need to be interested but not defensive. We need to say, "Can you tell me more about that?" rather than "Emily! How can you say it's boring?"

It makes perfect sense, of course, to use the "share session" format to create occasions for conversation about math and science as well as about writing. "What has it been like for you to do this work in fractions?" we can ask. "Do you have any ideas about what we might do in this class that could help you?"

Another format that some of us use often in share sessions is what I call "reading into the circle." If I wanted to encourage children to think about the language they use as they write, I might say at the start of a share session, "I have been dazzled by the way you are writing in fresh, brand-new ways. Can all of us take a few minutes to reread our notebooks, finding a sentence, a phrase, a paragraph, in which we love the words we've used?" Then, after a few minutes in which each of us leafs through his or her notebook, I'd say, "Put your finger on the spot if you found one (it's fine if you didn't), and let's do a reading-into-the-circle of these lines."

When this works well, one child reads . . . and there is silence. Out of that silence, another child reads. And another. I like this to be formal and ritualistic. If one of the readers begins with introductory comments such as, "This isn't *so* good but . . ." I intervene to talk about the eloquence of simply reading into the circle. If I see the readings moving in a round-robin fashion from one child to the next around the circle, I intervene to support voices coming in from different corners of the room.

Once children know how to participate in this reading-into-the-circle ritual, what a waste it would be to *not* use this across the curriculum. If everyone has just read a social studies chapter on the Civil War, we could say, "I know we've each learned some intriguing things about the Civil War; let's find one thing that fascinates us and do a reading-into-the-circle." We could use this strategy to savor the language an author has used in a shared book, to reflect on the crucial moments in a narrative, to gather together the attributes of a character, an era, an event.

Share sessions, then, like conferring and the "status of a class" roll call, can easily be used throughout the day. But isn't this true for all the structures in our workshop? We may want to take any one of the elements of writing workshops and imagine using that element across the day. I'd suggest we each begin with whatever structure works best in our writing workshop. How could we extend this structure? How could we use it throughout the day? If we were to use it often, if we could invest time in extending this strategy, what might we do?

IV

The Changing Curriculum
in the
Writing
Workshop

21

Developing a Curriculum for the Writing Workshop

Some time ago, Australian educator Di Snowball spent a few months as a visiting staff member with the Teachers College Writing Project. As she went from school to school working with teachers, she asked them, "What are you on about in your writing workshop?"

Often, teachers looked at her a little blankly as they stuttered out an answer. "You know, we're writing. Drafting, revising . . . you know."

"What will you be doing next?" Di asked.

"Next?" teachers would say, totally baffled by the question. "We'll keep on with the writing workshop."

Persistent, Di would ask something like, "How has the year proceeded so far?" and again, it was as if the question didn't make any sense to teachers. If Di changed her tack and asked to see the teachers' lessons or unit plans, the teachers seemed all the more confused. One teacher later confided, "I wanted to ask if she was from the principal's office." Another said, "I wondered, 'Whose side are you on?' " Sometimes teachers showed Di plan books with "writing workshop" written into each day of the week; sometimes they'd show her fake plans written to meet an administrative mandate; but only rarely did writing workshop teachers show her real plans.

Later, at a Project meeting, Di mused about this aloud. "Don't they have a curriculum?" she said. "Don't they plan?" Then she added, "I don't understand."

But I understood. When I first learned about the writing workshop, I saw it as a revolt against curriculum. I remember thinking that in this new paradigm, there was no place for "the curriculum," which I saw as the units, lessons, and topics that filled textbooks and teachers' guides. I knew the word *curriculum* came from the Latin word *currere*, "to run," but instead of running my class down a curricular track, I wanted to establish an ongoing, predictable studio in which youngsters could develop and pursue their own important purposes as writers. Because I hoped to teach into my students' own purposes, I remember thinking, "How can I have objectives for the whole class?" I figured that if I was forced to record my objectives and plans, I'd either put something generic like "Write and revise," or I'd list *thirty* objectives and *thirty* plans, one for each child. The whole idea of planning teaching harkened back to the old regime; it felt teacher-directed and top-down. I wanted, instead, to be child-centered and responsive.

I've grown wiser, thank goodness. *Of course* we can plan and live *toward* units of study in our writing workshops and still be student-centered. *Of course* we must approach our teaching with at least some sense of the possible course we may run with our students. *Of course* we can reject old notions of curriculum without rejecting our responsibilities as educators to dream, talk, think, fantasize, scheme, study, plan, worry, and write about our curriculum.

It's a fantasy—a dangerous fantasy—to think that brilliant teaching happens on the spur of the moment in response to particular children. Clearly, responding to individuals is at the heart of our teaching—but those responses happen in context, and we're responsible for the evolving context of our classrooms. I find it helpful to remember that when a basketball coach interacts with individual players, the coach doesn't use these brief interventions as a time to set up the entire game. The game first gets going, and then, in the midst of the ongoing game, the coach advises in a one-to-one way: demonstrating, cajoling, nudging, suggesting. When we expect all of what happens in the writing workshop to emerge in response to what individual students do, we end up relying too exclusively on conferring as our only vehicle for teaching. When all our teaching happens in one-to-one conferences, we sometimes end up ushering a few children through the process—acting like tugboats taking children through a canal—and inadvertently leave another twenty-five children "drafting and revising" in an aimless fashion. Alternatively, we sometimes bolt around the room, nudging each of our students into his or her own totally private course to run, and then find it impossible to sustain and guide each one.

We tend to blame either situation on the problems inherent in conferring, when the problem is actually curriculum. We tend to say, "The idea of conferring with each student isn't practical," when what isn't practical is the idea that all of our curricular development can happen on the spur of the moment and on a one-to-one basis through teacher-student conferences.

Yet the question remains, "How might I envision a year-long curriculum for a writing workshop?" So far, I've tended to emphasize the ongoing structures and expectations that are ever-present in our writing workshops, and this is certainly part of our curriculum. As teachers of writing, our first and most essential challenge is to establish an ongoing writing workshop in which we and our students initiate, pursue, and help one another on important projects. But I also think curriculum happens in a chronological fashion; it is something that occurs over the course of a school year and a school career. And I think we need to plan for variety as well as continuity. We need to plan ways to nudge students to try new modes of writing and to reach for new depth. In most of the workshops I know best, the year is sectioned into different "chunks" or "units."

At the beginning of the year, the focus in most classrooms is on creating a richly literate and trusting community in which youngsters can "carry on" with their own reading and writing. In the primary writing workshop, this means that children know where writing tools are kept and can choose paper and pens as well as topics and genres for themselves, they know that they can draw and write, spelling as best they can, and they know that they can interact with one another. This also means that they learn to go from completing one piece to beginning another without necessarily any intervention from the teacher. This kind of independence is equally important (and yet, ironically, harder to achieve) in the upper-grade writing workshop. If children keep notebooks, our first goal is not for them to write well but for them to write independently, moving fluently through the process of writing. Our goal is for youngsters to feel so at home with the rhythm of gathering entries, finding a kernel to develop, living with and gathering details around that kernel, and then drafting, revising, and editing a particular piece of writing, that they do this effortlessly, fluently, and flexibly. Sometimes the gathering happens in the mind's eye, and sometimes the work needs no drafting and revision. The process will not be the same for every writer or for every piece. But I think it's fair for us as teachers to insist that just as writers usually edit their work for errors, they also usually live with their subject for a while, collecting their thoughts around that subject. And they usually look at what they have to say, at their material, asking, "What might I make of this?"

In order for this to become second nature to children, we need to create an environment that supports our students in this work. We approach the year, then, knowing that in our conferences, mini-lessons, demonstrations, response groups, and share sessions, we'll encourage students to live with their notebooks, gathering volume and variety in their pages. All of this has already been described in some detail (Chapters 4, 5, and 8). But once our writing workshops are humming along, where do we go from there? What then becomes the source of our curriculum?

There is, of course, no one answer to this question. I think it's clear, however, that after a while, it's no longer helpful for us to focus our energies on what I regard as "beginning of the year" challenges. Once young writers can use their independent reading and their lives to help them find things to write about, we're spinning our wheels to continue devoting our interest, conferences, and so forth to *evoking* writing. Once youngsters can ask one another, "What are you writing about?" and can say, "Tell me about your dog," we, as teachers, can focus on new frontiers. I'd go further and say that if we don't move to new frontiers, our workshops will stagnate, energy will lag, and soon there will be a reason, a new reason, why we're back to cajoling students into writing. The reason, however, won't be that our students don't know how to initiate writing for themselves; it will be that if we don't take curriculum development seriously, if we don't help youngsters soar and reach and stretch as writers, their energy will lag. People get energy from taking on new challenges, new projects, new ambitions and from seeing themselves developing new abilities.

What, then, comes after the first phase of the writing workshop? Or, more important, how do we go about deciding this? What do we draw upon in making these plans? It is key to realize that the question is not "What else could we do in the writing workshop this year?" There are always any number of possibilities, and many of them might be "successful"—but successful in what way? Toward what end? The risk, among those of us who develop curriculum, is that we'll plan a set of activities rather than a framework, a philosophy, a set of beliefs. When curriculum becomes a set of activities, we find ourselves in what Kathy Short and Carolyn Burke describe in *Creating Curriculum: Teachers and Students as a Community of Learners* as "an unending cycle of coming up with new theme units, new projects, new reading and writing activities, and new 'experts' who [can] provide us with yet more activities and procedures" (1991, p. 2).

Our question in designing our curriculum must be, "Of all that I might do, what seems wisest?" As Short and Burke state, "For us, a curriculum involves putting into action a system of beliefs" (p. 6) and "a curriculum is a prediction concerning how people learn, what people should be learning, and the contexts that will support that learning" (p. 33). When we write or plan a curriculum, we are saying, "My hunch is that this is essential and that one way for this to happen might be. . . ." Clearly, creating a curriculum is something that individual teachers, and sometimes (when teachers share an educational philosophy) *groups* of teachers do. My point in this chapter is not to dictate how to design a curriculum, but to encourage all of us to take curriculum seriously. I find it enormously helpful to pull back from the busyness of my teaching and ask, "Of all the things I could do to help my students as writers, learners, and people, what might be the most important?"

Although curriculum development is something each of us does through a process of soul searching, we do not make these decisions in an isolated way. Our thinking is always shaped by the norms and goals and assumptions of the various "clubs" to which we belong. Our thinking about curriculum will be shaped by the faculty in our schools, by the parents in our communities, by the children with whom we develop that curriculum—and by the educational thought-collectives to which we belong. Many of us in the educational thought-collective to which I belong share certain assumptions, and these guide us as we imagine our writing workshops evolving over the course of a year. These include:

- *The belief that language skills develop through genuine, purposeful use and not through artificially contrived exercises.* If our district gives us a list of skills to cover, it's helpful to realize that the district's ultimate goal and ours are probably the same: to support our students' growth as writers, readers, and thinkers. Our focus needs to be on this end goal, not only all the 56 (or 156) component goals (paragraphing, alliteration, simile, metaphor, and so forth). If these truly *are* things writers need to know and experience, and our students are engaged in a rigorous writing workshop, then our students *will* work with these aspects of language as they come up. To study alliteration or parallelism as ends in themselves is to misunderstand these techniques, for their power comes from using them to create meaning. The wisest point to introduce a list of skills is *after* we have worked with students on their important projects for a few months. We and our students can look back on and record what we've done. The list may in this way serve to remind us all that the techniques we're inventing as we write are universal ones with official names, and that they are techniques we can use again. The list will also, of course, remind us of other bits and pieces of information about language we may want to tuck into our teaching.
- *The belief that writing will happen throughout the day, for many purposes and many varied shapes and genres.* If there is a time set aside twice a week for independent project work, each student may be expected to plan how he or she will use that time and later, to reflect on how the work is proceeding. The classroom or the

school may have mailboxes, with teachers, students, parents, and community members often writing back and forth to each other. One student may be the class chronicler for a week, maintaining records of the events of that week in a class log. The class may keep a huge calendar, with a different child each day recording a memorable event within each day's square. Students may keep a self-standing log in math or science, or they may keep a learning log that moves at different times of the year into different curriculum areas.

- *The belief that, at least for most of the year and in most classrooms, it's helpful to have a block of time (an hour a day?) set aside for a freestanding writing workshop.* If we merge the writing and reading workshop under the umbrella of a thematic study, we would do so only for a month or two, because we believe there is something fundamental and essential about the process of turning one's life experience into literature. For similar reasons, we would not want all of our students' writing to be in the service of their reading (literary criticism, book reviews). For a time, most of their writing might be about their reading, but only for a time.

- *The belief that it's helpful for the structure of our writing workshops to be fairly consistent over the course of the year.* It is sometimes useful for us, before the year begins, to imagine a timeline of how this structure might develop as the year proceeds, knowing the students will alter and add to our expectations. For example, we might begin with a set time in which all class members hold peer conferences, with us, as teachers, often shaping what happens in those conferences. Later, peer conferences might be scheduled by the writer any time he or she needs one during the workshop, and one response group comprising four or five students might meet under our watchful eye during the time once allotted to peer conferring. Once that response group is going well, another might form. In a similar way, we might imagine mini-lessons moving from being teacher-led to being student-led, we might imagine students' daily records moving toward larger reflective work and towards portfolios, and so forth.

- *The belief that consistency is important in the writing workshop, but so, too, is variety.* Part of our responsibility as teachers is to plan for variety. We'll probably want to be sure, for example, that students experience different forms of publication over their school careers, so that they know what it is to submit their writing to a literary magazine, to turn their writing into bound books, to perform their writing, to read it aloud to an audience, to circulate it among readers. We'll probably want our students to have some experience not only with finding their own topics, but also with writing toward an assigned topic, as when a class of students writes toward a final assembly for the school on a particular shared topic. We will certainly want our students over the course of several years to write within a wide range of genres including, probably, the short story, memoir, poetry, journalism, the book review, literary nonfiction, and the opinion essay.

After reading this chapter, a colleague remarked, "You talk about curriculum as if we develop it all on our own. For so many of us, the curriculum comes from the district, from the state education department." It is true that many of us are given "a course to run." But in the end, our teaching needs to grow out of our beliefs. We need to know these beliefs in order to articulate them, and we need to reconsider them often. The process of discovering what we believe, of thinking critically about these beliefs, of putting them into practice—this, to me, is curriculum development. At times, curriculum development becomes a political affair, involving meetings and negotiations, but as richly literate people, we know how to read, listen, speak, and write for real-world reasons. Could there ever be a more important reason to read, listen, speak, and write than to do so in order to teach according to our best current hypotheses about how young people learn and according to our sense of what matters?

Resource on Curriculum for the Writing Workshop

Short, Kathy G., and Carolyn Burke. *Creating curriculum: Teachers and students as a community of learners.* Portsmouth, NH: Heinemann, 1991.

22
Genre Studies

My colleagues and I often shape our curriculum around the idea of genre studies. We regard genre as primary, and therefore we not only encourage a wide range of genres, we also tend to spend some chunks of the year focusing in a whole-class way on specific genres. The emphasis we place on genre is, in fact, one of the distinguishing characteristics of the work we do, one of the things that sets our work apart from the work of many other educators. For many other educators, the focus of the curriculum is apt to shift not from one genre to another, but from one topic to another: from weather to transportation, from Egypt to South America. My concern with this approach is that if students write a poem, story, and picture book about Egypt, and then a poem, story, and picture book about Brazil, I'm not sure they will be growing as poets or as fiction writers. If the focus is always on the topic—the country or the dinosaur—when will children inquire about line breaks, meter, and repetition in poetry, or about developing a character and staging a story in fiction?

Because the forms in which we write become lenses that affect our way of seeing the world, it is tremendously important that we not allow our writing workshop to become a place in which children write over and over in the same genre. Student writers must be nudged to extend their repertoire. As Tom Newkirk reminds us, "any system of education that limits children to one genre, even one as powerful as the fictional story, may also limit the vantage points that children may assume" (1989, p. 5).

Of course, each of our children will come to school with different knowledge about genre, and the first thing we'll want to do is to discover and tap into that knowledge. We need to know that some children have a sense of what phone books, coupons, and letters are like, and others, of mysteries, poems, and journalism.

Over and over, I find myself dazzled by the amount of knowledge about genre even very young children already have. One morning, as I chatted with my son Miles, I investigated his genre knowledge.

"Miles," I said, and put a plate of pancakes in front of him, "Would you try something? If I tell you a *kind* of writing—like a poem, a joke—would you pretend you're writing and do that kind?" Before he could ask me to leave him alone with his pancakes, I said, "Can you tell me an epitaph, like for a gravestone?"

Miles didn't pause for an instant before answering:

> Here lies Evan,
> Four years old.

Next I asked for a joke. Miles immediately took on the different voices of a knock-knock joke.

> Knock, knock.
> Who's there?
> Fa.
> Fa-who?
> Fa-rt in your face, that's who!

I kept going. "How about a newspaper article?"

Miles still didn't miss a beat. "*President has a job problem,*" he announced, and then, after a moment of hemming and hawing, continued to dictate the article.

> Today President Clinton announced that to solve the army's no-job problem, he'll send people to other countries to get jobs.

Miles had no problem inventing an instant recipe:

> Bowl of vanilla yogurt. Add blueberries. Stir and taste. Yummy, yummy.

He was equally confident in giving directions:

> Take one mile four,
> then go 2.7,
> then take a left. Go up Nod Hill.
> The house before you go down the biggest hill,
> 18 Pelham Lane.
> Go in the driveway.

When Miles writes in school, he often writes genreless "pieces." These "stories," as they are called, feel like school writing, like compositions, because he hasn't asked the question that is so essential to writing: "What kind of thing am I making?"

Miles is not exceptional in his knowledge of genres. In many of the primary-level classrooms throughout New York City even very young children demonstrate that they already have a sense of the different voices and forms of various genres. The writer of the following piece, for example, knows and uses the conventions for word problems in math (see also Figure 22–1):

> Me and Daphne was married and we had 5 children and we gave 3 of them away. How many that we got?

$$\begin{array}{r} 5 \\ -3 \\ \hline 2 \end{array}$$

And in the single piece of writing, shown in Figure 22–2, the author shows that she knows and differentiates between the genre of advertisements and the genre of stories:

> [On the television:]
> Tired of being harassed by your stepparent? Move out, get a job, pay your own bills.

> [Text of story:]
> One day my sister Courtney was asleep. Then she yelled "Kelly" because she was having pain. So we put her on the couch. Then we called my aunt Salas. She said, "Breathe in, breathe out."

Clearly, we'll want to use and extend whatever genre knowledge our students bring with them. One of the best ways to do this is to be sure that the classroom is filled with real-world reasons to write and that we are capitalizing on these opportunities. If visitors often come to the classroom, a few children may want to study visitors' guides and write their own. If two

FIGURE 22–1   A word problem in math

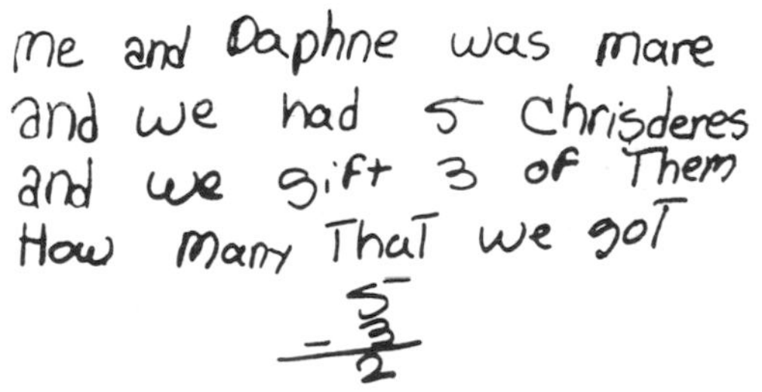

me and Daphne was mare
and we had 5 Chrisderes
and we gift 3 of Them
How many That we got

$$\begin{array}{r} 5 \\ -3 \\ \hline 2 \end{array}$$

FIGURE 22–2   Ads and stories

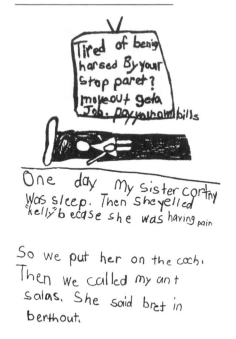

children know how to work the tape recorders and earphones in the listening center and are expected to teach others what they know, they can be
encouraged to study the genre of written directions and then write their
own. Many classroom jobs will create real-world reasons to write. If there
are librarians in the classroom, these children might publish a monthly
"Book Review," complete not only with book reviews but with author
profiles and a list of the classroom "best-sellers." If there are mail carriers,
these children might write to the local post office in order to learn about the
postal system, make their own stamps, and plan their own postal routes. In
More Than Stories, Tom Newkirk describes second graders in Kathy
Matthews's classroom who wrote "job descriptions" for their classroom jobs
(and of course, each job has its own opportunities for writing):

> The News Reporter: The news reporter should watch the news and
> write the news every day on the newspaper.
>
>   He or she should write the date on the top of the newspaper.

> The Mathematician: The mathematician has to do a graph every
> morning.
>
>   The mathematician has to keep the math area clean. He or she puts
> things away if they aren't in the right place.

The Meteorologist: Every day, the meteorologist writes the temperature, the precipitation, the air movement, the sky conditions, the forecast, and the outlook.

The meteorologist writes about the moon, too.

The Horticulturalist: The horticulturalist has to water the plants in the class. The horticulturalist has to spray them and take care of them and not give them a whole lot of water.

He or she has to try not to break the plant. Dead leaves and flowers have to be picked off.

The horticulturalist has to feed the plants, too. (1989, p. 165)

Newkirk goes on to say (pp. 165–66):

The writing associated with the jobs actually begins as soon as children enter the classroom. The mathematician picks up a clipboard with a sheet of paper containing a survey question; within the next twenty minutes, the mathematician has to ask every class member the question, record the answer, and write a statement summarizing the results. One difficulty with this job is keeping track of who has been surveyed, so that no one is left out. One student, Debbie, decided that she needed another student to help her, and so, with Kathy's encouragement, she wrote two "Help Wanted" signs, which she posted on the classroom walls. One read:

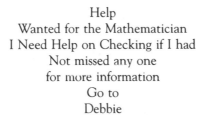

Help
Wanted for the Mathematician
I Need Help on Checking if I had
Not missed any one
for more information
Go to
Debbie

Inviting Students to Explore a Wide Range of Genres Within the Writing Workshop

We will not all teach in classrooms that feel as close to real life as Kathy Matthews's classroom. For some of us, instruction in different genres happens exclusively within the writing and reading workshop. There will probably be a time when we simply encourage our youngsters to choose from a wide range of genre possibilities. We may want to begin this by doing something my colleague Georgia Heard and a first-grade teacher did recently. They took a big plastic laundry basket to the school library and filled it with different kinds of books: cookbooks, riddle books, "how-to" books, anthologies of poems and short stories, alphabet books, retellings of traditional fairy tales, "all-about" books, biographies. Then, back in the classroom, they simply emptied the basket, saying as they did so, "You may want to write an alphabet book, as this author has. . . ."

It's important to consider how these genres fit with the notebooks our students may be keeping. Typically, some genres tend to be written without the benefit of a collection of notebook entries. For example, when we write directions we are not apt to collect entries, and the same is true when we first write recipes or brochures. Most genres, however, will clearly grow out of entries. Sometimes a genre emerges after the material, "the blob of stuff," as Isoke Nia calls it, has been gathered and the writer asks, "What might I make of this?"

At the start of the year, I'd expect that one writer might turn his material into a poem and then remake that same material into a toast to deliver at his big brother's wedding. Another writer might write a letter, another, a personal narrative, another, a song. In order to do this, writers will need to reread their collection of entries on a topic and then imagine, in their mind's eye or through a sequence of lead paragraphs, how their quarry of material could be shaped into a song, a mystery story, a joke, a picture book. Because students may not know how to imagine different genres for their "blob of stuff," I sometimes take a collection of entries I've gathered on a subject and, standing at the chalkboard, say, "I *could* write this as a poem." Then, I reread the entries aloud, commenting on the parts that feel like a poem, and soon I'm drafting a poem on the chalkboard. After a few minutes, I stop and say, "I could, on the other hand, write this as a letter." Sometimes, instead of doing this in front of children, I do it collaboratively with them. If the children have copies of my entries or of a classmate's entries, they can—for a few minutes—work in pairs, reading the material over and asking, "What genre possibilities do I find here?" Then, working together, we might as a class imagine the ways the entries might be shaped into different genres.

By doing this work together, I think we begin to realize that the material of our lives can be fashioned into different shapes. When we write, we don't just record "what happened" or "what I know." Our writing is not a mirror image of life. When we write, we take what happened and sculpt it, as a jeweler takes gold and shapes it. As I mentioned in my discussion of design conferences (Chapter 14), children need to learn that our material doesn't control us; we control it. What a lesson this is! So often, when I ask young writers, "Why did you decide to start with this?" they look at me, startled by the question, and say, "Because that's how it started." I want youngsters to know that, as craftspeople, we can make choices.

Donald Murray recently demonstrated another way to help writers see how we can shape and reshape our material. When Murray worked with my colleagues and me on our writing, he began by reminding us that, as writers, we each probably have a few topics we continually explore. He asked us to put those topics on the page. Then he suggested that we take one topic and think about that topic in writing. "Just write whatever you want to write," he said.

After ten minutes, Murray stopped us. "Now let's take that same material that is now on your page and reimagine it in a different form. If you've written a narrative, write a poem . . ."

After another ten minutes, Murray again stopped us. "Now let's again reimagine what we've written. This time, let's try it in yet a different genre." This continued for an hour, and what a lesson it was!

Designing a Whole-Class Genre Study

For most of us, genre is not something we think about at the very end of the writing process, as when we look at a collection of entries and ask, "What might I make of this?" Usually in writing it's primary. The forms in which we write shape our entire process of living-toward-writing. Donald Murray explains:

> Most writers view the world as a fiction writer, a reporter, a poet, or a historian. The writer sees experience as a plot or a lyric poem or a news story or a chronicle. The writer uses such literary traditions to see and understand life. (1982, p. 36)

My colleagues and I are therefore apt to spend several six- or seven-week chunks of the school year on inquiries into particular genres. During these stretches of time, the whole community reads and writes poetry, for example, or journalism, or short fiction. "Does this mean *everyone?*" teachers sometimes ask, and their inflection suggests that they find the idea of an entire class writing within a common genre to be problematic. My answer is yes. We regard genre studies as fundamental enough to shape our curriculum around them. We find that when an entire class inquires into a genre, it is life-giving. It opens doors and leaves a lot of room for variety and choice, while also allowing the classroom community to inquire deeply into something together. We want our students to know what it is not only to fashion the material in their notebooks into a poem or a newspaper article, but also to read and live as poets or as journalists.

The idea of a community of people immersing themselves in the world of one genre fits with what we know about writers. Writers tend to choose one genre for themselves and then to live inside that genre. Poets hang out with other poets; they go to poetry readings together and workshops in which they talk about digging into the images of their lives, and they live looking at the world through the lens of poetry.

When the entire class pulls together into a shared inquiry into one genre, we might read and write picture books or drama, short fiction, letters, literary nonfiction, memoir, or poetry. Oftentimes, when I talk about these genres, teachers come to me with pencil and paper saying, "Will you give me a list of the genres?" Sometimes they ask, "Would you regard folktales as a genre? Tall tales? Haiku?"

I don't think there is any one magical list of "genres" or that it's helpful to try to nail this issue down. I sense that, in part, the questions I'm asked come from teachers considering whether the genres that fill their students' reading programs can also be the genres of their students' writing lives. I'd caution people against lining up a writing curriculum that matches a pre-existing reading curriculum. I question the authenticity of having students *write* folktales, for example, for these tales generally grow out of an oral tradition; they aren't produced by a writer sitting at a desk. For similar reasons, I might be skeptical of the idea of writing tall tales or fairy tales.

Let me be clear. I do not intend to dampen any reader's interest in devising a genre study of his or her own. In fact, I want to encourage readers to join with their students in inventing new genre studies. My colleague Randy Bomer has suggested that if I want to help readers do so, I might uncover some characteristics of genre studies in general, and he has helped me think about what they might be.

What Happens in a Whole-Class Genre Study?

Whatever the genre, I'd probably begin by finding an example of it that "knocks my socks off." I'd read that example aloud and hope that it would evoke a powerful response in students' lives and in their notebooks. I'd do this as a way of drawing all of us under the genre's spell, but also as a way of demonstrating that our goal in a genre study is not to collect facts about the genre but to inhabit it. Soon, I'd hope that students would join me in searching for, sharing, and writing in response to powerful examples of the genre. I'd also want students to live with the genre in whatever ways feel authentic, from doing choral readings and making anthologies of poems to reading picture books aloud to young children. Once we were doing what readers do—laughing, crying, wincing, arguing, remembering—in response to the texts (and doing all this in our notebooks), I'd want students to join me in turning around and asking, "How does the writer create these responses in me?"

In this and in other ways, then, genre studies are not unlike the reading-writing connections I described in Chapter 17. In most genre studies, we begin by immersing ourselves in the genre and gathering entries that we write in response to our reading. As we do this, there will always be a few texts that evoke particularly strong responses within the classroom, and these become our touchstone texts, the texts we examine and reexamine, talk about, and admire and learn from. A genre study is a structure we create in order to scaffold and support reading-writing connections. Our students read and evaluate, muse over and analyze, learn from and model themselves after texts that are like those they will write.

Recently, Randy Bomer reminded me and the teachers in our community of another significant thing that happens in a genre study. We, as teachers, try to create conditions that encourage our students to live like poets or journalists or short story writers. For example, if we decide that the sound of a text is crucial to picture books and our students are writing picture books, we may want to bring a storyteller into our classroom to talk about how he or she uses voice as an instrument in creating a story. We may want to bring in tape recorders and encourage students to make books-on-tape recordings of their favorite published picture books or of their own early drafts. The point is that we can introduce elements into the classroom environment that encourage our students to listen to the sounds of their entries.

In almost any genre study, we'll reread lots of old notebook entries looking for seed ideas, and we'll also live with our notebooks, collecting new entries, new seed ideas. The nature of what we gather in our notebooks will change with the genre, but this does not mean that our entries will be *drafts*. If we're living toward writing poems, we'll gather images, wonderful words, lines for poems, responses to poetry, and notes on poetry. If we're living toward fiction, we'll have details about our characters in our notebooks: what they do, think, care about, wonder, fear. We'll have family webs and explorations of the people in our characters' lives. We'll have timelines, with single moments of tension blocked out. We'll have lead sentences, too. If we're living toward journalism, we'll have story ideas, times and places for interviews, transcripts of interviews, lead paragraphs.

Once we've moved from notebooks into first drafts, we'll study our few touchstone texts with a new purpose. On a particular day, for example, I might suggest that students studying memoir work in their response group to find the places where the author of a touchstone text moved between telling the external story (what happened) and the internal story (how their characters responded to what happened). Then I might ask students to look at their own drafts to identify ways in which *they* switch between the two. What might they learn from how their mentor author made these moves?

The characteristics of any particular genre relate to the purposes and the audiences for whom that writing is destined. When our children finish their work in a genre, it will be important that they publish their texts in appropriate ways. They'll want to read their picture books aloud to young children who are snuggled close. They'll want to perform their plays, write musical accompaniments for their songs, do choral readings of their poems, have readers for their short stories.

At the conclusion of a genre study we need to stand back and talk together about what we've discovered. We'll also want to talk in general about what we've learned about taking on a new genre. Any school-sponsored genre study should enable students to conduct their own independent study when they want or need to write in a new genre. A little while ago, Angelica, a fifth grader in one of our writing workshops, told me, "When I decided to write journalism, I didn't know how to do it. The only nonfiction I knew was encyclopedia writing, and that wasn't for me. So I watched the newscasters."

Listening to Angelica, I thought of how similarly we both dealt with the challenge of writing in a new genre. A few years ago, Georgia Heard asked me to write the foreword to *For the Good of the Earth and Sun.* When the time came, I thought, "I don't know how to write forewords," so, like Angelica, I went out in search of models. I made copies of six or seven forewords. Angelica did even better. She found the discourse community in which journalism functions and then pretended that she was an insider in that community. As she explained,

> When I watched the newscasters, there was one little part where they were telling about the riots in Bensonhurst; I pretended I was writing that down, what they said. I put down what happened at the rally just to practice being a journalist. In my mind, I thought, "There was a rally in Bensonhurst . . ." and I kept writing it, and after a while it was easy because I got the hang of putting down what people said, then what happened, and then, when I watched the newscasters, they often put just little bits of description in with the facts, so I did that too.

Margaret Meek, author of *On Being Literate,* says that in schools, most children do learn to read and write. The distinction between one person and another centers on what we do with the skills we acquire. Some readers and writers, but not all, grow up to be curious about language. Some people, like Angelica, enjoy language. "They use it with feeling and flair when they talk, tell jokes, invent word games and do crossword puzzles. They are, in a sense, in control of language, as a skilled player manages a football, a versatile violinist interprets a score, or a racing driver handles a car" (Meek 1992, p. 54). We develop such control from experience and from reflecting back on that experience. This is what happens in a genre study.

Recommended Literature

Benedict, Susan, and Lenore Carlisle, eds. *Beyond words: Picture books for older readers and writers.* Portsmouth, NH: Heinemann, 1992.

Bomer, Randy. *A time for meaning: Learning literacy with people aged 10–20.* Portsmouth, NH: Heinemann, in press.

Calkins, Lucy McCormick, with Shelley Harwayne. *Living between the lines.* Portsmouth, NH: Heinemann, 1991.

Clark, Roy Peter. *Free to write: A journalist teaches young writers.* Portsmouth, NH: Heinemann, 1987.

Newkirk, Thomas. *More than stories: The range of children's writing.* Portsmouth, NH: Heinemann, 1989.

Shulevitz, Uri. *Writing with pictures: How to write and illustrate children's books.* New York: Watson-Guptill, 1985.

Wilde, Jack. *A door opens: Writing in fifth grade.* Portsmouth, NH: Heinemann, 1993.

Zinsser, William. *On writing well: An informal guide to writing nonfiction.* New York: Harper & Row, 1985.

See also the resources listed at the end of Chapters 23, 24, and 25.

23
Poetry
It Begins in Delight and Ends in Wisdom

When I think of the Writing Project's involvement with poetry, my mind is filled with the image of poet Elizabeth Henley bringing first graders from a Greenwich Village school outside on an early spring day. The children lay on huge sheets of brown paper and with big, brilliant-colored marker pens and spring sunshine, made a mural filled with poems.

When I think of our Project's involvement with poetry, my mind is also filled with the image of Isoke Nia holding Jerome's torn bit of notebook paper in her hand as if it were made of the finest silk in all the world and saying, "A poem like this needs to be heard, and it needs to come from all corners of the room." Soon the room was edged with children standing on chairs and desktops and crowding into corners, creating an orchestrated rhythmic reading of "The Dumptruck and the Crane."

I have images of poems given as gifts: sent to grandparents in Yugoslavia and to fathers in the Dominican Republic, placed under a rock on a fresh grave, read aloud at a wedding, captured on audiotapes and given as Christmas gifts. And I have an image of Tómas inscribing intricate margins alongside his poems about his baby sister. "I'm going to hang these beside her crib," he said. "I know she can't read yet, but she'll feel them there."

Then, too, when I think of the Project's involvement with poetry, I have images of the Project staff during our Thursday study group taking a sheet full of rainy day poems and in groups of three and four pulling those poems together to recreate the sounds of rain and thunder. In my group, snippets of poems were read against a recurring backdrop of "It's raining, it's pouring, the old man is snoring . . ."

I have images of children meeting in huddles at the start of a writing workshop to choreograph their reading of Eloise Greenfield's "Things" and then, with high fives and good-natured punches on their backs, moving up front to perform, to celebrate their poem and their solidarity.

It seems to me that in our Project we've loved our way into poetry. We've danced and sung, painted and performed poetry. And we've come to believe that poetry may be our favorite genre for children.

Why Poetry Makes an Ideal Genre Study

"Poetry," Eudora Welty has said, "is the school I went to in order to learn to write prose." Poetry can also be the school our children go to in order to write prose. Early on in the workshop our children often write bland pieces of reportage on their lives, pieces that sound more like written-down versions of "show-and-tell" than literature:

> Yesterday I went to the park and we did a lot of things. We played and we saw a squirrel . . .

The problem with this writing is not that the writer has failed in her attempt to write literature, but that she never dreamed she was writing literature. She just told what she did yesterday. There is nothing deliberate or crafted about the piece. The author never paused for an instant to think, "How shall I write this?" or "What would sound good?" or "What's a good way to start?" Her attention was on what she did yesterday, on the events themselves.

Poetry repositions us in relation to our subject. A child who writes about the park is more apt to make that essential literary pause if, for example, as she writes she has in her mind the memory of Aileen Fisher's rendition of her visit to a park (Bauer 1986, p. 15):

> SNOWY BENCHES
>
> Do parks get lonely
> in winter, perhaps,
> when benches have only
> snow on their laps?

Poetry is also a powerful genre because of its condensed nature. Because poems can be very short, every child in every classroom can be a poet. The genre is accessible even to five-year-old writers who labor over the mechanics of putting pen to paper. Shelley Harwayne recently visited a classroom and watched, when a little girl sat in the author's chair, how the other children rolled their eyes at each other as if to say, "Oh no," and snickered.

Samantha held her paper about an inch from her nose, peered ominously at it, and in a halting, belabored whisper read, "I like green. I like black. I like blue and yellow."

With the brilliance of all good teachers, Shelley found a miracle in the moment. "Samantha, it sounds just like a jazz chant." She said,

> I like green
> I like black
> I like blue and yellow

Soon everyone had made a space on the floor in front of them and was beating out the jazz chant. The class then became an orchestra with three sections, one group beginning very softly and the others joining in.

"Do you have any others like that?" Shelley asked the bewildered but delighted Samantha, who said, "Sure," and produced pages and pages of three-line ditties. The class spread into different corners of the classroom and each group performed a different poem.

The condensed nature of poetry not only makes it more likely that a child like Samantha will be successful, it also means that all children will be able to do more with words. Poems can move through four drafts in less than a page or two. At the same time, poetry offers a powerful forum for teaching young writers to make reading-writing connections. When students read Judy Blume novels, it's not easy for them to match their writing to their reading, but when they read an Aileen Fisher poem, reading-writing connections feel far more possible.

Poetry is powerful because of the ways it can enrich people's lived lives. Poems can be read aloud at Thanksgiving dinner or at a baby's baptism. Poems can be put onto greeting cards or framed and given as gifts. Poems can also be woven into the life of a classroom community—posted next to the aquarium, chanted as a ritualized opening to every day's math class, hung on the classroom door as a motto for the community.

Helping Children Fall in Love with Poetry

As Randy Bomer has reminded me, the way we learn poetry is no different from the way we learn language. Whether we're learning to talk or to use punctuation or to write poems, the conditions for our learning are always the same. Brian Cambourne has listed those conditions, and educators the world over return to his list time and again. If we adapt his list specifications to poetry, we can say that we learn poetry when we are *immersed* in meaningful examples of poetry; when teachers, authors, and peers *demonstrate* the ways they live as readers and writers of poetry; and when we are *expected* to read and write poetry and are *engaged* in doing so, given *responsibility* for reading and writing poetry in our own ways, and given time to *use* what we know—*approximating* as best we can—with others who *respond* to what we do.

I love the image of launching a genre study in poetry by *immersing* ourselves in a sea of poems. There are countless ways to begin doing this. Georgia Heard, the first poet to work in our Writing Project and the person who introduced me to the power of this genre, often began her work by asking children about his conception of poetry. Once she told a group a of fifth graders about how she'd gone into another classroom and introduced herself as a poet only to find the children sticking out their tongues at her and rolling their eyes. "I didn't think it was me," she said, "and so I figured it was poetry they didn't like." Then Georgia asked these children whether they felt the same way. About a third of the class, the students who had written silly nonsense poetry that year, said poetry was okay; it was easy. The others hated it. "It's boring," they told Georgia. "It's for girls." "It is too hard to understand." "Poetry is for rich people, it's for snobs," Vanessa said and then explained, "They are talking above us and about us. They don't want us to understand."

Georgia's quiet attention during all this seemed to dissipate the negative views of poetry. The children were warming toward Georgia, if not toward her subject. Some even moved closer as she began quietly telling them about her poetry. "For me, poems have to be about something that is so important to me, I need to have a physical feeling of that topic inside me." Then she explained, "You know how when you are scared, really scared, you can feel it in your body, or when you are so, so happy, and your body sings? Well, when I have a physical feeling like that about my topic, I know I have a poem."

No one giggled and no one rolled his eyes. Instead, the thirty-six pre-adolescents, most of them boys, listened spellbound. Georgia continued speaking in her honest, serious way, commanding their attention by giving them hers. "Feelings are the source of a poem, but you can't just write the feelings onto paper," she said. "Instead of trying to tell the reader my feelings, I go back in my mind's eye and locate the feeling in specific, concrete things that we see and hear. I get a picture in my mind and then re-create that picture so the reader can feel what I felt."

Listening to Georgia, I was reminded of a description of poetry by an anonymous author from the eleventh century:

Poetry presents the thing in order to convey the feeling. It should be precise about the thing and reticent about the feeling, for as soon as the mind connects with the thing the feeling shows in the words; this is how poetry enters deeply into us.

Once we know the images our students already have of poetry, we can be sure to bring in poems that push back the boundaries of their definitions of poetry. If our children think poems are for rich kids and snobs, we'll want to bring in poems that might have grown in a crowded city apartment or a shelter for the homeless. If our children think poems are about unicorns and rainbows, we'll want to bring in poems about tractors and oil spills, homework and baby sisters. If our children think all poems rhyme, we'll want to bring in poems that are held together with repetition and rhythm rather than with rhyme. If children think poems are silly, easy ditties, we'll want to bring in poems that open our hearts to the deepest, truest parts of who we are.

When I talk about bringing in poems, I don't have any single image of how that might best be done. After Georgia launched the class into poetry, she brought in a poem she'd written, "Oldfields," and pulled the class together around drafts of that poem. Georgia told the children that the poem began while she was sitting at work. She had an image of how as a little girl she'd gone into the woods with a spoon to dig up an Indian grave her grandfather had shown her. "I kept the picture in my mind until I got home and then, concentrating on the image, I wrote and wrote and wrote, just trying to get the image and the feeling onto paper, not worrying if it was good." Then, after she had put away the draft, other images came to mind somehow connected to the first. "I put them down too, the images of my grandfather walking around in his now empty house, and of the clocks he always loved ticking in that empty house." She added, "I didn't interpret or explain how the images were connected. I never explain in my poems, I just present the images and trust that the subtle connections will be there."

I was sure Georgia was talking over the children's heads, but the children didn't seem to think so. Their attention was, if anything, growing stronger. I have since come to suspect that part of Georgia's power is her implicit belief that children can understand poetry in all its subtlety. They may not follow everything she says but they feel its magic, and they sense the seriousness and authenticity of it. Georgia made these fifth graders feel important. She made them take poetry seriously. "Read your poem to us," they said. Georgia read her second draft, in which three images were combined and the lines were divided so they looked like poetry:

OLDFIELDS

1

I went out to see the Indian grave
my grandfather told me about
at the edge of the woods
near the burning field.

I picked off the leaves and stones
that covered the mound
and dug all afternoon
until the woods grew dark
and the kitchen light of the house
behind me came on.

I expected to find jewels,
pots and arrows
or an Indian headdress
with feathers on it.

Except for the dirt
that filtered through my hands,
the grave was empty.

2

I am standing near the wall
at the edge of the burning field.
I see my grandfather
walk around the rooms
of the empty summer house.
He has been dead for years.
Hunched over, thin as air
he walks a path from the kitchen
through the dining room.

3

Years ago,
up the front staircase
in my bedroom in the summer house
I lay in bed awake
listening for the clock
downstairs to strike midnight.
I saw the spirits fly out of the clock
like black smoke going up a fan.

4

In the living room
the grandfather clock
is still ticking.

Any hour now,
it will break into chime.

When Georgia finished reading there was a silence. Then the children had questions. "Did you use particular writing strategies?" Michelle asked, and Georgia answered that concentrating on the image was a strategy, as was free writing, and that there were other strategies she'd tell them about in future mini-lessons. One youngster commented that "Oldfields" was like a story, and when Georgia explained that it was a narrative poem, the boy wanted to know how narrative poems were different from stories. This led into a discussion of the characteristics of poetry. When Diana asked whether Georgia had used set rhythms, Georgia told the children, as she had told the teachers, about formalist and free verse poets. "I am a free verse poet," she said. "I know I have rhythm in my voice and often, after my first draft, I go back and find that rhythm. Usually, for me, one line has three beats, but this rhythm is set from inside of me. If you write a lot of poetry, you'll find your own rhythm." By then, it was time to write. Georgia reminded the children where poetry comes from and urged them not to censor their first drafts. The room was filled with a workshop hum.

If I wrote poetry, I would certainly bring the drafts in, as Georgia did, and use those drafts and the decisions behind them to show children how poems are made. But I'm scared of poetry, and feel clumsy and inept when I try to write it. As teachers, we need to use whoever we are in our teaching, so I have sometimes brought my insecurities to a class knowing others would share these feelings and that together, we could begin outgrowing them. Once, I gathered students around me and told them about how Georgia had tried to teach me to write poetry.

"Think of an image, Lucy," she said. "Let a powerful image come to mind."

I thought very hard, my face scrunched, my mind grasping for something that would qualify as a powerful image. "Nothing, Georgia. I don't think in images, I'm lousy at description. See, I told you I can't write poetry."

"You can, you've just decided that you can't."

"Okay, I'll try again," I said, and this time I thought, "An image? Of what? Our house? My dog?" Then, remembering a poem I'd written long ago at a workshop, I seized upon that image. "I've got one, Georgia," and I told her about how I rode a motorcycle when I taught in England.

"Okay, make a picture in your mind and tell me what you see."

I cleared my throat and began. "Down the road / I go. / Grayness around me. / The air, lushness melting into grays . . ."

Georgia was quiet for a moment. "Lucy," she said, "Can I ask you a question? How come you say it so, so funnylike. 'Down the road / I go . . . ' Why don't you say it in a more regular way?"

I was stunned. "But then what would make it into poetry?" That was the question I asked Georgia, and it was the question I posed to my students. "Let's investigate together," I said. "Let's read and read and read poems, and see if we can learn for ourselves what it is that makes something into poetry."

All our genre studies will begin with the question "What's essential in this genre?" Teachers who read this chapter or Georgia Heard's brilliant book, *For the Good of the Earth and Sun*, will learn about how some poets, teachers, and children have answered the question of what's essential in poetry, but rather than *telling* our students these characteristics, we'll want to invite them to join us in finding out what they are.

Some teachers have invited their whole class to join an inquiry into poetry by pushing all the desks to the edge of the classroom and then putting a mountain of poem books on the floor at the center of the room. "Let's wander through these books with a friend, read poems aloud and silently, swap and share poems, looking for poems with which we are in love," these teachers have said. "As we explore the nooks and crannies of these books, let's each look for a small handful of poems that make us gasp, that make us stop. Let's look for poems that affect us like those Emily Dickinson talks about: 'If I read a book and it makes my whole body so cold no fire can ever warm me, I know that is poetry.' "

It's tremendously important, of course, that we aren't reading the poems silently, but that we're actually voicing them and lingering to talk about them. Once we have found the poems we love best, our touchstone poems, we'll want to find ways to hold onto them. After an hour of meandering among poetry anthologies, some of us will copy poems into our writer's notebook, perhaps creating a special place at the back or perhaps deciding, instead, that they belong in the midst of the stuff of our lives. Oftentimes, children in Writing Project schools have made anthologies of their best-loved poems. Georgia Heard helped us realize we can study the anthologies others have made and read what anthologists say about their craft. In his foreword to his anthology, *Pocket Poems* (1985), Paul Janeczko likens collecting poems to collecting baseball cards: The fun is in trading them, in categorizing and recategorizing them. "Poems aren't meant to be kept in a shoe box all banded together," he says. "They need to breathe." He goes on,

> But folders of poems do not an anthology make . . . I want the reader
> to think about how the book was put together and why poems are where
> they are. . . . I discovered, too, while working on *Don't forget to fly* that
> groups of two to six poems work better for me than larger groups. . . . Of

course, this makes the anthology more difficult to organize because I must connect all the sections as well as the poems. (p. iv)

When we study anthologies, we find that some are organized by theme, as in Lee Bennett Hopkins's *Click, Rumble, Roar: Poems About Machines,* or Caroline Feller Bauer's *Rainy Day: Stories and Poems.* Sometimes poems are selected for an anthology because of the ways they sound, as in Paul Fleishman's *Joyful Noises: Poems for Two Voices.* Some anthologies have sections organized by theme or by author. Sometimes photographs or paintings or quotes or comments or vignettes from the author's life accompany each poem. Often there is a foreword written by the anthologist, and when children compile anthologies they also write forewords, such as this one by Naomi Rose:

> Poems are nature,
> In her loveliest way,
> Like a bright green
> Rusted leaf falling from a tree.
>
> Poems are beautiful words,
> put together to form something you wouldn't see by yourself.
> Poems are mysteries which take time to solve.

All of our effort should go to ensuring that children are invited inside poetry and made to feel at home there. When I was in school, my teachers fenced me out of poetry. They taught me that poetry was too complicated for me. One of the characters in Jean Little's wonderful *Hey World, Here I Am* writes about her experiences with poetry, and they were my experiences as well:

> I used to like "Stopping by Woods on a Snowy Evening."
> I like the coming darkness,
> The jingle of harness bells, breaking—and adding to—the stillness,
> The gentle drift of snow. . . .
>
> But today, the teacher told us what everything stood for.
> The woods, the horse, the miles to go, the sleep—
> They all have "hidden meanings."
>
> It's grown so complicated now that,
> Next time I drive by,
> I don't think I'll bother to stop. (1986, p. 28)

As we join our children, immersing ourselves in a sea of poetry and finding the poems that will be our touchstones, we will invent ways to feel at home with poetry. Everyone in the room can join in writing the curriculum.

A child might one day put two lines of poetry on the chalkboard, and by accident they look as if they were written as part of that day's agenda. If we are amazed and delighted by the brilliant idea of finding a poem for each day, a new classroom ritual will be established. Soon there will be more children inventing ways to weave poems throughout the school day. A child might suggest that just as the class uses a choral reading of a poem to call together the reading circle, poems can also launch the science workshop or end the day or start the week. Another child might suggest forming a greeting-card center, complete with art supplies and poetry anthologies. Children might want to find poems that can be turned into songs or big books. They may want to borrow Charlotte Zolotow's idea and put poems that speak to particular novels inside the back cover of these books. Children will probably want to learn the poems they love by heart, and I think we should encourage and support this effort. In his memoir, *Wordstruck* (1989), Robert MacNeil reminds us of what it means to learn poems by heart. "By heart," he says, "is a perfect expression." We learn poems because we love them, because we want to carry them in our hearts.

Once we have dwelled in the house of poetry, we'll also want to circle around to study it, to ask, "How has the poet done this?" We'll want to look at line breaks and structure, at images and metaphor. But this analysis comes later. A poetry genre study is itself like a poem. As Robert Frost has said, "It begins in delight and ends in wisdom."

The Stuff of Poetry

In Chapter 3, I quoted Naomi Shihab Nye's "Valentine for Earnest Mann," an exquisite poem that can remind us that poems are not made of pretty words but of the stuff of the world. Similarly, our poetry workshops need to be full not only of posters and quotes and pretty sounds of poetry, but also of fossils and sprouted acorns, photographs of the moon and clippings from the newspaper. When Georgia Heard asked the poet Stanley Kunitz for advice on what to do after she left his graduate writing program, her mentor answered, "Go be an archaeologist, go be a potter. Grow plants, watch the stars. You have to have another field because it will give you your metaphors."

And so I think in a poetry workshop, we need to invite careful study of a seedling, of a horned toad. These things hold poems for those who have the eyes to see. In order to see, we need to look and look again and then look some more. We need to follow Byrd Baylor's advice in *The Other Way to Listen*:

> Do this:
> go get to know
> one thing
> as well
> as you can.
>
> It should be
> something
> small.
>
> Don't start
> with a mountain.
>
> Don't start
> with the whole
> Pacific Ocean.
>
> Start with
> one seed pod
> or
> one dry weed
> or
> one
> horned toad.

As writers we look not only with our eyes but also with our hearts and minds. We look and ask questions. We look and make comparisons, as this five-year-old poet has done (Figure 23–1):

FIGURE 23–1   A five-year-old's poem

Spring
flowers
lean
when they lean
they look like chickens
leaning to get their food

We look inside and under, and we let what we see remind us of forgotten glimpses. We look in all the ways Gary Paulsen describes so eloquently in his novel *Monument,* the story of Mick, an itinerant artist who is brought to a small midwestern town in order to create a monument. Like a poet, he doesn't begin by sitting at his desk trying to put feelings into a form. Instead, he takes his notebook into the town. He sketches the corner of an abandoned house and a tiny popsicle-stick cross the Walther kids made when they found a dead bird, and the swirl of sparrows at the grain elevator. Trailing behind the artist is a young girl, Rocky, who sees his sketch of the sparrows, spots in the trail of dust, dancing swirls of birds. She watches the artist see things, see *inside* things, and says, "I want to see like you. Teach me to draw."

The artist gives her a sketchpad (a notebook) of her own, and the two of them, the teacher and the student—two artists, two poets—head off into the world. They mosey through the old section of a graveyard, where Rocky finds she cannot take her eyes off a small stone.

CLAIR MILLER
BORN MAY 5, 1887
TAKEN OCT. 9, 1890
SHE BIDES IN HEAVEN,
AT PLAY WITH ANGELS DEAR

"She was just a baby," Rocky said.
Mick nodded. "Draw."
Rocky drew the headstone, and Paulsen describes the incident from her point of view:

So I drew the headstone and it was going fine until I started on the little curled-up lamb on top. It was so small and alone. I remembered the orphanage and how it had been sometimes alone in the room when I didn't think I would ever get adopted, alone like the little lamb. I wondered how Clair Miller had come to die and I started to cry.
"Ahh, yes, there it is, isn't it?"
"It's not what you think."
"Well, of course it is. You're crying, and that's the way it should be."

"I'm not crying. I don't cry." Not at the orphanage and not since the orphanage. I didn't cry. Not ever. And here I was crying.

"It's all right to cry," he said. "I cry each day—my soul weeps. It means you're seeing something as it is, as it's meant to be seen, doesn't it? Oh, yes, crying is the thing to do." He smiled. "As long as you keep on drawing. Know the line, always that, know the line."

And I kept drawing and only dripped a little on the paper. (1991, pp. 92–93)

Like the artist in Paulsen's novel, we will want to take the young apprentices in our classrooms into the world to see the littlest particulars that are there and be moved by them.

Cynthia Rylant, whose anthology of poems, *Soda Jerk,* is written from the point of view of a young boy who works as a soda jerk in a small-town pharmacy, says this about that boy and about poets:

A lot of people think they can write poetry, and many do, because they can figure out how to line up the words or make certain sounds rhyme or just imitate the other poets they've read. But this boy, he's the real poet, because when he tries to put on paper what he's seen with his heart, he will believe deep down there are no good words for it, no words can do it, and at that moment he will have begun to write poetry.

Writing Poetry

One child may write the first draft of a poem as she sits, clipboard in hand, watching a beetle burrow into a rotting log. Another may write her first draft of a poem in the wake of one her teacher has read aloud. Still another will gather images and words from the newspaper and construct a poem out of them, or eat an orange and reach for the words to capture its taste and smell and presence. There is no one way to write poetry, and we'll probably want to open up lots of avenues into the genre. Almost always, however, there will be the magic combination of tiny sensory specifics and of the big feelings they hold.

In *For the Good of the Earth and Sun* Georgia Heard describes how she helped lead children into "the deep water" of poetry:

I gathered the students on a rug and talked to them about making poems. The kids' faces were so small; they were so young. . . . I told them exactly what was essential for me to make a poem.

"All my poems start with a strong feeling I have about something," I said. "Then usually I try and get a picture of it in my mind. Let me give you an example. This summer a bat got into my house. I walked across the living room, and all of a sudden this huge . . . what looked like a shadow . . . came flying toward me."

Excitement leaped into their faces. Hands started going up. "I've seen a bat." "One time a bat got into my house. . . ." They all wanted to talk about bats. I listened to their stories, then continued.

"I was so afraid, I ran into the kitchen and hid in a corner. Then a friend of mine hit the bat with a broom and got it into a box to let it outside. I remember how it crawled out of the box. It was only about as big as a mouse. And it kind of turned around and looked at me as it was crawling on the stone wall. What was I afraid of? I felt sorry for it. The picture of the bat will never leave my mind." (1989, pp. 10–11)

Then Georgia read them the poem she'd written about that bat. Her goal was not to invite them to write about the bat but to let them know that we write by taking an image from our own lives and picturing it. She said, "That's something that happened to me, that I wrote about. Why don't you all close your eyes and think about what's important to *you*—something that's happened to you, something you care about, anything."

That day, Laura raised her hand. "All I see are stars," she said. "Stars, stars everywhere. They look like they're brand new. Sometimes when I look at stars I get afraid. Stars. Stars everywhere."

What she said sounded like a poem to Georgia, who is able to see poems that others don't. Now more children had images, and what they said sounded like poetry, too. Georgia, like my son's swimming teacher, dives into the deep water herself, and then beckons youngsters to join her there. I'm less able to dive into the deep water of poetry and say, "Join me," and so I'm apt to tell children about a poet I know who said, "I try and get a picture in my mind," and who began with an image of a bat.

When our children first write poetry, we can predict that despite all our teaching some of them will write out of their old images of what poetry is. When Georgia worked with me in Rose Napoli's sixth-grade class, Devon, for example, wrote this:

LUNCH

These peas are fit for a dog!
The stew is swamped in a fog!
Oh no! I reached for the chicken in the back
and the ugly lady gave me a smack.
I swear, in the spaghetti I saw a rat.
That ain't soup I'm looking at.

Georgia therefore spent her second day in this classroom emphasizing the need for important topics. She read poetry to the children and discussed the problem she found in many of their papers. Many agreed that their concern for rhyme sometimes made them forget what they wanted to say. As one child put it, "You lose your mind, all you think about is rhyming the words." Even when she wasn't directly talking about the importance of taking poetry very seriously, Georgia's assumptions and her presence continued to convey this message. Later that second day, when she had again gathered the children together, this time for a closing meeting, she talked with them about the centrality of *image* in a poem but did so in ways that continued to say, "This is deep, this is big." She told the children that when she had been writing "Oldfields" (it's significant that Georgia cycles back to this touchstone text), after she got down the three images, she read through the poem and knew it wasn't finished. "The feeling didn't seem to come across," she said. "Poetry has to hit a person right in the heart or it won't work." The children once again listened with great care to what she said. "If some of your poems don't work, then you have to ask whether you are committed enough to your topic. If you are, what I do is close my eyes again, get the image, and then free write, only this time my first draft has given me a head start." Georgia ended the meeting by reading Philip Levine's poem "Starlight" aloud to the class, letting it cast a spell over the room. She read the poem twice, and when she finished, she sent the children off to their own writing. She spoke in whispers and the children did too, as if none of them wanted to break the mood. Georgia's first conference was with Ying.

"This poem I wrote, this doesn't have that much feeling in it," Ying said, her voice so soft I could hardly hear it. "There is another feeling I get but I can't put it into words. It is when I get home from school and I am changing my clothes. I don't know what it is, but it is in my stomach. I can't put it into words."

"You can say just that, Ying," Georgia replied, touching the child's arm as she spoke. "You can say, 'I can't put it into words, this feeling that is in my stomach,' and then you can explore the feeling."

Later that day, Ying came to us with a poem in hand saying, "I want to know if you get a feeling when you hear it." This is what we heard.

A FEELING

Echoes of voices my friends
Going through my ears,
While traveling to

My own bitter world
I see only a blur
I feel my heart will burst into
a million pieces.
A feeling I can't get rid of
And I can't hold back my tears
My stomach growls
My heart is ready to tear
But there is something
I just don't know.

"I got the feeling, Ying, it was a very strong feeling. It was a feeling of anxiety."

Ying nodded. She started to leave us, then stopped and hesitantly said, "I get the same feeling when my brother and father fight, and when my grandfather died." By the time Ying left the conference, she had learned that just as Georgia put several images into "Oldfields" she could combine the images of her father and brother fighting and of her grandfather's death with the feeling she had after school. Back at her desk, Ying began to write, adding lines to her initial draft:

I see my mother trying to separate my father and brother
It feels like dying, to have a terrible family.
I ask the holy heaven for help
But I get no answer
I'm falling . . .

I do not entirely understand what poets mean when they talk about the central role of *image* in their poetry. But I've watched Georgia conferring and talked with her about her conferring enough to know that the way she helps children ground their poems in an image is by saying, "Can you picture that? Close you eyes and see if you can get a picture in your mind. Tell me what you see and feel." My favorite example of this is one Georgia tells about in *For the Good of the Earth and Sun*. Jason brought Georgia a poem:

Cats are cute
Cats are great
Cats can't be beat.

Georgia saw and (in her brilliant way) celebrated how much Jason knew about poetry. He understood the power of repetition, of rhyme. Then, hoping to locate the poem's significance in his life, Georgia asked Jason why he'd decided to write about cats. Once she learned that he had a cat, she was on her way. She describes the episode this way (p. 41):

"Will you close your eyes again, and tell me what you see in your mind, what you saw before when you saw your cat?"

His eyes close tight, and he speaks slowly. "Well, I see my cat. He's curled up on my bed. I love him. I pretend that he's my son." He quickly opens his eyes.

"I pretend that he's my son," I say back to him. "You know, what you just said sounds like poetry. You really helped me *see* your cat. I wrote down what you said; let me read it back to you." After, I continue.

"A lot of poets do what you just did: first they put their ideas down, then they go back and think again and see if there's anything else to say. Closing your eyes seemed to help you really see your cat. You don't have to stop there; you could keep thinking, and you might want to write down more things that come to your mind. That's how a lot of poets write their poems. You might want to try it. . . . "

When I return later, Jason has finished again, this time for good.

My Cat
My cat is black and white.
I pretend that he is my son.
I love him.
His feet smell like popcorn.

After I had read an early draft of Georgia's book, I teased her, "Georgia, you have yourself closing your eyes to picture things in so many conferences . . . It's as if you're teaching with a blindfold!" And, of course, whenever we, as teachers, do something often, children soon begin to mimic us. Inna wrote four lines and then didn't know what else to write. Instead of conferring with Inna herself, Georgia asked Tara if she would help her.

"Make a picture with your mind," Tara said to her friend. "What do you see?" Inna was able to respond with the following:

As I looked out the window
I saw a bird on a raspberry bush
As bright as a rainbow

That strategy doesn't work for every child. Jeffrey, for example, described his mental picture by saying, "One day last summer, I was with my dad and went in a tiny boat." His voice lacked the urgency and immediacy of poetic language; there was a once-removed quality to it.

Georgia said, "Jeffrey, I want to try something with you that I often do with myself when I want to write a poem. Would you pretend that I'm your best friend and you've just come rushing into the room, and you are telling me, quickly, about the fishing . . . blurt it out to me, what you would say."

This time Jeffrey's beginning was more immediate and had the makings of a poem. "We went fishing, Dad and me, in this tiny boat. Thousands of fish were splashing around." Georgia later helped Jeffrey break his sentences into lines and soon he had a draft of a poem:

> We went fishing,
> Dad and me, in a tiny boat.
> Thousands of fish were splashing around . . .

In her conferences that day, Georgia helped other children put their images onto paper in their own words. Tara's first draft seemed contrived, as if her concept of poetry was getting in her way:

> Riding my bike down the hill,
> I saw headstones
> and a beautiful sky.

In their conference, Georgia asked Tara to bring to mind the picture she was describing and then to talk about it. As Tara talked, Georgia interrupted once or twice, softly asking questions that elicited more details. Tara's next draft used language that was more natural, and she had added the image of a gate and the smell of freshly cut grass:

> TARA—DRAFT 2
>
> I ride down the hill
> I look across
> I see a black gate
> and lots of headstones.
> The freshly cut grass fills my nose
> I see a beautiful sky
> of pink
> blue
> and white
>
> I stop. . . .
>
> Am I looking at the sky
> or is the sky looking at me?

When children gathered for the share meeting at the end of the day, Georgia suggested that they listen for three things:

1. The overall image—was it clear?
2. Did they get a strong feeling? What was it?
3. What strategies did the author use in writing the poem?

Georgia decided the children were ready to take another step. The next day she introduced the concept of form. I already knew that early in a poetry genre study she would not talk about the terms many of us most associate with poems: rhyme, haiku, sonnet, ballad. Georgia had explained to the teachers with whom she was working that in poetry there are two camps, the formalists, who teach and write poetry in terms of fixed forms, and the free verse poets, who find their forms in the rhythm and content of what they are saying. Georgia belongs to the latter camp, and she believes it is easier for children to begin with free verse. "If the fixed forms were to come first," she said, "it would be like, in September, teaching children that their narratives must contain two paragraphs, with nine sentences in each one, and that six of the sentences must begin with an article, and two with a proper noun. Think what that would do to the writing." She continued, "Children would spend their time trying to remember and to follow the rules, and they'd lose the urgency of what they had to say. They would get the wrong idea of what it means to write."

Georgia's point, I noticed, was not that form is unimportant or that fixed forms don't belong in the elementary grades. She was only pointing out that an early emphasis on fixed forms can distort what it means to write poetry.

Now as the children settled into their circle, Georgia said, "There are two aspects to a poem: the content, which we've talked about, and the structure. After I have written a draft and sometimes during the drafting, I think about the structure of my poem. Just like buildings have architecture—some are tall and thin, some are short and wide—poems also have to be built according to a design that works."

Georgia began with the issue of line breaks. She told the children that her first drafts often look proselike but that afterward, she rereads the drafts aloud, adding slashes at the places where her voice naturally pauses. "Then I type it up and see how it looks and hear how it sounds," she said. "Usually it isn't right and so I do it again and again, making the lines longer and smoother, or shorter, more punctuated."

Wanting the children to understand that the form can reinforce the content, Georgia gave the words of William Carlos Williams's poem "The

Red Wheelbarrow" to them and asked them to divide it into lines. Some divided it like this:

so much depends upon
a red wheelbarrow
glazed with rain water
beside the white chickens.

Others had different ideas, but none of them spread the poem out as the poet William Carlos Williams had done.

THE RED WHEELBARROW

so much depends
upon

a red wheel
barrow

glazed with rain
water

beside the white
chickens.

In talking about Williams's decision, the children could see that the line breaks reinforced the author's message. Then they looked at two ways Whitman could have divided the beginning lines in "Song of Myself" and tried to guess which he had chosen. Most of the children were able to see—and hear—that the second version, Whitman's own, was a more joyful one, and that it was more appropriate for the poet's message:

SONG OF MYSELF

1
I celebrate
myself,
and sing
myself,
and what I
assume
you shall assume.

SONG OF MYSELF

1
I celebrate myself, and sing myself,
and what I assume you shall assume.

Then the children looked at other poems and began to sense the different visual effects an author could create and to see that creating a structure is part of creating a poem.

Georgia's first conference that day was with Kim. "I don't like my poem," Kim announced, pushing the paper toward her.

"Why don't you like it?"

"There are too many 'frees.' " Kim read a stanza aloud to illustrate the problem. Each line began with "Free" and this repetition held the poem together.

Instead of responding individually to Kim, Georgia asked the class if they would put down their pencils. Then she told the whole group about Kim's dilemma, explaining, "It doesn't have to be a problem because in some poems, and even in some prose, repetition is an important part of the text's structure." She told them that using the same word in every line was a technique called parallelism, that it was even used in the Bible, especially the Psalms. After a few minutes of discussion she let the class return to their work.

Kim understood, she said, but she still thought the poem sounded funny with so many "frees." Georgia accepted her judgment, and we moved on. Joseph was writing about Mars and had decided that instead of repeating a word he would repeat the first four lines. "They are the most important lines," he said. "If I tell them at the beginning and at the end, they will stay in people's minds."

Next we listened as Michelle discussed the poem she had just finished with Thyessa. "I've worked on it for four days, and that's about fifteen minutes a word," Michelle said. "I like it, but it goes by too fast. Nobody will notice my words." The girls wanted us to solve the problem, but we assured them they could find a solution, and they did, as was evident in the difference between Michelle's third draft and her final one.

The energy in the classroom that day was tangible. Several children were frenetically copying and recopying their poems, trying them first in quatrains, then in couplets. Some banged away at the old typewriter Rose had brought from home. A few children had thesauruses on their desks, and they searched through them for the best possible words. Others looked through anthologies of poetry, comparing their own work with the poems in the books. Many children wrote silently, earnestly. Still others listened to a friend's poem. Everyone was talking poetry, writing poetry, and listening to poetry.

In the share meeting that day, Morat asked the class for help. "I don't have enough description," he said, and read through his first draft:

In the sky I see a bird
it's coming down

What should I do
no time to think

I got to get her
I got you little fellow

Why did you fall
to be with me

I guess I'll never know
But know I'll take you home

Tara raised her hand. "I think it was good, I could see it. I saw an eagle
and a mountain, and the eagle was flying over the mountain."

Robert interrupted. "No, I see you walking in the woods."

Morat held his head, as if dizzy from his classmates' comments. "Whoa,
hold it. It wasn't in the woods or the mountains, it was in a grassy plain. It
wasn't an eagle, it was a bluebird."

"Why didn't you say that?"

"I didn't know until now." The next day, Morat produced another draft,
and this one made the image clearer.

I'm lying on the grass plains.
I see a Bird!
it's circling above me
it's a beautiful Bird
it's Blue like the sky
it's hard to see her in the sun

"Oh no"
It's falling
I got to get it

I got you little Fellow
you're safe
I wonder why you Fell
could it be because of me
Well, no matter, as long as we are together
don't be scared I won't leave you
we will be together little Fellow

Georgia was pleased with what she had begun in Room 413, and she felt
confident that with a little help, Rose could now take over the poetry
workshop. That afternoon, Rose and Georgia spent a few hours thinking

about possible mini-lessons. The next day it was Rose who gathered the children together.

Rose had decided that for a few days, her mini-lessons would be very simple ones. The children were already juggling a huge amount of new information, and she didn't want them to focus more on technique than on their content. For her first mini-lesson, Rose read William Stafford's poem, "Traveling Through the Dark." The poem is a sad one, and Rose read it well. It seemed to me that some of the children were teary-eyed when Rose finished reading it. The children began talking, first about the subject of the poem and then about the author's choice of words. One youngster noticed how Stafford used tiny details such as "By the glow of the taillight" to convey the general information that they were driving behind another car. Then Rose gave each child a copy of the poem and suggested that they scatter around the room and take turns reading it aloud to each other. All through the room, clusters of children pored over the poem. Some read it quickly, others slowly. They compared their pauses and wrestled with meaning. In retrospect, Georgia, Rose, and I now realize that poetry, like a musical score, is meant to be presented. We could have done a great deal more with having children read aloud their favorite poems. The children could have organized choral readings of poetry—their own, or someone else's—and the unit could have ended with a poetry reading; but there will be other opportunities.

Later the children would tell me how much Stafford's poem "Traveling Through the Dark" had influenced them. When Morat wrote, "I wish I had a friend / who cared for me / Who loved to spend some time with me / Who stuck up for me in a shyish way," he told me that the sad, touching feelings in his poem came from Stafford's poem. Jung told me that "Traveling Through the Dark" taught him about poetry. "I learned that in a poem, you can get all these feelings out in a little bit of words, like you have mystery in one word."

Another day Rose began the workshop by asking her young writers to tell the others about their writing process: what they had been doing and what they planned to do next. Some children reported that they were turning their poems into songs. Others were on their second or third poem. Several had left poetry and were working on fiction or personal narratives. Most, however, were still deeply immersed in their first poem: drafting, revising, sharing with friends, rewriting, refining.

The next mini-lesson was particularly effective. Rose read Gwendolyn Brooks's poem "We Real Cool" to the class, and as she read it the children laughed . . . until she reached the last line.

THE POOL PLAYERS.
SEVEN AT THE GOLDEN SHOVEL.

We real cool. We
Left school. We

Lurk late. We
Strike straight. We

Sing sin. We
Thin gin. We

Jazz June. We
Die soon.

There was a hush over the room.

"At first it seemed like a funny poem, but the ending makes it sad," Hasun said.

"Yeah, the last line changes everything," the others agreed.

Marsha quietly said, "That's how a poem is, everything has to fit like a puzzle, all the pieces fitting together, and if you change one thing the whole poem is changed."

The children began thinking a great deal about endings, and their focus on endings helped them grasp the notion of form. "When I write my poems," Michelle said, "every line has a meaning in it and then at the end, the closing lines tie in with all the meanings of the other lines. See, poems have to have something to cover the whole thing with, something has to hold it all together."

I think the most powerful lesson about endings—and indirectly, about form—came not during the mini-lesson but during the share time when Gregory and Omope read their poems aloud and the children saw the power of their endings. After this, Rose was careful to include the children's own pieces in mini-lessons as well as in share meetings.

CLOWNS
by Omope

When I see clowns they make me
feel like I'm a giggling hyena
because they make
me laugh so much
As I see them I think
I'm in another world
A world that is full
of clowns
And clowns spinning in my head
saying "Be one,

be a clown." But my mouth
says, no
　　No No No No
　　　I don't want to be a
　　　　clown

POEM
by Gregory

As I strolled through the
open alleyway looking at the
stars above that gleam happily
I stare down at debris
below me in disgust
knowing that some day
I will reach the stars

When Cindy finished her poem, "The Mirror," that day's mini-lesson focused on the poem. Cindy is tall for her age, and presents herself as tough and cynical, although she is actually quite the opposite. Here is her poem:

THE MIRROR

I stare at the face,
I see mean eyes, tight look.
Whose face is it?
I turn my head
and realize the face is mine.

The class was stunned by what Cindy had written, and for a long while they responded to the content of it. Then, with an overhead projector, Rose displayed the poem and asked the class to think about Cindy's use of the white space. The spaces make the reader pause, and this nudges a reader to *do,* in our mind's eye, what Cindy has said. "I stare at my face," she writes, and in our minds we stare at a face. "I see mean eyes . . ." and we picture those eyes. "I turn my head . . ." and in the pause provided by the white space, we turn our heads, "and realize the face is mine." It would have been an entirely different poem had Cindy written it like this:

THE MIRROR

I stare at the face,
I see mean eyes, tight look.
Whose face is it?
I turn my head and realize the face is mine.

My last day in the poetry workshop was June 13. It was a hot, sticky day. The children had all worn shorts and T-shirts, and their clothes stuck to their damp skin. We all felt sweaty, yet somehow this added to the mood. Everywhere writers toiled over their drafts. The classroom felt, sounded, smelled like a newsroom. Many of the children were still working on their poetry. Six or eight were compiling a book of poems to give to the principal, several others were typing up final drafts, and still others were into new poems. When Morat saw me, he motioned for me to come over when I had a chance. When I got to him, Morat handed me a little scrap of paper. "It's a poem in Russian," he whispered, not wanting to distract the others.

At the end of that workshop, Rose told the class that Morat had brought something special for the share meeting. Morat sat in the author's chair, looking very shy and embarrassed, and in Russian, he read a poem he'd brought with him when he moved to America. He read it several times, and the class marveled at the sound of the poem. "It's so beautiful it hardly matters that we don't know the meaning," they said. Again and again the class listened to it, admiring its sounds. Watching all of this, I thought of how embarrassed Morat had been at the start of the year about the Russian language. "It's the worst punishment in the world when my parents make me practice my Russian," he had told me, and now, here he was, reciting this beautiful Russian poem to all his friends and sharing their pleasure over the sound of his language. Later, Morat would translate the poem into English, struggling with the issues any translator knows. Before the year ended, other children would bring in poems from their homelands. Watching all this and thinking back to it now, I have an unbelievably strong response to the entire poetry workshop.

The feeling is a physical one. In my heart, I have such a feeling of pride and warmth, such a sense that this is so important, I almost feel ready to write a poem.

Recommended Literature

Abercrombie, Barbara, ed. *The other side of a poem.* New York: Harper & Row, 1977.

Arnosky, James. *A kettle of hawks and other wildlife groups.* New York: Lothrop, Lee & Shepard, 1990.

Baylor, Byrd. *Desert voices.* New York: Charles Scribner's Sons, 1981.

Baylor, Byrd, and Peter Parnall. *Your own best secret place.* New York: Charles Scribner's Sons, 1979.

Booth, David, ed. *Til all the stars have fallen.* Ontario: Viking, 1990.

————. *Voices on the wind: Poems for all seasons.* New York: Morrow Junior Books, 1990.

Chandra, Deborah. *Balloons and other poems.* New York: Farrar, Straus & Giroux, 1990.

Ciardi, John. *You read to me, I'll read to you.* New York: HarperCollins Children's Books, 1987.

Coleman, Mary Ann. *The dreams of hummingbirds.* Morton Grove, IL: Albert Whitman & Co., 1993.

Degen, Bruce, ed. *Jamberry.* New York: HarperCollins Children's Books, 1993.

Demi. Trans. by Tze-Si Huang. *In the eyes of the cat.* New York: Henry Holt & Co., 1992.

Elledge, Scott, ed. *Wider than the sky: Poems to grow up with.* New York: HarperCollins, 1990.

Fleischman, Paul. *Joyful noise: Poems for two voices.* New York: Harper & Row, 1988.

Gordon, Ruth, ed. *Peeling the onion.* New York: HarperCollins Children Books, 1993.

Greenfield, Eloise. *Honey, I love and other love poems.* New York: HarperCollins Children's Books, 1986.

————. *Night on Neighborhood Street.* New York: Dial Books, 1991.

————. *Under the Sunday tree.* New York: HarperCollins Children's Books, 1991.

Hopkins, Lee Bennett. *Pass the poetry please.* New York: HarperCollins Children's Books, 1987.

Hughes, Langston. *The dream keeper and other poems.* New York: Alfred A. Knopf, 1932.

Janeczko, Paul B., ed. *Look for your name: A collection of contemporary poems.* New York: Orchard Books, 1993.

————. *The place my words are looking for.* New York: Macmillan Children's Book Group, 1990.

Kennedy, X. J. *Knock at a star: A child's introduction to poetry.* Boston: Little, Brown, 1985.

Kennedy, X. J., and D. Kennedy. *Talking like the rain.* Boston: Little, Brown, 1992.

Kuskin, Karla. *Dogs and dragons, trees and dreams.* New York: HarperCollins Children's Books, 1980.

————. *Near the window tree: Poems and notes.* New York: HarperCollins Children's Books, 1975.

Lewis, J. Patrick. *Earth verses and water rhymes.* New York: Macmillan Children's Book Group, 1991.

Livingston, Myra Cohn. *Celebrations.* New York: Holiday House, 1985.

————. *Sky songs.* New York: Holiday House, 1984.

————. *There was a place and other poems.* New York: Macmillan Children's Book Group, 1988.

Margolis, Richard. *Secrets of a small brother.* New York: Macmillan Children's Book Group, 1984.

Martin, Bill, Jr., and John Archambault. *Listen to the rain.* New York: Henry Holt & Co., 1988.

McCord, David. *All small.* Boston: Little, Brown, 1986.

Merriam, Eve. *Fresh paint.* New York: Macmillan Children's Book Group, 1986.

————. *The singing green.* New York: Morrow Junior Books, 1992.

Moore, Lilian, ed. *Sunflakes.* New York: Clarion Books, 1992.

Morrison, Lillian, ed. *Rhythm road: Poems to move to.* New York: Lothrop, Lee & Shepard, 1988.

————. *Whistling the morning in.* New York: Boyd's Mills Press, 1992.

Prelutsky, Jack, ed. *Random House book of poetry for children.* New York: Random Books for Young Readers, 1988.

Ryder, Joanne. *Inside turtle's shell . . .* New York: Macmillan Children's Book Group, 1985.

Rylant, Cynthia. *Waiting to waltz: A childhood.* Scarsdale, NY: Bradbury Press, 1984.

Worth, Valerie. *Small poems.* New York: Farrar, Straus & Giroux, 1972.

Recommended Professional Literature

Graves, Donald. *Explore poetry.* Portsmouth, NH: Heinemann, 1992.

Heard, Georgia. *For the good of the earth and sun: Teaching poetry.* Portsmouth, NH: Heinemann, 1989.

————. Living like a poet. *The New Advocate,* vol. 6, no. 2 (Spring 1993).

Livingston, Myra Cohn. *Climb into the bell tower: Essays on poetry.* New York: Harper & Row, 1990.

24
Making Memoir Out of the Pieces of Our Lives

When I was a little girl, I loved the day-long drives home from Michigan, with five of us kids in one station wagon and four in the other. When I rode with Dad, just as we turned from the dirt road onto the pavement, he'd say, "So, what were the highlights of this summer?" and then we'd begin spinning our experience into memories.

"The storm on Fox Island," I'd say, and someone would add, "when we had to cross the lake in the storm, with the sheets of rain, the thunder and winds, singing songs to stay warm."

As we drove on and on, we'd story through the summer, through making blackberry tarts, watching the cows be milked, the sound of Ellen's belly flop. Then we'd story through our lives, our family's life. "Tell us about Grandfather," we'd say to Dad. "Tell us about you and Mum."

Each year as we drove past fields and farmyards, we'd hear again about how, when Dad was courting Mum, she'd suggested they take a midnight dip and swam clear across the lake. Each year we heard again about the cake she'd baked with a pot holder between the layers.

I loved those stories, and I needed them. "Stories . . . create our first memories," Margaret Meek says. "From the stories we hear as children we inherit the ways we talk about how we feel, the values which we hold to be important, and what we regard as the truth" (1992, pp. 105, 103). When I later headed off on my own journey—to summer camp, to school, to create my own family—I brought those Calkins stories along. "This is who we Calkins kids are," I said. The challenge of my life has been to say, also, "This is who I am."

"Tell me the story again of how I got my name," the child says, leaning against a parent's knee. "Tell me the story of how I was born." "Tell me about when I first went to school." I used to think that we write memoir when our lives are done and we want to give one last, loving look back, but now I know that it is by looking back that we create our lives, our selves. The instinct for memoir is there whenever we return to a remembered place, catch a whiff of a childhood smell, feel nostalgic over a photograph. The seeds of memoir are there when we listen to stories and say, "That reminds me of when. . . ." The seeds of memoir are there when we draw pictures of our old house, of the tree that used to grow near the fence, of the dog we used to have. The seeds of memoir are there in notebooks, in entries that begin, "I remember . . ." or "Once, when I was little . . ." or "One time, a long time ago . . ." or "In my family, we usually. . . ."

When I was new to the writing workshop, I regarded most of what my students wrote as "personal narratives," only I called them "pieces." As I think about it now, it seems fitting that I spoke of those narratives as "pieces." They *were* pieces, pieces that could have been developed and shaped to make autobiography or memoir, speeches or poems, short stories or personal essays.

Let's look at some of the "pieces" I included in the first edition of this book. In "Wonder," Rebecca lingers over a tiny, fleeting moment of her life. The writing—and the self-consciousness it shows—is impressive. But what *is* this? Where in the library, in the world of publications, would one find such a kind of writing?

> I stare blankly at my math. "How do I do this?" I wonder. I scold myself: "Rebecca! You've done things like this lots of times!" But I can't remember how to do this. I try to force my brain back to a little while ago. I can't remember. I ruffle the pages of my math book, looking for when I did something like this before. Nothing. I turn back to my empty math paper. My mind is erased.

My hunch is that it's most accurate to call this an entry, anecdote, or vignette and that one would be most apt to find it embedded in a fuller text. It could be part of a memoir, or a short story about a little girl sitting in front of an empty math paper, or a personal essay on math, or a letter to the teacher, but as it stands now, it's a fragment that hasn't yet found its shape, its purpose, its audience.

The same is true for Kristen's "piece," entitled "Hero," cited in the first edition of *The Art of Teaching Writing*:

> I got on the bus. I couldn't find a seat to sit in. The only place I could find was one with a boy a sitting on it. And as I got on the seat he said "Get out and sit somewhere else."
>
> "I can't," I said. My little brother Matt came up to him and hit him on the head lightly with his lunchbox. The boy jumped over to the next

seat. I was ashamed that I couldn't handle it myself. My brother sat down with me. I was glad he did it and I thanked him.

Earlier, we examined another "piece"—Philip's "The Splashing Roaring Rapids":

> Kersplash! "Oh boy I'm as wet as a . . . Oh no!" "A waterfall!" I said to my brother . . . "Uh bye." "Oh no!" I forgot! "I'm seatbelted! I'd better cover my head!" Ninety seconds later . . . "Whew." "We are lucky we missed that waterfall." Kerplunk! "We hit a rock." "We kept on going until . . ." Shlunk! "We hit the side of a cliff. "Awww it's over." "Now I know why they call it the Roaring Rapids." I said to my brother, "I'm soaked to the bone."

In this chapter, I want to consider this question: "If we were to help Rebecca, Kristen, and Philip develop these fragments—these seed ideas—into a memoir, how would we proceed?"

Virginia Woolf provides us with one important answer. "A memoir," she says, "is not what happens, but the person to whom things happen." When children put their lives on the page, they often leave out one person—themselves. Philip, in the example above, does not show us *his* experience of the waterfall or how that moment fit into the rest of his life. If I were to help Philip begin to grow this incident into a memoir, I'd probably begin by telling him that readers need to understand what the experience was like for *him*. I might show Philip how another child took a chronological "just the facts ma'am" account of an episode and added a layer of reflectiveness to it. Jesse Weiss, for example, first wrote a blow-by-blow account of going to the hospital with a broken arm. Then, in a later draft, he tried to bring out his observations and thoughts. In one section of his new version, he wrote:

> I didn't think I'd broken my arm. At least it didn't feel broken. After all, all I'd done was to trip over the sidewalk!
>
> I was put on some kind of a rolling table. "What's going to happen to me? Where am I going?" I asked myself.
>
> A chubby man with brown hair began pushing the cart and a lady with blonde hair and spectacles joined him, pushing it. As we turned a corner, the man said to the lady, "What are you doing tonight?"
>
> The lady answered back, "I have to go to my parents' house. Sorry."
>
> The man started to blush and I said in my mind, "That guy must be embarrassed." They went on talking, and in my mind I thought, "These two people are taking their time, walking very slowly when a little boy

is in pain and agony." I didn't show what I thought. "They don't care. They probably have situations like me every day." I didn't say anything, but I remember the feeling.

This scene is more memoirlike than the waterfall story, because Jesse is not only telling about an event, he is also aware of himself as the person to whom the event happened. But the writing still doesn't feel quite like a memoir to me because it leaves it unclear how this broken arm episode reveals Jesse, how it is connected to him today. Later, Jesse jotted a few marginal notes in order to explore why this moment mattered to him. He wrote, "I learned that my whole family likes keeping feelings in." Once Jesse had written—and discovered—this idea, he was able to collect other moments that illustrated it. He wrote next about moving day and how he and his family all waved a cheerful good-bye to their old house, pretending not to care. By this time, he'd moved from writing isolated *pieces* toward writing memoir.

Launching a Memoir Genre Study: Responding to Literature and to Our Lives

I would probably not begin a study of memoir with a definition, trying to answer the "What is memoir?" question. I wouldn't want to launch the genre study by having students collect disconnected facts about the genre. Instead, I'd want us to immerse ourselves in an experience of the genre. I might therefore begin by reading aloud a short memoir selection, one I'd chosen because it left me speechless and because I figured it would do the same for my students. "After I read this," I'd probably say, "let's write and write about a moment, a scene, from our own lives." And then, when the room grew quiet, I'd read. I might read a passage from Maya Angelou's *I Know Why the Caged Bird Sings,* from Jean Fritz's *Homesick,* or from Eva Hoffman's *Lost in Translation.* I might read "Eleven" from Sandra Cisneros's *Woman at Hollering Creek,* or I might read this selection from Eloise Greenfield's *Childtimes:*

MAMA SEWING

I don't know why Mama ever sewed for me. She sewed for other people, made beautiful dresses and suits and blouses, and got paid for doing it. But I don't know why she sewed for me. I was so mean.

It was all right in the days when she had to make my dresses a little longer in the front than in the back to make up for the way I stood, with my legs pushed back and my stomach stuck out. I was little then, and I trusted Mama. But when I got older, I worried.

Mama would turn the dress on the wrong side and slide it over my head, being careful not to let the pins stick me. She'd kneel on the floor with her pin cushion, fitting the dress on me, and I'd look down at that dress, at that lopsided, raw-edged, half-basted, half-pinned *thing*—and know that it was never going to look like anything. So I'd pout while Mama frowned and sighed and kept on pinning.

Sometimes she would sew all night, and in the morning I'd have a perfectly beautiful dress, just right for the school program or the party. I'd put it on, and I'd be so ashamed of the way I had acted. I'd be too ashamed to say I was sorry.

But Mama knew. (pp. 142–43)

If the memoir study occurred in the middle of the school year, students would already be familiar with the process of writing in response to literature. We wouldn't need to spend time distinguishing it from writing *about* literature. Instead, we could begin to use literature to ignite memories.

I would probably spend several days reading selections from memoirs aloud and inviting children to join me in responding to these texts, because I'd know this would be one of the most powerful ways we would have to experience the material. And while I'd want to do the same general thing for a few days, I'd probably also want to make small, significant changes between one day and the next.

If we wrote in response to an excerpt one day, another day we might tell stories in response literature. What I like best is to sit on the floor in a circle when we do this, so we can see one another's faces and watch the way stories evoke stories, the way they move around the circle. If my students seemed to feel self-conscious, vulnerable, and exposed in such a circle (as some adolescents are apt to feel), we might tell stories from behind the safety of desks, and we might even have the storytelling happen in small groups.

Whether we are sitting and sharing in a whole-class circle or a small group, oftentimes students come to the circle feeling it's inappropriate to carry on about their stories for too long, and so they're apt to give only quick summaries. "It reminds me of how my brother used to tease me," one child recently said.

"Can you, in your mind, picture one particular time when your brother teased you?" I asked.

"Yes," she answered, and then after I cajoled her to continue, she said, "Once, I opened the door to my bedroom and found my brother had hanged my baby dolls; each doll was hanging there with a noose around its neck."

The entire room gasped audibly. In that moment of response, every one of us in that room was reminded that we can render the details of our lives in such a way that they make others gasp and wince and remember. We were reminded of the power of the story. Later, when we were deeply involved in writing and revising our own memoirs, the story of those baby dolls, each hanging from a noose, would become a touchstone moment. "You're still writing it in general terms. You're still writing like 'My brother used to tease me,' " I'd say. "Describe the scene; make a particular picture and help us see it."

There are other ways to intervene in storytelling, to raise the level of what's happening. "Ramon," I recently said to a very small child, "tell it so we feel how hard it was. Give us goosebumps." Sometimes it's enough to say, "Pass the microphone to Rosa," and then, passing an imaginary microphone to Rosa, we might add, "Wait until you feel the silence, Rosa, until we're brimming over with readiness for your story."

On other days, I might read two or three memoir selections, one on top of the next, until we were all filled to the brim with images of childhood, and only then would we have the relief of writing. Or I might read aloud a selection from a memoir that gathers in lots of memories rather than one that lingers on a particular scene and suggest that we use the structure of the memoir and compile our own list of images. For example, I might read aloud this selection from Paul Auster's *The Invention of Solitude*, suggesting that afterward we all begin writing our own collection of "She remembers . . ." or "He remembers. . . ."

> He remembers that he gave himself a new name, John, because all cowboys were named John, and that each time his mother addressed him by his real name he would refuse to answer her. He remembers running out of the house and lying in the middle of the road with his eyes shut, waiting for a car to run him over. He remembers that his grandfather gave him a large photograph of Gabby Hayes and that it sat in a place of honor on the top of his bureau. He remembers thinking the world was flat. He remembers learning how to tie his shoes. He remembers that his father's clothes were kept in the closet in his room and that it was the noise of hangers clicking together in the morning that would wake him up. He remembers the sight of his father knotting his tie and saying to him, Rise and shine little boy. He remembers wanting to be a squirrel, because he wanted to be light like a squirrel and have a bushy tail and be able to jump from tree to tree as though he were flying. He remembers looking through the venetian blinds and seeing his new-born sister coming home from the hospital in his mother's arms. He remembers the nurse in a white dress who sat beside his baby sister and gave him little squares of Swiss chocolate. He remembers that she called them Swiss although he did not know what that meant. He remembers lying in his bed at dusk in midsummer and looking at the tree through his window and seeing different faces in the configuration

of the branches. He remembers sitting in the bathtub and pretending that his knees were mountains and that the white soap was an ocean liner. (1982, pp. 8–9)

Then, too, I might suggest that we all simply read published memoirs with our notebooks beside us knowing that the texts we read will unlock our own long-forgotten memories. It's a powerful thing to read a book-length memoir with our notebooks at our side, because this way, each of us can select for ourselves the moments that resonate and fill us with stories. I would never have known, for example, that the passage that would especially speak to Lila in Jean Fritz's *Homesick* was one about how her baby sister died. When young Jean first heard that her baby sister had died, and for long afterward, she felt "wooden." And then, in an instant, that changed:

> When the coffin was out of sight, my father put his arm around me. "You know, Jean," he said, "you have been very, very good through this."
>
> Suddenly something inside me exploded. I wheeled around at my father. "*Good!*" I shouted. "That's all anyone can think about. *Good!* I haven't even thought about being good. I haven't tried to be good. I don't care about being good. I have just been me. Doesn't anyone ever look at me?"
>
> My father had sat down in a rocking chair and had pulled me onto his lap. I was crying now. All those tears that had been stored up inside were pouring out. My whole body was shaking with them. My father held me close and rocked back and forth.
>
> "You don't understand," I cried. "You and Mother will never understand. I was waiting for Miriam to grow. I knew she'd understand. She was the only one. I was counting on her. I needed her."
>
> I looked up at my father. His head was back on the headrest, his eyes were closed. Tears were streaming down his cheeks. "I do understand, Jean," he said. And we went on rocking and rocking together. (1982, p. 76)

Lila, too, had felt "wooden." Reading this passage she was reminded of those times and was comforted by knowing that Jean Fritz understood her. Lila began by quoting from Fritz's *Homesick,* and then wrote from her life.

HOME SICK

"You don't understand," I cried. "You and Mother will never understand. I was waiting for Miriam to grow. I knew she'd understand. She was the only one. I was counting on her. I needed her."

I felt the same way about my brother Bryan who died before he was born. I often think if he were alive, he would be right here playing with me. Or right now he would be sleeping in his crib. Right now I miss him. He and I would have so much fun together. I could babysit him sometimes. I could give him a bottle or feed him. I feel there is a big hole in my life that Bryan disappeared from. I think I needed Bryan just like Jean needed Miriam. I needed to take care of him. I need another family member. Especially since my aunt died. This family has a lot of people who died. He would sort of be like Evan, Kathryn's little brother.

What Is Memoir? Using Literature to Inquire into the Genre

Once we had begun inhabiting the genre of memoir and living under its influence, my next priority would probably be to invite students to join me in an exploration of the genre. One of the easiest ways to do this is to encourage all the members of the class to roll up their sleeves and begin searching for examples of memoir. As one child and then another brings texts into the classroom, we'd gather around those texts asking, "Is this memoir?" Is Cynthia Rylant's *When I Was Young in the Mountains* memoir? Is Jane's Yolen's *Owl Moon* memoir? Is Gary Paulsen's *Cookscamp* memoir?

When I first began studying memoir, my central question was "How is memoir like—or unlike—autobiography?" In his book *Inventing the Truth: The Art and Craft of Memoir*, William Zinsser has an answer: "Unlike autobiography, which moves in a dutiful line from birth to fame, omitting nothing significant, the writer of a memoir takes us back to a corner of his or her life that was unusually vivid or intense" (p. 21). Then he adds, significantly, "Memoir is a window into a life." Memoir is not a life; it's a window into a life. It's a perspective on a life. It is, as Jean Little, author of two memoirs (*Till All the Stars Come Out* and *Little by Little*) says, "not the whole head of hair, but one or two strands of hair."

"When you are writing about yourself," Russell Baker says in his chapter in *Inventing the Truth*, "the problem is what to leave out." This is an entirely different problem from what you encounter when writing a biography about someone else. "The biographer's problem is that he never knows enough. The autobiographer's problem is that he knows too much" (1987, p. 49). Jean Little solved the problem of selection by leaving out everything from her life except the moments and images that followed her two chosen "strands of hair." She told about those that fit into how she grew to be a writer and those that showed her learning to deal with becoming blind.

Even if we have only a beginning sense of what memoir is, it's wonderful fun to rummage among picture books asking not only, "Would *this* qualify as memoir?" but also, "Why?" or "Why not?" It's intriguing, also, to begin thinking, "What are the different *kinds* of memoir?"

We need to remember, however, that if we do this inquiry in a teacher-led whole-class way, with our students together on the carpet or in a meeting area and with us at the front of the circle, there may be only a very few in the group who are actually inquiring. I love classrooms that bustle and hum with a *spirit* of inquiry. For this to happen, we will probably want to invent a structure to support small-group inquiry.

"But when I let small groups go at this on their own," one teacher said to me, "they decide that *Where the Wild Things Are* is a memoir."

My response was, "Is that so bad?" Good fiction will often read as if it is memoir; and memoir, on the other hand, will often feel very much like fiction. I think the important thing is that these children are focusing on Sendak's story and asking, "Is this true?" "Does this show one strand, one part of a life?" The important thing is the inquiry, not the answers.

Bringing the Concept of Emblematic Moments into Our Classrooms

In Chapter 23, we thought about how we might create a place for poetry by inviting children into chants and choral readings, songs and collections of favorite words. We do this because the sounds of language are particularly important in poetry and because we hope that by living inside poetry, children will learn to delight in and listen for the sounds of language whenever they write.

What are the characteristics that are as basic to memoir as language and image are to poetry? How in a memoir course of study do we create an environment in which *these* characteristics will flourish?

In writing memoir, we select moments that reveal our own experiences of our lives. My emphasis is on two words, *select* and *reveal*. How do we issue a generous invitation for children to join us in doing this? I would probably begin by suggesting that the children and I focus on selecting. For example, if we anticipated visitors in our classroom, I might seize the opportunity to suggest that we try to convey the spirit of our class by each finding a single item from the classroom that best represents the whole of the classroom. Once we each had our object we could share them in small groups and ask the others in our group to help us explore ways our object might be emblematic of the classroom. We could also bring our notebooks home with the assignment of recording very specific observations about a single person in our lives—a parent, a caretaker, a grandparent—and then we could tell about that person by selecting one detail that seems to us to "say it all." We could follow the same process of gathering details and selecting one that is particularly emblematic in order to depict our home, our dinner table, the front foyer of our school.

I would also suggest that we encourage writers to select something that reveals who we were as children. For example, we might bring a single photograph into the classroom and then tell stories and write about and discuss the question "How does this photograph convey the whole of my childhood?"

Children will need help if they are to write and tell stories in response to a single object, a single photograph. Some children resist the notion of selection. In order to tell the whole story, they want to bring shoeboxes full of photos or albums stuffed with pictures, but memoirists know that the whole story is, in a sense, contained within any one moment. Kathy Doyle helped her fifth graders build meaning around single photographs or images when she read with them a section from Patricia MacLachlan's novel *Journey*. On this particular page, the boy Journey is looking through a photograph album and reminiscing nostalgically about the days when his family was still intact. He does this as part of an effort to resolutely convince himself that his mother will return soon. The scene opens with Journey's grandmother, with whom he is now living, looking at a photograph and nodding. "The camera knows," she says.

Journey doesn't understand what she's saying. He looks at the picture.

In the picture the girl who was my mama sat behind a table, her face in her hands, looking far off in the distance. All around her were people laughing, talking. Lancie, Mama's sister, made a face at the camera. Uncle Minor, his hair all sunbleached, was caught by the camera taking a handful of cookies. In the background a dog leaped into the air to grab a ball, his ears floating out as if uplifted and held there by the wind. But my mother looked silent and unhearing.

"It's a nice picture," I said. "Except for Mama. It must have been the camera," I said after a moment.

Grandma sighed and took my hand.

"No, it wasn't the camera, Journey. It was your mama. Your mama always wished to be somewhere else."

"Well, now she is," I said.

After a while Grandma got up and left the room. I sat there for a long time, staring at Mama's picture, as if I could will her to turn and talk to the person next to her. If I looked at the picture long enough, my mama would move, stretch, smile at my grandfather behind the camera. But she didn't. I turned away, but her face stayed with me. The expression on Mama's face was one I knew. One I remembered.

Somewhere else. I am very little, five or six, and in overalls and new yellow rubber boots. I follow Mama across the meadow. It has rained and everything is washed and shiny, the sky clear. As I walk my feet make squishing sounds, and when I try to catch up with Mama I fall into the brook. I am not afraid, but when I look up Mama has walked away. Arms pick me up, someone else's arms. Someone else takes off my boots and pours out the water. My grandfather. I am angry. It is not my grandfather I want. It is Mama. But Mama is far ahead, and she doesn't look back. She is somewhere else.

I walked to the window. Birds still sang, flowers still bloomed, cows still slept in the meadow, and I ate soup—now cold—as if my mama hadn't ever gone. (1991, pp.11–13)

"Let's do what Journey did," Kathy said to her students. "Let's take one photograph—or one entry, if you'd like—and hold it in our hands as Journey did and *really* look. What do we see? Wonder? Feel? Remember?"

Jesse Weiss, the boy who wrote about breaking his arm and being wheeled in to the doctor, took an entry from his notebook and next to it wrote what he noticed, wondered, thought.

JESSE'S ENTRY	JESSE'S REFLECTIONS AS HE LINGERS WITH HIS ENTRY
"You could give me your phone number and I'll give you mine," my friend said. "That won't work, Eli," I answered. "We can still be friends after you move," he said. But I saw the expression on his face and knew we would be passed forever. I didn't say anything. "Come on, Jesse," my mother called. "It's time to leave." I climbed in the car, and we drove off. When I looked at my new house, I said, "It's nice," and so did everyone. I'd have to deal with it, because New York was lost to me.	I don't say what I feel aloud. When someone suggests our reading club does an activity, I agree out loud, but inside the idea disgusts me. In my reading club, the leader makes a suggestion, and all the rest of us agree, but inside I don't agree, and I always wonder if there are other people thinking like me . . . I always think differently than everyone else, and I wonder why. Really, I don't even know if I think differently or not, because everyone else may also be keeping their feelings in as well.

Andrew Lindner, like Jesse, decided to linger over an entry—a written-out scene—rather than an actual photograph. In the entry he selected, Andrew had written about finding solace in the quiet of the forest. The entry begins,

The forest near my house is dark, but the sun manages to get through. A sharp cliff goes down slowly if you go down any path. The path is smooth from years of stomping down it to a place of mystery. . . . I first discovered the woods in a search for quiet.

The entry ends with Andrew describing a special tree, "my climbing tree."

It is the biggest tree in the forest. It resembles me.

Now, at his teacher's suggestion, Andrew tried to look at and into and around this scene to remember and question. Next to his original entry, Andrew wrote:

It surprised me that I said I'm like the tree, wanting to be the biggest, because when I'm in the forest I'm a different person.
    In different places in my life, I act totally different. In the woods, it's a different me than in school.

Over the next few weeks, Andrew would write and talk again and again about how those places in the forest called forth one Andrew while school called forth another Andrew. Rereading his first entry, he said, "I like to be the biggest, the best in life, but in the forest it doesn't matter. I can just mix in with the group, not really the group but with what's there in the forest." Then he added, "I feel freedom, I feel content, in the forest. In some ways I'm the king of the forest and in some ways I'm not. I'm the king of myself in the forest."

Eventually, in the final draft of his memoir, Andrew set the peacefulness of the forest vignette against a very different moment outside the forest in which he competes with his little brother. Andrew juxtaposed the two moments and used them to represent two sides of himself. As he walks through a gate between the world and the forest, he moves between one Andrew and the other. He wrote:

I walked through the gate, the gate that changed the world. The Forest is dark, but the sun manages to get through.
    A sharp cliff becomes gradual if you go down my path. The path's smooth from years of stumping down it to a place of mystery.
    I find bottles, shopping carts, doors, even a house, but it's really a special place. I walk slowly there, for the quiet of the wood commands respect. I first discovered the wood in a search for quiet.
    In the forest there's a special tree, my climbing tree. It is the biggest tree in the Forest. The tree, like me, thinks you should be the biggest, but in the forest being the biggest doesn't matter to me or the tree.

When I am in the Forest, I feel contented, I feel Freedom, I am the King of the Forest. I bring my Friends to the Forest but they don't understand, they don't know why I whisper. I am glad of that.

In the Forest I am free from my other life as Andrew Lindner.

Andrew's process of pearling an image—a bit—of his life is, I think, an essential part of memoir. This process can begin in very small ways when we take a moment, a scene, an episode, and say, "How does this fit into the whole of my life?"

In a recent memoir workshop, I was reminded of a photograph from my childhood in which all nine Calkins children sit clustered in front of the fireplace, with a row of nine Christmas stockings hanging from the mantle. In each stocking, there is a little white standard poodle puppy. "What does this photograph have to do with the whole of my life?" I asked, and then wrote one entry after another about that one photograph: about the braces on my teeth and the awkward hairstyle, about family traditions—including the Christmas card photographs—and my efforts now to continue these traditions with my sons. In that photograph, as in any photograph, there were many, many stories. I wrote an entry about my mother's love for her dogs. That entry began with how she put the puppies in the Christmas stockings and ended with how, in a "family portrait" that appeared in our church bulletin after the nine of us kids had left home, Mom and Dad sit with two beaming "children," Cracker and Sparky, my mother's dogs.

In addition to gathering stories such as these, it's sometimes interesting to ask, "How are these stories connected?" In the end, memoir is not only about emblematic moments, it's also about the themes, the strands, that run through our lives. Sometimes, when we begin with bits that feel separate, something amazing happens if we assume they are not and ask, "How do these tie together?"

The work we can do with a single photograph or entry can instead be done with a treasured object, with a remembered place. "What does that window in my third-floor bedroom have to do with the whole of my life?" I ask. "What does that window say about who I was as a child?"

"I remember my bedroom because I liked to be alone," Marissa told me. "My bedroom showed what I am like because it had posters of my heroes," she said. Her comments are not unlike those many children say or write. Our job will be to help children go deeper, to help them say more. Instead of telling young writers to add more feelings, I encourage them to add more concrete details.

"Can you picture yourself, there in your bedroom?" I asked Marissa, trying to help her trust that the details of her life matter. "What do you see? Make me feel as if I am there with you and tell it to me *exactly.* " I could also have said to Marissa, "I like to be alone too . . . but I know it was different for you. I need to experience what your bedroom was like *for you.* What did you think about up there alone? What did you do?"

I want my students to understand how a detailed vignette can make readers relive the feelings of the moment. Often, the children and I return to the memoir we've read earlier for an example of an emblematic moment. Studying Eloise Greenfield's "Mama Sewing," which I quoted earlier, I may ask, "Which parts of this made your heart feel differently? Which parts made you know how Eloise Greenfield felt?" Youngsters often speak of the image of Eloise's mother, kneeling on the floor with her pin cushion, frowning and sighing and working away with the pins. We talk, then, about how it's the little details in "Sewing," and in all of literature, that convey an author's feelings.

Finding—and Making—Plot Lines in Our Lives

While our students talk, read, and write about emblematic moments, we can help them find the thematic strands that run through their own lives and through the memoirs they read. One of the best ways I know for doing this is to suggest that they make timelines of particular life strands. I could easily, for example, make a timeline of key moments in the relationship between me and my hair. I'd include in it the au pair who used to brush my hair, and my early, awkward efforts to curl my hair. I'd include desperate experiments with beer and egg, and the feeling that if I could only get my hair to shine, then maybe I'd have a date for the junior prom. I'd include, too, my more recent struggles with gray hairs and all that they mean about my life.

There are endless topics for timelines; my relationship with the clarinet, with my body, with my brother, my life as a writer. Because each dot on each timeline, like each single photograph, contains endless stories, a timeline of any one of these strands can function as a table of contents for many future entries. Sometimes we may want to find our life strands by beginning with just a single moment. "What other moments somehow fit with this one?" we ask. It's particularly important to take a moment from long ago and attach it to a moment from today (or vice versa). Two points determine a line. When there is a now and then, there is a lifeline (a potential memoir) between them.

It is also helpful to look at the published memoirs that have become touchstones in our classroom and ask, "Is there a theme in this memoir?" Inevitably, a person deals with some particular aspects of his or her life in a memoir. In Jean Fritz's *Homesick,* we know from the title and from the opening image that the memoir centers on the fact that, growing up in China, Jean felt homesick for America. It begins:

> In my father's study there was a large globe with all the countries of the world running around it. I could put my finger on the exact spot where I was and had been ever since I'd been born. And I was on the wrong side of the globe. I was in China in a city named Hankow, a dot on a crooked line that seemed to break the country right in two. The line was really the Yangtse River, but who would know by looking at a map what the Yangtse River really was?
>
> Orange-brown, muddy mustard-colored. And wide, wide, wide. With a river smell. . . . I loved the Yangtse River, but, of course, I belonged on the other side of the world. In America with my grand-mother. (p. 9)

One way to think about the themes of memoir is to categorize memoirs according to their central subject. Some center around a relationship, such as that between a grandparent and a child, as in Dayal K. Khalsa's *Tales of a Gambling Grandma* and young Heather Aark's memoir about her relation-ship with her cousin:

SHE WAS JUST LIKE A SISTER

When I was born, my cousin Joanne helped to take care of me. When I got a little older, she used to dress me up in fancy lace dresses with silk on top. We even got in fights sometimes about if we should go to expensive shopping malls or tempting movies. Joanne taught me how to dance in ballet, tap, and jazz. She also taught me how to do my hair in curlers and crimps, and with her touch it came out perfect.

Every weekend she would take me roller skating and I would look forward to it. I remember once Joanne took me roller skating for the first time. Joanne ties my shoe in a double knot in two loops. She thought my skate size was 13½. I was wearing brown skates that looked like mud with an orange bow that looked like the sun. I fell 123 times. I got up and slipped 436 times. Then I got up and held Joanne's hand. She told me to hold my hands up and balance. We went around the rink so many times I was about to drop.

I know it can't ever be the same again, because I know that one day I will lose her, and that I won't do as much with her as she has done for me.

Joanne developed cancer. I visited her in the hospital in Florida. I made chicken noodle soup for her. It smelled delicious. When I found out she will pass away, I took my mom and hugged her tight!

Some memoirs center around memories of a place, as in Anna Egan Smucker's *No Star Nights*, a portrait of a steel mill town. Some center around a moment, as in Clyde Bulla's *A Grain of Wheat*, and ten-year-old Lila's memoir, which includes this section:

> I lay awake for what seemed like a hundred years, waiting for my parents to come home. I couldn't fall asleep until I knew what was going on between them. I got up out of bed and snuck over to the window watching for the blue station wagon to creep up the driveway. I heard the motor of the car long before I saw it. When I heard the screen door open, I pictured my mother and father in the doorway. They would have made up by now.
>
> But I was wrong, completely wrong. Only my mother had come home. I heard her bid my grandmother good night, and started walking up the stairs. Before she had gotten up the last step, I was fast asleep.
>
> The next morning, I woke up to hear birds singing, and a quiet house. I got out of bed, and walked out of my room barefoot. I decided to play with someone, so I went downstairs looking. I walked into the playroom, greeted by the sight of the coffee table littered with peach pits and empty peanut butter jars. My father was sleeping on the couch.
>
> I ran upstairs and checked my parents room, seeing Genevieve sleeping there. I ran into Genevieve's room not really noticing the brown shelves with the porcelain doll on the top shelf. My main focus was on my mother sitting at the desk drawing something.
>
> "What are you doing?" I asked.
>
> "Oh! You startled me!" she said with a little laugh.
>
> "What are you doing?" I asked a second time with a touch of impatience in my voice.
>
> "Drawing a picture of the new house we are going to live in," she said humming a tune under her breath.
>
> "What!!! We're moving?!!" I screamed.
>
> "Yes we are," my mother said in a soothing tone.
>
> "Why?" I asked.
>
> "Lila, I think you have noticed how much your father and I have been fighting," she said in a stern voice.
>
> "Yes," I said uncertainly.
>
> "Well, we have decided the only solution is a divorce."
>
> "What?" I whispered as I crept out of the room. I was really feeling horrible so I went into my bed. I lay awake thinking so many thoughts. Where were we moving to? Was it far away? Is everyone going with us? I only knew two things, we were moving and that one parent was staying behind when they did move because parents who are divorced don't stay together. My eyelids drooped down and before I knew it, I

was fast asleep. The next thing I knew it was morning and I felt as if a steam roller had rolled over me.

What we look for in the texts we read will probably match what we look for as writers. When we are trying to collect entries for our memoir, for example, we'll tend to look at the material other authors have used.

- Memoirists often write about the places of their lives. For Jean Fritz, the place that matters is China. For Madeline L'Engle, the place that matters is a house. Either way, place often plays a big role in memoir.
- Memoirists often write about their imaginations, about what they fantasize and fear, about their private, subjective experience of events.
- Memoirists often place themselves within their family tree, telling something about their familial roots. One way to do this is with grandparent stories; another way is with stories about how they came to be given their names or stories of their birth.

When our focus as writers shifts from collecting toward asking "How can I combine these pieces? How can I shape this blob of stuff?" we will tend to look at texts to see how the author links memories together.

It is helpful to reread memoirs, characterizing them according to their shape. Cynthia Rylant's *When I Was Young in the Mountains* is like a photograph album, each page holding a different snapshot of Rylant's childhood. Her book *Birthday Presents* has a similar shape. "On your first birthday," Rylant said, "we made a star cake, but since you had only four teeth, you just sucked the icing off our fingers. . . . On your second one, we made a clown cake. We invited our friends, but you ignored everybody." Jean Whitehouse Peterson's *I Have a Sister, My Sister Is Deaf* is also a collection of vignettes. This time there is no recurring phrase such as "when I was young in the mountains" but the vignettes are organized around the theme of what it's like to have a sister who is deaf. Anna Egan Smucker's *No Star Nights* begins with the same accumulation of images, most of them having a quality of "Every day, when we were little. . . ." In *No Star Nights*, as in many memoirs, after an accumulation of little images about everyday life, the rhythm shifts to a slower pace, and the book ends with a long, detailed story of *one* day.

Some writers tell their story in a way that creates a unifying link. In Sharon Mathise's *The Hundred Penny Box*, for example, the great grand-aunt, who was one hundred years old, kept an old box with pennies, one for each birthday. In the book, the grand-aunt counts the pennies, telling the story of each one. Those pennies bring together a lot of stories, just as the photo album in Rylant's *Birthday Presents* does for a lot of birthday stories.

Of course, it's not important that our students find the shapes and structures we find in books. The important thing is simply that all of us are poring over examples of the genre, talking about the kinds of things memoir writers often do.

In Jean Little's memoir *Little by Little,* the title and an early scene combine in a similar way to establish a unifying theme. Early in the book, Jean sets out to climb a tree, and her neighbor, Marilyn, restrains her from doing so, saying, "You have bad eyes."

> "I do *not* have Bad Eyes," I told her defiantly. "If your mother said that, she's wrong. My mother never said so and *my* mother is a doctor so she'd know. My father is a doctor, too, and he never said so, either. They both said I can climb any tree I like." (1987, p. 3)

Marilyn, however, is persistent. She continues to taunt Jean, "You do so have bad eyes!" until Jean runs into the house to her mother.

> "What is it, Jean?" she asked in a quiet, calming voice.
> "Marilyn says her mother says I have bad eyes," I burst out, my words sputtering in their rush to get said. "She said I can't climb the tree because it's dangerous if you have bad eyes. I don't have them, do I? I can climb the tree, can't I?"
> Mother did not hesitate. I can still hear the words that set my world turning on its axis again.
> "You do have bad eyes," she said, "but you go right ahead and climb the tree." (p. 4)

And in her life and in her memoir, Jean does climb—to the top—little by little.

Youngsters will find that as they try to design and shape their drafts, they are reexamining their lives in order to discover—or, more accurately, to invent—the themes of their lives. Bo Ram's sense of a life theme grew out of an entry she cherished in which she described standing outside her dying grandmother's bedroom. In order to "grow a memoir," Bo Ram first wrote long, detailed entries about that one moment. Then she asked, "While I waited outside Grandma's room, what did I think? What did I remember?" These questions led her to write entries about other moments she and her grandmother had shared. In her final memoir, she found a way to combine the single moment outside her grandmother's bedroom, and the other memories that "hang on the clothesline" of her relationship with her grandmother. Bo Ram's memoir begins like this (see also Figure 24–1):

> As I tried to listen to every word my youngest uncle and mother were saying, I forgot all about the colorful blocks on the floor lying in front of me, waiting to be made into a small house. I could not take my mind off what I call a secret talk going on in my grandma's room. I got up and went through the wood hall to grandma's room.
>
> Grandma lay on the only bed in the house, with my uncle and mother on their knees at each side. I could not understand why she was sleeping on the bed. In Korea we use blankets as mattresses too.
>
> I took a step into the room with my right foot. Nobody noticed. I lifted my left foot when my uncle told me to stay in the hall with a soft voice. I could not understand why I could not go in.
>
> Every morning I was welcome to go in, to play Korean cards and sing songs with her. Soon I would miss all that. I would miss the times we played every morning Korean cards, how my hand fit inside her wrinkled, worn hands and we would skip outside our gate to ride the fake horse the horse man brings almost every morning.
>
> Thinking about this made my legs tired. I looked around and sat on the wood stairs that led up to the second floor . . . As the house grew into silence the front door opened and in came grandpa . . .

Bo Ram didn't just stumble upon the idea of embedding her memories in the scene in which she stands outside her dying grandmother's bedroom. She'd written memories of her grandma in her notebook, and she'd also written about the scene outside the bedroom. I showed her how she could combine the two. This happens fairly often when students gather entries around a subject. They sense that the entries should end up in a single piece of writing, but they don't know how to stitch them together. I think it's fine to show them ways of doing this, but this doesn't mean children can necessarily learn from our demonstrations. I tried to show Bo Ram how to link her entries in ways that would help her another time, when she worked on another piece, but I'm not sure she can yet do this on her own. It's important, therefore, to let students know that there are some very easy ways of putting related entries side by side in a single piece of writing.

In Jean Little's memoir, the moment-by-moment details of the climbing the tree scene are set against another very different scene in which Jean is learning to play the piano. There is no effort at a transition between the two moments because each moment is placed in a different chapter. Because I find that young writers often have difficulty making transitions, I've

FIGURE 24–1   The beginning of Bo Ram's memoir

As I try to listen to every word my youngest uncle and mother was saying, I forgot all about the colorful blocks on the floor lying on front of me, waiting to be made into a small house. I could not take my mind off what I call a secret talk going on in my grandma's room. I got up and went through the wood hall to grandma's room.

Grandma lay on the only bed in the house, with my uncle mother on their knees at each side I could not understand why she was sleeping on the bed. In Korea we use blankets as matterese too.

I took a step into the room with my right foot. Nobody noticed, I lifted my left foot when my uncle told me to stay stay in the hall with a soft voice. I could not understand why I could not go in.

Every morning I was welcome to go in, to play Korean Cards and sing songs with her. Soon I would miss all that. I would miss the times we played every moring Korean Cards, how my hand fit inside her wrinkled, worn hands and we would ship outside our gate ride the fake horse the horse man brings almost every moring.

Thinking about this made my leg tired. I looked around and sat on the wood stairs that led up to the second floor...As the house grew into silence the front door opned and in came grandpa.

encouraged some children to do as Jean Little did, or to use little stars to separate scenes. In a later section of Bo Ram's memoir (see Figure 24–2), she uses stars to help her switch from climbing the mountain toward her grandma's grave to being at the grave:

> I wished for once that mother would notice that I was brave but I knew she would ask what had happened and why I did not tell her.
>
>   *   *   *   *   *
>
> By the time my legs were loosened up, we were there. The tomb was round and there was something round behind it as if it was holding up the mountain so it would not fall on the tomb. The tomb was on top of some rocks that were put neatly on top of each other.

Drafting and Revision

I've described some of the ideas that are central to memoir, but I have been less clear, I think, about how work in our classrooms may proceed as our students develop their memoirs. In a sense, what I have tried to suggest is that as we launch a genre study in memoir, our workshops will have two strands:

FIGURE 24–2   A later section of Bo Ram's memoir

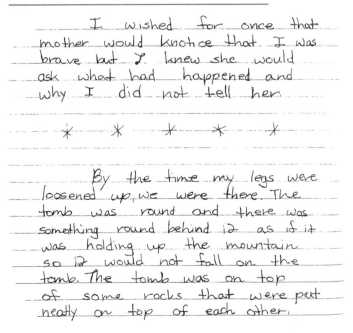

READING MEMOIR

Hearing memoirs and excerpts of memoirs read aloud.

Thinking about familiar books and asking, "Could this be regarded as memoir? Why? Why not?"

Reading book-length memoirs (perhaps independently chosen).

Finding favorite excerpts from the above.

Finding one's own, and the class's, touchstone texts.

Noticing the way memoirists write with emblematic moments.

Revisiting memoir to find themes that hold these published memoirs together.

Studying jumps in time in memoirs.

Studying the external/internal stories in memoirs.

Etc.

WRITING MEMOIR

Writing in response to memoirs (and later doing this with more detail, doing it to "give us goosebumps," etc.).

Storytelling from memoirs (and later doing this with more detail, doing it to "give us goosebumps," etc.).

Bringing in selected photographs, objects, etc., and storytelling/writing in response to them. How do they reveal who we were? How do they link with the whole of who we are?

Rereading previous notebooks and entries for memoir-like bits and perhaps for big ideas—strands— that keep recurring.

Gathering more entries, more material for a memoir.

Making multiple timelines of different strands in our lives, writing many entries about a selected moment or two in a timeline.

Taking one moment and writing about another that somehow belongs alongside it.

Circling narrative entries with musings on "what this means about me" and "how this fits with the whole of my life."

Bringing out the internal story in entries for one's memoir.

Making outlines, plans of how the memoir may go.

Etc.

By this point, if not before, our students will probably need to move out of their notebooks and onto yellow paper in order to write a first draft. It's important to nudge children to do these drafts on paper outside the notebook because the paper itself carries a message. "This will be for readers," it says. "This is meant to be literature."

My colleague Randy Bomer describes his teaching at this stage of the process as "shoving kids out of the nest." It's true, I think, that it sometimes comes down to forcing kids to make the move from a notebook into a draft. The easiest way to do this is to set a deadline. "By Friday, all of us will need to be working outside our notebooks on drafts."

Some will write an entire draft on yellow paper and then reread their notebooks asking, "What else could I have included?" Some will begin by recopying a cherished entry and then writing in the gap between that entry and the next. Some will begin by mapping—or outlining—the possibilities. Sometimes, particularly in the upper elementary and secondary school grades, we will want to nudge students to write several outlines of different possibilities for memoir as a way of nudging them to consider several different options. This may not be helpful to all of them, but the task of jotting down several possible outlines isn't an onerous one, and at some grade levels it may be advisable to encourage all our students to do this.

As soon as children begin to write a draft, I anticipate that I'll stop some of them and encourage them to write with far more detail. I think the task of writing one's life feels so big, it's hard to believe that it's appropriate to write with small details. Most of my favorite selections from children's literature are effective because the author puts everyday occurrences into words, and I'd share these with young memoirists. I love Byrd Baylor's description, in *The Best Town in the World*, of the field of wildflowers. "There were all shades of lavender and purple and orange and red and blue and the palest kind of pink. They all had butterflies to match" (1982, p. 10). I love Cynthia Rylant's description in *The Relatives Came* of what it's like to sleep in a house full of aunts and uncles and cousins: "It was different, going to sleep with all that new breathing in the house." Most of our students, and most of us, would never dream of writing about flowers that have butterflies to match or the sounds of new breathing when company stays over in our house. In order to write memoir, we need to see that literature is made out of the everyday stuff of our lives. I would go as far as to say that the contribution memoir-writing makes to our lives is that it helps us to be moved by the fine details of our lives. These are not writing lessons alone; they are also living lessons.

Telling children that details matter doesn't necessarily enable them to write with detail. Showing children the way details contribute to great literature helps, but this, too, is not necessarily enough. I think we also need to give students strategies—tools—for writing with details. One strategy is to take an entry, a vignette, and deliberately assign oneself the task of writing it "long." Shaunda began with this small entry:

OVERHEARD CONVERSATION

I overheard my father say in the nighttime "These are family matters, I'm calling the police."

I had to go to the bathroom but I was afraid that the police would see me in my PJ's.

This is a longer version of it:

When I see them fight, even over the telephone I get scared and worried because they could abuse each other's mind and I just get scared. I have to find the right words how to explain my feelings. I get upset, and scared, when I hear them raise their voices. Once, my father started hitting my mother, and my mother started yelling, "Call the police, Lila!" I got so upset, thinking the police would arrest him. That was a heartbreaking thought, that my own father would go to jail. I remember once, it was a hot summer night, and I was at my grandmother's house going to sleep in my underwear (I was much younger), and I pretended to go to sleep, and my father and grandma and my father started yelling about how they are our family problems, and then: I'm calling the police. I fell asleep for half an hour, and when I woke up, I had to go to the bathroom, but I thought the police was there, and I didn't want him to see me in my underwear.

Maybe my idea of abuse is my parents having a divorce. It is like sort of mind abuse to me, because the fighting is abuse to the feelings, heart, and brain. It's also abuse to me.

If we are, as Jean Little suggests, going to "tell the truth but tell it like fiction," we need to realize that our memoir will come not only from our memories but also from our imaginations. If we recall an episode that happened in early spring, we recreate the setting by drawing on all the early springs we've ever known—we add the worms lying on the driveway on a wet spring morning, the yellowish-green daffodil shoots we found when we pulled aside the thick layers of leaves. As Jean Fritz says of her process of memoir writing, "I lace memories together with fictional bits when memory doesn't give me what I need."

Often, when children write memoir, many of the details come later as they rewrite their first drafts or as they gather entries around an emerging theme. Dori Kavanaugh began her work with memoir by writing about a time when her grandma was taken to the hospital with a stroke. I asked, "What does this story about your grandma show about you?" She answered by explaining that she feels close to her grandmother and tried to help her when she was in the hospital.

"I don't really get the sense that you felt that way," I said, looking over Dori's draft. Then I suggested Dori read the draft aloud and stop every few lines to tell what *she* was thinking and feeling and noticing. Dori read this section of her draft:

> "I have some very upsetting news, honey," Mom said.
> "What wrong, Mom?" I asked.
> "Grandma had a stroke and she's going to be in the hospital for a couple of weeks," she said.
> "When can we see her? Is she going to be O.K.?" Tears came to my eyes.

Later, when she revised the section to add all that she said that day, Dori wrote:

> My Mom was on the phone with my Grandpa.
> "Mom," I said.
> "Shh! I'm on the phone!" she yelled.
> That made me mad. So I ran into the den and turned on the TV, and waited for my Mom to tell me what was wrong.
> "Dori," she called.
> "I'm coming," I replied anxiously.
> "I have some very upsetting news, honey."
> I knew it was going to be something I didn't want to hear.
> "What's wrong, Mom?" I asked.
> "Grandma had a stroke, and she's going to be in the hospital for a couple of weeks," she said sadly.
> The word "stroke" slowly brushed over me like a soft fan. I hardly knew what a stroke was.
> "When can we see her? Is she going to be O.K.?" I said. Tears came to my eyes. My Grandma was the second closest relative I had.

"I think we can see her in two days. We need to let her rest," my Mom said.

Now tears came to my Mother's eyes. My Mom has been through a lot with my Grandparents. My Grandfather had been sick for a few years and now it was my Grandmother's turn.

Maxine Kumin, after rereading her own writing, once said, "I realize very little of my inner material is showing as yet in this journal." Then she said—and I think her image is a brilliant one—"I am too much living a life of mother and wife now to unfold. It is all . . . in the pleats."

Dori's interior life was in the pleats, too, but she was able to reveal it. She read another section of her draft aloud to me:

A lady came when Grandma was in the hospital.

"Snacks," she yelled, and Grandma bought me some graham crackers. I was upset because she didn't want anything.

Later, Dori rewrote this section so it read:

"Here, let me get you that," I said to my Grandmother trying to be helpful.

She was in the Hospital and she really did look ill.

"No, it's O.K., I'll try to reach it," my Grandma said.

It seemed that everything I wanted to do, she ended up doing. I wanted to help her out so badly, but I guess she didn't need help from a little kid like me.

"Are you sure?" I asked nicely.

"Ya, Hon, it's O.K.," she answered.

Then a lady came.

"SNACKS!" she yelled, as if we couldn't hear that well.

"Grandma, when are you coming home?"

"Ya, I'll have a pack of graham crackers with apple juice," she said, ignoring me.

I never knew she ate that stuff.

"I'm not sure. Here, Dori," she said, handing me the food.

Why was she doing so much for me? I thought I was supposed to help her, wasn't I? I wanted to cry right there, but I held it back because I didn't want to act like a baby in front of my family.

"Thanks," I said, trying to accept it.

I began to unwrap the red package that held the graham crackers when I felt sick to my stomach. I looked at her pale, sad face and tried to smile back, but couldn't. Her hair was all tangled and flat from not going to the Beauty Parlor, she had intravenous in her arm to give her nutrition, and the sad part was she couldn't get out of bed and be flexible like she used to, because she was so sick, she really couldn't hold herself up.

By this time, Dori had realized that her memoir was going to be about how much she wants to help people. Rereading her notebook, she found an entry in which she'd described (in a tangential, offhand way) a time when she helped a homesick friend at camp. "This goes with the scene of me in the hospital, wanting to help Grandma," she said, as she looked over the camp entry. In the camp entry, however, the fact that Dori helped another camper was buried under a lot of extraneous detail. It began

> "Bye!" I screamed as the bus was about to take off.
> "Remember to take a shower every other day!" said my mom.
> It was June 27, 1991. We were leaving to go to camp, so I was a little nervous, but I knew I was going to have fun. The girl who I sat next to was a year younger, but she was really nice. We played crazy eights the whole time. Her mom was a head counselor for the older girls, and she was nice also.
> When I got there, a counselor who I had no idea was, helped me off the bus.

It was a major breakthrough for Dori to find, buried in this narrative, a section about helping another camper. Just as she'd rewritten the hospital scene to bring out the idea of how much she wanted to help her grandma, Dori now rewrote the camp scene.

Dori still faced the challenge of somehow combining the two scenes—the hospital scene and the camp scene—into one unified piece. It would not have been easy for her to move gradually between the two scenes, so she borrowed a technique she'd seen Bo Ram use earlier of putting a little row of dots between two separate but related vignettes. For Dori, the line of dots was almost a place holder for the transitions she would someday write. This is "the joint" Dori made between the hospital scene and the camp scene:

> "Bye," I whispered.
> I didn't want to leave her alone. The look on her face made me want to cry. I didn't want to leave for camp. I wanted to be with Grandma.
>
> .   .   .   .   .   .
>
> Soon I left for camp and, wouldn't you know it, someone else needed me. Her name was Laura, her bed was next to mine, and she was homesick.

"I hate to see people feel bad," Dori explained. "It's also good because Beverly Cleary goes to different subjects in one story like I do. She goes, 'As the years pass, blah, blah, blah, like I do.'"

Dori was quiet for a moment. Then she added, "I put the camp part in because I realized while I was working on this memoir, all of a sudden I dug into my life, and I realized that all of these things make one. And I never knew I was such an outgoing person (outgoing as in helping people and trying to make them laugh a little bit). I don't know why I'm this way. I guess I was born like this."

Dori looked up and said, "It's pretty amazing. You find a treasure bank."

And she had.

Recommended Literature

Memoir-like Picture Books

Blume, Judy. *The pain and the great one.* New York: Dell Publishing Co., 1985.

Brinckloe, Julie. *Fireflies.* New York: Macmillan Children's Book Group, 1986.

Clifton, Lucille. *Everett Anderson's nine month long.* New York: Henry Holt & Co., 1988.

Cooney, Barbara. *Hattie and the wild waves.* New York: Viking Children's Books, 1990.

Crews, Donald. *Bigmama's.* New York: Greenwillow Books, 1991.

———. *Shortcut.* New York: Greenwillow Books, 1992.

de Veaux, Alexis. *An enchanted hair tale.* New York: Harper & Row, 1987.

Dorros, Arthur. *Abuela.* New York: Dutton Children's Books, 1991.

Dragonwagon, Crescent. *Home place.* New York: Macmillan Children's Book Group, 1990.

Hendershot, Judith. *In coal country.* New York: Alfred A. Knopf, 1987.

Khalsa, Dayal Kaur. *My family vacation.* New York: Tundra Books, 1988.

———. *Tales of a gambling grandma.* New York: Clarkson N. Potter, 1986.

Levinson, Riki. *I go with my family to grandma's.* New York: Dutton Children's Books, 1990.

———. *Watch the stars come out.* New York: Dutton Children's Books, 1985.

Marshall, James. *Rats on the roof and other stories.* New York: Dial Books, 1991.

Miles, Miska. *Annie and the old one.* Boston: Little, Brown, 1971.

Naylor, Phyllis. *How I came to be a writer.* New York: Macmillan Children's Book Group, 1987.

Patrick, Denise L. *Red dancing shoes.* New York: Tambourine Books, 1993.

Pomerantz, Charlotte. *The chalk doll.* New York: HarperCollins Children's Books, 1989.

Rylant, Cynthia. *Appalachia: The voices of sleeping birds.* San Diego: Harcourt Brace Jovanovich, 1991.

———. *But I'll be back again: An album.* New York: Orchard Books, 1989.

———. *When the relatives came.* Scarsdale, NY: Bradbury Press, 1985.

———. *When I was young in the mountains.* New York: Dutton, 1982.

Shreve, Susan. *Family secrets.* New York: Dell Publishing Co., 1983.

Smucker, Anna Egan. *No star nights.* Illustrated by Steve Johnson. New York: Alfred A. Knopf, 1989.

Stevenson, James. *Don't you know there's a war on?* New York: Greenwillow Books, 1992.

———. *Higher on the door.* New York: Greenwillow Books, 1987.

———. *July.* New York: Greenwillow Books, 1990.

———. *When I was nine.* New York: Greenwillow Books, 1986.

Thomas, Jane Resh. *Saying goodbye to grandma.* New York: Clarion Books, 1988.

Turner, Ann. *Dakota dugout.* New York: Macmillan Children's Book Group, 1989.

Williams, Vera B. *A chair for my mother.* New York: Greenwillow Books, 1982.

Yolen, Jane. *Owl moon.* New York: Philomel Books, 1987.

Memoir-like Chapter Books

Bulla, Clyde Robert. *A grain of wheat.* Boston: Godine, 1988.

Byars, Betsy. *The moon and I.* Englewood Cliffs, NJ: Julian Messner, 1991.

Cisneros, Sandra. *The house on Mango Street.* New York: Vintage Books, 1989.

———. *Woman hollering creek and other stories.* New York: Random House, 1992.

Cleary, Beverly. *A girl from Yamhill.* New York: Morrow, 1988.

Clifford, Eth. *The remembering box.* Boston: Houghton Mifflin, 1985.

Dahl, Roald. *Boy: Tales of childhood.* New York: Penguin, 1988.

Fritz, Jean. *Homesick: My own story.* New York: G. P. Putnam's Sons, 1982.

Geras, Adele. *My grandmother's stories.* New York: Alfred A. Knopf, 1990.

Greenfield, Eloise, and Lessie Jones Little. *Childtimes: A three-generation memoir.* New York: HarperCollins, 1979.

Hunter, Mollie. *A sound of chariots.* New York: Harper & Row, 1972.

Kincaid, Jamaica. *Annie John.* New York: Plume, 1985.

Little, Jean. *Hey world, here I am!* New York: Harper & Row, 1986.

———. *Little by Little: A writer's education.* Ontario: Viking, 1987.

———. *Stars come out within.* New York: Viking Children's Books, 1991.

Lord, Bette Bao. *In the year of the boar and Jackie Robinson.* New York: HarperCollins Children's Books, 1984.

Maclachlan, Patricia. *Journey.* New York: Doubleday, 1991.

———. *Sarah, plain and tall.* New York: Harper & Row, 1985.

Margolis, Richard. *Secrets of a small brother.* New York: Macmillan Children's Book Group, 1984.

Meltzer, Milton. *Starting from home: A writer's beginnings.* New York: Puffin Books, 1991.

Naylor, Phyllis. *How I came to be a writer.* New York: Four Winds Children's Books, 1978.

Nhuong, Huynh Quang. *The land I lost: Adventures of a boy in Vietnam.* New York: HarperCollins Children's Books, 1990.

Nye, Naomi. *Yellow glove.* Portland, OR: Breitenbush Books, 1986.

Paulsen, Gary. *Woodsong.* New York: Puffin Books, 1991.

Rosen, Michael. *Home: A collaboration of thirty authors and illustrators to aid the homeless.* New York: HarperCollins Children' Books, 1992.

Rylant, Cynthia. *But I'll be back again: An album.* New York: Orchard Books, 1989.

Shreve, Susan. *Family secrets.* New York: Dell Publishing Co., 1983.

25
Literary Nonfiction

Nine-year-old Debbie explained to me, "When my teacher told us to write a report, I got goosebumps and butterflies in my stomach and everything. I knew this time would come because all the kids write real reports in fourth grade, but when it was here I didn't know what to do. I was so scared. On Saturday I went to the library like my sister used to do, and I got the encyclopedia and put down the facts: people, places, dates, Indians, wars. Then I wrote it up."

Debbie is only in fourth grade, but many older students have similar anxieties. One of Tom Romano's high school students described the research report she was doing for another class by saying, "Our grades will be determined by how closely we follow our outlines. . . . I feel bound, prisoned, and dull. As if the wings of my mind and pen have been clipped" (1990, p. 139).

One of my assistants, after hearing these stories, told me about a college student who phoned to ask my assistant if he would type a ten-page report for her. The student arrived twenty minutes later with a musty old book in hand. "Just take ten pages from the book," the student said. "But do me a favor. When you come to big words, change them to small ones." As she turned to leave, she added, "Don't worry, the book is out of print now so they'll never know."

Something is dreadfully amiss. In the first edition of *The Art of Teaching Writing* I suggested that these pervasive problems with nonfiction writing begin when young children like Debbie go to the library on a Saturday morning "to copy down the facts." But I've come to believe that the problem begins earlier, after show-and-tell time in the kindergarten classroom when we tell children, "Okay, now, clear your desks off so we can get started," and when we say, "Put your stuff—your rocks covered with barnacles, your baseball cards—into your cubbies so they won't get lost." As a result, after our children spend two minutes sharing what they find interesting in their lives, they put away their barnacles and baseball cards. As a result, their projects do get lost. It's hard for nonfiction writing to thrive when our children's treasures and collections, hobbies and projects get lost in teacher-designed studies and state-controlled curricula. How much better it would be if, instead of bringing their projects in during show-and-tell time, children knew there was a time in school when centers of inquiry could form around their treasures and interests. If children in the primary grades were examining, drawing, measuring, mulling over, and investigating milk pods or the blueprint of a building (or whatever else they have brought in), this would provide a foundation for nonfiction writing. Out of what comes to school in children's pockets and backpacks, out of what they see and wonder about and poke into, their nonfiction writing emerges.

The impulse toward research and nonfiction writing needs to be nurtured during the early childhood years. No one has more hobbies and projects than the very young child. When my son Miles was three, he found a boulder in the woods that had veins of marble and bits of glistening mica in it. Miles rolled the boulder down from the hill and onto our deck, where it became the first exhibit in his rock museum. Over the next year, he dragged other special rocks into his museum. Some came by way of a wheelbarrow, others on toboggans. He studied each with a magnifying lens and then labeled it. When we moved from one house to another, Miles insisted that his rock collection be loaded into the moving van and brought along.

My son's fascination with the world is not unusual. Earlier, I told about how Georgia Heard and her young nephew spent the Fourth of July waiting for the slugs to come out and watching as each slug left a little trail of ooze behind. Those of us who live and work with very young children know that it was Georgia's nephew who lured Georgia onto the porch to study and celebrate slugs. Those of us who know the young child's willingness to linger and look, to watch and wait, know, too, that although Jane Yolen writes her beautiful book *Owl Moon* as if it was the *father* who takes his child out in the midnight woods to search for owls, truly it was the *child* who pulled the father away from the phone, the desk, and the television into the winter's night. Children's curiosity and their passion to explore the world are the greatest resources we could ever hope to draw upon in teaching nonfiction writing.

Robert Francis's poem "Summons," which was, I think, written from one lover to another, could easily be my poem to my sons.

SUMMONS

Keep me from going to sleep too soon
Come wake me up. Come any hour
of Night. Come whistling up the road
Stomp on the porch. Bang on the door
Make me get out of bed and come
And let you in and light a light
Tell me the northern lights are on
And make me look. Or tell me the clouds
Are doing something to the moon
They never did before
See that I see. Talk to me and show me till
I'm half as wide awake as you are.

My children are so wide-awake it is exhausting. While we were driving recently to the grocery store, Evan picked up a cassette tape and started to finger it. "Evan, sweetie," I said, "Don't touch the black part of the tape."

"Why not?" he asked, moving his hand onto it.

For an instant I wondered what to reply. "You'll rub the music off," I said, aware as I spoke of the inadequacy of my answer.

Evan peered at the tape more closely, turning it this way and that. "How did the music get *on*?" he asked.

Afterwards, I wondered the same thing. "How *does* music get affixed onto an audiotape?" I thought. But, of course, for me the more important question was "Why have I stopped asking these questions?" Our children haven't stopped asking questions. "I know the equator is a hot line—but do you step *over* or *under* it?" Miles asked. Looking up from a chart illustrating human evolution he said, "So we used to be gorillas. What will we be next, Mom, huh?" Then, answering his own question, he said, "I guess eagles." When I tucked Miles in that night, he looked up at me and asked, with a touch of worry in his voice, "Mom, when *will* I be an eagle?"

Those of us who care about nonfiction writing need to know that the impulse toward nonfiction writing is there when a child finds a rock covered with barnacles at the beach and decides to bring it to his classmates, or when Georgia's nephew researches the slime trails of slugs. When David Macaulay, the award-winning author of *The Way Things Work*, was asked why he creates nonfiction books, he said, "Much of the answer lies in my own childhood." He explained, "I played outside a lot . . . I watched frog spawn grow into frogs and hid in the root systems of the larger trees. I went to school through those woods **every** day, looking for unusual rocks, setting paper on fire with my magnifying glass and finding, on very special occasions, bits of animal skeletons, moles and mice, mostly" (Hearn 1993, p. 153).

The roots of nonfiction writing for Annie Dillard, one of America's finest nonfiction writers, began in a similar fashion. In *An American Childhood*, Dillard writes, "The attic bedroom was a crow's nest, a treehouse, a studio, an office, a forensic laboratory, and a fort." When the paper boy gave young Annie Dillard three heavy grocery bags filled with a rock collection, she became a detective, putting each of her rocks through a series of diagnostic tests to determine what it was. "Can you crumble it in your fingers? It's soft. What you have there is talcum powder. Can it scratch a fingernail, a copper penny, a pane of glass, and a knife blade? It's quartz" (1987, p. 137).

Dillard says she was all for cracking open ordinary New England granite like a piñata and laying bare clusters of red garnets on topaz. Once she realized that even the dull rocks along highways held miracles and mysteries, everything in life became potentially fascinating to her. As she explains, "Everything in the world, every baby, city, tetanus shot, tennis ball, and pebble, was an outcrop of some subtle and hitherto concealed vein of knowledge, opportunity, that had compelled people's emotions and engaged their minds in the minutest detail. . . . There must be bands of enthusiasts for everything on earth. . . . There was no one here but us fanatics; bird-watchers, infielders, detectives, poets, rock collectors" (1987, p. 159).

My dream is that all our classrooms will be filled with fanatics: with bird-watchers, detectives, rock hounds, star-gazers, with bands of enthusiasts that form around submarine models, sprouted acorns, and a barnacle-covered rock.

In many of the classrooms I know best, teachers say to parents during Open School Night, "Please, please, encourage your child to have interests and hobbies and obsessions—and to bring them into the classroom." When children's interests and observations are invited into the classroom, the writing workshop will contain information writing and children will move easily between nonfiction and all the other genres—poetry, memoir, fiction, and so forth. We need to let our children know, for example, that when Ronald writes a book that begins with the two pages shown in Figure 25–1, he is writing an information book. Ronald's book is not unlike Margery Facklam's *And Then There Was One* or Helen Sattler's *Giraffes*. If Ronald sees that these books have tables of contents containing lists of chapters, he may decide that what he's written so far is not an entire book, but the first chapter ("Kinds of Dogs") of a book.

FIGURE 25-1   Two pages that may become a chapter in Ronald's book

TRS PUPES

There are shepherd puppies.

AÏR AP V

And there are American puppies.

Nonfiction writing, then, will already be happening in our classrooms when we decide to bring the whole class together around a shared inquiry into this genre. But what might it mean for the whole class to focus together on nonfiction?

The Relationship Between Thematic Studies and a Nonfiction Genre Study

Until recently, when I tried to focus on nonfiction writing, I incorporated it into a thematic study. Several years ago, for example, I worked with Judy Davis and her fifth graders. Together we immersed ourselves in a thematic study on the homeless. The children, their teacher, and I interviewed homeless people, directors of shelters, journalists, and social workers. We all read and collected newspaper and magazine articles. We took notes from radio and television broadcasts, searched for children's literature about the homeless, and tried, through all of this, to get a sense of the lay of land on our topic. It was tremendously exciting work, and I learned a great deal about thematic studies from it (see Chapter 13 of *Living Between the Lines*). The only problem was that we never managed to weave a genre study on nonfiction writing into our inquiry into the homeless. Although we'd intended to study wonderful nonfiction writing in order to learn about the genre as well as about the topic, in the end the work on the homeless was so complex and rich we didn't have much time or attention left over to look *at* nonfiction as a kind of text. Instead, we looked *through* nonfiction texts to the information they contained. We considered stopping the work we were doing on the homeless to examine good nonfiction texts, but it wouldn't have worked to bring all the momentum of our research to a halt in order to conduct a study-within-a-study. In the end, Judy Davis's students used what they already knew about writing to write in whatever genre they chose. Some wrote chronological personal narratives about the process of researching the topic; some wrote poems and stories about the homeless. Some used what they already knew about nonfiction to write in that genre and did good work, but it was not a genre study in nonfiction.

At the time, I thought our inability to study the qualities of effective nonfiction was a personal failure, and I vowed to do better. Since then, however, a team of Writing Project colleagues led by Randy Bomer and Shirley McPhillips have spent several months on an exploration into nonfiction genre studies. They've come away from this work believing that a genre study—a shared inquiry into, in this instance, nonfiction writing—is totally different from a thematic study, which is shared inquiry into a topic, not a kind of writing. Judy Davis, her fifth graders, and I had been inquiring into a topic, the homeless, not a kind of text. In our mini-lessons during the homelessness study, for example, we had focused not on the qualities of good nonfiction writing, but on tools and techniques for investigating a subject (interviews, surveys, observations, and so forth). As Randy Bomer points out in A *Time for Meaning,* in a genre study on nonfiction writing we need to focus not on ways of investigating a subject but on ways of informing readers about the subject. He suggests, therefore, that students may want to write about subjects on which they already have expertise. Miles, for example, may want to write about his rock collection and Georgia's nephew about his study of slugs. Each child will draw on what he or she already knows, and together the class will inquire into how they can write effectively about these various areas of interest and expertise.

In thinking about the characteristics of such a genre study, it's helpful to remember what we know about genre studies in poetry and memoir. From these we can infer that in a nonfiction genre study:

- Teachers and children will begin to live like nonfiction writers. This will probably include using a notebook to gather observations, details, thoughts, and questions about a subject as well as notes and observations on the genre.
- Teachers and children will listen to, collect, share, respond to, sort through, categorize, and study examples of very short nonfiction. As we do this we'll ask, "What seems to be true about this genre?" and "What might it mean for us to write nonfiction?"
- Each writer rereads his or her notebook, finds a seed idea, and begins to live and research and write around that idea.
- Each writer rereads his or her collection of entries thinking, "What will I make out of this?" "How might I shape this?" "What kind of nonfiction text might I make?"

- Teachers and children will find a few shared touchstone texts. These we respond more deeply to and study more closely. As we do so we'll ask, "How does this text affect me? How did the author accomplish this purpose? What can I learn from this text that will help me with my writing?" We then refer to these texts in our own efforts to research, write, and revise.
- Teachers and children begin to draft a piece of nonfiction writing, referring often to the lessons we have learned in studying the qualities of good writing in touchstone texts.
- Our texts are published in ways that are appropriate to the genre.
- Teachers and children look back on their reading and writing to assess and articulate what we have learned about literary nonfiction.

Living Like Nonfiction Writers

When our students are immersed in nonfiction writing, they live obsessed by a subject they care very much about and see that subject everywhere. Because Jackie plans to write an article for *Cricket* magazine about her Maine coon cat, she listens even to the different kinds of purrs her cat makes. In her notebook, she tries to understand and to explain those sounds. Does each sound have its own decipherable meaning? What about the different squeaks her guinea pig makes? Do they, too, have meanings? Is there a hunger squeak, a scared squeak, a squeak of greeting?

When Jackie uses her notebook to investigate her subject in these ways, her teacher makes a big fuss over what she's done. Jackie's teacher has a lot to celebrate, because Jackie is demonstrating a very sophisticated under-standing of research. When I was a child I researched a subject by going to the library and reading the appropriate section of the encyclopedia. Now, of course, I research very differently. This book is a research report on teaching writing, but I did not do my research by going to a library and pulling the W volume of the encyclopedia from the shelf. Instead, I began with what I experience and know. Then I sought out new life experiences and relation-ships that would help me learn more. My exploration has involved extensive reading, certainly, but equally important have been observations, inter-views, discussions, arguments, fantasies, free-writing, photography, and so forth. And although I have now written quite a long text on this topic, over the past two decades I have also written many shorter nonfiction pieces: notes to myself, letters to friends, workshop plans, speeches, research memos, articles, chapters.

Jackie's research on Maine coon cats was sophisticated not only because she drew on personal experience and observation as well as library research. It was also sophisticated because although she already knew her topic well, she was truly engaged in inquiry. In a mini-lesson Jackie's teacher said to all the writers in the class, "Jackie reminds me of a very famous writer, Eudora Welty, who says, 'I write what *I don't know* about what I know.' Jackie knows *so much* about her cat, but instead of just telling all she knows, she's puzzling over questions that intrigue her and investigating the mysteries of her topic!"

Jean Fritz, the author of some of our best historical nonfiction for children, emphasizes the importance of inquiry—and surprise—for nonfiction writers:

> Good nonfiction is invariably related to *story* and, like fiction, it travels from the known to the unknown . . . and here, I think, is where the world of education goes wrong. Whenever it glides over surprise, whenever it ignores suspense, whenever it insists on presenting pat answers instead of probing into questions, it is weakening the power of nonfiction on which much of education is based. (1993, p. 164)

She goes on to add,

> As human beings, we thrive on astonishment. Whatever is unknown quickens us, delivers us from ourselves, impels us to investigate, inspires us to imagine. (p. 185)

I remember my introduction to this kind of research. When I first apprenticed myself to Don Murray, he suggested in a graduate seminar on nonfiction writing that we list the topics we knew and cared about; then he asked us to begin researching something we didn't know about one of those topics. What I learned was that an unfamiliar topic—dragonflies, for example—would have been much easier for me. I decided to research the Vermont Writing Project, a project both like and unlike others I knew. The research was enormously thought-provoking. I found that because I knew a lot *around* my subject but not *about* my subject, I needed to constantly integrate new information with old, book information with life experience, the ideas of others with my own ideas, abstract notions with concrete facts. Then, because I cared so much about the topic, I also needed to make my truth beautiful. A topic like dragonflies would have been much easier!

Living like a nonfiction writer, then, means watching for surprise and perplexity and mystery. It means knowing that even the subjects we know very well can be endlessly new to us.

Immersing Ourselves in the Genre

If we and our students are going to immerse ourselves in examples of good nonfiction writing, we need to begin by clarifying what we mean by nonfiction writing.

David Macaulay, Jean Fritz, Lois Lowry, and Milton Meltzer have each written about nonfiction writing, yet none of them can define it. The dictionary claims that nonfiction is "prose works other than fiction," but this isn't very helpful. "Are the numbers on the elevator buttons nonfiction?" Macaulay asks. "The dictionary's definition makes nonfiction sound like non-books, like the other-than category," Lowry complains.

The genre of nonfiction contains a huge breadth of forms. Directions are nonfiction, as are brochures, recipes, biographies, travel logs, essays, editorials, feature articles, and so forth. If we are going to study the genre, we will probably want to focus on one of its subsets.

In order to select the form of a nonfiction genre study, we will want to consider the context and purpose for the writing we will do. If a school visiting day is approaching, there might be good reason to read and write guidebooks. If the class wants to protest a school policy, there may be good reason to write editorials. If many students are acting as teachers to each other, informing others about their areas of expertise, these students may want to read and write encyclopedia-like writing in which they note many facts about a subject. This is the kind of nonfiction writing my son Miles often writes. In a book titled *Army Book* he lists facts about aircraft carriers on one page and about submarines on another. When Miles writes books such as this, he seems to truly believe that his five-line-long books will become resources for all the kids in his class. It is good for him to claim this authority as an expert on his topic. Miles's delight in listing facts is not unlike his delight in gathering pretty rocks or shells. He is a collector. He loves to line up what he knows, to count the amount he has collected, to sort his stuff into piles, to share his loot with others.

By the time children are in fourth or fifth grade, however, they are less apt to believe that their books about army boats or horsemanship will be used as sources of information by others. My colleagues who have studied nonfiction suggest that rather than trying to convince kids that their report on rocks will become a resource for rock collectors the world over, we may want to agree that library books will probably contain more information about a subject. If our students' goal for their writing is not to inform but to share their fascination with a topic and their ideas about it, then instead of writing like encyclopedias, they'll be writing in the literary nonfiction tradition of John McPhee and E. B. White.

Once we and our children have decided on the form of nonfiction we will be writing, we'll want to search for the very best examples. Everyone needs to be invited in on the search, and everyone needs to become a critic of what is found. We'll all begin clipping articles out of newspapers and children's magazines and finding good nonfiction books. My colleagues discovered that in order to be good critics of the writing in nonfiction picture books, it helped to look at the written texts apart from any accompanying photographs and ask, "Could this text stand on its own?" Articles tend to be more helpful than books, because they more closely match what children will be able to write. "Is this beautiful writing?" we'll ask. "Is this the kind of thing I want to write?"

As Kathy Doyle's fifth graders pored over examples of nonfiction writing, they kept a giant chart to record what they learned. On one page they listed "unique features" of nonfiction:

- Point of view: Sometimes the author uses an interesting point of view.
- Subtitles help to organize the text.
- Sometimes the author first convinces you to care, then either something happens or information comes.
- Often, the author brings you into the scene in a "you are here" way.
- Some include the questions you might be asking.
- Some have graphs, charts, photographs, illustrations.

In thinking and talking about this chart and the other charts her students compiled, Kathy was ambivalent about whether the charts had helped. "Charts of 'Ways to Begin a Nonfiction Article' and 'Observations' made my students read more actively," Kathy said. I was sure she was right. Because the children had places to record what they noticed, they had paused to articulate the fact that nonfiction writers often use subheadings, indexes, captions, charts, cross-references, diagrams, bibliographies, quotations, statistics, personal vignettes, colorful leads, and so on. It was therefore somewhat helpful for the class to work together to make lists about the characteristics of their genre. On the other hand, a writer can't produce good nonfiction simply by putting all the listed ingredients together on a page. Once made, these lists had almost nothing to offer to the process of writing nonfiction, nor had they necessarily yielded deep insights about nonfiction.

When Kathy and I talked more about the lists, we realized how easy it is in studying nonfiction writing to bypass the centrality of response. When reading poetry or memoir, Kathy's students first responded as human beings: they cried and laughed and marveled and winced and remembered their own lives. Only later did they turn around and ask, "How did the author create this effect?" In learning from fiction, poetry, and memoir, we had always tried to be sure that our students *first* responded as human beings, returning to analyze or to label or to list the components of effective writing we saw in the texts. "What would it have meant," Kathy and I wondered, "if we had first been *responsive* readers of literary nonfiction?"

Over time, Project teachers have begun to say to our students, "When we find ourselves *really responding* to a text, when we find ourselves drawn in, surprised, mystified, filled with wonder, beginning to understand, able to envision something, let's mark those sections. Later, we can return to those sections to ask, 'What was I thinking or feeling or learning?' and 'How did the author create this effect?' "

Ariana knew right away that the page of Lasky's *Think Like an Eagle* that really affected her was the one "where she has Jack, who's a nature photographer, seeing a bear and rushing down the river, to get a picture of the bear." When I asked Ariana to tell me why that page mattered to her she said, "To me, the book is not just about Jack and not just about nature; it's about how Jack is affected by nature. This page shows that." She looked at the page for a while. "I think the camera is how *he* connects with nature. He used to be a hunter; now this [photography] is his way to connect. It's like in *Journey* when the grandfather uses picture-taking to connect with his family. Jack uses it to connect with nature."

This sort of reflectiveness may not have given Ariana something to add onto a "Features of Nonfiction Writing" list, but her thoughts about how Jack connected with his topic led the class to talk about how many nonfiction writers take readers along as they tell the story of how they became connected to a subject. As we watch authors come to know and care about their subject, we too are drawn into a relationship with the subject. Ariana and her classmates notice, for example, how George Laycock opened his *Boy's Life* article "Valley of the Cranes."

> Early on a black, cloudy night, I crouched in my hiding place beside the river and waited. Suddenly, a dark and ghostly island seemed to take shape before me. The whole island was alive and creeping downstream.
> Gradually, I figured out what was happening. Through my binoculars, I could see that my "island" was really a mass of giant birds. They

moved like silent ghosts—a crowd of hundreds of sandhill cranes wading slowly through the darkness on their long, thin legs. . . .

I had come to Nebraska, in the heart of America, just to see this carnival of cranes. Some naturalists call it the world's greatest spring bird show.

Later, I realized that in a similar way, Bruce Brooks draws us into his fascination with the designs of nature:

One evening, when I was about five, I climbed up a ladder on the outside of a rickety old tobacco barn at sunset. . . . I was allowed to roam, poke around, and conduct sudden studies of anything small and harmless. On this evening, as on most of my jaunts, I was not looking for anything; I was simply climbing with an open mind. But as I balanced on the next-to-the-top rung and inhaled the spicy stink of the tobacco drying inside, I *did* find something under the eaves—something very strange.

It appeared to be a kind of gray paper sphere, suspended from dark planks by a thin stalk, like an apple made of ashes hanging on its stem. (1991, pp. 3–4)

Brooks goes on to say, "The troubling thing was figuring out who had designed it, and why."

I assumed the designer was a human being; someone from the farm, someone wise and skilled in a craft. . . . Even when I saw wasps entering and leaving the thing, it did not occur to me that the wasps might have fashioned it for themselves. (pp. 3–4)

My point is not that nonfiction writers often bring readers in on their own growing obsession with a topic, but that in studying nonfiction, we can easily come up with lists of trivia. Probably our biggest and deepest learning about the genre will come if we begin instead by letting it matter to us and then later try to understand what it is that the author has done.

Exploring and Experimenting with the Tools of a Nonfiction Writer

In nonfiction writing as in other genres, young writers probably learn the most from a close study of a few carefully selected texts. The texts that made Isoke Nia's third and fourth graders stop in their tracks included Barbara Bash's *Urban Roosts*, Yukio Tsuchiya's *Faithful Elephants*, and a one-page article about popcorn. When the children studied these pieces, they saw that the authors combined information and experience, that they wove together "memoir-ish stuff and facts." Isoke's fifth and sixth graders had no problem doing this, but for her younger writers especially, it was not an easy thing to move back and forth between their lives and the external information. To help these children, Isoke asked the class to pretend that they were researching a topic—rain clouds, perhaps—and she gave each child a packet of texts about the subject. In the packet, she included personal vignettes as well as statistics and related facts. "Let's imagine that this was our topic and this was what we'd collected," she said. "Can we work in pairs to see if we can combine these bits into one, unified piece?" Later the class worked together on the chalkboard to share and discuss the ways in which they'd tried to integrate the various kinds of information.

Kathy Doyle's fifth graders noticed something very different in the touchstone texts they studied. "All the writers had a way of organizing what they saw," one child told me. "Like in *Sagura Cactus*, Barbara Bash writes about all the different things that happen to and in and around the roots of the cactus, then the stem, then the flower. And in *Peeping in the Shell*, Faith McNulty tells the facts inside a little story about breeding a whooping crane. Each author sort of decides on the *way* to tell the story." To help her students experience the moment of decision for themselves, Kathy asked them to spend an hour in different rooms of the school, with each child choosing a point of view from which he or she would write about that room.

Emily said, "When I did it, I learned a problem about observing. Where to begin. I was in Mr. Fann's room, and there was so much I could have written about, and I *really* had to decide." She added, "I decided to compare Mr. Fann's class to Mrs. Doyle's, but I still had to decide how to start, what to compare, in what order."

Kate added, "I went to the library, and it was kind of hard because the fourth graders were talking and everything, and it was hard to observe them because they were so fast. I ended up observing the books because they didn't move, and I watched this one shelf and wrote who did what to it, or at it."

Ariana was surprised that Kate found that having a roomful of people made observing hard. "I was in the gym, and to me it was hard because people *weren't* there, so I was thinking about how the gym is a place to do things, and all day it gets a lot of wear, and when I was there, the gym was taking a break and relaxing and stretching out."

Kathy's students didn't spend long writing about rooms in the school; this was a small exercise alongside their ongoing efforts to find and develop subjects of their own. Once they had these subjects, Kathy suggested that her students deliberately try out different points of view and different voices in the entries they were gathering about them. Alice, for example, was gathering entries in order to write an article about orchestra rehearsals. In her notebook she tried to write first a humorous entry about one rehearsal, then a pensive, thoughtful entry about the same rehearsal, then another in which she emphasized the personalities of the instruments, and yet another in which she emphasized the people in an orchestra and their different jobs.

In similar ways, we can help our students not only explore issues of voice and point of view, but to also experiment with issues of focus. When I first began working on my writing with Don Murray, he knew intuitively that after five years of classroom teaching I was so full of stories that if left on my own, I would probably blurt out all I knew onto the page in a giant tangle of ideas, experiences, and emotions. Murray wisely insisted that I *not* begin writing until I'd developed lead paragraphs for each of twenty different articles I might possibly write about my teaching.

"Twenty articles?" I thought. "Twenty, twenty," I said over and over to myself, and I remember purposefully keeping each idea tailored and small so that I would still be able to produce nineteen others. What a wonderful hands-on exercise in narrowing one's topic!

Most of our students will need similar help if their nonfiction is going to be focused. Often, students enter our classrooms expecting to write a two-page essay on topics as broad as "America," or "the solar system," and it's no wonder that they have this expectation. In a survey of American secondary schools, Arthur Applebee (1981) found that teachers have often assigned topics that could be the subject of a whole book, a series of books, or even an entire library—topics on which students would need a lifetime of research before they could develop a sense of expertise. It is not unusual, Applebee says, for teachers to ask for a two-page report on topics such as twentieth-century American architecture or the diesel engine.

Although a five-year-old and a fifteen-year-old are similar in that they will both approach nonfiction writing intending to "tell the whole thing," children of different ages often seem very different in their ability to understand focus. For five-, six-, and seven-year-olds, it's progress indeed to sort what they write into sections. We celebrate when a book titled *My Cat* has separate chapters on "Feeding My Cat" and "Can My Cat Talk?" Older children, however, will also understand that an entire article can be written in response to the question "Can My Cat Talk?" and that there are many possible ways to focus such an article. The author may want to stress the humanlike characteristics of her cat, and especially, of her cat's "language." Then again, her focus on her cat's language might also lead her into a discussion of communication among chimpanzees and dolphins.

Drafting

When I was a child I thought that "writing in your own words" was quite literally a process of translation. You turned the big vocabulary words, the ones that didn't sound like you, into smaller words and you rephrased everything else so you weren't copying.

If our students have been poring through old copies of *Boy's Life, Ranger Rick,* and *Cobblestone* and clipping, saving, and savoring the feature articles they admire most, if they've been critiquing what my colleagues call information-in-the-raw books such as Seymour Simon's photograph essays (*Snakes, Whales, Earthquakes*) for being "like an encyclopedia," we probably need not worry about reminding our children to write "in their own words." If they are writing about topics they've experienced as well as studied, if they've gathered pages and pages of entries about their topic, if they've chosen a specific form and voice and angle after trying other possibilities, we probably will not have to worry about our children writing "in their own words."

In a genre study on nonfiction writing, children will learn that the process of writing literary nonfiction is not at all one of translating someone else's words, that nonfiction writing begins with living immersed in one's topic, letting everything in life remind you of it. It's about probing the topic, asking questions of it and exploring its mysteries. It's about letting exploration become a journey to new places.

Debbie began studying hotels for the homeless and then suddenly realized how silly it was for her to study hotels without drawing on what she already knew about them: Her father is a caretaker at a very posh New York City hotel. But how could she combine what she knew about fancy hotels with hotels for the homeless? They were worlds apart . . . and that became her point. With her notebook in hand, Debbie spent time at both the posh hotels and the hotels for the homeless. Her scrawled entry begins:

> Well I'm standing here on a marbled floor with mirrors in back of me and wall lamps and there's a statue of what looks like a cupid, fresh flowers, old-fashioned clocks, painted walls, antique rugs, leather seats. Piano playing in the restaurant, big dining room, everything is spic & span clean, ritzy marble lamps, paintings, antique furniture, brass doors, neatly dressed waiters, all tables have candles, reception desk, info desk, classical music, lots of doormen (3), walk down series of steps, and it's so warm in here. Chandelier in the dining room. . . .

Later, Debbie drew on what she'd seen and read in order to write an essay that begins:

I live next to the Plaza Athénée, one of the most beautiful hotels I've ever seen. It's the only connection I've ever made to the word "hotel."

But now I realize that hotels mean different things to different people.

To me, the lobby of this glorious hotel means a place of fantasy where I visit and see antique furniture so old I'm afraid to sit on it. There are waxed floors you could see your reflection in, and I'm too scared to run because I might put a mark on it. There are marble columns taller than I am, and flowers almost too expensive to smell.

To Rachel and her children the lobby of the Martinique hotel means old cracked tiles popping up if you step wrong, smells of alcohol and beer in the air from the night before, smells of roach spray from an exterminator that recently came.

To me hotel elevators mean clean carpeted places with velvety seats and polished panels that smell like lemon. The ride feels so smooth, it's like the elevator is staying in one place.

To Rachel and her children it means broken-down elevators with graffiti. To Rachel it means not being able to finish her children's laundry on time because she is too scared to take the elevators and too tired to walk the 13 flights of stairs.

Debbie has learned not only about hotels but also about writing literary nonfiction. She has learned that she can be a primary researcher on the topics she has experienced. Our children can bring their notebooks and pencils; they can watch, look, and listen. What our children will also learn is that as nonfiction writers they can respond—by remembering, laughing, weeping, disagreeing, questioning. Literary nonfiction is not just about a collection of facts, it's about the author's relationship to those facts and about the meaning an author builds from and around and despite those facts.

As we immerse ourselves in a nonfiction genre study, most of the writing we and our students will do will be precursors to our rough drafts. As we follow our topics, we will need to write constantly in order to gather ideas and unravel mysteries. We may decide to keep double-column entries in our notebooks, one side for recording facts, statistics, and bits of information, and the other for wondering and speculating and asking questions. We may nudge ourselves to write entries that begin with "thought starters," such as "What I wonder about most of all is . . ." or "The thing I can't understand is . . ." or "The part that really gets to me, that makes my heart feel differently, is. . . ."

Of course, it's no easy task to take all of this gathering and turn it into what Isoke calls a "blob draft." For some students, drafting can be a process of copying and combining entries. But often students will need to put their notebooks aside and try to write a draft in which they find their voice.

Don Graves tells the story of how he agonized over the first draft of his Ford Foundation report, *Balance the Basics*. "I had reams and reams of data, and the data made me feel as if I had to write in a sterile, objective tone. I was suffering from an acute phase of 'Dissertation Donny,' he says. Then, as the story goes, Graves finally went to Don Murray for help, bringing with him the two overworked pages he'd managed to produce. Murray looked at them, sighed, and said, "Wait a moment." Several minutes later he returned from the cellar with a cardboard box, some black paper, tape, and scissors. He proceeded to work for fifteen minutes, and then he handed Graves a black box with one small hole in it. "What you're to do," he said, "is to go home and put aside every single note. Then begin writing as if you were telling folks what you've learned. After you've written each page, slide it through the hole, and when the paper is done, we'll open the box."

Not everyone needs a black box, but all of us *do* need to learn how to write with voice and energy when we work on nonfiction texts. For some students, it will help if teachers suggest, as Murray did, that first drafts be written without notes. The goal is fluency, voice, and an organizing image. Later the authors can reread their drafts, adding in bits and pieces from their entries. Others may find it helpful to draft several leads before proceeding to the body of their reports. These are some of the leads fourth graders wrote:

> A beam of sunlight shone through the crack in the red foxes den. The fox opened his eyes just a slit and looked around his den. It was a cozy stump . . .   *Amy*

> In the stillness of the dark, a 170–200 pound St. Bernard lay on its side, curled to fit on the mat. Looking at him, I wondered if he was dreaming about long winters of rescuing lost travelers. Just that year he'd dug some out with his huge paws, licking their face afterwards to keep them warm.   *Hope*

> The boat started with a sputter as I, Celia Thaxter, and my family left for the Isles of Shoals . . . I couldn't wait to see the island we would live on. Nearer and nearer we came until . . .   *Melissa*

It's not only upper-elementary children who can write with a clear voice. Listen to the "song" in Figure 25–2, an extraordinary piece of nonfiction written by a kindergartner.

> One day—well, if there was a day—there was sand and dust and rocks
> and stones and some other things. And it was a *thunderclaps*!
> And a planet began to rise.

FIGURE 25-2 Nonfiction by a kindergartner

And they called it Earth.

And do you know what? It rained and rained and rained for thirty days in the big holes.

And see? We began to grow.

And the first animal was a little dinosaur. . . .

When the Earth turns around the sun, the sun turns around the Earth. The sun isn't really a big ball. It is really a giant star. It is really far, and so it looks like a circle.

Don't listen to the newspaperman, all that about the sun. Don't be afraid because the sun will last forever.

That's all there is.

Nonfiction Writers Become Teachers—and the Learning Continues

When our children become nonfiction writers, when their work is published, they become teachers within the classroom and school community. What an important thing it is to give children this chance to claim and develop, share and become famous for what they know about. Soon one child becomes famous as the grasshopper catcher, another as the rock climber, the stamp collector, the inventor, the Italian chef, the interior decorator.

By giving each child the opportunity to claim and share his or her individual area of expertise, we do far more than teach children another genre. We also foster each child's independent interests, and we invite each one to act as an authority. In doing so, they lay claim to their own voices. I recently attended a large conference in a field other than my own. Sitting amid that crowd of people exchanging pleasantries with those around me, I had a faceless feeling. No one knew who I was or what I did. They didn't know my family, my work, my life stories. If I'd been able to teach others what I know, I would have felt more present. Many students spend years in classrooms without ever being able to teach others what they know. The bottom line in teaching writing is that we must know what it is that our students know. The British educator Harold Rosen has said, "Every child has a story to tell. The question is, will they tell it to us?" I think we can also say, "Every child has lessons to teach. The question is, will they teach them to us?"

When our students become teachers, they also become learners, filling up their notebooks and their minds with new ideas and observations. Not long ago I asked a group of student teachers how they liked teaching. I expected them to talk about their roles in school and their relationships with students and colleagues, but what they wanted to tell me about was the effect of teaching on the rest of their lives. "I think about teaching all the time," one said, and the others agreed. "Even at the theater, I find myself drawing connections to whatever I'm teaching." Another added, "Whenever I read the newspaper, I keep cutting things out to share with the kids." For these student teachers, teaching is a lens that changes the way they see everything.

And isn't—or wasn't—it that way for all of us? Have we begun to take for granted the transforming power of teaching? Listening to those student teachers, I felt as if they were articulating something I'd long forgotten. On the topics I teach, I am a magnet. Any related information sticks to me and to my notebook. When I know I will be teaching a class on a particular topic, I become a powerful learner. Everywhere, I see related anecdotes, ideas, and quotations. Because I teach, I learn. "We are the teaching species," Erik Erikson has written. "Not only do the young need adults, but adults also need the young." He adds, "Human beings need to teach not only for the sake of those who need to be taught but for the fulfillment of our identities and because facts are kept alive by being shared, truths by being professed."

Erikson is right. I need to teach because my ideas are kept alive by being shared. And I am not alone—we are the teaching species. What we sometimes forget is that our students are also part of the teaching species. They, too, need to keep ideas alive by teaching them to others.

Literary Nonfiction

Bash, Barbara. *Tree of life: The world of the African baobob.* Boston: Little, Brown, 1990.

———. *Urban roosts.* Boston: Little, Brown, 1990.

Baylor, Byrd. *The desert is theirs.* New York: Charles Scribner's Sons, 1975.

Brooks, Bruce. *Nature by design.* New York: Farrar, Straus & Giroux, 1991.

———. *Predators!* New York: Farrar, Straus & Giroux, 1991.

Cameron, Ann. *The most beautiful place in the world.* New York: Alfred A. Knopf, 1983.

Dewey, Jennifer Owings. *At the edge of the pond.* Boston: Little, Brown, 1987.

Facklam, Margery. *And then there was one: The mysteries of extinction.* Illustrated by Pamela Johnson. Boston: Little, Brown, 1990.

French, Vivian. *Caterpillar.* Cambridge, MA: Candlewick, 1993.

Goffstein, M. B. *A writer.* New York: HarperCollins, 1984.

King-Smith, Dick. *All pigs are beautiful.* Cambridge, MA: Candlewick, 1993.

Lasky, Kathryn. *Dinosaur dig.* New York: Morrow Junior Books, 1990.

———. *Sugaring time.* Photographs by Christopher G. Knight. New York: Macmillan, 1983.

———. *Think like an eagle.* Boston: Little, Brown, 1992.

Lauber, Patricia. *Dinosaurs walked here . . .* New York: Bradbury Press, 1987.

———. *Volcano: The eruption and healing of Mount St. Helens.* New York: Bradbury Press, 1986.

Lipsyte, Robert. *Assignment: Sports.* New York: Harper & Row, 1984.

MacNeil, Robert. *Wordstruck.* New York: Viking, 1989.

McNulty, Faith. *The lady and the spider*. New York: HarperCollins
    Children's Books, 1987.

————. *Peeping in the shell*. New York: HarperCollins Children's Books,
    1987.

Parnall, Peter. *Winter barn*. New York: Macmillan, 1986.

————. *Woodpile*. New York, Macmillan, 1990.

Paulsen, Gary. *Woodsong*. New York: Bradbury Press, 1990.

Reit, Seymour. *Behind rebel lines*. San Diego: Harcourt Brace Jovanovich,
    1988.

Russell, William, ed. *Animal families of the wild*. New York: Crown Books
    Young Readers, 1990.

Rylant, Cynthia. *Appalachia: The voices of sleeping birds*. San Diego:
    Harcourt Brace Jovanovich, 1991.

Sattler, Helen Roney. *Giraffes, the sentinels of the savannas*. Illustrated by
    Christopher Santuro. New York: Lothrop, Lee & Shepard, 1989.

Schlein, Miriam. *Pigeons*. Photographs by Margaret Miller. New York:
    Thomas Y. Crowell, 1989.

Siebert, Diane. *Sierra*. New York: Harper & Row, 1991.

Winter, Jeanette. *Follow the drinking gourd*. New York: Alfred A. Knopf,
    1988.

Professional Literature

Barzun, Jacques, and Henry G. Graff. *The modern researcher*. New York:
    Harcourt Brace Jovanovich, 1957.

Bomer, Randy. *A time for meaning: Learning literacy with people aged
    10–20*. Portsmouth, NH: Heinemann, in press.

Fletcher, Ralph. *What a writer needs*. Portsmouth, NH: Heinemann, 1992.

Fritz, Jean. The known and the unknown: An exploration into
    nonfiction. In *The Zena Sutherland lectures*, ed. Betsy Hearn. New
    York: Clarion Books, 1993.

Graves, Donald H. *Investigate nonfiction*. Portsmouth, NH: Heinemann,
    1989.

Hearn, Betsy, ed. *The Zena Sutherland lectures*. New York: Clarion Books,
    1993.

Lasky, Kathryn. Reflecting on nonfiction. *The Horn Book Magazine*,
    September/October 1985: 527–32.

Macaulay, David. The truth about nonfiction. In *The Zena Sutherland
    lectures*, ed. Betsy Hearn. New York: Clarion Books, 1993.

Zinsser, William. *On writing well*. New York: Harper & Row, 1990.

26
Theme Studies
Reading the World, Reading the Word

In his book *Schoolteacher,* Dan Lortie (1975) says that although there have been radically new methods in almost every other occupation—agriculture, business, medicine, and accounting—in education our principal methods of instruction (recitation, lecture, seatwork) have remained the same since colonial times. This resistance to change in American schools exists alongside a frenzy of surface-level changes. Every year, central office staff, building administrators, and Board of Education members announce that a district has taken on new priorities, acquired new programs, hitched itself to new stars, and yet, as teachers know all too well, in some ways nothing ever changes. When we hear of yet another new program, new initiative, or new aim, we sigh "Here we go again." We shrug off whatever new demands come along, thinking "These, too, shall pass" and "Whatever comes around goes around."

Every once in a long while, however, an idea comes along that has the power to alter the entire landscape of our classrooms. For many of us, the writing workshop has been such an idea. Now, another idea is changing the classroom landscape.

I remember the social studies and science classes I experienced when I was a child. Mr. Reinhardt put a big stack of textbooks on the first desk in each row of our classroom, and we passed the books down the row. I wrote my name in the box inside the back cover of my copy, and that weekend I made a book jacket out of a paper bag. The book jacket was the best thing I can remember doing with that textbook. After that, I copied vocabulary words and definitions out of it, answered questions at the ends of chapters, and studied for tests. When we studied the Civil War, I read and answered questions about dates, battles, and generals. How differently some children today go about studying the Civil War! In classrooms with theme studies, children read and discuss and write in response to Jim Murphy's *The Long*

Road to Gettysburg, Paula Fox's *The Slave Dancer,* Mildred Taylor's *Roll of Thunder, Hear My Cry.* In some classrooms, students research what their neighborhood might have looked like during the Civil War, compare Abraham Lincoln's and Bill Clinton's inaugural addresses, explore similarities and differences between the American Civil War and the civil wars that are wreaking havoc in so many countries today. What a different tone and spirit there is in these classrooms than in the classrooms I remember from my childhood!

The idea with the power to change everything in our classrooms is called "theme studies" or "interdisciplinary education" or "thematic studies" or "scholarly pursuits" or "theme cycles." The label probably doesn't matter. What *does* matter is that this idea can radically alter the tone, texture, and structure of our entire day, our entire classroom. The writing workshop has often been inserted into a traditional school day, but the entire day changes when along with the writing workshop we and our students also have theme studies. Relationships change. Students begin saying things like "I have an idea. Let's . . ." and "But what *I* wonder is. . . ." Students begin bringing plans and projects, questions and expertise into the classroom. In his study of American schools, John Goodlad said that although what students like best is to build, plan, make, enact, instead they tend to sit passively, filling in blanks, answering short-answer questions, and copying from the chalkboard. All this changes in a theme study. When one realizes how resistant American schools are to change, it's absolutely miraculous that the idea of theme studies is sweeping through so many of our schools.

A Critique of Published Theme Studies and an Effort to Form Guidelines

New math started out as a wonderful new idea, one that was going to bring creativity and energy and collaboration into the math curriculum. But as Seymour Sarason has shown, new math ended up looking very much like *old* math. The same could happen to theme studies if we're not careful. The idea has such promise that we need to take great care to preserve its integrity. In education, we tend to take radical new ideas and stretch, chop, twist, and splice them until they fit into the existing norms of the school day rather than alter those norms. But just as revision is a complement to good writing, so too is revision a complement to good teaching. When we write something that has great promise, we look at it and ask, "What's working that I can extend? What's not working that I can discard or rethink? Where is this leading me? What really matters in what I've said?" These are also questions we need to ask of what we are doing with theme studies.

At a recent staff development workshop at Teachers College, I suggested that workshop participants join me in a critical look at some published theme studies. We looked, for example, at a diagram like the one in Figure 26–1.

"Tell me what you think when you look at this," I said to the teachers at the workshop. "I feel exhausted," one woman answered, and the room broke into laughter. She'd spoken for us all.

FIGURE 26–1   Flow chart for a theme study

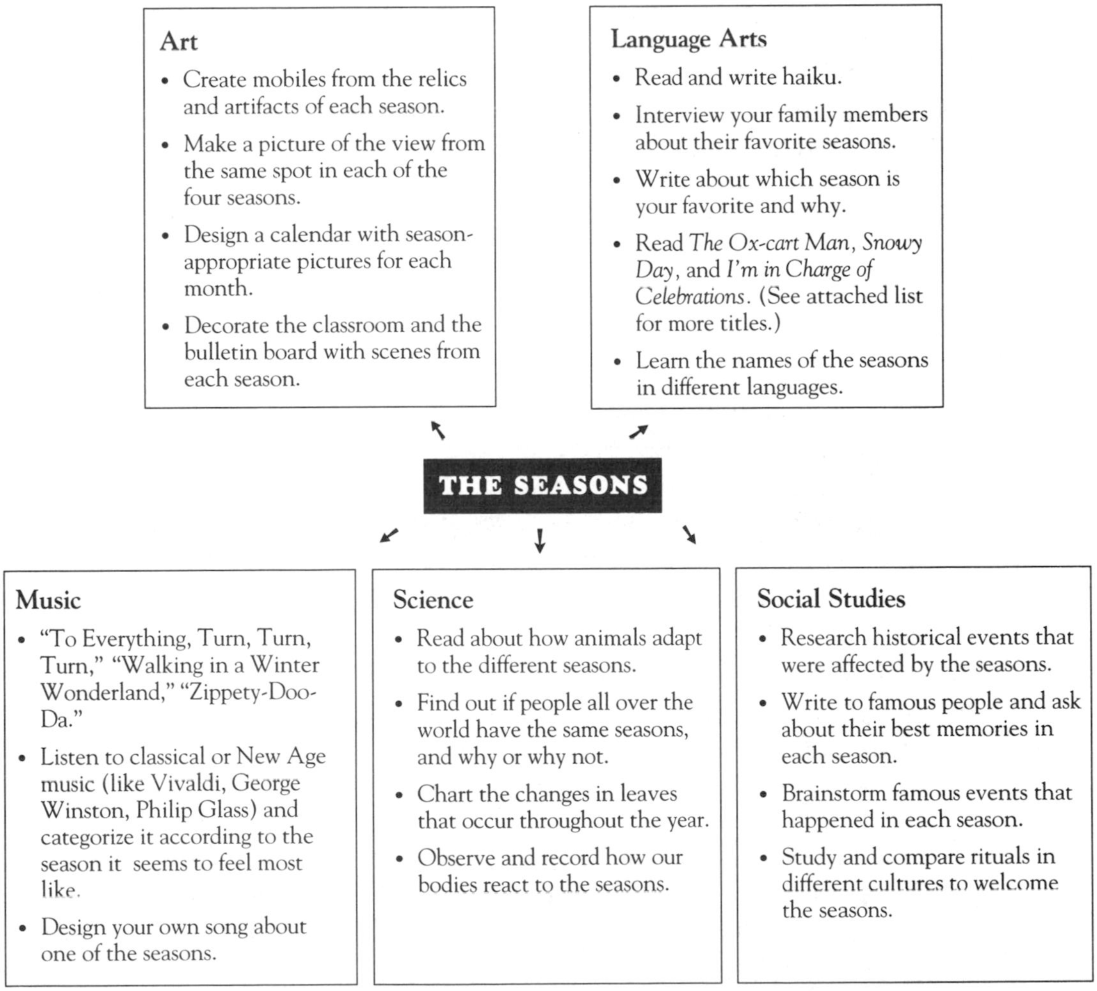

Art

- Create mobiles from the relics and artifacts of each season.
- Make a picture of the view from the same spot in each of the four seasons.
- Design a calendar with season-appropriate pictures for each month.
- Decorate the classroom and the bulletin board with scenes from each season.

Language Arts

- Read and write haiku.
- Interview your family members about their favorite seasons.
- Write about which season is your favorite and why.
- Read *The Ox-cart Man, Snowy Day*, and *I'm in Charge of Celebrations*. (See attached list for more titles.)
- Learn the names of the seasons in different languages.

THE SEASONS

Music

- "To Everything, Turn, Turn, Turn," "Walking in a Winter Wonderland," "Zippety-Doo-Da."
- Listen to classical or New Age music (like Vivaldi, George Winston, Philip Glass) and categorize it according to the season it seems to feel most like.
- Design your own song about one of the seasons.

Science

- Read about how animals adapt to the different seasons.
- Find out if people all over the world have the same seasons, and why or why not.
- Chart the changes in leaves that occur throughout the year.
- Observe and record how our bodies react to the seasons.

Social Studies

- Research historical events that were affected by the seasons.
- Write to famous people and ask about their best memories in each season.
- Brainstorm famous events that happened in each season.
- Study and compare rituals in different cultures to welcome the seasons.

It seems that publishers no sooner get their hands on a subject for a thematic study than they break it into a million tiny pieces. The irony is that for many of us, the whole point of doing thematic studies is so that we can finally stop racing between one tiny subject and another. Although we turn to thematic studies as a way of simplifying our curriculum, developing expertise, and probing a topic, we may be so accustomed to racing through the little bits and pieces of preset curricula that we unknowingly recreate in our thematic studies exactly what we set out to avoid.

In the schoolyard behind the local elementary school where a group of well-intended parents have built an adventure playground, I sometimes watch children playing. They line up and then race, one by one, up the steps, down the slide, along the beam, across tires roped into a bridge. . . . If a child stops to do acrobatics on the beam or to play the Three Billygoats Gruff trip-trapping across the bridge, the others in line call out, "Hurry up" or "Get going."

When I was young, we played on a stump at the edge of the playground. That stump was our chariot, our podium, our throne, our nature center, our castle. I composed more stories, considered more careers, and conducted more investigations around that stump than I ever did in the classroom. Watching my son and his classmates hurrying through the apparatus on their fancy new playground, I can't help but wonder, "Where is the adventure in the adventure playground?"

My real concern is that this kind of well-intended "adventure playground" also exists inside the school. When I see students hurrying through a huge list of activities that we well-intended teachers have assembled, I cannot help but ask, "Where is the *study* in this thematic study? Where is the inquiry, the probing, the investigation?"

If I were to create a list of criteria for an effective theme study, it would include the following.

1. *A theme study should encourage depth, thoughtfulness, and focused inquiry.* If we value depth and thoughtful inquiry, then I think we need to reconsider several popular assumptions. One is the misconception that our goal in a theme study is to link together as many disciplines as possible. When this is the goal, the result is often a hodgepodge of vaguely related activities. One publisher, for example, suggests that we can connect the abacus with a theme study on families if we use it to record how many false teeth each child's grandparent has. We can link learning to tell time with our theme if we make paper plate clocks and use them to illustrate what our grandparents do at different times of the day. Such a hodgepodge is a far cry from a genuine inquiry.

If we really believe that knowledge is integrated, why can't we trust that a deep investigation of one particular topic will lead us naturally across subject divisions? How much better it would be for students to pursue a trail of thought about a selected area of interest and to learn by doing so that investigations can lead us to many unforeseen territories and ways of knowing.

Of course, it would be hard to imagine a deep inquiry into a subject as broad as "families." I suspect we as teachers choose broad topics in part because our curriculum requires that we convey broad concepts to our students. The important thing here is that overarching concepts reside in particular instances. If we feel responsible for teaching our students broad ideas about transportation, for example, it does not mean that the topic of investigation must be as big as transportation itself. We and our students could pursue a topic as focused as the traffic problems in an overcongested intersection near our school, and within this case in point wrestle with concepts as large as public financing of transportation or the way civilization grows out of systems of transportation.

My sons have lured me into an interest in elementary school science. Several years ago when I heard that Mary Ellen Giacobbe was studying science education with the renowned Eleanor Duckworth, I phoned Mary Ellen to ask what she was reading in the course.

"We're reading the moon," Mary Ellen answered.

"*The Moon,*" I repeated, adding it to my book list. "By whom?"

"The moon, Lucy," she answered. "We're reading *the moon. The moon.* By God."

It didn't make things any clearer when she explained, "Every night, each of us watches the moon for half an hour."

"What's there to watch?" I wondered, and I wondered this again when I learned that Eleanor Duckworth has been watching the moon for sixteen years and meeting for week-long retreats with a study group to make sense of all that she and the others see. Duckworth says, "We're surprised to find that . . . everything that seems simple has depths unimagined for investigating and finding more about. . . . You just look at the phenomenon; and if you ask yourself what you can find out about it, you notice all kinds of things which keep leading to deeper understanding" (in A. Meek 1991, p. 32). When teachers in Duckworth's courses first begin recording whatever they see when they look at the moon, they tend to enter into the activity believing they already knew about the moon. "Very soon," Duckworth says, "they find out things that surprise them. Like, sometimes, on bright, starry nights, there's no moon to be seen. How come? . . . And sometimes, you see it tonight, and you go out a couple of hours later, and it's not there any more" (p. 32).

If Duckworth can spend sixteen years observing the moon, then surely we and our students can spend two months studying the traffic congestion outside our schoolhouse. When we do so, we will find, as Duckworth suggests, that a seemingly simple topic has depths unimaginable.

What I am saying is that if we want our students to study something in depth, we need to focus on a particular topic. But I'm also saying that researching something "small" doesn't prevent us from working with the broad concepts of our curriculum. Duckworth's moon watchers will probably wrestle with all the concepts of space that are covered in our curricula. They'll think about rotation and revolution, day and night, seasons and leap years and time changes, gravity and weight and orbits and planets and stars . . . but they'll do this while also maintaining "a governing gaze" on the moon as they see it in their own lives.

In a similar way, fourth graders at P.S. 148 studied the major concept of immigration, but they did so while focusing on the question of how they could make it easier for an immigrant to enter into their school community and their neighborhood. Fifth graders in Kathy Doyle's classroom studied the world's different ecosystems (bog, desert, rain forest, and woodlands) by learning from these ecosystems as they existed in their own homemade terrariums.

But let me return to the idea of a teacher who decides to do a theme study on transportation. If the teacher doesn't focus on a small subtopic (such as the traffic problems outside the school), she is apt to divide her class into subgroups, one studying airplanes, another studying the railroad. Until the members of a class have spent a lot of time learning, and learning how to learn, together, I think we need to avoid dividing the class into subgroups each pursuing a different subtopic, or we end up devoting a good percentage of our teaching time to choreography.

Recently, I watched some first graders at P.S. 148 work on a theme study of babies. The teacher, Laurie Pessah, gathered the children's questions. They were interested in how babies learn to talk, how babies are born, babies' toys, what babies eat. Typically, each of these interests becomes a subgroup, and the teacher in a theme study on babies, like the teacher in a theme study on transportation, runs among the study groups like the circus performer trying to keep plates spinning on the ends of sticks. "Here's another book," we tell one group as we rush on to the next group. "Why not take notes on that?" we urge them, hoping to keep them productive. A third group seems to be wobbling off course. "Settle down," we remind them. If we're running between different groups in this way, I don't think it's very easy to support students as they frame an investigation, compare information from one source with that from another, and invent ideas.

Laurie decided not to use her students' early questions as the frame for the investigations for another reason. She realized that when we organize our entire curriculum around questions students raise at the start of their inquiry, we forget that until they have immersed themselves in a topic for a while, they don't know the significant questions to ask. Kathy Short recently reminded us that doctoral students spend as much time finding the question they'll explore as they spend conducting their research. It takes a lot of knowledge before a person can identify the really interesting loose ends to pursue, the gaps to fill.

The first graders at P.S. 148 ended up focusing their research on the topic of babies' toys. They brought baby brothers and sisters into their classroom and recorded how long it took each of the babies to approach and engage with particular toys, and how long each toy sustained each baby's interest. Soon they were questioning published recommendations about which toys were appropriate for which ages, They ended up inventing their own toys as well as their own chart of appropriate toys for different ages, which they mailed to the authors of several books on babies. Meanwhile, the children began thinking about gender issues related to toys, and this led them to investigate violence on television shows. As these first graders pursued a line of investigation, they ended up using math and art and writing and reading and experimentation as tools of inquiry, but their investigation was not chopped up into these areas from the start. If one were to draw a diagram of this research about babies, it would look more like Figure 26–2B than Figure 26–2A.

2. *Ideally, in theme studies youngsters are invited to take on an inquiry stance like that of a field scientist, anthropologist, or historian.* In the thematic studies I've discussed thus far, children not only learned about a subject, they also became insiders, learning from within a discipline. When the first graders observed and documented how babies interacted with different toys, the young investigators were acting as developmental psychologists. When Kathy Doyle's fifth graders observed and investigated their miniature ecosystems, they acted as field scientists. When students study the congested traffic outside their school, they act as city planners. When Duckworth's students puzzled over the patterns in the sky, they did so as astronomers.

FIGURE 26–2A   An interdisciplinary unit on babies

Math:
ages, weight

Music:
lullabies

Nutrition:
the food groups

Art: *collages, paints,*
pictures of babies   **BABIES**

Science: *babies*
of many animals

Literature: *poems,*
stories, chants
about babies

Social Studies:
caring for babies
around the world

FIGURE 26–2B   The same topic, but with an emphasis on inquiry

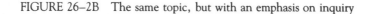

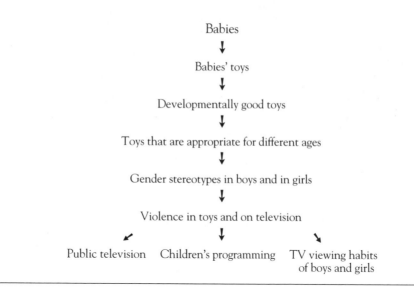

Babies
↓
Babies' toys
↓
Developmentally good toys
↓
Toys that are appropriate for different ages
↓
Gender stereotypes in boys and in girls
↓
Violence in toys and on television
↓
Public television   Children's programming   TV viewing habits
of boys and girls

Instead of reading an encyclopedia entry about other people's ideas on the moon, they observed the moon and then developed and tested their own ideas. As developmental psychologists, field scientists, and astronomers, these teachers and children became idea-makers.

Duckworth, whose books include *The Having of Wonderful Ideas* and *Science Education: A Minds-On Approach for the Elementary Years* (with Jack Easley, David Hawkins, and Androula Henriques), says that she will never forget the first time she was invited to learn in this way: "It was the first time . . . I got excited about my own ideas. I had been excited about ideas before, but they had always been somebody else's ideas. . . . This was the first time that I had a sense of what it was like to pay attention to my own ideas." She continues, "It is, of course, exhilarating to find that your own ideas can lead you somewhere."

If we are going to invite our students inside a discipline, then even those of us who love the smell and feel of a new book more than anything in life must realize that reading and writing are not the only ways of learning about the world. If we are investigating spiders, we must learn not only from poems and stories and fables, nonfiction books and newspaper clippings, diagrams and charts about spiders, we must also learn from the spiders themselves. We must write down other people's ideas about spiders, but we must also write down our own. We need to search for, watch, categorize, count, compare, diagram, and feed spiders; and in doing this hands-on, primary research, we will originate and pursue our own ideas. Of course, not all subjects are conducive to primary research, although with ingenuity we can often find ways into a primary investigation. How easy it would have been for Kathy Doyle, for example, to decide that there was no way to study ecosystems like the desert or the rain forest from within the confines of her New Jersey classroom!

The idea that children might learn about a subject by taking on the habits of a discipline has other important implications. If our students are acting as astronomers, for example, then they will probably not be spending a great deal of their time writing fake diaries as if they were spacemen living on Jupiter. As Carol Edelsky, Bess Altwerger, and Barbara Flores suggest in their important book, *Whole Language: What's the Difference?* (1991), we need to remember that just as the author Katherine Paterson doesn't use story starters and Anne Tyler doesn't put her hand in a paper bag to feel different textures and then write down texture words, so, too, child writers don't need to do these things. "We know this for writing," Edelsky and her colleagues write. But then they add:

> Somehow we forget the lesson when it comes to natural and social sciences. But it's the same thing. Historians don't answer a list of someone else's questions so they can be checked on their knowledge of Civil War facts. Anthropologists don't do clever follow-up activities like conducting a pretend interview with their favorite informant. It doesn't matter if such activities are fun and if children like them. They aren't honest science.

3. *In a theme study, learning should be purposeful.* One of the most important things that distinguishes whole language classrooms from traditional ones is that in whole language classrooms, language is used, skills are developed, and information is learned for *real* purposes. Students learn the difference between a fact and an opinion not because it is in the curriculum, but because they are submitting an editorial to the local paper. Similarly, in a good theme study, students don't chart distances between planets just to have done so. They may do it because they are creating a planetarium for the younger grades in the school or because they are investigating the possibility that there may be life on other planets, but they don't chart these distances as part of a trivial pursuit research project. A sense of purpose comes first from having a real, passionate interest in the subject and then from having goals and plans and real-world audiences. It helps, therefore, as we select and focus on subjects for a thematic study, if we and our children imagine what we might aim toward in our learning. Might we organize students to join the shopkeepers on our city block in helping the homeless from our area? Might our investigation of pollution lead us into a save-the-river project? Might our study of weather lead us to create a school-based weather station?

4. *I wouldn't want, in a theme study, to contradict my beliefs about writing and reading.* Because I believe that a fiction writer needs to develop his or her characters slowly, out of a lot of writing and living, I wouldn't want children in a thematic study to read historical fiction about colonial America and then immediately write their own such story. Because I don't believe writers go around writing new endings to other people's texts, I wouldn't encourage this kind of writing within a thematic study. Because I believe in having authentic contexts for writing, I wouldn't want the entire class to spend much time writing pretend diaries as if they were sailing the seas on the Mayflower. But this does not mean I wouldn't use writing in a thematic study. When I'm investigating a subject, I use writing as I collect information—concepts, questions, quotations, and statistics—in a notebook, and I know students will want to do this as well. More important, however, I also use writing in order to think about the information I am gathering, and I would especially want to encourage students to do likewise.

Then, too, in a good theme study, I wouldn't want to contradict my beliefs about reading. Because I believe that we need to read fiction *first* for all the millions of meanings it will have in our lives, I wouldn't want students to read a particular novel in order to find out about the clothes worn during a particular era or about the life cycle of a spider. They may, perhaps, *reread* a book looking for such particulars, but literature should first be read aesthetically.

I should add here that although reading and writing will *enrich* a theme study, I wouldn't dream of having my entire reading/writing workshop subsumed in a theme study. I've recently been dumbfounded by the realization that some school systems are moving from a basal reading program toward literature-based thematic units, as if the thematic unit can be a vehicle for teaching all of the language arts. It's wonderful when you are inquiring about colonial America to read a bit of historical fiction, but students also need opportunities to read and write texts for all the many meanings those texts might have in their lives.

Choosing a Subject for a Theme Study

Although some educators claim that the subjects for theme studies must emerge out of the interests of a particular group of students, I think it's more realistic and more prudent to assume that teachers as well as children will have a major role in determining the subjects for whole-class theme studies. I want to emphasize that this decision will need to be in the hands of teachers and students working collaboratively, and not in the hands of district curriculum. Even when a school district lays out the territory a teacher must explore in a given year, the individual teacher will need to consider it carefully: "Which of these subjects might become areas for deep inquiry and which might be better covered in a more cursory fashion?" A teacher recently told me that she dealt with the human body, a required subject, by spending three entire days in June on the subject, thus allowing her students to devote more time, over more months, to a thematic study on another topic.

But how do we decide which topics will be particularly suited to a theme study? These are some of the questions I consider:

- If I have a curriculum I am expected to follow, which subjects within it (or which aspects of which subjects) might capture the imagination, interest, and energy of my students and of me?
- What resources (other than and including books) are available if we do a theme study on one of these topics? For the subjects I'm considering, are there experts, sites for field trips, people to interview and survey, things to observe, brochures, pamphlets, maps, music, newspaper clippings, radio broadcasts, and accessible nonfiction books?
- Within which of these subjects might students be able to conduct hands-on primary research? Which research tradition might they participate in? Would they be field scientists? anthropologists? city planners? historians?

- If my students develop an expertise in one or several of these topics, will it have real-world payoffs for them? Will they find themselves understanding current events differently? talking about the subject with adults around them?
- Which of these topics (or which aspects of these topics) might help my students think critically about the issues of a democratic society? Which topics would foster greater compassion, understanding, social consciousness, and justice?
- Of the topics I'm considering, are some more developmentally appropriate for the age groups I teach than others?
- What kinds of final projects and purposes can I imagine the students pursuing?

It's not likely that I would ever decide to do a theme study on teddy bears. I suspect that my students don't have a deep interest in learning more about teddy bears, and even if they do, the subject is not high on my list of interests. There are few resources, other than books, songs, and chants, available on the topic. I can't envision teddy bears as the subject for primary research, and if my students became experts in teddy bears, unless the topic led us into environmental or consumer issues, they probably wouldn't listen to the news differently or participate in the conversations around them differently. Most of all, an investigation of teddy bears would probably not do a great deal to help my students and me live more socially conscious or compassionate lives.

Other subjects are more complicated. Animals, for example, is a topic that has a lot of advantages, but it also has some problems. One of the biggest problems with a research project on animals is that the temptation would be great for the class to divide up into subgroups, with a cluster of children studying horses and another studying dolphins. There is nothing wrong with this, but it's hard to imagine how we could bring in experts, conduct hands-on research, and work toward major real-world purposes on each subject. If students studied an issue such as communication between animals, however, one could easily imagine how we might conduct primary research with our cats, dogs, guinea pigs, and parakeets, and we might indeed invite experts into the classroom, watch films together, and so forth. Furthermore, an investigation of communication between animals might well lead us into an involvement with animal rights, for example, or into a project bringing together animals and the elderly.

A topic such as colonial America raises a new set of questions. It's hard to imagine how a class might conduct primary research on such a subject.

There are no survivors to interview, and it's not easy for youngsters to do much firsthand research on the Pilgrims. This doesn't disqualify the subject; every topic has its own set of possibilities and constraints. But I do think teachers who are approaching a thematic study on colonial America will want to think through possible ways of approaching the subject. Is colonial America best learned about through reading and writing historical fiction? If so, the subject might fit better a genre study on historical fiction rather than a thematic study. Alternatively, is there an angle on the subject that might allow for some primary research? Might it be possible to focus on America's frontier then and now? Could the colonial era be investigated through a study of how our patch of earth has changed through the past few centuries?

Launching a Theme Study: The Immersion Phase

Anyone who has ever led a theme study in the classroom knows the fun of the immersion phase. We remember poring over books to find the really good ones, rereading our poetry anthologies to find the relevant poems, cutting clippings from newspapers and magazines, phoning experts and arranging field trips, finding free brochures and pamphlets, writing off for more information.

My first bit of advice seems fairly obvious: We need to let our students in on the fun. We need to turn responsibility for gathering resources over to them, and we need to bring the phone books, stationery, stamps, maps, newspapers, poetry anthologies, and magazines they'll need into our classrooms.

In *Living Between the Lines* I tell about a teacher who turned this phase of the research over to her students. Judy Davis, a fifth-grade teacher at P.S. 183 in Manhattan, told her students that the project they were doing on the homeless belonged to everyone in the classroom, that they'd all be gathering resources together, and that it wouldn't be easy because there aren't a lot of books on homelessness. Each child promised to do something each night to secure resources on the subject, and soon they were transcribing news from the radio, writing journalists for more information, and arranging for speakers and field trips.

After a week of this work, Judy said to me, "If something happened and we had to end this whole thing right now, I'd still look back—even on just this week of research—and think of this as one of the best parts of our year."

I knew what Judy meant. Students who'd been disengaged all year had become hooked into this work. Every day Reginald walked a half-mile to the police station until finally, on a Saturday, he interviewed a policeman whose beat included areas where the homeless congregate. Chris tried to volunteer to work in a soup kitchen. Debbie took her notebook with her to the fancy hotel in her neighborhood and wrote about the flowers, the plush elevator, and the marble floors, juxtaposing these observations with those she made in hotels for the homeless (see pp. 445–46).

In *Living Between the Lines* I talked about the importance of involving children in this immersion phase.

> To me, it felt enormously important that classrooms were filled with phone directories, files of addresses, brochures, newspapers, subway maps, and graph paper. It felt important that children were listening to the news with pen in hand and phoning each other afterward to ask, "Did you get that reporter's name? We should write to her." It felt important that every morning in Judy's classroom there was a mail call and that the teacher across the hall, whose classroom held the fifth-floor extension telephone, would often stick her head into Judy's room to say, "Sabrina, a woman named Susan Martin phoned to say she's bringing two homeless people in tomorrow for you to interview. She'll call you at home tonight," and, "Anabelle, you have a phone call in the office." And it was absolutely extraordinary to have Anabelle return to the classroom flushed with excitement saying, "I've got a speaker for us. His name is Mr. Wilkerson and he runs a family shelter and he's coming next Thursday at one o'clock." (p. 197)

Anabelle began by investigating the concept of shelters for homeless people, but soon she was writing a portrait of a man who'd devoted his life to public service. When we involve students in this phase of the research, time and time again they'll find that behind all the important issues there are people. William Zinsser writes about this in *On Writing Well.*

> Often, in fact, you will find yourself embarking on an article so apparently lifeless—the history of an institution, perhaps, or some local issue such as storm sewers—that you will quail at the prospect of keeping your readers, or even yourself, awake.
>
> Take heart. You will find the solution if you look for the human element. Somewhere in every drab institution are men and women who have a fierce attachment to what they are doing and are rich repositories of lore. Somewhere behind every storm sewer is a politician whose future hangs on getting it installed and a widow who has always lived on the block and is outraged that some damn-fool legislator thinks it will wash away. Find these people to tell your story and it won't be drab. (1990, p. 81)

But let me make one final and, I think, crucial point about the immersion phase of research: Students, from the first, need to gather resources, but they also need to find meaning in those resources. Anyone who has ever done research knows that analyzing and understanding is easier if we don't wait until we're buried in mountains of stories, essays, interviews, and statistics before we begin to reflect on and relate what we are taking in.

Helping Students Make Meaning from All They Gather

As soon as we and our students begin to live like magnets, gathering anything related to our subject we can possibly find, we need to set up ways to respond to the incoming data. In his book *Science and Human Values*, Jacob Bronowski points out, "There is nothing on the face of a fact that tells you what it means," and our students need to know this. Cutting an article out of the newspaper is not research, it's an invitation to *do* research.

"Scientists look for order," Bronowski says, but adds, "Order doesn't display itself. It's not there for the mere looking. There is no way of pointing a finger at it—or a camera. It must be discovered, in a deep sense, created." Then he uses a fable by Karl Popper to illustrate his point.

> Suppose that someone wished to give his whole life to science. Suppose that he therefore sat down, pencil in hand, and for the next twenty, thirty, forty years recorded in notebook after notebook everything that he could observe. He may be supposed to leave out nothing: today's humidity, the racing results, the level of cosmic radiation and the stockmarket prices and the look of Mars. . . . Dying in the calm certainty of a life well spent, he would of course leave his notebooks to the Royal Society. Would the Royal Society thank him for the treasure of a lifetime of observations? It would not. . . . It would refuse to open them at all, because it would know without looking that the notebooks contain only a jumble of disorderly and meaningless items. (1972, p. 14)

When I began conducting classroom-based research, I expected that my observational notes on students should be strictly descriptive, that I should record exactly what I saw and only that. What a surprise it was to have my professor tell me that one-third of my notes should be about my research plans, and one-third should be about my reactions to what I observed. Our students need to be told the same thing. Our notes mustn't be "just the facts." What we see and hear and notice must lead us to wonder and to plan new lines of investigation. An investigation is different from a wide-awake life because when we investigate, we set out to inquire in a deliberate, planful fashion. This happens in our notes.

As we enter the immersion phase of our research, we need to be very careful lest we drown in all that comes into the room. Systems must be established early on for making something of the incoming information. Some classrooms turn their bulletin boards over to this purpose. If the class is studying winter, one child may bring in and post a news clipping about the beaver's fur coat. Other children then post *related* clippings in a clump around the first. Meanwhile, yet another clump—this one about winter storm forecasts—begins to grow on another section of the bulletin board. In other classrooms, there is a time called "Pair and Share" in which students meet with classmates to read and talk about what each brings to the class. Often file systems are set up, with categories that are reconsidered every few days. Children can hold seminars to teach each other what they are learning, even when their ideas are still half-baked and inaccurate.

This informal opportunity for data analysis can steer young researchers in new directions, as it did nine-year-old Birger, when he was given the chance to tell the class about his topic. Standing in front of the class during the share meeting, Birger spoke about the grey squirrel's diet, mating habits, appearance, enemies, and so forth. The class was particularly interested, however, in a curious statement he made about how squirrels squeak when they are cold and how this saves their lives.

Diane raised her hand. "Does the squirrel squeak even if he's sleeping?"

Birger nodded, adding, "Only if his body temperature goes below forty degrees and the squeak saves his life."

"You mean he automatically squeaks?"

Birger nodded, and then Brad asked, "How does the squeak make its body temperature go up? Is it like a thermostat?"

Birger wasn't sure, and so the meeting ended with Birger promising to do more research and to report back his findings. The process, then, is one of collecting, connecting, and then collecting again, of shifting between learning, teaching, and learning. In this way students develop the expertise from which they will write. By talking about something, they begin to identify what they know and what they don't know.

Helping our students develop ideas and participate actively in the immersion phase of research, then, has a number of benefits:

- By telling our students that the project, from the start, belongs to all of us, we invite them to share in the ownership of a thematic study, to feel that they are makers rather than merely recipients.

- We provide opportunities for an enormous amount of functional, real-world reading and writing. Students write business letters and read phone books and see the benefits of these literate engagements.
- We help students imagine how to pursue a subject. They learn how to open up a subject, how to find the interesting questions, how to understand the lay of the land. By guiding the whole class in learning how to learn, we equip children to do this immersion phase on their own next time. That "next time" may come later in the thematic study when each child has his or her own focus to pursue.
- If, early on, we encourage students to make something of what they learn in their research, they develop a meaning-making stance. This stance is easiest to develop when one has only a small amount of new information, but once developed, it will serve the researcher well.
- When students act as co-researchers and colleagues during the immersion phase of a research project, it's quite natural that they'll play a major role in shaping the direction of the research as they begin to close in on a particular focus. It's crucial for students to learn that researchers overview a subject, asking themselves what might be an interesting thing to pursue. If the teacher alone does this work, we're taking over the most important intellectual moves in a research project, and our students won't be learning how to learn.

As we all hone in on a subject, we'll probably shift from simply reading about it to gathering some of our own primary data. Whether we are talking about Kathy Doyle's students studying their ecosystems, first graders observing babies' interactions with toys, Eleanor Duckworth's moon watchers, or the hypothetical students studying congested traffic outside their building, observation is one of the first and most essential ways of making meaning.

Reading the World: Making Meaning from Observation

Fifteen years ago, when Don Graves invited me to join him as a research associate in one of the nation's first observational studies of children and their writing, I knew nothing about research. I'll never forget how foolish I felt during my first days with my researcher's clipboard. "What do I record?" I wondered. On my second day as a researcher in Pat Howard's classroom,

Don Graves joined me. The children weren't writing, they were doing math—actually, copying things out of their math books—but Graves suggested that we stay. I walked up and down the rows, looking for data about writing. There was nothing for me to record anywhere. Finally, I went to the back of the room and leaned against the radiator to wait for some data. I waited but nothing happened. After what seemed like an eternity, I signaled Graves, who'd been scurrying about, and we left.

Before I could let out a weary groan, Graves burst out with, "Zowie! What a gold mine. Wasn't that *amazing?*"

"Uhhh . . ." I said, and then, hiding my amazement, I nodded in agreement. "Yeah, amazing. . . .What'd *you* see?"

Graves couldn't wait to spill out his observations. "Wasn't it something the way some kids had chairs so low and desks so high . . . or the others, with chairs so high and desks around their knees. Imagine what that does for penmanship." Graves added, "How'd you suppose that kid up front could write with a two-inch-long pencil? And that guy with the eraser the size of a golf ball—zowie!"

Over the years, working alongside Don Graves, I received a lot of instruction in observation. Once Don and I interviewed a teacher in Brooklyn together. She was reading through her mail when we arrived. "Just a sec!" she said, and after quickly skimming memo after memo, she deposited the entire stack in the wastepaper basket. Then, apologizing for the delay, she said, "Let's start." I opened my notebook and began my notes. A few hours later, Graves started a speech by telling about that teacher's trash can full of memos. "We have to do something about the clutter that fills our mailboxes, our trash cans, and our curriculums," he said. What a lesson! If we're going to observe well, we need to become people who can watch a colleague going through her mail and say, "Zowie!" In order to do this, we need to realize that meanings come not from events themselves, but from what we bring to them.

A year ago, the writer Jean Craighead George and Carolee Matsumoto, a science educator, joined me in leading a day-long workshop on science education at Teachers College. My plan in approaching the day had been to bring the entire auditorium full of teachers outside to observe pigeons, but as Jean George and I walked toward the auditorium, I realized to my dismay that there weren't any nearby pigeons.

"What'll we observe?" I said to Jean, frantic.

"Let's observe the sidewalk," she answered. She spoke with such self-assurance that I didn't want to question her suggestion. But an hour later, standing in front of the auditorium full of teachers, I could hardly get the words out of my mouth. "After a fifteen-minute break for coffee," I said, "let's all take our paper and pens and spend ten minutes observing the sidewalk."

Nothing happened on my sidewalk square during these ten minutes. And so, when we gathered inside the auditorium to share our observations with each other, I asked Carolee Matsumoto to begin. This is what she'd written:

> I chose 1 block of sidewalk and recorded the time and gave myself 10 minutes. I drew a sketch. My sidewalk square is new compared to others, it's more white and bumpier, rough, not worn down. I did a texture rubbing and noted there are stridations in 3 directions. I measured it and found it 6 of my feet minus one big toe × 6 of my feet up to the ball of my foot. I noted a crack next to the brick wall. In it there were 10 plants (3 different species). These reminded me of Einstein's story—he was unsure whether to leave Princeton or to stay and was talking through the issue with a friend as they strode along the sidewalk. Suddenly he knelt down beside a little blooming flower wedged into a crack of the sidewalk. "That's it. Bloom where you are planted!" he said. I found 18 tar spots and wondered, "Where did they come from?" The street? Why? How? I found rocks in the sidewalk—pink, white, black, translucent. Where did they come from? Was the cement a mixture? Is other cement similar? I found a smashed piece of paper towel, a staple, a little piece of gold tin foil—cigarette pack?—and a used match and some cellophane. These all fit together with the idea of cigarettes. I also found a bit of Styrofoam cup and a plastic container which says something like Burke restaurant. Where is it? I noted the leaves of the sidewalk (see attached collection). In 1 block there were 10 different kinds of leaves. Where did they come from? There aren't many trees nearby. I saw a green patch across the street and tried to calculate whether the wind could blow leaves from there to here. I listed the kinds of leaves. One is from my favorite tree—the ginkgo—and I thought of its great history and stories and made a note to later search for the tree.

Later, Kathy Doyle and her students (who had all been present that day) studied Carolee's observations and realized that she had done the following:

1. She noticed ways in which her subject (the chosen square of a sidewalk) was like and unlike others from the same general category (other sidewalk squares). She drew some tentative conclusions about what the similarities and differences might mean.
2. She noticed the patterns (stridations in three directions) of her subject and made a visual depiction of it (a texture rubbing).

3. She measured the dimensions of her subject.
4. She noticed components of her subject (the crack next to the wall) and recalled relevant stories.
5. She made four different collections (of the tar spots, stones in the cement, leaves, and plants in the cracks), categorized each by color or species, asked questions about them, especially about their origins, and began to imagine possible ways to pursue some of these questions.
6. She pieced separate items together into overarching concepts (cigarette pack) and again raised questions and offered tentative answers.

Students from other classrooms have taken lessons from mentor observers. They have, for example, noticed Peter Parnall's observations in his book *Woodpiles*. Parnall opens the book by telling about the kinds of wood he has in his woodpile. He discusses the oak, maple, ash, and eventually he says, "Most woodpiles are made of wood, if you think of them that way. Mine is made of the spaces between: the aisles and runways that are a world for many creatures soft and warm" (1990, p. 4).

Parnall pursues this line of investigation throughout his book. This is an important lesson for those of us who want to learn from the world. When my colleagues and I try our hand at observing, for example, I find that we tend to jump from one quick observation to another. We may write notes like these about a construction site:

The men's hands look cold. The pulley is making a lot of noise. There seems to be some sort of a lever on top of the building.

What happens, I think, is that we notice one thing ("The men's hands look cold") and then censor ourselves. We think, "That's not a very scientific observation" or "That's not important," and we immediately transfer our attention to a machine. The secret of observing well, however, has everything to do with lingering longer, with following up on our initial observations. And indeed, as Eleanor Duckworth showed through moon watching, almost any subject has depths unimaginable. If we could only trust in what we notice, if we could only learn to sustain our governing gaze, we might go from an observation about the men's cold hands to asking questions: Are there any sources of heat? Where are they? Who gets to be near and far from the heat? Do the managers stand nearer to the heat? Does anyone wear gloves or mittens? Who are these people? What are the gloves like? Why might they be like this? Do the construction workers seem to feel cold? If not, why not? Are the people working higher up colder?

In Kathy Doyle's fifth-grade classroom, children began each day's theme-study workshop by making some general, meandering observations of their terrariums. Dori noticed the plants, the temperature, the creatures, and the changes in her desert terrarium. After ten minutes she and her classmates were expected to give themselves a focus. On this particular day, Dori decided to observe one of her lizards, the gecko. She followed its movements, recording them as she did so. This was what most of Kathy's students did when they observed, and it's what I did when I set out to observe my sidewalk square. We wait for something to happen. We *follow* our subject. But Peter Parnall would not have had much to say about his woodpile had he only recorded the plot line of the woodpile's adventures, nor would Carolee Matsumoto have had much to say about her square of sidewalk if she had only told what happened as she watched it. In order to make meaning, we need instead to follow *our ideas*. We can't look at a subject and expect that an idea will jump up (from the lizard, the sidewalk, the woodpile) and hit us on the head. We have to *make* ideas. Carolee did not sit beside her sidewalk and wait for the lightning bolt of inspiration. She collected things and counted them and categorized them; she used her feet to measure things. She *acted* on the sidewalk.

When I met with Dori and a few of her friends, we talked about how Dori might act in ways that would sustain her interest in the gecko. We came up with this list:

1. Dori could carefully draw or diagram her gecko, thinking about things such as how its body is designed to fit its life, its ecosystem. Alternatively, she could focus on a part of the gecko, like its legs, drawing them carefully, watching them, comparing them to legs of other desert and nondesert creatures. She could do an inquiry on legs-across-the-world, with careful drawings of how legs vary in different ecosystems.

2. She could read a book on the gecko and then look to see ways in which her gecko matched (and did not match) what the book said.

3. She could try to figure out why the gecko needs the desert environment. What does it do in the desert that it couldn't do in the other environments? She could look at the bog and at the woodlands and try to imagine the gecko living there.

4. She could brainstorm all the questions she has about the gecko and then choose one (how is the male different from the female) and investigate that question.
5. She could read a book on some other, somewhat related subject, like frogs, and use that book to get her thinking about the gecko.

Dori ended up looking at a book about frogs. She began this somewhat halfheartedly, not expecting it to jog any ideas about her lizard. The book had a picture of a frog's head on its cover. Dori flipped past the cover and on to page one. "Wait, wait," I said, returning to the cover photograph. "Let's just look at this photograph and use it to get us thinking about the gecko."

Dori commented first on the frog's eyes, which rose like giant lumps above his head. How different they are from the tiny little slit-like eyes in the middle of a gecko's face! "Why are the frog's eyes so different?" she wondered. "Is it that the frog needs to see in all directions—behind him, on the side—because that's his form of protection? Does the gecko have other forms of protection? Do the frog's eyes, in fact, allow it to see enemies more quickly?"

Soon Dori and a friend had framed an investigation for themselves. Diana slowly and silently approached the frog (and then later, the gecko), while Dori measured how close the intruder was able to get to each creature before she was seen.

I was dazzled by how easily these fifth graders learned to be active meaning-makers. A few weeks later I brought visitors to the classroom. Just before the visitors came, I gathered the children together and said, "I know these visitors are going to wonder how you can sustain an interest in your ecosystems for so long. Most people would think you could only observe a terrarium for a few minutes and then there would be nothing more to see. Can you tell me how you are able to continue being *so* interested?"

The children began talking. One of them said, "Say you see a spore in the moss. Every day it could be different, if you look close."

"Or different things happen to it, around it."

"You ask questions and you try to answer them."

"You get clues."

"Like, you ask, 'When did it start growing?' You can't really *know* how it started growing before now, but you can get clues. You can measure and graph how fast it grows now, and then count back."

"Or there might be spores forming on other moss."

"You can ask about how animals react to it. Do they go around it? Stay near it? Not notice it? Is it in anyone's food chain?"

"And do other plants have spores, or anything like spores, or instead of spores?"

"You can take it out and look at it under a magnifying lens and a microscope."

"You can look at what's around it, under it. You can pull up the moss and brush off the dirt that clings to the moss and see. . . ."

Finally, a child said, "And you can look in books to see if they are wrong or right."

It's not surprising that when children read the world like this, they read words differently as well.

Making Meaning Through Reading

"How can we keep children from copying out of the encyclopedia?" teachers often ask. "How do we get them writing reports in their own words?" These are age-old questions.

When I was in fifth grade, I knew more about plagiarism than about research. In *Living Between the Lines*, I wrote:

> Over and over I'd been told, "It's against the law to copy. It's stealing." I imagined the police coming with handcuffs to carry off anyone who forgot to change the big words into smaller ones. I remember explaining to my younger brothers and sisters, "You can get kicked out of college for plagiarism." I still recall our solemn, big-eyed awe at the thought that there could be criminals right in our own classrooms . . . and I recall my own private unspoken fear that I myself might be caught. (1991, p. 200)

Books about nonfiction writing in the classroom are full of suggestions for ensuring that students don't copy. Some people suggest enforcing the rule "Your books must be closed during note-taking." Others suggest telling students that they should only take notes after their reading is done or insisting that notes must be fragments of sentences. I think all of these suggestions miss the point. As I suggested in Chapter 24, the important thing is not that students translate the author's words into their own, but that they become authors, that they become meaning-makers. The question we're asking should not be "How do we keep students from copying?" but instead, "How do we help students to be active, invested learners of their subjects?" If students are questioning, reflecting, comparing, connecting, probing into, puzzling over, envisioning, and imagining, they *will* write in their own words. Perhaps the best way to help our students to be active, assertive readers of *words* is to have them first be active, assertive readers of the *world*. Dori will read about desert lizards very differently once she has made meaning from her own experience of them.

Dori and her classmates will be very different readers if they know they are expected not only to record but also to muse over what they read. We find it helpful, therefore, to teach students that the strategies they've used to develop their personal narrative notebook entries are also strategies they can use to develop entries about their reading. They can, for example, put a single line or a single statistic from a reference book at the top of a notebook page and then spend the page "getting to the bottom" of that issue. They can jot marginal questions about the incoming information. They can keep a two-column notebook, with one column for the facts themselves and one column for their reactions to these facts.

One of the most effective ways to galvanize students into taking an active, meaning-making stance while they read is to be sure that their reading is interspersed with opportunities for talking with one another about their subject. In some instances, the shift between reading and talking will happen every few minutes as a reader moves down the page.

If youngsters read nonfiction in pairs, they can practice a strategy that Harste, Short, and Burke call "Say Something." I tried it recently when I read McNulty's *The Lady and the Spider* with my son. After a meaning-chunk, which for us was a page of text, we stopped and "said something." I began by reading aloud the page shown in Figure 26–3A. Evan was silent. The page had seemed a bit sparse and I wasn't at all sure there was much to be said about it. I wanted to go on, to get more text under our belts before we tried to talk about it, but I forced myself to pause, look expectantly at the page, and wait. Evan was still silent. Then he pointed to the head of lettuce and said, "It looks like a big fish." He showed me the imagined fins, eye, mouth. I was silent. "Notice," he continued, pointing to the worm in the soil, "it's camouflaged." Then he pointed to the little plant. "Is it a weed or a baby lettuce?" He pointed to a spider on the lettuce and to an ant. "It's called *The Lady and the Spider*, but there are a lot of insects."

We turned to the next page (Figure 26–3B) and read the text. This time it wasn't hard for me to pause after reading it. "The baby lettuce is growing," Evan said. "They're not hills, they're lettuce. They call it hills because they are so big for her. . . . Virginia [Evan's grandmother] has spiders, she has thousands in her house." Then he peered again at the spider. "Are these legs or antennae in the front? Do they come out of the head?"

FIGURE 26–3 Pages from *The Lady and the Spider* (McNulty)

A

B

Writing for Publication

In a theme study, the goal is not to produce a research paper complete with subheadings and footnotes and a bibliography. The goal is to open up the world to investigation. It is to know what it is to live like field scientists, historians, anthropologists, to know what it means to develop an area of expertise.

We and our children will read and write throughout the theme study for all the reasons that learners the world over read and write. We'll read and write to understand, to probe a subject, to pursue our questions, to figure out what we know, to organize our learning, to solicit new knowledge, to clarify our ideas, to feel, to remember, to plan. . . . We will also, at some point, begin to read and write as experts on a subject. Our investigations will continue, but we'll also become teachers of a subject. We'll write letters to members of congress and journalists and people who need to know about the subject. We'll sketch out plans for speeches and workshops. We'll write brochures, manuals, editorials, personal essays, articles, historical fiction, poems, announcements.

Much of what we and our children write within theme studies will be nonfiction. Although during the theme study itself, the focus will not be on learning how to write nonfiction well (that is, the focus of a genre study on literary nonfiction writing, as explained in Chapter 25), nevertheless, the theme study will give students many opportunities to use what they already know about nonfiction writing toward important purposes.

Laurie Pessah's first graders wrote guidelines for selecting toys, charted how a baby's needs change as the baby grows older, wrote letters to experts on child development, and wrote an editorial about the toys in stores. Kathy Doyle's fifth graders wrote editorials about pet shop owners who do not know the animals they sell, speeches asking members of their school to purchase acres of the rain forest, a field guide to the plants and animals around their school, and the script for a play on endangered animals. From these theme studies, then, students learned not only about the joy of pursuing a subject but also about the responsibilities that come from a knowledge of the world.

Literature on Theme Studies

Altwerger, Bess. *The theme cycle: Creating contexts for literacy.* Katonah, NY: Richard Owen Publishers, 1994.

Dillard, Annie. *An American childhood.* New York: Harper & Row, 1987.

Dorris, Ellen. *Doing what scientists do: Children learn to investigate their world.* Portsmouth, NH: Heinemann, 1991.

Duckworth, Eleanor Ruth. *The having of wonderful ideas.* New York: Teachers College Press, 1987.

Edelsky, Carole, Bess Altwerger, and Barbara Flores. *Whole language: What's the difference?* Portsmouth, NH: Heinemann, 1991.

Fulwiler, Toby, ed. *The journal book.* Portsmouth, NH: Boynton/Cook–Heinemann, 1987.

Harlen, Wynne, ed. *Primary science: Taking the plunge: How to teach primary science more effectively.* Portsmouth, NH: Heinemann, 1985.

Harlen, Wynne, with Sheila Jelly. *Developing science in the primary classroom.* Portsmouth, NH: Heinemann, 1990.

Manning, Maryann, Gary Manning, and Roberta Long. *Theme immersion: Inquiry-based curriculum in elementary and middle schools.* Portsmouth, NH: Heinemann, 1994.

Rynerson, B. "This fish is so strange to me": The use of the science journal. In *Workshop 4: The teacher as researcher,* ed. Thomas Newkirk, pp. 88–99. Portsmouth, NH: Heinemann, 1992.

Zinsser, William. *Writing to learn.* New York: Harper & Row, 1988.

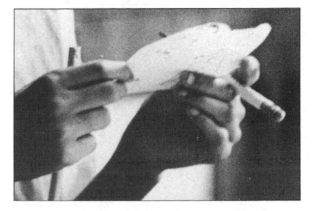

V

Writing Workshop Teaching in a Larger Context

27
Writing to Learn Throughout the Day

Some time ago, my husband John and I were watching a television show in which people were making a movie. When the cameras were focused, an actress took out a fake gun and pretended to shoot one of the actors. He fell down, pretending to be dead. The camera people called, "Retake," and again the actress took out a fake gun, pretended to shoot the actor, and again he fell down, pretending to be dead. This continued until the actress interrupted filming to say, "I have to fix my face."

As she walked off to the dressing rooms, my husband muttered, "She's going to switch guns." I glanced sideways at him, perturbed by his morbid notions. She was following a script. Of course she wouldn't substitute a real gun for the fake one. The actress returned, filming resumed, and all was well. Once again she took out her fake gun and pretended to shoot the actor, and once again he pretended to be dead . . . only this time, he didn't get up.

Startled, I turned to my husband. "Have you seen this before?" I asked. "How did you know? There wasn't any bad music. . . . "

My husband shook his head. "Lucy," he said, "it was obvious." Then, after a long pause, he asked, "When you watch television, Lucy, what are you doing?"

"I'm watching television," I answered, the inflection of my voice showing that I thought it was an obvious answer. But in retrospect, I realize that John does something quite different when he watches television. He is asking questions, searching for answers, posing new questions, building hypothetical answers to those questions, and looking for confirmation. I wait for things to happen.

My husband's prediction about the actress and her fake gun illustrates a crucial difference between us. When John watches television, he is a problem-finder, a question asker; I am not. In his book, *The Informed Vision,* David Hawkins (1974) notes that few people are problem-finders. Hawkins suggests that this is particularly true when it comes to dealing with the scientific, technological world in which we now live. We spend two minutes admiring scientific products—airplanes, computers, engines—and then pass from excitement to boredom. Hawkins's comment hits home for me. If I ask for a window seat on an airplane, it's because I can sleep more easily leaning against the window. I don't wonder at the interactions of wing and atmosphere. I don't look out the window and speculate about whether space is a kind of fullness or emptiness. I don't marvel at vapor trails. I live too much of my life in exactly the way I watch TV . . . and many of our students do the same.

Writing Can Turn Passive Students into Active and Engaged Learners

As teachers, we have seen our students watching our classes as I watch television. With glazed eyes, they wait for information to come to them. We see their glazed eyes and think, "I've got to be more stimulating." Our lessons become more animated, more varied—anything for a flicker of interest. Of course, we've fooled ourselves. We've bought into the notion that we can "learn them." This is not only bad grammar, it is impossible. Learning isn't something we can do for (or to) our students. Learning requires an act of initiative on their part. We can only create conditions in which learning can happen.

Writing can help create those conditions by encouraging students to ask questions, to notice and wonder and connect and inquire. One of the wonderful things about writing is that even just five minutes of it can move us from watching a television show, reading a book, listening to a lecture, or participating in a discussion in a passive way, to doing these things with active, hypothesis-developing, idea-building engagement. Writing can lead us to generate ideas, observations, questions. In this chapter I want to explore ways in which students can use writing to develop meaning—to compose ideas—about volcanoes, weather, Brazil, the Bill of Rights, multiplication of fractions, and all the world.

I need to write, in part, because writing is my way of staying wide awake in my life. I think with pencil in hand. When a student comes to my office to talk with me, I often say, "Wait, let me get a pencil." The pencil allows me to listen better, to structure what I hear. Because my fingers itch for the pencil, I carry pencils in my car, and when I plan speeches or rehearse chapters, I sometimes jot a word or two down on nearby scraps of paper. I do not care about neatness or word choice; I am writing to think. Writing gives me awareness and control of my thoughts. It allows me to hold onto ideas long enough to scrutinize them, to think about my thinking. Toby Fulwiler (1982), an influential scholar on this topic, points out that only in peculiar circumstances such as some English classes, is the precision, shape, and correctness of the writing act viewed as more important than the thought it engenders. He writes, "Scientists, artists, mathematicians, lawyers, and engineers all 'think' with pen on paper, chalk on blackboard, hands on terminal keys" (p. 19). Like these people, I think by writing and I want students to do likewise.

Fulwiler has helped teachers of history and chemistry, business and math change their classrooms (and their images of learning). These changes have occurred as people keep "writing-to-learn" journals. These journals can be used in teacher-directed, whole-class ways, and yet they can bring new levels of student engagement to even these fairly traditional classrooms. In "Journals Across the Curriculum," for example, Fulwiler (1980) tells of an American history teacher who periodically interrupts his lectures to ask students to write for a few minutes on a particular point. "In discussing the railroad system of the state," Fulwiler says, "he asks students to write for five minutes about their knowledge of trains—whether from personal experience, movies, or books" (1980, p. 15). In the same article, Fulwiler tells of a geography professor who uses journals to teach his students about observation. His students look more carefully and closely because they are keeping journals. A drama teacher asks a student actor to live with a consciousness of his or her character, recording what the character would see, think, and feel, in various situations. A metallurgy professor asks students to write about each day's lecture topic prior to attending class and then, after class, to write either a summary of the lecture or questions about it.

Because these assignments to write, as Fulwiler says, "clear out a little space" for students to interact with the ideas thrown at them, many people agree with him that we, as teachers, will want to weave short journal writing assignments throughout all of our teaching. "Too often instructors lecture right to the bell, trying to make one last point, while at the same time realizing by the rustle in the room that the students are already mentally on their way to lunch. Better, perhaps, to cover less lecture teaching and to end class with students recording their own observations and summaries. This final act of writing/thinking helps students to synthesize material for themselves, thereby increasing its value" (1980, p. 17).

There are many other ways to insert this kind of writing into a subject-area class. If many students seem to have tuned out of a whole-class discussion, we might interrupt the discussion to suggest that we all take a few minutes to write down what we're thinking. This act of writing can nudge passive observers into a participant role, reengaging them in the topic. Then, too, if the class seems to have lost its bearings in a discussion, we might invite everyone to summarize the essence of the issue and use these written summaries to regain our bearings. If it seems that students aren't listening to one another in a discussion but are only waiting for a chance to put their own ideas on the table, we might suggest that we all use writing to keep track of the times we feel our ideas changing, the times when someone else's thinking affects our own. Before we and our students read, watch a film, or listen to a lecture, we could suggest we write down what we already know on a subject or what we wonder about it. At the end of the book, film, or lecture we might write about what we learned or what we now wonder.

Let me pause to point out that in each of these instances, the goal has not been for students to write in more of their subject-area classes. Students already spend 44 percent of their classroom time writing (Applebee, Lehr, and Auten 1981). But only 3 percent of this writing involves composing ideas on the page. The goal, in the instances I've described, has been to use writing to scaffold more thinking. This means that the writing these students do is very different from the writing students usually do in subject areas. Most of the writing that students do is the kind of writing I did when I was in school. I wrote to reveal to teachers what I knew and didn't know. I wrote essay exams, answers to questions, words to fill in the blanks, and book reports that proved I'd read the book. I also took notes, knowing that later I would have to demonstrate to others that I knew the information teachers and encyclopedias and textbooks provided on a topic. By recording facts on the page, I intended to inscribe them into my mind. With luck, when the time came, I would be able to shake all the prerecorded information out onto the blank page.

My experiences with writing across the curriculum were not unusual. People often ask students to copy off the chalkboard, record definitions, list key dates, copy notes, and so forth. When we ask students to do this writing, our hope is that writing will help them acquire information. We want to fill our students' brains with the facts they need to know. Then, in essay questions and homework assignments, we hope students will reproduce that information on paper, thus demonstrating what they have recalled.

The ways in which we think about writing within subject areas grow out of our models of learning. When writing happens across the curriculum, all too often it happens in ways that reflect the metaphor of students as blank slates or empty vessels. Learning, according to this metaphor, happens when teachers (or books, films, etc.) write on the students' blank slate minds, pouring information into the students' empty brains. According to this transmission model, learning is a process of *receiving* and *reproducing* information.

Fulwiler's use of writing-to-learn logs represents a very different image of learning, as does my own. Many of us who are interested in writing as a vehicle for learning agree with Piaget, who says, "To understand is to invent." According to this constructivist image of learning, we *develop* rather than *acquire* ideas. We learn as we build personally meaningful representations of what we are coming to know. James Britton (1970), one of the leading researchers in the area of writing to learn, uses the metaphor of a map-maker in order to describe the active and experiential process of learning:

> From a childhood in city suburbs, I went at the age of fourteen to live on the outskirts of a town. I could walk into the country. On Saturdays we did, my brother and I. As we explored the area we drew a map of this precious bit of countryside, and I can recall one name on it—there was a long winding lane called Hobbleythick Lane. With the name comes a picture of a tall, ragged hawthorn hedge: one only, though I suppose there may have been a hedge on the other side also.
>
> The map was a record of our wanderings, and each time we returned we added it to or corrected it. It was, though a crude one, a representation of the area; we valued it as a cumulative record of our activities there. Furthermore, looking forward instead of back, the map set forth our *expectations* concerning this area as we approached it afresh each time. By means of it we might hope to move around more purposefully, more intelligently. . . .
>
> I have arrived at this general point: . . . that we construct a representation of the world as we experience it, and from this representation, this cumulative record of our past, we generate expectations concerning the future; expectations which, as moment by moment the future becomes the present, enable us to interpret the present. (pp. 11–12)

When we ask students to write about what seems to be most central to a story, to reflect on a class, to brainstorm and explore questions, to keep double-entry journals with one column for what happens and one for what they make of it, we are encouraging them to be map-makers. A particular view of teaching and learning shines through these uses of writing to learn. In the examples I've mentioned, learning is regarded not as acquiring and reciting someone else's information but as making representations—making maps—of that information. When students do short stints of writing, it can switch their brains from off to on. It can nudge them to question, summarize, notice, categorize.

When Our Students Are Engaged Learners, They Use Writing as a Tool for Thought

It is a step ahead to move from note-taking, copying off the chalkboard, filling in the blanks, answering questions, and writing essays and reports toward using writing to gather ideas for a discussion, to summarize what's been said, to reflect on the day's lesson, and to generate questions. Although I celebrate these ways of using writing to nudge students to interact personally and actively with the material, I also believe that these methods represent both a new image of teaching and learning, and an old one. I believe we can learn from these methods and then extend them.

In many of the examples I've cited so far, we don't see learners leaning forward to learn and using writing as part of that effort. We don't see learners grappling with new ideas and using writing as a way of throwing a rope around the information. Instead, we see students sitting passively before the teacher's information, and we see the teacher requiring whole-class short-term moments of writing as a way of turning brains from "off" to "on."

Nothing in my experience tells me that our students' brains are "off" to begin with. Content-area classrooms *can* be places in which students sit passively, but they don't need to be. One of the things that has astonished me most as a parent has been my sons' fascination with learning about everything—spaceships and thunder, gravity and planets, Egypt and China. Why should we not teach in ways that allow youngsters to bring their wide-eyed curiosity about the world into our classrooms? There is so much to learn, the world is so fascinating, that we can quite easily help young people care about rivers and electricity, numbers and geography. We teach best when we assume that our students will be passionate learners. We already teach reading and writing as if our students can't possibly *not* fall head over heels in love with both processes. If we assume this also of math and science, music and history, then we won't expect our students to be sitting passively in front of textbooks.

If our ideas about writing across the curriculum emerge out of the image of learning represented by the writing workshop, then we can begin with the premise that because we and our students live like writers, this will affect all that we see, think, feel, and remember throughout our lives. When Cynthia Rylant said writing "is about going fishing as an artist, having relatives over for supper as an artist, walking the aisles of Woolworth's as an artist," she could have added, "studying the Mayflower as an artist, learning about latitude and longitude as an artist." I use a notebook not only for "creative writing" but also for my "content area" research. For me, life is all of a piece. When I write to notice and remember what my sons say it is not separate from how I write to notice and remember what other researchers say. I write to "grow" all of these observations, to make something of them, and whether I'm writing about personal or professional issues, I do this by asking questions, making connections, looking closely.

Fifth grader Katie is no different. Like me, she uses a notebook not only for "creative writing" but also for her content-area studies. Her entries (examples of which are shown in Figure 27–1) emerge out of her science

FIGURE 27–1 Katie's notebook entries

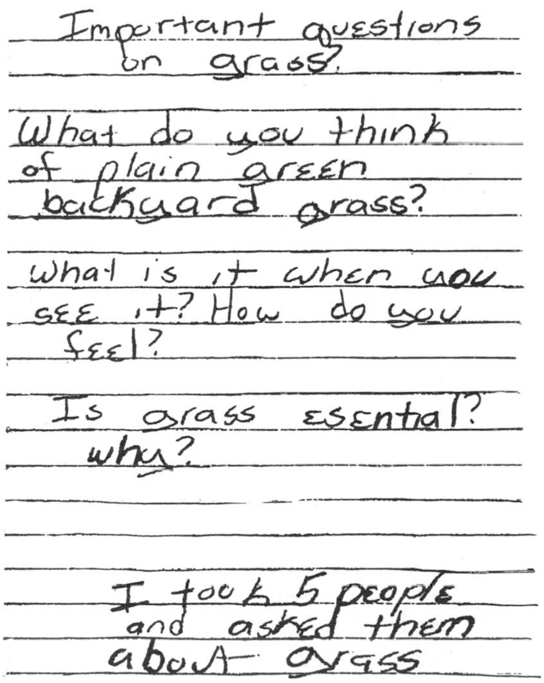
Important questions on grass.

What do you think of plain green backyard grass?

What is it when you see it? How do you feel?

Is grass esental? why?

I took 5 people and asked them about grass

classroom and have the same reflective quality as the entries she writes in the writing workshop.

What I am suggesting is that there needn't be a Great Divide between the way we write in a writing workshop and the way we write in a class on Colonial America. In both instances, the writing process may begin with what in Bloom's taxonomy may be called "lower level" thinking: recording what we recall, hear, see, and notice, whether the information is from our weekend experiences or from a book we've read. Then we need to dig deeper, writing to probe into, puzzle over, muse about, imagine, feel.

I am not necessarily arguing for a single notebook that accompanies students throughout the curriculum. I've tried this and find that one subject often drowns out the others, that the "subjects" tend to overwhelm writing-out-of-our-lives. But I do think students need to know that there are strategies for thinking while they write, for turning on their own minds, and that whether they are writing about their families or about the different kinds of clouds, they can use these strategies. Just as Geirthruder Finnbogadottir took a line from her life that mattered to her ("I've never known anything but childhood, and one day it will all be gone") and put that line at the top of a page and wrote in response to it, we can do the same with a quote from a book, a statistic, a definition. Just as Megan wrote marginal questions ("Why do I do weird things like this?") next to her entry about accidentally shaving off her eyebrow, we too can write marginal questions alongside our notes from lectures and films.

Strategies from writing to learn in the content areas can also be used in writing about our lives. As I mentioned earlier, when a class discussion has lost its bearings, it's sometimes helpful for everyone to take a moment and write "The main thing we're talking about is. . . ." When we gather lots of material in our notebooks about a subject from our lives, we often lose our bearings. It's helpful sometimes to take time out, to break away and write "The main thing I'm talking about is. . . ."

My point is that when Toby Fulwiler suggests we ask students to write at particular junctures in our classes, I think our goal must be not only to improve that day's discussion but also to demonstrate ways writing can help with future learning. Students need to know that their teacher is nudging them to try a strategy for thinking while they write, for using writing to turn one's brain from "off" to "on," and they need to know that each of us can use these writing-to-learn strategies whenever we are writing to think.

If we want to begin a class on railroads by asking students to write for five minutes about trains—whether from personal experience or from movies or books—as Fulwiler's history teacher did, our goal should be to help students learn not only about railroads but also about the value of taking the time to incorporate one's personal knowledge into a topic of study. If we want our students to spend time each night writing a summary of a class on metals, as does Fulwiler's metallurgy professor, then our goal should be that our students learn not only about metals but also about the power of writing as a tool for integrating new information.

Third-grade teacher Terry Moore has used writing in these ways throughout his reading curriculum. Early in the year Terry asks his students to try particular ways of writing in response to their reading. Later, he knows they will choose from the ways he has demonstrated and from others they have invented as they assign themselves the task of doing different kinds of writing in response to reading. Because many of his third graders aren't yet fast and fluent writers, when Terry models ways of writing to learn he tries to demonstrate those that invite a maximum amount of thinking and a minimum amount of writing. For example, one day, after telling his students that Mortimer Adler once said, "Some people think a good book is one you can't put down, but I think a good book is one you *must* put down—to muse over, to question, to think about," Terry suggested that his students insert stick-on notes in their books whenever they found themselves putting the book down to think. Later, his students used what they wrote on the stick-on notes to initiate small-group book talks. Another day, Terry suggested that they might find the one word or sentence that captured what the book was really about and gather some notes about why that section seemed so central to them. Yet another day, Terry mentioned that it's helpful to reread a story thinking about the turning points for a character and suggested that each member of the class choose a character and record the page numbers of sections of the text that were turning points for that character.

For the first few weeks of the year, Terry assigned ways of writing to learn, but his purpose is to demonstrate to his students ways in which they can independently use writing to explore texts. From the beginning, his students know he will expect them, as members of a response group, to decide for themselves what kind of writing will generate good talk about books. By November they are expected to read and to write about their reading each night, but the specific nature of the writing they do is usually left in the hands of the response group. Some days the children use and adapt techniques Terry has demonstrated for them. Other days they invent their own ways of writing about a text. At the end of each response group's meeting, the members talk over what kind of writing they want to do during the upcoming night. Do they want to read Chapters 6 and 7 and jot down all their questions, starring the one that most intrigues them? Do they want to predict what will happen in the story and list the pages on which they found the clues that support their predictions? If writing is going to become part of children's lives, if it is truly going to become for them a tool to think with, then it is very important that *they* be in charge of deciding the forms of and purposes for their writing.

Sometimes colleagues have asked me to suggest writing-to-learn strategies like those Terry Moore and Toby Fulwiler use. I tend to think it is more important to nudge people to imagine their own strategies. When I do talk about strategies for writing in the content areas, I begin by thinking, "What are the learning strategies I want to share?" Learning in any subject consists of similar activities: asking questions, making guesses, gathering information, assimilating it, and so forth.

Using Writing to Support Asking Questions

Writing can encourage students to ask questions, just as John asked questions of the television show. I can't stress enough the importance of problem-finding and of question-asking. Certainly the ability to ask appropriate and probing questions is a crucial part of comprehension, and this is true whether comprehension involves a book, film, lecture, math problem, or life situation. Yet we do not teach question-asking in schools. Often we do not even allow for it. In most classrooms, students rarely ask questions, they only answer them. Over the course of twelve classes, for example, Arno Bellack (1963) found only nine instances of pupil-initiated sequences of thought. Discussions were all led by teacher initiative. Yet asking questions is often the most challenging and important part of thinking. As Wertheimer writes, "Often in great discoveries the most important thing is that a certain question is found. Envisaging the productive question is often more important then the solution of a set question."

Writing can provide students with a forum for asking questions. There will be times when we ask all the members of a class to use logs to generate questions. For example, before showing a film on the Civil War, we might ask students to record the questions they have about the war. Or, if we were showing the film as an introduction to a particular topic—perhaps the causes of the Civil War—we might ask for questions relating to that topic. Similarly, we might begin a lesson on long division or a reading assignment on clouds by having students jot down their questions. After the film, lesson, or reading assignment, students could look back at their list of questions, checking off those that had been answered, crossing out those that now seemed irrelevant, and adding the new questions that had emerged from the activity. But asking questions is one thing, and learning to ask more probing and more appropriate questions is another. We might go a step further and ask students to think about their questions: Which ones were best? What makes one question more effective than another? They might meet in groups to compare their questions and to select a single important question that could then become the basis for class discussion.

In Kathy Doyle's classroom, fifth graders spend some time each day writing about whatever they are investigating. As I mentioned in Chapter 26, early in the year groups of her students make terrariums to represent woodlands, deserts, rain forests, and bog ecosystems, and these ecosystems are the subjects of their research. Sometimes Kathy will suggest that all students write using a particular strategy, such as asking questions, but on most days, students select their own ways of exploring their ecosystem. These are Jesse Weiss's questions about his snail:

1. Why do the snails' shells change color when the jar is out of water?
2. Why do the snails like only half of the water in their tank?
3. How can you tell if a snail is mating?
4. How can you tell a male from a female?
5. Do snails mate?
6. How much water do the plants need?
7. How long should we leave the light on for the plants?
8. How much sunlight do the snails need?
9. Are the plants and animals going to follow the same routine?

Each of Kathy's students also selects a bit of the world around their school and observes that patch of world throughout the school year. Andrew Lindner didn't set out specifically to raise questions about the moss on his tree, but that's what he did nevertheless, as shown in Figure 27–2.

FIGURE 27–2 Andrew's observations and reflections

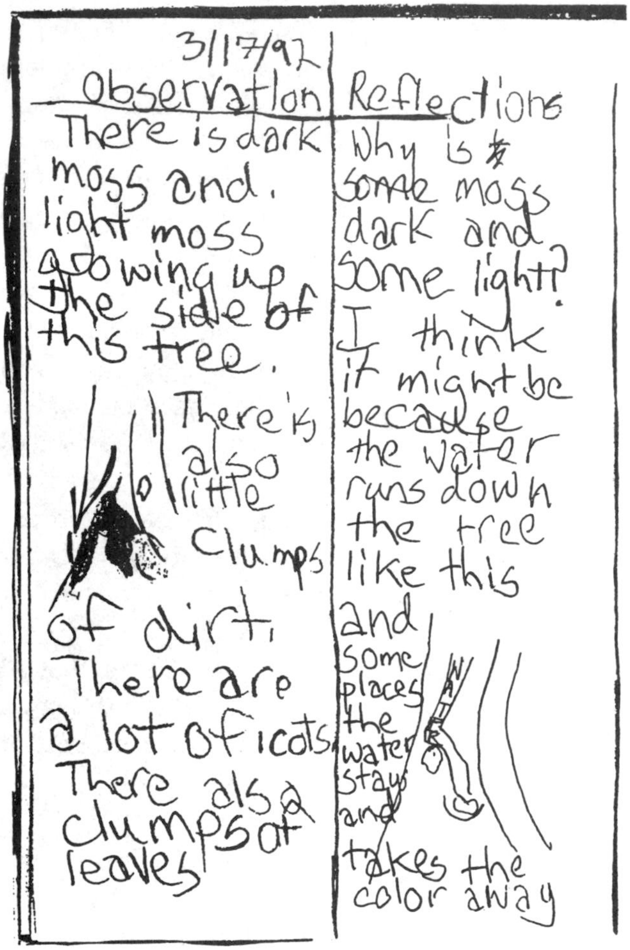

Using Writing to Support Making Guesses

Not long ago I observed a science resource teacher working with a group of third graders. "What do all living things need in order to survive?" she asked the children. The youngsters were silent. Then a hand shot up. "Skin?" Tracey suggested. "If you don't have skin then your heart will pump and it will go all over the place." The class enjoyed Tracey's guess, but the resource teacher did not. She sighed loudly and looked for a better response. Hesitantly, Noah asked, "Is it mothers?" No, the science teacher told him, it began with F. "Fathers?" The expert turned and on the board she wrote: Food, air, water.

What that expert forgot is that in science, guessing is called forming hypotheses. In reading, it is prediction. In either case, guessing, like asking questions, is a crucial part of learning. Yet often, like the resource teacher, we inadvertently dismiss children's guesses. "You're guessing" has come to be a negative expression meaning "Don't guess." Logs can help undo the damage we've done.

Before students watch the Civil War movie, we could ask them to jot down what they imagine might have caused the Civil War. "Pretend to be an expert on the topic and make up some causes for the war," we could tell them. Peter Elbow calls this an instant version:

> Simply deny the need for research, thinking, planning and turn out an instant version . . . Pretend you know things you don't know, act as though you have made up your mind where you're uncertain, make up facts and ideas . . . and you will be able to get much more out of any reading and research you (eventually) do. (1981, p. 64)

Such an "instant version" can catapult students into a position of initiative and control. They'll watch a movie differently because they've made an investment in the topic. "I guessed right!" they'll say, or "I didn't think of that."

Halfway through, before all the causes of the Civil War are revealed, students could go back and revise their instant version in light of what they have already learned. Or the film could be shown straight through, with time reserved afterward for reflecting on the strategy of making guesses. Some students will have based their instant versions on a remembered story, the words of an old song, or their knowledge of other wars. Others will not have thought to make connections or to search through their minds for clues but will instead have made "wild guesses."

Writing can be used similarly within a literature workshop, and once again there could be time for students to reflect on their guesses and their predictions. Were they wild guesses, or did students base their expectations on clues provided by the author? What clues did the text provide? Good guessing is a skill, and students can use logs to develop that skill.

In Summary: Writing and Thinking

Eve Merriam's picture book *The Wise Woman and Her Secret* acts, I think, as a wonderful metaphor for writing to learn. The story opens with a group of people from the village hearing tales of the wise woman who lives on top of the hill and deciding to travel to see her in order to learn the wisdom of the world. They hurry, faster and faster, up the hill. Only little Jenny dawdles behind. "Don't lag, don't loiter, don't dawdle," the people call to her, and hurrying on and on, they finally arrive at the old woman's house. When they ask her to tell them the secret wisdom, the old woman, rocking in her chair on the porch of her home, says, "You will have to discover it for yourselves."

The villagers tear off, looking under the hay in the barn, in the fruit trees . . . and then one of them spots a well. Surely the wisdom will be here! They pull up a bucket of water, dump it out with care, then see with dismay that there is only a tarnished penny at the bottom of the bucket. Throwing the penny on the grass, they hurry off to find the secret of the wisdom of the world.

Jenny comes along and sees the penny, covered with a dew drop, lying on the wet morning grass. She picks up the penny and, peering at it, goes to show it to the woman rocking on the porch.

> The wise woman was there, and as she rocked, Jenny nodded her head in rhythm. The wise woman changed to another silent tune and asked, "What do you have in your pocket, little girl?" . . .
>
> Jenny handed over the coin, and the wise woman held it up to her eyes, peering closely. Then she turned it over and peered at the other side, then flipped it back again and spun it around and around in her hand. . . .
>
> Jenny took the coin and held it close to her eyes the way the wise woman had. She peered at one side and then at the other. "Why," she wondered aloud, "does it look green instead of copper-colored? And what are the Latin words? How do they fit into such a small space? What do the numbers mean? Why did they put the face on the coin? What kind of building is that on the other side?"
>
> The wise woman listened, and laughed. "My dear child, you have found the secret."
>
> Jenny was puzzled. "How can I have found it?"
>
> "Because, you see, the secret of wisdom is to be curious—to take the time to look closely, to use all your senses to see and touch and taste and smell and hear. To keep on wandering and wondering."
>
> "Wandering and wondering," Jenny repeated softly.
>
> "And if you don't find all the answers, you will surely find more to marvel at in this curving, curling world that spins around and around amid the stars." (1991, p. 16)

If we want to help our students know the wisdom of the world, we'll want to invite them to use writing to explore the obsessions of their lives. Writing can be a way to puzzle over why one baseball team trades a particular player for another player, to think through which quilting design would be best for a new quilt.

Our hopes for this writing will not be the same as my teacher's hopes for the essays and answers to questions I wrote when I was a student. We'll want to ask students to look back over their writing asking any one of these (or similar) questions:

- What new ideas have I come to by writing this?
- In what ways have I changed my initial idea about the subject?
- What has surprised me as I write?
- What new ideas of my own have I invented?
- What idea am I beginning to grow that might be important?

These questions do not need to wait for the end of the semester grading-time. These will be the daily questions, the questions that help our students go from writing to talking. If the members of a response group or a class have just written a two-column entry (what they see in their ecosystem in one column and what they wonder about in the next column), and we hope they will now talk about this writing, the best way to avoid long, tedious round-robin readings of all the entries may be for each child (or perhaps for pairs of children) to reread what they've written and to make some notes in response to a question, such as "What observation or idea intrigues me the most and why?" These can then be shared. This becomes a wonderful plat-form from which the group can move between observations and theories.

Once we've nudged students to use their notebooks as forums for making guesses, we can encourage them to see this as an option whenever they write to think about a subject. In this entry, Diana Lee, for example, goes from raising questions to making questions (or framing hypotheses) to mounting investigations:

FREE WRITING

Why did Chubs, the fish, die?
Did he not like the food?
Was he just old?
Was there something wrong with the water he swam in?
All these questions ran through my mind about Chubs, my favorite fish.
I wonder if there was anything to stop Chubs from dying. But Chubs did
not show any signs. He was sick, so I answer that question with a no.
When I think of the tropical environment, I think of colorful fish and
chameleons. Our group had a chameleon, but it ran away through a
crack on top of our terrarium, and I think how he got out of the top was
by first climbing on the air pump which Noah let me borrow. I put the

air pump in my tank for the fish, so she could breathe better. Without the pump, the fish looked unhappy, but when we put it in, the fish looked happy and started to swim around in the water happily.

In one of our experiments, we put the frog into deep water. Everybody said he would die, but he looked happy, and when he needed air, he swam to the top. Can frogs breathe under water? The air smelt really bad in our terrarium when there was mold in there. I think the mold was caused by the hermit crab cakes the hermit crab eats, because the mold was all around the hermit crab cakes.

Sometimes I worry about the hermit crab. I don't know if he is alive or dead, because he buries himself under the dirt and hasn't come up to eat at all for two weeks. I wonder if the hermit crab can eat some particles in the dirt. I think our group will dig him up today. Oh, I just thought of a good experiment for my group to do. Here is the question: What would happen if we put the hermit crab into water?

Here is the plan: We put the hermit crab into water. He can stand and then have a big rock in the middle of the water. If the hermit crab doesn't like the water, he will climb onto the rock, but if he does like the water, he will stay in it.

The frog sits in the plants a lot, and I worry about the plants, because if the frog jumps on the plant too much, they will get weak and die. I am sort of glad the hermit crab is under ground, because he used to dig up the plants.

The important thing about Diana's entry is that she clearly has a repertoire of ways to push an idea around and develop it. From her teacher and classmates she has learned not only the strategies themselves, but also she has learned to be a strategic writer. One can almost imagine Diana saying to herself, "Now I'm going to try this kind of thinking." At home, when Diana snuggles down with a novel, one can imagine her saying, "I'm going to guess what it will be about," and then proceeding to collect the clues that will confirm or challenge that guess.

There is an old saying, "If you catch someone a fish, they eat for a day. If you teach someone to fish, they eat for a lifetime." If we teach children the power of writing to learn across the curriculum, we will also teach them the power of writing—and of thinking—across their lives. Could anything matter more?

Recommended Professional Literature

Fulwiler, Toby, ed. *The journal book.* Portsmouth, NH: Boynton/Cook–Heinemann, 1987.

———. Journals across the disciplines. *English Journal,* Vol. 9 (December 1980), pp. 14–19.

Martin, Nancy, Bryan Newton, Pat D'Arcy, and Robert Parker. *Writing and learning across the curriculum.* Portsmouth, NH: Boynton/Cook–Heinemann, 1976.

Zinsser, William. *Writing to learn.* New York: Harper & Row, 1988.

28

The Home–School Connection
Composing Literate Lives in Homes and Neighborhoods

I didn't notice Daniel until I'd been in his fifth-grade classroom for a week. Even then, what I noticed was his easy nonchalance and his self-sufficiency as he sat with his baseball cap on, his chair tipped back, and his feet on Andrew's desk surveying the classroom. If someone had asked me then to select one child from the Maugham School who would teach me about the home-school connection, Daniel would have been the last person on my list. He seemed too big for that.

Then, in October, after Daniel reread an entry in which he'd described the tight quarters of his old apartment, he surprised himself and us by writing these marginal notes:

> It was a cozy crowded apartment and back then my family was close but when we moved to our new house we began to break up.

Daniel sensed there was something important in his marginal notes. He went on to write entries about the old apartment and the old intimacy. In one of them, he imagined a scene in which he, as a five-year-old, was trying to write his name at the kitchen table while his mother cooked supper:

> I put my pencil to the paper. "Daniel, Daniel," I said as I listened to the sounds and came up with the first letter. "D." I said the letter aloud to make my mom proud of me. "A."
> "Right," my mother answered, quick and sparky. Times like these I cherished. I was feeling so close to her. "E then I," I said, too proud. "No, it's I then E," she said, speaking so softly that it seemed I hadn't made a mistake. She went off to check the chicken supper, and I finished writing and then looked at my name on the paper. It was all squished together and crooked but me and my mom made it. My name on that paper was exactly like my apartment.

Daniel wrote about how the move to a big new house in suburbia changed everything:

> Tenafly was supposed to be bigger and better, but instead it was just bigger. . . . The rope that held my family together was loosening, loosening drastically. I didn't do my homework in the kitchen anymore because I could do it in the study or family room. I didn't ask my mom for help anymore because she was too busy with Ben, the baby. . . .

Daniel also wrote an entry he later described as the most important paragraph he'd ever written:

> The other day I asked my mom the biggest question of all. "Mom, can I have a cat?"
> "You already have a toad and two frogs," she said.
> "Please, Mom, I need a cat. I *need* one."
> She shook her head. "Daniel, I don't have time to take care of a cat," she said.
> "That's why I need one," I answered quietly.

"Before I wrote this I was as blind as a bat," Daniel said, without elaborating. "I've learned that details, feelings, and memories are full."

It wasn't hard for Daniel to assemble the various entries into a single memoir, but he sat for a very long time over the ending. "I'm good at *writing* endings," he told me, "but this one has to *happen*. I don't know how it will turn out."

Then one day, in the midst of a literary discussion about the settings and characters in Patricia MacLachlan's *Journey*, Daniel suddenly sat up from his normal slouched-on-the-carpet position and said, "I just realized something." In what seemed to be a total non sequitur to the conversation, he explained, "You have to *wait* to drive and to get a job, but you don't have to *wait* for your family to get closer."

"Know that cat's cradle we did?" Daniel asked the class a few days later. "I was showing it to my dad and he had a different one and he came behind me." Daniel held his hands out, as if they were laced into an invisible string, and as he spoke, we imagined his father standing behind him. "He put his hands on mine, and I looked down and saw our hands, and the string, and thought, 'This is the string that'll bring us closer.'"

Another day Daniel told us that he'd convinced his father to read a chapter of Patricia MacLachlan's *Journey* with him. *Journey* is the story of a boy who is abandoned by his mother. When cajoled to share whatever anecdotes the story evoked in him, Daniel's father told his son about how, growing up on a kibbutz, he'd felt abandoned because all the older children had grandparents near them. "I adopted my aunt and uncle and pretended they were my grandparents," he said. Later, in his notebook, Daniel mused, "I wanted to push Dad to tell more details but it was good. We don't have many talks. He always comes home late and he reads his own books while I watch TV. We got to talk this time."

Until I worked with Daniel, I had assumed that the home-school connection was all about bridging the communications gap between school and home. I'd assumed it was about sending letters to students' parents and sharing writing samples and portfolios with them, and about holding parent workshops. And I had assumed that this chapter about the home-school connection would be full of tips on how we can anticipate and deflect the parental "Are they learning anything?" angst that inevitably occurs when school is exhilarating and fun. Daniel made me realize that, as important as all of these concerns may be, something far bigger is at stake in the home-school connection. Daniel reminded me that if we and our children are going to know the power of reading and writing we need to know what it means to have great books and great conversations be part of our lived lives. We need to feel how a letter can be a bridge over troubled silences. We need to sense the way a shared story can act as shared adventure, inviting us to journey together, and to yearn and hope and worry and weep together, too.

What could be more important than finding ways to help children weave reading and writing into the fabric of their lived lives? Robert Coles addresses this in his book *The Call of Stories* (1989). Although Coles brings literature into hospitals, not homes, the effect is the same. A medical student, reflecting on what it means to read and write at the center of one's life, at the places in which we human beings struggle with the deepest issues of humanity, says, "It's one thing to read Tillie Olsen or Ralph Ellison or William Carlos Williams in a literature course; it's another to read them now." Then he says, "I've never thought of stories or a novel as a help in figuring out how to get through a day . . . but now, when you're coming back from the work we do in a clinic and you pick up those stories, you feel as if the author knows you personally." Picking up a specific book, he said, "The story I read merges with the situation I'm in . . . and it all becomes part of me" (pp. 181, 182).

It was not only the physicians who were reading literature in the midst of their lives; the patients were as well. A cancer patient, fighting a life-and-death battle against a tumor growing inside him, said, "I used to be 'interested' in Hemingway's stories, but when I read them after getting sick, I was into them, so much into them that I'd read a page or so and stop and think . . . I could see Hemingway's 'old man' fighting for his last victory of that boat . . . fighting it out with the sharks, pulling on it [the marlin] and taking it in, finally, even though his skiff is half destroyed and the fish mostly eaten by the sharks . . . and I wonder whether I'll win my big struggle with 'it' " (p. 187).

When I read and write with the people I love, I experience for myself the power of bringing literacy home. Texts become charged with new significance when they are set into the relationships of my life. When Daniel said of his father, "We got to talk this time," his words echoed in my mind. Two years ago, when my father turned seventy and was temporarily forced to retire, he began writing his memoir. "It will be a gift to the grandchildren," he told me; but I knew it was also a gift to himself. I knew he was looking back to find the plot line, the larger meanings, an ending that would work.

After I put the boys to bed at our lakeside cabin that summer, Dad and I would often sit at the end of the dock. We'd watch the sun set over the lake, and Dad would read bits of the memoir to me and we'd talk. Once, thinking of the memoir as a whole, I asked Dad why his father wasn't more present in the story. Dad had a ready answer, but apparently weeks later, when he'd finished the memoir, made copies for each of his children, and put them into mailing cartons, the question was still there for him.

When Dad and I next met, he told me as we drove from the airport to my home that after he had wrapped a copy of his memoir for each of us and taped the last box, he'd sat on the floor, the box between his legs, with a palpable sense that he'd left a story out. "I hadn't just *left* it out, I'd boxed it out, taped it out," he told me. His voice cracking, he began to tell me the missing story. Each of my father's childhood summers on Cape Cod had ended with a townwide sailing race. One year, when he was only eleven, my dad had skippered the winning boat, with his father acting as crew for him. After my father and my grandfather had won the Labor Day sailing race together, the cheering crowd tried to hoist my dad into the sea. Dad, then a skinny, awkward kid, made feeble protests, hiding behind an excuse about having athlete's foot, but they'd thrown him in anyway, and he had emerged from the sea like a wet cat. My grandfather, watching the scene, had said nothing. They walked home, my Dad's sneakers squishing, without a word. Remembering the walk, my father said, "Not a word about the race!" and hit the dashboard of the car to add an exclamation mark to his sentence, his memory. "Not a word about 'What a way to end the summer!' " (wham, wham). "Not a word about them heaving me into the sea" (wham).

This time when I asked my father about his father there was no ready answer. He wondered and circled around, unsure, reaching. Remembering that conversation now, I can't help but think, "We got to talk that time."

My father's memoir sits on my bookshelf now. It is not the one he boxed up that day. Instead, one section begins with the sailing race and the silence. In it, Dad writes,

> The story, as I write it, fills me with intense sadness. The most important part of the story may not be the episode itself, but the fact that I rejected it from the initial log. I didn't include it because it was just *so* sad. When my daughter Lucy read over an early draft of the log and asked, "Where is your father in this story?" my answer was to add him in. But now I know he was missing from that draft of the log because he was missing from my life.
>
> For all that I was given in my childhood, one thing was missing—a father who understood and cared for me, not just in a collective sense as one of his brood, but for me as a person. What was missing was a father who understood and cared for his skinny second son. I do not remember my father giving me a single bath, I do not remember him reading to me, or coming into the shop to inspect and admire the boats I made, I do not remember camping out together, sleeping under the canvas together. . . .
>
> I can write this now because I know that in some other ways I *am* like my father; in my love of my work, in my attitudes about marriage. I now know, too, that my father's role in my life helped me know I wanted a very different role in my children's lives.

Joanne Hindley, a colleague of mine at the Writing Project, recently lost her mother. A few months before her mother died, Joanne gave an exquisite keynote address at Teachers College. Her mother was there to hear the speech, in which Joanne spoke of a childhood of learning and loving with her mother. Now Joanne holds on to the memory of those shared words like a lifeline, and I know I will do the same when my father is gone.

Sitting in Room 113 listening to Daniel's earnest voice as he told about his somewhat blundering and deeply tender efforts to find in reading and writing threads that might draw his family closer together, an idea began to grow in my mind. As teachers, many of us *say* that our goal is lifelong literacy for our children. It's a convenient goal because we cannot hold ourselves to it. We cannot know today whether our students will love reading and writing throughout their lives. And yet, if we think of the phrase "all through their lives" horizontally rather than longitudinally, we *can* know if a love of reading and writing lasts throughout all the aspects of our students' lives today. Shouldn't we then live toward the goal of "life-*wide*" literacy?

Lifewide literacy has big implications for homework. For too long, we have sent home the vocabulary drills and questions at the ends of textbook chapters, the ditto sheets on syllabicating spelling words. We've relegated these things to homework as our way to clear them out of the school day. How can we do this and still say our goal is for children to live richly literate lives? Isn't it a waste to have syllabicating spelling words be the literacy kids bring home to do in their lived lives? Isn't it a waste to have vocabulary drills and textbook questions be what families congregate around, to have these be what kids do together in the evenings over the phone, to have this be what they carry in their backpacks? And if our goal is for children to live richly literate lives, isn't it a waste to suggest that what children should do at home is to close themselves in their bedrooms and read and write alone?

In schools, we know reading and writing flourish when they happen in richly interactive settings. If we want children to be lifelong writers, doesn't this mean we need to encourage them to create these same richly interactive conditions in their homes and neighborhoods? If we want them to be lifelong readers and writers, don't we need to help them compose lives that support their literacy? A child may choose to read or write with a grand-mother, a cousin, a buddy, a neighborhood grocer; a child may center his or her literacy around an effort to build a spaceship or to save a swamp or to share a novel. But one way or another, shouldn't we suggest that along with spending time on independent reading and writing, children might also consciously and deliberately weave literacy into the passions and projects and people of their lives?

When Kathy Doyle, her colleague Shirley McPhillips, and I shared these thoughts with Kathy's fifth graders, Andrew Lindner grasped what we were saying right away. "I think the way schools usually do it, there is no such a thing as homework," he said. "Home is where the *family* is. Most homework is done away from the family, apart from the family. Mostly it's not *home*work, it's just *later-*work."

And we usually don't even stop to imagine that it could be other-wise. When Shirley McPhillips began asking parents about their expecta-tions about homework, it seemed that even the parents who were most supportive of inquiry-based schools had very traditional expectations. "Homework should give students a chance to practice what they did in class." Homework, they felt, "is a way to drill in the basics," "a way to reinforce what was going on during the day." Many of the parents thought *more* homework was in order, so they bought workbooks at grocery stores or designed their own workbook pages for their children. "The added practice will prepare them for middle school," they explained. How ironic to think these well-intentioned parents create more and more school-like homework in an effort to prepare children for middle school when the reason to have school at all is to help children live richly literate lives independently, outside of school, at home.

It was clear to Shirley, Kathy, and me that if we were going to help Kathy's students reimagine homework, we also needed to do this with their parents. We gathered the parents together one evening. "Your child's reading, writing, and theme studies will spill over into your home this year," we said, "and we want their obsessions and passions and projects to spill over from the home into the classroom as well." Then we asked the parents to tell us about their children's home projects. I had brought a tape recorder as well as a notebook. I didn't want to miss a word of their observations. "We need to hear from you," I said. "Tell us about the interests and projects they pursue at home."

The room was silent. My tape recorder hummed quietly, recording silence. Finally, one mother broke the awkwardness. "Well, my Beth plays volleyball in the intramural on Saturdays. She enjoys that," she said.

There were a few other reports on children's participation in intramural sports and music lessons, but that was all. "What do your children collect?" I asked, prompting them.

The parents, for the most part, weren't sure.

"What are their hobbies? What fills their free time?" I wondered.

One or two parents had an answer—horses, baseball cards, lessons—but for the most part, they didn't know what to say. "When they were younger, we did more with them," a mother said, as if speaking for all the parents. "Now that they're older, it's mostly the peer group they want."

I wasn't so sure, and I don't think the parents were either.

After a while, the parents, Shirley, Kathy, and I began to really talk. What I learned that night was that these parents knew how to support their children's literacy when they were very young: they'd read bedtime stories to their children, they'd hung their children's first drawings and stories on the refrigerator, they'd bought tickets to make-believe zoos and museums. But they did not know how to support their children's literacy now. Many tried, but what they did was revealing. They bought workbooks and software programs, enrolled their children in computer or math camps, drove their children to after-school classes in science or foreign languages. Many of them supervised their children's homework and talked to them about the importance of "study habits."

Later, my colleague Lydia Bellino helped me see all this in a new light. The interesting thing is that in wonderful primary classrooms throughout the world, we have begun to use what happens at *home* as a model for what should happen at school. We try to make our classroom read-aloud sessions have the intimacy and interactive quality of bedtime stories. We try to let children's questions and collections and obsessions drive the classroom's science and social studies inquiries. Why, when children reach the middle childhood years, does the direction of the home-school connection change so radically? Why, in the middle grades, do we begin to fashion our home learning in the likeness of school learning? Is this because we have trouble really recognizing the intellectual value of free exploration, of independent projects, of self-initiated work and play?

That evening, I should have told those parents that it was curious and sad for me to see that all of their efforts were geared toward bringing school-like instruction into their children's weekends and after-school hours and vacations. Those parents need to know that there is no better place for their children to learn to live inquisitive and richly literate lives than in their homes and neighborhoods.

In her study of creative thinkers across a range of disciplines, Vera John Steiner (1985) researched people who have grown to be successful scientists and artists and found that during their youth, these people "pursued their play with intensity and determination." Steiner cites a study of creative thought, done by Jacob W. Getzels and Philip Jackson, that found that what distinguishes creative individuals is more "an openness to experience" and "an interest and enthusiasm for life" than any particular set of skills. They said, "The home atmosphere supported the adventurous spirit of those young people. . . . It was the parents' enthusiasm rather than specific instruction in art and science that first helped their development" (Steiner 1985, pp. 60–61).

The important thing for us, as parents and as teachers, to remember is that our children need to discover their own interests and passions. We cannot do this for them. Our role is to watch for the glimmers of a project and then get behind those glimmers. When Miles was two and Evan newborn, they both spent several days a week at Teachers College's Center for Infants and Parents. Often during each day, I'd go to the Center to nurse Evan and watch the scene. Once I watched Miles roam about the Center absentmindedly banging two blocks against each other. "Oh," one of the caretakers said, "Miles is making a parade!"

Miles looked up, startled but pleased to learn that he was making a parade. Instantly he began lifting his knees high and marching about as if he were indeed the parade master. Soon the caretakers had ushered other children into the parade and joined in themselves, carrying the infants. Miles broke into his own rendition of "Seventy-Six Trombones Led the Big Parade."

Watching this, I thought, "That's what we, as teachers and parents, must do." We need to watch for parades. Often, children will not even know they're leading a parade, but we can say what we see, and we can get behind their parades.

Kathy Doyle was in a sense "getting behind her children's parades" when she scheduled time at the beginning of each day for the home-school connection and organized share sessions in which class members shared their home-school projects with one another. Just as the caretakers at the Center for Infants and Parents had not planned to get behind Miles's parade on that particular day, so too, Kathy's students led her and the class into projects she'd not anticipated. For example, when her children brought treasures from home to school, instead of saying, "Put that stuff in your cubby so it doesn't get lost," Kathy said, "Bring that stuff out—your collections and projects and stories—or it might get lost." Her students' treasures didn't become objects for show-and-tell times, but rather for "explore and investigate" groups. Sometimes, a hornet's nest or a book of maps would catch the children's attention for only a little while, and sometimes, they'd lead to a big project. In the home-school work, as in the notebook work, the question "Is this something I want to pursue more deeply?" was always in the air. When Shan brought a centipede to school inside a tiny glass box with a lid that magnified it, a cluster of friends joined him in drawing and reading about the small creature. When Kathy saw their hubbub of excitement, she asked questions she might have asked in writing conferences: "Are you going to stick with this for a bit?" and "What might you make of this?" Soon Shan was collecting and studying more insects in order to write *A Field Guide to Insects from Home and School.*

Meanwhile, David wrote songs for his guitar and worked with a neighborhood friend to turn his back lawn into a nature preserve, complete with rotten logs and berry bushes for attracting wildlife. Dori organized an environmental club, "Save the Spotted Owl," and worked to raise people's consciousness about the environment. She also read dog obedience books in order to learn how to train her dog. Sam and Elias designed an improved hamster cage.

Above all, what the children did was to read, write, and talk—about reading and writing and about life itself—with members of their families. For Kathy's children, as for me, this often led to a new intimacy between parents and children. Brian Jacobs, for example, decided he wanted his dad to know what it was like to gather childhood memories and shape them into a memoir, so he began having a series of conversations with his father. Shirley McPhillips (in press) writes about one of these conversations:

> Brian asked his dad to sit with him for a series of talks about his childhood memories. A tape of the first conversation reveals the poignancy of this moment.
>
> BRIAN: "This is *our tape*. Brian Jacobs and his dad" (both laugh).
> DAD: "Brian tells me that I'm supposed to talk about something in my life when I was small that is important to me. I was born in 1942, which is a *long* time ago—'The Acres Apartments.' My brother and I, alone with Mom. My dad, a captain in the war, was *away*. When we would ask about him, Mom would hold up a picture of a man in uniform. He was just away. . . . Then one day we were taken over to Grandma's. Dad was coming home *that day*. . . . Late in the afternoon, we were brought to our apartment. It is still such a *vivid* memory, seeing him for the first time. . . . ."
>
> Brian's Dad describes in detail coming into the front hall, looking down the little corridor, his father coming around the corner—"a big, big guy." He doesn't remember much after that except that from then on, "life seemed a little different, more military." He envies his own children "growing up in a family where Mom and Dad were always there."
>
> DAD: "Is this the kind of memoir you want?"
> BRIAN (Softly): "Yeah."

Daniel scheduled once-a-week field trips with his little brother to the Flatrock Brook Nature Reserve. In his notebook, Daniel wrote about what it was like to be a mentor for his brother.

> It was good. He was always following me, turning over rocks and looking in the sand. If I was disappointed that we didn't find anything, he was upset, too. When we did find things, he knew how to notice, and he didn't want to go until he'd seen everything. I wonder, can he keep himself interested if he's alone?

Andrew, like Daniel, invented a learning adventure with his little brother. Six-year-old Peter, according to the school, was a struggling reader. Andrew brought a small pile of picture books to each of his sessions with Peter, and observed and recorded Peter's strategies for choosing a book. After each session, Andrew reflected on the sessions on an audiotape and in his notebook. One day Andrew said on the audiotape: "Peter asked me to read him the names of the authors this time. Now that's a definite change— to be choosing books by authors. Peter also pointed out he knows a dog like the one on *When I Was Nine*'s cover. That's very good, because he's relating something from the story to his life. It's only a little thing, not a big explosive thing . . . but he also read a five-line page and it had huge words like 'locomotives went steaming past.' When he read 'locomotive,' I was sort of sleeping and I went, 'Whoa!' Reading that page with 'locomotive' for Peter was like us reading a really hard book."

Later, musing on this, Andrew said, "It's not like Mrs. McCabe told him, 'Okay, now Peter, your homework tonight is to read a five-line page.' Nobody tells him what to do. He just thinks it up. That's self-learning." Then he said, "Now, how can *I* push myself to do something way past me, like he did?" He added, "It really pushes you to see your little brother or sister do that."

Later, in talking to Shirley McPhillips about these learning adventures, Andrew continued to think about the idea of self-learning. He said, "Kids have to be part of their own education. That's it."

29

Do I Dare to Care So Much?

I remember, when my son Miles was a newborn, leaving the beauty parlor with my hair still wet in order to hurry home to him. Driving home that afternoon, I passed a woman standing by the side of the road. I drove on, hurrying, hurrying. I passed another woman standing beside the road, and another. As I sped home to baby Miles, it dawned on me that these were mothers waiting for the school bus. They'd always been there, but I'd never seen them. "How can the kids be coming home *now?*" I thought. The afternoon shadows were already long.

Then a yellow bus came into view. A little towheaded fellow got off wearing a huge bus tag and carrying a bag almost as big as he was. His mother knelt down, touched his face, and, as I imagined, said, "Tell me." I drove on to my newborn son with tears streaming, thinking, "They're right about my hormones; I see a mother waiting for a school bus and *I'm crying?*"

But now, for the first time, I wait at the end of the driveway to catch that glimpse of yellow as the bus rounds the bend in our road. And when Miles gets off the bus, with his bus tag and his paper sack, I crouch beside him, hold his face in my hands, and say, "Tell me."

I hear that Gordy has sneakers that light up when he walks, Chris has a black belt in karate, Mrs. Robinson's cat had to be put to sleep, and then Miles scampers off to his brother. I wipe away my tears and know it's not that my hormones are out of sync. It's that it is huge—giving your child to school today and tomorrow, this year and next year, until they are all grown up.

I know the worlds Miles has built at home. I know about how he puts chisels and hammers, books and magnifying lenses into his red wagon and goes bumping through the woods to a little rock outcrop he calls "My Mining Center," where there's a crevice in which he stores his chips of mica and marble, and a tree that becomes his pole, allowing him to slide from one level of the Mining Center to another. And I know about Story Rock, which stands at the crest of the hill behind our house. When we reach Story Rock, Miles, Evan, and I lean back, with the trees overhead and the world below, and from that vantage point we tell stories.

I know the worlds Miles has built at home, but I also know that the world he is building at school, with his teachers and his friends, will affect him far more than the Mining Center and Story Rock. I see the effects of school every day. It has given Miles a whole new discourse. On Miles's first day of kindergarten, he leaned back in his chair after dinner and said, "Whoever wants a popsicle, raise your hand." Then John, Evan, and I were told to "line up, girls first" beside the refrigerator. Later that evening, Miles brought me one of his drawings. "Do you like it?" he asked. When I assured him that I loved it, he pressed on. "Is it good enough for a sticker?"

The power of school became particularly clear to me when Melissa, a new school friend, first came over to play. For weeks I'd been running along behind Miles as he pedaled down the road on his two-wheel bicycle. By the time school started, Miles could wobble along by himself for a little bit as long as I got him started and there were no turns in the road. On this particular afternoon, Melissa jumped on Miles's bike and began spinning tight little eight's on the driveway. Leaving the bike in a tangle at Miles's feet, she headed off somewhere else. Miles eyed the bike for a moment, then sprang aboard and, in an instant, the dust was flying as he spun tight circles on our driveway.

That night, I saw Miles peer at a picture in his comic book of some superhero doing wheelies on a motorcycle. Early the next morning, Miles jumped aboard his bike and started riding over our lawn, down the hill, over rocks. As he rode, he jerked up on his handlebars.

I watched in amazement. I'm supposed to know how to teach. Despite all my best teaching and all my labor, it was Melissa who, in ten minutes of her time, had gotten my son doing wheelies across the lawn.

I shouldn't have been surprised. "We get our identities," Frank Smith has said, "through the company we keep, the clubs we join, the communities we belong to." At school, Miles was finding clubs to join, and those clubs were already shaping his identity.

My mother tells me that I've got it wrong, that it's the home that has the lasting impact. For years I think I believed the same thing. But last year I observed and participated all year in a wonderful classroom, and I saw one child, and another, and another, changing under the influence of that classroom community and that teacher, Kathy Doyle. I saw these children deciding who they wanted to be in life. I saw them taking their lives in their hands, making themselves into themselves. And by June, as I watched, I found myself wiping away the tears and thinking, "I *never knew* school could matter *this* much."

I think of Andrew. At the end of fifth grade, Andrew reread a story he'd written a year and a half before about sleep-away camp. In it, he told of being chased by a wild-eyed, drooling raccoon, and of fishing stained underpants out of a swamp. "The truth is, camp was nothing like this story," Andrew said as he reread his piece. "I wrote it in fourth grade, and back then, I acted completely different than I really am in school, or no one would like me. In second grade kids called me a nerd, and after that there were two Andrews—a school Andrew and a home Andrew. Now there's just one Andrew."

Now that Andrew felt comfortable bringing his "real self" to school, he returned to the subject of his summer at sleep-away camp. This time he wrote about how, on the last day of camp, he'd paused to say goodbye to the goats and the gravel driveway. The memoir ends:

> "No, no, it can't be time to go yet!" I ran around the rec hall and saw the cars coming to get us.
>
> We took pictures and cried until finally Soren joked, "Now we're all peeling onions!"
>
> Driving away, we stopped to say goodbye to the goats who had been with us the whole time. We drove up the gravel driveway, still crying. I thought the magic was gone. At the end of the gravel driveway, just before the paved road began, we stopped to pick flowers and to wave goodbye to the goats and to the gravel driveway.
>
> In the car, I knew one thing. I could never truly explain what happened at camp. I couldn't explain the magic. I'd try to explain, to tell my parents what it had been like, how we'd felt, but I would never really explain and secretly, I didn't mind that. These were *my* friends; these were *my* memories.

When Andrew learned that he needn't rely on rabid raccoons or dirty underwear to hold his reader's attention, that he could take the fine details of his life and imbue them with significance, he learned a lesson that changed not only his writing but also his living. When Andrew and his classmates began to realize their lives were worth writing about, they experienced things differently. One of Andrew's classmates, Steven Halleck, traveled to Arizona for a cousin's wedding. When Steven's mother told him to pack his suitcase, he carefully stacked his church shoes so that he could fit a small plastic aquarium beside them in the suitcase. Then he packed a magnifying glass, knapsack, net, plastic bags, and his notebook. "I figured

I'd wear the suitcoat to make space," he said. In Arizona, instead of the normal "Here we are at the airport" photography shots, Steven took pictures of flowers, trees, rock formations, and desert creatures. "The sun is always out there," he said later, as he went through the photographs with me. "The sun keeps everything in a sharp view. The shadows are really shadows. It's never dull outside; there's lots to celebrate there."

Pausing over one photograph, Steven said, "The trees surprised me. I didn't think there'd be trees there. But in Arizona, you can always see through the trees and there'd be mountains back there, and the sky. Sometimes the sky is whitish blue and sometimes solid blue. It looks good behind the cactus, the plants, and the rocks."

Laying out five or six flower photographs, Steven explained, "There's a lot of patterns on the flowers. They bunch up in purples, blues, reds, and the blues are the same height, and the reds. I couldn't figure that out. One purple flower looked furry from a distance; it wasn't like the others. My mom had no idea what it was."

I do not know if the wide-awakeness and curiosity Steven has learned in the writing workshop will stay with him for his whole life, but I do know it went with him to Arizona, and I am amazed that one year of school can matter so much.

What an awesome responsibility this is, knowing our teaching matters this much. How do we live with this knowledge? I believe that when we recognize how much our teaching matters, we become activists, defending, with all our might, our right to teach wisely and well.

I recently asked a teacher to explain her daily schedule to me. "I like to start every day with reading, and then move into writing," she said. "But this year, because our scores on the citywide math exam were low, we have to do math and reading before eleven."

You *must* do this?" I said, open-mouthed. "Who said so?" Even before she could answer, I added, "*Everyone* in the school must teach math and reading before eleven? What if you believe it should be done differently?"

I was startled to learn of the new mandate but even more startled to learn that the teacher hadn't even questioned the policy. She didn't like it, but she'd shrugged it off with a sigh and proceeded to revamp her schedule. As we spoke, she was intrigued by my response. "You think it's *that bad* to start with reading and math?" she asked. But my point, of course, wasn't that one schedule is better than another. My point was that our teaching matters.

We need to be able to teach according to our beliefs. If our teaching doesn't represent our best current notions about what matters in classrooms and in life, if our teaching doesn't represent our most cherished hypothesis about education, then how can we hold ourselves responsible for and learn from the results of our teaching? Roland Barth was wise indeed when he said, "The greatest tragedy I know is to be caught up in the position of doing something one does not want to do or does not believe in." If that teacher wants to begin her day with reading and writing, it is tragic to imagine that instead she must follow someone else's image of how her day should proceed.

We may not always be able to bring all of our dreams into the classroom, but we need to remember those dreams. If we want to begin our day within the intimacy of our own classroom rather than with announcements over the public address system, we need to say so. If we want to keep our students for two years so that we can know their lives and support their intentions better, we need to propose this. My point is not in the particulars of these policies. My point is that we need to hold on to our dreams. We need to hold on to them for dear life.

If we can begin to fathom how much our teaching matters, then perhaps we will begin to take more responsibility for nourishing ourselves as teachers and as people. In the end, what we bring to our classrooms is ourselves. Because our teaching matters so very much, we have a responsibility to take care of ourselves as learners and hopers and dreamers. "We cannot create what we cannot imagine," Lucille Clifton has said, and her words are wise. Because our teaching matters, we need to nourish our imaginations by visiting other classrooms and by listening to the stories of other teachers.

Seymour Sarason was wise when he said, "The notion that teachers can create conditions which are alive and stimulating for children when those same conditions do not exist for teachers has no warrant in the history of mankind." Why is it that we give our students opportunities to read and write, time to pursue their own important projects, mentors who inspire and coach, chances to work in small response groups . . . and yet we do not give these same things to ourselves? When will we take our own learning seriously?

As I end this book, I want to say one thing to the teachers of my children and of all children: Let's not *ever* fool ourselves into thinking that our time with students does not matter that much, that it's only the home that makes the difference. Our teaching can change what kids pack in their suitcases; it can help them cherish the intersection of a gravel driveway and a paved road; it can invite them to do wheelies as writers, readers, and learners. Our teaching matters more than we ever dreamed possible.

READER'S GUIDE

What are all my students doing while I move around the classroom conferring with them individually?
See Chapters 11 and 21 and pages 46–47, 88, 98–102, 115–16, 170, and 389.

I sense that the chemistry in a writing workshop is everything. How do I help my group of students come together as a close-knit, trusting, and energetic community?
See pages 14–19, 139–48, 175–76, 231, 249–51, and 253–54.

I sound like a broken record during my conferences with students. How can I expand my repertoire of things to say?
See Chapters 4, 13, and 14.

What do I do with the youngsters who continue to resist writing? How might I lure them to become deeply involved in the workshop?
See Chapters 2, 15, and 16 and pages 29, 44–46, 118–19, 160–61, 168–69, 171–72, 433–34, 439, and 449.

We began the year with a burst of energy, but now we're all dragging a bit. How do I get back on track?
See Chapters 16, 22, 23, and 24 and pages 11–12, 171–76, 203–5, and 251–52.

My problem is time. How can I possibly fit everything in?
See Chapters 3, 11, 20, and 29 and pages 3, 11–12, 63, 115, 163, 185–88, and 355.

My students have grown accustomed to collecting entries in their notebooks. How do I help them take the next step, moving from entries towards drafts?
See pages 41–49, 123–27, 130–35, 416–26, 442–47, 467–68, and 470–75.

When my kids ask how to spell a particular word, may I tell them the correct spelling?
See pages 68, 74, 89–90, 201–2, 289–95, and 301–3.

I need to know more about qualities of good writing if I'm going to invent mini-lessons day after day. Where might I turn for help?
See pages 5–7, 44, 100–101, 133, 149–50, 153–54, 326, 401–2, 404, 407–9, and 440–45.

To be honest, my students' writing seems boring. Their minor revisions don't make much of an impact. What can I do to help them dramatically improve their drafts?
See pages 44–46, 100, 113–17, 139–45, 150–53, 208–18, 249–53, 269–70, 326, and 384–85.

Do I need to write in order to teach writing well?
See pages 3–4, 11–19, 27–31, 54, 70, 144–45, and 168.

What's your understanding of the ways writing can be used in the literature classroom?
See pages 12–13, 22–24, 77, 153–54, 165–66, 175, 203–5, 251–52, 255–58, 277–78, and 376–77.

Please help me understand better what may happen when my group of students gathers for a whole-class share session.
See pages 32–34, 46–47, 69, 123, 127, 142–48, 153, 169–70, 190, 253–54, 372–74, and 383.

Which excerpts from this text might be especially relevant to parents?
See Chapters 28 and 29 and pages 11–16, 21–23, 53–57, 71–73, 77, 110–13, 225–26, 231–38, 268, 273–77, 281–82, 338, 342–45, 390, and 432–35.

I want to help my students write more and more thoughtfully throughout the day.
See Chapters 26, 27, and 28 and pages 4, 24–29, 60, 62, 65–66, 77, 109–13, 172–74, 360–61, and 379–81.

When I ask my students to revise, they resist. When I insist, they make only minor changes. Help!
See Chapters 3, 7, 8, 13, and 24 and pages 44–46, 130–35, 203–18, 231, 266–71, 326, and 421–26.

Should I grade my students' finished drafts? If so, on what basis?
See Chapter 19 and pages 245–47, 265–71, 366–67, and 371.

How can I increase the likelihood that when my students talk during peer conferring, their talk will support their writing?
See pages 30–31, 40–47, 99–100, 115–17, 169–71, and 205–7.

I am a kindergarten teacher and I want to read the sections of this book that apply most directly to me, and then return to read the entire book. Which sections should I turn to first?
See Chapters 3, 6, 7, 11, 12, 13, 22, 23, and 25 and page 231.

I am a K–6 resource room teacher and I work with small groups of students away from their regular classroom. I want to begin by reading the sections of this book that are most directly pertinent to me. What should I read first?

See Chapters 3, 7, 8, 13, and 24 and pages 44–46, 130–35, 203–18, 231, 266–71, 326, and 421–26.

I am a secondary-school teacher and I'd like to begin by reading the sections of this book that most directly address the challenges of teaching at the secondary level. What should I read first?

See Chapters 1–4, 10–14, 16, and 24.

ANNOTATED BIBLIOGRAPHY

Aragon, Jane Chelsea. *Salt hands.* Illustrated by Ted Rand. New York: E. P. Dutton, 1989.
When we write, we often hurry past the details of our lives. It's enormously important for a writer to be able to slow time down, to write and live as if in slow motion, and this is what Jane Aragon has done in this story. This is not the story of a winter full of adventures. It is instead the story of a moment when a wild deer licks salt off the hands of a little girl. "He lowered his head calmly," Aragon writes, "and sniffed my hands. Then he tasted the salt." The girl held her breath and didn't move. Then she says, "His whiskers tickled my fingers." For children who are fed a steady diet of television dramas, this quiet story demonstrates an entirely different kind of drama and strength.

Atwell, Nancie. *In the middle: Writing, reading, and learning with adolescents.* Portsmouth, NH: Boynton/Cook–Heinemann, 1987.
This award-winning classic is a testimony to the power of wonderful teaching. It brims over with stories of eighth graders and of their teacher, Nancie Atwell, who learns alongside and from them. The book is divided into two sections, one on teaching writing and one on teaching reading. Although it is aimed especially for teachers "in the middle," in grades 7–9, the methods of teaching are those that teachers of grades K–6 regularly use in their reading/writing workshops.

Banks, Lynne Reid. *The Indian in the cupboard.* New York: Avon Books, 1980.
This is an exquisite story about Omri, a ten-year-old boy who puts a plastic figure in a particular cupboard. The two-inch-high figure emerges from the cupboard as a minuscule, but very much alive, Indian named Little Bear. Omri keeps Little Bear a secret from everyone except his best friend, Patrick, who eventually brings a second plastic figure, a cowboy, to life. The book becomes a story of relationships between Omri and Patrick, and between an Indian and a cowboy, and of people caring for each other. This story ambles along from one adventure to another, in somewhat the same fashion as *Stuart Little.* It is my sons' favorite read-aloud, and it is equally popular among fifth and sixth graders.

Barth, Roland S. *Run school run*. Cambridge, MA: Harvard University Press, 1980.

This is one of several books that have been enormously helpful to me as I think about the culture of schools. Barth writes as a building principal, but he speaks to all who are interested in reforming schools. He wants schools to become places of learning for all of us, teachers, principals, and children alike. Barth is particularly insightful in describing how professional development can happen from *within* a building.

Barth, Roland. *Improving schools from within: Teachers, parents, and principals can make the difference*. San Francisco: Jossey-Bass, 1990.

All over New York City, small circles of building principals have met in study groups in response to this exquisite book. Roland Barth, a former principal and the director of a Principal's Center, has enormous empathy for principals, yet he holds steadfastly to his vision of the principal as the chief learner in a school and to the importance of collegiality, risk-taking, and professional growth.

Baylor, Byrd. *The best town in the world*. Pictures by Ronald Himler. New York: Macmillan, 1982.

This collection of stories and conversations celebrates memories and the stories our parents tell to us and the little things a person never forgets. It celebrates wildflowers in all shades of lavender, purple, orange, red, blue, and the palest kind of pink, with butterflies to match. And people who can tell time without wearing a watch. It's a patchwork quilt of memories, a bureau drawer filled with old treasures, a photo album, a notebook.

Baylor, Byrd. *Everybody needs a rock*. Pictures by Peter Parnall. New York: Aladdin Books, 1974.

Ralph Peterson, in *Life in a Crowded Place*, tells of a teacher who builds a beautiful ritual around this book. Whenever a new child moves into her classroom, the children gather in a circle and hear this story. The new child chooses his or her very own rock from a collection, and as the rock is passed among other class members, each says what he or she will do to make the new child's experience a happy one.

Baylor, Byrd. *The other way to listen*. New York: Charles Scribner's Sons, 1978.

The message of this book, like the message of Eve Merriam's *The Wise Woman and Her Secret*, is that we need to take the time to look closely, to listen. The wise older man tells the child, "Do this. Go get to know one thing as well as you can. It should be something small. Don't start with a mountain. Don't start with the whole Pacific Ocean. Start with one seed pod." This is, of course, wise advice to a writer, or to a teacher, or to a learner of anything.

Baylor, Byrd, and Peter Parnall. *Your own best secret place*. New York: Charles Scribner's Sons, 1979.
Walking through a tangle of shadowy thickets and tall river grass, salt cedars and willow trees, the heroine finds herself a secret place. The place, in the hollow of a cottonwood tree, had been someone else's secret place before it was hers. William Cottonwood had left notes saying, "No matter how long I am gone, this is still my tree." Reading this book, we are reminded of how we've all declared places to be ours, named them, and found small treasures in them. No matter where we go, those places are, in a way, still ours.

Bissex, Glenda. *GNYS AT WRK: A child learns to write and read*. Cambridge, MA: Harvard University Press, 1980.
In this unusual book, Bissex provides detailed documentation of her son's independent growth as a reader and a writer. The book is beautifully written and solidly grounded in theory. It is particularly helpful as a statement on invented spelling and on purposes for writing.

Blos, Joan, and Stephen Yammell. *Old Henry*. New York: Mulberry Books, 1987.
This picture book, like *One Hundred Dresses* or *Crow Boy*, is one I read early in the year as I try to help my students respect each other and the people in their lives.

Bomer, Randy. *A time for meaning: Learning literacy with people aged 10 to 20*. Portsmouth, NH: Heinemann, in press.
There are so many books on methods of teaching reading and writing that new books are easily lost. This book will not be lost. It will stand out because of its depth and substance. Reading it, one has a heady feeling. Bomer expects a lot of his readers, and indeed, each page and paragraph convey new and substantial ideas. The book assumes general knowledge of the writing process à la Graves/Atwell/Calkins, and it takes the reader a great deal farther. The books opens with chapters on the teaching of English, then moves into insightful chapters on writing and reading workshops, including major chapters on genre studies with

secondary-level classrooms. This book is honest, probing, important, and clear. I predict it will become one of the most often referred-to books in the field.

Brinckloe, Julie. *Fireflies.* New York: Macmillan, 1985.
This is the story of a young boy who sees tiny lights flicker in his backyard. "Fireflies!" Soon he and his friends have assembled, jars in hand, and they dash about waving their hands in the air like nets. The story is a beautiful example for our youngsters to study as they put into words the vignettes of their own lives.

Bunting, Eve. *The Wednesday surprise.* Illustrated by Donald Carrick. New York: Clarion Books, 1989.
Secretly, on Wednesday nights, seven-year-old Anna teaches her grandmother to read. Together, Anna and Grandma give the surprise away on Anna's father's birthday. Grandma reads and acts out one book, and another, and another. "Are you going to read everything in that bag?" Dad asks her. "Maybe I will read everything in the world," Grandma answers.

Cisneros, Sandra. *The house on Mango Street.* New York: Vintage Books, 1989.
If I had money enough to bring just one bit of literature into my classroom and I was teaching writing to people aged 8 through 80, this would be the book I'd buy. In searing, clear, startlingly original prose, Cisneros writes short vignettes about the everyday moments on Mango Street.

Collins, Pat Lowery. *I am an artist.* Illustrated by Robin Brickman. Brookfield, CT: Milbrook Press, 1992.
This simple picture book can be a perfect introduction to writing. "I am an artist," Collins writes, "when I find a face in a cloud, or watch the light change the shape of a hill . . . when I name the colors inside a shell . . . or discover pictures in drops of rain." It would be good to have another version of this, set in a city, for, of course, the artist sees art also in a snow-capped fire hydrant, in the faces of people on a crowded city street.

DeFelice, Cynthia. *When Grampa kissed his elbow.* Illustrated by Karl Swanson. New York: Macmillan, 1992.
This celebration of the everyday magic in our lives is a perfect introduction to the writer's wide-awakeness. The book is the story of a girl, her grandpa, and their imaginary play, which allows them to see more keenly the magic

snowballs of a hailstorm, the miracle of a bird family living in Grandpa's old boot, a shooting star in the night sky.

Elbow, Peter. *Writing with power: Techniques for mastering the writing process.* New York: Oxford University Press, 1981.
Elbow's book is a smorgasbord of ideas and metaphors on teaching writing. In a style that is recursive and full of voice, Elbow portrays writers and their ways of working. He suggests an array of composing strategies that are invaluable to teachers of writing.

Fletcher, Ralph. *What a writer needs.* Portsmouth, NH: Heinemann, 1992.
Don Murray begins the foreword to this book by saying, "UNIQUE. *What a Writer Needs* by Ralph Fletcher is unique." I agree. It is a book for teachers about the qualities of good writing, organized into rather predictable chapter titles, such as "Creating a Character," "Voice," "Beginnings," "Endings," and so forth. What makes the book unusual is that Fletcher resists talking about these components of writing in reductionist ways. Instead, he brings them to life with long, intimate, honest stories, written in searingly beautiful prose.

Fox, Paula. *Monkey Island.* New York: Orchard Books, 1991.
This is a masterpiece. It's the story of three homeless people, two men and a boy, "trying to find better ways of sleeping on stone" at the entrances of buildings. It's the story of literacy and love, too, in the lives of these people. The book was published in the same year as Jerry Spinelli's *Maniac Magee,* and both deal with old and young people, with white and black, with homelessness and literacy.

Gardiner, John Reynolds. *Stone Fox.* New York: Thomas Y. Crowell, 1980.
How can a little book hold so much? This powerful story is full of characters who will stay with us for life. It's also full of drama and adventure. A young boy's grandfather lies dying of a broken heart because he knows his debts will force him to lose his farm. The boy is determined to save the farm, and this eventually leads him to enter a sled-dog race, and to race against Stone Fox, the giant, silent Indian. It's the story of a boy and his dog, racing against all odds. It is also the story of determination and heartbreak and tenderness. A touchstone text.

Gardner, Howard. *Artful scribbles: The significance of children's drawings.* New York: Basic Books, 1980.
Readers will learn from Gardner not only about children's development in art but also about artistic development in general. Gardner speaks about the

artistic flowering of the six-year-old, and about the dogged realism that inhibits the drawings of many older children and adolescents. This is only one of Gardner's many books on development, and each is important.

Goodman, Ken. *What's whole in whole language?* Portsmouth, NH: Heinemann, 1986.
This is the most succinct, clear statement I know of about whole language. It is the perfect book to use for educating parents, colleagues, and, when necessary, administrators on the language learning theory behind whole language, and on what whole language is—and is not.

Graves, Donald H. *Writing: Teachers and children at work.* Portsmouth, NH: Heinemann, 1983.
Graves wrote this book out of our two-year-long study of children at Atkinson Academy. Concrete and practical, this book has been an invaluable guide for teachers of grades K–6 who are new to the idea of the writing process. With chapters entitled "Survive Day One," "Help Children Choose Topics," and "Publish Writing in the Classroom," the book has, for more than a decade, helped teachers as they begin turning their classrooms into writing workshops. This book is a classic, and Graves has done more than any person alive to reform the teaching of writing in the elementary grades.

Graves, Donald H., and Bonnie S. Sunstein, eds. *Portfolio portraits.* Portsmouth, NH: Heinemann, 1992.
Doctoral students from the University of New Hampshire, along with their professors and teachers, collaborated on this book, in which they argue for less standardization of portfolios. Contending that a writer's portfolio should be that person's individual, idiosyncratic way of saying, "This is who I am," Graves et al. describe ways to blur the boundaries between classroom instruction and portfolio. This book is particularly helpful for individual teachers who want to incorporate portfolios into their writing workshops.

Greenfield, Eloise. *First pink light.* Illustrated by Jan Spivey Gilchrist. New York: Black Butterfly Children's Books, 1976.
A gentle story by one of my favorite authors, this book shows how we can make art out of the littlest moments of life. The plot is similar to that of Rachel Isadora's *Crossroads* and *Journey to Jo'burg*. A child waits and waits and waits for his father to return home. Perhaps because the story is about how time slows down when we wait, Greenfield slows time down as she

writes. This is something children, who tend to write in quick summaries, need to learn to do. "As soon as he saw the first pink light, he would get in his hiding place. And when he heard the key in the door, he would call his daddy."

Greenfield, Eloise. *Honey, I love and other love poems*. New York: Harper-Collins Children's Books, 1986.
This is one of my favorite poetry anthologies. The poems can be woven into writing workshops in innumerable ways.

Grover, Mary, and Linda Sheppard. *Not on your own: The power of learning together*. Toronto: Scholastic, 1989.
In this short (42-page) book, colleagues Glover and Sheppard give a portrait of a reading-writing K–1 classroom and an overview of the essential characteristics of that classroom. Nothing is more important to the authors than establishing a sense of community, and they show ways of weaving reading and writing throughout the life of the community. The book is dedicated to Ralph Peterson, author of *Life in a Crowded Place*, and his emphasis on rituals, celebrations, and community building can be seen throughout the book.

Hale, Nancy. *The realities of fiction*. Boston: Little, Brown, 1961.
This is not a new book, but it is one that deserves to be taken down from the shelf. Hale's insights provide a fresh perspective on fiction writing. The book is particularly helpful to teachers of upper elementary and secondary school.

Harste, Jerome C., Virginia A. Woodward, and Carolyn L. Burke. *Language stories and literacy lessons*. Portsmouth, NH: Heinemann, 1984.
This award-winning book has been heralded as a major breakthrough in our understanding of developmental issues in writing. Written by some of the best known teachers in literacy education, the book is an important theoretical text. Although it focuses on young children, it's a significant book for anyone interested in the teaching of writing.

Harwayne, Shelley. *Lasting impressions: Weaving literature into the writing workshop*. Portsmouth, NH: Heinemann, 1992.
This book is jam-packed with classroom vignettes and teaching ideas. Set in New York City classrooms, it is particularly helpful for teachers of grades 2–6 who want lots of suggestions for ways to use literature in the writing workshop. Readers will come away with a long list of recommended titles, as well

as with powerful strategies to try right away. One of the special strengths of this book is that the author is willing to talk about students who struggle.

Heard, Georgia. *For the good of the earth and sun: Teaching poetry.* Portsmouth, NH: Heinemann, 1989.
In this inspirational book, Georgia Heard helps us to remember what is essential in writing, teaching, and living. The book is an eloquent introduction to a genre study in poetry, and it is so beautifully written that it is equally appropriate for teachers of kindergartners and teachers of graduate students.

Heide, Florence Parry, and Judith Heide Gillilan. *The day of Ahmed's secret.* Illustrated by Ted Lewin. New York: Lothrop, Lee and Shepard, 1990.
Ahmed carries his secret with him all day as he moves through the bustling city of Cairo. All kinds of sounds are tangled together in Cairo: "trucks and donkeys, cars and camels, carts and buses, dogs and bells, shouts and calls and whistles and laughter." But loudest of all is the silent sound of Ahmed's secret, which he has not spoken. Finally, at home, Ahmed says to his family, "Look, I have something to show." He holds out a piece of paper on which, in Arabic, he has written his own name. What a beautiful way to celebrate literacy, and to invite children to begin telling each other the history of their lives as writers and readers.

Hoffman, Mary. *Amazing Grace.* Pictures by Caroline Binch. New York: Dial Books, 1991.
The book opens, "Grace was a girl who loved stories. She didn't mind if they were read to her or told to her or made up in her own head." This is a joyous celebration of a child's imagination, an imagination that brings her into battles as Joan of Arc and leads her to sail the seven seas with a peg leg and a parrot. Above all, it's an imagination that allows her to believe she can do anything she wants to do.

Isadora, Rachel. *Ben's trumpet.* New York: Mulberry Books, 1979.
This splendid, simple story illustrates the mentorship model of teaching and learning. Ben listens to the music from the Zig Zag Club and joins in on a trumpet no one can see —except one man, the trumpeter for the club, who takes Ben's dream seriously and invites him to become part of the world of music.

Jaggar, Angela, and M. Trika Smith-Burke, ed. *Observing the language learner*. Newark, DE: International Reading Association; Urbana, IL: National Council of Teachers of English, 1985.
This book is particularly important to teachers who are interested in the theoretical underpinnings of an integrated approach to the language arts. Although each of the articles in the anthology is written in simple, clear language and filled with anecdotes, the articles are far from lightweight. Each is written by a leading researcher and grounded in theoretical ideas on language learning.

Janeczko, Paul B. *The place my words are looking for*. New York: Macmillan Children's Book Group, 1990.
I cannot say enough about this beautiful anthology of poems. My colleagues and I use this as one of our touchstone books.

Lionni, Leo. *Tico and the golden wings*. New York: Alfred A. Knopf, 1964.
This is, on one level, the story of a bird who gives away the feathers of his beautiful, golden wings until he resembles all the other blackbirds. The other birds are delighted that he is now the same as they. "Now you are like us," they chirp, but the bird who has been through all of these changes thinks, "Now my wings are black . . . and yet I am not like my friends. We are *all* different. Each for his own memories, and his own invisible golden dreams."

Lowry, Lois. *Autumn Street*. New York: Dell Publishing Co., 1980.
Because this novel is written in the first person from the point of view of a child, and because of the author's gifts as a writer, it can be a powerful resource for young writers. Youngsters read passages of this book, passages about school milk, about caring for one's grandfather, about what a child sees in a clothes closet, and says, "I want to write just like that." I would probably use excerpts as a resource in grades 1–3, and I'd consider using the entire book as a touchstone for grades 4–8.

Lowry, Lois. *Number the stars*. New York: Dell Publishing Co., 1989.
The Horn Book describes this novel as "seamless, compelling, and memorable—impossible to put down; difficult to forget," and I agree. The story takes place in 1943, when Nazi soldiers move into Copenhagen. It's a tense, fast-moving story of friendship, dangerous missions, courage, and people who live bravely for their ideals and their friends.

MacLachlan, Patricia. *Journey*. New York: Doubleday, 1991.
This little gem of a book was an essential volume in Kathy Doyle's fifth-grade class during the year I spent in that room. It became our reference point whenever we talked about qualities of good writing; we used it to learn how to develop a single dramatic scene, how to make characters live, how to jump from one moment and place to another. It was an excellent book to study. It can be read aloud and then pored over, circled around, admired, questioned.

MacLachlan, Patricia. *Through Grandpa's eyes*. Illustrated by Deborah Kogan Ray. New York: HarperCollins, 1980.
When I was young, a teacher of writing blindfolded my classmates and me, took us out of doors, and told us to *really* listen. This book accomplishes those same purposes and more. A child tells about how his blind grandfather teaches him to hear and feel and smell his house, and to savor what he sees. Grandpa teaches him to hear the wind in the grass, to distinguish the call of a red-winged blackbird from that of a sparrow, to smell the wet earth by the river.

Margolis, Richard. *Secrets of a small brother*. New York: Macmillan Children's Book Group, 1984.
The poems in this book are vingettes about sibling relationships. Many young people write about their siblings, and for them, this book can be an important resource.

Mathers, Petra. *Sophie and Lou*. New York: HarperCollins Children's Books, 1991.
Because we try, in our classrooms, to support children who learn from mentors, who risk trying new things, who develop learning partnerships with friends, a picture book such as this one (and the discussions it evokes) can go a long way toward helping us to establish a safe, supportive learning community in our classroom. A dancing school opens across the street from Sophie's apartment. Painfully shy Sophie gradually becomes drawn in by the classes she observes as she peeks out from behind her curtains.

Mayher, John. *Uncommon sense: Theoretical practice in language education*. Portsmouth, NH: Boynton/Cook–Heinemann, 1990.
This book won the most significant award given by the National Council of Teachers of English, and for good reason. It is a probing, ambitious, comprehensive overview of current reforms in English education. Mayher's back-

ground is in teaching English in the secondary schools, and teachers of this age level will especially appreciate this richly theoretical book.

McLerran, Alice. *Roxaboxen.* Illustrated by Barbara Cooney. New York: Lothrop, Lee and Shepard, 1990.
When Marian dug up a tin box filled with round black pebbles, everyone gathered around and declared it "treasure." After that there were treasure-hunting days on the desert hill across from their homes, and soon a miniature town grew with streets lined with white stones, and with a town hall, a cemetery, a jail. Children who hear this story will have their own stories of make-believe forts and spaceships, of treasures they've found on hillsides and in attics.

McNulty, Faith. *The lady and the spider.* Illustrated by Bob Marstall. New York: HarperCollins Children's Books, 1987.
In this simple little book, McNulty helps readers envision a head of lettuce through the eyes of a spider and see the valleys of green, the leafy den, the tiny pools of water in the head of lettuce. It tells of the lady who takes the time to see the spider clinging to the lettuce leaf and to think, "Isn't it wonderful that a creature so small can live and love life, find food, and make a home just like me!" This could be a powerful source of lessons on point of view.

Merriam, Eve. *The wise woman and her secret.* Illustrated by Linda Graves. New York: Simon & Schuster Books for Young Readers, 1991.
I cannot imagine a writing workshop (or a science lab or a reading community) without this book as one of its touchstones. Villagers hear about the wise woman who lives on top of the hill, and they hurry to learn from her the secret of the wisdom of the world. "*You* must find it," she tells them, and the people rush hither and yon, searching everywhere. But it is a small girl who lingers over a tarnished penny who finds the secret. "Why does it look green instead of copper-colored?" she asks. "What do the numbers mean?" The wise woman, rocking in her chair, says, "My dear, you have found the secret . . . for it is to be curious, and to take the time to look closely."

Moffett, James. *Teaching the universe of discourse.* Portsmouth, NH: Boynton/Cook–Heinemann, 1983.
Densely written and theoretical, this book presents the author's comprehensive theory on how one learns discourse. Moffett suggests a curriculum based on his hierarchy of abstraction. Students move from personal toward abstract writing, from an audience that is intimate toward one that is distant.

Murray, Donald M. *Expecting the unexpected: Teaching myself—and others—to read and write.* Portsmouth, NH: Boynton/Cook–Heinemann, 1989.
Don Murray, the father of writing process, is a Pulitzer Prize-winning writer. It's no surprise, then, that his prose is strong, intimate, fresh, courageous. Murray's books are always studded with insights about writing and living. In this book, he is especially clear about the value of surprise in writing, about the need sometimes to write badly and to form new thoughts as one writes. Chapters 1 and 10 are favorites of mine. This book fits especially well with working with notebooks.

Murray, Donald M. *Learning by teaching: Selected articles on writing and teaching.* Portsmouth, NH: Boynton/Cook–Heinemann, 1982.
————. *Write to learn.* New York: Holt, Rinehart and Winston, 1984.
————. *A writer teaches writing.* 2nd ed. Boston: Houghton Mifflin, 1985.
Don Murray is a leading mentor for teachers of writing. Each of these books is beautifully written. On every page readers will find lines they will want to pin onto their bulletin boards and excerpts they will want to share with colleagues and students. Murray's trust in his students and his involvement in his craft are infectious. *Learning by Teaching* is an anthology of his articles; *Write to Learn* is a guide for people wanting to begin their own writing; *A Writer Teaches Writing* is an overview of his ideas on teaching writing in secondary schools and colleges. All three are invaluable.

Myers, Walter Dean. *Scorpions.* New York: Harper & Row, 1988.
Many of the youngsters I work with in New York City applauded when *Scorpions* was selected as a Newbery Honor Book. It's a book about likable boys whose lives are tragically changed after they acquire a gun. It's a story about friendship and family— and about gangs, weapons, showdowns in the park, jail. This book could easily become a touchstone book for a class of fifth, sixth, seventh, or eighth graders.

Newkirk, Thomas. *More than stories: The range of children's writing.* Portsmouth, NH: Heinemann, 1989.
Written by one of the most probing and original researchers in the field, this book focuses on young children's nonnarrative writing. Newkirk explores the dazzling, diverse range of children's writing and probes the early development of their abilities within the modes of argumentative and explanatory writing.

Paterson, Katherine. *Lyddie*. New York: Lodestar Books, 1991.
This is one of my favorite of Katherine Paterson's books, and, of course, Katherine Paterson is one of everyone's favorite authors. *Lyddie* is historical fiction. The year is 1843, and the setting is the mill town of Lowell, Massachusetts. The issues revolve around laborers banding together to improve working conditions. But this is also a story of friendships between very different people, about people uniting and finding solace and strength in their relationships.

Paulsen, Gary. *The monument*. New York: Delacorte Press, 1991.
An artist is brought to a small midwestern town and commissioned to create a monument. He does so by first moving through the town with his notebook and charcoal, catching glimpses and recording vignettes and emotion and truth on the page. A girl, Rocky, apprentices herself to the artist, and both she and all of us who read this story learn from the way in which the artist sees, feels, and makes meaning. For those of us who draw and/or write, and particularly for those of us who keep notebooks, this book will enrich and deepen our understanding of both drawing and writing.

Perl, Sondra, and Nancy Wilson. *Through teachers' eyes: Portraits of writing teachers at work*. Portsmouth, NH: Heinemann, 1986.
Sondra Perl and Nancy Wilson lived in a suburban school district for a year, documenting what they saw in six of the school's K–12 writing classrooms and helping teachers and students to document and learn from their journey. The result is an uneven but rich collection of portraits of writing classrooms. One, written by Sondra, tells the compelling story of Diane Burkhardt's eighth-grade classroom, and another tells an unusual and wrenching portrayal of a classroom that fails.

Peterson, Ralph. *Life in a crowded place: Making a learning community*. Portsmouth, NH: Heinemann, 1992.
In this little book about a big idea, Peterson examines what teachers have called the "chemistry," the magic that makes everything else possible in our teaching. He articulates the heartaches we experience as we try to create communities within our crowded classrooms and suggests that as cultural engineers we can use rituals, celebrations, and rites to create small civilizations in our classrooms.

Reid, Margarette S. *The button box*. Illustrated by Sarah Chamberlain. New York: Dutton Children's Books, 1990.
I can envision two ways to use this straightforward tale about a boy who pores over his grandma's button collection, imagining stories to accompany

the buttons. The idea that even tiny buttons hold stories could remind children that there are stories in all that we collect. Then, too, the structure of the book, with all of the buttons presented early, and then the stories of each following, shows children a possible way to link their entries together into a unified shape.

Rosen, Michael. *Home: A collaboration of thirty authors and illustrators to aid the homeless.* New York: HarperCollins Children's Books, 1992.
This is a collection of poems, pictures, and stories, contributed by thirty of our greatest artists and writers, with proceeds going to help the homeless. But the proceeds also go to those of us who read, reread, and study these short, intense bits of literature.

Routman, Regie. *Transitions: From literature to literacy.* Portsmouth, NH: Heinemann, 1988.
Teachers who are considering incorporating more whole language into their K–2 classrooms are comforted and informed by Regie Routman's chronicle of changes in her own primary-level classroom. Routman's writing program differs in significant ways from that described in *The Art of Teaching Writing,* and these differences will pose interesting and, I believe, significant questions for readers of both books. Many readers praise *Transitions* for the sheer amount of helpful information it contains, not the least of which is a series of long reading lists.

Shaughnessy, Mina. *Errors and expectations.* New York: Oxford University Press, 1977.
In this classic, Mina Shaughnessy helps us see the logic behind the errors that often swamp us in our students' writing. The book is based on her work with adult basic writers, but much of it (especially the opening chapters) is relevant to teachers at most grade levels.

Short, Kathy G., and Carolyn Burke. *Creating curriculum: Teachers and students as a community of learners.* Portsmouth, NH: Heinemann, 1991.
In this brief volume, the authors argue for a collaborative approach in which teachers and students join in curriculum development. They argue that curriculum development is all about creating social structures that support learning. They make a particularly powerful plea for readers to resist thinking of curriculum as a set of activities. This view of curriculum, they claim, led us to be in "an unending cycle of coming up with new theme units, new projects, new reading and writing activities, and new 'experts' who could provide us with yet more activities and procedures." Curriculum reform,

under this old view of curriculum, is merely "additive." Instead, curricular reform should involve rethinking one's beliefs. "A curriculum," they say, "is a prediction concerning how people learn, what people should be learning, and the contexts that will support that learning."

Smith, Doris Buchanan. *A taste of blackberries*. New York: Thomas Y. Crowell, 1973.
The book opens with a shocking, sad story of friends playing together, and of one of them dying from a bee sting. In an understated and simple way, the author moves from this opening into a gentle, strong story about a boy who is learning to live with and in spite of loss. A beautiful book.

Smith, Frank. *Insult to intelligence: The bureaucratic invasion of our classrooms.* Portsmouth, NH: Heinemann, 1986.
In this book, one of the world's most thoughtful authorities on the teaching of reading launches a powerful critique of the "drill and skill" approach to teaching language arts. Smith provides a checklist for parents who want help knowing what to look for in classrooms.

Spinelli, Jerry. *Maniac Magee*. Boston: Little, Brown, 1990.
This is a book that has carried away all the honors. It was the Newbery Award winner in 1990, and also the winner of the Boston Globe–Horn Book Award for fiction. The book opens, "They say Maniac Magee was born in a dump. They say his stomach was a cereal box and his heart a soft spring." It's the story of a boy who was a legend because he ran faster than anyone dreamed possible, a boy who becomes even more of a legend because of the way he brings two sides of a town together. This book could easily become a touchstone book for a class of third, fourth, or fifth graders.

Steiner, Vera John, ed. *Notebooks of the mind.* Albuquerque: University of New Mexico Press, 1985.
In this extraordinary book Vera John Steiner suggests there are some habits of mind that characterize creative thought across all the disciplines (science, dance, writing, art, mathematics, music). These include wide-awakeness and the willingness to hold onto and pursue an idea, to have obsessions.

Temple, Charles A., Ruth G. Nathan, and Nancy A. Burnig. *The beginnings of writing.* Boston: Allyn and Bacon, 1982.
This is a clear, detailed description of the growth in primary children's ability to spell and, to a lesser extent, to write. Anyone interested in

undertaking a detailed study of children's early spellings will benefit from this carefully researched text.

Van Manen, Max. *The tone of teaching.* Portsmouth, NH: Heinemann, 1986.
This book could be retitled *The Essentials of Teaching,* for it is about all that matters most in our work with children; it's about the power of a true handshake, of a wink, a look. It's about the way a teacher watches a child skipping rope and sees much more than a passerby could see. My colleagues and I ordered thirty copies of this 50-page book recently, and spent six weeks (and will spend the rest of our lives) living with it.

Waber, Bernard. *Ira says goodbye.* Boston: Houghton Mifflin, 1988.
This story is as artfully designed and as poignantly written as its better-known mate, *Ira Sleeps Over.* It should be read when children move out of a class. It deserves to be a classic.

Waber, Bernard. *Ira sleeps over.* Boston: Houghton Mifflin, 1975.
In this classic story, Ira struggles over whether to bring his teddy bear when he sleeps over at his friend's house. "Will Reggie laugh?" is his question, and it is the question our children ask when we encourage them to bring *their* teddy bears, and life stories, and memories, and dreams to the writing workshop. Reggie doesn't laugh, for he has a teddy bear of his own, and the two boys become closer.

Wilde, Sandra. *You kan red this! Spelling and punctuation for whole language classrooms, K–6.* Portsmouth, NH: Heinemann, 1991.
Somehow parents and even some educators have developed the mistaken notion that in writing workshops, there is little emphasis on spelling, that children spell "freely," that there is no instruction in spelling and grammar. It's essential that we correct this notion without retreating to weekly spelling lists and vocabulary ditto sheets. Wilde's book is grounded in informed theory; it's a reliable, scholarly, and practical overview of spelling and punctuation in the whole language classroom.

Yashima, Taro. *Crow boy.* New York: Puffin Books, 1976.
This is a moving tale about a slow, quiet little boy who walks miles and miles to school from his country home and is taunted by his classmates and left behind in his lessons. Then a special teacher helps everyone to see and to celebrate the boy's extraordinary talents, unnoticed for so long, and we are reminded of the hidden talents in all our classrooms. This is a wonderful

book to read aloud at the start of the year, or at any other time when we want to pay particular attention to the importance of seeing and celebrating the diverse gifts in all of us.

Zinsser, William. *On writing well.* New York: Harper & Row, 1990.
With chapters on travel and sports writing, on the lead and the ending, on clutter and simplicity, this book offers us a treasure chest of mini-lessons. Zinsser writes in the clear, simple, honest way that has become his trademark, and he offers suggestions for helping students write similarly.

Zinsser, William, ed. *Inventing the truth: The art and craft of memoir.* Boston: Houghton Mifflin, 1987.
This favorite book contains a collection of essays about memoir, written by Russell Baker, William Zinsser, Toni Morrison, and others. I particularly value Morrison's essay.

Works Cited

Applebee, Arthur. 1981. *Writing in the secondary school: English and the content areas.* Urbana, IL: National Council of Teachers of English.

Applebee, Arthur, F. Lehr, and A. Auten. 1981. Learning to write in the secondary school: How and where. *English Journal* 70:78–82.

Atwell, Nancie. 1987. *In the middle: Writing, reading, and learning with adolescents.* Portsmouth, NH: Boynton/Cook–Heinemann.

Auster, Paul. 1982. *The invention of solitude.* New York: Viking Penguin.

Avi. 1987. Speech, National Council of Teachers of English conference. Boston, MA. November.

Baker, Russell. 1982. *Growing up.* New York: New American Library.

———. 1987. Life with mother. In *Inventing the truth: The art and craft of memoir,* ed. William Zinsser. Boston: Houghton Mifflin.

Bauer, C. F., ed. 1986. *Rainy day: Stories and poems.* New York: Harper Trophy.

Baylor, Byrd. 1978. *The other way to listen.* New York: Charles Scribner's Sons.

———. 1982. *The best town in the world.* New York: Macmillan.

———. 1986. *I'm in charge of celebrations.* New York: Charles Scribner's Sons.

Bellack, Arno. 1963. *Theory and research in teaching.* New York: Teachers College Press.

Bereiter, Carl. 1982. From conversation to composition: The role of instruction in a developmental process. In *Advances in instructional psychology,* ed. R. Glasser, vol. 2. New Jersey: Lawrence Erlbaum Associates.

Bolton, Faye, and Diane Snowball. 1993. *Teaching spelling: A practical resource.* Portsmouth, NH: Heinemann.

Bomer, Randy. In press. *A time for meaning: Learning literacy with people aged 10–20.* Portsmouth, NH: Heinemann.

Braddock, Richard, Richard Lloyd-Jones, and Lowell A. Schoer. 1963. *Research in written composition.* Champaign, IL: National Council of Teachers of English.

Britton, James. 1970. *Language and learning*. London: Penguin.

Bronowski, Jacob. 1972. *Science and human values*. New York: Harper & Row.

Brooks, Bruce. 1991. *Nature by design*. New York: Farrar Straus & Giroux.

Brooks, Gwendolyn. 1959. We real cool. The pool players. Seven at the golden shovel. In *The world of Gwendolyn Brooks*. New York: Harper & Row.

Brown, Roger. 1968. Introduction. *In Teaching the universe of discourse* by James Moffett. Boston: Houghton Mifflin.

Bruner, Jerome S. 1966. *Toward a theory of instruction*. Cambridge, MA: Harvard University Press.

Bulla, Clyde Robert. 1988. *A grain of wheat*. Boston: Godine.

Byars, Betsy. 1991. *The moon and I*. Englewood Cliffs, NJ: Julian Messner.

Calkins, Lucy McCormick. 1980a. Punctuate, punctuate? Punctuate! *Learning* (February): 86–89.

———. 1980b. Research update: When children want to punctuate. *Language Arts* (May).

———. 1983. *Lessons from a child: On the teaching and learning of writing*. Portsmouth, NH: Heinemann.

———. 1986. *The art of teaching writing*. (1st ed.) Portsmouth, NH: Heinemann.

Calkins, Lucy McCormick, with Shelley Harwayne. 1991. *Living between the lines*. Portsmouth, NH: Heinemann.

Cazden, Courtney. 1972. *Child language and education*. New York: Holt, Rinehart and Winston.

Cheever, John. 1991. *The Journals of John Cheever*. New York: Alfred A. Knopf.

Chittendon, Ted. 1991. Speech for Educational Testing Service conference. Columbia University Teachers College, New York.

Chomsky, Noam. 1980. In *Thought and language/language and reading*, ed. M. Wolf, M. K. McQuillan, and E. Radwin. Cambridge, MA: Harvard Educational Review.

Ciardi, John. 1987. *You read to me, I'll read to you*. New York: HarperCollins Children's Books.

Cisneros, Sandra. 1992. Eleven. In *Woman hollering creek and other stories*. New York: Random House.

Clifton, Lucille. 1991. *Quilting: Poems, 1987–1990*. New York: BOA Editions.

Coles, Robert. 1989. *The call of stories.* Boston: Houghton Mifflin.

Cowley, Malcolm, ed. 1959. *Writers at work: The Paris Review interviews.* New York: Viking Press.

Csikszentmihalyi, Mihalyi, and Reed Larson. 1984. *Being adolescent: Conflict and growth in the teenage years.* New York: Basic Books.

Dillard, Annie. 1987. *An American childhood.* New York: Harper & Row.

Duckworth, Eleanor, Jack Easley, David Hawkins, and Androula Henriques. 1990. *Science education: A minds-on approach for the elementary years.* Hillsdale, NJ: Erlbaum.

Dyson, Anne Haas. 1989. *The multiple worlds of child writers: Friends learning to write.* New York: Teachers College Press.

Edelsky, Carole, Bess Altwerger, and Barbara Flores. 1990. *Whole language: What's the difference?* Portsmouth, NH: Heinemann.

Edelsky, Carole, and Kelly Draper. 1983. Hookin 'em in. *Anthropology and Education Quarterly* 14: 260–81.

Elbow, Peter. 1981. *Writing with power: Techniques for mastering the writing process.* New York: Oxford University Press.

English profiles handbook: Assessing and reporting students' prgress in English. 1991. Victoria, Australia: School Programs Division, Ministry of Education and Training.

Erikson, Erik H. 1964. *Insight and responsibility.* New York: W. W. Norton and Co.

Fisher, Bobbi. 1991. *Joyful learning: A whole language kindergarten.* Portsmouth, NH: Heinemann.

Fox, Mem. 1990. *Mem's the word.* Victoria, Australia: Penguin.

Francis, Robert. 1966. Summons. In *Reflections on a gift of watermelon pickle and other modern verse,* ed. Stephen Dunning, Edward Lueders, and Hugh Smith. Glenview, IL: Scott Foresman.

Fritz, Jean. 1982. *Homesick: My own story.* New York: Dell Publishing Co.

———. 1993. The known and the unknown: An exploration into nonfiction. In *The Zena Sutherland lectures,* ed. Betsy Hearn. New York: Clarion Books.

Fulwiler, Toby. 1980. Journals across the disciplines. *English Journal* 9, 9 (Dec.): 14–19.

———. 1982. Writing: An act of cognition. In *Teaching writing in all disciplines,* ed. Kenneth Erle and John Noonan. San Francisco: Jossey Bass.

Gardner, Howard. 1980. *Artful scribbles: The significance of children's drawings.* New York: Basic Books.

————. 1982. *Art, mind and brain: A cognitive approach to creativity.* New York: Basic Books.

Getzels, Jacob W., and Philip Jackson. 1985. Quoted in *Notebooks of the mind*, ed. Vera John Steiner. Albuquerque: University of New Mexico Press.

Goodlad, John. 1984. *A place called school: Prospects for the future.* New York: McGraw-Hill Book Co.

Goodman, Kenneth S., Yetta M. Goodman, and Wendy J. Hood. 1989. *The whole language evaluation book.* Portsmouth, NH: Heinemann.

Graves, Donald H. 1983. *Writing: Teachers and children at work.* Portsmouth, NH: Heinemann.

Graves, Donald H., and Bonnie S. Sunstein, ed. 1992. *Portfolio portraits.* Portsmouth, NH: Heinemann.

Greenfield, Eloise. 1986. "Harriet Tubman." In *Honey, I love and other love poems.* New York: HarperCollins Children's Books.

Greenfield, Eloise, and Lessie Jones Little. 1979. Mama sewing. In *Childtimes: A three-generation memoir.* New York: HarperCollins.

Hawkins, David. 1974. *The informed vision.* New York: Agathon Press.

Heard, Georgia. 1989. *For the good of the earth and sun: Teaching poetry.* Portsmouth, NH: Heinemann.

Hearn, Betsy, ed. 1993. The truth about nonfiction. In *The Zena Sutherland lectures.* New York: Clarion Books.

Hoetker, James. 1982. A theory of talking about theories of reading. *College English* 44, 2 (February): 175–81.

Holdaway, Don. 1979. *The foundations of literacy.* New York: Ashton Scholastic. (Distributed in the U.S. by Heinemann, Portsmouth, NH.)

Howard, Elizabeth Fitzgerald. 1991. *Aunt Flossie's hats and crab cakes later.* Boston: Houghton Mifflin.

Inner London Education Autority. 1988. *The primary language record: Handbook for teachers.* London: Centre for Language in Primary Education. (Distributed in the U.S. by Heinemann, Portsmouth, NH.)

Janeczko, Paul, ed. 1985. *Pocket poems.* New York: Bradbury Press.

Khalsa, Dayal Kaur. 1986. *Tales of a gambling grandma.* New York: Clarkson N. Potter.

Laycock, George. 1993. Valley of the cranes. *Boy's Life:* April.

Lindbergh, Anne Morrow. 1965. *A gift from the sea.* New York: Random House.

Little, Jean. 1986. After English class. In *Hey world, here I am!* New York: Harper & Row.

———. 1987. *Little by Little: A writer's education.* New York: Viking.

Lortie, Dan. 1975. *Schoolteacher.* Chicago: University of Chicago Press.

Lowry, Lois. 1980. *Autumn Street.* New York: Dell Publishing Co.

MacLachlan, Patricia. 1991. *Journey.* New York: Doubleday.

———. 1993. Speech at Teachers College Writing Project's Summer Institute, New York. July.

MacNeil, Robert. 1989. *Wordstruck.* New York: Viking Press.

McLerran, Alice. 1990. *Roxaboxen.* New York: Lothrop, Lee & Shepard.

McNulty, Faith. 1987. *The lady and the spider.* New York: HarperCollins Children's Books.

McPhillips, Shirley. In press. Untitled article.

Meek, Anne. 1991. On thinking about teaching: A conversation with Eleanor Duckworth. *Educational leadership,* March, pp. 30–34.

Meek, Margaret. 1992. *On being literate.* Portsmouth, NH: Heinemann.

Merriam, Eve. 1984. A lazy thought. In *Jamboree: Rhymes for all times.* New York: Dell Publishing Co.

———. 1991. *The wise woman and her secret.* New York: Simon & Schuster Books for Young Readers.

Morrison, Philip. 1964. The curricular triangle and its style. *ESI Quarterly Report* 3, 2: 63–70.

Murray, Donald M. 1968. *A writer teaches writing: A practical method of teaching composition.* Boston: Houghton Mifflin.

———. 1982. *Learning by teaching: Selected articles on writing and teaching.* Portsmouth, NH: Boynton/Cook–Heinemann.

———. 1984. *Write to learn.* New York: Holt, Rinehart and Winston.

Newkirk, Thomas. 1985. On the inside where it counts. In *Breaking ground: Teachers relate reading and writing in the elementary school,* ed. Jane Hansen, Thomas Newkirk, and Donald Graves. Portsmouth, NH: Heinemann.

———. 1989. *More than stories: The range of children's writing.* Portsmouth, NH: Heinemann.

Newkirk, Thomas, with Patricia McLure. 1992. *Listening in: Children talk about books (and other things).* Portsmouth, NH: Heinemann.

Nye, Naomi Shihab. 1990. Valentine for Ernest Mann. In *The place my words are looking for,* ed. Paul B. Janeczko. New York: Bradbury Press.

Parnall, Peter. 1990. *Woodpiles.* New York: Macmillan.

Paulsen, Gary. 1991. *The monument.* New York: Delacorte Press.

Peterson, Ralph. 1992. *Life in a crowded place: Making a learning community.* Portsmouth, NH: Heinemann.

Pritchett, V. S. 1991. *The cab at the door.* London: Hogarth Press.

Rief, Linda. 1991. *Seeking diversity: Language arts with adolescents.* Portsmouth, NH: Heinemann.

Rist, Ray. 1973. The urban school: A factory for failure. In *Risk makers, risk takers, risk breakers,* ed. Jo Beth Allen and Jana M. Mason. Cambridge, MA: MIT Press.

Romano, Tom. 1987. *Clearing the way: Working with teenage writers.* Portsmouth, NH: Heinemann.

———. 1990. The Multi-genre research report. In *The writing teacher as researcher,* ed. Donald A. Daiker and Max Morenberg. Portsmouth, NH: Boynton/Cook–Heinemann.

Rose, Mike. 1989. *Lives on the boundary: A moving account of the struggles and achievements of America's educationally underprepared.* New York: Viking Penguin.

Rylant, Cynthia. 1985. *The relatives came.* Scarsdale, NY: Bradbury Press.

———. 1987. *Birthday presents.* New York: Orchard Books.

———. 1990. *Soda jerk.* New York: Orchard Books.

Shaughnessy, Mina P. 1977. *Errors and expectations.* New York: Oxford University Press.

Short, Kathy G., and Carolyn Burke. 1991. *Creating curriculum: Teachers and students as a community of learners.* Portsmouth, NH: Heinemann.

Smith, Frank. 1982. *Writing and the writer.* New York: Holt, Rinehart and Winston.

———. 1983. Reading like a writer. *Language Arts* 60: 558–67.

———. 1986. *Insult to intelligence: The bureaucratic invasion of our classrooms.* Portsmouth, NH: Heinemann.

———. 1988. *Joining the literacy club: Further essays into education.* Portsmouth, NH: Heinemann.

Squire, James. 1984. Composing and comprehending: Two sides of the same basic process. In *Composing and comprehending,* ed. Julie M. Jensen. Urbana, IL: ERIC Clearinghouse on Reading and Communication Skills, and NCTE.

Stafford, William. 1986. *You must revise your life.* Ann Arbor: University of Michigan Press.

Steiner, Vera John, ed. 1985. *Notebooks of the mind.* Albuquerque: University of New Mexico Press.

Ueland, Brenda. 1938. *If you want to write.* St. Paul, MN: Graywolf Press.

Vygotsky, Lev Semenovich. 1962. *Thought and language.* Cambridge, MA: The MIT Press.

Welty, Eudora. 1984. *One writer's beginnings.* New York: Warner Books.

Whitman, Walt. 1949. Song of myself. In *Leaves of grass and selected poems.* New York: Holt, Rinehart & Winston.

Wilde, Sandra. 1991. *You kan red this! Spelling and punctuation for whole language classrooms, K–6.* Portsmouth, NH: Heinemann.

Williams, William Carlos. 1938. The red wheelbarrow. In *Collected earlier poems.* New York: New Directions Publishing Corp.

Zemelman, Steven, and Harvey Daniels. 1988. *A community of writers: Teaching writing in the junior and senior high school.* Portsmouth, NH: Heinemann.

Zinsser, William. 1990. *On writing well.* New York: Harper & Row.

————, ed. 1987. *Inventing the truth: The art and craft of memoir.* Boston: Houghton Mifflin.

CREDITS

Thanks to the following for permission to reprint previously published material:

Excerpt from "Valentine for Ernest Mann" by Naomi Shihab Nye in *The Place My Words Are Looking For,* selected by Paul B. Janeczko. Published by Bradbury Press, an affiliate of Macmillan Publishing Company, Inc. Reprinted by permission of Naomi Shihab Nye.

Excerpts reprinted by permission of Wendy Hood. In *The Whole Language Evaluation Book,* edited by Kenneth S. Goodman, Yetta M. Goodman, and Wendy J. Hood (Heinemann, A division of Reed Elsevier Inc., Portsmouth, NH, 1989).

"A Lazy Thought" from *JAMBOREE Rhymes for All Times* by Eve Merriam. Copyright © 1962, 1964, 1966, 1973, 1984 by Eve Merriam. Reprinted by permission of Marian Reiner.

Excerpt from *Aunt Flossie's Hats (and Crab Cakes Later)* by Elizabeth Fitzgerald Howard. Text copyright © 1991 by Elizabeth Fitzgerald Howard. Reprinted by permission of Clarion Books/Houghton Mifflin Company. All rights reserved.

"Invitation" from *Where the Sidewalk Ends* by Shel Silverstein. Copyright © 1974 by Evil Eye Music, Inc. Reprinted by permission of HarperCollins Publishers.

From *If You Want to Write* copyright © 1987 by the Estate of Brenda Ueland. Reprinted with the permission of Graywolf Press, Saint Paul, Minnesota.

"After English Class" from *Hey World, Here I Am!* by Jean Little. Text copyright © 1986 by Jean Little. Reprinted by permission of HarperCollins Publishers, New York, and Kids Can Press Ltd., Toronto, Canada.

Excerpts reprinted by permission of Georgia Heard: *For the Good of the Earth and Sun* (Heinemann, A division of Reed Elsevier Inc., Portsmouth, NH, 1989).